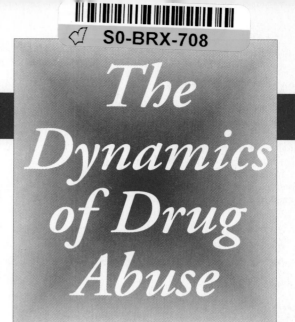

The Dynamics of Drug Abuse

Diana H. Fishbein
U.S. Department of Justice

Susan E. Pease
Central Connecticut State University

Allyn and Bacon
Boston London Toronto Sydney Tokyo Singapore

Executive Editor: Karen Hanson
Vice President: Susan Badger
Editorial Assistant: Jennifer Jacobson
Marketing Manager: Joyce Nilsen
Production Administrator: Mary Beth Finch
Editorial-Production Service: Thomas E. Dorsaneo
Text Designer: Andrea Miles/Menagerie Design & Publishing
Cover Administrator: Linda Knowles
Composition Buyer: Linda Cox
Manufacturing Buyer: Megan Cochran

The views expressed herein do not necessarily reflect the views of the U.S. government.

Copyright © 1996 by Allyn & Bacon
A Simon & Schuster Company
Needham Heights, Massachusetts 02194

Library of Congress Cataloging-in-Publication Data
Fishbein, Diana
    The dynamics of drug abuse/Diana Fishbein, Susan Pease.
    p. cm.
    Includes biblographical references (p.   ) and index.
    ISBN 0-205-13967-1
    1. Drug abuse—Physiological aspects. 2. Drug abuse—Social aspects.
        3. Drug abuse—Treatment. I. Pease, Susan. II. Title
RC564.F57 1996   95-24215
616.86—dc20   CIP

Printed in the United States of America.
10 9 8 7 6 5 4 3 2 1   99 98 97 96 95

As an expression of our devotion, we dedicate this book to John B. Pease and John Pease Love, and Howard, Daniel, and Alana Shapiro, and to all of the world's children hoping that, in the near future, no child will have to endure the tragedy of drug abuse.

CONTENTS

PREFACE

As a result of media hype, government attention and public distress, the nation has become obsessed with the apparent epidemic of drug abuse and its association with crime. Although this is not the first such "crisis" and will not be the last, there is some validity to the perception that drug abuse has become a plague on society. Drug abuse has contributed to an increase in child abuse and neglect, domestic violence, gang activity, youth violence, and various forms of psychological and behavioral pathology. Corresponding with this resurgence of a drug problem are other social ills that are certainly compounding and perhaps exacerbating the incidence of drug abuse. Unemployment, lack of low paying jobs, poverty, destitution, homelessness, dissolution of community resources, decentralization of government, and growing discontent with present policies and outcomes all play an interactive role with the drug abuse phenomenon. Not only do they increase the likelihood that more people will abuse drugs, but in turn, drug abuse also increases the prevalence of these social ills. The result, according to many experts, is the break-up of the family structure, believed to be the basis for much of our present nation-wide instability. In simple terms, the more individuals who feel hopeless, destitute and incapable of upward mobility or self-improvement, and are without access to the means to attain their goals, the more likely drug abuse and criminal activity will ensue. Other nations experiencing similar conditions are also witnessing this trend.

These perceptions, whether true or not, have made this book necessary. As drug abuse researchers, professors and community service providers, the authors are of the impression that the public and policy-makers alike are subject to a great deal of misinformation, mythical beliefs and misdirected solutions. Consequently, this book is designed to provide a more accurate and rational picture of the nature and extent of drug abuse in the United States.

A host of authors have chosen to write on this topic, resulting in several texts dealing with drug abuse. This book, however, differs in a number of ways. Our overall goal is to make available a book that offers comprehensive coverage, providing all relevant information in one source. Unlike most other drug texts on the market, this book includes all of the following: 1) social and cultural issues are addressed; 2) genetic and biological conditions associated with drug abuse are viewed in interaction with social and environmental factors; 3) discussions of law enforcement, drug trafficking, and social drug policy are presented with critiques and recommendations for future directions; 4) a multitude of theories of addiction from various disciplines are reviewed and critiqued; 5) an individualistic assessment of drug abuse is given; 6) the social context within which drugs are used is described; 7) there is less of a concentration on the pharmacology of drug actions and more on individual differences, what drug abuse constitutes, and how society responds to drug use that students will find both relevant and interesting; 8) there is continuity throughout the text along with an overview to introduce the student to the field of drug abuse; and 9) we deal with various topics that have direct bearing on drug abuse generally and criminal activity specifically.

In short, *The Dynamics of Drug Abuse* is a comprehensive text that addresses all aspects of the drug abuse field. A multidisciplinary view of drug abuse keeps the reader up-to-date in a field that is rapidly changing. For the first time, an explanation is offered of how sociological, psychological, and biological factors interact to influence drug taking behavior and the societal response to such behavior. There is not an abundance of detail to bog the student down in minute facts that do not facilitate an understanding of the field. Case studies and examples of real people and situations are presented to ease the reader into the field and generate interest and enthusiasm. There are various exercises and illustrations that help students personally relate to the material. This book is written for students of sociology, psychology, criminal justice, criminology, drug abuse, pre-med, nursing, and social work.

We provide evidence that a rational rethinking of drug policy using solid scientific work along public health lines could enable us to understand and control the relationship of specific drugs to antisocial behavior. Programs generated from this approach would incorporate well-founded treatments to reduce unwanted behaviors rather than a vague moral condemnation of some drugs and their users. There is no question that certain types of drugs produce behaviors that are antithetical to social life. However, the decision that criminal justice agencies constitute the only segment of society to control these behaviors has been made often on the basis of fear and misinformation.

This book includes a contemporary literature review and observations and conclusions based on our present knowledge base to better educate the drug abuse student. Importantly, the book also presents a research plan that provides direction for a comprehensive approach to the study of drug abuse and antisocial behavior. In addition, policy and programmatic recommendations are presented with respect to reducing demand for drugs and curbing related antisocial behavior, emphasizing the importance of treatment and prevention. The authors present evidence that the involvement of related public health agencies, school systems, communities, and parents will greatly enhance the ability of the criminal justice system to manage and circumvent these problematical behaviors. Once the generating conditions of drug-related antisocial behaviors are identified, preventative programs and treatment interventions will be recognized as better suited to control the problem. Resulting from this public health approach is the potential to detect early warning signs of a problem *before* it is necessary for the criminal justice system to intervene. Furthermore, information pertaining to the origins of drug-related antisocial behavior will enable us to develop global programs within communities that effectively prevent the very onset of these problems.

The Plan of the Book

The first chapter, Drug Abuse: Social Contexts and Individual Consequences, discusses macro-level aspects of drug-taking behaviors. In essence, the overall nature and extent of drug abuse in the United States is reviewed and an understanding is instilled that drug abuse does not occur in a vacuum. In other words, the reasons for drug abuse are based both on global socio-cultural and economic conditions, and on personal circumstances. Those generating conditions in any given case determine, in great part, the impact drug abuse will have on the individual.

The second chapter on history details drug abuse trends in our society and leads into a discussion of how these trends have directed drug abuse policies. In particular, the development of drug schedules and penalties for possession and distribution are very much a function of historical patterns and present fears.

The third and fourth chapters on brain structure and function, and pharmacology, present fundamental information on how the brain looks—its anatomy—and how it works—its function. Details included about neuroanatomy and neurochemistry are exclusively those related to drug use: which parts of the brain are influenced by psychoactive drugs, which chemicals are influenced, and how is brain function altered to produce behavioral changes. The pharmacology chapter explains how psychoactive drugs change the brain's activity to contribute to tolerance, withdrawal, dependence, and behavioral disturbances. In this chapter, the foundation is laid for understanding the following chapters on individual drugs.

The fifth chapter provides a review of theories of addiction, from the sociological to the genetic. Each one is critiqued, leading to a closing discussion of how they may be integrated to better understand the phenomenon of drug abuse.

From the sixth chapter to the fourteenth, individual drugs are discussed with respect to their properties, effects, abuse potential, toxicology, social context, and behavioral and psychological results. In addition, each drug chapter contains a section on the nature and extent to which its use is associated with criminal or antisocial behavior. Finally, a treatment section concludes each chapter by discussing specific treatments available for those who abuse that particular drug. Treatments discussed include social, psychological and pharmacological in approach.

Chapter 15 on treatment approaches provides a general overview of treatments available to drug abusers, independent of the particular drug of abuse. This chapter lists various modes of treatment and enumerates the characteristics of these various modalities. Importantly, a discussion of who is a candidate for treatment, what type of treatment is appropriate, and other controversial issues is included. Subsequently, classifications of treatments are presented according to the theoretical model on which they are based, from the pharmacological to the social.

Chapter 16 reads almost like an exciting novel. Drug trafficking is defined and true stories pertaining to major drug cartels and their distributors are conveyed. Chapter 17 on law enforcement techniques details the many sorts of strategies used and evaluates their effectiveness. From street level narcotics law enforcement to international interdiction efforts, law enforcement tactics are reviewed.

Finally, Chapter 18 concludes the text with recommendations for future social drug policy based on the contemporary knowledge base presented throughout the text. Once again, it is the authors' assertion that as we become more familiar with current findings in the field of drug abuse, future policy decisions will be more rational and effective.

We would like to thank those professors who read and commented on earlier versions of this work: David Mason, Northern Illinois University; Joe Terhaar, Eastern Washington University; David M. White, East Carolina University. Special thanks are extended to Dr. Clarence S. Greene, Jr., Vice Chairman, Department of Neurosurgery, Chief of Pediatric Neurosurgery, University of California, at Irvine Medical School; and Dr. Craig T. Love, Research Psychologist, Center for Alcohol and Addiction Studies, Brown University Medical School, for their valuable insight and critical review. And our personal thanks for their assistance to Betty Sue Benson, Texas Christian University; Charles Faupel, Auburn University; John C. Hardgrave, California State University, Fresno; David Mason, Northern Illinois University; Joe Terhaar, Eastern Washington University; and David M. White, East Carolina University. Finally, we wish to thank Deborah R. W. Gamzon, who provided many of the photographs within this book.

CHAPTER 1

Drug Abuse
Social Contexts
and Individual Consequences

Objectives

1. To provide an overview of the book.
2. To discuss the extent and social implications of the drug abuse problem.
3. To explain how definitions of drug abuse differ among people of diverse backgrounds.
4. To describe the social nature of definitions and proscriptions attached to drug abusers.
5. To introduce an integrated approach to understanding drug abuse that includes both medical and social explanations.
6. To provide a historical context of the drug problem.
7. To understand why we target certain groups and drugs based on the social status and characteristics of the user.
8. To contrast concerns between illegal and legal substances.
9. To discuss drug abuse as a symptom of underlying social and medical pathology.

Drug abuse and addiction are costly and destructive behaviors that many contend afflict our society like a disease. Drug abuse is no longer considered a victimless crime in that the loss of productivity, disabilities, welfare needs, children born to drug users who are in need of special services and their increased risk for antisocial behavior, and the loss of productivity are examples of how drug abuse impacts us all. Columbia University's Center on Addiction and Substance Abuse recently reported that one in five Medicaid dollars are spent on hospitalizations attributable to drug abuse and that 70 percent of these costs involve hospitalizations for diseases that allege substance abuse as a major risk factor. If these figures are correct, then we do indeed have a social obligation to identify effective ways of managing drug abuse. To accomplish this ideal, we must first attempt to assess the scope of the problem and understand its nature.

Understanding drug use, abuse, and addiction is such a complex undertaking that it is difficult to simply formulate the questions requiring address. What constitutes drug abuse? This question has been asked for centuries, but even today the answers are not consistent or clear. For some, drug abuse may include drinking alcohol occasionally or using marijuana at a party a few times a year. For others, an individual is a drug abuser when he or she drinks alcohol regularly or uses other illicit drugs as a social lubricant. While still others believe that one is a drug abuser only at the point of dependency, either psychological or physical, on an illegal drug, many people do not think alcohol can be abused simply by virtue of its legality. The arguments are numerous and are frequently based on moral beliefs, upbringing, and emotional reactions, rather than on facts and well-informed opinions. Although emotional arguments can be considered superfluous or misleading, popular sentiments about drug abuse are largely a function of gut level, personal feelings because we lack stringent criteria and standards by which to categorize the drug user. As a consequence of our confusion over definitions, we are not able to present a definitive position on the issue. Nevertheless, through our discussion of the controversy and introduction of those facts we have accumulated, the reader will be able to develop an informed opinion of what constitutes drug abuse.

What leads people to use drugs? Why does only a subgroup of users continue on to abuse drugs, and, within this population, why does an even smaller subgroup eventually become drug dependent? These questions have generated scores of investigations and theories in an attempt to explain why most people do not become drug abusers,

and why even addictive drugs do not entrap all those who try them. Given that drugs of abuse can produce euphoria, pleasure, and escape from problems and bad feelings, why don't more people engage in drug use? On the other hand, given that drugs of abuse have unpleasant side effects that are, in some cases, quite insidious, undesirable, and dangerous, why does anyone use them at all? There seems to be some sort of balancing act that occurs between the forces that encourage drug abuse and the forces that discourage it. Most likely these forces are numerous and multidimensional and include drug properties, genetic and biological conditions, learning experiences, personal traits, neighborhood conditions, family environment, and even global societal and political events. In essence, therefore, humankind has pursued the answers to two queries: What conditions protect people from abusing drugs, and what conditions are conducive to abusing drugs? Throughout this book and particularly in Chapter 5, theories that consider these questions will be discussed along with evidence that both supports and refutes each of them. It is our contention that no one theory of drug abuse or addiction can adequately explain this complex and dynamic phenomenon; thus we consider an integrated approach to the study of drug abuse taking into account a multitude of factors from various behavioral science fields.

The Extent of Drug Abuse

The National Institute on Drug Abuse (NIDA) and the Substance Abuse and Mental Health Services Administration (SAMHSA) conduct nationwide surveys to estimate the extent of drug use in the United States. Although these surveys have inherent limitations, as do all self-report studies, it is believed that they do provide a barometer by which we can measure trends since the same limitations exist from survey to survey. Throughout this text, references will be made to two major volumes of surveys conducted by NIDA and SAMHSA. First is the annual National Household Survey on Drug Abuse (NHSDA), which presents data regarding illicit drug use (including the use of prescription drugs without a doctor's permission), alcohol, and tobacco use among members of the household aged twelve and older (SAMHSA, 1994). The NHSDA provides information concerning drug use in the respondents' lifetime, in the year preceding the survey, and in the past month preceding the survey. For some categories of drugs, respondents are asked about their weekly use and whether they used a particular drug twelve or more times during the year.

The NHSDA produces estimates of prevalence rates for different drugs. These estimates are based on in-person interviews with a large national probability sample taken from the entire U.S. population.

There are some limitations inherent in these self-report surveys. For example, their accuracy is based on the truthfulness of the respondents and how well they can recall past behaviors. About 2 percent of the population is not represented in the sample. Excluded from this survey are persons living in military installations, college dormitories, group homes, prisons, nursing homes, and treatment centers as well as those with no permanent homes, such as the homeless and residents of hotels. As a result, there is probably some degree of constant underestimation of drug use.

Despite these limitations, the household surveys do provide a means of gauging drug trends in the United States.

Table 1.1 presents data showing the prevalence of drug use among Americans between the ages of twelve and thirty-five during 1993. Each drug is presented by whether the respondent ever used, used it during the past year, or used it during the past month.

The NIDA publication measures the prevalence and trends of drug use among high school seniors, college students, and young adults up to the age of thirty-two who are high school graduates (Johnston, O'Malley, & Bachman, 1993). The survey does not include dropouts who represent 15 to 20 percent of each age group. However, change estimates should not be affected by dropout rates. Since 1975, prevalence of illicit drug use, alcohol, and tobacco use among American high school

Table 1.1 *Drug Use Among Americans Ages 12-35; Percent of Respondents in 1993 Reporting Frequency of Use for Specific Drugs*

DRUG	Ever Used	Use During Past Year	Use During Past Month
	RATE ESTIMATES (PERCENTAGES)		
Marijuana	33.7%	9.0%	4.3%
Cocaine	11.3	2.2	0.6
Crack	1.8	0.5	0.2
Heroin	1.1	0.1	-
Hallucinogens	8.7	1.2	0.2
PCP	4.1	0.2	-
Inhalants	5.3	1.0	0.4
Stimulants	6.0	1.1	0.3
Sedatives	3.4	0.8	0.3
Tranquilizers	4.6	1.2	0.3
Analgesics	5.8	2.2	0.7
Anabolic Steroids	0.4	0.1	-
Needle Use	1.4	0.3	-
Alcohol	83.6	66.5	49.6
Cigarettes	71.2	29.4	24.2
Smokeless Tabacco	12.8	4.0	2.9

- = Rate too low to estimate. See original for full explanation

Source: Substance Abuse and Mental Health Services Administration, *1993 National Household Survey on Drug Abuse.*

seniors has been studied. College students and other young adults were added later.

The proportion of college students using any illicit drug in the prior year dropped steadily from 1980 to 1984 (from 56 percent to 45 percent), followed by a leveling off from 1984 to 1986 (at around 45 percent) and then a significant decline between 1986 and 1990 (from 45 percent to 29 percent). (See Figure 1.1.) However, in 1992, use of any illict drug increased to 31 percent. These trends are similar for high school seniors and other young adults one to four years beyond high school who are not currently enrolled full-time in college (Johnston, O'Malley, & Bachman, 1993, p. 161). Whether or not the trend towards increased drug use will continue beyond 1992 remains unknown.

Use of any illicit drugs other than marijuana declined more steadily between 1980 and 1986 (with annual prevalence among college students dropping gradually from 32 percent to 25 percent) but showed an accelerating decline

(to 13 percent) between 1987 and 1991 and leveled in 1992. Again, this trend is consistent with the high school seniors and the young adults (Johnston, O'Malley, & Bachman, 1993, p. 167). (See Figure 1.1.) Although there appears to have been some steady decline in drug abuse, recent evidence suggests that the incidence of drug abuse in these groups of youths may be rising somewhat in the 1990s. Specific trends for each individual drug of abuse will be discussed in the chapters that follow.

The Prevalence and Social Experience of Drug Abuse

So are we or are we not experiencing a drug epidemic unlike any before? The figures cited above are somewhat elusive and don't provide a broad historical perspective. We are bombarded daily by reports of the increasing number of children using drugs; of drug use at earlier ages than

Figure 1.1   *Any Illicit Drug: Trends in Annual Prevalence Among College Students vs. Others 1-4 Years Beyond High School*

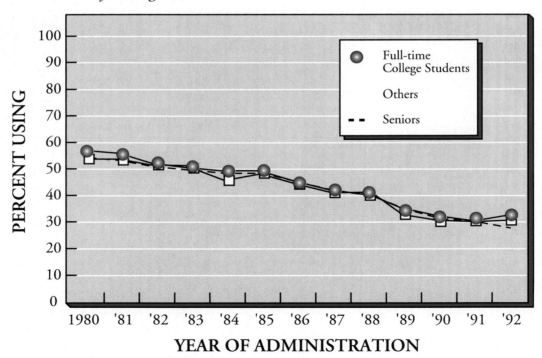

Source: National Institute on Drug Abuse, *1990 National Household Survey on Drug Abuse.*

ever before; of the number of crimes committed either while under the influence, to purchase drugs, or to protect the territory of drug sellers; of the number of criminal offenders who are drug addicted; of the number of babies born drug exposed or addicted; of exorbitant costs to society of drug abuse; and so forth. Most people in the United States are under the impression that drug abuse is rampant and out of control like never before. Has a massive drug problem swept America? It is true that the use of drugs to alter consciousness is replete in our history— most societies have utilized mind-altering and addictive substances, suggesting that drug use is a cross-cultural behavior. Even some lower animals go out of their way to ingest plants that provide a chemical high. Furthermore, we have experienced numerous and periodic epidemics in drug abuse throughout the history of this country in spite of stringent legal remedies. We sometimes lose sight of these historical trends, believing that previous experiences could not possibly compete with present circumstances.

Presently, we are in the midst of a drug epidemic, but of a somewhat different kind. Use among middle-class youth has declined, presumably due to educational campaigns. Use among lower-class youth has increased, however, particularly within areas that are considered crime infested and problem ridden. Thus, the link between drug abuse and crime has grown quite a bit stronger, is no longer behind closed doors, and has contributed to a widespread public fear of drug use as a whole. This so-called epidemic is discriminatory, not a global color-blind or classless phenomenon; there are class distinctions between types of drug use, extent of use, and consequences of use. By virtue of the fact that the drug problem has worsened in low-income areas, we are forced to consider the social conditions that may play a role in the problem. Even though we have all been hit by economic hardships in the past fifteen years, the lower classes had very little to lose in the first place and are suffering more severely. The economy, therefore, is probably a major player in the drug abuse phenomena. Moreover, because a quarter of the children in this country live below the poverty level and many are homeless, we are faced with a new, ever-increasing generation of individuals at great risk for drug abuse.

Individuals of all social groups and colors abuse drugs; however, we are rarely made aware of the consequences of alcoholism or drug addiction in the upper echelon of our society. Why is that? Do we tolerate or accept drug abuse within certain groups? Do we define it differently when a physician becomes dependent on morphine, when an unemployed poor minority man begins using heroin, when a lonely frustrated housewife turns to alcohol or Elizabeth Taylor goes to Betty Ford? Yes! We have a tendency to classify drug users according to their social standing, even though the consequences of their drug abuse may be quite similar. One reason for this inadvertent response is that drug use within low-income areas is more visible; drugs are purchased and used on the street, there is more outside activity of all sorts, and drug use is more associated with unemployment, disability, overt child abuse and neglect, emergency medical situations, and crime. Individuals in higher-income areas are more likely to purchase and use drugs behind closed doors. They are less likely to openly discuss their use. They have access to community and medical services, such as private physicians, psychiatrists and psychologists, medical insurance, and other supportive resources to attend to problems that result from their drug use and maintain an air of secrecy. Does that make drug abuse in "good" neighborhoods better or more acceptable than drug abuse in "bad" neighborhoods? Absolutely not. Instead, we are simply able to ignore or trivialize the problem in higher-income areas because we know less about it. Thus the second reason for our differential response to various drug users is lack of knowledge.

What is also true is that attitudes and societal responses to drug use have also varied widely across cultures and across historical time zones. The use of narcotics and even cocaine was not an issue at the turn of the century, and many respectable people legally administered them. Now heroin and crack use in particular is most highly concentrated in lower-income minority areas of our cities. Early in this century, marijuana was considered the work of the devil, and believed to contribute to violence, sexual depravity, and mental illness. Now medical professionals are considering legalizing the substance for glaucoma and cancer sufferers. Alcohol and nicotine are the most widely used substances today and are conclusively known to cause more damage (medical, personal, legal, and societal) than heroin and cocaine combined. And, ironically, they are both legal. These mixed messages are confusing to laypersons, youth, scientists, and policymakers alike. It is apparent that drug use concerns us most when low-income groups are the primary users. In fact, it is evident that we legislate most stringently against drugs and their users who are concentrated in lower-class, minority areas.

Integrating Social and Medical Perspectives of Drug Abuse

All cultures, throughout history, have tolerated and accepted the use of certain psychoactive (mind-altering) drugs under certain conditions. Hashish has been condoned in the Middle East, psychedelic mushrooms are used for religious and spiritual purposes in various Indian cultures, South Americans chew leaves of the coca plant, and, of course, those of us in the United States drink alcohol, smoke nicotine cigarettes, and drink caffeinated beverages. In each of these instances, society has established rules and guidelines that govern which substances are used, by whom and when. And over time, these rules are subject to change depending on social conditions and political tides. As a result, we have never been entirely opposed to the altering of consciousness, and we have exhibited a proclivity to pursue such a mental state on occasion. In accordance with the social order, we are simply instructed to follow the rules and adhere to prevailing social definitions of acceptable drug use.

We are presently of the mind-set that all illegal drugs are bad and should be banned, irrespective of their pharmacological properties and their association with medical, personal, or societal damage. Public fear has fueled this reaction. This mind-set is not entirely logical, particularly given that many legal drugs are dangerous and that some illegal drugs are relatively benign. Thus, the rules of the game have become less clear and many people are confused by conflicting messages. We strongly deplore the use of marijuana, even for medical purposes, and continue to condone the use of alcohol, a drug associated with crime, violence, disability, unemployment, and death. It is time that we evaluate the actual pharmacological properties of drugs and the consequences of their use so that we may come to an informed opinion. It is also time that we take into consideration sociological perspectives on drug use, including an assessment of society's definitions of, reactions to, and theories about drug abuse. "Sociological perspectives provide a framework for understanding the processes by which societies determine legitimate or illegitimate drug usage, respond to 'illegitimate' usage, and influence the propensity of individuals and groups to utilize particular drugs in particular historical periods" (Richman, 1985). Integrating pharmacological and sociological perspectives are essential to set our priorities, concentrate our energies, develop techniques, and formulate policy decisions that are likely to effectively deal with the drug crisis we currently perceive. This strategy will minimize our emotional and moral input and maximize our intellectual contribution to the drug problem.

As a nation, our lack of perspective regarding the origins and social context of drug abuse can be cited, in part, for our present ineffectiveness. First and foremost, we must come to terms with the notion that drug abuse is only a symptom of an underlying problem. To employ a medical analogy, drug abuse is not itself the disease nor is it the source of the disease. There is underlying pathology on both a personal and societal level that results in drug abuse; drug abuse is, only one symptom of a disease that afflicts us all as a society. Rampant drug abuse is a reflection of social ills—it is an indication of society's failure to satisfy basic needs and care for the welfare of its citizens. Specifically, the social contribution to drug abuse is very much a function of poverty, social immobility, unemployment, lack of community services, isolation, deprivation, poor educational systems, urban decay, deterioration of the family unit due to social stressors, unavailability of medical services, social interventions and treatment, and many other harsh conditions. Geographical areas characterized by these conditions have the most alarming rates of drug abuse and crime. In recent decades, policymakers and citizens alike have permitted the dissolution of vital resources that kept families afloat and have taken a punitive, rather than corrective, approach to the problem. Each of us must recognize the role we play in contributing to the drug abuse crisis, even if it is simply our ignoring or downplaying it. Unless we take a stand and attempt to rationally understand the issues, drug abuse will continue to plague our country. We are all part of the social process underlying present social ills.

Notwithstanding, drug abuse is also very much a reflection of personal tragedy. Individuals who are satisfied with their lives, who feel empowered to make improvements, who have self-respect generally are at low risk for becoming dependent on abusive drugs. Conversely, those who would like to make personal or lifestyle changes but lack the means, the self-esteem, or the support and those who have acquired feelings of helplessness in their worlds are at quite high risk for drug abuse. Although we cannot mathematically calculate who will eventually use and who will not, weighing both the social and personal advantages against the disadvantages provides some measure of how likely drug abuse, or other antisocial behaviors, is to develop. Child physical and sexual abuse, personality disturbances, learning disabilities, genetic or biological liabilities, social deprivation, and many other conditions frequently not under an individual's control dramatically increase the risk. People must possess the will not to use drugs, and "the will" is at least partially a function of what they perceive they may lose if they do partake in drugs.

The critical point in understanding an individual's final decision to use drugs is that many of these conditions are correctable. Rebuilding urban areas; enhancing the job market; providing occupational training, parenting classes, and medical and prenatal services; revitalizing social services and foster care programs, educating children and the public at large, and increasing the availability of treatment services are only a few approaches that may have a significant impact on the incidence of drug abuse. It is our responsibility to become informed of the nature and scope of drug abuse in our communities and prepare the social climate for corrective, nationwide changes. We have been lulled into thinking that the drug war was successful in reducing the problem; however, we are now witnessing a relapse. We have slacked off in our efforts to curb drug abuse and are, again, experiencing a trend in the wrong direction.

▦ Summary

Given that both the public and policymakers are relatively unfamiliar with the findings and facts pertaining to drug abuse in America, this book will educate people with the goal that better informed opinions will result. The study of drug abuse is an unusually diverse and complex field and requires that examination of the issues include an integration of sociological, psychological, epidemiological, and biological knowledge. We have attempted, therefore, to present discussions on all aspects of drug abuse, including a history of drug laws, drug trafficking, drug properties, theories of drug addiction, treatment, social drug policies, and law enforcement efforts. This book is unique in its inclusion of both social and biological perspectives, in addition to its discussion of how these forces interact in a dynamic system. And, because of the intrinsic link between drug abuse and criminal activity, particular attention is given to discussions of that relationship and how it influences how we, as a society, function. We expect that it will be useful to the student of sociology, social work, psychology, criminology, medicine, nursing, psychopharmacology, and behavioral genetics.

The overall purposes of this book are to:

- *dispel myths about drug abuse, such as beliefs that drug dealers strike it rich, that drug users are vicious criminals, that so-called soft drugs are benign, that treatment does not work, and that the war on drugs has been successful*
- *provide accurate information reflecting our present state of knowledge*
- *discuss controversies and debates in the field*
- *evaluate scientific findings, both those well founded and those that remain speculative*
- *integrate theories to provide a multidisiplinary perspective*
- *contribute to better informed public opinions*
- *enhance decision-making ability among policymakers*
- *increase the potential for the development of effective social policies*
- *provide an update of contemporary treatment strategies*
- *emphasize the need for further research*

We have made the following assumptions, strongly supported by scientific evidence, throughout this book. These assumptions are based on the concept of "individual differences," a significant determinant of behavior but not a simple concept to measure and evaluate. First, some individuals are biologically predisposed to drug dependence. There are documented individual differences in genetically influenced personality and temperamental traits; in physiological, metabolic, and biochemical processes; and in the body's reaction to drug exposure. Second, some drugs are more addicting than others, in particular, nicotine, cocaine, heroin, amphetamines, and alcohol. Third, some drugs are more attractive to some individuals than others. As a result of both personal and social influences, some users have a "drug of choice" and resort to other drugs only as a default measure when their preferred drug is unavailable. And fourth, drug-taking behavior is acquired and maintained through learning experiences.

Although we have addressed many pertinent issues and provided contemporary information reflecting the state of our knowledge, there remain many questions that have yet to be fully answered. Why do some individuals initially take drugs while others never reach that stage? Why do some continue to take drugs while others discontinue use after only a brief period? What is the mechanism that transforms a drug user into a drug abuser? What strategies effectively stop drug abuse? How does relapse occur for some and not others? Perhaps by the next edition we will have additional answers to these unresolved queries.

CHAPTER 2

History of
Drug Use and Legislation

Objectives

1. To discuss the attitude toward and prevalence of drug use in the United States before the enactment of drug legislation.
2. To highlight the reasons why drug legislation was enacted.
3. To review the impact of drug legislation on arrests, rate of incarceration, and social acceptance of drug use.
4. To shed light on the current trends in drug use and drug legislation.

he use of drugs as a means of altering consciousness appears to have a history longer than the written record. For example, archaeologists uncovered a three thousand-year-old opium pipe on the island of Cyprus near Turkey. Assyrian tablets, circa 700 B.C., describe the method of collecting opium from the opium poppy, which is similar to the way opium is still collected today. Egyptian records from 1500 B.C.. indicate that opium was used as medicine to soothe crying babies and was also used by Pharaoh Rameses II who lived from 1292–1225 B.C. (Latimer & Goldberg, 1981, p. 19). Most cultures have chosen some drug as a socially acceptable way of altering consciousness. For example, many Peruvian Indians chew the coca leaves containing cocaine, Native Americans use mescaline, Middle Easterners prefer opium and hashish, and Americans drink alcohol. Some researchers argue (Siegel, 1989; Weil, 1986; Zinberg, 1984) that to seek an altered state of consciousness is a natural drive with drug use as a logical means to achieve this state.

Table 2.1   *Time Line of Drug Development and Legislation*

YEAR	EVENT
1806	Morphine developed by a German pharmacist's assistant
1831	Morphine accepted by medical community as efficient and effective pain relief
1832	Development of codeine
1848	Invention of the hypodermic needle, Freud wrote about cocaine's medical value
1861-1865	Widespread use of morphine during the War Between the States
1885	Parke-Davis manufactured cocaine for use as medicine, Freud wrote about cocaine as a cure for morphine addiction and as a treatment for depression
1898	Bayer Company markets heroin as a cough suppressant
1899	Bayer Company markets aspirin
1903	Cocaine removed from Coca-Cola
1906	Pure Food and Drugs Act (ingredients must be listed on the product's label)
1908	Opium smoking outlawed in the United States
1914	Harrison Act passed (tax placed on manufacture and sale of opium products)
1914 - 1918	World War I
1919	Volstead Act (beginning of Prohibition)
1922	*United States v. Behrman* (medical doctors can no longer prescribe opiates to addicts)
1933	Prohibition ended
1937	Marijuana Tax Act (tax placed on manufacture and sale of marijuana)
1938	Food Drug and Cosmetic Act (drugs must be tested for safety)
1939-1945	World War II
1956	Narcotic Drug Control Act (selling heroin to someone under 18 could result in the death penalty)
1970	Comprehensive Drug Abuse Prevention and Control Act (possession and sale of controlled substances specifically outlawed)
1971	Widespread use of marijuana in the United States
1984	The appearance of crack cocaine
1984	The Comprehensive Crime Control Act of 1984 (first significant drug legislation since 1970)
1986	Anti-Drug Abuse Act of 1986 (increased criminal penalties for drug offenses)
1988	Anti-Drug Abuse Act of 1988 (increased criminal penalties for drug offenses involving children)
1989	The appearance of ice and crank
1990	President George Bush employs the military in "Drug War"

Regardless of whether the use of mind-altering substances is a natural human pursuit, societies have universally attempted to regulate the use of various drugs. In all societies, some drug use is acceptable, depending on the extent to which the drug is used and the drug's effects. Some drugs are outlawed or at least socially condemned. And as established in Chapter 1, which drugs we choose to outlaw changes over time as a function of prevailing belief systems, political trends, and perceived social needs. These choices are frequently not based on the drug's chemical properties or its health effects.

The manner in which American society selected and controlled acceptable psycoactive drugs and outlawed others was not always accomplished by logical and rational decision-making processes. During the early 1900s, ignorance, hysteria, politics, racism, corruption, and self-aggrandizement by some seeking to further their political careers influenced twentieth-century drug policy. Although we cannot deny that some writers, politicians, and scholars were concerned about the health of Americans, the primary factors that shaped American drug laws were based on issues other than the public health. This point is best illustrated by the fact that alcohol, one of the most addictive and damaging psychoactive drugs, was made legal again following the end of prohibition. On the other hand, the opiates, highly addictive but less dangerous in pure form in terms of the number of unhealthy side effects, remained illegal. Moreover, those who used opiates were considered degenerate criminal "dope fiends" by the rest of society. Early in the twentieth century, an association between the stigma of drug addict and the labels criminal or immoral was formed.

Before Drug Regulation

During the nineteenth century and early twentieth century, Americans had fairly easy access to drugs of their choosing. There was little regulation of any kind with regard to the content of medicines, the claims made by their purveyors, or the manner in which they were dispensed. Medical schools were not accredited (Musto, 1987) and the Rush Medical College of Illinois issued degrees through the mail (Latimer & Goldberg, 1981). Since there were no regulating agencies and doctors and pharmacists were unlicensed, nearly anyone could call him- or herself a doctor and market his or her miracle cure-all medicine. The lack of licensing made it difficult to pass laws restricting or controlling drugs because viola-

tors could not be threatened with loss of license (Musto). According to Musto (p. 40),

> The status of legislative control of dangerous drugs during the nineteenth century may be summed up as follows: The United States had no practical control over the health professions, no representative national health organization to aid the government in drafting regulations, and no controls on the labeling, composition, or advertising of compounds that might contain opiates or cocaine. The United States not only proclaimed a free marketplace, it practiced this philosophy with regard to narcotics in a manner unrestrained at every level of preparation and consumption.

Probably the two most important factors that set the stage for drug regulation were the increasing and alarming rates of narcotic addiction and the association of drug use with minority groups. These issues are examined below.

Drug Use and Levels of Addiction Before Drug Regulation

The early colonists who arrived in America from Europe were interested in individual freedom. The Magna Carta (1215) was the embodiment of English common law and the colonists abided to live by that decree. Individual rights were revered as reflected in this document and, in accordance with this philosophy, individual drug use was not directly regulated. That would have been considered an invasion of privacy and governmental intrusion. Instead, the colonists attempted to control the *influences* of certain drugs. Translated into practical terms, that meant they were more interested in regulating the amount taken by an individual to prevent a level of intoxication that might lead to disruptive behavior or a lack of productivity. Rather than mandate no alcohol use, "drunkenness" was outlawed. Controlled drug use was acceptable. Because the colonists dreamed of building a new homeland and leading a civilized life, their goals were threatened by those who became ineffective and lazy as a result of their drug use. Records indicate that alcohol was the only drug of concern and that, although other psychoactive drugs were available (e.g., cocaine and marijuana), they were used primarily for medicinal purposes.

Toward the end of the nineteenth century, social and economic conditions changed drastically and forced a new evaluation of existing drug laws. A move toward the West had ensued and several political and social battles had been fought, including the Civil War. Cities began to form and people began to migrate to industrial areas instead of living in rural farm lands. Crowding and increased interaction and contact with neighbors contributed to contagious diseases, pollution, contrasting lifestyles, crime, and value conflicts. The workplace was more competitive but without direct regulation or monitoring. As a result, there were no rules about who could work where, for how long, and for how much. Children were employed by companies that provided substandard, unhealthful conditions. Medicines and foods were not monitored, and people became sick from them. Given the harsh way of life that had developed around these new urban areas, citizens began to realize that restrictions and regulations were necessary for a better quality of life.

The first narcotics laws in the United States were city ordinances on the West Coast. San Francisco in 1875 was one of the first cities to regulate drug use. These ordinances marked the beginning of a trend toward the prohibition of opiates and eventually other drugs. When the Reform Movement developed in 1887, drug laws were revamped and a federal initiative emerged to provide national guidelines for drug use and possession. Initially, the design of these laws was to regulate the health effects of certain drugs. But as the Reform Movement developed and gained speed, drug laws began to reflect efforts to ensure social conformity and religiosity and to oppress groups of individuals considered "undesirable."

Although most writers agree that there was a significant addiction problem in the U.S. at the turn of this past century, inconsistent estimates of the extent of the problem have been cited. For example, Musto (1987, p. 42) estimates there were 250,000 addicts among the U.S. population of 76 million. In 1871, Dr. George Calkins estimated in his publication *Opium and the Opium Appetite* (cited by Latimer & Goldberg, 1981, p. 190) that 20 percent of Americans were addicted to opiates in one form or another, and King (1972, p. 18) references the 1890 census as estimating 2.5 million addicts, a figure ten times Musto's estimate. On the other hand, the U.S. Narcotics Bureau provided a figure of 1 in 400 addicts (about 1,900,000) (cited by Lewis & Zinberg, 1964). In 1919, government documents claimed 1,000,000 addicts (Courtwright, 1982, p. 9), whereas *The Literary Digest* (American enslavement to drugs, 1919) estimated

1,500,000 in that same year. Clyde L. Eddy, vice president of the American Pharmaceutical Association in 1923, claimed there were one million addicts in the United States. (One million drug addicts, 1923.) On the basis of a historical analysis of surveys of physicians and pharmacists, records of maintenance programs, military medical examinations, and opiate import statistics, Courtwright (p. 9) estimated there were about 4.59 addicts per thousand persons in the 1890s amounting to about 313,000. Courtwright believes this figure represents the highest number of addicts before 1914. As a point of comparison, present estimates (1995) indicate that about 2 million use opiates occasionally and that about 500,000 are addicted. Evidently, the opium epidemic in the late 1800s was severe and could be considered somewhat comparable to the drug problems of today.

One reason for the difficulty in providing accurate estimates can be attributed to a lack of sophistication of survey techniques and data analysis. Definitions of what constituted drug use, abuse, and addiction were also quite variable and dependent on the social conditions and concerns of the time, resulting in different estimates of prevalence. Most influential in determining how many addicts there were and which drugs were the most popular was the government and other special interest groups, which often fabricated figures in order to support a particular viewpoint. The oppression of certain types or classes of people was at times the intent, and in other instances the desire was to save souls and reform people who had gone astray. Even in modern times, for example, cocaine use was somewhat overlooked when it was used primarily by upper- and middle-class folks in the 1970s and early 80s. When it became cheap enough for lower-class folks to purchase, however, we began to focus on cocaine use and include a great many more users in our numbers of addicts. Accurate estimates, therefore, have been hard to come by.

Unlike today's heroin addict who usually begins opiate use in search of the perfect high, the typical nineteenth-century morphine addict was a white middle- or upper-class housewife who received her first dose in the course of legitimate medical treatment (Courtwright, 1982). King (1972, p. 18) cites one physician who observed, "Thousands of women were addicts of opiates, with no thought of wrong-doing, who would have gone on their knees to pray for a lost soul had they seen cigarette stains on the fingers of a daughter."

Several factors are believed to have contributed to changes in the rate of addiction:

1. *the development of such "new" drugs as morphine, codeine, and heroin and the initial belief that they were not addictive.*

2. *the invention of the hypodermic needle, which delivered these narcotics in a rapid and effective manner.*

3. *the use of morphine during the American Civil War.*

4. *the marketing of patent medicines containing such addictive substances as alcohol, cocaine, and the opiates in their various forms.*

Although opium had been used for thousands of years as a pain killer, it was not until a German pharmacist's assistant, Frederich Serturner, developed morphine in 1831 that the medical profession began to use it on a widespread basis. Morphine was considered ten times more potent than opium (Ray, 1990). Shortly thereafter, in 1848, the hypodermic needle was invented by Dr. Alexander Wood of Edinburgh. Physicians were now able to deliver the drug through subcutaneous (under the skin) injections and provide relief more efficiently and rapidly than oral ingestion of opium (referred to as opium eating) (Latimer & Goldberg, 1981). Doctors also erroneously believed that injecting morphine would be less addicting than eating opium since they believed that the alkaloid that caused addiction was removed from the opium when it was converted into morphine.

Doctors were able to make widespread use of the injection method of morphine during the American Civil War (1861–1865). The injections delivered immediate pain relief on the battlefield and were used to control "the ubiquitous dysentery" that plagued both the Union and Confederate armies (King, 1972, p. 16; Lewis & Zinberg, 1964; Ray & Ksir, 1990). (Note: Latimer & Goldberg disagreed and said that morphine was not used extensively until five years after the Civil War. They further asserted that blaming addiction on the war experience was more credible than simply admitting that you fell victim to the drug due to moral weakness.)

Following the Civil War, anyone could purchase a hypodermic needle from the drugstore "along with specially-prepared patent vials of injectable Magendie's Morphia Solution" and by the 1870s and 1880s self-injection of morphine hit an all time high (Latimer & Goldberg, 1981, pp. 186, 188).

It was not until about 1871 that the medical profession recognized a problem of addiction to morphine by a significant proportion of the population (Latimer &

Goldberg). In 1898, the German pharmaceutical company, Bayer Laboratories, marketed heroin, a drug three times as potent as morphine, as a cough suppressant and cure for morphine addiction. By about 1910, it was generally known that heroin was addictive.

Furthermore, confounding the medical profession's attempts to determine what effects opiates had on people was the fact that doctors did not yet know to sterilize needles and used the same one to inject several patients. As a result, many diseases and abscesses were then attributed to the drug instead of the lack of sterilization (King, 1972, p. 17). This medical ignorance and the resulting confusion retarded the development of an understanding of the addictive properties and effects of opiates. The misinformation generated during this era provided grist for many myths about opiates still prevalent today.

Another factor that led to the high rate of addiction was the pervasive use of patent medicines. Alcohol, opium, morphine, heroin, cocaine, and cannabis were popular ingredients in patent medicines (Chase & Schlink, 1927), which carried names such as "Smith's Revivifier and Blood-Purifier," "Doctor Pierce's Favorite Prescription," and "Pond's Extract, the Universal Pain Extractor" (J.H. Young, 1961). For the most part, the patent medicines were advertised as a cure-all for virtually any ailment known to man, woman, or child. The term patent medicine does not really provide an accurate reflection of what these medicines were; we generally think of a patent as a formula or product registered with the government that gives the producer the exclusive right to sell the product for a limited period of time. The turn of the century patent medicines were not registered with the federal government and their formulas were secret. They could be purchased through mail order catalogs, from the local drug store, or from hawkers who sold them from the back of wagons while staging elaborate shows (LeBlanc, 1925; J.H. Young). Before 1906 these medicines were sold without their contents listed on a label. When contents did appear on labels, they were often intentionally misleading. For example, a particular potion would be advertised as a cure for morphine addiction and claims were made that it contained no opiates when in actuality chemical analysis would show that morphine was the primary ingredient. As a result, those who purchased the drug expecting to withdraw from morphine with a minimum of discomfort were partially correct in their assumption. They felt no discomfort, but neither were they being cured of morphine addiction. There were no laws against false or misleading advertising, and the prevailing attitude was that of "consumer beware" (J.H. Young).

Doctors and pharmacists did feel some responsibility for protecting the public from quackery, and articles did appear in the professional journals concerning these medicines. However, there was little incentive for these organizations to police themselves. Medical journals received large advertising revenues from the drug companies (as they do today) and advertising was often presented in the form of an "article" or "editorial" (J.H. Young, 1961). Pharmacists felt they were caught in somewhat of a bind. On one hand, they recognized that many of the patent medicines were either ineffective or made the patient feel better because of the prevalence of psychoactive drugs that could lead to addiction. On the other hand, the sale of these drugs made a significant contribution to the pharmacist's profit margin. If he did not sell the drugs, his customers would simply patronize a pharmacist who did (J.H. Young).

Another factor that made regulation of these patent medicines difficult was the fact that their manufacturers were a powerful group of investors who bought a lot of newspaper ads. Each contract with newspapers contained what was known as a "red clause." Printed in red ink was a statement to the effect that if the state passed a law that in any way restricted the manufacture or sale of patent medicine then the contract was automatically voided. Such a clause also prevented newspapers from reporting any controversy or criticism concerning patent medicines such as might be reported as part of the paper's coverage of meetings of the American Medical Association. Therefore, the concern of the medical profession regarding these products was not brought to the public's attention through the newspapers (J.H. Young, 1961, p. 211). It was not until 1905 that the dangers of patent medicines containing alcohol, cocaine, cannabis, and opiates were reported to the public in a series of articles by Samuel Hopkins Adams entitled "The Great American Fraud" published in *Collier's* magazine. The series began with the following quote (Adams, 1905, cited by J.H. Young, p. 219).

Guillible America will spend this year some seventy-five millions of dollars in the purchase of patent medicines. In consideration of this sum it will swallow huge quantities of alcohol, an appalling amount of opiates and narcotics, a wide assortment of varied drugs ranging from powerful and dangerous heart depressants to insidious liver stimulants; and, far in excess of other ingredients, undiluted fraud. For fraud, exploited by the skillfulest of advertising bunco men, is the basis of the trade.

Racism and Drug Laws

Racism was probably one of the most important variables associated with the passage of drug laws in America. As argued by Latimer and Goldberg (1981, p. 200) ". . . the Chinese had been hauled into it all. Whole volumes of horror about the health hazards of morphine couldn't have done it—health is about the last thing anyone considers in deciding whether or not to abuse any drug—but prejudice persuaded people to go for the cure right away." Opium smoking was associated with the Chinese, cocaine use with Southern blacks, and marijuana smoking primarily with Mexicans but also with blacks. Restricting the drug using behavior of these groups through law enforcement tactics was one method to suppress them as a social class and limit their ability to become upwardly mobile.

The Chinese and Opium Smoking

It was accepted without question in the 1860's, then, then that the Chinaman had robbed the whites of rightful employment on the new transcontinental railroad system. In fact, one of every five Chinese in the West was involved in railway construction, spanning ravines with trestles, blowing tunnels through mountainsides, shoveling level grades out of vertical mesa slopes, and laying endless leagues of steel rail across the salt flats and prairies. It was the Chinese who were trapped in the high Sierra blizzards, decimated by the Indians, bitten and stung and eaten by the wildlife; Vanderbilt simply couldn't find white workers crazy enough to take the job, especially at coolie rates, and so it was the coolies who built the railroads. The whites, feeling vaguely robbed of an epoch of heroism and sacrifice equal to that of the great 1850's covered-wagon migrations, never entirely forgave the Chinese. They were accused of robbing jobs no one else would have taken while they were available, and revenge was duly forthcoming. (Latimer & Goldberg, 1981, p. 204).

The revenge referred to by Latimer and Goldberg involved tremendous violence and discrimination against the Chinese during the latter part of the nineteenth century and early part of the twentieth century. The Chinese came to the United States during the mid-nineteenth century as indentured servants to work on the railroads or perform other menial labor eschewed by whites. The Chinese intended to stay in the United States temporarily until they earned enough money to return to their families in China with significant savings (Courtwright, 1982). They brought with them the practice of opium smoking. The American employers sold opium to their Chinese employees thereby encouraging opium smoking and further indebting the Chinese. Such an arrangement ensured that the Americans would have a steady supply of poorly paid workers because the Chinese could never pay off the debts for drugs nor could they return home to their families (King, 1972).

As the economy took a turn for the worse during the 1870s the Chinese were seen as taking jobs from whites. Samuel Gompers, in his attempt to organize a national labor coalition, publicized the fact that "the big bosses" used Chinese labor as a means of preventing union organization (Latimer & Goldberg, 1981, p. 206–207). Hostility and violence against the Chinese became commonplace. Opium smoking was viewed as a "disgusting habit" and the Chinese as "disgusting people."

Newspapers and magazines reported that many white gamblers and prostitutes smoked opium although there was also a fear that the idle rich would take up the habit for lack of anything better to do (Courtwright, 1982). Rumors also abounded that beautiful, innocent, young white girls were seduced into the low life (meaning prostitution) through indoctrination to and subsequent addiction to opium (Courtwright; Latimer & Goldberg, 1981).

Opium smoking was subsequently outlawed in 1908. The net effect was that an otherwise law-abiding group of people who primarily kept to themselves in their own community was now a criminal class. "In an exquisite refinement of cultural sadism, it was decreed by the health department [of San Francisco] that all jail prisoners wearing knotted pigtails must, for sanitary reasons, have said pigtails removed; a sacrilege comparable to shaving a Lubavitcher rabbi" (Latimer & Goldberg, 1981, p. 206).

Not only were the users of opium considered criminals, but a new class of Chinese criminals emerged, those who trafficked in the illegal importation and distribution of opium. As is the case with all illegal drug operations, the Chinese organized crime syndicates engaged in violent competition thus fueling law enforcement and the press with additional material for stories about the Yellow Peril.

Blacks and Cocaine

In 1900, the American Medical Association sought to remove cocaine from the patent medicine industry via federal legislation. They met resistance from southern politicians who saw the passage of a federal narcotics law as yet another intrusion of the federal government into state affairs. Southerners were still sensitive to federal intervention in view of the Civil War and its aftermath. Southerners were particularly concerned that enforcement of the federal narcotics laws, which were enacted for moral purposes rather than procurement of tax dollars, would inevitably lead to the protection of voting rights for blacks (Musto, 1987, p. 55).

In order to overcome anticipated resistance from southern politicians, cocaine use became associated with unruly behavior on the part of southern blacks. The propaganda included reports of cocaine-crazed blacks exhibiting uncontrollable acts of aggression and superhuman sexual prowess, including the rape of white women (Latimer & Goldberg, 1981, pp. 227–228; Musto, 1987, p. 55). An article appearing in the *New York Times Sunday Times* best illustrates the prevailing view of the effect of cocaine on blacks (E.H. Williams, 1914, p. 12).

> *A recent experience of Chief of Police Averly of Asheville, N.C., illustrates this particular phase of cocainism. The Chief was informed that a hitherto inoffensive negro, with whom he was well acquainted, was "running amock" in a cocaine frenzy, had attempted to stab a storekeeper, and was at the moment engaged in "beating up" the various members of his own household....But when he arrived there the negro had completed the beatings and left the place.... The man returned and entered the room where the Chief was waiting for him concealed behind the door. When the unsuspecting negro reached the middle of the room, the officer closed the door to prevent his escape, and informed him quietly that he was under arrest.... The crazed negro drew a long knife, grappled with the officer, and slashed him viciously across the shoulder.*

Knowing that he must kill the man or be killed himself, the Chief drew his revolver, placed the muzzle over the negro's heart, and fired "intending to kill him right quick," as the officer calls it. But the shot did not even stagger the man. And a second shot that pierced the arm and entered the chest had just as little effect in stopping the negro or checking his attack.

Meanwhile the Chief, out of the corner of his eye, saw infuriated negroes rushing toward the cabin from all directions. He had only three cartridges remaining in his gun, and he might need those in a minute to stop the mob. So he saved his ammunition and "finished the man with his club."

Stories such as these, served to perpetuate the fear that blacks presented a clear and present danger to society. Since it was unpalatable for Southerners to accept that an "inferior black" mortal could threaten their safety and security, it was necessary to add the idea of a new drug that prevented bullets from penetrating their bodies, and blacks were accorded superhuman powers. The rest of the country could hardly blame southern law officers for killing these drug-crazed demonic monsters in cold blood.

Marijuana, Blacks, and Mexicans

According to Sloman (1979, p. 29) marijuana was probably brought to the United States by three sources: U.S. sailors who frequented South and Central American ports; the black cavalry stationed along the Mexican border; and Mexicans who worked in the beet fields in the United States. Slaves may have also brought the practice from Africa. During the early 1900s recreational use of marijuana was most prominent among southern blacks and New Orleans and New York jazz musicians as well as other theatrical types.

During the 1920s, a period of economic prosperity, Mexican laborers were brought to the United States to work in the beet fields and in selected factories (Musto). Similar to the Chinese laborers, the Mexicans were hired to perform labor that white workers refused to do. However, it was not until the start of the Great Depression that marijuana smoking and its link to Mexicans became a prominent concern of Americans. The Mexicans became a convenient scapegoat for the eco-

nomic problems facing America. The jobs in the beet fields and factories that whites were previously unwilling to consider began to look good. Public opinion supported sending the Mexicans home because they were taking jobs from whites. This sentiment was fueled by an association with Mexican use of marijuana. Stories began to circulate linking marijuana use with crime and insanity. Claims were made that marijuana caused people to become violently insane and sexually stimulated. Homosexuals were said to be particularly vulnerable to the sexual and violent stimulation of marijuana. Reports of Mexicans giving the drug to white school children also began to surface (Musto). The following quote from a session of a Montana legislative committee summarizes the prevailing attitudes toward Mexicans during this period.

There was fun in the House Health Committee during the week when the Marihuana bill came up for consideration. Marihuana is Mexican opium, a plant used by Mexicans and cultivated for sale by Indians. "When some beet field peon takes a few rares of this stuff," explained Dr. Fred Fulsher of Mineral County, "he thinks he just been elected president of Mexico so he starts out to execute all his political enemies…" Everybody laughed and the bill was recommended for passage. (Montana Standard, 1929, January 27, cited by Sloman, 1979, pp. 30–31.)

Much of the impetus for the beginning of drug regulation then was due to the increasing rates of addiction to narcotics among white Americans as well as the association of minority groups to drug use and subsequent criminal behavior. It is important to note that the forthcoming drug legislation was based on ignorance concerning the effects of drugs.

The Pure Food and Drug Act

Not only were Americans concerned about what was in the drugs they were taking, but as a result of *The Jungle,* an exposé on a Chicago meat packing firm by Upton Sinclair, Americans were becoming interested in government regulation concerning what they ate. The book depicted gruesome stories about tubercular cattle and hogs, as well as human parts, being included in packaged food.

...as for the other men, who worked in tank rooms full of steam, and in some of which there were open vats near the level of the floor, their peculiar trouble was that they fell into the vats; and when they were fished out, there was never enough of them left to be worth exhibiting—sometimes they would be overlooked for days, till all but the bones of them had gone out to the world as Durham's Pure Leaf Lard! (U. Sinclair, 1950, p. 99.)

In 1906, Congress passed the Pure Food and Drug Act requiring all packaged food to carry a label listing its contents. In addition, the law required that all patent medicines containing alcohol, cocaine, cannabis, or any of the opiates including heroin, opium, morphine, and laudanum list the ingredients on the label. However, this law only applied to drugs that were transported across state lines. Following the implementation of the Pure Food and Drug Act, one-third of Americans stopped using patent medicines (Latimer & Goldberg, 1981).

The Harrison Act

One way Americans could bring themselves fame or power was to identify a real or imagined evil, stir everyone up about it, then offer their services as protection from the evil. This strategy was used by J. Edgar Hoover (former director of the Federal Bureau of Investigation), Joseph McCarthy (former United States Senator), and Harry Anslinger (former director of the Federal Bureau of Narcotics).

Campaigns against drugs were also a way to get your name into the society pages. Nancy Reagan was not the first woman of social prominence to chose the repression of drugs as an issue to bring herself personal publicity. In 1912, the public relations firm for the second Mrs. William K. Vanderbilt chose the repression of narcotics as an issue for their client. "...thanks to the bottomless reservoir of Vanderbilt funds, [the public relations firm] launched telegram and letter campaigns to lawmakers in Albany and Washington on the theme that helpless people of the lower classes had to be protected from this 'poison'" (King, 1972, p. 24). The cause was a means of keeping her name in the society pages, and her social status served to influence law makers.

As World War I approached, the belief surfaced that addiction was caused by America's enemies in Europe.

The idea of the oppression of drugs was tied to patriotism (King, 1972). By the end of the war in 1918, drug hysteria ran rampant with reports of school children going to class stoned on heroin (King).

In 1910, Dr. Hamilton Wright, who was employed by the State Department as a "drug adviser" to President William Howard Taft, became instrumental in the passage of the Harrison Act. The United States was interested in opening up trade with China. However, due to the poor treatment of Chinese in the United States, China refused to purchase American goods. At the same time, China was attempting to deal with its own opium problem. Wright began to portray the Chinese as innocent victims of the Arabs who initially introduced opium to the Chinese and then blamed the British for continuing the sale of opium to the Chinese. The United States needed to stop using the American Chinese as scapegoats since they wanted to trade with China. Americans had always deplored the Chinese and their habit of opium smoking, but at the same time the United States wanted to show China its goodwill. Under the guise of helping the Chinese, opium smoking was outlawed, having the secondary effect of creating a new class of Chinese criminals (Latimer & Goldberg, 1981).

In 1914, the Harrison Act (later, often referred to as the Harrison Narcotics Act) was passed, and with it began a new era of governmental control over citizens' lives. This law mandated that all opiates and coca imports be taxed and that doctors and pharmacists who prescribed and sold cocaine or narcotics be registered with the Treasury Department and keep records of their transactions. The purpose of the law was to control the drugs, not to penalize the doctors or the users. The method of acquiring drugs was changed by this law, which was not intended to stop drug use or punish the users or suppliers. Furthermore, the law was not intended to improve public health; rather, it was politically motivated. Physicians, now entirely responsible for opiate-dependent people, were allowed to prescribe narcotics to addicts and treat patients as they saw fit. Ironically, those who supported the Harrison Act opposed liquor prohibition and even Frances Harrison himself, the congressman sponsoring the bill, was labeled as "a notorious congressional drunkard" (Latimer and Goldberg, 1981, p. 230).

Shortly after the passage of the Harrison Act, an article in the *Literary Digest* quoted a member of the Public Health Service as saying this about the new law, "If the law be strictly enforced, and the supply of 'dope,' through other than proper channels, absolutely cut off, the medical practitioner has an opportunity such as he has never before had...." The prevailing belief on the part of the American Medical Association and other health practitioners was that if the medical profession controlled the supply of opiates, then addicts could be treated and cured of their addiction and opiates would be used only in the course of proper medical treatment.

The Harrison Act had an unforeseeable effect on the medical practitioner, one probably not anticipated by the various organizations that endorsed the law. The physician became the target of law enforcers and new restrictions were placed on how they could practice medicine as it pertained to opiate-using patients. When they erred, by monitoring and maintaining addicts or violating other newly made rules, they were routinely investigated, arrested, and convicted. In effect, the Harrison Act of 1914 contributed to the development of the underground drug market. Some physicians felt it necessary (or perhaps lucrative) to dispense these drugs to maintain an addict and were compelled to seek illicit sources to avoid scrutiny. Users were commonly drawn away from a physician's care in an attempt to avoid being scrutinized and resorted to unregulated, illegal markets. Once drug users were forced underground, their associations with the criminal element grew. As a result, instead of simply being labeled as drug addicts, users and suppliers were also considered criminals.

Law enforcement officials felt that the new law was not strict enough. New York's Narcotic Squad was quoted in the New York *Herald* as saying in reference to the state and federal laws:

> *The only criticism of [the new State and Federal laws]...is that they are not more sweeping and more drastic. As these laws stand now only certain of the habit-forming drugs are under the ban. Others just as baneful and far more cheaper in cost are exempt, and the police are powerless to arrest those who have them in their possession.*
>
> *Give us power to arrest every dispenser of all habit-forming drugs as well as those having them in their possession, and we would put such a crimp in the curse here that it could never come back.(Federal aid in the antidrug war, 1915, p. 959.)*

Although law enforcement agencies were not given the legal authority to arrest dispensers and users following the law, they took the power and intimidated doc-

tors. In Cincinnati, in 1916, federal enforcement officers attempted to make a differentiation between curable addicts and noncurable addicts, a distinction best left to a medical professional. Doctors or pharmacists prescribing narcotics to curable addicts could be arrested and sentenced to prison ("Dope-cops" at work, 1916.) On the other hand, in 1919, as a result of the Supreme Court case Webb v. United States, doctors could only prescribe narcotics as a cure with the idea of eliminating the habit by reducing the level of the drugs over a period of time and were not allowed to prescribe to simply maintain habits. Musto (1987) believes this came about because of the fear that many soldiers would be returning from World War I addicted and the government did not want the addiction continued. There were exaggerated claims of more than a million addicts in the United States. Furthermore, as a result of prohibition, some thought that alcohol users would turn to other drugs and increase the narcotic drug use rate; thus, it was argued that stricter law enforcement was needed in order to control this new demand (Drug addicts in America, 1919). By making it illegal to prescribe narcotics to maintain an addiction, the government hoped that it would deter people from substituting narcotics for alcohol. Subsequently, narcotics could not be prescribed to maintain an addict.

As a result of these conflicting messages and subsequent arrests, physicians shied away from treating opiate addicts at all, thereby driving the addicts to seek drugs from the thriving black market. By 1922, the Court ruled in Behrman v. United States that narcotics could not be prescribed by any doctor to any addict. Narcotics could only be prescribed in the course of medical treatment for some condition other than addiction. The role of the Treasury Department expanded from enforcing and collecting the tax to arresting law violators and addicts. Today's doctors also practice medicine under threat and harassment from the Drug Enforcement Administration. Terminal cancer patients are often left to suffer incredible pain until their deaths because doctors whose prescriptions for pain killing narcotics are monitored by the DEA are afraid to prescribe "too much" of the narcotic and cause their terminally ill patients to become "addicted" (Trebach, 1987).

Perhaps as a concession to the drug companies who lost money as a result of the restrictions, additional laws were passed during the 1920s prohibiting the importation of such "finished" products as morphine or heroin or cocaine. Only crude opium and coca leaves could be imported, processed, and sold by American drug companies (J.H. Young, 1961).

By 1929, 75,000 people were arrested for violations of the Harrison Act and 25,000 of those were doctors (Latimer & Goldberg, 1981). In 1928, one-third of federal prisoners (2,529 of 7,138 prisoners) (King, 1972, p. 44) were held because of convictions under the Harrison Act and its subsequent revisions.

Although in Linder v. United States in 1925 the Supreme Court revised the Webb and Behrman rulings to state that doctors could prescribe narcotics to help addicts, Treasury agents continued to intimidate the medical profession by quoting the following from Webb and purposely failing to mention the later rulings.

> *An order purporting to be a prescription issued to an addict or habitual user of narcotics, not in the course of treatment but for the purpose of providing the user with narcotics sufficient to keep him comfortable by maintaining his customary use, is not a prescription within the meaning or intent of the ACT; and the person filling such an order, as well as the person issuing it, may be charged with violation of the law (Webb v. United States, cited by King, 1972, p. 46).*

By 1936, Lawrence Kolb, who headed the treatment component of Lexington Narcotics Farm, influenced the Kentucky legislature to pass a law making narcotic addiction illegal. Dr. Kolb was concerned because treatment for narcotic addiction was voluntary, and his patients were free to leave the institution before Dr. Kolb felt they were cured. Therefore, the penalty associated with the new law was a one year mandatory sentence designed to keep addicts incarcerated for at least six months in order to be cured of their addiction. However, there was no scientific evidence to indicate that those who remained incarcerated were any more cured than those who left (Latimer & Goldberg, 1981). Several other states followed suit by enacting laws specifying that addiction itself was a crime. Not until 1962 did the Supreme Court rule that addiction was not a criminal offense (Lewis & Zinberg, 1964).

In 1919, it was estimated that at least one million Americans used opium and other narcotic drugs and about 100,000 Americans were addicted to narcotic drugs. It would appear that the Harrison Act did little to control drug use and addiction but did much to create a new class of criminal addicts as well as a new market for organized crime.

The U.S. Narcotics Bureau and the Legacy of Harry J. Anslinger

> *Harry Jacob Anslinger, who ran the U.S. Narcotics Bureau for more than three decades, may well stand in our history as one of the most tyrannical oppressors of his fellow citizens ever to be sustained in public office by this republic. Like his counterpart John Edgar Hoover, Anslinger built an impregnable empire within the federal structure by portraying himself to members of Congress…as an indispensable defender against the forces of evil (King, 1972, p. 69).*

In 1930, when then Deputy Commissioner L.G. Nutt of the Treasury Department's Prohibition Bureau was removed after a federal grand jury's accusation that New York agents falsified records by reporting city police arrests as their own as well as the suggestion of corruption between federal agents and illegal drug traffickers, Assistant Commissioner Anslinger was appointed to replace Nutt. Shortly thereafter, the Treasury Department removed drug enforcement from Prohibition and created a separate agency, the Bureau of Narcotics.

Anslinger and the Marijuana Tax Act of 1937

The passage of the Marijuana Tax Act in 1937 best represents the tremendous power and influence of Commissioner Anslinger. In the mid-1930s the Federal Bureau of Narcotics began to report that marijuana was associated with violent crimes such as rape and murder as well as insanity. King (1972) argues that Anslinger used the marijuana issue to gain national attention since J. Edgar Hoover of the FBI was receiving considerable national attention as a result of the FBI's role in the apprehension of the Lindberg baby's kidnapper and encounters with such infamous organized crime characters as John Dillinger.

Passage of the Marijuana Tax Act would extend Anslinger's and the Bureau of Narcotics' power. Lacking any scientific support for his position, Anslinger testified before Congress by relying on sensational tales of murder, mayhem, sexual promiscuity, addiction, insanity, and suicide brought on by the "killer weed." He used racist tactics whenever possible. Also included were reports of school children attending class intoxicated on marijuana. Sloman provides some of the examples used by Anslinger.

> *Two Negros took a girl fourteen years old and kept her for two days in a hut under the influence of marihuana. Upon recovery she was found to be suffering from syphilis (Sloman, 1979, p. 59).*
>
> *An entire family was murdered by a youthful addict in Florida. When officers arrived at the home, they found the youth staggering about in a human slaughterhouse. With an ax he had killed his father, mother, two brothers, and a sister. He seemed to be in a daze....He had no recollection of having committed the multiple crime. The officers knew him ordinarily as a sane, rather quiet young man; now he was pitifully crazed. They sought the reason. The boy said he had been in the habit of smoking something which youthful friends called 'muggles,' a childish name for marihuana (Sloman, 1979, p. 63).*

Stories such as these ensured the easy passage of the Marijuana Tax Act of 1937. Similar to the Harrison Act, the Marijuana Tax Act required that a tax be collected on the manufacture and sale of marijuana in an effort to outlaw the drug. Before this act was passed, it was well known that marijuana had been used for hundreds of years, by otherwise law-abiding citizens, for its medicinal properties, rather than for its mind-altering abilities. In fact, it was rarely used recreationally, other than by some entertainers. As a result of reports that blacks and Mexicans, who were known to use marijuana, became violent due to the drug's effects, and because of the push to deport Mexicans to free up the labor force for more Anglo-Americans to acquire jobs, the Marijuana Tax Act was popular. Marijuana was, at that time, classified as a narcotic, despite the fact that its properties are in no way similar to that of any narcotic drug. Marijuana remains scheduled as a narcotic even today. An interesting academic question that has yet to be answered is whether or not the Marijuana Tax Act, and eventually the criminalization of marijuana, had an effect on its subsequent popularity as a recreational drug. Many experts believe that this law made it impossible to use marijuana for legitimate medical purposes and forced recreational users underground into a criminal subculture (McKim, 1991).

Comprehensive Drug Abuse Prevention and Control Act of 1970

During the tenure of President Richard Nixon, who ran under a platform of "law and order," stringent laws were proposed to tackle the crime problem and wage a "war on drugs" (sound familiar?). There was a prevailing belief that crime was committed primarily by drug users and that drugs directly contributed to the crime problem. The law that was finally enacted, the Comprehensive Drug Abuse Prevention and Control Act of 1970, was formulated, in part, by medical professionals and research scientists. This major piece of legislation resulted in major changes regarding the control of narcotics and other psychoactive drugs. All drugs listed under the act now came under the jurisdiction of the federal government, and law enforcement agencies were no longer empowered to decide which drugs to regulate but now acted simply to enforce the laws.

The manufacture, distribution, and possession of controlled substances were to be directly regulated by this act, rather than through the process of taxation. Enforcement of the new drug laws was changed from the Department of Treasury to the Department of Justice. First-time offenders were treated more leniently and would eventually have their records expunged if they stayed out of trouble, but drug dealers would receive harsher penalties. The 1970 law was considered a more scientific approach to deal with the threat of drug abuse.

Of direct relevance to today's regulation of drug use and possession is that five schedules of drugs were created by this act. Penalties for sale or possession were based on the classification of the specific drug. This schedule is relied upon today by law enforcement and the courts to target particular drugs and their users. It is not based on the pharmacological properties of the drugs (as mentioned in Chapter 1); instead, it is based on vested interests and beliefs of the public and politicians.

Drugs were classified into five schedules with Schedule I drugs being the most serious and Schedule V drugs the least serious. For example, the most stringent penalties for manufacture or possession were associated with Schedule I drugs, which were considered to have high abuse potential, no accepted medical use, and whose production were highly controlled. Heroin, marijuana, THC, LSD, and mescaline are considered Schedule I drugs. Schedule II drugs include morphine, cocaine, methadone, opium, and some barbiturates and amphetamines. These drugs have a high potential for abuse, an accepted medical use,

Table 2.2   *Drug Enforcement Administration Description of Each Schedule for Drug*
Classification

Schedule I
A. The drug or other substance has a high potential for abuse.
B. The drug or other substance has no currently accepted medical use in treatment in the United States.
C. There is a lack of accepted safety for use of the drug or other substance under medical supervision.

Schedule II
A. The drug or other substance has a high potential for abuse.
B. The drug or other substance has a currently accepted medical use in treatment in the United States or a currently accepted medical use with severe restrictions.
C. Abuse of the drug or other substances may lead to severe psychological or physical dependence.

Schedule III
A. The drug or other substance has a potential for abuse less than the drugs or other substances in Schedules I and II.
B. The drug or other substance has a currently accepted medical use in treatment in the United States.
C. Abuse of the drug or other substance may lead to moderate or low physical dependence or high psychological dependence.

Schedule IV
A. The drug or other substance has a low potential for abuse relative to the drugs or other substances in Schedule III.
B. The drug or other substance has a currently accepted medical use in treatment in the United States.
C. Abuse of the drug or other substance may lead to limited physical dependence or psychological dependence relative to the drugs or other substances in Schedule III.

Schedule V
A. The drug or other substance has a low potential for abuse relative to the drugs or other substances in Schedule IV.
B. The drug or other substance has a currently accepted medical use in treatment in the United States.
C. Abuse of the drug or other substance may lead to limited physical dependence or psychological dependence relative to the drugs or other substances in Schedule IV.

and controlled production. Penalties for the manufacture and possession of these drugs are not as serious as for Schedule I drugs. The act also limited the amount of scheduled drugs that a legitimate drug company could produce in an effort to control the amount of drugs funneled to the black market.

Comprehensive Crime Control Act of 1984

When the Comprehensive Crime Control Act of 1984 was signed, it had been almost fourteen since the

enactment of significant federal criminal law reforms. The act contained sections on bail reform, sentencing reform, expanded forfeiture authority, stricter penalties, amendments to assist in the investigation of international money laundering, and miscellaneous amendments pertaining to federal jurisdiction regarding violent crime (U.S. Attorneys, 1989, p. 53). Many of the changes contained in this act were designed to help the federal government apprehend, prosecute, and incarcerate drug dealers and users. In essence, regulations over drug use, possession, and trafficking were tightened and law enforcement remedies were expanded by this act.

Table 2.3   *Federal Trafficking Penalties*   *As of November 18, 1988*

| CSA | PENALTY | | Quantity | DRUG | Quantity | PENALTY | |
	2nd Offense	1st Offense				1st Offense	2nd Offense
I and II	Not less than 10 years. Not more than life. If death or serious injury, not less than life. Fine of not more than $4 million individual, $10 million other than individual.	Not less than 5 years. Not more than 40 years. If death or serious injury, not less than 20 years. Not more than life. Fine of not more than $2 million individual, $5 million other than individual.	10-99 gm or 100-999 gm mixture	**METHAMPHETAMINE**	100 gm or more or 1 kg[1] or more mixture	Not less than 10 years. Not more than life. If death or serious injury, not less than 20 years. Not more than life. Fine of not more than $4 million individual, $10 million other than indidual.	Not less than 20 years. Not more than life. If death or serious injury, not less than life. Fine of not more than $8 million individual, $20 million other than individual.
			100-999 gm mixture	**HEROIN**	1 kg or more mixture		
			500-4,999 gm mixture	**COCAINE**	5 kg or more mixture		
			5-49 gm mixture	**COCAINE BASE**	50 gm or more mixture		
			10-99 gm or 100-999 gm mixture	**PCP**	100 gm or more or 1 kg[1] or more mixture		
			1-10 gm mixture	**LSD**	10 gm or more mixture		
			40-399 gm mixture	**FENTANYL**	400 gm or more mixture		
			10-99 gm mixture	**FENTANYL ANALOGUE**	100 gm or more mixture		

	Drug	Quantity	1st Offense	2nd Offense
	Others[2]	Any	Not more than 20 years. If death or serious injury, not less than 20 years, not more than life. Fine $1 million individual, $5 million not individual.	Not more than 30 years. If death or serious injury, life. Fine $2 million individual, $10 million not individual.
III	All	Any	Not more than 5 years. Fine not more than $250,000 individual, $1 million not individual.	Not more than 10 years. Fine not more than $500,000 individual, $2 million not individual.
IV	All	Any	Not more than 3 years. Fine not more than $250,000 individual, $1 million not individual.	Not more than 6 years. Fine not more than $500,000 individual, $2 million not individual.
V	All	Any	Not more than 1 year. Fine not more than $100,000 individual, $250,000 not individual.	Not more than 2 years. Fine not more than $200,000 individual, $500,000 not individual.

1 Law as originally enacted states 100 gm. Congress requested to make technical correction to 1 kg.   2 Does not include marijuana, hashish, or hash oil. (See separate chart.)

Federal Trafficking Penalties - Marijuana   *As of November 18, 1988*

Quantity	Description	First Offense	Second Offense
1,000 kg or more; or 1,000 or more plants	Marijuana Mixture containing detectable quantity.*	Not less than 10 years, not more than life. If death or serious injury, not less than 20 years, not more than life. Fine not more than $4 million individual, $10 million other than individual.	Not less than 20 years, not more than life. If death or serious injury, not less life. Fine not more than $8 million individual, $20 million other than individual.
100 kg to 1,000 kg; or 100-999 plants	Marijuana Mixture containing detectable quantity.*	Not less than 5 years, not more than 40 years. If death or serious injury, not less than 20 years, not more than life. Fine not more than $2 million individual, $5 million other than individual.	Not less than 10 years, not more than life. If death or serious injury, not less than life. Fine not more than $4 million individual, $10 million other than individual.
50 to 100 kg	Marijuana	Not more than 20 years. If death or serious injury, not less than 20 years, not more than life. Fine $1 million individual, $5 million other than individual.	Not more than 30 years. If death or serious injury, life. Fine $2 million individual, $10 million other than individual.
10 to 100 kg	Hashish		
1 to 100 kg	Hashish Oil		
50 to 99 plants	Marijuana		
Less than 50 kg	Marijuana	Not more than 5 years. Fine not more than $250,000 individual, $1 million other than individual.	Not more than 10 years. Fine $500,000 individual, $2 million other than individual.
Less than 10 kg	Hashish		
Less than 1 kg	Hashish Oil		

* Includes Hashish and Hashish Oil   (Marijuana is a Schedule I Controlled Substance)

Anti-Drug Abuse Act of 1986

On October 27, 1986, President Ronald Reagan signed into law the Anti-Drug Abuse Act of 1986. In addition to considerably enhancing federal, state, and local drug abuse prevention and treatment efforts, this sweeping legislation provided the law enforcement community with significant new resources for its battle against the illicit manufacture, distribution, and consumption of drugs. This act substantially increased penalties in a variety of areas, including setting mandatory minimums for simple possession and doubling penalties for anyone who knowingly involved juveniles in drug activity. Under the drug "kingpin" statute in the act of 1986, the "principal managers/organizers" of drug trafficking organizations can be charged with operating a Continuing Criminal Enterprise (CCE). If convicted, they receive substantial prison sentences (in some cases, mandatory life imprisonment with no possibility of parole). The act also made money laundering a federal crime, strengthened banking regulations to help reveal money laundering, and provided for the forfeiture of laundered monetary instruments. The Anti-Drug Abuse Act of 1986 also established the "schoolyard" law, making it an offense to distribute drugs within 1,000 feet of a school. Other sections of this bill addressed international narcotics control, interdiction, demand reduction, and other aspects of the national war on drugs (U.S. Attorneys, 1989, pp. 53–54). The notion of drug-related activities as synonymous with criminal activity was further reinforced.

Anti-Drug Abuse Act of 1988

The Anti-Drug Abuse Act of 1988 was designed to complement earlier statutes and to provide for an omnibus federal, state, and local effort to combat the illicit importation, distribution, and use of drugs. This far-reaching legislation created a Cabinet-level position of Director of National Drug Control Policy and William Bennett was appointed to fill the position referred to in the media as "Drug Czar." It was Mr. Bennett's job to centralize and streamline federal activities with respect to both drug supply and demand reduction. The act expanded federal support to ensure a long-term commitment of resources and personnel for substance abuse education, treatment, rehabilitation, and enforcement activities (U.S. Attorneys, 1989, p. 54).

The Anti-Drug Abuse Act of 1988 went one step further than the "schoolyard" law within the Act of 1986, adding similar prohibitions regarding areas within 100 feet of playgrounds, parks, youth centers, swimming pools, and video arcades. The minimum sentence for a first offense under this statute is at least one year in prison and the maximum penalty is 40 years in prison. There is no parole in either case.

The Anti-Drug Abuse Act of 1988 reinstated the death penalty to be used by the federal government. Anyone convicted of a drug-related killing or anyone convicted as a "drug kingpin" can now be executed. The last federal execution had occurred in Iowa in 1963.

■ Summary

The human desire to alter consciousness with drugs appears to have a long history. Many cultures tend to approve one mind-altering drug and seek to control the use of other drugs. Since the turn of the century in the United States, the selection process of acceptable versus unacceptable drugs has often been politically motivated. Those in power regulated or outlawed the drugs of choice associated with certain minority groups while maintaining access to their own drugs of choice: alcohol, nicotine, and caffeine.

Since 1984 the federal government has increased efforts to control illegal drugs once again by enacting several pieces of legislation that increase penalties for drug use and trafficking and expand the powers of the government to enforce drug laws. During this same period, drug use has shown some decline in the United States. This trend has been primarily for middle-class youth; in 1993, middle-class use has increased again ever so slightly. Drug use tends to ebb and flow over the years so at this time it is impossible to say whether this is a trend or not. Nevertheless, the use of hallucinogens and marijuana has replaced the use of cocaine and other more dangerous drugs in the middle class, so we still have a great deal to concern ourselves with. In lower-class groups, drug use has not significantly declined. Given that drug laws have a greater impact on minority and lower-class populations (their drug use is more visible and law enforcement efforts are more concentrated in these areas), there is the glaring probability that stricter laws, more stringent law enforcement efforts, and mandatory sentences for drug users and dealers has not been a success in the war against drugs.

CHAPTER 3

Brain Function and Chemistry

Objectives

1. To provide an overview of how the brain and environment interact to produce inappropriate or maladaptive behaviors.

2. To familiarize the reader with the structure and function of the nervous system.

3. To explain in general terms how information travels through the brain and central nervous system.

4. To discuss the impact of social and personal stressors on brain function and behavioral responses.

5. To provide an overview of how drugs of abuse influence brain chemistry to alter behavior.

6. To identify brain sites and chemical processes that are affected by psychoactive drugs.

uman behavior in general, and drug abuse and addiction in particular, are the result of a dynamic interplay between genetic/biological and social/environmental forces. Taking drugs, especially illegal drugs, is a complex human behavior. Information culled from many disciplines helps to explain the reasons for and consequences of their use. For example, the cultural anthropologist examines the cultural context and traditions that influence both the choice of and accepted use of psychoactive substances as well as the societal processes that determine which drugs will be designated as illegal. A cellular biologist offers an understanding of the impact of drugs on the composition and biochemical stability of each cell. Neurophysiologists describe how drugs influence the nervous system and the operations of the brain. A sensation and perception psychologist concentrates on the subjective experience of the drug's effects, thereby helping to define the experiential (the perception of an experience) aspects of drugs and alcohol. A clinical psychologist examines the impact of consuming an abusable substance on the individual's social and family life. At the center of all these viewpoints, tying them inextricably together, lies the interaction between a drug's effects on the brain and body and the context within which a drug is used.

The brain is the physical point at which mind, body, and environmental substances merge and where we experience our internal and external world. Just as the pain of a cut finger is experienced in the central nervous system (CNS), so is cocaine in any form—smoked, injected, or sniffed. Understanding the physical events in the brain is one of the key elements in understanding the nature of substance abuse.

The structure and function of the brain are fundamentally responsible for the reward value of certain drugs thereby playing an important role in the development of drug abuse and addiction. The brain's pleasure and pain centers, as described in this chapter, provide biological rewards for drug use while learning, opportunity, circumstance, and a number of other important socioenvironmental factors reinforce drug-taking behaviors. An environment conducive to drug abuse may produce an addict through the drug's pleasurable effects even though the individual was not genetically predisposed to drug abuse and the brain was originally operating normally. Conversely, some biological disturbance or imbalance in the brain may place an individual at risk for drug abuse behavior even when the environment is not conducive to drug use. As illustrated in Figure 3.1, a greater number of risk factors present in the individual's environment increases the likelihood of drug abuse or other antisocial behaviors.

For example, in Chapter 6, evidence is discussed that genetic factors may play a role in the development of alcoholism; some people appear to have a genetic predisposition to alcohol abuse. Specifically, biochemical and physiological

Figure 3.1   *The Developmental Stages of Maladaptive Behavior*

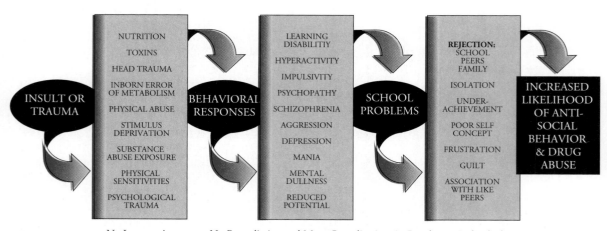

No Intervention ⟶ No Remediation and More Complications in Developing Individuals

conditions that are genetically designed may increase an individual's susceptibility to alcohol abuse by increasing sensitivity to alcohol, thereby enhancing alcohol's reward value, or by changing the metabolism of alcohol, causing an individual to need more to obtain a desirable effect. Whether alcoholism actually develops depends on environmental input: circumstances, opportunities, and learning experiences. Thus, when an individual is genetically at risk for alcoholism in the presence of an environment conducive to its development, there is a greater likelihood that the individual will become alcoholic.

Whether the environment or genetics more significantly influence drug-taking behavior, compulsive drug use is fueled by biological processes. Chemical imbalances in the brain are strong determinants of drug use and, in particular, continued use. The tendency toward compulsive use is partially a function of brain chemistry—both preexisting and resulting from drug use. Initial drug experiences have a profound influence on brain chemistry, which compounds the risk of further use. Some drugs exert such a strong effect that all individuals, whether predisposed to drug abuse or not, may be so reinforced by their effects that it becomes difficult to resist them. "Ultra-potent" drugs, such as crack cocaine and "ice" (crystallized methamphetamine), may substantially alter brain chemistry, increasing the perception of need for the drug or desire to continue using it. As well, learning experiences, the presence of severe life stressors, and the ready availability of drugs in the environment contribute in important ways to drug-taking behaviors.

In order to understand why certain drugs are biologically rewarding and, therefore, have high "abuse potential," it is necessary to present an overview of the structure of the brain and its operation. Mechanisms that are important in altering mood and producing human behavior are described to clarify how drugs of abuse impact on brain function and behavior. Changes in brain function do not only occur on a neurological level but also involve changes in learned behavior that become incorporated into the behavioral patterns of the user.

Basic Anatomy of the Nervous System

Historically, the brain was thought to be an organ strictly of intellect and cold logic. Similar to the heart and kidneys, the brain was believed to perform only functions that kept our bodies alive and permitted us to rationalize.

Following this view of the brain, humans should be rather "like the Spock character from Star Trek," responding only to logic and reason and demonstrating a lack of compassion, attachment, and emotion. Now we know that the brain is the seat of all our feelings, emotions, moods, cravings, and instincts.

If a specific region of the brain is stimulated with an electrical probe, known as "electrical stimulation of the brain" or ESB, the subject will experience feelings of rage, anger, or sadness, and may exhibit behaviors ranging from withdrawal to violence. The specific response depends on the area of brain stimulation. Each area produces an identifiable and consistent response. Memories, as well as the feelings associated with those memories, can also be produced by stimulation of appropriate areas. When a neurologist stimulates brain regions responsible for memories, the patient may, for example, convey sudden memories of the smell of honeysuckle from childhood and the emotions that once surrounded that smell. Because electrical stimulation of the brain is not painful to the individual—there are no pain receptors (nerve endings) in the brain—neurologists have been able to study the effects of ESB on mood and behavior. In fact, it is essential for a patient to remain awake during ESB and during neurosurgery. This way, the patient may describe to the physician any feelings or sensations to ensure that essential areas of the brain are not destroyed during the procedure. Individuals undergoing neurosurgery have provided information about brain function that was previously uncharted territory, so we now have a better understanding of how our brains allow us to experience emotions, memories, and drives that make us uniquely human.

The structure or anatomy of the nervous system provides the blueprint for various functions, while physiological and chemical processes determine which areas of this blueprint will be stimulated to produce a particular effect. The nervous system has two separate parts, each of which is composed of cells called neurons or neural cells. The central nervous system (CNS) houses all nerve cells and neuronal structures (groups of nerve cells functioning in combination) that exist within the skull and spine (see Figure 3.2). The peripheral nervous system refers to those neurons that exist outside the skull and spine. The peripheral nervous system can be further subdivided into the somatic nervous system and the autonomic nervous system. The somatic system consists primarily of sensory and motor nerves. Sensory nerves provide us with our conscious senses, such as sight, touch, and hearing, by connecting nerves from sensory receptors for these senses to

Figure 3.2   *The Central Nervous System*

The situation of the brain and spinal cord within the body (left) and the principal components of the central nervous system (right)

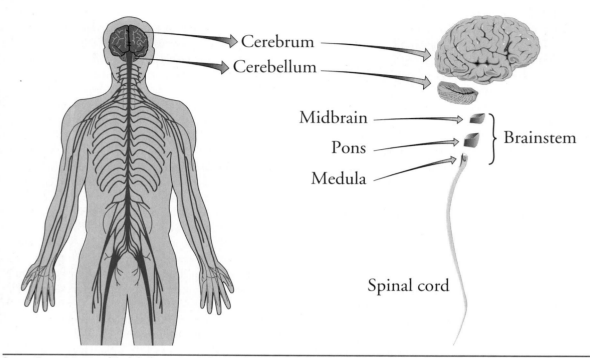

Cerebrum

Cerebellum

Midbrain

Pons

Medula

Brainstem

Spinal cord

the CNS, enabling us to become aware of sensory input. Motor nerves are housed in the spinal cord and send signals to muscle groups to become activated. The autonomic nervous system controls functions that are beyond our conscious control (for most people), including blood pressure, heart and intestinal activity, hormone levels, and other so-called vegetative functions. This part of the peripheral nervous system is discussed at length later in this chapter, under the subheading Endocrinology: The Body's Chemical Network, due to its importance in individual vulnerabilities to drug abuse.

The CNS may be further subdivided into two parts: the brain and the spinal cord. The human brain weighs approximately 3 pounds and contains billions of neurons entirely within the confines of the skull. A pragmatic design of the brain was presented by MacLean (1976) that described the brain as having three primary components: the brainstem, the limbic system, and the cortex (see Figure 3.3). Although we now know that the brain cannot be so simplistically depicted, these three categories still provide an instructive starting point for examining the operation of the brain.

Brainstem

The lowest part of the brain, called the brainstem, is attached to the top of the spinal cord. When information from the environment is received by the peripheral nervous system and relayed to the spinal cord, it must pass through the brainstem before entering higher centers of the brain, referred to as the cerebrum. Thus, all communication between the cerebrum and spinal cord is transmitted via the brainstem (see Figure 3.4).

The brainstem is responsible for physical survival; it controls breathing, heart rate, blood pressure, smooth

Figure 3.3   *The Triune Brain Model*

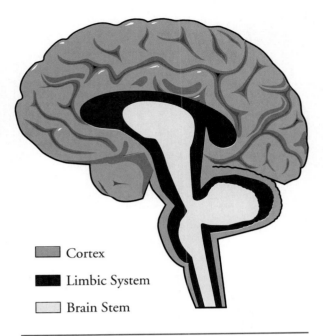

Cortex

Limbic System

Brain Stem

Source: Adapted from Dean MacLean's Model

muscle movement, and other activities that keep us alive without our conscious control. Because it regulates such fundamental, vital activities and is also present in reptiles, it has been called the "reptilian brain." All reptiles and animals have a brainstem; however, many do not have much above it. Reflexive and instinctual behaviors guide them, and they live without emotions, intellect, and other behaviors that become possible with additional brain tissue. One of the brainstem's functions in humans, perception of nonverbal communication, has its roots in more primitive species. These nonverbal functions establish the foundations for routine and ritualistic behaviors that all species perform, such as those associated with mating. When the brainstem is electrically stimulated, reflexive and instinctual behaviors will be displayed, such as the startle reflex.

Extensive damage to the brainstem generally causes death. In contrast, extensive damage to other parts of the brain, such as the limbic or cortical portions, may result in a loss of specific functions or abilities but certainly not death. In fact, when other areas of the brain have experi-

enced significant trauma, an intact brainstem will allow an individual to remain alive without life support systems. One can readily observe the importance of additional brain tissue in humans during a tour of a trauma center. Many patients, frequently the victims of drunk driving accidents, suffer from extensive damage to the higher brain centers that made them uniquely human, leaving only the brainstem intact. These individuals demonstrate no evidence of consciousness, rock back and forth, exhibit reflexive responses, and cannot respond to their environments. Injuries that affect the brainstem may result in paralysis, muscular diseases, and sudden infant death (Harmony, 1984).

An intricate network of cells and fibers extending upward from the core of the brainstem into higher centers is called the reticular activating system or RAS. It is believed that the RAS regulates sleeping and waking cycles and alerts the individual to incoming stimuli. The RAS serves as a sentry or early warning system that increases arousal levels when stimulated. If, for instance, you are sitting in a classroom, concentrating hard on the lecture materials, and the fire alarm goes off, your RAS comes to life. It allows the transmission of information that something novel is present and requires a response. If, however, the professor indicates that it is a false alarm and continues with the class, you will eventually tune out the sound of the alarm and once again concentrate on the lecture. The RAS has now habituated or adjusted to the sound and no longer sees the need to bore the brain with repeated messages of the alarm's sound. Once you have habituated to a stimulus, a response by the brain may no longer be necessary and the RAS will cease firing, reducing arousal levels.

Drugs, such as barbiturates, that depress the RAS, inhibit its activity and reduce the level of arousal, causing users to be relatively unaware of their surroundings. Stimulant drugs, such as amphetamines, act on the brainstem by stimulating the RAS, thereby increasing wakefulness and permitting the individual to engage in various behavioral activities.

Overall, significant drug effects on the brainstem are largely depressant in that they reduce the state of arousal of these vital centers. In particular, opiates and barbiturates produce this depressant effect and can be fatal if the doses are large enough to cause complete shutdown. Other drugs with stimulant properties are more apt to increase arousal levels of the RAS. The brainstem is also profoundly influenced by those psychoactive drugs that affect the subjective mood state or behavior of an individual.

Figure 3.4

Two Views of the Human Brainstem

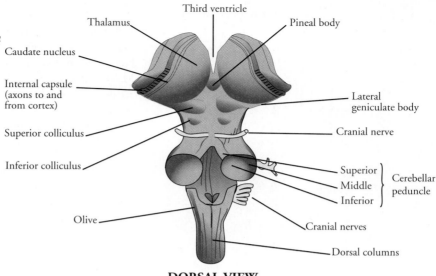

DORSAL VIEW

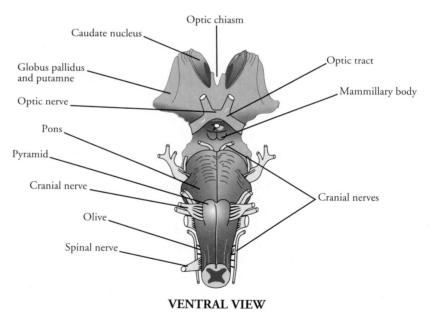

VENTRAL VIEW

Source: Adapted with permission from McGraw-Hill Book Company

Limbic System

Located above the brainstem is the limbic system. This primitive area of the brain is composed of many different structures that, in general, motivate us to respond to our environment and increase our chances of successful survival. Specifically, moods, hunger, thirst, reproductive and sexual behaviors, anger and aggression, memories, and many other feeling states that lead to survival-related behaviors are regulated by this region. (This system, by the way, is probably what Spock lacks.) Disturbances that involve this system, such as epilepsy, hormone imbalances, or low blood sugar, have been associated with affective disorders (depression), violence, sleep problems, memory lapses, sexual disorders, and other so-called mental disturbances (see Restak, 1984 or Snyder, 1980 for reviews).

Unfortunately, this emotional center of the brain is highly vulnerable to chemical and physical trauma that can result in psychiatric and/or behavioral disorders. Often it is difficult to determine whether the presence of behavioral or psychological symptoms actually disguise a biological malfunction. This difficulty can result in a failure to reach an accurate diagnosis concerning the cause of the problem. For example, individuals with limbic system abnormalities are all too often treated by nonmedical professionals who are trained to respond to the behavioral and psychological symptoms with counseling and who fail to identify possible neurological contributions to the disorder. An individual suffering from temporal lobe epilepsy, a condition resulting from electrical instability or a lesion within the limbic system, frequently manifests

inappropriate aggressive, sexual, or other excessive behaviors. These symptoms are often misdiagnosed as "psychological" rather than "neurological," and the condition remains untreated.

Several structures in the limbic system play a crucial role in the regulation of behavior and, in large part, are involved in a drug's rewarding effects (see Figure 3.5). Specific areas of the brain influence the operation of limbic structures. The specific operation depends upon which chemicals in the brain are most active and whether their effects are primarily excitatory or inhibitory. If a limbic structure that is essentially excitatory is activated by certain chemicals, activity of that limbic structure will increase and, generally, so will the individual's behavior. If an inhibitory structure is activated, neural and behavioral activity generally decreases. Similarly, drugs of abuse are essentially excitatory or inhibitory and selectively influ-

Figure 3.5   *A Cross Section of the Brain*

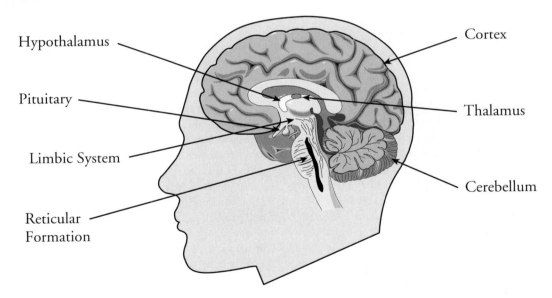

A cross section of the brain referring to several structures responsible for behavior, emotions, and intellect. The cortex represents the layer of neurons (brain cells) on the surface of the brain responsible for language, forethought, mathematics, and other higher intellectual functions. The cerebellum coordinates movement. The reticular formation arouses or alerts the individual to incoming stimuli from the environment. The thalamus relays sensory information and also involves attention and arousal. The hypothalamus acts to control eating, drinking, temperature, and other regulatory and behavioral functions. Finally, the pituitary is the "master" gland that interacts with the hypothalamus to regulate reproduction, tissue growth, temperature, water balance, and other body and behavioral activities. (from Teyler, 1975.)

ence brain regions responsive to the specific drug in question. The notions of excitability and inhibition are important to remember in developing an understanding of the various effects drugs can produce by their action on brain structures.

The thalamus, located centrally in the brain, provides a functional connection between the brainstem and the limbic system via the RAS. The thalamus relays information it receives from the brainstem, and the RAS in particular, to higher centers of the brain. It transmits sensory information to the cortex (central portion of the brain where sensory information is interpreted) and integrates incoming information to areas of the cortex involved in interpreting sensory stimuli. Basically, the thalamus receives RAS messages and makes the final determination of whether the information received is important enough to send up to the cortex for conscious inspection.

The hypothalamus, involved in limbic system function, is responsible for numerous vital functions that are necessary for survival. It controls hunger, thirst, temperature, sexual behavior and reproduction, and sleeping and waking cycles. The hypothalamus also controls the master gland, the pituitary. This gland sits at the base of the brain and releases a variety of sex, stress, and glucose metabolic hormones.

There are both excitatory and inhibitory areas of the hypothalamus that are specifically involved in the regulation of moods and behaviors. Due to the potential of the hypothalamus to elevate mood and modify behavior, the hypothalamus is particularly sensitive to several drug effects, both desirable and undesirable. Thus, stimulation of this structure may produce either approach or avoidance behaviors, as they are called by learning theorists. Individuals will either approach or avoid a stimulus depending on whether it produces an experience of pleasure or pain. Located within the limbic system is the pleasure and pain center that generates these sensations, thereby motivating an individual to avoid pain and approach pleasure. The hypothalamus, in conjunction with other centers in the brain, plays a crucial role in the activity of this pain and pleasure center.

Each psychoactive drug has multiple effects, both pleasant and unpleasant. Drugs with abuse potential (defined in Chapter 4) generally produce unpleasant effects that are initially weaker than those that are pleasurable and desired. When the drug stimulates areas of the pain and pleasure center, pleasurable effects usually overwhelm those that are unpleasant and the individual will approach or continue to self-administer the drug. Due to

the overwhelming pleasurable effects of cocaine, for example, some users will seek the drug and self-administer it for unlimited periods of time. If a drug stimulates areas that produce an overwhelming unpleasant effect (i.e., dysphoria or depression), the individual is likely to avoid self-administration of that drug. Nevertheless, even when a drug produces mostly pleasure, repeated use or overuse will eventually exhaust or deteriorate functions of the brain responsible for the pleasurable effects. At this point, unpleasant effects predominate and the individual may continue to use the drug simply to avoid the pain of withdrawal. In other words, people do not abuse drugs merely because the drugs' effects feel good. People begin to use drugs for their pleasurable effects. They continue to use them because, when they try to stop, they feel so bad: physically, emotionally, and spiritually. Thus, the way in which people respond to drugs is a function of the various effects of the drugs and the stage of their drug usage.

Normally, our behavior is reinforced on a biological basis by satisfying predetermined biological needs, such as hunger, thirst, sex, or sleep. However, electrical stimulation of the brain (ESB) provides an excellent illustration of how the pain and pleasure centers may be influenced by drugs of abuse to influence behavior. ESB that stimulates reward areas of the hypothalamus will cause an individual to continue behaviors leading to self-stimulation. Individuals continue to pursue the desirable effects, even when the pleasure experienced from this type of ESB causes them to ignore other essential biological needs. The only form of biological reward other than ESB that increases such extreme approach behaviors at the expense of other biological needs is the use of certain psychoactive drugs. Cocaine, for example, stimulates pleasure centers and may cause the user to chronically self-administer the drug while neglecting biological needs and causing physical, psychological, and social harm. Thus, obtaining a pleasurable drug effect (or ESB) replaces natural primary drives and may overwhelm better judgment.

The effects of ESB on feelings and behavior provide insight into how drugs affect feelings and behavior. ESB in portions of the hypothalamus outside of the pleasure center will produce extreme displays of rage, attack behavior, fear, or withdrawal. Chemicals in the brain that influence areas of the limbic system, such as the hypothalamus, appear to be responsible for the fight/flight/fright mechanism that motivates these reactions. The activation of this mechanism, as discussed later in this chapter, produces subjective feelings of anxiety, pain, and stress—all states that are preferably avoided.

Additional limbic structures and other regions that directly interact with the limbic system include the septum, amygdala, hippocampus, nucleus accumbens, locus ceruleus, medial forebrain bundle, basal ganglia, ventral tegmentum, and substantia nigra. Each area controls a variety of functions, and several of these structures comprise the reward system, thereby playing a major role in motivating organisms to behave in ways that will ensure their survival.

The septum is primarily involved in neural inhibition, behavioral suppression, and the experience of pleasure. When areas of this structure are stimulated electrically, the animal becomes passive, withdrawn, and may experience feelings of pleasure that are quite rewarding. Some animals so love having their septum stimulated that they forego other activities and ignore drives, such as eating, drinking, grooming, and mating to pursue septal stimulation. The amygdala is excitatory and may produce feelings of arousal, pain, and anxiety. It is associated with aggression and defensive behaviors. When certain areas of the amygdala are stimulated, the animal may display sham rage; behaviors and feeling states associated with anger, aggression, and pain are demonstrated, even in the absence of any provocation or external threat. Thus, a mouse receiving stimulation to these regions of the amygdala may attack a much larger animal, including a cat or even the researcher, without thinking twice about the consequences.

The hippocampus is primarily excitatory and is involved in memory processes and spatial awareness. Conversion of short-term information into long-term memory stores is believed to take place primarily in the hippocampus, while other regions of this structure are responsible for various feeling states. Damage to the hippocampus may result in the inability to retain new memories, even though old memories will still be intact. Recent evidence indicates that marijuana alters the ability of the hippocampus to retain memories.

The nucleus accumbens is a reward area deep within the limbic system that is rich in chemicals that, when stimulated, induce feelings of profound pleasure. Destruction of this structure in animals results in the elimination, or at least the reduction, of the reinforcing effects of commonly abused drugs. Activity within the locus ceruleus regulates sleep and arousal cycles. The medial forebrain bundle, which connects the hypothalamus with midbrain structures, plays a role in relaying positive reinforcement messages toward the forebrain and a portion of the brainstem. The basal ganglia (including

several structures) are concerned with motor control and emotional behavior. The substantia nigra is composed of a plate of nerve cells that extend from the tegmentum to the hypothalamus.

All of these limbic structures, and those they interface with that possess reward value and have a motivating influence, are responsible for the self-administration of electrical stimulation and of addictive drugs. The original purpose of many of these areas is to regulate the activities of eating, drinking, and sexual responsivity, behaviors that are essential to the preservation of the organism and, ultimately, the species. Discoveries that certain drugs stimulate these regions with more intensity and in a more concentrated fashion are, in part, responsible for the tendency to replace natural, primary drives with drugs of abuse. Pleasure centers were designed to ensure our survival; once exposed to more intense stimulation than can be achieved through natural means, pursuit of the drug may become, in and of itself, a primary drive.

In general, when the limbic system has been damaged, one of two outcomes is possible: inhibition or excitation of function. If the effects on the limbic system are inhibitory, the system is considered to be hypofunctioning. Reactions to environmental stimuli may be slowed or delayed. Drugs that depress the activity of the limbic system without depressing other brain regions may tranquilize or relax individuals so that they do not feel anxiety. This effect is typical of Valium or other tranquilizers and anxiety-reducing agents. If the effects on the limbic system are generally excitatory then it is said to be hyperfunctioning. Amphetamines and cocaine increase excitation in the brain, and users frequently display irritability, agitation, mania, hyperactivity, drastic mood fluctuations, or unusual elation.

The effects of damage to or a disturbance of the limbic system are usually limited to those behaviors and physical processes that are specifically controlled by this system. When disturbances of the limbic system are present, it is possible that higher intellectual functions may not be noticeably disturbed. Behavior appears to be well thought out and under the control of the individual when in actuality it is strongly influenced by limbic system dysfunction. Some examples might be depression or unprovoked and uncontrollable aggression. Such underlying and often hidden causes of antisocial behavior often confound the determination of criminal defendants' responsibility for their behavior. Defendants' behavior is perceived to be rational and premeditated in the absence of observable signs of a mitigating condition. In reality, individuals with limbic system disturbances—due to damage, instability, or drug use—are frequently overwhelmed by emotional urges generated by the pleasure center and are not sufficiently inhibited by the more rational cortex. This scenario also applies to drug abuse, as psychoactive drugs hyperstimulate the limbic system, overwhelming signals from the cortex to be more rational and inhibited.

Cortex

The cortex rests above the limbic system and is highly developed in humans. A common notion is that the more cortex present in a species, the more the animal is capable of complex intellectual functions. The cortex takes up about two-thirds of the human brain and is considered more sophisticated than in any other animal. This structure is responsible for higher intellectual functioning, such as problem solving, logic, forethought, insight, information processing, and decision making. Electrical stimulation or drugs of abuse may also generate feelings of pleasure and reward in various areas of the cortex. These regions tend to have connections with reward structures of the limbic system. There are four lobes of the cortex: frontal, temporal, parietal, and occipital as depicted in Figure 3.6. Each area is responsible for separate but overlapping activities.

There are also two hemispheres of the cortex that are believed to possess primary duties but can take over the duties of the other if necessary. The right hemisphere is primarily involved in creative, intuitive, and spatial abilities and has recently been thought to be the center of negative

Figure 3.6   *The Four Lobes of the Right Hemisphere of the Cortex*

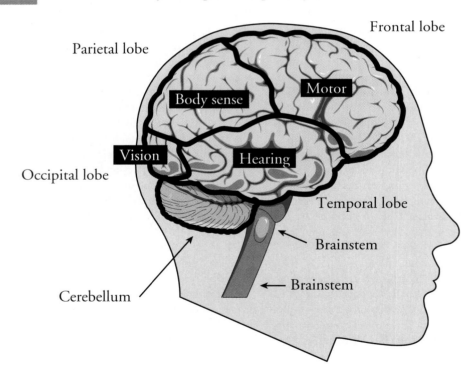

The frontal lobes are primarily responsible for goal-directed behavior and complex behavioral sequencing. The temporal lobes are involved in auditory perception, temporal sequencing, memory, and emotions. The central regions (not shown here) are responsible for skilled and gross motor movements. And the parietal-occipital regions are involved in visual perception, language, and abstract information processing. (From Teyler, 1975)

Figure 3.7

The Dual Brain: Right and Left Hemisphere Talents

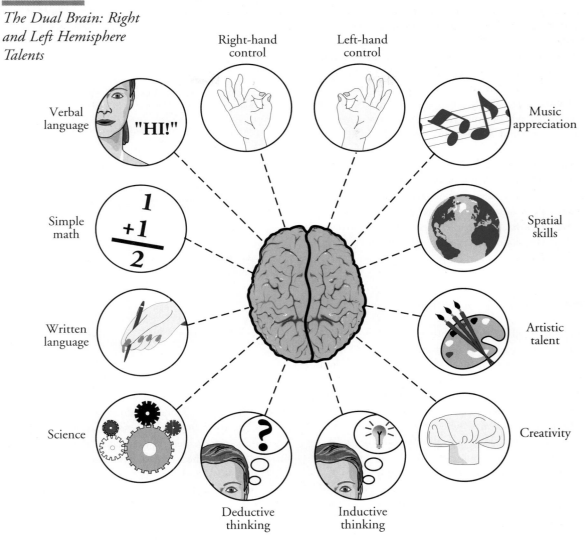

emotional experiences. The left hemisphere is essential in analytical, verbal, and sequential thinking (see Figure 3.7).

It is further believed that the left hemisphere is the center of positive emotional experiences. Thus, it has been asserted that activation of the left hemisphere produces pleasurable, uplifting sensations, while right hemisphere activity produces dysphoric, depressing feelings. We do not know, at present, if some drugs influence one hemisphere more than the other to produce a more positive or negative effect, but this possibility has been suggested.

Individuals who suffer from a disturbance within the cortex, depending on the region affected, may experience language disorders, impulsivity, reading or comprehension difficulties, and a variety of other cognitive or intellectual impairments. Many individuals with conduct disorders, antisocial behavior, hyperactivity, and other traits that place an individual at risk for delinquency or criminal behavior and drug abuse are believed to suffer from defects in the cortex, particularly within the frontal lobes (Hare, 1984; Luria, 1973; Nauta, 1971; Yeudall,

Fedora, & Fromm, 1985). Cortical deficits may stem from either environmental (i.e., head trauma), biological, or genetic causes, and include poor impulse control, problems anticipating consequences of one's actions, language difficulties, attention deficits, and irrationality. Because the cortex is primarily involved in learned behaviors, it is this region that is responsible for conditioned responses to drugs of abuse. Accordingly, when an individual begins to associate pleasurable or otherwise desirable effects from a drug, the cortex registers this association and initiates and maintains a pattern of behaviors that revolve around the use of the drug. The cortex, then, is at work when a smoker desires a cigarette while on the phone or after sex, when a cocaine user craves cocaine after seeing a dollar bill or a drug-taking peer, or when an opiate addict seeks heroin after watching a friend use a syringe. These are strictly learned behaviors based on conditioned responses that the cortex modulates.

Basic Brain Chemistry

The function of all these brain structures and regions are largely dependent upon brain chemicals. In fact, all brain activity is due to electrochemical impulses that are elicited by both bodily processes—including brain chemicals—and environmental stimuli. Numerous chemicals are present throughout the brain and body. Their precise physiological role is a function of where they are concentrated and what structures they are stimulating. Thus, the integrity of overall brain function is largely dependent on the presence and adequate supply of certain chemicals. Several different systems are responsible for producing and activating bodily chemicals, each having separate but interacting functions.

Endocrinology: The Body's Chemical Network

Endocrinology is the study of bodily glands that secrete hormones into the bloodstream to exert an effect either on an organ system or other glands in the body. Major endocrine glands include the pituitary, adrenal, thyroid, and pancreas (see Figure 3.8). The hypothalamus mentioned earlier is also considered a gland due to its direct chemical influence on the endocrine system, in particular, on the pituitary gland. The pituitary is the master gland as it regulates the function of the thyroid, pancreas, and

Figure 3.8   *The Endocrine System*

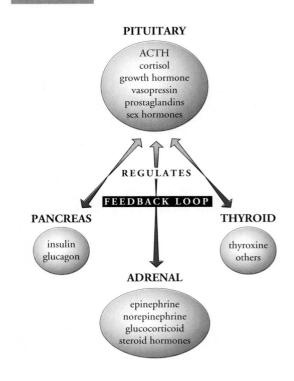

adrenal glands. Hormones produced by the pituitary are primarily those that regulate sex and reproduction, fluid regulation, growth, metabolic rate, and those released under stressful circumstances to influence coping responses.

The adrenal gland is located directly above the kidneys. It consists of a cortex and a medulla that releases adrenalin (or epinephrine) and noradrenalin (or norepinephrine). The adrenal cortex is a source of several hormones that are responsible for carbohydrate and protein metabolism and the balance of the acid/base characteristics of body cell fluids. Cortisol, a hormone that is released during periods of stress, is also produced by the adrenal cortex.

Adrenal hormones contribute to increased heart rate and blood pressure and feelings of anxiety, energy, stress, and aggression. The adrenal gland is responsible for the activation of the fight/flight/fright (f/f/f) mechanism. When an individual experiences a stressor in the environment, such as an attack or the loss of a spouse, the f/f/f mechanism is triggered by the hypothalamus, which organizes a response to a perceived crisis and sends messages to the pituitary, which, in turn, activates the adrenal gland. The adrenal gland enters a crisis mode by secreting large amounts of such stress hormones as adrenalin and cortisol. Ideally, this chain reaction improves an individual's ability to effectively respond to a stressor by calculating a path of least resistance, that is, to fight back or flee the situation. The emotional response is a feeling of fear to motivate one to quickly decide a course of action. Unfortunately, some individuals are subjected to continual stressors, and the stress response becomes overstimulated. With prolonged exposure to stressors, the f/f/f mechanism may break down.

The following scenario describes the biochemistry of this stress mechanism (see Figure 3.9). Assume an unarmed

Figure 3.9   *The Biochemistry of Stress*

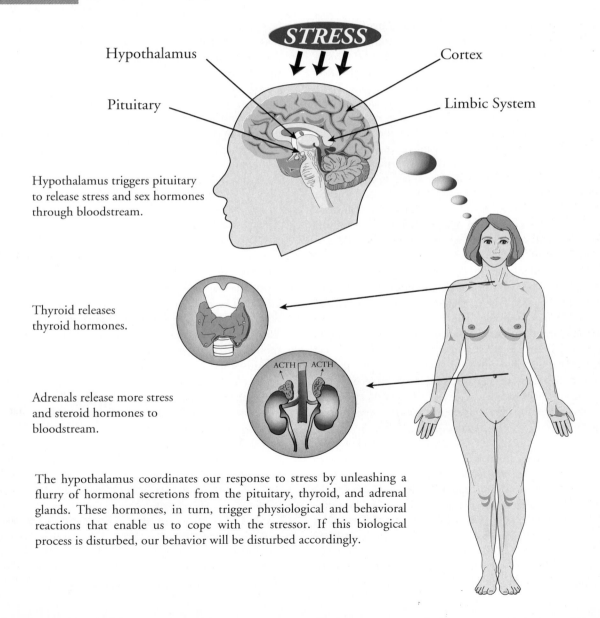

STRESS

Hypothalamus

Cortex

Pituitary

Limbic System

Hypothalamus triggers pituitary to release stress and sex hormones through bloodstream.

Thyroid releases thyroid hormones.

ACTH   ACTH

Adrenals release more stress and steroid hormones to bloodstream.

The hypothalamus coordinates our response to stress by unleashing a flurry of hormonal secretions from the pituitary, thyroid, and adrenal glands. These hormones, in turn, trigger physiological and behavioral reactions that enable us to cope with the stressor. If this biological process is disturbed, our behavior will be disturbed accordingly.

man enters a dark alley and notices a man with a weapon has followed him into the alley. During an acutely stressful event such as this, the initial CNS response is from the cortex. *Perception* of the stressor is achieved when the unarmed man's cortex has a cognitive awareness of the suspicious man. His cortex consciously *remembers* the dangerous nature of the situation and is the locus of his reasoning the best plan of action: fight or flight. The unarmed man's cortical functions will then *initiate* the necessary motor movement in the brainstem to act on this plan.

The limbic system is also activated and leads the individual in danger to experience *fear*. This emotion is necessary to evoke a sense of urgency for an immediate response. At this time the hypothalamus and endocrine system are stimulated into action to have a direct impact on hormonal pathways to a part of the peripheral nervous system called the autonomic nervous system (ANS)(see Figure 3.10). This system may be best remembered as an automatic nervous system as it is not normally under our conscious control and regulates vital functions and motor responses. A chain reaction of defenses is organized and triggers the activity of the ANS and the endocrine glands. The hypothalamus releases polypeptide hormones that signal the pituitary gland to produce ACTH, a stress hormone. Activation of the brainstem occurs almost simultaneously to alter motor activity and basic body functions, and the adrenal glands secrete noradrenalin, adrenalin, cortisol, and other hormones.

The physiological results of this dynamic process include an increase in heart rate and blood pressure, dilation of pupils (to allow more light into the eyes), relaxation of bronchial tubes (to obtain more oxygen), increase in blood glucose (for energy), slowing of digestion (to avoid interference with more vital functions), and a shift in blood supply to internal organs (for strength). These responses provide the person being pursued with the energy and wherewithal to fight back or get away. Absent these responses, the individual would lack the motivation, strength, energy, and resources to cope with a predator.

During this period of stress, people have been known to perform unusual feats of strength and endurance due to these dramatic physiological changes. Mothers have been known to lift cars to free trapped children. Normally, the strength needed to lift a car is absent, but under the influence of surges in our adrenal hormones, such strength becomes possible. The hallucinogen, phencyclidine (PCP), similarly activates this stress mechanism and users frequently demonstrate remarkable strength under unusual circumstances. In combination with the absence of pain

perception, PCP users may display extreme aggression. On a psychological and behavioral level, this process not only heightens our awareness and attention but it also causes us to feel fearful and stressed out.

The above sequence of physiological responses occur when the individual is normal and healthy. Such responses are generally specific to an acute, or temporary, stressful challenge. Frequently, however, stress may be chronic, and this process may malfunction. In the presence of several, severe stressors (e.g., death of a loved one, loss of a job, serious injury), it is possible that the stress mechanism may become exhausted and fail to produce sufficient amounts of hormones required to continually cope. Resistance to infections is lowered, glucose metabolism may break down decreasing the ability to absorb nutrients (and thus gain strength from food), the risk of heart disease increases, and behavioral problems may result from biochemical imbalances (e.g., manifest depression). As a result of this disruption in normal activities, stressful events frequently lead to the onset of psychiatric disorders to which the sufferer may be susceptible. Any drug that directly influences the limbic f/f/f response has the same potential to elicit various psychiatric disorders, depending upon the susceptiblity.

The Role of Learning

Some behavior is explained by biochemical and physiological responses to external compounds and environmental events that may lie beyond our control. It is also true that the individual learns to respond to environmental events so as to maximize the positive experiences (pleasure, good feelings, relief from a bad situation) and minimize the bad experiences (advent of pain, removal of pleasure). Obviously, stressful situations are painful for most people, and we attempt to avoid them. When a behavior results in the painful consequences of a stressful situation, the f/f/f system is activated. Most of us will be deterred from exhibiting that behavior in the future in order to minimize the possible negative consequences of the behavior. We feel anxiety due to the activation of the f/f/f mechanism when the threat of a negative consequence exists because of the learned association between the behavior and its likely result. This process of learning is called operant conditioning.

Most of us have learned that stealing is wrong. If we contemplate that behavior, it acts as a stressor by triggering the f/f/f mechanism, creating anxiety, and we are effectively deterred. On the other hand, when a specific stimulus is associated with a positive consequence involv-

Figure 3.10 *Sympathetic and Parasympathetic Divisions of the Autonomic Nervous System and the Target Organs It Serves.*

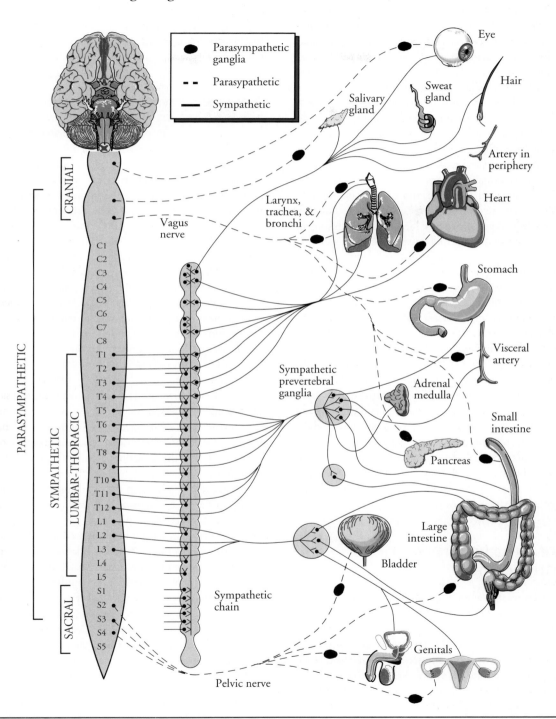

ing our behavior, we respond to maximize the positive consequence by repeating the behavior. When we experience a pleasurable consequence, as discussed previously with respect to ESB and drugs of abuse, we are conditioned to repeat the performance to elicit a positive result. For example, the person trying to quit smoking has drinks with friends, some of whom are smoking. This individual, like many other smokers, has always enjoyed sitting at a table smoking and drinking. Consequently, the person is very tempted to light a cigarette and is quite likely to do so. The circumstances, the presence of friends, alcoholic drinks and their effects, and secondary smoke from others are all stimuli associated with the pleasures of smoking.

No two individuals are born with identically functioning nervous systems. Therefore, the learning of behavior, the ability to be reinforced by pleasurable consequences, and the ability to be deterred by the threat of punishment occurs differently among individuals. For example, psychopaths (sometimes used interchangeably with the term *antisocial personality disorder*, ASP) are poor at emotional relationships, impulsive, immature, thrill seeking, and unable to learn through punishment. They have also been characterized as having low levels of perceptible anxiety and physiological responses during stressful events (Hare & Schalling, 1978; House & Milligan, 1976; Syndulko et al., 1975; Venables, 1987; Yeudall et al., 1985). Theoretically, psychopaths do not experience the discomfort of anxiety associated with a prohibited behavior because they have an underaroused autonomic nervous system and thus, are not easily deterred. As we will see later in this book, individuals identified as psychopathic or diagnosed with antisocial personality disorder are more prone to drug abuse because of their sensation-seeking behavior and their relative lack of anxiety. For them, there is little motivation *not* to misbehave, commit crimes, or use drugs.

Neurotransmitters and Neuropeptides

In addition to the endocrine system of hormones, other chemicals in the brain are neurotransmitters and neuropeptides (a few of which are referred to as opiate-like transmitters). Similar to the structures and hormones mentioned above, each transmitter serves different, albeit overlapping, functions. They are directly responsible for learning and many behaviors, emotions and moods. These chemical systems are the basis of all thinking and control bodily functions. Figure 3.11 depicts the func-

tional networks in specific brain regions that neurotransmitters operate from.

The mechanism of action by which transmitters and peptides transfer information in the brain establishes the foundation for drug effects on the brain—the basis of pharmacology.

Synaptic Transmission

Neurons in the brain number approximately twenty billion. The typical neuron consists of the following structures: The soma is the cell body, including the nucleus of the cell. Dendrites extend from the soma in the form of several branches to receive and respond to electrical activity of other neurons. The axon also extends from the soma to transmit electrical activity from the soma to other neurons, muscles, or glands. When an electrical impulse is conducted from the soma down the axon, it will reach the synapse which is the gap between cell bodies. The signal from the neuron is received by a receptor site on the dendrite of the neighboring neuron. The inset illustrates how neurotransmitters permit neurons to communicate.

Neurons are turned on and off by transmitters that act at the synapse to send signals from one neuron to another, allowing brain cells to communicate with each other. Some transmitters exert excitatory influences on the synapse and others produce inhibitory potentials, thus establishing a balanced system. When an action potential travels down an axon, specific transmitters are released from the axon into the synapse. These transmitters alter receptor sites on the dendrite's membrane of the adjacent neuron by exciting or inhibiting its activity. A new impulse, then, originates in the dendrite and is integrated by the soma to be transmitted down the axon to the synapse as another action potential.

Once a transmitter has been released into the synapse, postsynaptic receptor sites on the adjacent cell are stimulated and the transmitter is released back into the synapse. Some are metabolized, and the remainder are reabsorbed into the presynaptic nerve terminal. Each transmitter acts on the postsynaptic receptor in the same way that a key fits into a lock; specific receptors receive only those transmitters that fit that site. Thus, the requirement that transmitters can only exert an effect on a receptor site that is structurally compatible has been referred to as the lock and key mechanism.

Very few psychoactive drugs influence the axon. Anesthetics are the exception as they block the axons carry-

Figure 3.11a

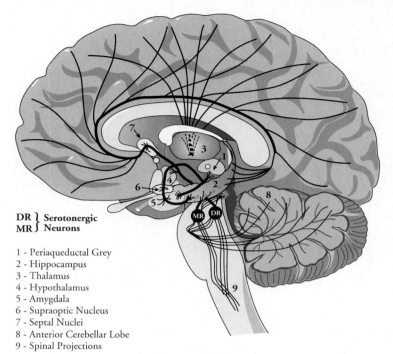

DR ⎫ Serotonergic
MR ⎭ Neurons

1 - Periaqueductal Grey
2 - Hippocampus
3 - Thalamus
4 - Hypothalamus
5 - Amygdala
6 - Supraoptic Nucleus
7 - Septal Nuclei
8 - Anterior Cerebellar Lobe
9 - Spinal Projections

Source: Valzelli, Raven Press, 1981

Figure 3.11b

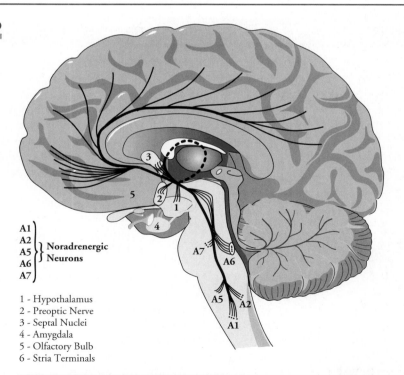

A1 ⎫
A2 ⎪
A5 ⎬ Noradrenergic
A6 ⎪ Neurons
A7 ⎭

1 - Hypothalamus
2 - Preoptic Nerve
3 - Septal Nuclei
4 - Amygdala
5 - Olfactory Bulb
6 - Stria Terminals

Source: Valzelli, Raven Press, 1981

Figure 3.11c

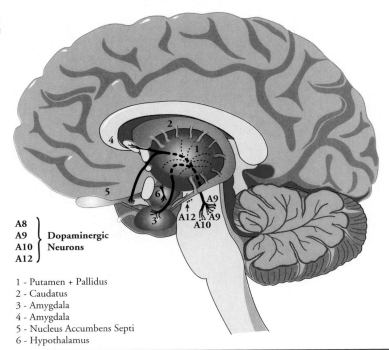

A8
A9 } Dopaminergic
A10 } Neurons
A12

1 - Putamen + Pallidus
2 - Caudatus
3 - Amygdala
4 - Amygdala
5 - Nucleus Accumbens Septi
6 - Hypothalamus

Source: Valzelli, Raven Press, 1981

Inset 3.1

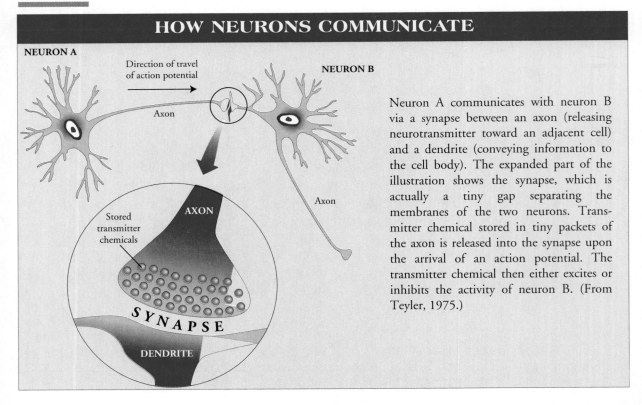

HOW NEURONS COMMUNICATE

NEURON A

Direction of travel
of action potential

NEURON B

Axon

Axon

Stored
transmitter
chemicals

AXON

SYNAPSE

DENDRITE

Neuron A communicates with neuron B via a synapse between an axon (releasing neurotransmitter toward an adjacent cell) and a dendrite (conveying information to the cell body). The expanded part of the illustration shows the synapse, which is actually a tiny gap separating the membranes of the two neurons. Transmitter chemical stored in tiny packets of the axon is released into the synapse upon the arrival of an action potential. The transmitter chemical then either excites or inhibits the activity of neuron B. (From Teyler, 1975.)

ing pain impulses. Psychoactive drugs exert their influence on the soma and dendrites by altering the excitatory and inhibitory balance controlled by synaptic processes. Virtually all psychoactive drugs exert their influence on neurotransmitter systems to produce physiological and psychological changes by either modifying their action or by mimicking them. In order to mimic neurotransmitters, psychoactive drugs must be either structurally similar to a transmitter or in some other way fit into a transmitter's receptor site, as seen in Figure 3.12.

Characteristics of Transmitters

Both deficiencies or excesses in neurotransmitter levels can produce profound disruptions in physical and behav-

Figure 3.12

Noradrenergic Synapse

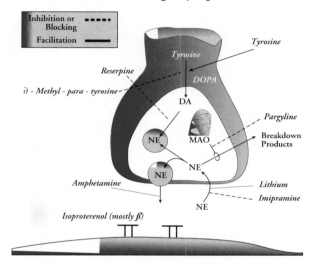

Dopaminergic Synapse

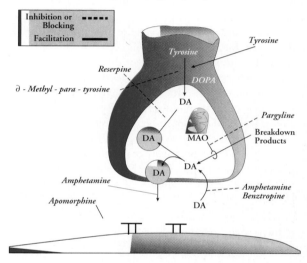

Cholinergic Synapse

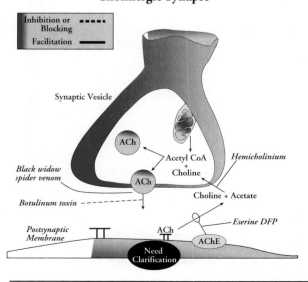

Serotonergic Synapse

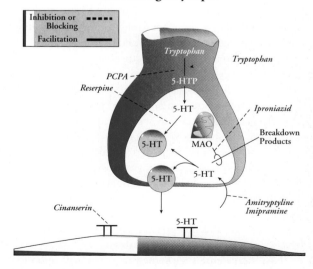

Source: Carlson, Allyn & Bacon, 1977

ioral processes (Coppen et al., 1972; Lieberman et al., 1982; Snyder, 1980). Modifications in these processes can be observed following natural changes in brain chemistry or artificial manipulation of neurotransmitters or the substances responsible for their production. The production of neurotransmitters is dependent, in large part, on the availability of certain substances that make up the foods we eat, including vitamins, minerals, carbohydrates, fats, and proteins (see Lovenberg, 1986 for detailed review). When the substance is an essential ingredient for the production of a neurotransmitter, it is called a *precursor*.

Many brain chemicals are synthesized in the brain without much assistance from outside sources since the necessary ingredients are available within the body. Other neurotransmitters, however, require supplies from outside the body for their production. If these supplies are reduced or insufficient, disease or disruption of a mental activity may result. For example, vitamin D is derived primarily from sunlight. Anemia or osteoporosis (bone thinning) may occur if an individual is deprived of even indirect sunlight. Many brain chemicals rely on components or constituents of the foods we eat. We quite literally eat to live (not live to eat as many of us behave). If it were not for these food constituents, our brains would be unable to manufacture adequate supplies of neurotransmitters that are essential to our existence and our performance.

The best understood transmitters with respect to drug influences and effects include GABA (gamma-aminobutyric acid), aspartic acid, glutamic acid, glycine, dopamine, norepinephrine, acetylcholine, and serotonin. The latter four neurotransmitters are involved with the experience of drug reward and pleasure, psychiatric and behavioral disorders. They play a prominent role in the understanding and treatment of drug abuse and addiction (see Table 3.1). Each of these transmitters, and others not mentioned, are profoundly altered when psychoactive drugs are taken. In fact, because the drug effects are a direct result of their influence on neurotransmitter activity, it is not surprising that chronic drug abuse can substantially and sometimes permanently disrupt how the brain utilizes these chemicals. Chronic cocaine use, for example, so profoundly increases levels of dopamine activity in the brain that damage is done to dopamine systems in that dopamine supplies and the number of receptor sites become depleted. As a result, cocaine abusers develop psychiatric conditions that, in many cases, did not previously exist. This scenario is true for many other psychoactive drugs.

Neurotransmitters are somewhat dependent upon the consumption of dietary precursors for their synthesis and use in the brain (Fernstrom, 1981a; Wurtman & Wurtman, 1979). Severe dietary restrictions can lead to insufficient neurotransmitter levels; however, psychiatric and behavioral disorders associated with neurotransmitter imbalances generally do not occur in the United States because of insufficient diet. Rather, inborn errors or irregularities in the way these chemicals are activated or external influences (e.g., drug use or pollution) are more commonly the culprit.

In either event, because drugs of abuse alter neurotransmitter activity levels and chronic use can deplete their supplies in the brain, neurotransmitter precursors have been included in treatment approaches for drug abuse and addiction.

Serotonin is primarily an inhibitory neurotransmitter that regulates sleep-wake cycles, relaxation, hunger, and psychic processes. Elevated serotonin levels have been found in individuals suffering from schizophrenia and are the result of certain drug effects and other related behavioral disorders (Green & Costain, 1981; Woolley & Shaw, 1954). Lysergic acid diethylamide (LSD) is structurally similar to serotonin and has the effect of increasing serotonergic activity. Because the LSD experience so closely resembles schizophrenia, both neurochemically and behaviorally, LSD was once used as a model to understand the biochemistry of schizophrenia. Many of the most popular psychedelic drugs directly influence serotonergic activity.

On the other hand, low serotonin levels have been related to sleep disturbances, anxiety, depression, obesity, and intellectual deficits (Coppen, 1967; Greenwood et al., 1975; Hartmann, 1977; Shopsin, 1978; Yogman et al., 1982). Of particular interest is the recent research on both violence and alcohol use. Individuals with a history of violence, including violent suicides and murders, and impulsive behavior patterns have been found to have abnormally low levels of serotonin activity (Brown, Goodwin, et al., 1979; Brown, Ebert, et al., 1982; Linnoila et al., 1983; Muhlbauer, 1985). Researchers first observed lower levels of serotonin in patients who had committed suicides; those who committed more violent suicides (by hanging, gun shot, or knife wound) had lower levels than those who had committed less violent suicides (by sleeping pills or gas). Obviously, these studies were conducted postmortem (after death). Additional studies began to focus on the relationship of serotonin to violence specifically since depression did not seem to be the only condition related to low serotonin levels. Examination of ex-marines who had been dismissed from the service as a result of their unruly and uncontrolled behavior provided further evidence for the

Table 3.1   *Table of Selected Neurotransmitters*

TRANSMITTER	AMINO ACID PRECURSOR	RELATED DISORDERS	AGONISTS	ANTAGONIST
Serotonin	Tryptophan	Impulsivity- Depression- Suicidal 　Behavior- Violence- Schizophrenia+ Anxiety	LSD Prozac Fenfluramine	Methysergide Alcohol Caffeine Lysergide Mescaline Marijuana Morphine 　Withdrawal
Dopamine Norepinephrine Epinephrine	Tyrosine Phenylalanine	Psychosis+ Schizophrenia+ Depression- 　Mania+	Bromocriptine Apomorphine Amphetamine Cocaine PCP Alcohol Lysergide Morphine 　Withdrawal	Most 　Neuroleptics Marijuana Desipramine Imipramine Trazodone Amitryptiline Bromocriptine
Acetylcholine	Choline	Alzheimer's 　Disease- Learning 　Disability- Violence+ Huntington's 　Chorea-	Nicotine Apomorphine Soman Physostigmine	Marijuana Atropine Neuroleptics Scopolamine

Key: - indicates low activity levels of the neurotransmitter are associated with the disorder
　　 + indicates high levels of the neurotransmitter are associated

role of serotonin in aggressiveness. Since then, many studies have found an association between low serotonin activity and both aggressiveness and impulsivity. Moreover, alcohol ingestion lowers serotonin, and there is evidence that those who are predisposed to problem drinking may have pre-existing low levels of serotonin. Therefore, alcohol use in certain individuals may, in part, provoke violent behavior by further lowering brain serotonin levels (Kent et al., 1985; Tarter et al., 1985).

Serotonin is produced in the body from the precursor tryptophan (Fernstrom & Wurtman, 1971), an amino acid found in protein foods such as eggs, dairy products, fish, and the muscle tissue of meat and poultry. Studies in laboratory animals show that brain serotonin levels can be influenced by diet and by the administration of pure tryptophan. When carbohydrates are ingested, insulin is released by the pancreas and blood levels of other amino acids fall relative to tryptophan. As a result, tryptophan is more readily transported into the brain, making tryptophan more available for serotonin synthesis. The administration of protein produces a fall in the blood level of tryptophan relative to other amino acids with the result that less tryptophan crosses the blood brain barrier into the brain. Given serotonin's proposed role in psychiatric and behavioral disorders, manipulation of tryptophan-containing foods, as well as carbohydrates, have been used to help manage these disorders.

Tryptophan supplements have been used with some success in the treatment of behavioral disorders for which serotonin insufficiency plays a role, particularly when used along with other forms of therapy. There may however, be adverse effects, such as nausea, headache, dizziness, and drowsiness when they are taken in large quantities for a long period of time (Leathwood, 1986). Moreover, tryptophan has been recently associated with a rare blood disorder, and the Food and Drug

Administration (FDA) has mandated its removal from the market. The possibilities of an allergic reaction to a contaminated batch of tryptophan or another unknown source of the disorder are being investigated. Nevertheless, assuming the safety of tryptophan is once again established, a tryptophan-rich diet or tryptophan supplements may be particularly effective in treating mania, certain types of hyperactivity, depression, alcoholism, or hyperaggression. In fact, tryptophan supplements have been shown to produce antidepressant, sedative, intellectual, and antiaggressive effects (Mizuno & Yugari, 1974; Moller et al., 1976; Nyhan, 1976; Weingartner et al., 1983; Young & Sourkes, 1977).

Because so many drug abusers suffer from a preexisting state of depression (e.g., Regier et al., 1990), many psychiatrists prescribe antidepressants. One major family of antidepressants includes serotonergic agonists, drugs that increase serotonin activity (e.g., amitriptyline, fluoxetine [Prozac], and trazodone [Desyrel]). Many of these agonist drugs influence the activity of transmitters other than serotonin, but the serotonergic effect is largely responsible for alleviating the depression. They operate by either inhibiting the reuptake of serotonin into the sending cell, causing serotonin to accumulate and continue to stimulate the receiving cells, or by directly causing the release of serotonin into the synapse. These antidepressants have become quite popular in the treatment of drug abusers for the following reasons: (1) chronic depression is pervasive among drug abusers, (2) drug withdrawal and long-term cessation frequently induce episodes of acute and chronic depression, and (3) serotonin is depleted by many drugs of abuse. For these reasons, such therapeutic drugs have proven effective for many patients.

Catecholamines are a group of structurally related chemicals that include adrenalin (epinephrine), dopamine, and noradrenalin (norepinephrine). Dopamine is an excitatory neurotransmitter that serves as a precursor for the neurotransmitter noradrenalin, and tyrosine is the dietary precursor to both. In turn, noradrenalin stimulates the production and release of the adrenal hormone, adrenalin. Adrenalin is not found in the brain but has the peripheral effects of maintaining blood pressure and regulating heart rate and glucose metabolism. The release of adrenalin is related to stressful conditions and contributes to feelings of anxiety and hyperactivity. Decreases in adrenalin release are associated with sedation and lethargy. Monoamine oxidase (MAO) is an enzyme that inactivates the catecholamines, thus, high levels of MAO are associated with a decrease in brain activity. Low levels, on the other hand, have been related to manic and sometimes violent behavioral states; relatively high, unchecked levels of catecholamines may contribute to feelings of being in a crisis mode.

Imbalances in either dopamine or noradrenalin contribute to a variety of behavioral and emotional disorders, including depression (Muscettola et al., 1977; Schildkraut, 1965; Snyder, 1980), psychopathy (Levander et al., 1980; Schachter, 1971), schizophrenia (Bellak, 1979; Bird et al., 1977; vanKammen et al., 1983), and mania (Coppen, 1967; Schildkraut, 1965). There is evidence that when the f/f/f mechanism is activated, noradrenalin and adrenalin respond similarly by increasing the level of arousal in the autonomic and central nervous systems. Amphetamine and cocaine both directly influence the activity of noradrenalin to create a manic, hyperactive state. Dopamine, in addition to its effects on motor activity, has been linked with the pleasurable effects of drugs like cocaine. Dopamine is concentrated in areas of the pain and pleasure center of the limbic system, and when stimulated, for example by cocaine, the increased activity of dopamine can produce profound feelings of pleasure and craving for more of the drug. Because neurotransmitters are found in a number of locations throughout the brain, where in the brain activity levels are altered influences the results. If they are altered in the limbic system, mood will change. If they are altered in the cerebellum, movement may change. If they are altered in the cortex, intellectual functioning may change.

Drugs that alter the synaptic activity of these transmitters can dramatically affect brain function and behavior. For example, Parkinson's disease is a motor disorder that involves atrophy of dopaminergic systems in the basal ganglia and hypothalamus. The treatment for this disease is the administration of L-dopa, the precursor for dopamine, to replenish supplies in the brain. As a result of evidence that dopamine is depleted by many drugs of abuse, in particular, cocaine, several dopamimetic agents, or dopamine mimicking agents, have been used in the treatment of substance abusers. Methylphenidate (e.g., Ritalin), commonly used for hyperactivity in children, bromocriptine (Parlodel) and amantadine (Symmetrel) are frequently prescribed for this purpose. These drugs have less abuse liability than cocaine or amphetamines and have a more rapid effect and a longer duration of action. Similar to the administration of methadone for heroin addicts, these drugs serve as substitutes for the more potent, addictive, and harmful illicit stimulants. Patients given such treatments respond with decreases in craving for a drug and do not relapse as often as those not given such treatment. On the down side, however, methylphenidate is mildly addicting and produces stimulation, an effect sought out by drug abusers. Bromocriptine, on the other hand, is a dopamimetic agent that has no abuse potential in humans. Nevertheless, there are some unpleasant side effects that limit its use in some patients. Amantadine is somewhat preferable to bromocriptine as it has fewer side effects and also has no abuse potential.

Also used in the treatment of drug abuse disorders are the tricyclic antidepressants that act on noradrenalin receptors by blocking its reuptake into the sending cell (e.g., desipramine and imipramine). The result is increased activity of noradrenalin at the synapse. This family of antidepressants, similar to the serotonin antidepressants, alleviate depression and elevate mood. The tricyclics have a low incidence of adverse effects, low toxicity, high patient acceptance, and no abuse liability. Their primary disadvantage is that it may take several days to a few weeks for these medications to take full effect. Several addictive drugs deplete noradrenalin supplies and, consequently, antidepressants that raise noradrenalin activity have become another option in the treatment of drug addiction. The choice between antidepressants that alter serotonin activity and those that alter noradrenalin activity depends on the particular drug being abused, the individual's psychological symptoms and history, and, to a great extent, trial and error results. In some cases, the precursor tyrosine has been included in a treatment regimen to naturally augment catecholamine synthesis and activity.

The neurotransmitter acetylcholine (ACh) mediates cholinergic nerve impulses in the peripheral and central nervous systems and is largely responsible for the processes of memory, learning ability and motor coordination (Davis & Berger, 1979; Green & Costain, 1981; Peters & Levine, 1977; Snyder, 1980). Acetylcholinesterase (AChE) is the enzyme that breaks down and deactivates acetylcholine. It will be discussed more thoroughly in Chapter 12. Diminishing brain levels of ACh are characteristic of the aging process and a form of premature senility, Alzheimer's disease (Bartus et al., 1982; Growden et al., 1977; Marsh et al., 1985; Perry & Perry, 1980).

It is not clear at this time whether ACh is essentially an excitatory or inhibitory transmitter, although there is evidence that it may have both effects depending on how it influences the postsynaptic membrane. Certain drugs act like ACh at the receptor site by producing effects similar to that of ACh. Nicotine, for example, alters cell activity and behavior in the same manner that ACh does. Other drugs, such as physostigmine and soman, inhibit the enzyme (AChE) that destroys ACh, thereby increasing the influence of ACh. Certain insecticides and nerve gases (sometimes used in chemical warfare) cause ACh to accumulate at the synapse. The result may be nightmares, confusion, hallucinations, and intellectual impairment. In one criminal case, a lawn specialist who had been working with insecticides for several months experienced an episode of extreme aggression, leading to the death of his client. His bizarre behavior was so uncharacteristic that evidence was presented in court to indicate that his violence was due to the build up of ACh (see Chapter 12). Several psychedelic drugs increase ACh activity directly or by inhibiting the action of AChE. These effects may be desirable to those using such drugs for their hallucinogenic properties.

ACh neurotransmitter is synthesized in brain cells from the dietary compound choline. Fish, poultry, and eggs are known as brain foods due to their high concentration of choline. Choline is widespread in both animal and plant products and is commonly found along with the vitamin B complex. Dietary sources serve as a primary supply of choline; in humans, the amount of choline in the diet determines the amount of choline in the blood that is delivered to the brain (Davis & Berger, 1979; Barbeau et al., 1979).

Pure concentrations of the choline complex are being administered to a variety of populations to examine its effects on brain functioning. Improvements in brain activity among normal populations and others with acetylcholine-related disorders are expected (Davis et al., 1979; Peters & Levine, 1977). Benefits to Down's syndrome patients have been suggested with ACh manipulations (Cantor & Thatcher, 1986). Of particular concern is the finding that elevated ACh activity is directly involved in the production of aggressive and violent behaviors in animals (Ijic et al., 1970; D.E. Smith, King, et al., 1970). As learning disabilities and cognitive deficits have been associated with antisocial behavior, choline supplementation may be beneficial in some cases.

Cholinergic agents are not generally used in the treatment of substance abusers because they are not specifically indicated and can be quite potent in producing undesirable effects. Instead, drugs that influence transmission of acetylcholine are used primarily in the treatment of certain motor disorders, bladder problems, and to reverse adverse effects of muscle relaxants used in surgery. Certain drugs that deactivate acetylcholine are currently being tested for their safety and efficacy as antidotes for chemicals used in warfare. Other than these uses, cholinergic agents are used illicitly by drug abusers for their hallucinogenic properties.

Neurotransmitter precursor therapies for the treatment of drug abuse have been tried with some success (Kleber & Gawin, 1986; Rosecan, 1983). Several popular drugs of abuse, such as opiates, PCP, and cocaine, ultimately deplete levels of dopamine, norepinephrine, and serotonin in the brain. The use of tyrosine and tryptophan with these drug abusers helps to restore supplies of the natural neurotransmitter. Thus, theoretically, the symptoms of withdrawal will be minimized and cravings for the drug reduced (Trachtenburg & Blum, 1988). The use of precursors, along with psychotherapy, is an accepted mode of treatment although there is no evidence that it is as effective as conventional medications. At this point in time, the administration of drugs that increase neurotransmitter activity (agonists) is more popular and less controversial in the pharmacologic treatment of drug abusers.

Opiate Transmitters

Opium, a powerful narcotic known since the classical Greeks, has proven to be the key to the latest discoveries regarding drug addiction. John Sydenham, a seventeenth-century philosopher and physician, once said

Among the remedies which it has pleased almighty God to give man to relieve his sufferings, none is so universal and so efficacious as opium.

Opium is known to relieve pain and induce euphoria, in part due to the action of opium on the pain and pleasure center of the limbic system. In the 1970s, researchers discovered that opiate drugs, such as morphine and heroin, exerted their effects within the brain at receptor sites that seemed to have an affinity for opiates. In other words, the brain was already equipped with receptor sites that were specifically designed to bind to opiate drugs, like a lock and key mechanism. Furthermore, these opiate receptors are located in those regions of the central nervous system that regulate the perception of pain and emotions.

These discoveries lead to an interesting question: Why would nature design receptor sites to specifically interact with the juice of the poppy? The search began for natural brain substances that bind to these receptors in order to explain the existence of opiate receptor sites. Investigations were successful in identifying what are now called neuropeptides or opiate peptides. These peptides are naturally occurring morphine-like substances that bind to opiate receptors to reduce pain and increase pleasure (see Snyder, 1978). Basically, three types of natural opiates, with various but overlapping functions, have been identified: endorphins, enkephalins, and dynorphins. Endorphins function to release chemicals and hormones to induce euphoria. Enkephalins suppress the release of neurotransmitters that convey the pain signal. Dynorphin is a pituitary and brain peptide that is quite potent, influencing a different set of receptors from the endorphins and enkephalins.

Several receptors for these neuropeptides have been located throughout the brain that mediate a variety of bodily and psychological processes. Opiate receptors are concentrated in the brainstem to produce general analgesia, reduce the perception of pain from the face and hands, and control the responses of cough, nausea and vomiting, blood pressure, and stomach secretions. The thalamus has opiate receptors to mediate deep pain that is influenced by emotional responses. The spinal cord contains opiate receptors to influence the process by which sensory information is received. Thus, the release of these chemicals reduce the transmission of painful stimuli. Finally, the limbic system contains the largest concentrations of opiate receptors where they mediate the influence of natural and external opiates on emotional behavior. Neuropeptides play a substantial role in stress responses and certain forms of mental illness (Green & Costain, 1981; Julien, 1988; Snyder, 1980).

In a sense, the activity of neuropeptides provide motivation for behaviors. Due to the ability of neuropeptides (or other external chemicals that are structurally similar) to induce pleasure and reduce pain, we are essentially motivated to increase their activity. The so-called addiction to exercise may exemplify this form of motivation. Exercise stimulates the activity of neuropeptides to suppress the perception of the pain exercise can produce. Regular and intense exercise can actually influence neuropeptides to the point that the body requires constant stimulation to maintain a balance in brain activity. Chronic exercisers report a "need" to exercise and a resulting "euphoria." If a regular exerciser stops, neuropeptide activity may be sufficiently suppressed to cause symptoms similar to withdrawal until neuropeptides can return to normal activity on their own.

A role has also been suggested for these neuropeptides in the tolerance and dependence that develops as a response to the use of external opiates, such as heroin, dilaudid, morphine, and codeine. The use of external opiates causes enkephalin receptors to becoming intensely stimulated. Due to the presence of opiates at the receptor sites, the activity of enkephalin neurons is subsequently decreased in order to maintain a balance of excitation and inhibition in the brain. The decline in enkephalin activity causes the user to require additional amounts of the external opiate to achieve the same effect of euphoria and pain reduction. Thus, tolerance to the external source of opiates develops. Once the user discontinues the drug, withdrawal symptoms occur from a deficiency of both external and natural opiates in the brain. The withdrawal symptoms indicate drug dependency. Withdrawal symptoms subside when enkephalin neurons become active again either on their own or via the stimulation of external opiates. The user is consequently motivated to continue drug usage to maintain a more intense level of opiate activity in the brain than is possible with only the natural opiates at work.

It has been hypothesized that acupuncture reduces pain by stimulating the release of natural opiate peptides. Thus, the perception of pain is suppressed in those with painful medical disorders or even those undergoing uncomfortable dental work. Investigators are presently considering the possibility that individuals with naturally low levels of neuropeptide activity may be more prone to substance abuse as a form of self-medication. We will discuss each of these theories and evidence to support them in the following chapters.

≣ Summary

Although the brain looks like a wrinkled, slithery cauliflower, it brings beauty and life to an otherwise mundane world. The brain gives us the ability to not only absorb information from our world but also appreciate and experience feelings about that information. As humans, our brains make the world multidimensional and provide us with the tools to manipulate our surroundings. All of our fear, love, hate, compassion, lust, and drives are regulated by our brains and provide us with the motivation to behave in ways that will ultimately enhance our chances of survival under normal conditions. When our bodies or our surroundings become dysfunctional, our brains may feed us misinformation or may operate inappropriately, thus providing an impetus for irrational or self-destructive behaviors. When judgment and perception of the world is impaired as a result of some brain irregularity, decision-making ability will be accordingly impaired.

Unfortunately, we may also intentionally change brain function to place us at risk for inappropriate or dysfunctional behavior. As a result of the intelligence and intense feelings our brains permit us to utilize, we have the capacity to alter the perception of our world by altering our brains. Thousands of years ago, humans discovered that certain consumable substances change our perception and our mood state by influencing the very chemistry that gives us reason to live and directions for doing so. Although we have the tendency to pursue change for the better, we are sometimes at the mercy of the substance. It may compel us to use more, given its ability to produce euphoria while we are actively using it and to produce dysphoria when we attempt to stop. At times, our brains can no longer make a willful decision to stop when a substance's effect is so powerful. It is these experiences that generate concern for the individual user regarding his or her health and well-being. We generally do not wish to lose control over our will or have our decision-making ability compromised. Drugs of abuse, however, may do just that.

CHAPTER 4

Pharmacology

Objectives

1. To explain how drugs exert their effects on the brain.
2. To present the methods of drug administration and summarize the advantages and disadvantages of each method.
3. To discuss the role of the blood-brain barrier and the placental barrier with regard to the impact of drugs on the brain and developing fetus.
4. To illustrate how drugs can affect fetal development and influence the developing child.
5. To provide definitions of drug dependence, tolerance, addiction, withdrawal, and abuse and to discuss the controversial nature of these definitions.
6. To understand how some drugs can block the effects of other drugs to achieve a therapeutic effect.
7. To understand how the placebo effect takes place.
8. To present social, psychological, and biological factors that may influence how individuals uniquely respond to a drug.

The field of pharmacology refers to the science of the nature and properties of drugs and their actions or, more specifically, the effects of drugs on the body, including the brain. In the previous chapter, we described how natural chemicals in our brains act on neurons and organs to subsequently alter behavior and mood. In this chapter, we will discuss how psychoactive drugs act on neurological systems and processes to cause pleasure, craving, dependence, aggression, and sedation, among other physical and psychological reactions. Psychoactive drugs have the ability to alter mood state or behavior by acting directly on mechanisms of brain function. Thus, it is not surprising that these drugs act in a manner similar to natural chemicals found in the brain, including hormones, neurotransmitters, and neuropeptides, that regulate our moods and behaviors. Both natural chemicals and drugs that are externally administered exert their effects on neural structures by influencing receptor sites and the activities of various brain chemicals.

To the drug user, the process of achieving a drug effect is simple: The drug is obtained, administered, and both desirable and undesirable effects are achieved. However, the actual processes of absorption, distribution, action, degradation, and excretion are highly complex. The field of pharmacokinetics is that subarea of pharmacology that describes these processes and the factors that affect them.

Most drugs do not have a global influence on all of the body's tissues. Instead, they become effective at particular sites of action. How they arrive at these sites—what factors interfere with or facilitate their arrival—depends on the drug used, the method by which it is administered, the user's constitution, other substances in the body, and a variety of other conditions. All of these influences are topics pertinent to pharmacokinetics. Because modes of administration are important determinants in drug effects, they will be discussed first. Once the various ways to introduce drugs into the body have been described, an explanation of the biological mechanisms underlying drug actions will follow.

Methods of Administering Drugs

There are many ways to administer a drug, and the method chosen will largely determine how quickly the drug will be absorbed, degraded (chemically broken down in the body), and eliminated. The efficiency of these processes will, in turn, determine the strength of the drug's effects as well as the length of time the drug remains in the body and continues to exert its effects. There are many ways of getting drugs into the body. Some are taken by

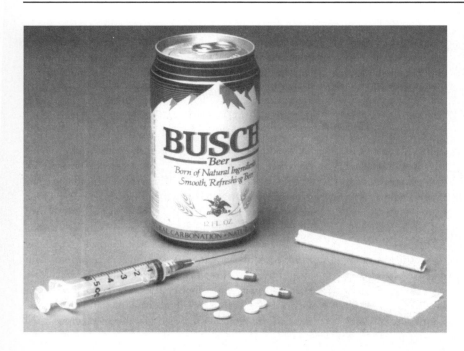

Routes of administration differ depending upon type of drug, desired drug effect and duration, and potential risks.

Table 4.1   *Routes of Administration: Disadvantages and Advantages*

METHOD	SUBSTANCE	DISADVANTAGES	ADVANTAGES
Oral			
tablets	aspirin	stomach problems	easy to use
capsules	amphetamines	unpredictable effects	readily crosses blood-
liquid	alcohol	degradation	brain barrier (if lipid
blotter paper	LSD		soluble)
solid	mushrooms		
Injection			rapidly absorbed
intravenous	cocaine	allergic reaction	quick response
intramuscular	barbiturates	overdose	avoids GI track
subcutaneous	heroin	site infection	
		infectious disease	
		collapse of vein	
		tracks	
Inhalation			rapid absorption
sniffing	amyl nitrite	dosage hard to gauge	quick response
smoking	nicotine	effects short lived	avoids GI track
inhaling into mouth	opium	irritate membranes	
	marijuana	and lungs	
	cocaine		
	cleaning fluid		
	PCP		

mouth in the form of a pill or liquid, whereas others are injected with a hypodermic needle or smoked. Some drugs can be absorbed by the mucus membranes in the nose (intranasally) or left to dissolve under the tongue (sublingually). Others may be rubbed on the skin or applied to the skin in the form of a patch and absorbed subcutaneously. Some drugs may even be taken in suppository form by placing it in the rectum. Once a drug has been taken and absorbed, bodily fluids transport it to the brain and other parts of the body in order to produce its effect.

Each route of administration is associated with particular side effects, dangers, and differences in how quickly and efficiently the drug is processed to produce the desired effect (see Table 4.1). Users select a preferred method of drug administration by considering the desired drug action, strength, and duration of the drug effect and the dangers they are willing to risk. For example, an individual about to use heroin may consider the intravenous route for its rapid and potent action. But the user must further consider the dangers inherent in administering a

drug by needle and may instead opt for sniffing. Not only must users choose the route of administration but they must also decide on the amount and the dosage form (tablet, capsule, liquid, powder) to take. Because there are so many decisions to be made, an unsavvy user may easily misuse a drug, possibly resulting in bodily harm.

Oral Administration

Oral administration of a drug (swallowing) is the most common route of drug ingestion. Alcohol is generally taken orally. (Some hard-core drug users have been known to inject alcohol into their veins with a hypodermic needle. An alcohol enema is another strategy.) When aspirin or cold medicines are taken, they are either swallowed as a tablet or drunk as a liquid. Psilocybin mushrooms are chewed and swallowed or brewed into a tea for drinking. LSD is generally blotted on a piece of paper or dropped into a sugar cube to be eaten. Chewing tobacco, on the

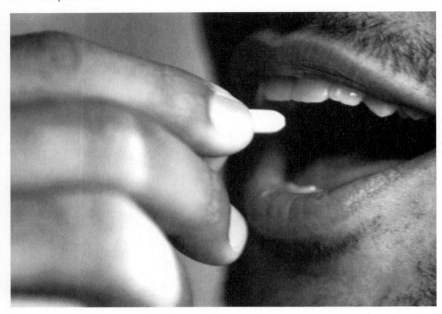

Many drug users prefer pill form due to the ease of administration and the absence of outward signs of the drugs presence; in other words, there is no residual smell, powder or bulkiness when carried.

other hand, is generally chewed but not swallowed and absorbed through the membranes of the mouth, although some may trickle down the throat into the stomach. Drugs that are administered orally must be metabolized by several organ systems before they become active. Stomach fluids break down ingested drugs and send the active ingredients to the intestine where they are absorbed by the wall of the intestine and dumped into the bloodstream. Thus, the amount of the drug that is absorbed and remains active is a function of how well the drug dissolves in stomach fluids and permeates the intestinal lining. Drugs taken in liquid form are more easily dissolved in stomach fluids than tablets or capsules.

A drug will exert its effects more quickly and with greater initial strength if the stomach is relatively empty. Thus, if the drug dispenser or user desires rapid absorption, the drug should be taken prior to meals. If a longer but less dramatic effect is desired, the drug should be taken immediately following a meal. Many drugs irritate the lining of the stomach and change the level of stomach acidity. These should be taken during meals. Some are available with a protective coating to alleviate stomach upset.

The absorption of alcohol is somewhat different from the process described above even though it is taken orally. At least 20 percent of the ingested alcohol is absorbed directly through the stomach walls into the blood, particularly if the stomach is empty. Thus, much of the alcohol

passes rapidly into the bloodstream, and its effects are felt almost immediately. The remainder passes into the upper intestine where it is absorbed readily into the bloodstream. When the stomach is full, the alcohol moves from the stomach to the intestine much more slowly and is more diluted by the stomach contents. Thus, the effect is somewhat delayed and muted.

Following this process of absorption or digestion, active metabolites (the active ingredients of the drug) enter the bloodstream and are circulated to sites of action. Most drugs are absorbed about thirty minutes after ingestion. However, if a drug has been poorly manufactured it may not be soluble (dissolvable) in stomach fluids. Instead, it will simply pass through the intestine and be excreted in the feces without being absorbed by the intestinal wall or entering the bloodstream. Moreover, if a drug readily binds to a food(s) or food constituent (e.g., fat or calcium), then very little of the active metabolites will enter the bloodstream. For this reason, some drugs should not be taken with food.

There are several advantages and disadvantages of oral administration. Drugs that are highly soluble in lipids (fats) target the brain due to its high lipid content and may easily cross the blood-brain barrier (described later). Consequently, an ingested drug that is lipid soluble will be readily absorbed from the gastrointestinal tract to influence brain activity. Drugs with high lipid solubility are generally not eliminated and begin to accumulate in the kidney to produce a greater effect. On the other hand, water soluble drugs are unable to penetrate the blood-brain barrier. These drugs may act on other organs or areas of the body and are eliminated rapidly by the kidneys (see Corry & Cimbolic, 1985).

Disadvantages of oral administration include an increased likelihood of stomach disturbances, including vomiting. Moreover, it is difficult to predict how much of a drug will be absorbed into the blood to become active. This unpredictable feature of drug ingestion may partially explain the differences in the ways individuals process drugs and their thresholds for drug effects. Other unknown genetic and/or constitutional variations may affect how an individual metabolizes drugs. Equally important is the variation in the way manufacturers produce drugs in terms of their molecular structure and the binding agents used. Finally, some drugs are degraded by the digestive juices in the mouth or stomach and may become inactive before they even reach the bloodstream.

Injection or Parenteral Administration

If a drug is largely destroyed by stomach acids, or if it is desirable to speed up the process by which a drug enters the bloodstream, injection or parenteral administration

with a hypodermic needle may be preferable to the other methods of administration. There are three common modes of administering a drug by injection: intravenous (into the vein), intramuscular (into the muscle), or subcutaneous (under the skin). All three methods achieve predictable results because nearly all of the drug is absorbed directly into the bloodstream. Accurate amounts of the drug can be administered quickly and inactivation by the gastrointestinal system and stomach is avoided.

The primary drawback of hypodermic injection is the risk of infection when the syringe and/or the injection site are not kept sterile. Other disadvantages include the inability to prevent an unexpected drug effect, such as an overdose or an allergic reaction to the substance. When using an oral method, the drug may be expelled by vomiting or stomach pumping. There is no such recourse after injection.

Intravenous Injection

Intravenous (IV) injection uses a hypodermic syringe to introduce the drug directly into a vein. On the street, this method is known as mainlining. Heroin and sometimes amphetamines, cocaine, and prescription drugs may be used intravenously. IV injection is considered the most effective and efficient way to deliver drugs to the system because of the rapidity with which they are absorbed and a response is achieved. Drugs that would either be destroyed

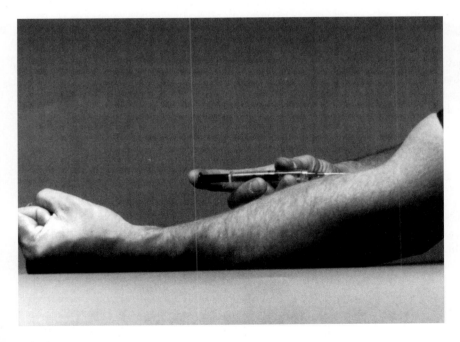

Intravenous (IV) use of a drug poses many hazards and requires some skill and discretion on the part of the user.

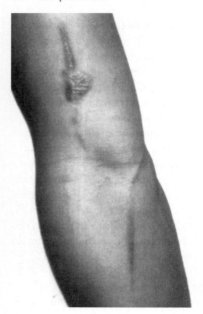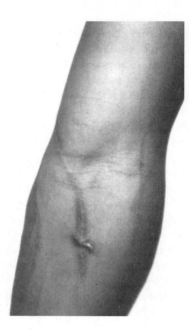

Track marks from frequent IV administration result from scar tissue that forms around a vein that has been repeatedly entered.

by the gastrointestinal tract or irritate the gastrointestinal tract can be more safely administered into blood vessels, which are relatively insensitive. In order for the drug to be injected safely, it must be prepared in a water-based solution. If the drug is in a fatty solution, the result may be a potentially fatal blood clot. The solution should be administered slowly to carefully control the dosage and to avoid any adverse reactions.

Repeated injections into the same vein may cause the vein to collapse. Chronic IV drug users frequently experience such collapse and must continuously change injection sites in various areas of the body (e.g., arms, hands, groin, legs, ankles, and under the tongue). Daily injections will cause the user's veins to develop scarring, called tracks, which can be seen. These thick tracks make continued injections difficult if not impossible, particularly for those not experienced with the IV method. Technicians or nurses not accustomed to caring for IV drug users may have difficulty finding a good vein to administer a drug in a medical emergency.

IV drug use may be particularly dangerous when a drug is given too quickly, even in usually safe doses; respiration can become depressed without warning, or the heart can be adversely affected. Finally, the risk of infectious diseases increases with IV drug use. Sometimes drug users will share the same needle to inject drugs and exchange blood from one user to another. AIDS (autoimmune deficiency syndrome), which results from exposure to the HIV, and hepatitis are two deadly diseases spread through the use of shared or contaminated needles. The largest group of individuals presently infected with the HIV contracted the virus from needle sharing. Injection is a most efficient way to spread the virus as traces of blood remain on the needle after each usage.

Intramuscular Injection

Intramuscular (IM) injections involve the introduction of the drug into a skeletal muscle—arm, thigh, or buttocks. This method is more rapid and efficient than oral administration but slower than intravenous injection. IM injections are used when a drug needs to be administered chronically, for example, for the long-term treatment of psychosis. The speed with which a drug is absorbed from muscle as well as the amount of the drug absorbed is a function of (1) the amount of blood circulated to the muscle where the drug is injected, (2) the solubility of the drug, and (3) the amount of the drug injected. The deltoid muscle of the upper arm is a popular site for injection because it has a large amount of blood, which contributes to rapid absorption of the drug. The buttocks have a poor blood supply, which results in slower absorption of the drug. When a large amount of a drug is needed, but a slow absorption rate is desired, the IM method is recommended. This method shares many of the disadvantages and dangers associated with the IV mode of drug administration. An added risk with IM injection is the danger of unintentionally hitting a vein rather than a muscle. When a vein is hit, the IM injection becomes an IV injection, thereby increasing the risk of blood clots if a fatty solution was used or the risk of rapid absorption of a drug meant to be absorbed slowly.

Subcutaneous Injection

The subcutaneous method involves the injection of a drug immediately under the skin, referred to by seasoned drug users as skin popping. This method shares many of the characteristics, advantages, and disadvantages of IM injections. The rate of absorption is slower than the other two injection routes, but there is less risk of adverse side effects or reactions. Because many drugs are irritating to the skin, this mode of administration may cause the skin around the injection site to die. Subcutaneous injection is not a common route used by physicians, but is frequently used by novice drug users becoming acquainted with narcotics.

Inhalation

Drugs can be inhaled by either sniffing them through the nose or inhaling them as smoke into the lungs. These two forms of inhalation are quite different and the speed with which the drug reaches the brain is much slower with sniffing than smoking. In fact, many users claim that smoking a drug is the fastest way to get it to the brain, which helps to explain why smokable drugs tend to have a greater dependence potential. Inhaling a drug in the form of a powder, gas, or particles carried in a spray or smoke is another method that avoids the gastrointestinal tract. As a gas, the drug penetrates the cell linings of the respiratory tract easily and quickly. Anesthetics are commonly administered in gas form. Drugs that are largely fat soluble and small in molecular size pass through the membranes of the lungs almost immediately. Since the capillaries containing blood and the membranes of the lung are in close proximity, absorption of the drug is rapid and complete. Although we know that the rate of absorption is efficient when active particles in smoke are inhaled (e.g., nicotine, opium, marijuana, or nicotine), there is very little information regarding the process of pulmonary absorption of these drugs.

In addition to tobacco, marijuana, opium, and the chemicals in cigarettes, another common drug of abuse that may be smoked is cocaine, freebased in the form of crack.

Butyl and amyl nitrites are drugs inhaled through the nose that are popular among youngsters and homosexuals. These drugs, packaged as aerosols, are legal and readi-

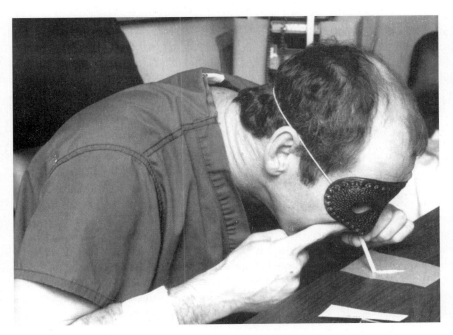

Inhaling a drug such as cocaine, nicotine or heroin, is the most powerful form of drug administration, leading to rapid effects.

ly available in "head shops" and hardware stores. They produce an immediate high that is described as a light-headed, dizzy, and giddy feeling. Some users enjoy the experience of a perceived heightened orgasm when these drugs are taken during sexual intercourse. The drugs also relax the sphincter muscles of the rectum, making anal intercourse easier.

Finally, cleaning fluids, gasoline, paint, paint thinner, shoe polish, acrylics, lighter fluid, household aerosols, and glue may be sniffed to produce a toxic, yet effective, high. Becoming more popular in the 1990s is the inhalation of common household products, which are readily available and provide a quick high. This activity is now called huffing and is known to produce more permanent brain damage than any other commonly abused drug. Teenagers report that it provides a powerful effect, helping them to escape from daily problems. Homeless people also engage in huffing, in particular choosing paint, which makes users easily identifiable by the specks of paint that cover their faces.

Powdered cocaine and heroin are routinely sniffed. These agents are absorbed through moist nasal membranes where they dissolve. Any mucus membrane in the body, in fact, is a potential locale for the administration of powdered cocaine, even when not inhaled. Placing cocaine on the tongue, eye, or even the genital area will produce a numbing effect as cocaine absorbs easily into the surrounding tissue.

There are several disadvantages to inhalation as a method of drug administration. First, it is difficult to gauge the dosage. Second, the drug effects are relatively short lived because these drugs are not easily stored in the body. Finally, many of these drugs irritate the linings of the nostrils and the lungs and may contribute to lung disease, asthma, allergies, cancer, and liver disease.

Drug Distribution

Following ingestion, by whatever mode chosen, drugs are absorbed into the bloodstream and routed throughout the body. Although psychoactive drugs may come into contact with most bodily tissues, they may only exert their action by locating sites of action that match their molecular structure. The user strives to take enough to achieve a desirable effect specifically on these sites. However, most of the drug settles in areas of the body other than these sites and is substantially diluted by the circulating blood and body fluids. If a drug can enter a cell within bodily tissue, then it is further diluted by the fluid inside.

Another reason that so much of a drug never reaches sites of action is that many drugs attach to protein molecules in the blood. How well the molecules of the drug bind to the molecules in the blood helps determine the overall drug effects. When most of the drug binds to protein, it remains inactive in the blood. Unbound or free components of the drug may cross the capillary walls to exert their effects on appropriate sites. Drugs that remain largely unbound more easily move out of the bloodstream to produce a more rapid effect that is shorter lived than that from drugs largely bound to blood proteins (Ray & Ksir, 1990). For example, alcohol is fairly evenly distributed throughout the body and has an effect on all bodily organs and tissues.

In order for some drugs to influence moods, behaviors, and emotions, they must be able to enter the brain. Many drugs are not able to enter the brain and, consequently, exert their effects on the peripheral nervous system and/or other organ systems. Access to the brain is restricted by the blood-brain barrier, a structural barrier designed to exclude certain intruders from entering the brain.

Blood-Brain Barrier

The blood-brain barrier serves as a functional obstacle to harmful substances attempting to enter the brain. It forms a wall between the brain's capillaries and brain tissue, allowing some substances from the blood to quickly enter the brain (see Figure 4.1). Other substances either enter the brain slowly or not at all. In fact, this barrier is more accurately referred to as a gate since many substances, both desirable and undesirable, enter and exit through this route. The blood-brain barrier reaches maturity after one to two years of age in humans. As a consequence, a fetus's or baby's brain is particularly vulnerable to exposure to psychoactive substances. Giving a baby a small bit of alcohol, for example, will exert a powerful psychoactive and toxic effect, because the drug so readily enters the brain and because it is broken down very slowly.

The blood-brain barrier is not well understood as it differs in structure from other areas of the body. For example, the capillaries of the brain do not contain pores like capillaries in other areas. Thus, water-soluble molecules, no matter how small, cannot exit these capillaries. Only lipid-soluble substances can pass through capillary walls. Once a substance escapes from the capillaries, it must be able to penetrate a thick, fatty covering of glial cells, called the glial sheath (Julien, 1988).

As illustrated in Figure 4.1, the blood-brain barrier can be a formidable impediment to unwanted substances. However, the barrier or, more appropriately, the gate permits many substances that are not essential for proper brain function to enter the brain and alter brain function. Other factors also determine whether a drug can gain entrance to the brain. For example, a brain injury or the presence of other drugs or chemical conditions in the brain may increase the absorption of certain drugs that would normally be excluded from the brain. Because psychoactive drugs frequently resemble natural brain chemicals, and because they are largely fat soluble, they generally pass through the blood-brain barrier rather easily.

Placental Barrier

The placental barrier functions to separate two distinct human beings: the mother and the fetus. This barrier is composed of a network of tissues that intervene between the fetal and maternal blood supply, preventing or hindering certain substances or organisms from passing from mother to fetus. On the other hand, a primary responsibility of the placental barrier is to transport essential nutrients to the fetus and allow waste products to be eliminated. Because the placental barrier must be permeable for such transportation purposes, many substances present in the mother's blood are mistakenly permitted to enter the placenta and potentially influence fetal development.

Pregnant women in the United States frequently take prescription, over-the-counter, and illicit drugs and, knowingly or unknowingly, exposure their unborn babies to these substances. Cold medications, antibiotics, pain relievers, antinausea agents, and other seemingly innocuous drugs are all routinely consumed by good-intentioned mothers. Some of these substances are able to cross the placental barrier and harm the fetus. Many other substances that we are all exposed to may also harm the fetus. For example, toxic substances in food (e.g., monosodium glutamate), caffeine, cigarettes (passive or active inhalation), cosmetics, household cleaners, and other environmental contaminants may affect the fetus in unknown ways. Fumes from gasoline contain benzene, a known toxin; thus, pumping gas at a self-serve station may be inadvisable for a pregnant woman. Many obstetricians also advise pregnant women against having their hair permed as the chemicals from the permanent solution soak into the bloodstream and may enter the placenta. Also, a mother who smokes cigarettes risks a smaller baby,

Figure 4.1   *Blood Brain Barrier*

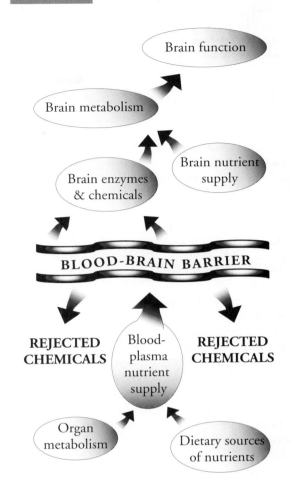

with smaller head circumference (somewhat reflective of intellectual capacity), and upper respiratory problems, including allergies, infections, and asthma.

Obviously, many pregnant women are not aware of some of the hazards in their daily lives that may affect their fetus. Furthermore, a woman typically discovers that she is pregnant three or four weeks (and sometimes months) following conception; at that time, much of embryonic brain development has already occurred. Although most babies exposed to these substances will appear normal and healthy, a few may not, and we will never be able to specifically pinpoint the cause. Many substances, including many drugs of abuse, are widely known to be toxic to a fetus, and the fetus receives approximately 75 to 100 percent of the drug concentration in the blood of the mother in a very few minutes. Exposure of a fetus to a drug with toxic effects can result in malformations, a process referred to as teratogenesis (literally meaning "formation of a monster"). This is most likely to occur when the mother takes a drug during the first trimester of pregnancy. During this period, major organs and bodily structures form so that the fetus is particularly vulnerable to gross deformities. Exposures later in pregnancy may result in late miscarriage, respiratory depression, early deliveries, low birth weight, abnormal brain function, cognitive or language impairments, and a host of other physical and behavioral problems. Newborn babies are unable to metabolize or eliminate drugs and, as a consequence, suffer more damaging effects than does the mother.

Drug Action

Once an unmetabolized drug or the active metabolite of a drug enters the brain, it may only exert an effect by increasing, decreasing, or somehow altering the activity of neural cells. The molecular structure of the drug or its metabolite determines which cells will be affected and in what manner. As discussed in the preceding chapter on the brain, the drug will target those cells that have an affinity for the drug or metabolite given its chemical structure. Those target cells become receptors for the drug. Even though the drug is evenly distributed throughout the brain, only receptor cells will receive the drug, produce an effect, and alter consciousness. Thus, the site of drug action is specialized according to features of both the drug and the cells involved (see Figure 4.2).

A drug may interact with the surface membrane of a cell, the cell body, or the synapse. If it acts on the surface of a cell's membrane, as does alcohol, it generally depresses the activity of the cell. It may act instead on the cell body by attaching to the membrane and changing its permeability. In this case, substances may be able to enter the cell more freely and their by-product may not be eliminated properly, or certain substances may not be able to enter that normally would be admitted. Depending on the scenario, the cell's activity may be either increased or decreased as a result (see Figure 4.3).

Most psychoactive drugs are thought to exert their effects on the synaptic membranes of neurons. As discussed in Chapter 3, some drugs are so structurally similar to natural neurotransmitters or peptides in the brain that they substitute for the natural chemical at the receptor site. When this substitution occurs, the drug may mimic the effects of the natural brain chemical by activating the cell, or it may suppress activity by blocking the site and preventing the attachment of the natural chemical. This is particularly true for the opiate drugs, which resemble neuropeptides, causing the brain to mistake the drug for its own chemicals.

Other drugs may influence the neuron's synaptic membrane in a host of other ways. Some may influence neurotransmitter activity by increasing or decreasing its deactivation rate. If a neurotransmitter's deactivation rate is increased, the activity of the neurotransmitter will cease more quickly. Conversely, if the deactivation rate is decreased, the neurotransmitter may be active longer. Thus, if the neurotransmitter is designed to stimulate, such stimulation may continue for a longer period than normal. Other drugs may evoke the release of neurotransmitters from neurons, while still others may prevent the reuptake of the neurotransmitter by the sending cell. In both of these cases, the drug is causing a sustained action of the neurotransmitter. Some antidepressants, for example, stimulate the release of norepinephrine while others may stimulate its release plus prevent its reuptake. Finally, other drugs may interfere with the ability of neurons to manufacture neurotransmitter substances by preventing the influx of enzymes or other substances required for production or by preventing the proper storage of neurotransmitters in the vesicles (the cell's storage facility)(see Figure 4.4).

As a rule of thumb, psychoactive drugs that alter the manufacture, storage, or release of neurotransmitters are called presynaptic drug effects (Ray & Ksir, 1990). For example, cocaine is thought to stimulate the release and interfere with the reuptake of the neurotransmitters norepinephrine and dopamine primarily at the presynaptic neuron. The sustained action of these neurotransmitters in the synapse results in an intense feeling of euphoria and heightened stimulation. Psychoactive drugs that act at neurotransmitter receptors have postsynaptic effects as they alter cell activity by mimicking or blocking a natural chemical (Ray & Ksir). The opiates, for example, substitute for the brain's neuropeptides because of their molecular similarity and produce the same effects at the postsynaptic site as the neuropeptides, only with increased intensity.

Deactivation and Elimination

After a drug has been distributed to various parts of the body via the bloodstream, it must be deactivated and even-

Figure 4.2 *Illustration of Drug Receptors*

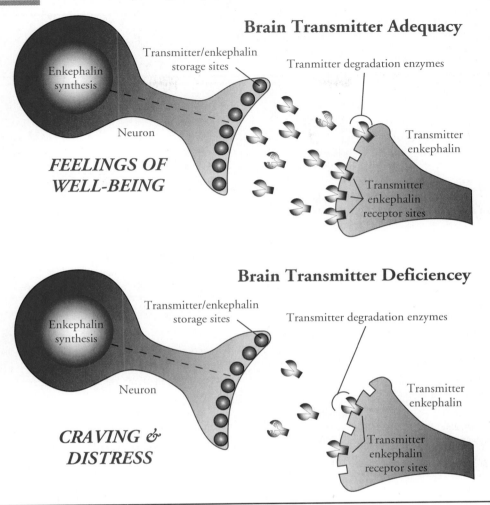

Brain Transmitter Adequacy

Enkephalin synthesis

Transmitter/enkephalin storage sites

Tranmitter degradation enzymes

Neuron

FEELINGS OF WELL-BEING

Transmitter enkephalin

Transmitter enkephalin receptor sites

Brain Transmitter Deficiencey

Enkephalin synthesis

Transmitter/enkephalin storage sites

Transmitter degradation enzymes

Neuron

CRAVING & DISTRESS

Transmitter enkephalin

Transmitter enkephalin receptor sites

Source: Neurogenesis, Inc. and Matrix Technologies

tually eliminated from the body. Drugs that are lipid soluble leave the bloodstream to alter behavior or consciousness in the brain. Lipid-soluble drugs will also be absorbed into body fat and may remain in the body for a longer period of time, potentially producing a sustained effect. This is true for phencyclidine (PCP), which is thought to remain in the fatty tissue of the central nervous system for an extended period of time. Fatty tissue does not receive a great deal of the blood supply, so when drug concentrations in the bloodstream diminish, the drug is released from fat in active form. This process accounts for why the percentage of body fat is an important determinant in drug effects. It also accounts for why lipid-soluble drugs may be

potentially dangerous. Although there are medical procedures that help to eliminate drugs from the bloodstream during a drug overdose, it is impossible to rid the body's fatty tissue of a drug that may eventually be released into the bloodstream in potentially fatal doses. As discussed in Chapter 12, it is believed that, as a result of being stored in fatty tissue, some psychedelic drugs are eventually metabolized or released to cause flashbacks in ex-users.

In addition to considering the lipid solubility of a drug in predicting drug effects, the amount of the drug that binds to protein is important. You may remember that part of the drug binds to protein and remains in the bloodstream as an inactive substance while the unbound

Figure 4.3   *Neurotransmitters and Sites of Action*

Neurotransmitter/ central action	Drug of abuse that affect neurotransmitter action	Central location
Aminobutyric Acid (GABA) General inhibition of other neurotransmitters	Alcohol Barbiturates Benzodiazepines Chloral hydrate Ethchlorvynol Meprobamate Methaqualone Phencyclidine	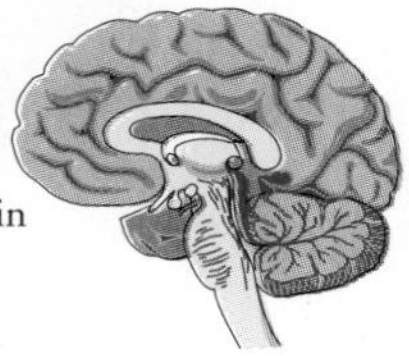 Throughout brain
Acetylcholine Counterbalances dopamine Maintains memory Initiates short-term memory	Phencyclidine	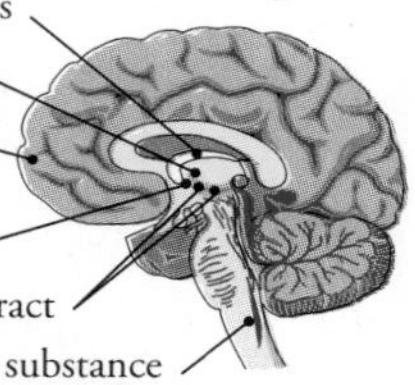 Caudate nucleus Lentiform nucleus Cerebral cortex Nucleus basalis of Meynert Nigrostriatal tract Reticular activating substance
Norepinephrine Modulates mood Maintains sleeping state	Amphetamines Cocaine Opiates Phencyclidine	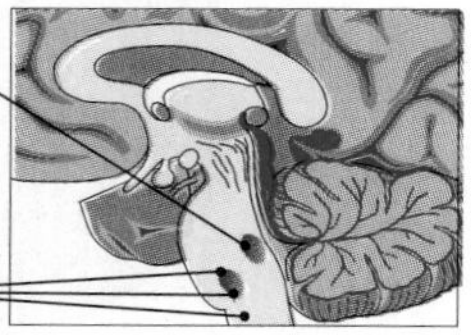 Nucleus locus ceruleus Pontine & medullary cell groups
Dopamine Counterbalances acetylcholine Stimulates pleasure center Modulates mood Affects intellectual processes Inhibits prolactin release	Amphetamines Cocaine Phencyclidine	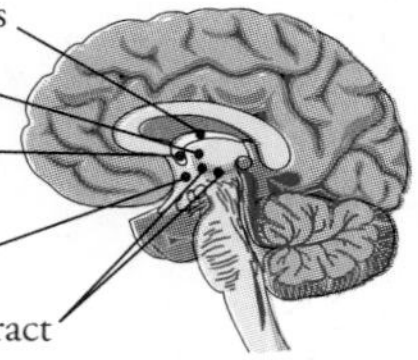 Caudate nucleus Lentiform nucleus Nucleus accumbens Tuberoinfundibular pathway Nigrostriatal tract
Serotonin Modulates mood Initiates sleep Involved in REM sleep	Psychedelic agents Phencyclidine	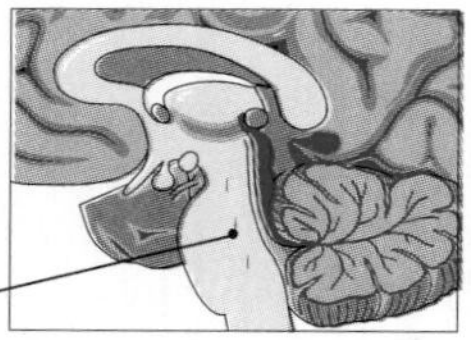 Pontine raphe nuclei
ßEndorphin Modulates mood Modulates pain perception Inhibits norepinephrine release	Opiates Phencyclidine	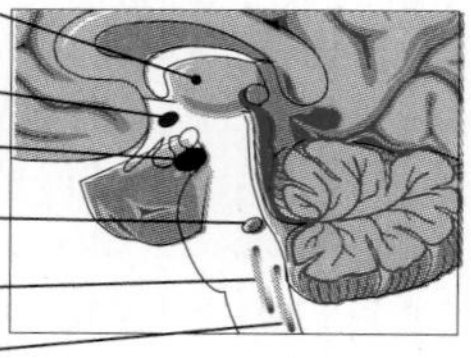 Thalamus Arcuate & premamillary nuclei Hippocampus Nucleus locus ceruleus Nucleus solitarius Substatia gelatinosa

Source: Beck Visual Communications, Inc.

Figure 4.4   *Receptor Blockage by Cocaine Keeps Dopamine in the Synapse to Enhance Its Effects.*

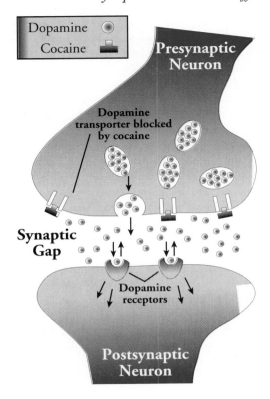

Table 4.2   *Common Drugs of Abuse*

Drug	Class	Street Names
Amphetamines	Stimulant	Black beauty Crosses Hearts
Barbiturates	Sedative/ Tranquilizer	Barbs Blue racers Yellow jackets
Benzodiazepines	Sedative/ Tranquilizer	"Roches" Tranks Pumpkin
Cocaine	Stimulant	Coke Crack Free base
Ethchlorvynol (Placidyl)	Sedative/ Tranquilizer	Green jeans Pickles
Fentanyl (Sublimaze)	Opiate	Six-pack
Glutethimide (Doriden, Doriglute)	Sedative/ Tranquilizer	Grays Seabees
Heroin	Opiate	Horse Skag Smack
Lysergic acid (LSD)	Psychedelic agent	Acid Blue Cheer LSD
Meperidine (Demerol)	Opiate	Banana
Meprobamate (Equanil, Miltown, Neuramate, etc.)	Sedative/ Tranquilizer	Bams
Mescaline	Psychedelic agent	Cactus Mex Peyote
Methamphetamine (Desoxyn)	Stimulant	Crystal meth Twenty-twenty
3.4 Methylenedioxy- methamphetamine (MDMA)	Psychedelic agent	Adam Ecstasy
Phencyclidine	Phencyclidine	Hog PCP Surfer
Propoxyphene (Darvon, Dolene, Doxaphene, etc.)	Psychedelic agent	Lilies
Psilocybin	Psychedelic agent	Mushroom Purple passion

Source: Giannini and Miller, 1989

or free part is activated, metabolized, and eventually eliminated. Each drug maintains a balance between its bound and unbound parts. This ratio becomes disturbed as the unbound parts leave the body. Thus, as the unbound portion is eliminated, portions of the protein-bound drug are released into the bloodstream in its free and active form. The result is a sustained drug action until all of the drug is released into the bloodstream as an active metabolite.

Most drugs are absorbed, distributed, metabolized, and deactivated before they are eliminated. Deactivation is largely the job of the liver, which produces enzymes that break down a drug and increase its water solubility. In most cases, this process produces a less active form of the drug called an end product. If a portion of the drug cannot be fully deactivated by the liver, it returns to the bloodstream to be recirculated and then again arrives at the liver for further deactivation. The efficiency of this mechanism

is contingent upon the health of the liver. For instance, some individuals in advanced phases of alcoholism are impaired in their ability to deactivate and excrete alcohol. The elderly also have difficulty in deactivating drugs as the liver no longer functions efficiently. Thus, toxic levels of a drug may accumulate and cause damage.

It is important to note that many psychoactive drugs actually increase the rate at which liver enzymes metabolize the drugs, causing the drugs to be eliminated more rapidly. The development of tolerance to a drug (discussed in the following section) is influenced by this mechanism. As the individual continues to use a drug, enzyme levels rise to deactivate the drug. Larger doses of the drug are then needed to achieve the same effect as smaller doses did earlier.

Once the drug has been deactivated biochemically, it is eliminated from the body through several routes. The kidneys can excrete drugs through the urine. This process is further influenced by the pH balance of the urine (the acid/alkaline ratio). If a drug is primarily basic (or alkaline), an acidic urine will enhance its elimination. If a drug is primarily acidic, a basic urine will enhance its elimination (Corry & Cimbolic, 1985). Some drugs are eliminated relatively unchanged in saliva and perspiration. Anesthetic agents may be exhaled through the lungs, as are small amounts of alcohol (hence, the unpleasant odor emanating from a drunk). Although cannabinols (from marijuana), nicotine (from cigarettes), and constituents of opium are absorbed into the lungs to exert their effects, they are eliminated in the urine. Drugs are also found in nursing mother's milk. Although amounts in breast milk are quite small, an infant can ingest active drugs through the mother's milk and the effects can be quite pronounced. Infants have not developed a fully functioning liver with the ability to deactivate the drug and may experience drug effects even when the mother no longer feels intoxicated. Finally, some of a deactivated drug may reach the bile, for example certain antibiotics, where it is sent to the intestine. If the drug is fat soluble, once it travels from the bile to the intestine, it may be reabsorbed into the bloodstream and eliminated by the kidney. If, on the other hand, the drug is mostly water soluble, small amounts of the drug may be detected in the feces.

Drug Dependence

Drug dependence is what most clinicians refer to as the final stage of drug use. The onset of a drug dependency becomes apparent when users are no longer in control of their drug-taking behavior. They are under the control of the drug—a chemical need for the drug. In 1950, the World Health Organization (WHO) defined drug dependency (called at that time drug addiction) as (1) an over-

whelming desire or need (compulsion) to continue taking the drug and to obtain it by any means, (2) the tendency to increase the dose, and (3) the psychic (psychological) and physiological dependence on the drug. The first criterion of drug dependence is a behavioral and psychological habit or perceived need for continued drug use and may be largely a function of the second and third criteria. Compulsion to take a drug is also, essentially, a function of learned experiences with previous drug effects. The user associates the drug with pleasurable or desirable effects, in addition to other environmental conditions, thereby becoming preoccupied with obtaining and using the drug. There is a general consensus that the latter two criteria of dependence are essential for a diagnosis of drug dependence: tolerance, established by WHO as the second criterion, and withdrawal, the third criterion.

Inset 4.1 illustrates the Diagnostic Statistical Manual's (DSM-III-R) established criteria for a psychiatric diagnosis of psychoactive substance dependence.

"The essential feature of this disorder is a cluster of cognitive, behavioral, and physiologic symptoms that indicate that the person has impaired control of psychoactive substance use and continues use of the substance despite adverse consequences" (APA, 1987: 167-168). These criteria for drug dependence are widely adhered to by practitioners and researchers alike.

Tolerance

Although one may develop tolerance to a drug without being dependent, tolerance is a necessary condition of drug dependence or addiction. Tolerance to a drug occurs when larger doses are required over time to produce the same effect originally achieved by a smaller dose. The user becomes less responsive to the effects of the drug for a number of reasons. Tolerance is not an all-or-none phenomenon. Rather, tolerance is a matter of degree with some drugs producing immediate and profound levels of tolerance, and other drugs producing only mild tolerance that is barely perceptible. It is also possible for tolerance to actually plateau over time; after the user reaches a particular dosage level, the effects remain the same given the same dose. The nature of the drug itself, the dosage taken, the frequency of use, the mode of administration, and individual physiological traits all determine the extent to which physical tolerance will develop.

If the drug remains active in the bloodstream for a long period of time (perhaps twelve hours or more), tolerance

Inset 4.1

DIAGNOSTIC CRITERIA FOR PSYCHOACTIVE SUBSTANCE DEPENDENCE DSM-III-R (APA, 1987)

A. At least three of the following:

1. substance often taken in larger amounts or over a longer period than the person intended

2. persistent desire or one or more unsuccessful efforts to cut down or control substance use

3. a great deal of time spent in activities necessary to get the substance (e.g., theft), taking the substance (e.g., chain smoking), or recovering from its effects

4. frequent intoxication or withdrawal symptoms when expected to fulfill major role obligations at work, school or home (e.g., does not got to work because hung over, goes to school or work "high", intoxicated while taking care of his or her children), or when substance use is physically hazardous (e.g., drives when intoxicated)

5. important social, occupational, or recreational activities given up or reduced because of substance use

6. continued substance use despite knowledge of having a persistent or recurrent social, psychological, or physical problem that is caused or exacerbated by the use of the substance (e.g., keeps using heroin despite family arguments about it, cocaine-induced depression, or having an ulcer made worse by drinking)

7. marked tolerance: need for markedly increased amounts of the substance (i.e., at least a 50 percent increase) in order to achieve intoxication or desired effect, or markedly diminished effect with continued use of the same amount

Note: The following items may not apply to cannabis, hallucinogens, or phencyclidine (PCP):

8. characteristic withdrawal symptoms

9. substance often taken to relieve or avoid withdrawal symptoms

B. Some symptoms of the disturbance have persisted for at least one month or have occurred repeatedly over a longer period of time.

is less likely to develop. Those drugs that become inactive more rapidly do so because they increase the number and activity of enzymes in the liver, which degrades the drug. Thus, they are more likely to produce a form of tolerance known as metabolic tolerance. This phenomenon is directly influenced by a drug's half-life—the amount of time that is required for half of the active portion of the drug to be metabolized or excreted. Short acting drugs are more likely to produce tolerance since they may tend to activate more enzymes. However, tolerance will diminish quickly once drug use ceases. For example, cocaine has a very short half-life and tolerance develops rapidly. Once the effects of cocaine have declined and the drug is no longer administered, tolerance disappears, and the user needs to start with the original dose when use resumes. If the amount of cocaine used after a week's rest equals the amount used during the last binge, the dose may be lethal. Thus, a drug with a short half-life will shorten the life of tolerance and determine how soon after drug use ends withdrawal symptoms will begin.

Another form of tolerance, cellular tolerance, develops when CNS cells attempt to compensate for drug effects. If a drug is designed to stimulate cell function, the cell will try to compensate for that stimulation by depressing its activity. Accordingly, stimulation by the drug during subsequent uses will be somewhat reduced, causing the drug user to increase the dose in order to heighten the drug experience. This cell reaction may be considered a biological defense mechanism mobilized by the body to ward off unfavorable drug effects. Enzymes are produced to inactivate the drug, and brain cells attempt to override drug effects. This mechanism causes the user to perceive a need for increased quantities of a drug to achieve the desired effect.

In sum, there are two types of tolerance that cause users to raise dosage levels. Metabolic tolerance refers to the greater efficiency of enzymes to degrade the drug with repeated use. The chronic user will have lower blood and brain levels of active drug than the novice drug user, even though both have taken the same amount. The second form of tolerance is cellular. Target cells in the brain develop an insensitivity to drug effects when drug use is chronic. As a result, drug effects are diminished even when levels of drugs in the blood and brain are high.

Tolerance develops differently depending on the particular drug taken and its unique effects, suggesting that there are several mechanisms involved in the development of tolerance. As a rule, tolerance will eventually disappear after the drug has been discontinued. How long this will take, again, depends on the particular drug, the mode of administration, and the length of time the drug was taken.

Cross tolerance occurs when tolerance to one drug diminishes the effect of another drug, indicating that the two drugs may exert their effects by the same mechanisms. Cross tolerance generally occurs when the drugs taken are members of the same family of drugs. All opiates will produce cross tolerance, even when they are not chemically identical; their effects are similar, and they all tend to be attenuated by opiate antagonists. Also, withdrawal symptoms from one opiate tend to be terminated by the administration of another opiate. This means that if a heroin user switches to methadone, another opiate, larger amounts of methadone will be needed to exert an effect than would be required for a nonuser, and the methadone will prevent the onset of withdrawal symptoms, thus maintaining the opiate dependency. Cross tolerance may also develop between LSD and other psychedelic drugs, such as mescaline. Drugs within the sedative-hypnotic family also share the ability to produce cross tolerance.

Reverse tolerance, or sensitization, occurs with only a few drugs and is characterized by increased effects of a drug after it is used repeatedly. This seems to be in stark contrast to the tolerance produced by most drugs. Marijuana, for example, is reported to produce more noteworthy effects after it is used several times. Amphetamines may also produce reverse tolerance. Something about the drug's properties, in interaction with the user's condition, causes the user to become more sensitive to the drug with repeated administration. As discussed in Chapter 6, some individuals believed to be biologically prone to alcoholism exhibit signs of sensitization; rather than becoming insensitive to alcohol over time, they actually become more sensitive.

Withdrawal

The third criterion for drug dependence cited by the WHO refers to the occurrence of withdrawal symptoms at drug use termination. Withdrawal symptoms are a direct result of drug dependence. They are frequently associated with tolerance (although they are separate phenomena) and may vary in severity depending on the level of physical dependence.

Due to the cellular tolerance that tends to result from chronic drug use, withdrawal symptoms are prolonged repercussions of the cell's attempt to compensate for drug effects. The result generally includes symptoms that are opposite to the effect produced by the drug and, as in rebound (defined later), drug cessation may actually exacerbate those symptoms that the user was originally attempting to suppress. An individual who has taken sleeping pills (barbiturates) for a period of time and terminates their use will experience unusual excitation and agitation as the cells remain highly active to override the drug's effects. Furthermore, the ex-user will experience an overwhelming desire to resume drug usage, known as craving, in order to quell withdrawal symptoms.

Opiates, barbiturates, and amphetamines produce symptoms of withdrawal that further motivate individuals to continue drug administration. In severe cases of withdrawal from drugs, such as alcohol and barbiturates, death may result. Dependence on alcohol is considered to be one of the most insidious addictions based on the high frequency with which death results from alcohol withdrawal among chronic alcoholics. This condition, known as delirium tremens (DTs), will be described in more detail in Chapter 6.

Although most incidences of drug dependence are self-induced, there is a growing recognition of a condition known as iatrogenic dependence. In these cases, the user becomes dependent on a prescription drug through inducements by a physician. Diazepam (Valium) is one example of a prescription drug that has been widely prescribed by physicians in the past, particularly to women, to reduce anxiety. With its properties of euphoria and relief from psychic pain, Valium has high abuse potential. Numerous other drugs with high abuse potential have been sought by patients from willing physicians, particularly the narcotics codeine, morphine, propoxyphene napsylate (Darvon), and meperidine (Demerol). Iatrogenically addicted patients are generally first exposed to prescription drugs for a legitimate medical purpose. Their use eventually becomes compulsive. These patients have been known to access several prescribing physicians to ensure a constant drug supply and continually phone these physicians with chronic, generalized complaints, indicating a need for more drugs. Impairments in daily activities develop, such as the inability to drive properly or to perform at the office, and the user becomes dysfunctional. Sometimes users are arrested for forging prescriptions. In recent years, the anxiety-reducing agent alprazolam (Xanax) has also been widely prescribed. Xanax has abuse potential and when iatrogenically addicted patients attempt to terminate their drug use, insomnia, severe anxiety, and sometimes panic attacks may result.

Drug Interactions and Effects

There are several ways a drug may have effects that were not predicted or desired, particularly when used in combination with other drugs. A cumulative effect will result when subsequent doses of a drug are taken before the initial dose has been deactivated and eliminated from the body. Levels of the drug may accumulate in the bloodstream, posing a potentially dangerous situation. The half-life of a drug becomes important in avoiding a toxic build-up. If a drug's half-life is relatively long, the next dose must be gauged so an adequate period of time elapses between doses. Heroin, for example, enables the user to experience the full effect of the drug and even sleep between doses to avoid a toxic build-up. On the other hand, cocaine, a drug with a short half-life, stimulates the user to stay awake. Thus, the user is more likely to administer doses in quick succession. In fact, with cocaine, the shorter the time between administrations, the greater the desired drug effect.

Another interactional effect is called displacement. When a drug that is substantially protein-bound has been taken and a second drug is introduced that displaces the first, large amounts of the first drug will be released into the bloodstream in active form. Displacement may produce a more intense effect of the first (or both) drug as more becomes available to the receptor and a potentially toxic situation may arise.

The term antagonism refers to the property of a drug to block another drug's receptor site. Once the site is blocked, the drug will not be able to access the receptor in order to produce an effect. Naloxone and naltrexone are opiate antagonists. Both of these drugs sit on the opiate receptor sites in the brain and either displace opiates currently occupying the site or prevent additional opiates from occupying the site. Since naloxone and naltrexone quickly displace opiates from the cells, they are often used to revive individuals who have overdosed on heroin.

A second way a drug may antagonize another drug is by somehow making the enzymes that are necessary to produce an effect unavailable or by interfering with the absorption of the drug. Antagonism may also refer to the ability of a drug to block the receptor site needed for a natural brain chemical, making it (the brain chemical) relatively ineffective.

Finally, a drug that acts as an agonist (also called a potentiator) either directly stimulates a receptor site to increase cell activity or enhances the effects of another drug or of both drugs. For example, opiates known as agonists stimulate either mu, kappa, or sigma receptors. Each of these receptors are located in various regions of the brain and spinal cord and are associated with various effects that are discussed more thoroughly in Chapter 7. When a drug agonizes the effects of another drug, in a sense, the result is synergistic; the user does not simply experience the effects of both drugs as they would function alone. Instead, the cumulative effects of the drugs are greater than the sum of their parts. The Karen Quinlan

Inset 4.2

TEST YOURSELF FOR ADDICTION

1. Do you have to use larger doses of cocaine to get the high you once experienced with smaller doses? (This means that you have developed a tolerance to the drug; you need more of it by a more direct route to achieve the same effect.)

2. Do you use cocaine almost continuously until your supply is exhausted? (This is called bingeing, and it signals loss of control over drug use.)

3. Is the cost of cocaine the major factor limiting your use, and do you wish you could afford more? (Your internal controls are virtually gone. The drug is in charge, and you will find yourself doing anything to get it.)

4. Do you use cocaine two or more times a week? (If you do, you are in the highest risk group for addiction.)

5. Do you have three or more of the following physical symptoms? Sleep problems, nosebleeds, headaches, sinus problems, voice problems, difficulty swallowing, sexual-performance problems, nausea or vomiting, trouble breathing or shortness of breath, constant sniffling or rubbing your nose, irregular heartbeats, epileptic seizures or convulsions? (Three or more of these indicate severe loss of bodily function related to coke abuse or addiction.)

6. Do you have three of more of the following psychological symptoms? Jitteriness; anxiety; depression; panic; irritability; suspiciousness; paranoia; difficulty concentrating; hallucinations; (seeing things that are not there); hearing voices when there are none; loss of interest in friends, hobbies, sports, or other noncocaine activities; memory problems; thoughts about suicide; attempted suicide; compulsive or repetitive acts like combing the hair, straightening of clothes or ties, tapping the feet for no reason. (Cocaine abuse is causing psychological problems that are not within your capacity to control.)

7. Have any or all of the problems specified in the previous two questions caused you to stop using cocaine for a period ranging from two weeks to six months or longer? (If not, the acquired disabilities are not strong enough to overcome the addiction.)

8. Do you find that you must take other drugs or alcohol to calm down following cocaine use? (You are trying to medicate yourself so as to maintain your cocaine habit without suffering the terrible side effects of addiction. You are, of course, flirting with becoming addicted to the second drug.)

9. Are you afraid that if you stop using cocaine your work will suffer? (You are psychologically dependent on the drug.)

10. Are you afraid that if you stop using cocaine you will be too depressed or unmotivated or without sufficient energy to function at your present level? (You are addicted and afraid of the withdrawal symptoms.)

11. Do you find that you cannot turn down cocaine when it is offered? (Use is out of your control.)

12. Do you think about limiting your use of cocaine? (You are on the verge of addiction and are trying ration use of the drug.)

13. Do you dream about cocaine? (This is related to compulsive use and the total domination of the drug.)

14. Do you think about cocaine at work? (This is also a part of the obsession with the drug.)

15. Do you think about cocaine when you are talking to or interacting with a loved one? (Obsession with the drug dominates all aspects of living.)

16. Are you unable to stop using the drug for one month? (This is certainly a sign of addiction.)

17. Have you lost or discarded your pre-cocaine friends? (You are stacking the deck in favor of cocaine by reducing negative feedback.)

18. Have you noticed that you have lost your pre-cocaine values, that you don't care about your job or career, your home and family, or that you will lie and steal to get coke? (Addiction causes slow but steady changes in the personality and the approach to life so as to reduce intrapsychic conflict.)

19. Do you feel the urge to use cocaine when you see a pipe or mirror or other paraphernalia? Do you taste it when you are not using it, or feel the urge to use it when you see it or talk about it? (This is called conditioning and occurs after long-term, heavy use.)

20. Do you usually use cocaine alone? (When addiction sets in this is the pattern. Social use ceases.)

21. Do you borrow heavily to support your cocaine habit? (You can be pretty sure you're addicted if you are willing to live so far above your means to get the drug.)

22. Do you prefer cocaine to family activities, food, or sex? (This is a sure sign of addiction. Cocaine need overrides fundamental human needs for food, sex and social interaction.)

23. Do you deal or distribute cocaine to others? (This kind of change in behavior signals addiction because it is an accommodation to the need for the drug.)

24. Are you afraid of being found out as a cocaine user? (Addicts usually live a double life, preferring not to choose one or the other alternative.)

25. When you stop using the drug, do you get depressed or "crash"? (This is a sign of withdrawal—a symptom of addiction.)

26. Do you miss work, or reschedule appointments, or fail to meet important obligations because of your cocaine use? (The drug has taken over your life.)

27. Is your cocaine use a threat to your career or personal goals? Has your cocaine use caused you to lose interest in your career? Has cocaine caused you job problems? Has the drug caused you

to lose your job? Has your cocaine use caused you to lose interest in or to have violent quarrels with people you love? Has your cocaine use caused you to lose your spouse or loved one? (You would hardly sacrifice so much if you were not addicted.)

28. Do people keep telling you that you are different or have changed in a significant way? (Addicted people are indeed different from the way they were pre-cocaine. Such comments are a clue to addiction.)

29. Have you used more than 50 percent of your savings for cocaine? Has your cocaine use bankrupted you and caused you to incur large debts? Have you committed a crime to support yourself and your cocaine habit? Have you stolen from work and/or family and friends? (If you are not addicted, would cocaine be worth these dreadful problems?)

30. Do you believe that your cocaine use has some medical value in treating a problem you have with energy, motivation, confidence, depression, or sex? (Users who believe this are most likely to develop addiction.)

31. Do you think you have had withdrawal symptoms when you stopped using cocaine? (Only addicted persons experience withdrawal.)

32. If you had $100 to spend, would you spend it on cocaine rather than on something for your house or apartment, on a gift for someone you love, or theater, records, movies, going out with friends or family? (Addicts become fixated on their drug they think of nothing else, no one else, and no other form of entertainment.)

33. Do you think that you are addicted? (If you think so, you probably are.)

34. Do you use cocaine compulsively despite your recognition that the drug is a very real threat to your physical and psychological well-being, relationships, family, and job? (This is addiction.)

35. Did you ever enter psychiatric treatment or therapy for a cocaine-related problem and not tell the doctor or therapist about your cocaine use or how current or recent it is? (When an addicted person is pressured into getting help, that person may not only try to cover up the extent of drug abuse but may also use treatment as a cover for continued use of the drug.)

36. Did you have a cocaine problem that was cured either through your own efforts or with the help of friends or with professional treatment? (The critical word is "cured." No addict is really cured—rather addicts have a remission of a chronic disease that can recur should they become users of cocaine again.)

37. Have you ever used cocaine and had hallucinations, a convulsion or seizure, angina (severe pain around the heart), loss of consciousness, the impulse to kill yourself or others? And when any of these side effects passed, did you figure that you would use less next time or use a purer quality of the drug? (These side effects are related to addictive use, but the addict prefers to ascribe them to overdose or to the adulterants used to make the drug go further. The user then can continue to use the drug under the illusion that it will be OK the next time.)

38. Do you leave paraphernalia or a supply of cocaine at work? (This may be a call for help by person who feels life is out of control. It is like a suicide note left so that people will find it and prevent the act.)

39. Do you sometimes wish that you would be discovered as user by someone who would see to it that you got into treatment and recovered? (If so, you know you need help and want it.)

40. Do you use cocaine three times a week, or even more often, and still try to maintain an interest in diet, health, exercise, and fitness? (The interest may be there, but the fact is that such heavy use of the drug makes it virtually impossible to act on the interest. There is too great a conflict in values.)

41. Have you switched from intranasal use to freebasing or intravenous use? (This usually means that tolerance to the drug has developed, and it is very likely that you will binge and become addicted in short order.)

42. Have you been using cocaine more than once a week for three or more years? (With this much use, any stress or change in your life can turn you into a daily user with a high probability of addiction resulting.)

43. Do you find yourself choosing friends or lovers because of their access to cocaine or their cocaine use? (This kind of behavior usually indicates a life out of control.)

44. Do you wake up in the morning and wonder how you could have let cocaine gain control over your life? (You are addicted if you have these thoughts.)

45. Do you find it almost impossible to fall asleep without a drink or sleeping pill or tranquilizer? (You now have a second addiction.)

46. Since you started using cocaine, have you ever wondered whether you would be able to live without it ? (We find that people who raise this question are generally hooked on the drug.)

47. Have you wondered whether you would be better off dead than continuing to use cocaine? (This question usually suggests an addiction so profound that the addict feels terminally ill.)

48. Have you ever wished that you would die of an overdose in your sleep? (Same as above.)

49. Do you use cocaine in your car, at work, in a public bathroom, on airplanes, or on other public places? (You are so desperate you want to be caught —and helped.)

50. Do you use cocaine and then drive a car within six hours after use? (Cocaine has impaired your judgment and you are out of control. Don't wait to get help until after you have injured or killed a pedestrian.)

case is one example of this action. She reportedly took barbiturates and alcohol simultaneously, which placed her in a coma that eventually caused her death. If she had taken either drug alone, that fatal outcome would probably not have occurred.

Finally, some drugs are called mixed agonist-antagonists. This means that the drugs stimulate one type of receptor while blocking another type. Opiates in this category, for example, include Nalbuphine, butorphanol, pentazocine, and buprenorphine. As an aside, some drugs that stimulate more than one type of receptor have a much higher affinity for certain receptors than others, thus, having greater drug effects associated with the choice receptor than with the secondary receptor.

Dose-Response Relationship

The dose of the drug taken is a critical consideration in determining the intensity of the response. Because a single drug will produce many different effects or responses, various dosage levels predict the intensity of each response differently. Barbiturates, for instance, may produce relaxation at a low dose, sedation at a moderate dose, and coma and death at a high dose. Barbiturate effects on mood state, however, differ entirely; in low doses there is mild euphoria and disinhibition, while in higher doses the individual will become behaviorally depressed.

For any given drug, there is a dosage level that will produce no response. With increasing doses of any drug, responses will generally become more intensified. If only a slightly increased dose of a drug produces much more intense effects, then there is little difference between what it takes to go from a minimal response to a maximal effect. Such drugs may be considered potentially unsafe, and great caution must be used when formulating the dosage. The potency of a drug is a function of the dose given; a very potent drug would be one that produces an intense response with a very small dose. LSD, for example, is considered extremely potent; minute amounts exert intense effects. On the other end of the spectrum, there are doses so high that no greater effect can be achieved. This is called the maximum effective dosage of a drug. No matter how much aspirin is taken, for example, the analgesic effects of morphine will never be reached.

Finally, it is important to note that individuals vary significantly in the way each responds to any given drug. The *Physician's Desk Reference (PDR)* provides recommended dosage levels based on average responses of a number of individuals who participated in studies of the drug. These averages do not always apply to individual cases; one person may have a low threshold to certain drugs necessitating that lower doses be taken, while another person may have a high threshold requiring higher doses to achieve a desirable effect.

Because there is so much variability in drug effects between individuals using the same drug at the same dose, the therapeutic index is used to determine what the effective dose is relative to the toxic dose. This index is calcu-

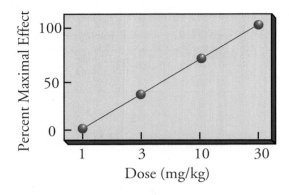

Figure 4.5   *Dose-Response Curve*

lated by determining the median dose that produces a desired effect in 50 percent of those who use it (effective dose, ED). Then, the median dose that causes death in 50 percent of subjects (lethal dose, LD) is calculated to create a ratio of LD:ED. (For those of you feeling squeamish about participating in drug studies, remember that these particular studies to formulate drug safety guidelines are performed only on mice.) A high therapeutic index, indicating a high ratio of LD to ED, suggests a greater safety margin.

As an example, let's consider the relative safety levels of morphine. Morphine's desired effect for most legitimate purposes is pain relief. Amounts greater than indicated, however, may produce respiratory depression. Thus, a dose of 10 milligrams may provide pain relief to 50 percent of subjects while a dose of 100 milligrams may kill 50 percent. The ratio, in this example, is 100:10 or 10, indicating that 50 percent of mice will be killed if ten times the average dose is administered. On the surface, determining dosage level seems elementary—one should simply take the recommended dose and not exceed it. But in reality, determining lethality and effectiveness is quite imprecise. There is a certain degree of overlap between these two results. Some subjects (mice or people) will die even with a recommended dosage. We can expect that a certain percentage of the population will be on either extreme with respect to drug responsivity. Certain individuals will respond to a much lower than average dose while others are able to take much higher doses than recommended without harm. Still others may suffer adverse consequences from taking only what has been recommended. It is also important to keep in mind that the therapeutic index applies selectively to particular drug effects, while all drugs have several effects that must be tested. Individual variability may be due to genetic factors, weight, age, gender, expectations, stomach contents, brain chemistry, psychological state, and much, much more. No matter what the cause, individual variability compromises our ability to exactly gauge safety levels of any given drug for any given person.

Placebo Effects

Because an individual's belief that a drug will produce a particular effect may be so convincingly strong, it is possible for an inactive, inert substance to produce a similar effect. This is known as the placebo effect. A placebo is commonly a sugar pill or some other inert substance that is administered to a subject or patient who believes the pill is an active drug. Given a sugar pill and told that the pill is an amphetamine, an individual may be likely to speed up, become agitated and hyper, and display behaviors typical of amphetamine users. The mere belief and knowledge of what the drug is supposed to do can completely alter behavior and mood state. Given a nonalcoholic drink and told that it is vodka and orange juice, people are known to become more sociable and uninhibited due to their tendency to associate alcohol consumption with such behaviors.

In medical research, placebos are used to counteract the influence that the experiment alone has on the individual that cannot be attributed to the experimental stimulus. Without the use of a placebo, an investigator may not know whether a drug is responsible for the changes observed in a subject or whether merely participating in the research or receiving a pill caused the changes. In a double-blind experiment, either a drug or placebo is administered to separate groups, and neither the experimenter nor the subjects know which group is receiving which pill. Under these conditions, changes observed in those who received the actual drug that are over and above those changes incurred by those receiving placebo can be considered a drug effect, rather than a placebo effect (Ross & Olson, 1982).

Placebo effects are surprisingly strong and sometimes effective. Studies have shown that acute pain can actually be relieved or the immune system boosted under the "influence" of a placebo (Fields & Levine, 1981; Gerald, 1981). There is apparently some biochemical process that is mobilized when a belief system, or the power of suggestion, is strong enough to have physical manifestations. For some

individuals, in certain circumstances, a placebo may exert its influence by releasing the natural opiates of the brain—the endorphins. In fact, the drug naloxone, which blocks the effects of morphine (structurally similar to the endorphins), also appears to block the placebo effect! Other neurotransmitters have also been implicated in the placebo effect, including serotonin and the catecholamines.

An interesting observation of individuals who are classified as thrill or sensation seekers involves their response to an alcohol placebo. When sensation-seeking subjects are given a drink that they are led to believe is alcohol, they are more prone to reckless driving than when they are not "drinking." Instead of thinking, "I've been drinking, so I'd better be careful driving," as most of us do, sensation seekers who merely think they have had alcohol engage in potentially destructive behavior. Indeed, the effects of a placebo can be dramatic.

Other Factors Influencing Drug Effects

In addition to the pharmacological properties of a psychoactive drug, there are many other physical and external conditions that may influence or modulate drug effects. Age, for example, determines to a great extent a drug's metabolization rate, duration of action, potency, elimination time, and effects. Small children tend to metabolize drugs more quickly and, therefore, need smaller, albeit more frequent administrations to maintain blood levels. Largely because children have less body fat, drugs are eliminated from their bodies more rapidly. They also tend to experience fewer and less severe side effects from many drugs. Paradoxical effects, which are effects opposite to those expected or experienced by most people, are more likely to occur among children. Stimulants, for example, frequently calm the hyperkinetic child, whereas in an adult the result is more commonly observed as hyperactivity.

The elderly generally experience the opposite consequences of those experienced by children. Because their organs do not function as well as a younger person, their bodies tend to eliminate drugs more slowly and drug effects last longer. They have a larger proportion of body fat, resulting in the accumulation of drugs in fatty tissue. Their circulation is poor and their brains have lost cells. There is a growing awareness that many elderly folks suffer from problems related to their drug use. In the past, physicians frequently chalked these problems up to depression, lethargy, and other disorders and prescribed more drugs! Beta blockers, used for certain heart conditions to reduce adrenal output, are widely used in the elderly. Because so many heart patients also have depression, physicians have assumed that they are depressed due to their failing condition and family circumstances, and prescribe antidepressants. Physicians are becoming increasingly aware that many of these problems are a direct result of the drugs being taken and are now either eliminating their use or, at a minimum, tapering back on the amounts given. Beta blockers, for example, have been shown to contribute to depression, so instead of prescribing antidepressants, reductions in the amount of beta blockers administered should be considered.

How massive an individual is should also be considered in determining dosage level and frequency of administration. Children, for example, must be weighed in order to determine dosage. Also, large people tend to metabolize drugs more slowly and retain the drug for a longer time. Drugs will be retained longer in fatty tissue. Although this is not universally true, people with a slight build tend to be more sensitive to drug effects.

Only recently have we discovered that race is an important determinant in drug effects. As you will read in Chapter 6, alcohol is metabolized differently by Asians than by Caucasians or African Americans. The National Institutes of Health are presently conducting studies to evaluate the effects of certain medications on various ethnic groups so that dosage levels can be carefully gauged and drug effects can be more accurately predicted.

Similar to race, gender also seems to play a role in drug effects. We know that women have more body fat and, consequently, tend to store more drugs in their systems. They also tend to be more sensitive to certain drugs, thereby experiencing greater drug effects. Some of this may be due to expectations, but other aspects of physiology are more important in male-female differences in drug response. Most drug research is conducted using male subjects. As a result, we do not know nearly as much as we should about gender differences in drug responsivity, so we are unable to accurately predict drug effects in women.

Drug Set and Setting

For years we have recognized that certain conditions not directly related to the drug's pharmacology or the user's biology may also profoundly influence and determine drug effects. A user's expectations for a drug-related experience is called the set. As described in Chapter 6, if individuals believe that alcohol will act as a social lubricant, they are more likely to become party animals. If, on the other hand, a person expects to become uninhibited and perhaps aggressive, a fight is more likely to ensue under the influence of alcohol. Expectations for a drug-related experience are very much based on what we have observed while others are using the drug; if Dad becomes angry or violent when drinking, we probably will also. Thus, modeling the behavior and moods of others who have used the drug helps determine our set. Expectations are also guided by what friends and others tell us about their experiences. If we are told that marijuana is sedating and causes users to become couch potatoes, we will probably become just that. Those who are told that marijuana unleashes social inhibitions and makes us giggle and become more amiable are more likely to become so. Another determinant of set is the user's fear. Those who are weary or anxious about their pending drug experience, particularly those who are naive users, are more likely to become distraught or have a "bad trip" than those who are experienced with drugs or have more positive expectations.

Obviously, some drug effects are so strong that our set will have only minor influences; for example, heroin is sedating, and it is hard to get around that. Amphetamines are profoundly stimulating and one would be hard pressed to find an amphetamine-intoxicated person who experienced sedation. Some drugs are more amenable to the user's set than others. Observers have noted that marijuana and the hallucinogens are more affected by the set than heroin, amphetamines, barbiturates, and PCP. Nevertheless, in sometimes subtle and sometimes potent ways, set or expectations can influence drug effects. Placebo effects are classic examples of how expectations can influence drug reactions; if a sugar pill is thought to be morphine, we may actually experience pain reduction.

Setting refers to the social context in which the drug is used. If the surroundings are unfamiliar or hostile, the user may become fearful, uncomfortable, or have a "bad trip." In the presence of friends or alone, on the other hand, the user will more likely be relaxed and the drug experience pleasant. In addition to the immediate surroundings, the setting contributes to the expectations for drug effects. As described in Chapter 13, Becker (1963) illustrated the significance of how we learn to respond to a psychoactive drug, in his example, marijuana. We must first learn how to use a drug properly to achieve a desirable effect. Then we must learn how to recognize the drug's effects. And finally, we learn how to identify the drug-induced changes as pleasurable. When someone first tries marijuana, he or she may not hold the smoke in long enough to achieve an effect. This must be learned. Frequently, novice users report that they did not become high after the first use. According to Becker, we must learn to recognize the effects so that, in a way, we can mentally expand upon them by focusing our attention on them. Sometimes, first users do not find certain psychoactive drugs pleasant, including marijuana, heroin, and cocaine. Over time the user begins to make positive associations with the drug effects. These are learning or conditioning experiences that allow a determined user to maximize the pleasurable effects and minimize the unpleasant effects.

Drug Use, Abuse, and Dependency

Drug use, abuse, and dependency are distinctive concepts, yet there is no consensus concerning their definitions or diagnosis. In fact, definitions of various forms of drug use and abuse vary among cultures and even among the individual treatment professionals who evaluate users. The general term drug use may refer to the use of drugs either for therapeutic or recreational purposes. In some rare circumstances, individuals who take drugs for medical reasons may cross the line to drug abuse or even dependence. For example, the use of morphine for post-operative pain may develop into a chronic narcotic dependence. Most simple drug usage may not, however, become habit forming or may not create feelings of pleasure that reinforce continued use. An individual may use aspirin occasionally to relieve minor headaches but will not experience euphoria or the need to take aspirin when a headache is not present. More important, simple drug use may not contribute in any notable way to our crime rate.

On the other hand, even simple drug use may be powerfully reinforcing and become problematic. When individuals take a drug to bring relief from a medical condition, they may experience what is known as rebound effect. This is likely to occur when a drug temporarily relieves symptoms. When the drug is discontinued, the initial symptoms resurface more severely than prior to taking the drug. For example, caffeine is a stimulant largely found in coffee, chocolate, and some soft drinks. It boosts energy and may even help to relieve a headache (due to its vasoconstriction properties). Caffeine withdrawal in chronic users, however, is frequently associated with extreme fatigue and headaches. These symptoms constitute the rebound effect. Another medication taken more

directly for therapeutic purposes is antacids. Relief from indigestion and heartburn result from their use, but rebound effects can be observed when the medication is discontinued and stomach acids build to a higher level than in the predrug condition. Finally, sleeping pills are notorious for suppressing rapid eye movement (REM), a stage of sleeping characterized by dreaming. When the pills are no longer taken, REM sleep may return in abundance and the ex-user will report a fitful and unsatisfying night's sleep. In each of these examples, continued drug usage is psychologically and biologically reinforced to relieve a medical condition (or simply to elevate mood and behavior as in the case of caffeine) and to avoid worsening the original symptoms when the drug is discontinued.

The point at which drug use becomes drug abuse has not been clearly established. Some might take the view that ingesting any psychoactive drug for any reason other than medical would qualify as drug abuse. Ungerleider and Beigel (1980) present a classification scheme for identifying types of drug usage, excluding drugs used for therapeutic reasons.

1. *experimental drug use: participated in primarily by youth and motivated by curiosity*
2. *recreational drug use: indulged in by many for pleasure with one or more drugs*
3. *situational or circumstantial drug use: ingested for specific effects, for example, use of stimulants to improve short-term study effectiveness or athletic performance*
4. *intensified drug use: regular drug use that interferes with one's behavior and one's relationships at home, at work, and/or at play*
5. *compulsive drug use: obtaining drugs becomes the overriding concern of daily life*

The first three patterns are considered the least severe forms of drug use. Nevertheless, Ungerleider and Beigel point out that most of our media, funding, and criminal justice efforts target these groups. Furthermore, the last two patterns are frequently accepted in our society, as reflected in our attitudes toward drinking alcohol and taking certain stimulants (e.g., caffeine or nicotine). Thus, we can see that the distinction between drug use and abuse is hazy and biased by subjective value judgments and personal experience.

Drug use, abuse, and dependence can be distinguished by the original incentives for usage and the level of control an individual has over the drug-taking behavior. Simple drug use may be viewed as under the control of the individual, a voluntary behavior. In these cases, social factors may play a role in the drive to use a drug and, however strong that drive might be, changing motivations to use a drug may alter that drug-taking behavior. For example, the classic experimental drug user described above may be easily persuaded to discontinue his or her marijuana use given a changing peer group with different pressures and incentives.

Although social and environmental conditions substantially contribute to the use and abuse of drugs, the role of direct, pharmacologic drug actions cannot be underestimated. It is these drug effects that are ultimately pursued by the users. In pharmacology, three measures of a drug's abuse potential have been generated by animal experiments. A tube inserted in the animal administers a drug to the animal whenever it presses a lever. The animal will begin to continuously press the lever when the injection contains a drug known to be dependence producing (Brady & Lukas, 1984; Clouet et al., 1988). The first criterion of a drug's level of addictiveness is derived from how hard the animal works to obtain the drug—how many times it will press the lever to receive the injection. The second measure of addictiveness is the extent to which the animal becomes preoccupied with administering the drug to the neglect of other basic needs, such as eating, drinking, mating, and grooming. The third measure is how quickly the animal returns to a regular pattern of lever pressing following a period of forced abstinence. Animals, including primates, will continue to self-administer a highly addictive drug until they die. Interestingly, death typically does not occur from a drug overdose. It occurs from either starvation, dehydration, seizures, infections, or cardiovascular collapse.

With regard to humans, drug abuse is identified when the individual either loses control of the drug-taking behavior or loses control over behaviors that result from drug use. Drug use becomes habitual or compulsive in the same way that gambling or overeating can become self-destructive or abusive. As with monkeys, human users may ignore certain needs. Usually they begin by neglecting their personal appearance, family, and job responsibilities. They progress to the neglect of basic biological needs, including hunger, and lose interest in sex and intimacy.

When individuals exhibit behavior that is disruptive to themselves or others, we would identify their drug use as drug abuse. For example, some who drink alcohol may drink only occasionally during social events and are able to stop after one or two drinks. This pattern of drug use constitutes a controlled behavior. Others, however, may become destructive, obnoxious, or even violent when drinking. Although they may not be alcoholic (exhibit a dependent drinking pattern), their drinking behavior is certainly problematic and may be considered out of their control. In either uncontrolled situation, one may define these drug-taking behaviors as drug abuse. Therefore, there are at least two signs of drug abuse: (1) losing control over the amount of drug being used at a single session and not being able to stop, or, (2) the onset of problematic behaviors or deleterious consequences from using the drug. With respect to the second criterion, some individuals may use a drug in a controlled manner only occasionally, but if the drug is producing health problems or antisocial behaviors, then most professionals would call it drug abuse. And what about the little old lady who has a martini every night? Is this drug abuse? She has not increased the dose over the past forty years nor has she increased the frequency with which she drinks. When she temporarily stops the nightly drink because of a medication she must take, she shows no signs of withdrawal. Most people would agree that this does not constitute either abuse or dependence. There may be, however, a psychological dependency. In order to help differentiate between casual use and abuse, refer to the DSM-III-R criteria for psychoactive substance abuse displayed in Inset 4.3.

■ Summary

Pharmacological properties of drugs determine, in great part, a drug's effects, sites of action, metabolism, distribution, and elimination. But drug properties do not function in a vacuum. These properties are profoundly influenced by the particular individual using the drug—his or her constitution, genetics, surroundings, expectations, and a variety of other conditions. Thus, characteristics of the drug and the user operate in an interdependent fashion, not as separate entities.

Many individuals use drugs only recreationally or experimentally and discontinue use as they mature. What makes them different from those who continue their use and become dependent? Again, a large part of this process depends on the drug's propensity to produce dependence and the individual's propensity to become dependent. Although in this chapter we emphasized the importance

Inset 4.3

DIAGNOSTIC CRITERIA FOR PSYCHOACTIVE SUBSTANCE ABUSE DSM-III-R (APA, 1987)

A. A maladaptive pattern of psychoactive substance use indicated by at least one of the following:

  1. continued use despite knowledge of having a persistent or recurrent social, occupational, psychological, or physical problem that is caused or exacerbated by use of the psychoactive substance

  2. recurrent use in situations in which use is physically hazardous (e.g., driving while intoxicated)

B. Some symptoms of the disturbance have persisted for at least one month or have occurred repeatedly over a longer period of time.

C. Never met the criteria for Psychoactive Substance Dependence for this substance.

of biological factors in drug effects and in drug-taking behaviors, the tendency toward severe drug abuse in the United States has increasingly become a function of socioeconomic and cultural conditions. Specifically, conditions that characterize our inner cities have contributed substantially to the risk for drug abuse and dependence. Poverty, unemployment, lack of medical services and child care, unavailability of community resources, poor educational systems, and the wide availability of illicit drugs are now primary causes of our drug problem. Moreover, as a result of these conditions, child abuse and neglect and the incidence of drug-exposed babies has increased, further contributing to the eventual drug use of these children. In areas distinguished by economic sufficiency, more important determinants of drug abuse may be genetic and psychological factors. As a result, those who abuse drugs or become dependent may have preex-

isting personal traits that place them at risk for such behavior in the absence of environmental precipitants. But these traits are overwhelmed by profoundly adverse environmental conditions and become, in a sense, washed out by these more severe experiences. Individuals in the inner city have a sense of helplessness and little hope for upward mobility. Resources that previously kept them barely afloat have become nearly extinct and they have nothing to fall back on. Twenty percent of children in the United States presently live under the poverty level. There is a lack of supervision in these areas, family units are disintegrating, and there is boredom. Under such conditions, psychological and genetic conditions become less important. Instead, feelings of power, control, and escape from environment provided by drugs become powerful reinforcers of drug-taking behaviors.

CHAPTER

Theories of Addiction

Objectives

1. To provide an overview of the several theoretical frameworks that are applied to the study of drug abuse and addiction.

2. To summarize and critique the major biological, psychological, and sociological theories that address etiological issues in drug abuse research.

3. To present drug abuse as a complex and dynamic interaction among many variables and circumstances.

4. To distinguish between factors that precede drug abuse and those that result from drug abuse.

5. To introduce a comprehensive and multidisciplinary model that accommodates many theoretical perspectives to better explain why some individuals are more prone to abuse than others.

Although the search for a single comprehensive theory to explain why some people are more prone to drug abuse and addiction than others has been undertaken by numerous investigators, no such theory has yet emerged. Many theorists have presented models that attempt to explain addictive behaviors, but no one has developed a comprehensive theory that fully accounts for the multitude of variables, situations, and conditions that contribute to such complex behavioral patterns as drug use, abuse, and addiction. Theoretical perspectives have been discussed from several vantage points to explore what determines human behavior in general. One position advocates that addiction is a breakdown in moral standards based on personal inadequacies or failed teachings. A second view argues that addiction develops as a result of societal ills and socioeconomic inequities. These theories, which are primarily sociological, emerged after observations were made that drug abuse differs among social classes with respect to types of drugs abused, situations associated with drug use, drug availability, and related criminality. A third position states that those prone to addiction simply exercise a free will choice of this lifestyle over all others available to them. Individual choice theories place the blame on the user rather than on conditions beyond the user's control. And fourth, the biological model asserts that addiction results from an involuntary response of the user's body, the nervous system in particular, to drugs of abuse that accentuate the rewarding aspects of drug use. These responses override outside prevailing forces that may otherwise prevent addiction. Thus, the individual suffers from a preexisting biological disorder or imbalance. Once exposed to a drug of abuse, the user quickly adapts to its effects and rapidly develops a biological need, or craving, for more.

Each theory of addiction holds the user responsible to a different degree. The model postulating that users make their own choice obviously forces the user to become completely accountable for his or her behavior while the biological model removes all responsibility from the individual. The truth probably lies somewhere along a continuum with individual responsibility on one end and no individual choice at the other (see Figure 5.1).

The available literature presents evidence indicating that the user is neither entirely at fault nor entirely at the mercy of outside influences. Another model is needed to explain addiction that takes into account the dynamic interplay between numerous conditions (personal, situational, biological, and environmental) that play a role in addiction. The above mentioned theories each exclude relevant and critical variables by focusing exclusively on social forces or only on biological conditions. A new comprehensive model must be developed that integrates these factors in an attempt to understand how they interactively contribute to addiction. Such a development is crucial if we are to provide effective treatment for drug abuse and addiction. Treatment modalities are invariably based on some underlying theory of addictive behaviors. If the theory is inherently flawed or fails to account for relevant variables, then treatment will also probably fail.

The evidence accumulated to date does not allow us to present such a comprehensive theory of addiction in our review of existing theories. Nevertheless, we do know that no one set of influences stands alone —sociological and biological influences are equally important in predicting addictive behavior. We also emphasize the importance of individual differences in each of the theories reviewed. Unique characteristics of the individual determine to a great extent a person's vulnerability to abuse drugs and eventually become addicted. Consistent observations of users suggest that some are more susceptible to abuse due to a complex interaction of psychological, social, economic, familial, biological, and environmental influences. It is possible, of course, that an individual may be exposed to forces conducive to drug taking; however, if drugs of abuse are never used or if other protective forces are strongly in place (e.g., family stability, strong religious affiliations, or high IQ), then that individual may never develop addictive behaviors. Nevertheless, individuals who are exposed to forces conducive to drug taking but do not partake may suffer from other chronic problems (e.g., depression, impulsivity, criminality, financial instability, or marital discord) even in the absence of drug usage. Drug abuse may be only one form of compulsive behavior that results from existing psychopathology—the particular type of compulsion may be more importantly determined by environmental and social factors. Research demonstrating the important role of individual differences makes a strong case for the need to incorporate comprehensive and individualized treatments to address the unique conditions that influence each user.

The following sections categorize various theories of addiction separately on the basis of their primary orientation (i.e., biological, psychological, sociological). The theories are presented as though the factors discussed are independent of each other, and there is no overlap among theories. This presentation serves purely organizational

Figure 5.1   *Continuum of Addiction*

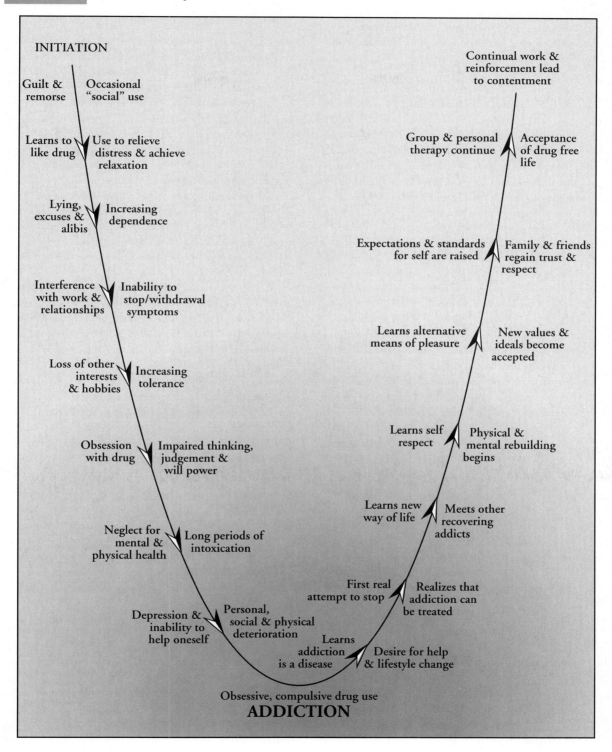

INITIATION

Guilt & remorse

Occasional "social" use

Learns to like drug

Use to relieve distress & achieve relaxation

Lying, excuses & alibis

Increasing dependence

Interference with work & relationships

Inability to stop/withdrawal symptoms

Loss of other interests & hobbies

Increasing tolerance

Obsession with drug

Impaired thinking, judgement & will power

Neglect for mental & physical health

Long periods of intoxication

Depression & inability to help oneself

Personal, social & physical deterioration

Learns addiction is a disease

First real attempt to stop

Realizes that addiction can be treated

Desire for help & lifestyle change

Obsessive, compulsive drug use
ADDICTION

Continual work & reinforcement lead to contentment

Group & personal therapy continue

Acceptance of drug free life

Expectations & standards for self are raised

Family & friends regain trust & respect

Learns alternative means of pleasure

New values & ideals become accepted

Learns self respect

Physical & mental rebuilding begins

Learns new way of life

Meets other recovering addicts

purposes. In reality, these theories must eventually be integrated and discussed as one dynamic force. An initial attempt is made to provide that glue in the final section in a discussion of the increasingly popular diathesis-stress model of psychopathology.

Theoretical Perspective

Many theories fail to address two critical issues with regard to drug use and addiction. First, many theories do not distinguish between those factors that contribute to the reasons to first use a drug, reasons to maintain drug use, and reasons for relapse. For example, Lindesmith (1947) proposed that there are different influences on each of these processes; drug availability and peer pressure may contribute most strongly to initial drug experimentation, while the reward value of the drug and the desire to avoid withdrawal may be more important in sustained usage. We will note whether each theory focuses primarily on initiation, maintenance, or relapse whenever possible.

The second issue pertains to the difficulty in distinguishing between factors that precede or cause drug abuse, those that result from drug abuse, and those that simply coexist with drug abuse as a constellation of personality traits possibly resulting from a common causal factor. Researchers tend to study those drug users who have been engaged in heavy drug use for a long period of time. As a result, it is difficult to identify and separate those factors that existed prior to drug use from those that occurred as a result of use. For example, depression is common among drug users. Were these users depressed before they initially used a drug? Was the depression instrumental (or causal) in their decision to use? Or did the depression result from the psychological and biological deterioration attributable to many years of drug abuse? Only those studies that are longitudinal in nature (that examine the individual prior to drug usage and follow-up over a period of years after drug abuse was established) or studies that examined at risk populations (that examined children considered vulnerable to eventual drug usage) can help us to distinguish the causal influences from the consequences of drug abuse. In any case, a number of common scenarios emerge from the literature that, at the very least, provide us with some understanding of the underlying mechanisms that appear to play a role in the development of addiction.

Biological Theories of Addiction

Theories suggesting a biological basis for the vulnerability to abuse or become addicted to drugs or alcohol take two interacting forms. First, there is convincing evidence that drugs of abuse act directly on brain mechanisms responsible for reward and punishment. Specifically, they stimulate those areas of the brain that create the sensation of pleasure and suppress the perception of pain, thereby reinforcing further drug-taking behaviors. Thus, the biological effects of abusable drugs encourage continued drug usage universally. Such theories, however, do not account for individual differences in the propensity to abuse drugs. They do not answer why some individuals experiment with abusable drugs and discontinue use after a short time, while others appear to be more intensely reinforced by the drug's effects and continue to become more serious, chronic drug users.

The second issue biological theories address is the possibility of inherited or acquired biological mechanisms that predispose some individuals to abuse drugs. Evidence exists that indicates some individuals may be more vulnerable to the rewarding effects of abusable drugs. Consequently, certain biological traits may increase the likelihood of eventual drug abuse or addiction, particularly in the presence of other external influences. We review environmental and sociocultural conditions later in this chapter that are equally conducive to drug-taking behaviors (e.g., drug-infested neighborhoods, family discord or disorganization, peer pressure, poverty, lack of employment opportunities, or poor education). In this section, we focus on findings that demonstrate the role biological systems play in the development of substance abuse.

Inherent Reward Value of Abusable Drugs

Part of the explanation for why drug use may become compulsive and self-destructive is found in the pharmacology of the drugs themselves. As discussed in Chapter 4, drugs with a high abuse potential, such as alcohol, heroin, and cocaine, stimulate reward systems of the brain. The resulting pleasure is so intense the user is tempted to seek a repeat performance. Such drugs are said to be reinforcing, to varying degrees because both animals and people will perform certain tasks or rituals to obtain the drug again. Cocaine, for example, has a high degree of reward value; animals will self-administer it until they collapse and die. Humans will self-administer it to the detriment of their health, fundamental personal needs, and family.

When the nucleus accumbens and prefrontal cortex of the brain are activated by a drug, for example, neurons within those regions turn on adjacent neurons, and a signal is consequently transmitted across a reward pathway to initialize feelings and thoughts of pleasure. Figure 5.2 depicts those pathways that are believed to be involved in reward and pleasure. These natural brain structures regulate motivations that encourage us to behave in ways that are fundamentally adaptive, thereby enhancing our survival. Thus, eating, exercise, sexual behaviors, and personal accomplishments all naturally stimulate these reward centers and motivate us to repeat the behavior. Related structures within the reward system help to control motor behavior so our movement may be directed toward these desirable behaviors. When all systems are functioning properly, motivations to eat or engage in sex do not pose

a problem by becoming compulsive. However, drug effects are much more intense than the influence of simple behaviors on these structures. The profound reward value of drugs may eventually supercede motivations to perform acts that enhance, rather than detract from, adaptation to our environment. The drug user will engage in maladaptive behavior in order to stimulate the reward centers of the brain.

The active properties of the drug itself have a great deal to do with their potential to produce addiction. Those drugs that provide an immediate rush, or intense euphoria, are more likely to be abused. Immediacy and intensity of effect are readily discerned by the user and may provide a powerful reinforcement for further use. In addition, drugs with effects that rapidly dissipate, encourage users to take additional doses to maintain their high. Thus, a behavioral pattern emerges that involves a high rate of repeat drug administrations during a single drug-taking session. Drugs that produce a high degree of toler-

Figure 5.2   *The Brain's Reward System*

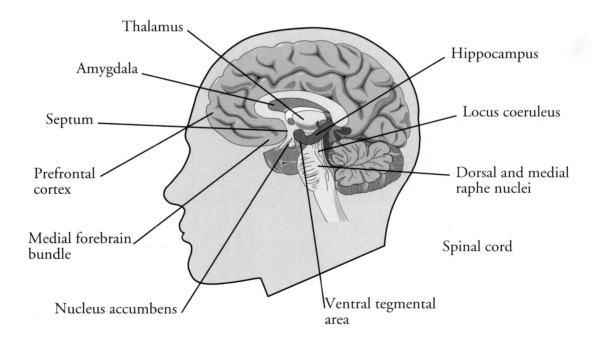

The brain reward system (in blue) is closely associated with structures of the limbic system.

Source: Adapted from *Brain, Mind and Behavior* by Floyd E. Bloom and Arlyne Lazerson. Copyright © 1988 by Educational Broadcasting Corporation. Reprinted by permission of W.H. Freeman and Company, with special assistance from L. Porrio and E. Palombo.

ance also contribute to addiction. The need for larger and larger doses with each administration more easily creates both a biological and a behavioral habit. Finally, those drugs that are associated with painful psychological or physiological withdrawal symptoms will more rapidly contribute to addiction. Users become motivated simply to avoid the unpleasant consequences of discontinuing the drug. For example, the depression (resulting from both psychological and physical influences) that follows abstinence from cocaine use is sufficient for many users to feel the need to readminister cocaine for relief.

Investigators (Goldstein & Kalant, 1990) have also suggested the use of certain behavioral criteria to judge the addictiveness or abuse potential of a drug. The first measure pertains to how hard an animal will work to self-administer the drug. Will an animal press a lever for an injection even though the drug may be delivered only once every 20 pulls? Will it jump through firey hoops or endure painful electric shocks in order to obtain the drug? Another measure is the degree to which the animal will ignore or neglect usual behaviors or routines in favor of drug self-administration. Will the animal ignore a member of the opposite sex in heat? Will it sacrifice food and water? Will it become stationary and forget to groom because of an obsession with obtaining more drug? The third criterion is how quickly the animal will return to the drug after the drug has been made unavailable for a period of time; in other words, how rapidly does the animal relapse? Obviously, the more quickly the animal reinstates previous drug-taking habits, the more addiction potential that drug is believed to possess. In humans, we see these same patterns emerge when drugs of abuse are available. Many users develop a compulsive preoccupation with certain drugs to the detriment of competing basic needs. Addicts have been known to use a drug despite an acute awareness that such use may have deleterious or even fatal consequences. These behaviors are reminiscent of animal experiments with monkeys who will kill themselves with a drug, particularly cocaine, through starvation, dehydration, infections, fatal seizures, or heart attack.

Theories that encompass the reward potential of a drug in determining the likelihood that a user will become addicted lead us to a consideration of how behaviors in general are learned. Because we will deal with learning theories toward the end of this chapter, we do not present a full review at this time. Instead, we summarily make note of the role that learning plays to emphasize the interaction between biological and psychological influences on drug-taking behaviors. When a drug produces pleasure

and reduces pain, it is said to be reinforcing. The inducement of pleasure is positively reinforcing while the reduction of pain is negatively reinforcing as it, in essence, eliminates an aversive stimulus. Therefore, positively reinforcing properties of certain drugs are defined by the euphoria, feelings of well-being, and elevated mood states, while negatively reinforcing properties refer to the relief from dysphoria or distress and a return to a normal or more positive mood state (see Wise, 1988 for discussion). Drugs with these two active properties readily instruct the user that behaviors revolving around drug use will lead to a more desirable state. Although these properties are inherently biological in that they depend on which parts and neurochemicals of the brain are activated, the user must first learn to associate these properties with the drug. When these reinforcing properties are perceived as intense and immediate, the user readily assimilates this information and is more likely to continue drug use. This process by which individuals learn to perform in a certain way to achieve a desirable consequence is referred to as behavioral conditioning. Unfortunately, the development of such conditioned responses to drug use complicates drug treatment efforts as we must deal with both the biological aspects of drug use and the complex learned behaviors that simultaneously develop.

Genetic Influences

In recent years, there has been a great deal of attention focused on the possibility that certain genetic traits contribute to substance abuse. Alcoholism is now thought to be more a result of genetic predisposition than environment, particularly among certain types of alcoholics (see Chapter 6 and Linnoila, 1986). The question of whether similar genetic mechanisms are at work in the development of other forms of drug abuse has not yet been answered, but there are some indications that certain inherited traits may make some individuals more vulnerable to substance abuse than others. Different strains of rats and mice, for example, have varying preferences for cocaine and similar genetic differences have been observed in animal studies where opiates are administered (George & Goldberg, 1989). We do not necessarily expect to find single genes or genetic traits that specifically predict vulnerability to abuse a particular drug, such as cocaine or heroin, as may be the case for alcohol. Nevertheless, we may eventually discover a constellation of genetic traits that globally predict predisposition to many forms of substance abuse.

Figure 5.3   *"Hooked" on Addictiveness*

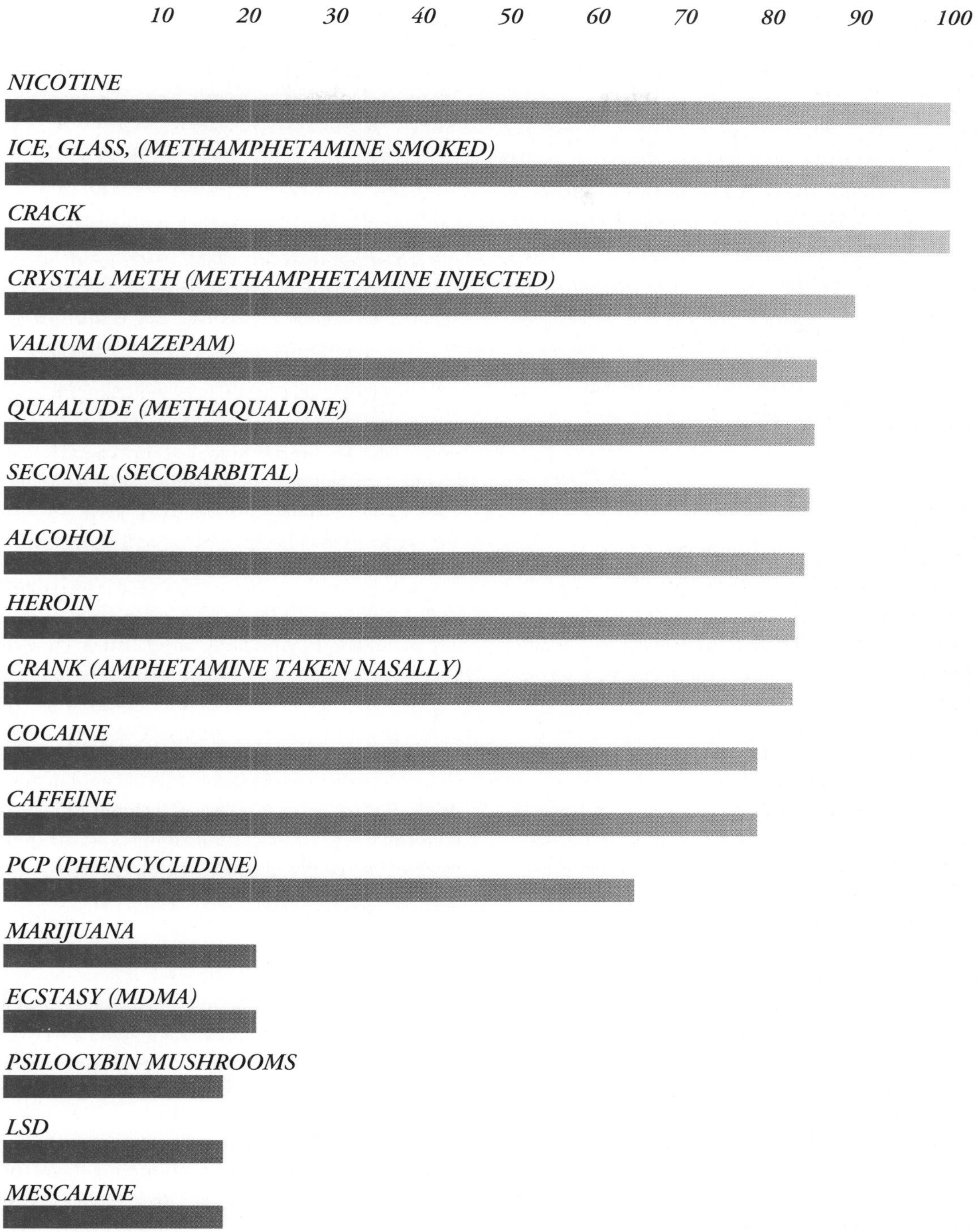

	10	20	30	40	50	60	70	80	90	100

NICOTINE

ICE, GLASS, (METHAMPHETAMINE SMOKED)

CRACK

CRYSTAL METH (METHAMPHETAMINE INJECTED)

VALIUM (DIAZEPAM)

QUAALUDE (METHAQUALONE)

SECONAL (SECOBARBITAL)

ALCOHOL

HEROIN

CRANK (AMPHETAMINE TAKEN NASALLY)

COCAINE

CAFFEINE

PCP (PHENCYCLIDINE)

MARIJUANA

ECSTASY (MDMA)

PSILOCYBIN MUSHROOMS

LSD

MESCALINE

Source: Researched by Valerie Fahey; reprinted from *In Health*, © 1990; by Anthony Schmitz; reprinted from HEALTH, © 1993.

Several investigators are attempting to determine whether other forms of drug abuse are equally likely to become manifest in children of drug abusers as in children of alcoholics. There is some evidence that this might be the case—examples of some findings in this area are as follows.

1. *Tranquilizer use in parents has been shown to be related to tranquilizer and marijuana use among their college-age children (Scherer, 1973).*
2. *Parents who use marijuana or hashish had more adolescent children who were drug users (Fawzy et al., 1983).*
3. *Abuse of various nonalcoholic substances was significantly greater in individuals with first-degree relatives who abused drugs than those that did not (Meller et al., 1988).*
4. *Alcohol problems in biological relatives are associated with other forms of drug abuse (Cadoret et al., 1986).*
5. *Marijuana use is more prevalent among college-age males with alcoholic relatives (McCaul, 1989).*
6. *First-degree relatives of heroin dependent individuals are more likely to be heroin-dependent (Maddux and Desmond, 1989).*

Although it is clear that environmental variables are important influences, these studies and others (Cadoret et al., 1986) have shown that environment is not the only important consideration in drug abuse —genetics plays at least an equally influential role. Perhaps an individual's initial decision to use an abusable drug is largely due to environmental influences while the propensity to become a chronic abuser and to develop a tolerance to and dependency on a drug is largely determined by his or her genetic makeup. In any case, it has been suggested that individuals may be either genetically protected from drug abuse by inherited adverse biological reactions to drugs or genetically more susceptible to the addictive and pleasurable reactions (Goodwin, 1980, p. 12). It is crucial that, in addition to family studies as the ones cited above, twin and adoption studies (described in Chapter 6) be carried out to determine the relative influence of genetics and environment. Such efforts at present focus on the study of alcoholism (Schuckit, 1987), but few studies have been done for substance abuse generally.

Once we have been able to establish the role of genetics in drug abuse, we must then identify the mechanisms by which drug abuse is transmitted from one generation to the next. The most likely candidates include the inheritance of particular biological systems and psychological traits that predispose vulnerable individuals to all forms of drug abuse and dependency. At present we are not able to predict a group's or individual's relative risk for drug abuse, however, when we know exactly what is being inherited, such prediction may become more viable.

Biological Systems

A number of biological factors more prevalent among alcoholics and their offspring or relatives than in nonalcoholic populations have been cited as markers or risk factors for alcoholism (see, e.g., Roy et al., 1987). Many of these markers are mentioned in Chapter 6, however others include low levels of the enzyme monoamine oxidase (MAO), neurophysiological irregularities as measured by the electroencephalogram (EEG or evoked potentials), neuropsychological or cognitive impairments, neurological abnormalities such as tremor and ataxia, and left-handedness (see Tarter & Edwards, 1987). Findings of differences between alcohol abusers, alcoholics, or children of alcoholics and nonalcohol abusing or low risk populations suggest two possibilities: (1) that the brains of the former group may be organizationally or functionally atypical, and (2) that these features may be genetically transmitted.

Very little research of this type has been done with a focus on forms of drug abuse other than alcoholism. Examples in each of the following chapters to show possible biological mechanisms in vulnerability to abuse drugs. For instance, there are indications of neurological abnormalities among some amphetamine-preferring users and low levels of neuropeptide activity among some of those who prefer the opiates. When the biological mechanisms are identified that predict individual vulnerability to abuse drugs, we expect them to be related to the sensitivity of those brain regions responsible for drug effects— both pleasurable and aversive. It is possible that individuals prone to drug abuse are more sensitive to the rewarding effects of abusable drugs or less sensitive to the drug's effects in general, thus they need to use larger and more frequent amounts to achieve an effect. It is, nevertheless, still possible that we will not discover specific biological conditions that predict specific types of drug abuse in any given individual, with the possible exception of alcoholism.

Another facet of biological approaches to explain addiction and abuse pertains to the notion that some drug users are attempting to self-medicate a preexisting disorder. The disorder may be considered either physical, as in pain or sleep disturbance, or psychological, as in anxiety or depression. Because many drugs of abuse often have some therapeutic potential, individuals with drug preferences may inadvertently or knowingly select those drugs that will specifically relieve their unwanted symptoms. There is some evidence, for example, that a subgroup of alcoholics suffer from anxiety disorder and find the depressive effects of alcohol reinforcing. Others with an anxiety disorder may choose benzodiazepines or barbiturates instead. Perhaps those prone to depression are more likely to become dependent on opiates or cocaine, there is a higher incidence of depression among these users than in the general population. Those who have difficulty sleeping due either to physical or psychological causes may readily find that a drink after dinner helps them to relax enough to fall asleep. Once they begin to associate the drink with the desired effect of sleepiness, they will be more likely to increase the dosage for a stronger effect and increase the frequency with which they use alcohol for a more long-term remedy. This type of use pattern may rapidly become compulsive and eventually produce dependence.

Psychological Theories

The search for an addictive personality that can reliably predict the abuse of drugs has failed to result in a profile of a typical drug abuser (see Sutker & Allain, 1988). Instead, individual studies report an association between particular psychological and personality traits with particular forms of drug abuse, but no one pattern stands out as a consistent theme in the literature. The one conclusion we can draw from a review of countless studies is that they all find a predominance of psychopathology among drug abusing populations. The presence of a psychological disorder along with an environment conducive to drug taking increases the risk of addiction, but we are not able to specify the particular individual features that will consistently result in addiction. It may be noted simply that addictive individuals have a tendency to excessive behaviors that may take the form of overeating, overexercising, unusual religiosity, overmedicating, or another all-consuming activity. The following sections describe the types of psychopathology that appear to play a role in the development of excessive drug-taking behaviors.

Psychological Predispositions

The most extensive research in the area of vulnerability to drug abuse and addiction has focused on personality traits and psychological disorders. Because psychological features that characterize an individual are relatively stable throughout a lifetime, tend to run in families, and have been associated with biological processes, psychological traits and disorders that are prevalent among drug abusers are considered to provide a link between genetic, biological, and psychological theories of addiction. Therefore, theorists believe that personality characteristics that predispose an individual to drug abuse are most likely transmitted from one generation to the next by genetic means in the form of biological irregularities with psychological manifestations. These personality traits, in turn, interact with the social and physical environment to finally determine whether drug abuse behaviors will result. Again, personality alone does not reliably predict the eventual abuse of drugs; the dynamic interplay between biological, psychological, and social factors predict drug abuse in ways not yet understood.

Several studies focusing on psychological traits have shown that antisocial personality, psychopathy, impulsivity, affective disorder, and anxiety are more prevalent among substance abusers than nondrug abusing populations (Alterman, 1988; Cristie et al., 1988; Shedler and Block, 1990; Tarter, 1988; West and Prinz, 1987). These traits may antedate drug usage and place the individual at risk for later drug abuse (Rounsaville, Anton, et al., 1991). As many of these traits and disorders have been associated with physiological and biochemical abnormalities and have a genetic component, we may eventually identify biological or psychological markers that help to distinguish those at risk from those not. Furthermore, identification of these markers may enhance our ability to more effectively treat the underlying causes of drug abuse.

Childhood Histories

A childhood history of hyperactivity, learning disabilities, cognitive deficits, and conduct disorder have all been cited as possible precursors or markers for eventual substance abuse. There is evidence that children with these problems suffer from a central nervous system disorder that prevents proper regulation over such processes as cognitive flexibility, attention, verbal fluency, and problem solving. These and other skills normally enable an individual to cope, make decisions, and mature at a reasonable rate. People with these disorders are characteristically immature, impulsive, uninhibited, moody, and have a high activity level and negative affect. Drug use by such individuals may be unusually biologically reinforcing because of the drug's effects on arousal levels and mood state, causing them to feel more stable. Further reinforcing their tendency to use drugs are the social circumstances that frequently lend themselves to involvement with peers who suffer from similar problems and are also abusing drugs.

It must be emphasized that the existence of one or more of these childhood problems does not destine a child to a life of drug abuse. Rather, we see a significant number of drug abusers with a history that may place the child at a disadvantage in our society, particularly when appropriate interventions are not available. Low self-esteem and motivation, and feelings of helplessness and failure resulting from these difficulties compound the problem, contribute to eventual drug abuse, and must be addressed in a comprehensive treatment strategy. Those children who are not offered treatment for their behavioral difficulties may be more likely to both seek the added physical stimulation they may need and escape from their disorder by using drugs.

Antisocial Personality Disorder or ASP

Almost invariably, studies have found a prevalence of substance users to fit the diagnosis of antisocial personality disorder (ASP), more so than one would expect to find in the general population (Regier et al., 1990). (A discussion of ASP as it relates to particular types of drug abuse are included within each drug chapter.) ASP is pervasive among alcoholics (Cadoret et al., 1987; Hesselbrock, Hesselbrock, et al., 1984; C.E. Lewis, 1984; Schuckit, 1985; Schulsinger, Knop, et al., 1986) and both ASP and alcoholism may be inherited together. ASP is equally common among opiate users and is disproportionately represented among all drug abusers (Collins, Schlenger, et al., 1988; Craig, 1988; Grande et al., 1984; C.E. Lewis, Rounsaville, Anton, et al., 1991). These findings are not suprising given the oft mentioned association between criminality and drug and alcohol usage. Furthermore, a substantial number of drug abusers and those with ASP are depicted with similar characteristics, including impulsivity, sensation seeking, immaturity, aggressive, risk taking, and a relative unresponsiveness to threats of punishment.

Individuals with ASP are more prone to commit crimes, presumably due to their increased need for stimulation, excitement, and danger. A significant proportion of the offender population has been labeled as ASP although the diagnosis is certainly not a necessary or sufficient condition for criminal behavior. It has been hypothesized that criminal behavior and substance abuse have one feature in common that may help to explain why ASP individuals are attracted to these activities—they both provide a heightened state of stimulation for individuals who are essentially sensation seekers. Because ASP individuals seek immediate gratification, have little self-control, and have greater physiological need for stimulation than others, they may be more likely to choose drug-related activities for the stimulation they provide.

Although the relationship between ASP, criminality, and substance abuse is strong, we do not know at this time what the precise mechanisms are that would explain their origins or their simultaneous development in some individuals. Antisocial traits and behaviors are frequently manifested prior to drug use, suggesting that drug use is only one symptom of ASP. Due to evidence that there may be genetic involvement and an increased incidence of brain irregularities within the drug-abusing group of antisocial offenders, it has been postulated that certain biological traits are, in part, responsible for the development of both antisocial and drug abuse behaviors.

In either event, it is critical to note that individuals with ASP are considered at higher risk for substance abuse than those without. We must attempt to distinguish those users with ASP from the others as the treatment modality chosen will depend on diagnostic traits. Drug users with ASP are widely considered by both scientists and clinicians as more difficult to treat for their drug abuse than non-ASP users, and they have a higher relapse rate once treatment has ended.

Anxiety

The personality trait of anxiety is believed to be associated with the tendency to abuse drugs and alcohol although results of several studies do not always agree. Anxiety disorders, especially phobias, are reportedly widespread among individuals who abuse drugs or alcohol (Regier et al., 1990). According to some self-reports, the first symptoms of substance abuse were preceded by phobias, indicating that the drug use may be an attempt to self-medicate an existing disorder. Evidence that individuals with anxiety disorders may be suffering from a neurochemical imbalance, in particular within the serotonergic system, and that drugs of abuse act on these neurotransmitter systems, provides further fuel for the argument that anxious people may be more likely to abuse drugs. The combined presence of heightened levels of anxiety and

Inset 5.1

DSM-III-R 301.70
ANTISOCIAL PERSONALITY DISORDER

A. Current age at least eighteen.

B. Evidence of Conduct Disorder with onset before age fifteen, as indicated by a history of three or more the following:
1.   was often truant
2.   ran away from home overnight at least twice while living in parental or parental surrogate home (or once without returning)
3.   often initiated physical fights
4.   used a weapon in more than one fight
5.   forced someone into sexual activity with him or her
6.   was physically cruel to animals
7.   was physically cruel to other people
8.   deliberately destroyed others' property (other than by fire setting)
9.   deliberately engaged in fire setting
10. often lied (other than to avoid physical or sexual abuse)
11. has stolen without confrontation of a victim on more than one occasion (including forgery)
12. has stolen with confrontation of a victim (e.g., mugging, purse snatching, extortion, armed robbery)

C. A pattern of irresponsible and antisocial behavior since the age of fifteen, as indicated by at least four of the following:
1.   is unable to sustain consistent work behavior, as indicated by any of the following:
   a. significant unemployment for six months or more within five years when expected to work and work was available
   b. repeated absences from work unexplained by illness in self or family
   c. abandonment of several jobs without realistic plans for others
2.   fails to conform to social norms with respect to lawful behavior, as indicated by repeated performing antisocial acts that are grounds for arrest, e.g., destroying property, harassing others, stealing, pursuing an illegal occupation
3.   is irritable and aggressive, as indicated by repeated physical fights or assaults, including spouse or child beating
4.   repeatedly fails to honor financial obligations, as indicated by defaulting on debts or failing to provide child support or support for other dependents on a regular basis
5.   fails to plan ahead, or is impulsive, as indicated by one or both of the following:
   a. traveling from place to place without a prearranged job or clear goal for the period of travel or clear idea about when the travel will terminate
   b. lack of a fixed address for a month or more
6.   has no regard for the truth, as indicated by repeated lying, uses of aliases, or conning others for personal profit or pleasure
7.   is reckless regarding his or her own or others' personal safety, as indicated by driving while intoxicated, or recurrent speeding

8.   if a parent or guardian, lacks ability to function as a responsible parent, as indicated by one or more of the following:
  a. malnutrition of a child
  b. child's illness resulting from lack of minimal hygiene
  c. failure to obtain medical care for a seriously ill child
  d. child's dependence on neighbors or nonresident relatives for food or shelter
  e. failure to arrange for a caretaker for young child when parent is away from home.
  f. repeated squandering, on personal items, of money required for household necessities
9. has never sustained a totally monogamous relationship for more than a year.
10. lacks remorse (feels justified in having hurt, mistreated, or stolen from another)

numerous environmental stressors (experienced by a significant number of serious substance abusers) makes the use of drugs that will alter consciousness, allow escape, elevate mood, and relieve anxiety even more attractive (see Ross, Glaser, et al., 1988).

Depression

As mentioned in each of the following drug chapters, affective disorders, such as depression, are disproportionately represented among substance abusing populations (Regier et al., 1990; Ross, Glasser, et al., 1988). Depression frequently exists prior to drug use, suggesting that it may play a causal role. Conversely, depression may result from heavy drug use (in particular cocaine; see Chapter 8), indicating that drugs at least exacerbate an existing depression in some cases while they may actually cause the depression in others. Evidence that depression is a result of an underlying neurochemical imbalance may help to explain why depressed individuals are more likely to abuse drugs. Several drugs of abuse act to elevate mood state by influencing brain chemicals responsible for depression. Consequently, not only is the user obtaining psychic relief from the mental pain of depression, but he or she is also receiving added biological reinforcement by stimulating those brain systems that may be causing their depression. In other words, they may be temporarily correcting an underlying imbalance.

The Role of Learning

The role of the learning process must not be underestimated in its contribution to drug abuse—biological and psychological tendencies to abuse drugs may be either diminished or reinforced by social learning. Drug-taking behaviors are acquired and maintained via the learning process in three ways: (1) through changes in social relationships, (2) by the formation of conditioned responses to both drug effects and drug-taking situations, and (3) by modeling or imitation of significant others (discussed in a later section). Relationships change gradually as individuals enter into a drug-using environment; they begin to associate more often with other drug users that will support their activities. This common scenario allows and even encourages users to maintain and perhaps escalate drug use. Users tend to sacrifice their own personal growth for the drug(s), and lifestyles begin to revolve around the purchase and use of drugs (Johnson, Williams, et al., 1990). Social support systems and lifestyles devoted to drug use pose a powerful obstacle to abstinence programs.

Compounding these contributions to drug abuse are conditioned responses to pain and pleasure (see Siegel et al., 1987 for review). Behavioral conditioning is a learning process of comparing new information with memories to produce a response. The two forms of behavioral conditioning, classical and instrumental, both directly contribute to drug abuse. Classical conditioning refers to the response elicited by a neutral stimulus that has been associated with obtaining a reward or avoiding harm; for example, a white laboratory coat is associated with food and elicits salivation or viewing drug paraphernalia elicits craving for a drug. Thus, painful and pleasurable situations eventually become associated with environmental cues that are simultaneously present. As a consequence, we will experience pleasure at the mere presence of an associated cue and perhaps crave the actual behavior that will allow us to experience a pleasurable or rewarding response. In the same way, drug users learn to associate the pleasurable drug effect with particular behaviors and paraphernalia and will likely experience craving when the cues are present even in the absence of the drug. Cigarette smokers, for example, commonly report difficulty abstaining when talking on the phone, when others are smoking, or after a meal as these are all cues that have become associated with the physiological effects of nicotine. Cocaine users also report extreme drug craving when they see a dollar bill, talcum powder, or a drug-taking peer. Heroin users find that viewing a hypodermic needle will initiate drug craving.

When an individual is instrumental in causing a stimulus to occur, instrumental or operant conditioning is at work. The stimulus elicited either satisfies a drive or permits us to avoid an unpleasant result. For example, if we learn through experience that the use of a drug is pleasurable, the behavior will continue. On the other hand, if we are consistently punished for such behavior (i.e., in the form of unpleasant drug effects, arrest, or disapproval), we are unlikely to repeat the action. Thus, both forms of conditioning revolve around the same conditions—the avoidance of pain and the search for pleasure—which function to reinforce our behavior. When the conditions are unfavorable to drug abuse, an individual is less likely to learn that drugs are reinforcing and is less likely to abuse them. On the other hand, when learning conditions are favorable to drug abuse, the individual may choose to experiment with drugs, making it more likely that abuse or addiction will eventually develop.

> As a consequence of their genetic or constitutional dispositions, their personal characteristics, and their learning experiences, humans seem to regulate their behaviors according to expectations for reward as adaptively as possible. It is reasonable to assume that people strive to achieve pleasure and to avoid unpleasant consequences and that learned habit patterns and personal traits may become maladaptive over time (Sutker & Allain, 1988)

Behavioral habits are equally as difficult to break as the pharmacological habit, and the behavior itself can become addicting. Treatment efforts are pervasively frustrated by the presence of social reinforcers that compound and exacerbate drug-taking behaviors.

Sociological Theories

Unlike biologists and psychologists who examine individual characteristics to explain drug use and addiction, the sociologist studies societal variables to explain drug use. Unfortunately, social theories are not well developed at this juncture, and many have yet to be directly applied to the field of drug abuse. Five perspectives generated from the field of sociology are presented. Each represents an area of inquiry that previous investigators concentrated on in attempts to explain antisocial behaviors and personalities in general. In recent years, these theories have been applied to an explanation of drug abuse. They include: (1) anomie theory, (2) strain theory, (3) control theory, (4) labeling theory, and (5) subculture theory.

Anomie Theory

Emile Durkheim, the father of sociology, developed the theory of anomie, which provides a strong foundation for strain theory and control theory discussed later. Durkheim viewed the inherent nature of humans as selfish with an unlimited capacity for wants and needs. It is society's function to place external limits on these wants, desires, and needs. Society clearly defines for its citizens what they can expect from life. Without this clear definition, people become frustrated and depressed because they want more than they can achieve. If an individual desires an unattainable goal, he or she works in vain because the goal can never be reached. "To pursue a goal which is by definition unattainable is to condemn oneself to a state of perpetual unhappiness" (Durkheim, 1951, pp. 247).

Even though many of those in the middle class might desire more wealth, expectations of great wealth by most people are not that common. Society attempts to socialize us to be relatively content to achieve within the limits set for us by the prevailing social structure. Therefore, society must limit people's expectations while simultaneously stimulating them to achieve and better their life within the limits set by the external social order.

However, during times of social upheaval, such as war, recession, or depression as in the 1930s, or even during times of rapid economic growth, society no longer clearly defines for its citizens what they can expect. During economic recession, many people find their income and standard of living suddenly declining. Their future becomes uncertain. Conflicting norms and values become pervasive throughout the social order, and individuals are thrown into a state of confusion concerning what is expected of them. They can no longer decide which goals are reasonable and achievable and which are not. When society no longer clearly defines for us what we can expect, we say society is in a state of anomie. During periods of anomie, crime rates, drug and alcohol use, depression, and suicide increase. Many people lose sight of their goals and are at risk of becoming detached or alienated from the mainstream of society. The less individuals feel they have to lose, the more likely they will pursue other avenues that are associated with some danger or negative consequences. Drug using and dealing, under such circumstances, allow anomic people an escape from reality and a chance to achieve, beyond their usual means, more wealth than is otherwise possible. Lacking realistic expectations and feelings of attachment to the community, these illegitimate means are more likely.

Strain Theory

Strain theory (Cloward & Ohlin, 1960; A. Cohen, 1955; Merton, 1938) makes the assumption that societal goals are clearly defined. Whereas Durkheim argued that anomie occurs when society fails to provide limits on its citizens' expectations, strain theorists believe anomie occurs when people are denied opportunities to fulfill needs and achieve cultural goals.

Generally speaking, cultural goals in America consist of the accummulation of wealth and the material symbols of status and success. The American dream consists of job security, home ownership, family, and a comfortable standard of living. Society has provided the means one needs to achieve those goals in the form of education and employment. The better one's education the more likely he or she will acquire the high-paying job necessary to purchase the symbols of success in American society. One must also possess certain social skills to acquire status and position in society. For example, one must obtain knowledge about how to interview for a job, dress appropriately, and display proper job ettiquette, such as being punctual for work and working hard. Certain segments of society are denied the same access as their counterparts to societal institutions that provide the necessary means to accomplish these objectives.

Merton (1938) proposed that there are five adaptational styles in coping with cultural goals and institutional means: conformity, innovation, ritualism, retreatism, and rebellion. The individual who accepts society's goals and the institutional means to achieve those goals is identified as a conformist and represents the majority of Americans. Most of us have accepted the culture's definition of success and by virtue of being in college, have accepted the institutional means to achieve the goal.

Others who reject the means but accept the goals fall into the innovation subtype. This group includes some people who commit crimes. They seek the material goals specified by society but use illegal means to achieve those goals. This segment of society generally comes from the lower classes. These people have been denied access to the institutionalized means to achieve cultural goals. For example, many inner-city children attend schools lacking the equipment and supplies necessary to provide a first-rate education. The family does not adequately prepare the child for school or emphasize the importance of the value of education. These children have difficulty competing for the high-status, high-salary jobs that define success in American society. Therefore, some may turn to crime as a means of achieving the cultural goals of wealth and power. Many children in the inner city see drug dealing as a way to acquire those symbols of social success, such as a fancy car, jewelry, and expensive clothes. Drug dealing is also a way of achieving power in the community. Drug dealers define ownership of territory and acquire weapons to defend their claims. Entire neighborhoods are held hostage to the intimidating tactics of the drug gangs. What they cannot attain through legitimate means, drug dealers attain through crime.

Those who adapt by way of ritualism tend to accept the means but reject the goals. This group might include bureaucrats who lose sight of the final goals when they find themselves absorbed in completing endless paperwork, day in and day out. Filling out the paperwork and going through the proper rituals become more important than the originally desired goal. Students sometimes encounter this situation during registration. Filling out the proper forms and getting the appropriate signatures becomes more important, despite the final result, than the goal of getting a course schedule that reflects the necessary courses for graduation.

Retreatists reject both cultural goals and the institutional means to achieve the goals. These people are considered the outcasts of society and include such groups as the homeless, hermits or recluses, psychotics, and street drug and alcohol abusers. The popular image of the heroin addict or crack addict whose life centers around drugs and the acquisition of drugs would be considered a part of this group. They have rejected societal goals as well as societal means and replaced them with the goal of drug acquisition. Oftentimes, members of this group commit crimes (a rejection of institutional means) to attain their goal of drug acquisition. Merton feels that some of these individuals may have lacked access through institutional means to achieve cultural goals. As a result of continued frustration and defeat, those in this group have given up altogether and rejected cultural goals.

The rebellious adaptation also requires that one reject society's means and goals. However, unlike the retreatist, the rebel seeks to replace the old means and goals with new ones. The drug-using hippies of the sixties are a good example of Merton's concept of the rebel. This group rejected society's values of material acquisition and monetary success and "dropped out." They even rejected the greater society's psychoactive drug of choice, alcohol, and replaced it with other psychoactive drugs, such as marijuana and LSD.

Cloward and Ohlin (1960) point out that rejection of accepted institutional means does not guarantee an individual admittance to the criminal subculture. Cloward and Ohlin argue that many young people who are denied access to institutional means enter the aggressive subculture. Their behavior is generally not goal directed but based on achieving such things as a tough reputation. From this group may be drawn possible applicants to the professional criminal organization. Professional criminals are organized and their behavior is goal directed. Those people who have been rejected from the professional criminal subculture slip into a retreatist subculture and tend to become chronic drug and/or alcohol users. They can be considered double failures. First they were unable to find success in the conventional social order, and second they were equally unable to find success in the criminal subculture.

Strain theory best explains the crime of drug trafficking as well as some forms of drug use. Many of the South and Central American cocaine traffickers use cocaine trafficking as a means to acquire the wealth and power otherwise denied them in these countries of limited social mobility. The same is true of other drug trafficking organizations such as the Italian mafia, the Jamaican possees, and the Crips and Bloods. Middle- and low-level traffickers in the inner cities of the United States often see drug trafficking as a way to escape their impoverished circumstances. Some do make enough money to live comfortably for the rest of their lives and leave the business. Others never realize their dream because they either get hooked on the drug themselves, are arrested, or are killed by rival groups. Still others lack the skill or contacts to find success in the underworld of drug trafficking and become retreatists (chronic drug users). Moreover, countries that tolerate, if not encourage, drug manufacturing and trafficking are commonly poor. They lack legitimate means to provide the necessities to their people in a fashion equal to that provided by the illicit drug market.

Control Theory

Travis Hirshi, a control theorist, attempted to explain conformity rather than deviance (Hirshi, 1969). He assumed our inherent nature was deviant and society would have to provide incentives for conformity. He identified four bonds that are responsible for conformity: attachment, involvement, commitment, and belief. When these bonds are broken people are free to deviate because there is nothing to ensure conformity. On the other hand, when an individual is strongly bonded to family, church, school, and community, that person is less likely to become delinquent.

Attachment relates to a close and caring relationship with significant others, such as parents, peers, and teachers. Individuals will conform because they seek the approval of these other important people and wish to avoid their disapproval. Without a close bond to these significant others, people are free to deviate.

The extent to which a people's behavior revolves around legitimate activities refers to their level of involvement as presented by control theorists. If most of their free time is taken up with conventional activity, such as sports, clubs, or acedemics, then there is no time to commit crime.

Commitment refers to the extent to which individuals feel they have something to lose by breaking the law. People conform because conformity pays off and lack of conformity might jeopardize something they value, such as their jobs or reputations. Ambition and aspiration also play a role with regard to conformity. For example, a young person refuses to use drugs in order to protect future job prospects. Therefore, middle-class drug users, in the absence of psychopathology, are the least likely to become addicted. "These individuals contain and control their use of all drugs because they have viable life investments (such as jobs, families, homes) to protect" (Rosenbaum & Doblin, 1991, p. 143). Those without jobs or the hope of obtaining a job may be more likely to find drug use a rewarding and low-risk behavior. "If I have no job, I have no job to lose through drug use, and the effects of the drugs make me feel better about not having a job."

Belief refers to a set of common moral values that people who relate closely to one another have, such as honesty, hard work, and respect for the law. If an individual internalizes the belief that committing crime is wrong, that person will probably conform.

Labeling Theory

The labeling theorist would argue that the user views his or her initial experimentation with drugs as normal. However, once that behavior has been brought to the attention of significant others, the user is labeled deviant (Becker, 1963; Erickson, 1962; Lemert, 1951; Schur, 1972; and Tannenbaum, 1938). Eventually, the user internalizes the label as deviant (Covington, 1987) and continues to use drugs because others expect this behavior. This process is known as the self-fulfilling prophecy. The individual changes his or her self-perception to fit with the expectations of others. Even those users who support their drug use with legal activities are viewed by society as criminals. Therefore, these users may carefully avoid stigmatization by maintaining conventional lifestyles and concealing their drug-taking behavior from friends and associates who do not use drugs (Covington). Others, however, are likely to develop a covert lifestyle to avoid confrontation or stigmatization, possibly forcing the user to affiliate more and more with an underground subculture.

Subculture Theory

Subculture theory assumes that we internalize the norms and values of our immediate environment. Much of this theory is predicated on the early work of Shaw and McKay (1942). These researchers discovered that criminal activity was largely contained within specific areas of the city of Chicago that were characterized by a physical and social design that perpetrated crime.

Edwin Sutherland (Sutherland & Cressey, 1978) argued that society is composed of conflicting norms and values that coexist in a culture. He believed that crime occurred most often in those subcultures where the values that support breaking the law were more prevalent than the values that support obeying the laws. For example, if children grow up in a family where the mother uses drugs and works as a prostitute and the father steals to obtain money, the children would not view drug use, prostitution, or theft as abnormal and will conform by imitating their parents and internalizing the deviant values as normal. This point was brillantly captured by a photographer for the newspaper *The Hartford Courant*. The *Courant* ran a series on the lives of drug users in Hartford, CT. The *Courant* photographer captured a shot showing a four-year-old girl pretending a kitchen match was a hypodermic needle and attempting to shoot heroin into her vein as she had seen her mother do many times before.

Children born into organized crime families see the criminal way of life as normal. They do not feel that selling or using drugs is wrong. Rather, this illegal activity is the means by which they accumulate wealth and become accepted in their subculture. However, since both deviant and nondeviant behavior is learned in close association with others, some people might not commit crime because they did not learn how to commit crime.

Social Learning Theory

The use of drugs is very much influenced by social learning experiences and cultural traditions. Drinking wine is part and parcel of the Jewish, Italian, and French cultures. From childhood, for example, a Jew learns how to partake in ceremonies that involve drinking small amounts of wine. Tobacco is included in Middle Eastern rituals, and chewing coca leaves is traditional within South American families. Marijuana and some hallucinogenic drugs are even standard in some native Indian tribes. Within the community, and particularly within the family unit, children either learn by example or by being included in activities that involve drug use. This scenario is also, unfortunately, true for those children whose parents abuse drugs and alcohol. All too often, children witness their parents' drug abuse or are even offered their first taste of drugs by family members. This behavior is likely to be repeated as they grow into adulthood. Families that maintain traditional values and rituals pertaining to the use of certain acceptable drugs and ethnic communities that remain relatively cohesive pass along these practices from generation to generation. Children reared in these environments generally adhere to the rules within their families and communities and are less at risk of becoming excessive or compulsive drug users. Taboos for drug-taking behaviors are well established and unambiguous. American society has become a melting pot, where communities and even families become diffused and culturally mixed. This situation is believed to contribute to some confusion about the rules for drug taking and may eventually lead to excessive drug use in vulnerable individuals.

Norman Zinberg (1984) feels there is a greater risk of drug abuse in a society that fails to teach responsible drug use. As pointed out in Chapter 6 with regard to alcohol, there are many formal (legal) regulations controlling alcohol use as well as many informal sanctions and rituals. For example, laws prohibiting sale of alcohol on Sundays or sale of alcohol to those below the age of twenty-one constitute formal sanctions. However, other informal sanctions and rituals—such as, never drink alone, don't drink before noon, know your limit—also govern the use of alcohol. These informal sanctions and rituals are primarily designed to control drug use.

As Zinberg points out (1984, p. 15) our culture does not support controlled use of illicit drugs and the federal government has refused to fund any research study that supports "responsible drug use." Children who observe parents drinking in moderation and only during special social events will learn the rules simply through their observations. Those who are further instructed in ways to control drinking behavior and are told about occasions when drinking is acceptable are much less likely to lose control. Children from homes where alcohol use is strictly forbidden, once they begin to experiment as teenagers, will not likely know the guidelines and limits. Excessive drinking, not knowing when to stop, and becoming disorderly when drunk may be, in part, a result of the teenager's lack of rules for drinking and role models to mimic. As well, young people who lack instruction or modeling but try illicit drugs, have not learned how to use the drug in a way that minimizes the chances of abuse and addiction. The peer group that introduces the user to the drug may consist of compulsive drug users who are unable to teach the new user controlled drug use.

It is important to note that subcultures of illicit drug users do maintain their own sanctions and rituals, which are often attempts to prevent addiction. Robins et al. (1974, 1980) show that many American soldiers used heroin during the Vietnam War without ever becoming addicted. Many were able to abstain once they returned home. Other subcultures teach young users the rituals and skills for successfully using drugs but do not protect them from becoming addicted. Thus, the novice quickly learns how to obtain drugs, how much they should cost, how to tell whether or not the drug has been cut with another substance, how to avoid detection, which drugs to combine and what combinations can be lethal, and many other aspects of the drug culture. Users become quite saavy and sophisticated in their drug purchases and uses and many, in fact, become amateur pharmacologists. These same users, however, do not necessarily learn the what dangers are, and many have distorted ideas about which drugs are addictive; for example, many still believe that cocaine is not addictive or at least that they are not addicted and can control its use. Cocaine users frequently report that they can quit at any time, but ask them to quit, and it becomes another matter.

Although there are many social influences on drug use, too numerous to include here, we do need to recognize the powerful influence of developmental pressures and peer groups. During adolescence, a whole host of developmental influences begin to rule our lives. As with most primate species, there is a need during adolescence to break free from our parents and to become more autonomous. Any parent will attest the fact that when so-called nice children reach their teen years, they can become monsters. All of a sudden, it seems, children no longer listen and mindlessly obey their parents. They question everything they are told, not only by their parents but also by all figures of authority. Teenagers are notoriously rebellious and experiment with alternative means to achieve those items or feelings that they desire. They want to explore their world and discover for themselves whether they wish to live as their parents do or if there are other more desirable, and perhaps more exciting, options.

During this experimental stage, adolescents will tend to engage in behaviors that they may not even consider later in life. Adolescents commonly feel immortal and invulnerable. So logically, this is the most likely developmental juncture for drug experimentation to take place. Drugs provide teenagers with a feeling of independence from their parents and an ability to explore alternative modes of behavior and perceptions of reality. For most teens, the allure wears off and a sense of obligation and future come into play once high school has ended and they turn eighteen. (It is probably no coincidence that at age eighteen an individual who commits an offense is treated as an adult by our legal system.) Thus, a majority only occasionally experiment with drugs for a few short years and then abandon them for larger personal and social aspirations. Those who continue to use and eventually become addicted are believed to suffer from personal, social, or biological disadvantages that may overshadow other legitimate aspirations. One influential social disadvantage is the presence of a peer group that accepts drug-related activities. Having friends that are heavily invested in the drug scene are likely to transmit the belief that drug use is normative behavior.

Morality and Values

Stanton Peele, a well-known addiction theorist, has proposed that we have lost sight of individuals' values in our fervor to discover a simple cause of and a magic cure for addictive behaviors (Peele, 1987). Unlike previous theories that seek to demoralize drug abuse and stop condemning addicts for their behavior, Peele contends that people should be held responsible for their moral qualities and addictive behaviors. Addictive behaviors, according to Peele, is influenced by preexisting values. Thus, society should attempt to instill values that are incompatible with addiction and substance abusing behaviors.

Evidence for the essential contribution of value systems to addiction include the following five areas of research. First, there are "large group differences in the successful socialization of moderate consumption of every kind of substance" (p. 188). Most people learn how to use potentially addictive substances in moderation. Peele believes their ability to moderate their intake is a function of cultural and group values, rather than some intrinsic feature of the drug or the individual. Second, there are "strong intentional aspects of addictive behavior" (p. 188). Those who do become addicted to a behavior or drug show their intentions to do so and appear to be strongly motivated in that direction. Third, there is a "tendency for some people to abuse a range of unrelated substances and to display other antisocial and self-destructive behaviors" (p. 188). Not only do individuals use a wide variety of substances to obtain a high, but they also display a number of other immoral or destructive behaviors. These observations suggest that drug abusers lack values conducive to moral behavior in a general sense. They feel, in essence, free to deviate from the norm and engage in hedonistic behavior no matter what the consequence for self or others as a result of their lack of an acceptable value system. Fourth, "developmental studies repeatedly discover value orientations to play a large role in styles of drug use in adolescence and beyond"(p. 189). In this statement, Peele argues that the drug abuser failed to learn prosocial values as a child and that the social learning process was inadequate during childhood. As a consequence, the door is left open to antisocial options. And finally, there is a "relationship of therapeutic and natural remission to personal value resolutions by addicts and to life changes they make that evoke values which compete with addiction" (p. 189). Many addicts are able to overcome their addictions, either with the aid of therapy or alone, by adopting value systems that conflict with their addictive behaviors and provide an alternative lifestyle (Peele, 1987).

Although this view blames addicts for their behavior and downplays the significance of biological and psychological conditions known to contribute to addiction, it provides an essential recognition of the role of individual decision making. Peele's view places full responsibility on the users, a tact found useful in therapy. Once users realize that they are ultimately in control, abstinence can be more readily achieved. We are all, essentially, responsible for our actions. Nevertheless, this strategy may only work if underlying conditions that were also influential in the addictive behaviors are identified and treated first. Unless we address these factors, focusing on values and responsibility alone may fail, and underlying problems will remain unattended. Furthermore, global primary prevention strategies to reduce child abuse, neglect, poor parenting and prenatal care, psychiatric illness, and other factors known to set the stage for drug abuse will never develop. The need to focus on all of these systemic and individual conditions does not, in any event, trivialize the role of values. As a society, it is essential that values conducive to health, achievement, work, self-control, and altruism are upheld and taught to our children.

Integrating Theories: The Diathesis-Stress Model

The diathesis-stress model is rapidly becoming the foundation for multidisciplinary theories of many forms of psychopathology (see Tarter & Edwards, 1987). This model attempts to demonstrate how various biological, psychological, and social factors interact to produce human behavior generally, and antisocial behavior specifically. According to this model, individuals vary considerably with respect to their biological strengths and weaknesses. Biological weaknesses, referred to as a vulnerability, act as influential conditions in an individual's risk for substance abuse. They are, however, only part of the story. Rather than acting alone, these biological features operate by setting the stage for how adaptively an individual will respond to personal stressors. Stress is more likely to contribute to some form of psychopathology when it is received by a biological system that is somehow compromised. Learning disability, brain damage or functional irregularity, drug exposure, genetic predisposition to temperamental disturbances, and other biological disadvantages lay the groundwork for a pathological response to stress. Prior learning experiences contribute further by either increasing or decreasing the risk.

Although the probability of a pathological response is a function of the number of these risk factors present, the probability is even greater in the presence of an adverse

Figure 5.4   *Interrelated Conceptual Domains of Risk Factors and Protective Factors*

A conceptual framework for adolescent risk behavior: risk and protective factors, risk behaviors, and risk outcomes.

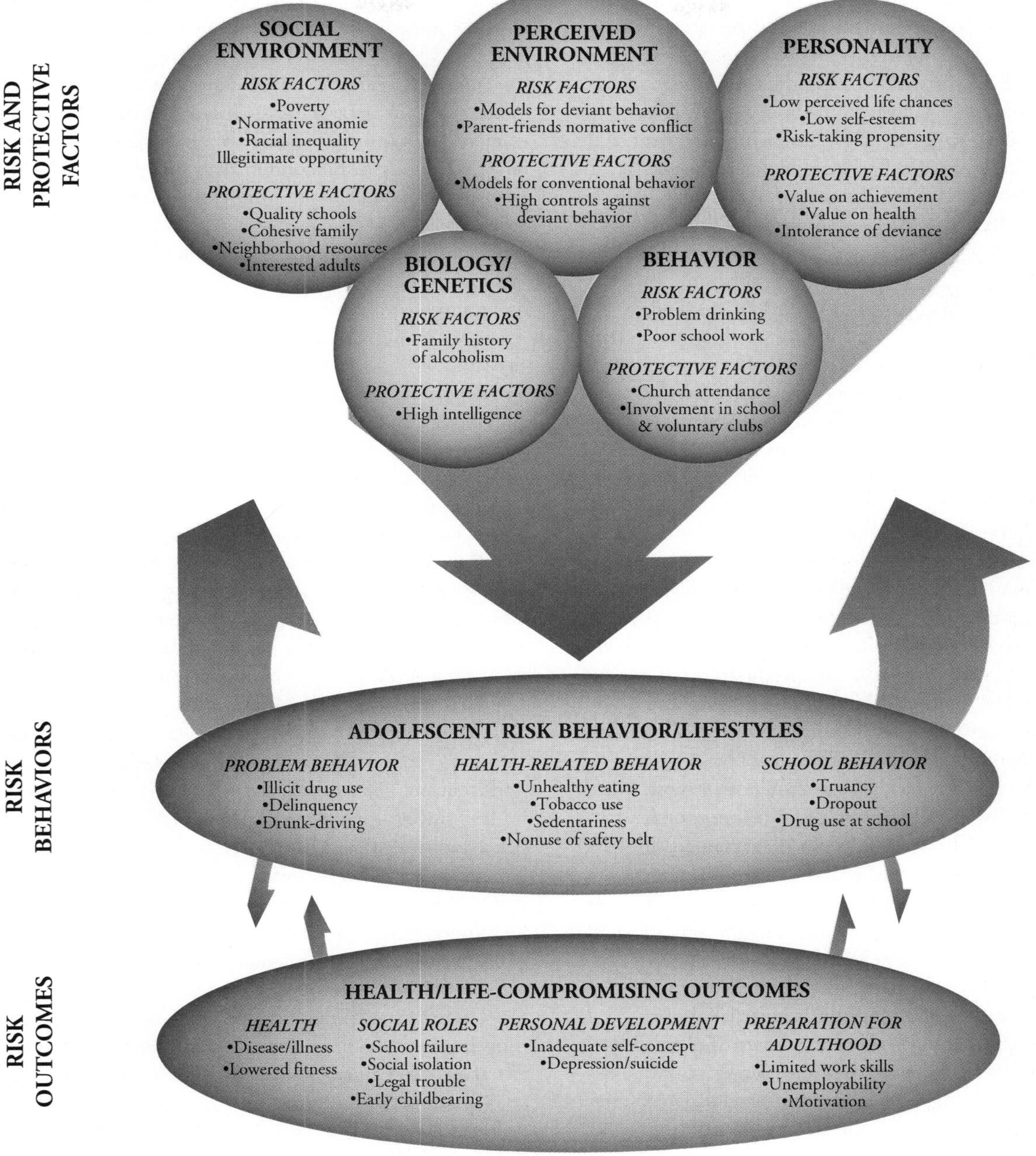

RISK AND PROTECTIVE FACTORS

SOCIAL ENVIRONMENT

RISK FACTORS
•Poverty
•Normative anomie
•Racial inequality
Illegitimate opportunity

PROTECTIVE FACTORS
•Quality schools
•Cohesive family
•Neighborhood resources
•Interested adults

PERCEIVED ENVIRONMENT

RISK FACTORS
•Models for deviant behavior
•Parent-friends normative conflict

PROTECTIVE FACTORS
•Models for conventional behavior
•High controls against deviant behavior

PERSONALITY

RISK FACTORS
•Low perceived life chances
•Low self-esteem
•Risk-taking propensity

PROTECTIVE FACTORS
•Value on achievement
•Value on health
•Intolerance of deviance

BIOLOGY/ GENETICS

RISK FACTORS
•Family history of alcoholism

PROTECTIVE FACTORS
•High intelligence

BEHAVIOR

RISK FACTORS
•Problem drinking
•Poor school work

PROTECTIVE FACTORS
•Church attendance
•Involvement in school & voluntary clubs

RISK BEHAVIORS

ADOLESCENT RISK BEHAVIOR/LIFESTYLES

PROBLEM BEHAVIOR
•Illicit drug use
•Delinquency
•Drunk-driving

HEALTH-RELATED BEHAVIOR
•Unhealthy eating
•Tobacco use
•Sedentariness
•Nonuse of safety belt

SCHOOL BEHAVIOR
•Truancy
•Dropout
•Drug use at school

RISK OUTCOMES

HEALTH/LIFE-COMPROMISING OUTCOMES

HEALTH
•Disease/illness
•Lowered fitness

SOCIAL ROLES
•School failure
•Social isolation
•Legal trouble
•Early childbearing

PERSONAL DEVELOPMENT
•Inadequate self-concept
•Depression/suicide

PREPARATION FOR ADULTHOOD
•Limited work skills
•Unemployability
•Motivation

Source: Reprinted from *Risk Behavior in Adolescence: A Psychosocial Framework for Understanding Action,* by Richard Jessor, 1992, by permission of Westview Press, Boulder, CO.

environment with severe stressors (e.g., poverty, unemployment, crime infestation, poor parenting, and lack of education). For example, individuals with hyperactivity may function well in society given appropriate attention. In the presence of family instability, lack of appropriate educational programs, and a delinquent peer group, however, the child may be more prone to antisocial behavior, possibly resulting in actions society considers criminal. Thus, environmental factors play a facilitating role in determining an adverse outcome (e.g., drug abuse) in vulnerable persons. In some cases, in fact, as when the environment is unusually harsh or conducive to drug abuse, environmental factors may be even more potent determinants of substance abuse than strictly biological vulnerabilities.

≡ Summary

Drug abuse and addiction are neither entirely inherited nor entirely acquired behavioral states. A theoretical focus on one set of influences to the neglect of the other precludes the development of a comprehensive understanding of abuse and addictive behaviors. Findings referred to in this chapter suggest that these behaviors are as much a result of a continuous and cumulative set of influences an individual is exposed to from conception on as are all other human behaviors. This view of drug abuse is consistent with the Development Course Model described in Chapter 3 which maintains that all forms of behavior, both social and antisocial, are products of numerous genetic and environmental process interacting over time.

A simple development sequence of influential events in the development of drug addiction may be illustrated by the following theoretical example. The son of an alcoholic father inherits a biological predisposition (or vulnerability) to problem drinking or alcoholism. This predisposition may take many forms, including the following: (1) an increased sensitivity to alcohol as indicated by differences in enzyme production, brain function, and physiological responsivity during alcohol intake, (2) cognitive or learning impairments (e.g., hyperactivity, attention deficit disorder, language delay, etc.), or (3) heritable psychological features such as impulsivity, sensation seeking, anxiety, or aggressiveness. These traits may increase the risk of alcohol abuse by exaggerating the rewarding biological and psychological properties of alcohol.

Environmental influences may further exacerbate the predisposition to alcoholism as the individual develops. Role modeling of the father's alcohol consumption and

other learning experiences both in the home and the community may reinforce a biological predilection to abuse alcohol. Problems in school may arise as a function of an existing cognitive or learning impairment, frequently present in children of alcoholics. Such cases of impairment require attention that most school systems are unable to provide in the form of an adequately stimulating environment and appropriate intervention programs. The presence of a disability, along with the lack of intervention, encourages the individual to interact more extensively with peers exposed to similar circumstances. Feelings of helplessness may surface as self-esteem and aspirations for future successes are undermined by an inability to perform competitively. Poor neighborhoods without adequate social support systems, community programs, and prospects for upward mobility (conditions significantly associated with the prevalence of alcoholism) may further advance alcohol dependence. Indeed, the father's alcoholism may increase the probability that the family will live in such disadvantaged settings. The incidence of these social and psychological disadvantages is greater among alcoholic populations; hence, they hypothetically function to reinforce alcohol tendencies in susceptible individuals.

This same scenario may apply to other forms of drug abuse. Future research efforts will investigate and attempt to estimate the relative contributions to drug abuse of genetic or biological conditions (e.g., inheritance of increased sensitivity to drugs, the inherent reward value of certain drugs, chemical or physiological irregularity, prenatal drug exposure), psychological features (early childhood deviance, antisocial personality traits, learning disability, conduct disorder), prior learning experiences (modeling, habit formation, conditioned responses), family circumstances (poor parenting skills, dysfunctional homes, abuse, neglect), environmental conditions and opportunities (urban life, poverty, lack of social mobility), and perhaps other as yet unknown contributors. Although previous studies have established that each of the above-mentioned factors play a role in the development of drug abuse, we have yet to estimate their relative significance or the manner in which they interact.

At present, these conditions appear to be nonspecific for numerous behavior disorders and, hence, we are not yet able to precisely predict the development of drug abuse as distinct from other behavioral or psychiatric phenomenon. With the discovery of traits or conditions that appear to be more prevalent among substance abusers when compared to other clinical and normal populations, specific prediction of drug abuse, as distinct from other behavioral disorders, will improve. It is possible that the ability to predict the abuse of a particular substance on the basis of these variables may never be realized. In some neighborhoods, drug availability is the strongest determinant of drug of choice. Nevertheless, there is hope of eventually understanding the development of drug abuse and addiction in terms of probabilities; the greater the number of risk factors and the more intense the exposure to these factors, the greater the likelihood will be of a resulting substance abuse disorder. It is also possible that the sequence of exposure is an important predictor of outcome. Once particular biological mechanisms, psychological traits, and social circumstances have been reliably identified among substance abuse populations, their relative contributions and dynamic interactions discriminating drug abusers from other populations can be estimated. Present efforts to prevent and treat drug abuse will subsequently improve by targeting those conditions, behaviors, and attitudes responsible for the onset and maintenance of drug abuse behaviors.

CHAPTER

Alcohol

Objectives

1. To discuss alcohol use in the United States as a major health problem, in spite of its legality.

2. To provide an overview of how alcohol is processed by the body to exert an effect.

3. To discuss the negative effects of alcohol on the brain, body, and psyche.

4. To explain how alcohol becomes addictive and in what ways alcohol is abused.

5. To describe the fetus and child who have been exposed to alcohol during pregnancy.

6. To identify the stages of alcoholism and diagnose the alcoholic.

7. To identify genetic, biological, and psychological traits that may place an individual at risk for a drinking problem.

8. To discuss the relationship between alcohol use and criminal and violent behavior.

9. To discuss the unique problems facing the families of alcoholics and how they attempt to cope.

10. To provide a summary of treatments that are used for alcoholism and alcohol abuse.

Alcohol is a drug that has been known since before the invention of the written word. Yes, it is a drug; it just happens to be a legal drug in most parts of the country. The active ingredient of alcohol, ethanol, is derived from the fermentation of grains (to make beer, gin, rye, whiskey, or vodka) or grapes and other fruits (to make wine, or brandy). Some enterprising individuals have even made wine out of dandelions. There must be something very special and desirable about alcohol to cause people to go to such great lengths to create it in such a wide variety of ways.

Indeed, the consumption of alcohol is part of many religious and cultural rituals (including communion in some Christian sects) and is a common social lubricant at gatherings. It is a lubricant because it seems to make the flow of conversation easier and smoother. Alcoholic beverages have such important functions in most world cultures that all societies have norms and laws dealing with the substance. For example, Americans have a loosely defined social structure associated with the type of alcohol consumed. The social structure is reflected in such distinctions as playing a higher status on champagne than beer. (Have you heard the phrase, "champagne taste on a beer budget"?) Within given alcoholic beverage categories, social status is also associated with the cost and uniqueness of the drink. Even beer, particularly expensive special or imported beers, can be considered high status. For example, beer from a small, independent brewery would carry a higher status than one from a larger, more commercial brewery. These descriptions of drinking customs are so well imbued in our cultural fabric that they constitute common knowledge and underscore the importance of alcoholic beverages to our society.

Nearly every culture in the world has laws and customs involving alcohol and its consumption, but they vary greatly from culture to culture. Some Muslim countries eschew public use of alcohol and have extensive laws detailing the prohibitions on drinking. It is considered legal to purchase and consume alcoholic beverages in most parts of the United States although this country also experienced a period of legal alcohol prohibition.

Laws governing the use of alcohol are often complex. Currently, alcohol purchases are restricted to certain times of the day and, with so-called blue laws, some states prohibit alcohol sales on Sunday. Children under twenty-one years of age are prohibited by law to purchase or consume alcoholic beverages. However, many of the Mediterranean European countries serve children wine at mealtimes and other family functions, clearly a violation of law in the United States. The recent legal trends in the United States suggest a movement toward less tolerance of alcohol consumption. This trend is seen in the implementation of

Drinking beer in some circles, particularly among college students, seems to be a national pastime.

increasingly punitive drunk driving laws and the growing implementation of drug testing of the American work force by employers.

Since the beginning of recorded history, there has always been a segment of the world population that has problems with alcohol. The Old Testament of the Bible includes stories of the Jewish people dealing with problematic consumption of alcohol. Plato, the great Greek philosopher, noted problems associated with public drunkenness and recommended some of the practices that serve as models for current laws in the United States (e.g., Plato recommended no alcohol for those under eighteen years of age). The Institute of Medicine (1990) based its discussions about needs for alcohol treatment on the tentative estimates that 25 percent of U.S. citizens consume substantial amounts of alcohol. (The Institute of Medicine recommends caution in using any specific estimates of the actual number of people with problems because the estimates vary widely based on definitions used.) According to their presentation, approximately 5 percent of the population are clearly dependent on alcohol while 5 to 15 percent are problem drinkers. Problem drinkers include those who have difficulty controlling or curtailing their alcohol intake, those who drink despite alcohol's worsening of health problems, and those who lose control over their behavior or mood state while drinking. Those who develop the extreme form of alcoholism suffer from numerous problems related to drinking. Many alcoholics, after as little as one drink, find themselves in the position of not being able to stop drinking. They frequently feel the need to consume alcohol and do so regularly. For others who are not alcohol dependent but occasionally drink heavily, the greatest problem they may face is missing a day's work after a "wild" party (assuming they don't drive under the influence). The remaining 75 percent of the population consumes small amounts of alcohol and these moderate drinkers are not considered problem drinkers or alcoholics.

This chapter will explore the way alcohol influences the body and what we understand about alcohol abuse and dependence. As you read the following pages, ask yourself how you would identify an alcoholic. Think about the nature of alcohol use and consider the danger of the beverage. Is alcohol any more or less dangerous to the body than other abusable drugs? How would you characterize the dangerous aspects of alcohol; is it a substance that can cause addiction or one that some people are already prone to becoming addicted to?

The Extent of Alcohol Use in the United States

In 1993, 83.6 percent of the American population aged twelve or over reported having tried alcohol at some time in their lives (see Table 6.1). In the twelve to seventeen age category 41.3 percent claimed to have tried alcohol at some time in their lives, 13.3 percent claimed to have used alcohol at least twelve times during the past year, and 4.0 percent claimed to have used alcohol at least once a week or more. In the eighteen to twenty-five age category, 21.5 percent of young adults responding reported using alcohol once a week or more. About a quarter (24.6 percent) of those between twenty-six and thirty-four years of age and 23.6 percent of those thirty-five and over also reported using alcohol once a week or more (Substance Abuse and Mental Health Services Administration, 1994).

In 1992, 88 percent of high school seniors reported having tried alcohol at some time in their lives (Johnston, O'Malley, & Bachman, 1993). Twenty-eight percent of seniors and 41 percent of college students reported drinking five or more drinks in a row at least once during the prior two-week period (see Figure 6.1). Twenty percent of high school females and 36 percent of high school males reported drinking five or more drinks in a row during the prior two-week period versus 33 percent of college females and 51 percent of college males.

Overall though, the trend appears to be one of decreasing drinking behavior among high school seniors and college students. Monthly prevalence of alcohol use among seniors had declined from 72 percent in 1980 to 51 percent in 1992. Daily use declined from a peak of 6.9 percent in 1979 to 3.4 percent in 1992 (See Figure 6.2). Consuming five or more drinks in row during the prior two-week interval fell from 41 percent in 1983 to 28 percent in 1992.

College students show less of a drop off in monthly prevalence since 1980 (82 percent to 71 percent in 1992) than do high school students and very little change in daily use or in occasions of heavy drinking which stands at 41 percent. This figure of 41 percent is higher than their age peers (i.e., those one to four years past high school) not in college (33 percent). Since the college-bound seniors in high school are consistently less likely to report occasions of heavy drinking than the noncollege-bound student, this figure reflects their catching up and passing their peers after high school (Johnston, O'Malley & Bachman, 1993).

In most surveys from 1980 onward, college students have had a daily drinking rate (3.7 percent in 1992) that is

Table 6.1   *Alcohol: Percent of population reporting use of alcohol ever, past year, and past month, 12 or more times during past year, once a week or more (1993) by sex and age groups for total population.*

	Ever Used	Used Past Year	Used Past Month	Used 12 or More Times During Past Year	Used Once a Week or More
	RATE ESTIMATES (PERCENTAGES)				
AGE					
12-17	41.3	35.2	18.0	13.3	4.0
Male	40.7	34.0	18.3	14.5	5.4
Female	42.1	36.5	17.7	12.0	2.7
18-25	87.1	79.0	59.3	49.2	21.5
Male	87.9	80.6	64.5	57.5	31.0
Female	86.4	77.5	54.3	41.0	12.3
26-34	92.4	81.0	62.8	50.4	24.6
Male	94.8	84.6	70.1	62.3	35.4
Female	90.1	77.5	55.7	39.0	14.1
35+	87.6	64.6	48.8	39.1	23.6
Male	94.6	72.6	59.1	52.1	34.9
Female	81.5	57.6	39.9	27.7	13.8
Total	83.6	66.5	49.6	39.9	22.5
Male	87.8	71.7	57.4	50.6	31.2
Female	79.8	61.7	42.5	29.9	12.6

Source: Adapted from Substance Abuse and Mental Health Services Administration, *National Household Survey on Drug Abuse:* Population Estimates 1993.

Figure 6.1   *Alcohol: Trends in Two Week Prevalence of 5 or More Drinks in a Row Among College Students vs. Others (1-4 Years Beyond High School)*

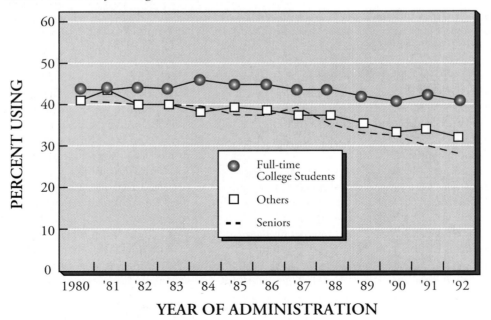

Source: Johnston, O'Malley & Bachman, 1993.

Figure 6.2   *Alcohol: Trends in Thirty-Day Prevalence of Daily Use Among College Students vs. Others (1-4 Years Beyond High School)*

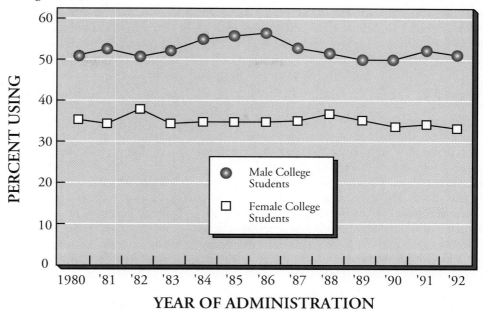

Source: Johnston, O'Malley & Bachman, 1993.

slightly lower than that of their age peers (4.0 percent in 1992), suggesting that they are somewhat more likely to confine their drinking to weekends, on which occasions they tend to drink a great deal. The rate of daily drinking has fallen among the noncollege group from 8.7 percent in 1981 to 4.0 percent in 1992. (Johnston, O'Malley & Bachman, 1993).

The great majority of young Americans are exposed to peers who drink alcohol. Many report they have friends who get drunk at least once a week; 80 percent of high school seniors, 77 percent of the nineteen to twenty-two year olds, 73 percent of the twenty-three to twenty-six year olds, and 66 percent of the twenty-seven to thirty year olds. In terms of direct exposure during the past year to people who were drinking alcohol "to get high for 'kicks'", such exposure is almost universal in these four age groups; 91 percent, 93 percent, 91 percent, and 87 percent respectively (Johnston, O'Malley & Bachman, 1993, p.135).

Although a clear majority of high school and college students do not drink to excess, there is a subgroup of these students who report intentionally drinking to the point of intoxication, and sometimes blackouts, several times a week. When asked why they prefer large quantities, these teenagers

and college students frequently state that they have more fun (although they generally don't remember what they did), feel more socially at ease, or forget their troubles more readily after ten or twelve drinks! Many of us experimented with alcohol in our teens, and most of us learned ways of drinking socially or stopped altogether by the time we completed college, if not way before. Always noticeable, however, were those friends who quickly found alcohol reinforcing, even when it made them sick, and did not stop drinking after one or two beers. Instead, they seemed to lose control and were unable or unwilling to stop after only a few drinks. These students appear to be on their way to a drinking problem if not full-blown alcoholism. Possible reasons for this predisposition will be discussed later in this chapter.

How the Body Responds to Alcohol

Varied Effects and Influences

Alcohol is quickly and completely absorbed into the body tissue (metabolized) like no other ingestable substance. In great part, the body absorbs alcohol directly into the bloodstream without any chemical changes. Alcohol's molecules easily travel across the blood-brain barrier and directly influence brain functioning almost immediately after ingestion. It also quickly crosses many structural barriers against large molecules, such as the placental barrier (separating the mother from her fetus); thus alcohol can influence fetal development at certain points in the pregnancy (see the section on fetal alcohol syndrome).

The speed at which the body metabolizes alcohol is modified by several factors. We can take advantage of these factors to slow down the impact of alcohol when we drink.

The stomach contents determine how quickly absorption will occur and what the immediate effects of drinking alcohol will be. When taken on an empty stomach, some of the alcohol will be absorbed directly through the stomach wall into the bloodstream. This is why the effects of alcohol appear to go "straight to the head" when a person drinks on an empty stomach. A full stomach will delay absorption by diluting the alcohol, particularly if protein foods, which tend to retain alcohol, are present. Munching on peanuts (a high-protein food) is a good way to slow the effects of alcohol.

The rate of alcohol absorption also depends on the amount of extra fluids taken immediately before and during consumption. When alcohol is used along with juice,

milk, or water, the effects may be somewhat delayed. However, carbonated "mixers" (club soda or cola) actually facilitate absorption and make the effects of alcohol occur faster. To slow the effects of alcohol, drinkers should also consume water or juice.

The concentration of alcohol in each drink also moderates the effects of alcohol on the body. The higher the concentration, the more rapidly the alcohol will be absorbed. Distilled liquors, including whiskey, vodka, and gin, range from 40 to 50 percent alcohol. Wine is approximately 12 percent alcohol while beer is only about 5 percent. All things being equal, a drink of distilled liquor will have a stronger effect than a glass of wine. However, all things are rarely equal. Beer may seem to be the safer drink due to its relatively low concentration of alcohol but beer is frequently consumed in larger quantities and more rapidly. The alcohol level in the body of such a beer drinker quickly matches or exceeds the level of a person drinking fewer glasses of whiskey (see Figure 6.3).

The physical size of the drinker also influences the effects of alcohol. In larger drinkers, alcohol becomes more diluted, less alcohol is found in the bloodstream, and it takes longer to become intoxicated. Alcohol is soluble in both fat and water and has an affinity for all fat and muscle tissue. Thus, larger individuals retain alcohol longer in fat and muscle tissue, but may not feel as intox-

Alcoholic beverages come in many forms, tastes, containers, and colors. They all, however, contain enough ethanol to cause inebriation.

Figure 6.3 *What's in That Drink?*

12 oz. beer	5 oz. wine	4 oz. wine	3 oz. sherry	1.25 oz. 80 proof
(4% alcohol)	(10% alcohol)	(12.5% alcohol)	(16.5% alcohol)	(40% alcohol)

Alcoholic drinks differ tremendously with respect to their alcohol content. Even though all these drinks are quite different in size, they all contain about half an ounce of pure alcohol, considered to be the size of an average drink.

icated. Small persons become intoxicated more rapidly due to their low body weight and fat mass. Women, for example, generally weigh less, have a higher percentage of body fat, and less body water than men. As a result, women retain higher concentrations of alcohol in the blood and in fat stores and, therefore, experience more potent effects. One must account for a variety of physical features to predict alcohol's effects.

Individual drinkers vary in their responses to alcohol because each has a different constitution and biochemical make-up that will determine how well that individual can tolerate alcohol. Drinkers also vary in the amount of alcohol they have consumed over the years, further modifying the effects of an alcoholic beverage. Those who drink only occasionally and who have not developed a tolerance to alcohol will metabolize about a third of an ounce of 100

Parties of all types often lead to excessive alcohol intake and uncharacteristic behaviors.

Drinking alcohol in a bar, rather than in the home or other social setting, has been associated with a tendency to drink more than one would normally.

percent alcohol per hour. This is equivalent to the amount of alcohol in one ounce of whiskey, 3 ounces of wine, or 12 ounces of beer, for example. If the drinker exceeds this amount per hour, intoxication will result. So, by drinking more alcohol than the body can metabolize over a period of time, the alcohol concentration in the blood will result in observable subjective effects (e.g., giddiness, body sway, uncoordinated movements, slurred speech). With increased tolerance, the experienced drinker will not become noticeably intoxicated as quickly.

It has been suggested that different susceptibilities to the effects of alcohol are inherited. The flush response seen in most Japanese when they drink alcohol is one of the clearest examples of the inherited responses to alcohol. This response is so unpleasant that this group is unlikely to drink much at all, even as teenagers in peer pressure situations.

Finally, the social circumstances in which the drinking occurs and the expectations of the drinker exert tremendous influence on the perceived effects of alcohol. Some individuals may have more control over alcohol's effects at a sedate cocktail party than at a hockey game, with the excitement of the competition and the cheering of the crowd. In the first instance, the drinker's social audience is less likely to tolerate loud, boisterous, drunken behavior. Although one may be forgiven once or twice, the known

drunk will probably receive fewer invitations to formal events. Also, when a drinker expects to become uninhibited, sexually stimulated, or aggressive when drinking, he or she is more likely to display that behavior under the influence of alcohol than the drinker without such expectations. These anticipated behaviors then become evident in individuals who believe they have drunk alcohol, but who actually received a placebo (Laberg & Loberg, 1989; O'Malley & Maisto, 1985; D.F. Ross & Pihl, 1988).

Responsible drinkers consider the effects of alcohol on the body. However, it is difficult for anyone to determine precisely how much alcohol has been consumed unless it is done in a scientific manner and drinks are consistently prepared. Bartenders and hosts do not use uniform proportions of liquor to mixer. Thus, unless undiluted glasses of wine or beer are consumed, the drinker may not be able to reliably predict alcohol's effect or prevent intoxication.

Alcohol's Effect on the Body

Enzymes in the body break down and excrete alcohol's toxic by-products. One of those enzymes, alcohol dehydrogenase, is located in the liver. Alcohol dehydrogenase helps metabolize alcohol to convert acetaldehyde, a by-product of alcohol, to acetate, which is subsequently excreted. If acetaldehyde is permitted to accumulate due to an enzyme deficiency, the individual will experience symptoms of toxicity, including headache, nausea, vomiting, sleepiness, and other hangover-like effects. However, it is not all bad; this negative response to alcohol can be induced by giving a drug called Antabuse to alcohol treatment patients. This drug (technically called disulfiram) has been successfully used in a variety of treatment settings. Antabuse works by inhibiting the synthesis of the enzyme alcohol dehydrogenase, which results in a build-up of acetaldehyde and causes the negative effects of nausea, vomiting, and so on. The effects of Antabuse are sufficiently strong to hamper the drinking of most alcoholics.

Approximately 95 percent of ingested alcohol is metabolized before it is excreted and the remaining 5 percent is excreted through the lungs and urine. Small amounts accumulate in the lungs and are exhaled during respiration. "Beer breath" is a result of this process. In fact, police rely on this process to determine alcohol levels in the blood of drivers they stop on the highway. If the officer suspects that a driver is intoxicated, a Breathalyzer test will be administered. The Breathalyzer measures the level of alcohol in the breath. Since breath alcohol levels are 5 percent of blood alcohol level, an estimate of alcohol consumption can be obtained.

Part of the variability between individuals in the extent to which alcohol is metabolized is a function of the liver enzyme, alcohol dehydrogenase. Those with high enough levels of the enzyme generally do not suffer from a hangover. The enzyme is about four times more active in males than females, so even if a man and woman weigh about the same, have the same amount of body fat, and drink the same amount, more pure alcohol is likely to reach a woman's blood and brain than a man's.

There is evidence that, as a whole, Asians have quite low levels of this enzyme, causing them to experience adverse effects, such as flushing and nausea, from even small quantities of alcohol (Newlin, 1989). Estimates are that 85 percent of Japanese carry an atypical liver alcohol dehydrogenase (Stamatoyannopoulas et al., 1975). This suggests that Asians may be more sensitive to alcohol from the accumulation of acetaldehyde, placing Asians at low risk for developing alcoholism. This is important ammunition for those who argue that at least for some, alcoholism is inherited. Other ethnic groups differ in their ability to metabolize alcohol, and it is possible that other ethnic groups differ in their ability to metabolize alcohol.

The only effective way of detoxifying an individual and eliminating the alcohol from the body is to simply wait for the alcohol to be metabolized, slowly and steadily. Common remedies, such as drinking coffee, walking, or breathing fresh air do very little to reduce the intoxicating effects of alcohol.

Negative Short-Term Effects

Alcohol is similar to sedative-hypnotic compounds that generally slow nerve cell activity in the central nervous system (CNS) (Julien, 1988). Thus, it is a general, nonselective CNS depressant. When taken initially, alcohol has the seemingly contradictive property of acting as a behavioral stimulant while inducing feelings of euphoria. However, this behavioral stimulation may occur due to the initial depression of inhibitory neural systems (see Table 6.2 for the chronic effects of alcohol). The first important influence of alcohol on the brain is to depress a part of the brainstem called the reticular activating system (RAS). The RAS is responsible for protecting us from overloading or underloading sensory receptors and arousing or focusing higher brain centers, such as the cerebral cortex, on relevant incoming stimuli. When the cortex no longer receives adequate guidance from the brainstem, the individual feels uninhibited and becomes more likely to exhibit uncontrolled emotional outbursts. These effects set the stage for some of the more extreme behavioral responses observed in certain individuals under the influence of alcohol, such as assaultive behavior, reckless driving, criminal activity, promiscuity, belligerence, and depression. As the individual continues to drink, increasing the dose of alcohol, excitatory neural activity becomes depressed. In sum, alcohol is a depressant; first, it depresses inhibitory centers leading to feelings of stimulation, and, second, it depresses excitatory centers leading to physiological and behavioral depression.

Drinking beyond that stage, further increasing the dosage, can result in "brain syndrome," otherwise known as Korsakoff's Disease, characterized by disorientation, mental clouding, impaired memory, decreased judgment, and labile (flat) mood. This occurs when alcohol dampens the activity of centers in the brainstem that control the cortex. Psychotic-like behavior, including hallucinations and delusions, may follow as the syndrome progresses. Usually, because brain syndrome is caused by the immediate toxic effects of alcohol, it may be reversed. Chronic heavy drinking, however, may cause permanent brain syndrome, a more long-term effect. A few people can drink themselves "crazy."

Table 6.2   *Medical Complications from Chronic Alcohol Use*

Behavioral and Psychiatric Disorders

"Brain Syndrome"

Central Nervous System Depression

Delirium Tremens

Hypoglycemia (leading to diabetes in susceptible individuals)

Heart Disease

Hypothermia

Korsakoff's Syndrome (organic brain syndrome associated with memory loss, confusion, amnesia, and disorientation)

Malnutrition

Seizural Convulsions

Sexual Dysfunction

Sleep Disturbances

Alcohol can suppress epileptic convulsions, at least for a while (Jaffe, 1985). This temporary anticonvulsant effect of alcohol is the result of an increase in the activity of an inhibitory neurotransmitter called gamma-aminobutyric acid (GABA). GABA serves as a brake on the rate of electrical activity of the brain to give our system a safety valve. However, when alcohol consumption ceases, the level of GABA suddenly declines and neural activity jumps to very high levels (called neural hyperexcitability). This is a dangerous state for epileptics as it may lead to seizures, possibly lasting for several days (Jaffe). But, hyperexcitability is not just a condition suffered by epileptics. It is particularly common when an alcoholic withdraws from alcohol. Brain seizures may ensue regardless of whether the alcoholic was initially epileptic and they are the primary feature of the DTs (delirium tremens), a potentially fatal condition.

On the other hand, some individuals are simply unusually sensitive to very small quantities of alcohol. A single drink may produce neural hyperexcitability in those with pre-existing CNS instability resulting from a discrete or "hidden" form of epilepsy, namely temporal lobe or psychomotor (Bach-y-Rita et al., 1970; Maletsky, 1976; Marinacci, 1963). In these cases, the initial depression of inhibitory centers allows excitatory centers to function unchecked, leading to excessive electrical discharges in the brain. Further reports suggest an association between this form of subcortical (below the cortex) epilepsy and psychopathic and/or violent behavior (see Herzberg & Fenwick, 1988; D.O. Lewis, 1981, p 39–55; Valzelli, 1981; Yeudall et al., 1985). The case of a mild-mannered, widely respected professor exemplifies this condition. He took his graduate students out each Friday for happy hour and engaging conversation. To the students' dismay and confusion, however, the professor became belligerent and unruly after only one beer! He was even involved in three known cases of sexual assault. On the following days, he had no memory of the details and would sometimes apologize for what he thought may have been inappropriate behavior on his part. After a while, students and faculty alike avoided his company where alcohol was being served. He eventually retreated to his office and stopped drinking altogether. Researchers have suggested that individuals, possibly such as this professor, with subcortical neural instability may experience blackouts, visual disturbances, dramatic personality or mood changes, and explosive episodes of rage after ingesting relatively small quantities of alcohol (Bach-y-Rita et al., 1970; Maletsky, 1976; Marinacci, 1963). This syndrome remains not well understood (Kligman & Goldberg, 1975; Stevens & Hermann, 1981).

Several other organ systems are deleteriously affected by alcohol. When alcohol is ingested and absorbed into the bloodstream, it rushes immediately to the heart and dilates blood vessels in the skin as if to facilitate its own transportation. The dilation of blood vessels is responsible for the warm flush experienced when drinking. Unfortunately, although we may feel warm, we are actually losing body heat more rapidly and lowering body temperature. Many people, from the homeless to downhill skiers, drink alcohol to keep warm, but the effect is just the opposite and in extreme cases can cause hypothermia (life threatening low body temperature) and possible death. We hear each year of homeless individuals found dead in the cold after becoming inebriated.

Alcohol affects the function of the kidneys by having a diuretic effect increasing fluid loss. The action of certain kidney hormones is impaired, and the large quantities of fluid ingested are difficult for the kidneys to handle. Because large amounts of liquids are taken in, the volume of urine increases as bodily fluids exit. (Remember, very little alcohol is eliminated this way so do not be fooled into believing that you are lessening alcohol's effect on the body by urinating more frequently.) Thus, the morning following a drinking binge, the mouth is dry and the individual is ravenously thirsty.

Another effect of alcohol is to interfere with sleep cycles. We must all complete several sleep cycles to feel refreshed in the morning. One phase of sleep is known as rapid eye movement or REM sleep. This phase is usually characterized by dreaming. Alcohol, tranquilizers, and barbiturates all suppress REM sleep, causing the user to awaken feeling fatigued and unrefreshed.

Finally, contrary to popular opinion, alcohol dampens sexual responsiveness. Alcohol has been considered an aphrodisiac because it lessens inhibition and restraint on behavior. Alcohol does initially provide the feeling of sexuality simply due to the lack of impulse control. Also, the expectation alone that alcohol is a sexual stimulant will provoke erotic feelings and sexual arousal in casual drinkers. In reality, alcohol depresses the ability to perform and be effective sexually. As Shakespeare wrote, "It provokes the desire, but it takes away the performance." As a result, people sometimes drink too much, get "in the mood," and find that it is difficult to maintain an erection or achieve orgasm. Heavy users of alcohol in particular suffer from long-term sexual dysfunction. Alcohol may cause atrophy of the testicles, and sperm production becomes impaired due in part to a lowering of testosterone levels.

The Hangover

A hangover is actually the result of several short-term effects produced by alcohol. It may occur when a person drinks more alcohol than his or her body is able to metabolize in a certain amount of time. The symptoms are widely experienced even by social or occasional drinkers: headache, nausea and vomiting, indigestion, diarrhea, fatigue, thirst, anxiety, or depression. The severity and longevity of symptoms are a function of the quantity and type of alcohol ingested and the sensitivity of the drinker. Some people develop hangovers more easily than others, and some forms of alcohol are more likely to produce hangovers than others. For example, wine more frequently produces a hangover than vodka, even when blood alcohol levels are the same.

The likelihood of experiencing a hangover is probably related to the reaction an individual has to the congeners in the alcoholic beverage. Congeners are natural by-products of the fermentation and processing of alcohol and may be quite toxic. They contribute to the differences between alcoholic beverages in taste, smell, and color. Beer contains a lower percentage of congeners while distilled liquors have much higher levels. The longer the alcohol is aged, the higher the congener level. Vodka, considered a purer form of "hard" liquor, has the same congener level as beer (see Ray & Ksir, 1990).

Other precipitants of hangover are dehydration, low blood glucose, stomach irritation, acetaldehyde build up, and depleted serotonin levels. Due to the diuretic effect of alcohol, the body's cells become dehydrated. More fluid is excreted than is taken in, causing extreme thirst and dry eyes. Low blood glucose or hypoglycemic episodes were described previously as a result of heavy drinking. The individual may awaken headachy, shaky, fatigued, and hungry. It is common to wake up in the middle of the night after drinking and feel anxious, sweaty, and shaky due to low blood glucose levels. Eating while drinking helps to minimize this effect. The stomach distress occurs because alcohol irritates the gastric lining. Acetaldehyde also accumulates, possibly causing headache and nausea. Finally, although serotonin levels rise initially, a subsequent decline of serotonin levels in the brain may contribute to feelings of depression, anxiety, and irritability and perhaps even a desire to drink again in an attempt to relieve the distress.

There is no simple cure for a hangover. Many people, particularly those with a drinking problem, believe that the "hair of the dog that bit you" is the best remedy and stir up a Bloody Mary early the next morning. This cure is not recommended. The only reason additional alcohol may relieve the symptoms of a hangover might be because it prevents the symptoms of alcohol withdrawal in the same manner a shot of heroin will eliminate its withdrawal symptoms. Curing a hangover with more alcohol may increase one's addiction to the drug. The only surefire cures for a hangover are rest, an analgesic such as aspirin for pain, liquids, sleep, and time. To minimize a hangover, it is helpful to drink only alcoholic beverages that are relatively low in congeners, to combine food and other fluids with alcohol consumption, to drink only moderate amounts of alcohol (obviously!), and to drink ample amounts of water before retiring for the night.

Finally, alcohol greatly impairs decision-making ability. Most people who drink until intoxicated report that they behaved in a way that they regretted and would not have considered had they not been drinking. This is a particularly disconcerting aspect of alcohol consumption in that many people place themselves or others at risk by increasing their sexual contacts. Impaired decision making may compromise the ability to say no, to practice safe sex, to remember contraception, or to judge partners adequately.

Negative Long-Term Effects

In spite of the wide variety of substances that are used to make it, alcohol contains virtually no nutritional value but is abundant in calories from glucose (simple sugar).

Each gram of alcohol contains seven calories and there are 28 grams per ounce! Beer, the king of alcohol as far as popularity goes, is especially caloric (see Table 6.3). That does not necessarily mean that heavy drinking will make you fat. Heavy drinkers may suffer from nutritional deficiencies because they substitute the calories in their drinks for more nutritive calories from food. Heavy drinkers lose their appetite because the body registers high levels of glucose in the blood from the alcohol.

Nutritional deficiencies resulting from the poor eating habits of heavy drinkers contribute to drastic fluctuations in blood sugar levels and changes in brain chemistry that control bodily function and behavioral responses. One particular condition, hypoglycemia—a chronic low blood glucose condition—may be caused by or contribute to problem drinking (Coid, 1979; S.Cohen, 1980; Wallgren & Barry, 1976). Alcohol intake enhances secretion of the hormone insulin to assimilate the large amounts of glucose (alcohol's calories are primarily sugar) entering the bloodstream. Insulin in the bloodstream results in a decline in blood glucose levels. When the decline is severe, the brain becomes involved by releasing a number of hormones to stabilize blood glucose (e.g., epinephrine, cortisol, ACTH). Such a crisis in blood glucose levels is worsened by a diet poor in the nutrients that are required to help stabilize glucose metabolism. Both the initial drop in blood glucose and the subsequent release of hormones by the brain have been associated in a few reports with a variety of behavioral disturbances which may include extreme aggression and other forms of criminal activity (see Fishbein & Pease, 1988; Prinz et al., 1980; Virkkunen, 1986). Apparently, only a subgroup of those suffering from hypoglycemia experience behavioral disturbances; however, alcohol consumption may further increase the risk.

Chronic alcohol intake may contribute to heart disease by damaging heart muscle and possibly causing heart failure. Small doses of alcohol, however, may actually improve circulation, lower cholesterol levels, and reduce the risk of certain forms of heart disease (Kaplan, 1991; Sheehy, 1992; Suh, Shaten, Cutler, & Kuller, 1992). Studies done in France (where a lot of wine and cheese is consumed) found that red wine, in particular, raises the good cholesterol (high density lipoproteins or HDL) and lowers the bad cholesterol (low density lipoproteins or LDL). After these findings were reported on the news, one of the authors discovered a maintenance man drinking red wine at 9:00 in the morning. He was overweight, had high blood pressure, and claimed that he had just discovered that drinking throughout the day would solve his

Table 6.3   Belly Up to the Bar? How Many Calories Are You Willing to Consume?

	Calories per serving	Alcohol in grams	Alcohol % by vol.
Regular beer (12 oz.)	143	16	4.6
Light beer (12 oz.)	108	14	4.2
Nonalcoholic beer (12 oz.)	68	1	0.3
Stout (12 oz.)	176	18	5.2
Malt liquor (12 oz.)	174	21	6.1
Ale (12 oz.)	172	19	5.6
Champagne (4 oz.)	95	14	12.5
Red wine (4 oz.)	90	14	12.5
White wine (4 oz.)	84	14	12.5
Light white wine (4 oz.)	52	8	7.4
Nonalcoholic white wine (4 oz.)	23	0.5	0.4
Nonalcoholic red wine (4 oz.)	20	0.5	0.4
Gin, rum, vodka, whiskey (80 proof, 1.25 oz.)	81	14	40.0
Low fat milk, 2% (12 oz.)	182		
Orange juice (12 oz.)	168		
Soft drinks (12 oz.)	150		

Source: Modern Brewery Age, Beer Institute, Beer Drinkers of America, Wine Institute, Distilled Spirits Council of the United States

medical problems. It is important to note that the studies' findings only apply to small doses, between one to two drinks per day, and do not apply to larger amounts ingested over a long period of time.

Alcohol's effects on the liver are profound. Chronic drinking can cause irreversible changes in its structure and operation, resulting in cirrhosis although one does not have to be an alcoholic to have cirrhosis. Cirrhosis of the liver causes 75 percent of all deaths associated with alcoholism (Julien, 1988). This disorder is insidious as there may be no signs or symptoms of its development for a long time. Eventually alcoholic hepatitis or other symptoms of liver dysfunction appear and cirrhosis may be properly diagnosed. Chronic alcohol ingestion leads to adaptation by the liver as the drinker develops an increased tolerance to alcohol although this does not offer protection from liver damage. The alcoholic will also develop a cross tolerance to sedatives and tranquilizers, thereby reducing their effectiveness. Alcohol also diminishes the therapeutic value of some antibiotics.

Psychoactive Effects

In low doses, the effects of alcohol are limited to the CNS. Generally, alcohol affects five main areas of brain function in graduated quantities: (1) 1 to 2 drinks (0.02 blood alcohol level [BAL]) affects reason, caution, intelligence, and memory but causes no discernible intoxication; (2) 3 to 4 drinks (0.05–0.09 BAL) affects self-control, and judgment with some signs of intoxication; (3) 5 to 6 drinks (0.15, BAL legally drunk) affects sensory perception with obvious signs of intoxication; (4) 7 to 8 drinks (0.3 BAL) affects coordination with obvious intoxication; and (5) more than 8 drinks (0.45+ BAL) affects vital centers with severe intoxication. The level of intellectual and behavioral disturbance as a result of alcohol intake is still largely unpredictable and varies greatly from one person to the next.

Alcohol-related behavior is a function of individual personality characteristics, prior learning experiences, and environmental conditions. In one setting, an individual may be relaxed and passive, whereas in another situation the same person may be easily provoked to aggressive or violent behavior. As the level of alcohol consumption increases, the environment will have less influence on the psychological or behavioral outcome. The individual will be increasingly intoxicated and less able to exert control over bodily functions as sedation sets in. In either case, alcohol is disinhibitory, meaning that the drinker will be less restrained in behavioral activities, psychological expressions, and physical functions. An individual who has consumed very large quantities of alcohol is more likely to be a danger to him or herself than to others. However, an individual who has ingested lower doses of alcohol is more likely to have the wherewithal to find his or her car, turn on the ignition, and then not have the capacity to drive effectively or safely. A severely intoxicated person is less able to inflict substantial harm, whereas a slightly less intoxicated person may still be quite dangerous in a brawl.

Pathological intoxication is a rare syndrome that may be seen in individuals who are extremely sensitive to the effects of alcohol. These individuals show signs of severe intoxication and impaired behavior after consuming only

Each individual has a unique reaction to alcohol as a function of preexisting constitutional, biochemical, and personality differences.

Source: Marc Holden

one or two drinks. They will also display repetitive and automatic movements and extreme excitement with aggressive, uncontrolled, irrational behavior (Berkow, 1982). As mentioned above, this disorder is more likely to occur when there is pre-existing CNS instability, possibly subtle subcortical epilepsy (Bach-y-Rita et al., 1970; Maletsky, 1976; Marinacci, 1963). The observer witnesses bizarre, uncharacteristic changes in mood or personality as the alcohol-sensitive individual begins to drink, as illustrated by the professor described earlier. The episode may last for minutes or hours and is followed by a lengthy sleep and amnesia.

Tolerance, Dependence, and Withdrawal

Ingesting alcohol regularly and in relatively large amounts will result in the development of tolerance. Those who drink irregularly or in small quantities may not develop any noticeable tolerance to alcohol. However, it is possible to become temporarily mildly tolerant to even small doses. The extent to which a drinker develops tolerance depends on the amount, pattern, and extent of alcohol intake.

Tolerance is a function of how well the liver metabolizes alcohol. As the liver accommodates alcohol introduced to the body, it become more efficient at synthesizing and releasing enzymes responsible for metabolizing the alcohol. Consequently, the more alcohol a person consumes, the more alcohol that person needs to produce the same effect; tolerance soon develops. Cell activity attempts to adapt to the alcohol by maintaining a balance between excitation and inhibition. As alcohol is neurologically depressing, the cells compensate by becoming more excited. When the alcohol has been metabolized and eliminated, the cells remain excited, and the drinker develops nervousness, shakes, and irritability. The drinker may then feel the need to drink more to relax and the cycle continues.

In occasional users, alcohol withdrawal is associated with hangovers in most people. Dependence on alcohol, however, is signified by more severe withdrawal symptoms when alcohol intake ceases. Delirium tremens (DTs) is a major abstinence syndrome mentioned earlier. When an alcoholic stops drinking, frightening hallucinations, agitation, violent physical symptoms, and uncontrollable behavior result. After this psychotic-like episode, sleep may set in while terrible nightmares and shakes occur. Confusion, disorientation, hallucinations, a high fever,

and profound perspiration may follow. If the individual has a high fever and becomes dehydrated, death may be imminent, sometimes even when treated in a hospital setting. Withdrawal from other drugs after chronic use, aside from barbiturates, does not produce such extreme, violent, and dangerous results.

The drinker may also develop a psychological tolerance and dependence. A psychologically tolerant drinker may not appear drunk even after large quantities are ingested, and we tend to think they hold their liquor better than most. They may not seem as physically impaired or show visible signs of intoxication. Psychological dependence is more directly related to the perceived need for alcohol. If we know something will give us a sense of euphoria or relax us when we are tense, we will desire that something. So it goes with alcohol. Many drinkers are self-medicating a psychological or psychiatric disorder with alcohol and, even before they have developed the disease alcoholism, they may become psychologically dependent on alcohol's effects.

Fetal Alcohol Syndrome

There has been much controversy about whether moderate amounts of alcohol can be taken safely during pregnancy. In 1981, the Surgeon General proposed that even small amounts of alcohol during pregnancy are not safe and may endanger the health of unborn children. The present consensus among medical professionals is that there is no safe amount and that pregnant women should avoid alcohol altogether. Research findings have been unclear, as women tend to underreport their drinking and small doses of alcohol may have only subtle effects that we are not able to discern. Due to the potential hazards of even small amounts of alcohol during pregnancy, and as scant as our knowledge may be at this time, it is generally recommended that pregnant women abstain entirely. Unfortunately, because alcohol is legal, many women do not see the dangers of drinking while pregnant. Of widespread concern is that some prenatal manuals only suggest limiting alcohol to one or two drinks per day while pregnant! We may never know whether a child's potential to grow and achieve has been even slightly undercut because of a mother's moderate indulgence. There is additional evidence that the reproductive system of animals is impaired as a result of in utero exposure to alcohol, causing them difficulties in conceiving offspring when they reach adulthood. This may also be true for people. In short, safe levels of alcohol during pregnancy have not been determined.

Although the detrimental effects of small quantities taken only infrequently are not entirely clear, in larger amounts the effects are obvious. Babies born to mothers who are chronic alcoholics suffer from a condition known as fetal alcohol syndrome (FAS). This condition is most notably marked by abnormalities in facial structure, limbs and the cardiovascular system. Children of alcoholic mothers have low birth weight, small eye sockets, a small head, and the bridge of the nose and the vertical groove between the nose and the mouth is flattened (see picture). And while chronic drinking during pregnancy poses a well-known hazard to the unborn child, binge drinking can be equally dangerous. A pregnant woman does not have to drink every day to damage her fetus—a drinking binge can be devastating to fetal development.

What is not so obvious during the initial months of life are the growth and developmental delays that result from brain damage incurred in utero. The stage of pregnancy during which alcohol is ingested determines what aspect of fetal development will be influenced. Large amounts of alcohol in early pregnancy is most likely to produce malformations in appearance. Many mothers-to-be are not aware of being pregnant during these early vital weeks and drink unknowingly. Brain development, however, occurs throughout pregnancy and may be adversely affected at any stage. Brains of children with FAS show gaping holes—the appearance is similar to a pretzel. Frequently, these children are mentally retarded or, at the very least, mentally dull, and they show severe developmental delays in neonatal and later mental and physical skills. Other defects may also be present in organs including the eyes, ears, heart, testicles, and skin. Although many of these abnormalities may be seen in other disorders, the presence of several of these symptoms and a known drinking history of the mother aids in an accurate diagnosis.

Even in the absence of gross mental retardation and physical deformities, more subtle effects due to lesser amounts of alcohol taken during pregnancy can occur. Neurological impairments in FAS children (who may not be easily identified as FAS) are the cause of a number of

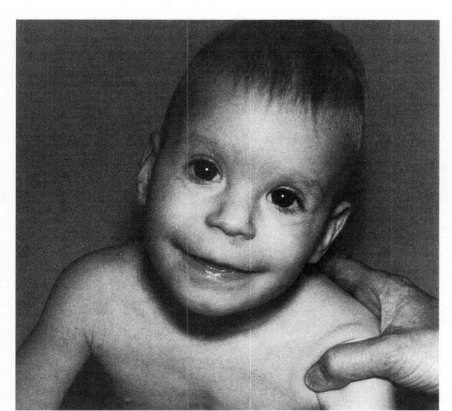

Fetal alcohol syndrome is characterized by facial deformities that are quite distinctive. Children exposed to smaller doses of alcohol during gestation, however, may not have overt signs of exposure but still may suffer neurological and cognitive impairment.

Source: Dorris, 1990

behavioral disorders that place them at risk for a lifetime of failure. They have memory impairments, a relative absence of abstract thought, and illogical thought patterns. They are unable to follow the rules of society or simple directions given them. One of the most disturbing aspects of FAS is the inability to assess the consequences of their behavior. It is, consequently, impossible to predict their behavior which tends to be impulsive and inappropriate. Due to this problem, FAS children and adolescents are prone to seriously delinquent and eventual criminal behavior. For example, there is a pervasive lack of understanding that taking things from others is stealing, so they do not experience remorse or self-control in such situations. Furthermore, they are gullible and tend to place their faith in those that are untrustworthy. These behaviors combined with their inability to think ahead and their tendency to wander off make FAS individuals vulnerable to mistreatment and abuse.

These traits alienate them from others, and as early as grade school they are shunned and pressured into befriending those who have similar behavioral disorders. As adults, FAS sufferers are likely to be drifters, criminals, homeless, prostitutes, mentally ill, or retarded. Early diagnosis of FAS can be critical to understanding an FAS child and providing the special attention he or she needs. FAS children are frequently adopted by unsuspecting parents who are unaware of the birth mother's drinking history or the telltale signs of FAS. Early diagnosis and intervention is especially helpful to confused and helpless adoptive parents who must deal with this difficult condition.

Unfortunately, until attention is focused on disorders found in children of substance abusers, many of these children will remain undiagnosed or improperly treated. With an absence of obvious physical deformities in some of these children, behavioral disorders resulting from neurological damage are repeatedly misdiagnosed. FAS children are commonly labeled conduct disordered or "bad" and may be sent to reform school or dealt with by social workers instead of gaining more appropriate medical assessment. Because proper diagnosis of FAS is so difficult, the known rate of FAS is grossly underestimated. FAS is the one cause of mental retardation in Western countries that is entirely preventable. However, once FAS has been inflicted, there is no cure or treatment—only understanding (see Dorris, 1990).

Alcohol can also be found in the breast milk of nursing mothers. After the mother ingests alcohol, the natural odor of breast milk changes. Nursing infants suck more but receive less milk. Infants also sleep more often for shorter periods of time on days when their mothers ingest alcohol (Mannella & Beauchamp, 1991).

Development and Diagnosis of the Alcoholic

Most of us have observed drunk or intoxicated people in numerous situations. They are mentally slow, motor movement and judgment is impaired, speech is slurred or uncommutable, coordination is off, the face is flushed, and there is a distinct odor of alcohol on the breath and skin. Not all individuals who are obviously drunk or intoxicated, no matter how severely, are alcoholic. In fact, it is possible to drink routinely and never become alcoholic (see Inset 6.1. Michigan Alcohol Screening Test, which includes common criteria used to determine alcoholism).

Alcoholism involves the development of characteristic deviant behaviors associated with prolonged consumption of excessive amounts of alcohol (Berkow, 1982). It is a chronic illness focused on the medical and the social implications of the disease. Alcoholism evolves slowly as tolerance and dependence, a number of behaviors, and situational and metabolic conditions develop. Although there is some disagreement about what constitutes alcoholism, it is generally recognized that eight symptoms aid in its diagnosis: (1) exhibiting frequent intoxication that is obvious and destructive and interferes with the individual's social life and work, (2) failing in marriage and increasing work absenteeism, (3) being fired, (4) seeking medical treatment for drinking, (5) suffering physical injury, (6) being arrested for driving while intoxicated, (7) being arrested for drunkenness, and (8) being hospitalized for DTs or cirrhosis of the liver. When these conditions occur regularly, alcoholism may be identified (Berkow).

The DSM-III-R (APA, 1987) suggests that there are three primary patterns of chronic alcohol abuse or dependence: regular daily intake of large amounts, regular heavy drinking limited to weekends, or long periods of sobriety interspersed with binges of heavy daily drinking lasting for weeks or months. "It is a mistake [however] to associate one of these particular patterns exclusively with alcoholism" (p. 173). According to the DSM-III-R, the critical distinction between abuse and dependence is the ability to control drinking behavior, which is still intact in alcohol abuse. Furthermore, the course of alcoholism appears to be somewhat different for males and females. The age of onset is generally earlier for males, occurring in the late teens or twenties, even though the drinker com-

Inset 6.1

MICHIGAN ALCOHOL SCREENING TEST

1. Do you feel you are a normal drinker? (If patient denies any use of alcohol, check here_____.)
2. Does your spouse (or parents) ever worry or complain about your drinking?
3. Can you stop drinking without struggle after one or two drinks?
4. Do you ever feel bad about your drinking?
5. Do friends or relatives think you are a normal drinker?
6. Do you ever try to limit your drinking to certain times of the day or to certain places?
7. Are you always able to stop drinking when you want to?
8. Have you ever attended a meeting of Alcoholics Anonymous (A.A.)?
9. Have you gotten into fights when drinking?
10. Has drinking ever created problems with you and your spouse?
11. Has your spouse (or other family member) ever gone to anyone for help about your drinking?
12. Have you ever lost friends or girlfriends/boyfriends because of drinking?
13. Have you ever lost a job because of drinking?
14. Have you ever neglected your obligations, your family, or your work for two or more days in a row because you were drinking?
15. Do you ever drink before noon?
16. Have you ever been told you have liver trouble? Cirrhosis?
17. Have you ever had delirium tremens (DTs), severe shaking, heard voices, or seen things that weren't there after heavy drinking?
18. Have you ever gone to anyone for help about your drinking?
19. Have you ever been seen at a psychiatric or mental health clinic, or gone to a doctor, social worker, or clergy for help with an emotional problem in which drinking had played a part?
20. Have you ever been arrested, even for a few hours, because of drunk behavior?
21. Have you ever been arrested for drunk driving or driving after drinking?
22. Have you ever been treated for any psychiatric or emotional problem unrelated to drinking?
23. Do you have a service connected disability related to any emotional problem?
24. Did you once feel that you had a drinking problem but no longer do?

monly doesn't recognize the problem until his thirties. Males typically do not develop alcohol dependence after the age of forty-five. Females, on the other hand, more often develop alcoholism later in age and show a history of depression or other mood disorders. This may be because females are more readily diagnosed with mood disorders than males. Males are also less likely to be diagnosed as depressed even when they are. The nature of female alcoholism remains much of a mystery since there is relatively little research on the subject.

Because the individual with the disorder virtually never sees it accurately, scientists and clinicians now recognize that denial is a hallmark of alcoholism. Denial is the alcoholic's major defense mechanism, and it often keeps the problem drinker out of treatment. When the alcoholic denies to significant others that drinking has become frequent and/or heavy and fails to admit that it is interfering with daily life, loved ones may believe the drinker and consequently do not intervene.

The developmental stages of alcoholism that reflect progressive levels of deterioration are as follows. The pre-alcoholic phase may be identified when the drinker engages solely in controlled social and cultural drinking patterns. For most drinkers, this pattern remains stable and drinking does not become a goal in and of itself. Pre-alcoholics may initially report drinking alcohol to be an occasional escape from tension, but the frequency of escape drinking may increase over time.

The early alcoholic phase is marked by a progressive preoccupation with alcohol. The drinker experiences guilt feelings about drinking episodes and begins to make excuses and to lie. Conversations about alcohol intake are avoided altogether unless it is with a drinking companion with similar habits. During this phase, the first blackout may be suffered.

The true alcoholic phase is reached when the lifestyle begins to revolve around drinking alcohol. The individual's appearance, home life, job, and belongings are all neglected. Consequently, personal and social relationships deteriorate and the individual's ability to perform adequately are impaired. At this point, the drinker finds that he or she cannot stop after only one drink; controlled drinking becomes difficult at best. Even at this stage, a diagnosis of alcoholism may be overlooked. Sometimes the symptoms of alcoholism are not visible, and in the midst of the drinker's denial, proper identification and intervention will not occur.

The complete alcohol dependence phase is the most severe, crippling stage of the disease. The alcoholic is now in danger of withdrawal symptoms if alcohol becomes unavailable. Without medical help, death may occur. Liver and brain tissues are damaged beyond complete repair.

Vulnerability to Alcohol Abuse and Dependence

Several differences in individual constitution were discussed previously that may increase sensitivity to alcohol. Vulnerability to alcohol dependence has also been linked with biological mechanisms and personality features that may increase alcohol's reward value to some people.

Biochemical Mechanisms

Animal studies have examined rats selectively bred for their alcohol preference and compared them with nonpreferring rats to identify biochemical differences. These findings have suggested that neurotransmitter systems play a role in alcohol preference (Murphy, McBride, et al., 1987; Weingartner et al., 1983). Serotonin has been particularly implicated because of its presumed modulating influence in excessive drinking behavior (Geller et al., 1973; Melchior & Myers, 1976; Myers & Melchior, 1977), and alcoholism has been associated with low levels of a serotonin by-product, 5-HIA. (Ballenger et al., 1979; Banki, 1981; Takahashi et al., 1974). Drugs that increase the concentration of brain serotonin decrease alcohol intake in rats (Amit et al., 1984; Murphy, Waller, et al., 1985; Rockman, Amit, Carr, et al., 1979; 1982) and possibly humans (Naranjo et al., 1984). Also, alcohol-preferring rats have lower amounts of serotonin in certain brain regions responsible for behavioral motivation and the brain reward system (Murphy et al., 1982, 1987).

Lowered serotonin turnover may contribute to alcoholism (Ballenger et al., 1979). Alcohol consumption immediately accelerates the rate at which serotonin is released and reabsorbed, but the rate eventually falls again, further depleting brain serotonin. Consequently, the alcoholic drinking pattern may develop in an unconscious effort to raise serotonin levels. These findings are noteworthy as several reports have shown that impulsive and aggressive or violent individuals also have low serotonin levels relative to others and are more prone to problem drinking and alcoholism (G.L.Brown, Ebert, et al., 1982; Fishbein, Lozovsky, & Jaffe, 1989; Siever et al., 1987; Virkkunen et al., 1987). While serotonin activity is responsible for inhibitory behaviors, a decrease in activity leads to lack of impulse control and unpleasant feelings. The chronic alcohol drinker may seek the immediate biological reinforcement provided by increased serotonin levels, yet suffer a subsequent decline following alcohol intake, producing more craving and, in some cases, more aggressive or impulsive behavior.

Cloninger (1987) expanded this line of reasoning by describing two types of alcoholics associated with specific personality traits that presumably reflect differences in neurotransmitter systems. Type I alcoholics begin drinking after age twenty-five and are passive or anxious. They tend to be reward dependent (sensitive and emotionally dependent), avoid harm (cautious, inhibited, and shy), and not seek stimulation (orderly and structured). Type I alcoholics find alcohol rewarding due to its antianxiety effects and rapidly become dependent. This primary form of alcoholism is not associated with criminality and is thought to be both genetically and environmentally determined (see Table 6.4).

Type II alcoholics have an early onset of alcohol-related problems and are antisocial, aggressive, and impulsive. This alcoholic subgroup more often has fathers with a history of criminality and severe alcohol abuse and sons who experience early onset of alcoholism. They are emotionally cool and detached, sensation seekers, and uninhibited. Alcohol provides more euphoria and stimulation to Type II alcoholics, although they tend not to lose complete control over their drinking. Indications are that early-onset alcoholism is more genetically determined than later-onset alcoholism.

Cloninger compared Type II alcoholics to alcohol-preferring rats by suggesting that both populations are unusually reinforced by the stimulating effects of alcohol. According to Cloninger's speculations, Type II alcoholics tend to have high levels of the neurotransmitter dopamine and low levels of norepinephrine and serotonin, possibly related to their antisocial tendencies. This biochemical imbalance is related to alcohol preference and may be genetically transmitted although the mechanisms are not as yet understood.

Genetic Aspects of Alcohol Addiction

For centuries, philosophers and scientists have noted that alcoholism runs in families. It has been observed that

Table 6.4   *Traits of Type I and Type II Alcoholics*

CHARACTERISTICS	ALCOHOLIC TYPE	
	Type I	Type II
	Problems Related to Alcohol	
Common age of onset	After 25	Before 25
Gender most afflicted	Male and female	Mostly male
Severity of alcohol dependence	Relatively mild	Unable to abstain
Fighting and arrests when drinking	Not common	Very common to be violent with or without alcohol
Psychological dependence (loss of control over drinking)	High	Not common
Guilt and fear about drinking problem	Common	Not common
Inheritance	Questionable	Most likely through father
Other drug use	Less common	More common
	Personality Traits	
Reward dependence eager to please, sensitive, dependent	High	Low
Harm avoidance cautious, inhibited, and shy	High	Low
Novelty seeking impulsive, excitable, distractible	Low	High
	Family History	
Criminal history	Less common	Common (especially father)
	Treatment	
Effectiveness	More successful	Resistant to treatment

alcoholics frequently have alcoholic fathers, mothers, grandparents, siblings, and children. Although there remains disagreement (Peele & Alexander, 1985), the evidence for a substantial genetic contribution is strong (Cadoret et al., 1987; Goodwin, 1986; Peele, 1986; Schuckit, 1986; Tarter, Alterman, et al., 1985).

There appear to be several inherited conditions mentioned previously that may predispose individuals to alcohol abuse and dependence. The way an individual metabolizes alcohol, how efficiently alcohol is degraded and eliminated, the tolerance level and many other biological factors that can be inherited may be partially responsible for the development of alcoholism. These are a few of the obvious constitutional differences that contribute to alcohol's ultimate effect and the potential to drink to excess. Temperamental traits (e.g., impulsivity), psychopathological disorders (hyperactivity), and personality features (psychopathy), frequently found among problem drinkers and believed to set the stage for problem drinking, may also be inherited. Finally, differences in brain function among alcoholics and their children have been found, providing further support for a genetic contribution, possibly to both alcoholism and the behavioral disorders associated with it.

As genetic influences are reflected in biological responses and temperamental traits, we may evaluate genetic influences in part by studying these characteristics and determining whether they are more common among blood relatives than in the general population (see Alterman & Tarter, 1986). There is evidence, for example, that a family history of alcoholism is related to the development of problematic drinking behaviors (Schuckit, 1976, 1982). Individuals who succumb more readily to excessive and problematic drinking are thought to have an increased susceptibility to alcoholism by virtue of both a positive family history of alcoholism and an early onset of deviant behaviors (e.g., conduct disorder). These individuals graduate more rapidly to alcohol abuse or dependence after their first exposure to alcohol and are, thus, considered at risk for alcoholism.

Specific neuropsychological, behavioral, and biological differences have been found between alcoholics or high-risk individuals and low-risk subjects. For example, intellectual and cognitive impairments are more prevalent in children of alcoholics relative to comparison groups. Several of these studies found significantly lower IQ scores (Aronson, Kellerman, et al., 1985; Ervin et al., 1984; Gabrielli & Mednick, 1983; Steinhausen et al., 1982; Streissguth et al., 1979). Others have reported that sons of alcoholics performed more poorly on cognitive function tasks (Alterman, Bridges, et al., 1986) and on vocabulary, categorizing, organization, and planning tasks (Drejer et al., 1985; Schulsinger, Goodwin, et al., 1985) than sons of nonalcoholics. The high-risk group had problems with goal-directed activities, and they demonstrated impulsivity in problem solving. In addition, the high-risk boys showed more deviant behavior at school.

Several studies examined metabolic and behavioral responses to small doses of alcohol consumed by subjects with and without alcoholism among their first-degree relatives. Findings suggest that individuals believed to be at high genetic risk for alcoholism based on their family history experience a greater sensitivity to alcohol's effects than others. Specifically, blood acetaldehyde levels were significantly higher, and they experienced more alcohol-related flushing and higher heart rate and skin temperature than low-risk subjects (Schuckit & Duby, 1982; Schuckit & Rayses, 1979). Also, autonomic hyperreactivity was observed (see Chapter 3 on autonomic nervous system responses) following alcohol intake (Finn & Pihl, 1989). Thus, it is possible that high-risk individuals are reinforced by these exaggerated physiological effects.

Studies of twins involve comparisons between identical (monozygotic or MZ) and fraternal (dyzgotic or DZ) twins. MZ twins are genetically identical while DZ twins are approximately 50 percent genetically alike, as are regular siblings. When MZ twins are found to resemble each other with respect to a trait to a greater extent than DZ twins, a genetic influence is at work. The extent that there is still some degree of DZ resemblance after genetic influences have been accounted for reflects the influence of a common environment on the trait.

Overall, twin studies indicate a greater resemblance rate for MZ twins than for DZ twins with regard to the frequency of alcohol use, severity of alcoholic symptoms (Kaij, 1960; Kaprio et al., 1987; Pernanan, 1976) and amount of alcohol consumed (Jonsson & Nilsson, 1968; Kaprio et al.; Pernanan et al.,). Alcohol elimination rates and other features of alcohol metabolism also appear to be largely controlled by genetic factors (Forsander & Eriksson, 1974; Vesels et al., 1971). These studies disagree as to precisely what extent environment and genetics contribute to the development and severity of alcoholism, deterioration from alcohol, and other social and physical consequences of drinking. Nevertheless, they all find evidence for genetic influences on the decision to use alcohol, the extent and pattern of use, and the metabolic and behavioral outcomes.

Adoption studies attempt to separate genetic contributions to alcoholism from environmental influences by comparing individuals who were raised from infancy by nonrelative adoptive parents with individuals raised by their biological parents. Biological sons of alcoholics are more likely to become alcoholic in early adulthood than are sons of nonalcoholics (Bohman, 1978; Goodwin et al., 1973; Cadoret & Gath, 1978). In a series of studies (Goodwin et al., 1973; 1974; 1975) of adopted-away sons with one or two biological parents diagnosed as alcoholic, the risk for alcoholism in the sons was three to four times higher than the risk for the general population of males. The risk was the same regardless of whether the son lived with an alcoholic biological parent, a nonalcoholic adoptive parent, or an alcoholic adoptive parent. In a separate study (Schuckit, Goodwin, et al., 1972), siblings with at least one biological parent with alcoholism were much more likely to become alcoholic than those with nonalcoholic biological parents, regardless of whether the biological or adoptive parent raised them.

Antisocial Personality and Alcohol Abuse

Studies have implicated antisocial personality disorder (ASP) as a factor in the development of alcohol abuse (Cadoret et al., 1984; Gottheil et al., 1983; C.E. Lewis, 1984). Alcoholics who are diagnosed as ASP tend to: (1) begin drinking at an earlier age, (2) progress to alcohol dependence more rapidly, (3) evidence greater impairment in social and occupational functioning associated with their drinking; and, (4) have an increased number of arrests associated with their drinking (Cadoret et al.; Drejer et al., 1985; Hesselbrock, Hesselbrock, et al., 1984; Schuckit, 1985; Schulsinger, Knop, et al., 1986).

Interestingly, relatives of individuals with ASP are more likely to be alcoholic, and there is a greater incidence of ASP among families with alcoholism (Lewis, Cloniger, et al., 1983). Furthermore, many of the genetic, physiological, neurochemical, and psychological conditions described above that characterize those at risk for alcoholism are found among those diagnosed with ASP. There is speculation that ASP and alcoholism are genetically related and may be due to the same antecedent causes.

Type II alcoholism, largely inherited (Cloninger, Bohmen, et al., 1981), is strongly associated with ASP. ASP alcoholics tend to respond to alcohol with higher lev-els of autonomic nervous system activity following alcohol intake (Cloninger et al., 1988; Finn & Pihl, 1987). Thus, alcohol intake among ASP individuals may stimulate neurological processes that are essentially rewarding or pleasurable, thereby increasing drinking tendencies. Those with ASP also find thrill-seeking activities particularly rewarding due to the stimulation of the autonomic nervous system. The likelihood of impulsive, aggressive, or criminal behavior increases even more in ASP individuals when drinking alcohol.

The pattern of alcoholism, related behavioral disorders, medical complications, and treatment results all differ between alcoholic subgroups. ASP alcoholics, in particular, have a greater incidence of other psychiatric symptoms, are more prone to abuse alcohol, receive more reinforcement from family members, and have a tendency to undergo more frequent treatment episodes. This group is likely to have a different prognosis and need a more comprehensive treatment approach.

Childhood Hyperactivity and Alcohol Abuse

There is a high incidence of childhood hyperactivity among adults with ASP and aggressive behavior (Guze, 1976). There appears to be an additional link between childhood hyperactivity and alcoholism (Hesselbrock, Meyer, et al., 1985; Wender, 1977; Wood et al., 1983). Similar intellectual impairments, for example, have been found in those with ASP, hyperactivity, and alcoholism. Families of hyperactive children have an increased incidence of alcoholic and ASP biological fathers (Cantwell, 1975). Type II alcoholics, in particular, report significantly more symptoms of childhood hyperactivity than Type I alcoholics (Alterman, Petrarulo et al., 1982; Tarter, McBride, et al., 1977).

The links between ASP, hyperactivity, and alcoholism are probably due to the contribution of impaired impulse control found in all three disorders (Schuckit, 1987). The offspring of alcoholics have a higher rate of hyperactivity, poor emotional control, impulsivity, and other management disorders (Aronson, Kyllerman, et al., 1985; Bell & Cohen, 1981; Fine et al., 1976; Landesman-Dwyer, 1979; Steinhausen et al., 1982). These findings provide evidence that ASP, hyperactivity, and alcoholism may be genetically related.

Aggressive and Criminal Behavior

Alcoholism, aggression, and criminal behavior have been repeatedly linked in the literature (Guze, 1976; McCord, 1981; Pihl & Ross, 1987; Schuckit, 1973) The majority of violent crimes are committed shortly after the perpetrators have consumed significant amounts of alcohol (Gary, 1976; S.W. Greenberg, 1981; Tinklenberg, 1973, 1981; Wolfgang, 1958). Prison inmates, when compared with a nonincarcerated population, display a disproportionately larger number of alcohol problems (Collins, 1981; Friedman & Friedman, 1973; Grigsby, 1963; Mayfield, 1976; U.S. Dept. of Justice, 1983). Furthermore, an individual with a drinking problem is more likely to have a criminal record than an individual without a drinking problem (Goodwin, Crane, et al., 1971; Petersilia, 1980). Even among juveniles, the seriousness of their offenses is related to their drinking habits (Temple & Ladouceur, 1986). Heroin addicts are more likely to be under the influence of alcohol at the time they commit crimes than any other drug of abuse and are just as likely to purchase alcohol as heroin following an income generating crime (Strug et al., 1984). In short, alcohol more profoundly influences aggressive and criminal behaviors than other drug of abuse (Collins, 1981; Pernanan, 1976; Mayfield, 1976; Tinklenberg, 1973). This relationship between alcohol and antisocial behavior can be attributed to a multitude of variables, including alcohol's effect on physiological condition, psychological or genetic predisposition, personal and cultural expectancies, and learning experiences (Pihl & Ross, 1987).

Three related mechanisms are responsible for the association between alcohol and aggressive or criminal behavior. First, it is possible that the inheritance of biological or physiological abnormalities that place individuals at risk for alcoholism are also responsible for their increased susceptibility to antisocial behavior. In the reports cited above, evidence was provided that alcoholism is largely genetic. Perhaps similar mechanisms that are inherited simultaneously place problem drinkers at risk for antisocial behavior when consuming alcohol.

Second, the direct action of alcohol on the brain sets the stage for alcohol-induced aggression in susceptible individuals through, (1) pathological intoxication, sometimes involving psychomotor epilepsy or temporal lobe disturbance, (2) hypoglycemic reactions, (3) alterations in neurotransmitter activity; and (4) reduced neurological and behavioral inhibition. These mechanisms do not completely account for the relationship as many drinkers do not become aggressive.

The third contribution to alcohol-related aggression attempts to account for the individual differences that influence alcohol's effects. Specifically, psychological states determine to a great extent whether an individual will aggress or not when drinking. Indications are, first, that alcohol changes psychological state and, second, that psychological state influences alcohol's behavioral effect. We have already provided evidence that alcohol dramatically alters moods, emotions, and behaviors through its pharmacology. In the second scenario, alcohol serves as a stimulus for a preexisting psychiatric condition or psychological predisposition (Pihl & Ross, 1987). Several such conditions have been associated with alcohol-related behavioral disorders, including impulsivity, depression, ASP, hyperactivity, and conduct disorder. Individuals with underlying emotional instability who drink alcohol are more likely to become antisocial than those without certain psychiatric conditions or personality traits. Additionally, psychological states that may facilitate the expression of alcohol-related aggression include personal expectations of how alcohol will influence behavior. Thus, many unruly drinkers may have a preexisting psychological tendency to aggress or be antisocial that is simply triggered or unleashed by alcohol (Alterman & Tarter, 1986; Tarter, Alterman, et al., 1985; Cadoret et al., 1987; Hesselbrock, Meyer, et al., 1985; Kofoed & MacMillan, 1986; C.E. Lewis, 1984)

Alcohol consumption is more likely to elicit aggressive or antisocial behavior in vulnerable individuals—those with specific behavioral or personality features that place them at risk for inappropriate behaviors in specific situations.

Alcoholism and the Family

Most research focusing on the effects of substance abuse on the family has dealt with alcohol as the drug of abuse and the family as consisting of a father, mother, and children (Finley, 1983). Although the chemically dependent parent may be the father, the mother, or both, the most common alcoholic family features the father as the alcoholic parent since women are much more likely to stay with alcoholic men than men are to stay with alcoholic women (Ackerman, p. 9). Twenty percent of alcoholic homes involve both parents suffering from alcoholism (Ackerman, 1983, p. 10).

Growing up in an alcoholic family can have profound effects on children. The family can be viewed as a system with each member contributing to the process of functioning. The chemically dependent family member drastically alters the way the system works and creates what has come to be termed the dysfunctional family. The functional family nourishes each member and allows each to grow. The dysfunctional family denies members a sense of self-worth and discourages growth. Ackerman (1983) feels that children of alcoholics are the invisible victims of abuse; therefore their problems are also invisible since the alcoholic is the one generally receiving all the attention.

The effect of the alcoholic on the child depends on the degree of alcoholism and the type of alcoholic. For example, the alcoholic parent who is violent and abusive while drinking will have a different effect on a child than the alcoholic who is sociable and happy after a few drinks (Ackerman, 1983). Some very general statements can be made, however, about the effects of living as a child in an alcoholic family.

Alcoholic families generally appear to be normal from the outside but are characterized by chaos inside the home. Very little is consistent and predictable in the alcoholic family, and children have difficulty learning to trust. The children often assume parenting roles and protect the alcoholic. Dishes still need to be washed, someone needs to get little Johnny off to school, fed and clothed, grocery shopping must be done, bills must be paid. All of these daily tasks, are taken over by the non-alcoholic spouse and the children. Sometimes even small children are required to care for younger ones, and find themselves performing household chores normally reserved for older individuals. In these cases, children grow up much too fast, taking on a parental role, without really being children and without mastering essential developmental stages.

The family may lie for the alcoholic to cover up his or her drinking and find that lying becomes a survival technique they incorporate into their lives (Woititz, 1990). Children of alcoholics learn that the truth is dangerous and may lie about other trivial matters when it would have been just as easy to tell the truth. But children of alcoholics learn that the truth can be dangerous and their most important task in the alcoholic family is hiding the truth. Therefore, this lesson is generalized to all situations and children of alcoholics learn it is always safer to tell a lie than to tell the truth.

The family becomes isolated as it protects the alcoholic's secret from extended family and friends. Families try to find ways to appear normal and avoid confronting the real problem head-on. Ackerman (1983, p. 17) believes that families feel silence might mean the problem will disappear. Maybe if no one talks about the problem for a long enough period of time, it will simply vanish.

Children of alcoholics spend so much time pretending to be part of a normal family, they never really learn what normal actually is. Therefore they guess at what is "normal" (Woititz, 1990). As a result, they may feel a need to take their cues from others concerning what is normal and may be susceptible to manipulation by others (Potter-Efron & Potter Efron, 1989). Children of alcoholics experience tremendous difficulty in establishing intimate relationships with others (Ackerman, 1983, 1987, 1989; Wegscheider, 1981; Wotitz, 1990). These children report greater self-depreciation and lower self-esteem than their peers, particularly the girls. Overall, as stated above, children of alcoholics are more likely than children of nonalcoholics to be hyperactive, antisocial, demonstrate low academic achievement, suffer cognitive impairments, and display other symptoms of negative feeling states and behaviors.

Everyone in the alcoholic home tends to "walk on eggshells" to avoid upsetting the alcoholic. Alcoholics commonly have hair-trigger tempers—even the slightest provocation will set them off and cause them to lose control. Family members fear verbal or physical beatings that they may receive if they make a mistake, fail to clean their room according to the alcoholic's specifications, speak when not spoken to, or perhaps even for standing in front of the television and impairing the view of the alcoholic. Because of the fear instilled in each family member by the possibility of an attack or outburst by the alcoholic, and because the behavior of the alcoholic is so inconsistent and unpredictable, the alcoholic wields tremendous control over the family unit. As a result, other family members sometimes develop symptoms of psychological trauma similar to the trauma experienced by soldiers during battle or children in war-torn areas (known as Post-Traumatic Stress Disorder, PTSD).

Wegscheider (1981) describes roles family members often assume as they try to cope with the chemically dependent family member. She presents these roles as the enabler, the hero, the scapegoat, the clown (or mascot), and the lost child. Family members may assume more than one role or even change roles.

The enabler is generally played out by the person closest to the alcoholic, most likely the spouse. This person steps in and takes on many of the responsibilities the alcoholic relinquishes as he or she spends more and more time drinking. If the alcoholic loses his or her job or drinks up the money, the enabler may become employed or work an additional job to make up the difference. By picking up the slack the enabler keeps the alcoholic from experiencing the negative consequences of his or her actions. As the alcoholic deteriorates, the enabler assumes more and more responsibilities.

The hero is generally played by the eldest child. Similar to the enabler, the hero also tries to make up for the family deficits by overachieving. By bringing attention to themselves for their successes, heroes divert attention from the alcoholic and feel better about themselves. But no matter how well they perform, they cannot change the alcoholic, and heroes are prone to suffer from guilt and feelings of inadequacy.

The scapegoat diverts attention from the dysfunctional family by acting out in an apathetic, hostile, and delinquent manner. Scapegoats fail in school, become pregnant or have repeated trouble with the law. Scapegoats often turn to chemical dependency to deal with alienation from the family (Wegscheider, 1981), that results when the family points the finger and calls the scapegoat the cause of the family's problem, thereby avoiding the real difficulty, the alcoholic.

The lost child withdraws from the family chaos. The lost child lives alone in a fantasy world much of the time. Pleasure is gained from material possessions, and he or she may be prone to overeating and substance abuse. The lost child does not cause the family any trouble, nor does the child receive any attention. Consequently his or her needs are rarely met because the child is ignored much of the time. This child may be particularly creative since he or she engages in long hours of solitary pursuits. On the other hand, the child has difficulty engaging in close relationships with others. "He has had little experience in either expressing his own feelings or handling such expressions from others; in cooperation or in negotiating disputes when cooperation breaks down; in sharing or in defending ownership; in assessing the real value of either material possessions or sensory pleasure. *He has had little experience in living"* (italics in original, Wegscheider, 1981, p. 129).

The mascot tries to divert attention from the family's dysfunction by playing the role of an amusing and entertaining clown or of an annoying, fidgeting, clumsy, attention grabber or by alternating between behaviors. The mascot, generally the youngest child, arrives in the midst of a dysfunctioning family. Although the family attempts to protect this child from its difficulties and assure him or her that everything is OK, the child knows it is not. This discrepancy between what is known and what is told causes the child a great deal of tension, anxiety, and fear that he or she is going crazy. Mascots release this tension by acting out and being funny. Through amusing displays of funny antics they divert attention from the dysfunction in the family, release their own tension, and receive a lot of positive attention. Sometimes these children are misdiagnosed as hyperactive and given the drug Ritalin (Wegscheider, 1981, p. 143).

Not only are children of alcoholics at risk in terms of learning maladaptive behavior patterns, but many are also at greater risk for physical violence at the hands of the chemically dependent family (see Potter-Efron & Potter-Efron, 1990). Parents (or spouses) may use alcoholics as an excuse to be abusive, "Yeah, I hit her, but I was drunk." Family members need to be protected from this added danger.

Literature on adult children of alcoholics is quite limited and is based primarily on clinical observations rather than actual studies. What little has been written suggests that there are long-term effects of growing up with an alcoholic parent that may influence decision making, psychological state, and behavior (see Tweed & Ryff, 1991). As children, these individuals tend to acquire particular survival roles in the family unit. Once they reach adulthood, there are indications that this adaptational stance breaks down, at which time they are more likely to manifest symptoms of depression, low self-esteem, guilt, inability to maintain intimate relationships and get in touch with their own feelings, and distrust of others. On the other hand, it is true that some adult children of alcoholics have actually been strengthened by the experience. Facing such hardship during childhood, for this subgroup, may enhance inner resources for coping with difficulties and facilitate personal growth. One finding is quite clear, however, and that is the elevated risk for alcoholism that offspring of alcoholics experience (see e.g., Sher et al., 1991). We are not certain, at this time, what the mechanisms are that may account for these observations, the familial risk for alcoholism is at least in part genetic. The effects of living with an alcoholic parent, an environmental influence, should not be underestimated. It appears that adult children of alcoholics are a quite diverse group; some become depressed, anxious or otherwise dysfunctional in adulthood, while others lead happy, well-adjusted lives in spite of their childhood experiences.

Codependency

The following poem distributed by codependents anonymous describes many of the characteristics associated with co-dependency. The author is unknown.

My good feelings about who I am stem
  from being liked by you and receiving
  approval from you.
Your struggles affect my serenity. My mental attention focuses on solving your
  problems or relieving your pain.
My mental attention is focused on pleasing
  you, protecting you, manipulating you
  to "do it my way."
My self-esteem is bolstered by solving your
  problems and relieving your pain.
My own hobbies and interests are put
  aside. My time is spent sharing your
  interests and hobbies.
Because I feel you are a reflection of me,
  your clothing and personal appearance
  are dictated by my desires.
Your behavior is dictated by my desires.
I am not aware of how I feel. I am aware
  of how you feel.
I am not aware of what I want. I ask you
  what you want.
If I am not aware of something, I assume.
My dreams I have for my future are linked
  to you.
My fear of your anger and rejection determine what I say or do.
In our relationship I use giving as a way of
  feeling safe.
As I involve myself with you, my social circle diminishes.
To connect with you, I put my values
  aside.
I value your opinion and way of doing
  things more than my own.
The quality of my life depends on the
  quality of yours.

Codependency refers to common methods people use to adapt to living with an alcoholic, other chemically dependent individual, or other abnormal person (Beattie, 1989). The codependent individual, in an effort to meet and respond to the needs and feeling of the alcoholic

denies his or her own needs and feelings. This self-defeating behavior helps the codependent cope with the alcoholic in the evolving dysfunctional system (Beattie, 1989, p. 13). After a period of time, the codependent person begins to deny he or she even has any feelings.

As the codependent person suppresses his or her true desires and feelings, a false self emerges which strives to please the alcoholic (Whitfield, 1989, p. 23). The codependent no longer develops independent opinions or interests. Rather, the goal of the codependent is the expression of opinions which will be approved by the alcoholic and to engage in behaviors which serve the interests of the alcoholic.

Other symptoms of codependency include workaholism, eating disorders, drug abuse, and the development of compulsive behaviors that may involve sex, spending, religion, achievement, or appearance (Beattie, 1989, p. 13). Codependents also experience such feelings as fear, anxiety, and shame, and experience an overwhelming need to control (Beattie, 1989, p. 17; Whitfield, 1989; Potter-Efron & Potter-Efron, 1989).

Those suffering from codependency should seek treatment from Codependents Anonymous, group therapy, or individual therapy with a therapist who is experienced treating codependent individuals. The goal of treatment is generally aimed toward helping the individual rediscover his or her inner self, recognize and correctly identify his or her feelings, and find ways to satisfy his or her own needs.

Treatment of Alcoholism

Many believe the alcoholic must hit bottom before he or she will seek treatment. Hitting bottom generally refers to the actual or threatened loss of job and/or family. Some alcoholics are able to reach a "high bottom" and seek treatment before their lives are totally destroyed. This high bottom can be brought on through intervention (Wegscheider, 1981). Intervention means that significant others in the alcoholic's life, such as family members, friends, or an employer, can create a crisis for the alcoholic that is so frightening and painful the person may be motivated to seek help (Wegscheider, p. 151).

Different types of alcoholic patients may respond to different types of treatment, and some alcoholics may be more successfully treated than others. A few clues are available to help predict which patients are more likely to respond to a particular treatment. In particular, alcoholic patients who are also diagnosed with antisocial personality disorder (DSM-III-R) are much less likely to remain in treatment very long or to remain abstinent for any period of time (Rounsaville, Dolensky, et al., 1987)— their prognosis is much worse. If other coexisting mental disorders (e.g., depression, anxiety, or borderline personality disorder) are present along with alcoholism, unless these are aggressively treated along with the alcohol problem, there is also a much worse prognosis.

Pharmacological Treatments

Pharmacological therapies play many roles in the management of alcoholics (see Malka, 1988 for review). Drugs, such as disulfiram (Antabuse), have been used to produce discomfort when alcohol is consumed so that the drinker will find alcohol offensive and eventually associate this unpleasant state with alcohol consumption. Psychotropic drugs including tranquilizers, antidepressants, beta-blockers, and neuroleptics, have been used with alcoholics and problem drinkers in an attempt to alter the effects of alcohol and to address possible underlying psychopathologies that drinkers may suffer from. Because the incidence of mental disorders, such as schizophrenia, anxiety/panic, depression, manic-depression, and psychosis is high among this population, it is expected that psychotropic medications will help to alleviate conditions that may have contributed to drinking problems and to prevent the worsening of mental symptoms during abstinence. Drugs are also widely used to manage the withdrawal episode (e.g., clonidine or diazepam), particularly if seizures are likely to occur. And finally, psychotropic therapies (e.g., lithium) are currently being tested to attenuate craving for alcohol in abstinent alcoholics to avoid relapse.

For the acute treatment of alcohol intoxication, there are a few promising experimental drugs that may have efficacy. A compound referred to as Ro-15-4513 appears to act on the receptor site for alcohol, thereby attenuating and actually reversing alcohol intoxication (Kolata, 1986). Because this drug is a convulsant, it has no clinical utility at this time but has, instead, aided in our understanding of alcohol's properties. Lithium, on the other hand, is one drug in particular that, in clinical trials, decreases drinking in depressed alcoholics and enhances abstinence from alcohol in recovering alcoholics. Furthermore, there is preliminary evidence that lithium, also used in the treatment of manic-depression, may have a direct effect on alcohol's ability to intoxicate. When lithium was adminis-

tered to alcoholics along with alcohol, these subjects reported that they felt less intoxicated and had less desire to continue drinking. It is possible that lithium either (1) acts to specifically block alcohol's effect on psychological and subjective states, or (2) that the effects of alcohol that alcoholics have become so accustomed to are quite different when combined with lithium and the experience is no longer considered pleasant or rewarding (see Judd & Huey, 1984 for a review of studies). Lithium's potential to normalize dysphoric or disturbed mood states in alcoholics and attenuate alcohol's acute effects may eventually have implications for new therapeutic options.

Buspirone, a nonbenzodiazepine antianxiety agent (discussed in Chapter 11), has been extremely successful and unusually safe in the treatment of anxiety disorders. There is also, importantly, little to no abuse potential or impairment associated with this anxiolytic (anxiety-reducing agent), unlike other depressants. Recent studies of the use of buspirone in alcoholics have been spurred both by evidence that anxiety and mood disorders are prevalent among alcohol abusers and the fact that buspirone does not interact with alcohol when taken simultaneously. These studies indicate that alcohol-abusive patients who receive buspirone remain in treatment longer than those patients who receive placebo. Furthermore, there is a reduction in alcohol consumption and craving and anxiety symptoms in these patients. Overall, patients improved with respect to all symptoms of psychopathology, an important finding given the role of mental disorders in the development of alcoholism (see Bruno, 1989).

Antidepressants are popular in the treatment of alcohol intoxication, alcohol-related psychopathology, withdrawal, and craving. Those antidepressants that act on norepinephrine neurotransmitter systems reduce the amount of alcohol drinking by alcoholics (see Sinclair, 1987 for a review) and aid in the treatment of depression that may coexist with alcoholism and alcohol abstinence. Antidepressants that function to enhance the activity of serotonin (e.g., fluoxetine) have also shown efficacy in the treatment of alcoholics. As described previously, serotinergic agonists (drugs that increase serotonin activity) suppress alcohol intake in animals and humans and also help to reduce mood disturbances, aggression, and antisocial tendencies alcohol abusers frequently display.

Even after a drinker has been able to abstain from alcohol for some time, the craving for alcohol can be intense and may quickly lead to relapse in those who cannot resist. Only recently, researchers have discovered a drug that may reduce an alcoholic's long-term craving for liquor. The medication naltrexone, is known to be an opiate antagonist and is widely available for the treatment of narcotic addiction. Estimates are that naltrexone, in combination with conventional behavioral treatments, reduces relapse from 50 percent to 20 percent. Naltrexone also appears to make it easier for alcoholics who relapsed into drinking while in a treatment program to once again return to treatment. Because craving for alcohol is responsible for the low numbers of alcoholics who seek treatment for their addiction, and many who do seek treatment drop out, resisting temptation may be easier with drugs like naltrexone.

Finally, Blum and Trachtenberg (1988) have devised a regimen consisting of vitamins, minerals, and neurotransmitter precursors to treat alcoholics. The idea behind this approach is to replenish the brain with the ingredients necessary to synthesize neurotransmitters and other chemicals that become depleted in alcoholism. In theory, once the brain has regained a chemical balance, the individual may not crave alcohol or experience the same reward value when alcohol is again consumed. The benefits of this approach is the use of nonaddictive substances in lieu of a powerful psychotropic medication; however, evaluation studies have yet to demonstrate its efficacy.

Detoxification

If a drinker demonstrates severe withdrawal symptoms when alcohol consumption stops, there is a need to detoxify the individual before any other form of treatment can be considered. As mentioned previously, withdrawal from alcohol in severe alcoholism can be deadly and needs to be carefully monitored by a medical professional. Mild symptoms of withdrawal, such as shaking, anxiety, insomnia, headache, cramps, irritability, and vomiting, can be tolerated by most patients. More serious symptoms requiring a formal detoxification effort include hallucinations, seizures, and psychotic symptoms. "Detox" programs range from a few days to a few weeks to rid the body of alcohol and stabilize the patient. Anticonvulsants and antipsychotic medications are commonly used while the individual is hospitalized. This is only the beginning of treatment for alcoholism, however, and is essentially the easiest stage to get through if proper attention is received. Once detoxified, the alcoholic now must travel down a long and difficult path to remain abstinent. Intensive, long-term treatment is now required.

Psychotherapeutic and Behavioral Programs

The most popular approaches to alcoholism treatment include behavioral modification, hypnosis, individual psychotherapy, group encounter programs, family therapy, and Alcoholics Anonymous. These programs evolved in an attempt to individualize the treatment of alcoholics and do not necessarily involve the administration of drugs unless specifically indicated—and even then, pharmacological treatments are only secondary. These programs are designed to address the unique problems suffered by each alcoholic and either target the individual, the individual's family, or the individual's environment. Each technique can be performed either in an inpatient or residential treatment facility or as outpatient treatment. Inpatient treatment involves the provision of housing and comprehensive services accommodating the needs of the alcoholic. Generally, as an inpatient, the alcoholic will remain in the hospital or facility for several months. Nearly every waking hour is spent in some type of therapeutic activity. Outpatient treatment involves visits to a private therapist or public facility for sessions devoted to developing new habits and relearning old behaviors. Although outpatient therapy is less comprehensive and intensive, it is cheaper and allows the patient to continue working and maintaining a home life.

Behavioral modification programs condition patients to associate drinking with undesirable consequences. One type of behavioral modification program, aversion therapy, is designed to substitute negative images or experiences for pleasurable feelings associated with alcohol. If something unpleasant happens each time a drink is taken, the individual is likely to learn that alcohol is responsible and will discontinue its use. When an individual drinks, for example, an electric shock administered each time a sip is taken will lead to negative feelings about alcohol consumption. In another instance, a drug may be given that produces physical discomfort when taken in combination with alcohol. Thus, every time the individual drinks, he or she gets sick and is less likely to continue drinking. Another form of behavioral modification is sensitization therapy. This approach teaches the patient to relax and then envision something terrible happening to them while drinking. For example, drinking alcohol and then vomiting, stripping, behaving irrationally, or otherwise making a fool of oneself in public is imaged. It is hoped that the patient will eventually associate these uncomfortable images with alcohol and abstain. Both forms of conditioning are based on the belief that attitudes about drinking alcohol will become more negative and no longer be associated with the positive images we so often see in beer commercials. Hypnosis is based on the same principles. While in a trance, patients are told to view alcohol with distaste and revulsion, and when awake, they will supposedly remember their new dislike for the substance. In all of these approaches, the disease of alcoholism is, however, not addressed.

Alcoholics Anonymous (A.A.)

Perhaps the most famous and widely used form of behavioral treatment for alcoholism is based on Alcoholics Anonymous (A.A.). This formal organization began in 1934 with the initial gathering of founding alcoholics who developed a way of returning to sober life (Alcoholics Anonymous, 1976). It has grown from 100 members when their Big Book was first published in 1939 to reach more than a million members worldwide in 1988. A.A. is both an organization designed to assist its members remain free from alcohol and a deliberately loosely established collection of alcoholics who continually encourage other alcoholics they encounter to join. The organization is not-for-profit and relies on contributions of its members and supporters. There are no directors in name. Rather, service boards made up of members are assembled when needed. As you will see, A.A. features spirituality, confession, and salvation as primary means of obtaining sobriety. Religion overtones are replete, however they do not cater to any particular religion, and the belief in God or a higher power are essential to this program.

Assumptions and Starting Points
In A.A., alcohol is the problem. Any suppositions about the path that led the individual to alcoholism is irrelevant until the individual gives up the use of alcohol. The basic goal of treatment is to stop drinking altogether and never again take that first drink that sends the drinker back down the path of no return.

"Once an alcoholic, always an alcoholic" (*Alcoholics Anonymous,* 1976, p. 33) is one of the basic operating principles in A.A. Thus, the goal of never taking another drink is part of the recognition of that operating principle. The successful member of A.A., one who no longer drinks, is described as a recovering alcoholic; never as a recovered alcoholic. It is assumed that the alcoholic has a special mental and physical reaction to alcohol that ren-

ders him or her unable to resist alcohol once drinking has begun. Alcoholics in this view are not social drinkers. This abusive response to alcohol is out of their control. In fact, the first step in the 12 steps toward recovery from alcohol is to admit that you are powerless over alcohol. An important implication of the concept of once an alcoholic, always an alcoholic is the notion that the alcoholic must remain active in resisting the desire to take that first drink. In fact, Alcoholics Anonymous advocates continual encouragement for alcoholics to become members and help fellow alcoholics resist the temptations to abuse alcohol as a means of resisting it themselves. The Big Book goes so far as to direct recommendations to spouses of A.A. members that will help accommodate the A.A. activities of the recovering alcoholic to allow him or her room to develop personal resistance.

It is suggested in the Big Book that only fellow alcoholics can understand the language and feelings of other alcoholics. The A.A. treatment specifically resists the use of treatment professionals because of the special perspective of the recovering alcoholic as well as the need of A.A. members to continue resisting alcohol through actively helping others. This approach has generally excluded professional treatment providers as legitimate participants in the A.A. program, unless the professional is also a recovering alcoholic. One major difficulty with that approach is that few treatment providers recognize the value of and need for constructive program evaluations. Thus, A.A. and the 12 Step Program have not been empirically demonstrated to be effective in treating alcoholics (Ogborne & Glaser, 1985).

The A.A. Treatment Process
A.A. members would argue that they are not in the treatment business but are rather a group dedicated to alcoholics' change in lifestyle to exclude the use of alcohol. Nonetheless, their approach is used as a treatment. It is not unusual for persons released from state supported programs and some private hospitals to include the recommendation of A.A. as a post-treatment maintenance program. The criminal justice system frequently includes A.A. as required conditions of parole, probation after criminal charges or, as part of driving while intoxicated (DWI) programs.

In spite of A.A. claims to the contrary, A.A. is the most widely available community-based treatment program today. A.A. frequently represents the only option for treatment in a given community. A.A. and its derivative organizations (Narcotics Anonymous, Al-Anon, and Alateen) play such a large part in the drug and alcohol treatment field that is important to understand how A.A.-type programs work.

The major components of the A.A. program are the group meetings and the one-on-one contacts among recovering alcoholics. The only A.A. membership requirement is a desire to stop drinking. The A.A. group has been deliberately organized to be a loosely connected collection of independent groups with no permanent staff, no professional counselors, no dues, no specific leaders. One of the 12 traditions includes the specification that any individual will be defined in public and in the press as "an A.A. member" rather than by individual names, hence the anonymous portion of the A.A. name. For the same reason, most meetings are closed, limited only to members, so that members are free to discuss personal problems. In open meetings, speakers and visitors are permitted to observe and ask questions.

Treatment involves proceeding through the 12 steps listed in Inset 6.2. These steps detailed further below, are presented to the reader as suggestions for a model for recovering from alcoholism (Alcoholics Anonymous, 1952, 1976). It should be kept in mind when reviewing them that an individual sponsor is available to each A.A. member to help him or her through the process. That sponsor is a fellow A.A. member and recovering alcoholic.

1. *Acknowledge powerlessness over alcohol.* The alcoholic must admit that life is unmanageable under present circumstances and admit defeat.
2. *Develop a belief that a greater power can restore the alcoholic.* This admission of dependence on a higher power is a key to developing an open mind and preparing the alcoholic to accept the extensive changes in lifestyle required.
3. *Decide to trust in the care of God.* It is important to note that Alcoholics Anonymous members consider their groups spiritual but not directly tied to any specific form of religion. Rather, they assume the presence of a God, however each defines God. This is a general call to be dependent on a spiritual being. One clear example of this position appears in the Big Book where family members are encouraged to give the recovering alcoholic room to relapse because "God has either removed your husband's problem or He has not" (Alcoholics Anonymous, 1976).
4. Make a "...*searching and fearless moral inventory of ourselves*" (Alcoholics Anonymous, 1952).

A.A. members are encouraged to examine their weaknesses and strengths in terms of moral character. These weaknesses represent the things that precipitate the self-destructive reentry into the alcoholic state. A.A. members are encouraged to find such things as sources of insecurity and resentment. According to the Big Book (Alcoholics Anonymous, 1976), resentment is the major cause of alcoholism. An individual who focuses on his or her vulnerabilities (eg. pride, self-esteem, insecurities, relationships) will create a spiritual deficit that subsequently leads to abuse of alcohol. Other faults, especially selfishness and self-centeredness, are also identified and tied to the tendency to drink. This task is presumably the baseline from which alcoholics begin to change their lifestyles.

5. *Once the list of character flaws is established, the alcoholic must admit these faults to God, the self, and one other person.* The admission of faults is of particular importance because the action of telling others helps relieve the alcoholic of guilt and sense of isolation. By sharing faults with others, the individual is drawn to them. It is also likely that the act of publicly admitting shortcomings and commission of stupid acts imposes a sense of commitment on the part of the alcoholic. In the world of clinical treatment such cathartic activity is described as part of the process of disposing of emotional baggage collected over time.
6. *The alcoholic must be "...ready to have God remove the defects in character"* (Alcoholics Anonymous, 1952, p. 63). This is a critical and difficult step in the process of spiritual redevelopment. It involves taking on an attitude of humility and accepting the idea of changing, becoming open-minded. Step 6, in the A.A. view, is an ideal state that the A.A. member continually strives to reach. The effect of this step is relevant to all the other shortcomings of the A.A. member: pride, lust, and so forth.
7. *"Humbly ask Him to remove...shortcomings"* (Alcoholics Anonymous, 1952, p. 70). Once the humility is established and the A.A. members accept the notion of being overpowered by alcohol, they ask to have the shortcomings that draw them to alcohol removed.

Inset 6.2

THE 12 STEPS FOR RECOVERY SUGGESTED BY ALCOHOLICS ANONYMOUS

1. We admitted we were powerless over alcohol-that our lives had become unmanageable.
2. Came to believe that a Power greater than ourselves could restore us to sanity.
3. Made a decision to turn our will and our lives over to the care of God as we understood him.
4. Made a searching and fearless moral inventory of ourselves.
5. Admitted to God, to ourselves, and to another human being the exact nature of our wrongs.
6. Were entirely ready to have God remove all these defects of character.
7. Humbly asked Him to remove our shortcomings.
8. Made a list of all persons we had harmed, and became willing to make amends to them all.
9. Made direct amends to such people wherever possible, except when to do so would injure them or others.
10. Continued to take personal inventory and when we were wrong promptly admitted it.
11. Sought through prayer and meditation to improve our conscious contact with God as we understood Him, praying only for knowledge of His will for us and the power to carry that out.
12. Having had a spiritual awakening as the result of these steps, we tried to carry this message to alcoholics, and to practice these principles in all our affairs.

8. *"Make a list of all persons...harmed, and [be] ...willing to make amends to them all"* (Alcoholics Anonymous, 1952, p. 77). The first priority after establishing the continuing struggle to be humble enough to have God remove shortcomings is to reestablish relationships. A.A. members must generate lists of people harmed by their morally bankrupt behavior. One of the biggest relational problems faced by alcoholics, according to the A.A., is isolation. This step is the beginning of dealing with that problem. Becoming willing to make amends to all harmed helps members accept their part of the blame for whatever has happened. Being willing to make reparations for the wrongs invloves visualizing meeting them face-to-face and determining what would be said. The task also forces A.A. members to understand the harm done to others by them from their victims' perspectives.

9. *"[Make] direct amends to such people wherever possible, except when to do so would injure them*

or others" (Alcoholics Anonymous, 1952, p. 83). This task usually starts with admitting to family and friends whatever wrongs the A.A. member has perpetrated and giving assurances that the member is attending A.A. and will no longer do those things. Whenever possible, the A.A. member makes amends directly to the victim. However, the A.A. member is cautioned to be prudent in expressing this restitution because it may harm others. For example, A.A. members are encouraged to not be too quick to discuss previous infidelities with unsuspecting spouses. The caveat is added because some members cite possible harm to others as an excuse to avoid performing of this task, particularly in very painful situations. A second reason for caution is that the task of making amends usually leads to euphoric feelings because the burdens of guilt and resentment are lifted.

10. *Continue to inventory personal lives and be quick to admit mistakes.* Keep in mind that A.A.

assumes that the alcoholic is always an alcoholic and membership in A.A. is a way of life, not just a treatment to complete. Step 10 represents the beginnings of a committed life to the A.A. way of living. It is a daily struggle to continue sobriety. Often the established A.A. member will spend a lengthy session with his or her sponsor conducting an honest review of recent activities. The sponsor is an ideal partner for this activity because he or she has followed the A.A. member through most of the course of their recovery (as has the sponsor with his or her sponsor) and already knows many of the A.A. member's weaknesses.

11. *Use prayer and meditation to improve contact with God.* This is a second step in the process in which A.A. members are reminded of their dependence on God to maintain sobriety. It is important to note that the eleventh step includes emphasis on the point that each person's version of God is valid. This meditation and prayer is to help individuals understand what God wants them to do and ask for the power to do it. The last three steps are all intended to help A.A. members stay sober, primarily through spiritual development.

12. *Carry the message to other alcoholics still suffering.* This last step is part of becoming a sponsor. It is driven both by the need of the spiritually renewed individual to attend to the spiritless as well as the need to keep moving, focusing on the needs of others to prevent A.A. members from losing sobriety. Helping other alcoholics through the process helps the A.A. member grow further.

In short, A.A. is a community of alcoholics working together to overcome their addiction. Using recovering alcoholics as counselors, members are able to relate to each other and understand each other's weaknesses and lifestyle complications that revolve around the excessive use of alcohol. Thus, there is a common bridge between members, creating a kind of community environment. Not only can this approach be beneficial for newcomers to the program, but it also has therapeutic value for those counselors diligently striving to maintain their sobriety. If individuals have the will and strength, A.A. provides a foundation and support network for rebuilding their lives.

Evaluation Studies of Alcoholics Anonymous

In spite of the relative lack of solid research on the effectiveness of A.A., the organization is both highly acclaimed and widely criticed (Ogborne and Glaser, 1985). Many clinicians, treatment professionals, medical doctors, and members, regale A.A. and believe that it is an essential component of any alcohol treatment regimen. Others, however, are not quite so convinced and point to statistical studies as evidence of its ineffectiveness. For example, the National Institute on Alcohol Abuse and Alcoholism (1989) reported that approximately 90 percent of alcoholics are likely to experience at least one relapse over the 4-year period following treatment. Similarly, Alibrandi (1978) reported at at least half of new A.A. members relapse within the first year. The following conversation took place with an alcoholic who was arrested and jailed for the twenty-fourth time:

"A.A. works for me. I don't know what I would do without it. I've been going for almost twenty years." When asked why he was in jail, he readily stated that he had been drinking and "got out of control." When asked why he was drinking if A.A. has been such a big help, the inmate responded that A.A. is always there to encourage him and provide him with the emotional strength and support he needs to go on. But apparently sobriety has not been a result of his membership.

Clearly A.A. works for some and not for others. There is no way at present to distinguish between those likely to succeed and those likely to fail; however, it is certain that those coerced or pressured into joining A.A. will probably not do well. Because A.A. relies on self-motivation and will, an alcoholic must first recognize the need to change, exhibit the desire to remain sober, and then devote him- or herself to the dictates of the program. Alcoholics mandated by criminal court to attend sessions, individuals on DWI charges, and those pressured by family members are not good candidates for an A.A. program. Stanton Peele, a well-known alcoholism researcher, is not impressed with A.A. given that, for one, individuals arrested for DWI get into less trouble afterward (e.g., fewer accidents and arrests) when they receive a punitive sanction, such as jail, than those who are referred to an A.A. program (Peele, 1989, 1991). Despite criticisms and negative findings, many A.A. members swear by the program and do remain abstinent as a result of their membership. Subsequent research should attempt to identify those who would benefit from A.A. so that alternative approaches could be utilized for those who likely would not respond to the A.A. regimen.

▮ Summary

Alcohol is, without a doubt, the most dangerous drug of abuse in the United States. Alcohol is responsible for more deaths due to disease, homicides, child abuse and neglect, crimes, and personal tragedies than any other substance. One of the reasons alcohol causes widespread destruction is that it is legal and difficult to regulate. Minors have ready access to it, and we cannot proscribe the behaviors of social drinkers or alcoholics until they become criminal.

Citizens are largely confused about the benefits and hazards of drinking alcohol. Several studies have shown that certain forms of heart disease may actually be controlled by drinking moderate amounts of alcohol. Some show an increase in good cholesterol and a drop in bad cholesterol, possibly contributing to a reduced risk of developing heart disease. And others show that drinking after menopause can raise estrogen levels and reduce the risk of heart disease and osteoporosis. Negative reports, however, warn that even small amounts may be detrimental to a fetus, and those who drink regularly may be at risk for the eventual development of heavy drinking and other health problems, such as ulcers. Also, people taking medications such as sleeping pills, neuroleptic drugs, painkillers, and antibiotics should definitely avoid alcohol as it may change effects of the medication.

This confusion has spurred renewed interest in the distinction between light drinking, moderate drinking, and heavy drinking. To one person, two drinks a day may be considered heavy drinking while to another, a bottle of wine or a six-pack of beer a day may be considered light drinking. Moderate drinking is often confused for social drinking, which has been defined as drinking patterns that are accepted by the society in which they occur. This obviously leaves the door wide open for tremendous variation in cultural and social conventions that differ throughout the world. Also, if a person is a party goer or a bar hopper, he or she is likely to consume more alcohol and still consider it only social drinking. A person who drinks only on special occasions, religious holidays, or at occaisional parties will drink far less and consider that

social drinking. And how about the little old lady who drinks a martini every night? Her drink is strong and the frequency of drinking is consistent. She has never increased the dosage over the past fifty years and can stop drinking while taking antibiotics for a flu without much ado. Is this the sign of a problem drinker or is this controlled or social drinking? There are vastly different conceptions of what constitutes acceptable levels of drinking. In a sense, this variation in drinking patterns has given way to the idea that "social drinking is in the eyes of the beholder."

Generally accepted at present by scientists and clinicians is the following definition of moderate drinking, which is thought to be different from social drinking: the daily amount of alcohol that can be consumed by an average heavy adult without untoward health effects. This translates to approximately two drinks a day for a man and one drink a day for a woman. However, if a person misses his or her daily ration, the person may not make up for it the following day by having one or two extra! Also, in calculating how much is acceptable, a person must not use an average—having two drinks a day is not the same as having fourteen drinks over a weekend. Such heavy but occasional drinking is called binge drinking, which can lead to alcoholism and cause severe health effects. Binge drinking can result in more serious, detrimental health and personal effects than small amounts of daily drinking. And finally, the size of a drink must be taken into consideration in determining how many drinks to consume. Two 32 ounce beers or 16 ounce daiquiris far exceed acceptable amounts.

Drinking remains widespread and does not discriminate between types of people. People from all walks of life can develop drinking problems and alcoholism. From high school students to doctors and lawyers, the consumption of alcohol can be problematic. Problem drinking and alcoholism are not restricted to skid row bums and criminal offenders; alcohol can become a hazard to almost anyone no matter what their background, upbringing, religious beliefs, or profession. And those who begin drinking early in life and quickly find that they cannot stop or lose control of their behavior are the ones we worry about the most. Included in this group is the typical high school or college student, the housewife, the professional, the athlete.

CHAPTER 7

Heroin and Other Opiates

Objectives

1. To provide a classification system for the opiates.
2. To illustrate how finished opiate products are derived from the opium poppy.
3. To differentiate among the various types of opiates.
4. To explain how opiates affect body and brain functions.
5. To provide a discussion of traditional medical uses of opiates.
6. To explain the process of addiction to opiates.
7. To provide a summary of the biological, psychological, and behavioral effects of opiates.
8. To discuss the relationship between opiate use, criminal or antisocial behavior, and the spread of AIDS.
9. To discuss various treatment options for opiate addicts.

Opiates are the best analgesics (pain relievers) known. Not only do these drugs alleviate pain, but they relieve anxiety and produce euphoria as well. The euphoria experienced by the user produces a relaxed feeling of well-being and indifference to anxiety-provoking stressors, overwhelming any pain that was present. Although the pain itself is not eliminated, the perception of pain is muted. The analgesic effects on pain and anxiety relief are the primary reasons for continued use of opiates. Their major drawback is the ease with which a user can become addicted.

Users generally refer to the "rush" that is experienced immediately after injecting heroin. This rush includes a sensation of extreme pleasure and tingling, warmth in the abdomen, and euphoria. One user described the experience as the feeling that warm water was being poured through his body, slowly filling his feet and then his body until it reached his brain. Others compare it with a sexual orgasm. Obviously, it is this very effect that addicts strive to achieve with each administration. Later, sedation and sometimes sleep set in, and the user may have vivid, pleasant dreams. Appetite for food and sex disappear and in the early stages of opiate use, nausea and vomiting may occur (Jaffe & Martin, 1985). Despite these obvious negative effects, users will compulsively seek these drugs, for the euphoria and pleasurable effects profoundly outweigh the unpleasant ones. As we will learn in this chapter, although the desire for pleasure and the avoidance of pain may initially seduce the user, subsequent uses cause brain chemistry changes that further motivate compulsive use. The decision to first use an opiate may be the individual's, but subsequent uses become less and less under the control of the individual's control and more a function of the chemical need to maintain an equilibrium in the brain. Once users are fully addicted, they will find themselves hard pressed to regain that profound feeling of pleasure they obtained during early sessions although they will try again and again. At this point, they are only trying to avoid the pain of withdrawal.

Opiates include both natural drugs derived from the opium poppy and synthetic drugs or opioids, produced in the laboratory to mimic natural opiates. Natural opiates include opium as well as morphine and codeine, the two principle ingredients of raw opium.

Raw opium is harvested from the opium poppy, or Papaver somniferum, a hardy plant that thrives in hot climates as those found in Turkey, India, and Mexico, or the areas known as the Golden Triangle of Southeast Asia (Myanmar, formerly Burma, Thailand, and Loas) and the Golden Crescent (Afghanistan, Iran, and Pakistan) (Cooper, 1990; U.S. Attorneys, 1989). The poppy must be planted each year, and the purple, white, or red petals of the poppy flower emerge during the spring season. In early summer, just before the poppy seed pod begins to ripen, the petals fall to the ground. The farmers then harvest the opium by making a small slit on the outside of the pod with a sharp knife. A white oozing sap is released, and the poppy is left overnight. During the evening, the white substance turns reddish brown in color and gummy in texture. In the morning, workers collect the gummy substance by rolling it into raw opium balls (The heroin trail, 1974; Levinthal, 1988; Theodore, 1988). About 3,000 poppies are needed to produce 1.6 kilograms of opium (Theodore, p. 4). Morphine and codeine are created from these raw opium balls. A slight additional chemical alteration of morphine creates heroin, the opiate most likely to be used recreationally.

In 1988, there were indications of increasing activity in heroin markets, and some experts believe heroin is making a significant comeback as the drug of choice among users of illegal drugs (Love, 1990; U.S. Attorneys, 1989). There has been an increase in the average purity level of heroin as well as a rich supply of the drug, possibly contributing to a larger population of drug addicts and health hazards.

Investigations by federal law enforcement agencies have confirmed the ready availability of relatively pure Mexican heroin in various forms, primarily on the West Coast. Southeast border seizures of heroin in 1988 were up 26 percent over 1987. Other areas of the country have also experienced either increased evidence of heroin addiction or increased levels of purity in the available supply of heroin.

New heroin distribution operations have been reported in Rhode Island. Providence has become a distribution center that supplies areas throughout New England. The high purity level of this heroin (40 to 70 percent) has caused overdoses throughout the region (U.S. Attorneys, 1989, p. 10).

Further contributing to the ready availability of opiates, a relatively new type of heroin is being imported from Mexico. This crudely processed, inexpensive, and potent heroin, often called "black tar", and less commonly "gumball" or "tootsie roll," is available in many areas of the country. Black tar heroin offers the supplier the convenience of easy transportation and primitive, easily performed processing. For the user, black tar heroin offers higher potency and a relatively inexpensive fix. Street sample purities have been registered at as high as 93 percent, and 60 to 70 percent purity is common. Mexican brown

A. *Incised opium poppy capsule.*
B. *Asian heroin*
C. *Mexican heroin*
D. *Codeine preparations*
E. *Morphine preparations*
F. *Meperidine Preparations*

Courtesy of the Drug Enforcement Administration

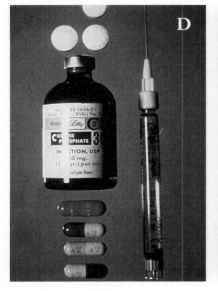

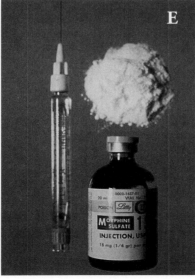

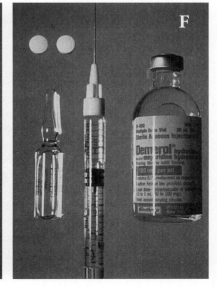

heroin, by contrast, often has purity levels in the 6 to 7 percent range. The ten-fold increase in purity and the relatively low price has also led to increased incidents of overdoses (U.S. Attorneys, 1989, p. 10).

About 60 percent of the heroin imported to the United States originates in the Golden Triangle with Myanmar (formerly known as Burma) leading the growth. Much of the heroin growth and processing is controlled by the half Chinese and half Shan general known as Khun Sa. Claiming that he and his well-armed army are fighting for independence of the Shan people, Khun Sa controls the largest heroin empire in the world (Shenon, 1995).

Mexican heroin production accounts for between 30 and 40 percent of heroin imports into the United States. It is estimated that in the period from 1983 to 1988, Mexican opium available for processing into heroin rose from 17 to 50 tons per year and that each ton of raw opium could be processed to yield about 100 kilograms of heroin. A combination of factors, including the expansion of opium production into the warm, fertile areas of central and southern Mexico, has caused this dramatic increase in Mexican heroin production (U.S. Attorneys, 1989, p. 10).

The Colombian drug cartels (noted for trafficking in cocaine) have also begun poppy cultivation in the Andean mountains of Colombia and have begun to move their manufactured heroin to the United States using New York City as the point of entry (Treaster, 1992a). Colombian heroin, nicknamed Colombian White, is reportedly quite pure and is often mixed with small amounts of cocaine to give it an added kick. Since the Colombian cartels already have well-organized distribution networks throughout the United States, Colombian heroin will soon flood the country. Expansion into the heroin market was a smart business move on the part of the Colombians since a kilo of heroin sells for as much as $200,000 in the New York market compared to $14,000 for a kilo of cocaine.

In addition to the growth of Mexican and Colombian heroin production and the spreading availability of black tar heroin, a new synthetic form, fentanyl, will contribute significantly to the drug problem in the United States. Fentanyl may be produced in forms a thousand times as powerful as any Mexican heroin (Freemantle, 1986). From the user's point of view, fentanyl and heroin are functionally interchangeable. Fentanyl can be packaged like heroin and cut with the same dilutents. Due to a lack of knowledge about safe dosage levels of this new and powerful opioid, a deadly ad hoc system of safe dosage testing is occurring in the streets among addicts and has resulted in a number of deaths from overdose (U.S. Attorneys, 1989, p. 11). Unfortunately, when addicts hear about deaths from heroin or fentanyl overdose, they often seek the same product as it promises a high often not achieved from the diluted drugs sold on the streets.

Prevalence of Heroin Use in the United States

Accurate estimates of heroin users are difficult to obtain because many hard-core addicts rarely possess a permanent address and are reluctant to identify themselves. The Substance Abuse and Mental Health Services Administration (1994) reports in the *Household Survey* that only 1.1 percent of Americans aged twelve to thirty-five have ever used heroin and 0.1 report having used it during the last year. Estimates of addicts range from 500,000 in the United States to about 1 million. Others, known as chippers, may use heroin occasionally and never become addicted. The annual prevalence of heroin use has been very steady since 1979 among high school seniors at 0.5 percent to 0.6 percent. Annual prevalence of heroin use among high school seniors hit its peak in 1975 at 1.0 percent. The annual prevalence rate of heroin use for young adults and college students have also remained quite stable in recent years at low rates (about 0.3 percent and 0.1 percent respectively) (Johnston, O'Malley, & Bachman, 1993).

Hard-core heroin use is largely a cultural phenomenon, observed primarily in this country's inner cities. Poor African Americans are disproportionately represented among heroin users, a reality that has led researchers to believe that the heroin subculture is, at least partially, a function of poverty, social immobility, destitution, and despair. It is in these impoverished pockets of the United States that heroin is most widely available, and drug availability is a condition that plays a strong role in drug usage. In urban areas, heroin use seems to correspond closely with socioeconomic status, including factors such as homelessness, unemployment rates, and urban decline. Also, women represent a significant percentage of heroin users. Having said this, we must emphasize that hard-core heroin use is not entirely restricted to these areas either. Physicians (Winick, 1963), nurses, and other so-called upstanding citizens are also addicted to heroin and other opiates.

Classification of Opiates

In an effort to find a drug that mimics the natural opiates' ability to attenuate pain and provide anxiety relief without their addictive properties, attempts to synthesize opiates have been made. Manufacturers have discovered, unfortunately, that it is difficult to synthesize opiate-like drugs with analgesic effects but without the euphoria and addiction potential. Other less scrupulous individuals have set out to capitalize on the euphoric properties of synthetic opiates, called opioids, and intentionally produce cheap opiate imitations to market in the illegal drug world. Table 7.1 lists the various forms of opiate drugs. Heroin, the most abused of the opiates, is a semisynthetic derivative of morphine.

Synthetic opiates include meperidine (Demerol), methadone (Dolophine), propoxyphene (Darvon), fentanyl (Sublimaze), and hydromorphone (Dilaudid).

Under the street name "China White," fentanyl has emerged on the illicit drug market as a "new" designer drug that produces short-term analgesia and euphoria. In addition to fentanyl, sufentanil and alfentanyl are also being touted on the street for their intense effects, which are considered ultra-potent (from 200 to 1000 times more potent than morphine). In the operating room, these drugs are used carefully in small doses to promote short-acting analgesia. Unfortunately, however, China White has become quite popular among street users in some areas throughout the country, contributing to a number of deaths. In dosages only slightly higher than those used in surgery, China White can produce respiratory depression and sometimes cause the muscles of the chest wall to spasm. Because these adverse effects can occur quite quickly, there is generally not enough time to administer an antidote to revive the street user.

Table 7.1   *Opiates: Names and Uses*

DRUGS	TRADE/OTHER NAMES	MEDICAL USES	DEPENDENCE PSYCHOLOGICAL	PHYSICAL
Opium	Dover's Powder Paregoric Parepectolin	Analgesic Antidiarrheal	High	High
Morphine	MS-Contin Roxanol	Analgesic Antitussive	High	High
Codeine	Tylenol w/codeine Empirin w/codeine Robitussan A-C Fiorinal w/codeine	Analgesic Antitussive	Moderate	Moderate
Heroin	Diacetylmorphine Horse Smack Dope	None	High	High
Hydromorphone	Dilaudid	Analgesic	High	High
Meperidine (Pethidine)	Demerol Mepergan	Analgesic	High	High
Methadone	Dolophine Methadose	Analgesic	High-Low	High
Other Narcotics	Numorphan Percodan Percocet Tylox Tussionex Fentanyl Darvon Lomotil Talwin	Analgesic Antitussive Antidiarrheal	High-Low	High-Low

All opiates are considered narcotics. Taken from the Greek word for "stupor," the term narcotic refers to any opiate analgesic. However, because early substance abuse research efforts and law enforcement concerns focused on opium and heroin, the term *narcotic* was used universally to also include nonnarcotic substances that were also illegal, such as cocaine, marijuana, amphetamines, and LSD. In fact, any drug that met with public disapproval and showed a capacity for abuse or addiction was called a narcotic. Narcotic and "dangerous drug" became interchangeable in the law, even when the identification was not based on pharmacological properties. As a consequence, penalties for the distribution of narcotics (including the erroneously labeled nonnarcotic drugs) are more severe, in spite of evidence that many nonnarcotic drugs (such as alcohol, nicotine, and cocaine) are more dangerous to users and those with whom they interact than narcotics. The misapplication of the term remains a problem today, and for that reason we specify that, throughout this book, narcotic will refer exclusively to natural or synthetic opiates.

Physiology and Metabolism of Opiates

About 10 percent of the weight of raw opium consists of morphine and about 0.5 percent is codeine. With the addition of two acetyl groups (a cluster of atoms comprising acetic acid) to the morphine molecule, heroin is produced (diacetylmorphine). This molecular change in morphine permits heroin to more readily cross the blood-brain barrier causing almost instantaneous effects. Since heroin reaches the brain in a shorter period of time, it is considered more potent than morphine. Hence, substance abusers are more likely to choose heroin over other opiates. Opiates are primarily metabolized by the liver and are then eliminated by the kidneys (Julien, 1988). This process is quite rapid, which means that the effects of opiates last for about four to five hours. At some point during this time, the addicted user must obtain and administer more drug. Thus, a great deal of the user's life is spent in drug-related activities.

Pain relievers synthesized to resemble morphine remain prescription only as chemists have failed to manufacture a nondependence producing narcotic. In the process of searching for new narcotic compounds, chemists discovered narcotic antagonists, drugs that block the effects of opiates and other narcotics by attaching to opiate receptors. Use of these agents have been shown to reverse acute adverse reactions, such as those associated with overdose, and to hasten withdrawal in an effort to control physical dependence. The action of these antagonists will be described in more detail with respect to pharmacologic treatment approaches.

Morphine and codeine can be detected in a urine screen for two to four days after use. Because heroin is metabolized to morphine and codeine, heroin use may not specifically be detected. Other urine screens will detect synthetic opiates. Trouble with urine surveillance of opiates may occur when an individual has been taking a cough syrup or analgesic substance for medical purposes. The urine screen will not be able to distinguish intermittent use of legitimate opiates from illicit or chronic abuse. Also, poppy seeds contain small amounts of morphine; thus, it is possible to eat a poppy seed bagel in the morning and show positive results for opiates that afternoon.

Natural Opiates in the Brain

In 1973, Snyder and Pert at Johns Hopkins University discovered that the brain contains cell receptors with a special affinity for opiates. Morphine-like drugs fit into these receptors like a lock-and-key mechanism to activate them. When this discovery was made, scientists asked, "Why would nature provide us with the brain receptors for the juice of a poppy?" There must be a reason for their presence other than to be "turned on" by an opiate! The supposition was made that a chemical substance must exist naturally in the brain that normally occupies and activates these sites. No neurotransmitter substance had yet been identified that locked into these opiate receptors.

In 1974, workers in England and Sweden succeeded in isolating a pair of molecules, leu-enkephalin and met-enkephalin. These molecules had morphine-like properties, however they were much more potent. Shortly thereafter, a group of endorphins (morphine-like chemicals within the brain) were identified in brain tissue and found to have a powerful opiate action. Beta-endorphin is specifically associated with opiate receptors. These three molecules are all amino acids from the peptide family of chemicals and are very similar in structure to the opiates.

Endorphins and enkephalins are housed within neurons and released to behave like neurotransmitters or to modulate neural activity. They are particularly responsible for the perception of pain and mediation of stress, emotions, and mood. The receptor sites that receive these

Foods and medicines that may produce a positive urine screen for opiates even in the absence of illicit use.

peptides integrate the information they contain and regulate pain, stress, emotion, and mood. Areas of the brain where opiate receptors are concentrated include the brainstem (which has analgesic action), the medial thalamus (which influences deep pain), and the spinal cord (to dampen the effect of incoming painful stimuli). The greatest numbers are located in the limbic system (to influence emotional behavior).

There is also evidence that endorphins are released from the pituitary gland and that enkephalins are released from the adrenal gland under conditions of stress and possibly exercise (Akil et al., 1976; Mayer et al., 1977; Pomeranz et al., 1977; Pomeranz & Chiu, 1976). Explanations for this phenomenon are not well established at this time; however, investigators believe that glandular release of these peptides serves to suppress pain in the brain's attempt to cope with stress and survive. A woman, for example, in Baltimore was shot in the hip while trying to escape from a drive-by shooting with her grandchild. She perceived no pain, only the terror that something may happen to her grandchild. As soon as she was able, she ran into her apartment and up the stairs to flee from the shooters. Her son found her there attending to the grandchild, who had also been shot. He noticed blood coming from her dress and inquired about her condition. She was not even aware she had been shot! The stress of both the situation and the physical trauma probably caused her brain to release large amounts of neuropeptides to strengthen her coping skills and prevent her from being distracted by her own pain. Once the situation was over, however, the pain became

quite perceptible, perhaps because the release of peptides once again diminished.

There is some speculation that the frequently reported runner's high may be a result of peptide release, providing both pain relief and a subjective feeling of being high. Many runners and other athletes refer to a second wind they experience shortly after they begin their sport. It is possible, albeit not well tested, that this second wind is their bodies' release of neuropeptides in response to the stress of exertion, giving them the extra boost necessary to complete the task.

Methods of Administration

Synthetic and natural opiates alike may be administered by different routes: oral, hypodermic needle injection, or inhalation. The most efficient modes are injecting the drug into the cardiovascular system and inhaling it into the respiratory system; absorption from these systems into the gastrointestinal tract is more rapid and complete than when drugs are taken orally. Opiates present in the stomach are fat-soluble so they are poorly absorbed into the bloodstream. Consequently, blood levels of the drug taken orally are at most half of that achieved when injected with a hypodermic needle. The only possible advantage of oral administration is that the drug will remain in the system for a longer period of time, exerting its effects more slowly. Nevertheless, the drug's action is reduced and may be somewhat unpredictable.

Most illicit heroin users begin their initial use of the drug by inhaling it in powder form. Another popular method of inhalation is called "chasing the dragon" (Schuckit, 1995). After placing the heroin on a piece of aluminum foil, a flame is held under the foil. The heroin turns to liquid and the vapors are inhaled through a tube. This method of heroin ingestion provides a rapid high.

In medical settings, drugs are generally administered into the muscle, under the skin, or through the vein via injection. Street users generally employ the subcutaneous method (skin popping) or the intravenous method (mainlining). Unlike narcotic injections by a medical professional, street users mainline the drug by drawing their own blood up into the syringe or eye dropper, mixing it with the heroin, and injecting it back into the vein slowly, a process called booting. Addicts believe that this process prolongs the euphoric effects of the drug although some of this effect may be due to a conditioned response, as playing with the drug and its paraphernalia frequently elicits a pleasurable response from an addict simply as a function of associating these cues with the pleasurable drug effects. Chapter 4 described the problems sometimes associated with both skin popping and intravenous injection, including overdose, adverse drug reaction, and infection from unsterile needles. Because IV users draw blood into the syringe, the possibility of contracting infections like HIV when needles are shared is quite high. Inhaling opiates bypasses some of these disadvantages and drug effects tend to be quicker and more complete. Inhalation of heroin has become more popular by users concerned about the possibility of contracting the HIV virus (leading to AIDS) via a contaminated needle. Nevertheless, inhalation also bypasses some of the perceived advantages of injecting opiates. Fat-soluble opiates, like heroin or fentanyl, cross the blood-brain barrier easily and rapidly reach substantial levels in the brain. When they are injected, the subjective experience may be so intense that the user feels a rush of sensation, sometimes even before the injection is completed. Users have been known to sit for a few minutes with the needle still in their arms while they sit back and experience the rush.

Medical Uses of Opiates

Relatively low or therapeutic doses of opiates may be administered for a number of medical purposes. The most common use is for analgesia, or pain relief. Doses below those that would normally cause sedation or respiratory depression may be administered to relieve pain without untoward side effects. Even though these drugs can be used without causing the patient to sleep, a feeling of slight seda-

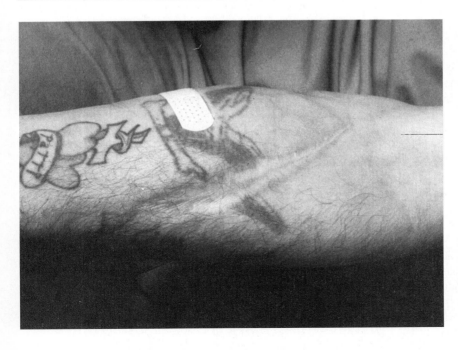

This heroin user has many tracks. Although he claimed that the long scar is from heroin use, it has the appearance of a knife wound.

tion or sleepiness is frequently reported. Aside from not directly inducing sleep or a loss of consciousness, another advantage in using opiates for pain relief is that impairment of mental and physical functions is less severe than with pain killers in other families. Although the painful stimulus and the pain impulse in the CNS is still there, the perception of pain is attenuated and feelings of anxiety associated with pain disappear. Thus, the suffering caused by pain relief is alleviated by suppressing the patient's awareness of it and distress resulting from it. The patient may even still be aware that the pain is there but not be particularly bothered by it as tolerance to pain increases dramatically. Morphine drugs are sometimes administered to women in the throes of labor and delivery to minimize the pain. These mothers have reported an awareness of the pain, but felt somewhat removed from it and less anxious about delivery. Because of the potential risk to the newborn (e.g., slowing the fetal heart rate) and the mother (not fully able to function or respond during the birthing process), however, morphine is not commonly used today. There are related reports that acupuncture works to relieve pain by triggering the release of natural opiates in areas similarly responsible for the perception of pain.

When opiates are given to individuals without pain, they may produce dysphoria (an unpleasant experience). Common effects in the pain-free person are nausea, vomiting, drowsiness, inability to concentrate, difficulty in thinking, apathy, reduced physical activity and visual acuity, and lethargy (Jaffe & Martin, 1985). In postaddicts, those who have successfully conquered a past addiction, the mental impairment is less pronounced and euphoria more noticeable due to previous experience with the drug—as if the brain has a memory for the drug or has been permanently altered.

For centuries, opiates have been used to control chronic, sometimes life-threatening, diarrhea. Particularly in countries where the food and water supply is contaminated with bacteria, opiates have provided relief to millions of people, including children, in danger of death from dehydration. In order for food to be transported through the intestines, peristaltic contractions occur within the gastrointestinal tract. Narcotics operate to decrease these contractions and are, therefore, responsible for the constipation that both heroin addicts and pain patients experience. When an addict withdraws from a narcotic, diarrhea results as a part of the withdrawal experience.

Finally, opiates have antitussive characteristics; they suppress the cough response. When an individual is suf-

fering from congestion or post nasal drip, coughing is a natural response by the body to eliminate irritants and other agents from the respiratory system. This is called productive coughing. Nonproductive coughing occurs when there are no irritants to remove and the cough is more of a reflex than a functional response. In such cases, prescription cough suppressants that contain codeine are generally used to effectively control this response. If the cough is productive, an expectorant is much preferred over an opiate-containing remedy so the body can cleanse itself properly.

There has been some enthusiasm in the clinical and scientific communities for the use of natural and synthetic opiates in the treatment of certain psychiatric disorders. Because of their anxiety-reducing and uplifting effects, they have been considered for the management of panic disorder, psychosis, depression, and manic-depression (see Kreek & Hartman, 1982). Compared with conventional medical treatments for these disorders (i.e., neuroleptics, antidepressants, tranquilizers, and others), opiates seem to produce relatively few side effects, even following long-term treatment.

Addictive Properties of Opiates

Opiates tend to be addictive in that they produce profound degrees of tolerance and psychological and physiological dependence, which are powerful motivating factors for compulsive use and abuse of these substances. Furthermore, the depletion of the brain's natural chemicals from repeated opiate use contributes to difficulty in abstaining over the long run, causing relapse.

Tolerance

Users of opiates quickly find that they must increase the dose of narcotic drugs to obtain the same effect, whether the drug is used legitimately for pain relief or recreationally for its euphoric effects. When an opiate is used often, its action on the brain and body begins to decrease, and the dose must be raised to achieve a desired effect. In particular, tolerance to the effects of respiratory depression, analgesia, euphoria, and sedation will develop to all opiates. The ability of opiates to constrict pupils and to constipate, however, are not compromised by tolerance. Thus, it is clear that tolerance is not an all or none phenomenon—it may develop for some effects but less so or not at all for other effects.

When the drug is used only occasionally, tolerance may be minimal. It is possible to maintain small dosage levels when only using recreationally on the weekends or when chipping. Thus, the same dose of opiates used on the previous occasion may be sufficient to achieve its desired effect. This scenario, however, is not the most commonly observed among opiate users involved in antisocial lifestyles. More frequently, the intermittent use of opiates quickly develops into regular, chronic use, and tolerance will develop accordingly. In fact, studies commonly reveal that drug-using subjects tend to receive either a full psychiatric diagnosis (DIS; DSM-III-R) of dependence on opiates or no diagnosis, even though the structured interview normally also includes a middle category called symptoms of dependence for drugs of abuse.

The phenomenon of cross tolerance to all other opiates, develops in the user even to those opiates that have never been tried. Thus, an individual who has developed a tolerance to heroin will find that tolerance has also developed to all other natural and synthetic opiates.

Physical Dependence

Because the opiates are so similar in structure to the natural opiates of the brain, drugs such as heroin have an affinity for these receptor sites and readily produce dependence (Jaffe & Martin, 1985). The use of opiates over a period of time causes the brain to produce smaller quantities of the natural peptides because the presence of an external source more than compensates for the required supplies of natural opiates. As the natural amounts of these transmitters decrease, opiates provide the primary supply of peptide-like substances available. When the individual discontinues opiate use, the brain experiences a deficiency of opiate-like substances. After a period of time without opiates, both the experience and perception of pain and anxiety becomes exaggerated, thus motivating the individual to seek more of the drug.

In addition to direct interference with natural opiate-like chemicals in the brain, opiates alter other neurotransmitters as well. Specifically, they serve to inhibit dopamine and acetylcholine. When the activity of these two neurotransmitters is low, many of the body's functions, such as heart rate, blood pressure, and neural transmission become depressed. These effects add to the feeling of relaxation, although psychological depression may result when their activity is chronically low. During withdrawal from heroin, the activity of dopamine and acetylcholine increases dramatically, intensifying many of the unpleasant withdrawal symptoms (see Table 7.2).

Until recently the concentration of heroin in street drugs has been relatively low, which means that the degree of addiction may not have been as high as one might expect.

Table 7.2 Opiates: Toxic Effects, Overdose, and Withdrawal

Toxic Effects	Effects of Overdose	Withdrawal Symptoms
Hypotension	Slow and shallow breathing	Watery eyes
Drowsiness	Clammy skin	Runny nose
Respiratory depression	Convulsions	Yawning
Constricted pupils	Respiratory arrest	Loss of appetite
Nausea	Seizures	Irritability
Allergic reaction	Coma	Tremors, panic
Constipation	Possible death	Cramps, nausea
Lowered sex drive		Chills & sweating
Insomnia		Diarrhea
Infection from contamination		
Deteriorated lifestyle		
Fetal damage		

Many users could go cold turkey (withdrawing without the assistance of other drugs) and not suffer the extreme withdrawal symptoms commonly associated with cessation. Nevertheless, the user's belief that symptoms will occur is sometimes enough to make the withdrawal a painful one. On the other hand, the belief that withdrawal will be symptom-free is often sufficient to minimize the untoward effects.

Withdrawal symptoms begin about four hours after the last injection; users begin to feel severe anxiety and craving for the drug. At eight hours, users will yawn repeatedly, perspire heavily, and experience flu-like symptoms such as teary eyes and runny nose. This is a result of histamine release, a neurotransmitter responsible for symptoms of allergy. Twelve hours after the last injection, the pupils dilate, muscles twitch, bones and muscles ache, and body hair stands on end. Eighteen to twenty-four hours later, blood pressure, pulse, breathing rate, and body temperature all rise while vomiting and diarrhea begin. Between thirty-six and seventy-two hours later,

symptoms subside. You will notice that these are characteristic responses of the flight and fight mechanism activated under periods of acute stress.

It is possible that some people attracted to heroin either produce excessive amounts of dopamine and acetylcholine or fail to metabolize these transmitters properly. An accumulation of these substances can partially explain the perception of physiological pain and feelings of anxiety that may lead some persons to abuse heroin in an attempt to seek relief. Another possibility is that some opiate users may be compensating for an inborn or acquired biochemical deficiency. They may produce low levels of the natural opiates found in the brain and spinal cord (Goldstein, 1976; Snyder, 1977, 1980). Therefore, exogenous opiates provide a state of normalcy that mimics the biochemical balance of individuals with sufficient endogenous opiates. On the basis of this assumption, some addicts need opiates in the same way a diabetic needs insulin—to correct a metabolic defect (see Figure 7.1).

Figure 7.1   *Opioids and Alcohol Craving*

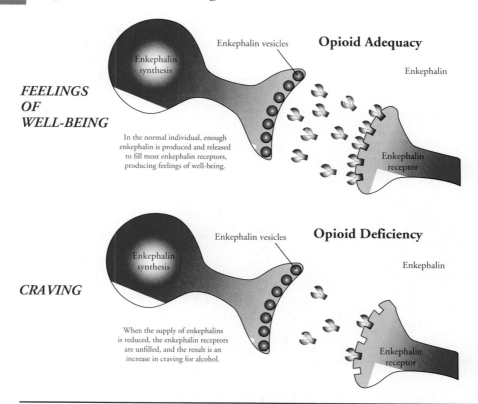

Psychological Dependence

When the use of a drug becomes associated with a pleasurable response, there is always the danger of psychological dependence. The process of becoming compelled to continue using due to learned association is called behavioral conditioning. It works in two ways. The first part of the conditioning process occurs when the individual reliably experiences a pleasurable stimulus following a particular behavior, called positive reinforcement. In the case of opiates, immediately following injection, the user, particularly the experienced user, feels a rush of sensation and euphoria, although some first time users actually experience dysphoria, including lethargy, anxiety, sedation, mental clouding, or nausea. The drug causes a general feeling of well-being and relief from any existing physical or psychological pain, such as anxiety. Even among those who "control" their opiate use by administering small quantities to maintain a constant but subdued state of relaxation, the relief from stress and the escape from the realities of life are profoundly reinforcing. These results contribute to a powerful compulsion to seek and readminister the drug.

The second aspect of the conditioning process is called negative reinforcement. The development of physical dependence to opiates is, as described above, associated with withdrawal symptoms. In order to eliminate the possibility of this unpleasant result, users readminister the drug. Once these symptoms are removed, the drug-using behavior is reinforced, further strengthening the drug habit.

The more quickly a drug produces euphoria, alleviates pain, and suppresses withdrawal symptoms, the more likely it is to rapidly produce psychological dependence. Eventually, even the activities surrounding drug use become reinforcing. For example, users report experiencing pleasure and sometimes euphoria simply by preparing their needles for injection. In fact, there are even reports that some of the physiological results of opiate use, such as pupil constriction, occur during the process of preparing to use opiates or following the injection of a placebo. The treatment of opiate dependence is complicated by this learned, psychological process. Although we may be able to administer a substitute drug like methadone or help an individual through withdrawal until the physical dependence is eliminated, the routines and rituals associated with drug use remain compelling. It is recommended that these users be deprogrammed so that the behaviors surrounding opiate use are no longer pleasurable in and of themselves. Certain places and friends must be avoided and the psychological response to the use of a needle must be extinguished. One way to do so is to administer an agent that blocks the euphoric effects of opiates so that when the drug is used, the individual no longer experiences the pleasurable response. Eventually, the association between drug injection and a positive stimulus is eliminated.

An ex-drug addict leaving jail is more likely to overdose since the last dose taken is frequently used after a period of abstinence.

Long-Term Opiate Addiction

Long-term addiction to opiates is relatively harmless to individuals provided that acquisition takes place in a non-threatening environment and that they can obtain the drug in its pure form. Unfortunately, the environment of street users is not generally conducive to relatively safe use; rather, street heroin users tend to live in filthy environments, their heroin is frequently contaminated, their diets and health are poor, and their neighborhoods unstable and dangerous. The three long-term side effects of prolonged use are constipation, lowered sex drive, and insomnia. When compared with the effects of long-term nicotine addiction (i.e., lung cancer, heart disease, throat and larynx cancer to name just a few) or alcoholism (i.e., cirrhosis of the liver, heart disease, cancer, and early death) opiate addiction is relatively benign.

Because heroin is illegal and prepared by drug dealers, users may experience other effects, caused by the additives rather than the opiates themselves. Street heroin has been known to be cut with talc, quinine, and rat poison as well as other unidentified substances. Talc, when injected into the veins, can cause blindness and quinine may cause a severe allergic reaction in some users. These users sometimes die before the needle is removed from the vein, as their lungs quickly become congested with fluid. Since addicts rarely have access to the knowledge or materials to sterilize their paraphernalia, they may inject drugs with dirty needles or share needles and promote the spread of such diseases as hepatitis, tetanus, and HIV.

Since heroin users can never be sure how much actual heroin is present in the supply purchased from a dealer, they may inadvertently die from an overdose of the drug if a larger amount of pure heroin than expected is present. Deaths from heroin overdose may also occur after a user has spent enough time in jail or elsewhere to withdraw from the drug. After a period of abstinence, users are no longer tolerant to heroin although they expect the same dosage used before withdrawal will still be necessary to produce the desired effects. The fatal dose is, therefore, the same dose the individual used previously. Heroin causes death by depressing respiration and may occur several minutes or hours after an overdose.

Toxic Effects of Opiate Use

Acute drug side effects include nausea and vomiting as opiates stimulate the area of the brain responsible for these symptoms. Even chronic street users experience nausea and vomiting shortly following injection. Other short-term effects are primarily behavioral, and none of them are particularly dangerous. Injecting heroin results in a phenomenon called nod, where the user falls asleep for a very short time and experiences a rich dream world. Users also find it difficult to concentrate. Heroin suppresses the sex drive, and some males even suffer from temporary impotence and women may experience a cessation of their menstrual periods (Rosenbaum, 1995),while the drug is present. A few of the opiates (i.e., Demerol) produce allergic reactions in some, including classic skin rashes, itching, and hives. Orthostatic hypotension is also commonly seen after use of certain opiates; blood pressure drops, particularly upon standing up, causing sweating, shakiness, dizziness, and faintness. See Table 7.2 for a list of the toxic effects of opiates and their causes.

In addition to experiencing the behavioral and physiological side effects, drug users frequently become involved in legal complications and lifestyle changes. Maintaining an opiate addiction is frequently associated with increased interactions in an underworld environment, characterized by crime and poor living conditions. Engaging in a deviant lifestyle devoted to the purchase and use of drugs contributes directly to poor health, improper diet, poor hygiene, and, consequently, early death. Obviously, there is also the possibly of arrest and incarceration.

Pregnant or nursing women using opiates encounter other more disturbing side effects. Because opiates pass through the placental barrier, babies born to addicted mothers are similarly addicted and must suffer the same withdrawal symptoms. These babies demonstrate irritability, excessive crying, increased breathing, tremors, increased bowel movements, and sometimes vomiting and fever. The long-term effects on the developing child are not well understood. Opiates may also be found in the breast milk of nursing mothers and, therefore, ingested by the infant. Unfortunately, the infant's body is not capable of efficiently metabolizing and eliminating the drug.

An overdose of opiates is truly life threatening. Opiates have the direct effect of depressing respiration by their action on the brain. Death may result from respiratory arrest when the brain becomes less sensitive to carbon dioxide levels in the blood and doesn't realize it needs more oxygen. Because the effects on respiration are additive when sedative-hypnotics are used in combination with opiates, overdose and death are commonly related to multiple drug use. Many heroin users who die from overdose also have elevated levels of alcohol in their blood.

The same scenario is observed when sleeping pills or quaaludes are combined with heroin.

Chronic opiate use is not associated with any known medical problems involving tissue or organ damage, quite unlike alcohol. It is apparently possible to maintain a long-term addiction to heroin without particularly undue consequences if pure supplies with known concentrations of opiate are used carefully. Nevertheless, it is important to note that injecting heroin is frequently associated with dire medical consequences, especially from "sepsis" or nonsterile conditions. Tetanus, infection of the lining of the heart, abscesses in the lungs, pneumonia, and tuberculosis are other conditions resulting in sepsis. Furthermore, the threat of contracting AIDS and hepatitis is formidable in these groups as contamination due to needle sharing is extremely common. In some areas of this country and others, clean needles are distributed to high-risk individuals by organizations concerned about the unbridled spread of these deadly diseases. At this time, the organized distribution of clean needles is not a widely accepted practice in many cities due to the belief that drug use is symbolically being condoned.

Opiate Use, Psychopathology, and Criminal Behavior

The opiates tend to be the most misunderstood of all the addictive and abused drugs. There are many behavioral and pharmacological effects of opiate use, some of which are strictly related to the impact of opiates on biological and psychological systems and others which are more directly a result of its prohibition and possession. These various effects can be attributed to the following conditions. First, the direct pharmacologic drug effects obviously lead to behavioral and psychological alterations that have been discussed. Second, the psychological and biological condition of the user plays a direct role in how the opiate will influence the user's brain and behavior. Third, the illegality of the drug itself encourages those who wish to purchase and use opiates to go underground, lead a double or secret life, and associate with illicit drug dealers. Behavioral habits and lifestyles change accordingly as an indirect effect of opiate use. And fourth, conditions under which the drugs are prepared are often unsanitary, causing the drugs to be exposed to contamination. This may lead

Heroin addicts on a street corner in Baltimore.

to unexpected drug effects and health hazards. Thus, drug effects on the brain and behavior may be due to a variety of conditions other than the drug's immediate pharmacologic properties.

Also commonly confused is the association between opiate use and aggressive behavior. It is important to note that not all opiate users commit crimes. But when aggression and criminal behavior are associated with addiction to heroin, these behaviors are primarily economically motivated and supported by environmental and subcultural systems. These behaviors are further reinforced by learned contingencies; the user begins to associate criminal activity with the eventual acquisition of a drug that produces pleasurable effects. Someone addicted to heroin might commit an act of aggression to obtain money to buy the drug, but there is no known relationship between the pharmacologic effects of heroin and aggressive behavior.

There is additional research suggesting that individuals prone to abusing opiates (and possibly other drugs) may require a level of neurologic stimulation over and above that which is normally provided by conventional appetitive behaviors (i.e., eating, sleeping, having sex). Due to an unusual need for stimulation and excitement, these individuals may be satisfied only when they engage in thrill-seeking or risky activities. This can be achieved by both the use of drugs, in this case opiates, and certain types of criminal activity. The excitement of a criminal lifestyle frequently precedes opiate use. Drug use in general is part and parcel of that lifestyle and frequently accompanies criminality. Opiates may become the drug of choice under these circumstances simply as a result of subcultural encouragements or availability. The proposition that individuals who have adopted criminal lifestyles are more prone to drug abuse may help to explain the prevalence of violence and criminal behavior among many opiate users.

One common misconception about the nature of the relationship between opiate addiction and crime is that otherwise law abiding individuals try heroin, become addicted, and then find that they must commit crimes in order to raise the cash needed to sustain the addiction. Most heroin addicts displayed antisocial behavior first and addictive behavior second (Inciardi, 1986; Nurco, 1989). For example, women appear to be more likely to become addicted after becoming a prostitute despite the common belief that women become prostitutes in order to pay for a heroin habit. On the other hand, there is further evidence that offenders commit a much higher rate of crime after becoming addicts. Thus, it appears that opiate addiction furthers an already established "criminal career." Inciardi's

(p. 126–127) sample of 573 narcotics users admitted responsibility for 215,105 offenses during the twelve months prior to being interviewed. "Of the 215,105 offenses, only 609 resulted in an arrest." Inciardi goes on to state "narcotics users, at least those studied in Miami but most likely others, are highly successful criminals that systems or urban law enforcement are unable to control" (p. 128). Ball, Rosen, et al. (1981) found that 243 heroin addicts were responsible for more than 473,738 offenses during their criminally active years. These crimes did not include possession or use of illegal drugs. Therefore, there appears to be merit to the argument that control of the addiction would result in a lowering but not elimination of the crime committed by addicts.

In strictly pharmacologic terms, opiates tend to reduce aggressive and hostile tendencies; aggressive behaviors may actually be attenuated by direct drug effects, and a feeling of calm and sedation minimize the chances of violent behavior (Finestone, 1967; Greenberg and Adler, 1974; Inciardi and Chambers, 1972; Julien, 1981; Kozel et al., 1972; Wikler, 1952). There is evidence, however, that opiate users have a higher incidence of psychopathic behavioral disorders (see Craig, 1988) and that during active opiate abuse periods, users commit significantly more crimes, including violent crime (Gropper, 1984). As the biological effects serve to directly suppress aggression, circumstance and other social properties of a drug-using environment may contribute more substantially to criminal behavior in opiate users.

Persons experiencing chronic anxiety and/or pain may be more inclined to abuse heroin or other opiates due to their ability to reduce pain and anxiety and generate euphoria. Affective disorders (i.e., depression and anxiety) and personality disorders (i.e., borderline personality disorder and antisocial personality) are the most frequently documented psychiatric diagnoses among opiate users (Khantzian & Treece, 1985). There is a large incidence of psychopathy and antisocial personality among opiate addicts (Sutker & Archer, 1984). As opiates are known to attenuate aggression and anxiety, initial use may have been reinforced by the resulting suppression of or escape from depression, anxiety, or antisocial and aggressive tendencies that disrupt users' lives. Theorists postulate that such disorders predispose individuals to drug dependence.

The high incidence of violence and crime among active addicts (Gropper, 1984) suggests that antisocial behavior among opiate users is not strictly modified by opiates' pharmacologic effects. If this were true, psychopathic users would tend to aggress less often when under the influence of opiates than when the drug is withdrawn. It is instructive to consider that individuals with these personality disorders have been characterized as thrill seekers, risk takers, impulsive, and sensation seekers (Ellis, 1987; Fishbein, Lovosky, et al., 1989; Zuckerman, 1978). It has been further suggested that, in general, exercise, stress, and other forms of excitement increase production of the natural opiates found in the brain (Pargman and Baker, 1980; Rivier and Vale, 1988; Sacks and Sacks, 1981). Engaging in risky, criminal activities may, therefore, increase the perception of pleasure via endogenous opiate mechanisms, particularly for those individuals who require an unusual amount of physiologic stimulation (as described in Chapter 3). Thus, psychopathic individuals would be more likely to find criminal activity rewarding in a biological sense. Opiate use, similar to the use of other drugs, may serve as an additional source of stimulation. Stimulation of both forms influences neurological reward centers in the brain, reinforcing the continuation of that behavior. According to this scenario, opiate users may be, "by nature," more involved in aggressive and criminal activities generally, explaining why their criminality precedes their drug abuse. Hence, individuals who use heroin and participate in high-risk criminal activities may be essentially self-medicating pre-existing pathology (Khantzian, 1985; Pervin, 1988).

Injectable Drug Use and AIDS

Not only is opiate addiction associated with crime and violence, but injectable drug use has contributed to a significant number of AIDS (Acquired Immunodeficiency Syndrome) cases. AIDS is caused by infection with a virus called the human immunodeficiency virus (HIV). HIV attacks important white blood cells known as T lymphocytes. Following this attack a person's immune system can no longer fight off infections associated with usually harmless microorganisms or unusual cancers that a person with a normal immune system is able to ward off (Institute of Medicine, National Academy of Sciences, 1986, pp. 5-6). The virus is a particularly insidious one since "a person infected with HIV may not show any clinical symptoms for months or even years but apparently never becomes free of the virus. This long, often unrecognized period of asymptomatic infection, during which an infected person can infect others, complicates control of the spread of the virus" (Institute of Medicine, National Academy of Sciences, 1986, p. 6). There is no evidence

that AIDS is spread through casual contact; rather, it is spread through anal and vaginal intercourse, intravenous blood transfusions of infected blood and sharing needles to inject drugs. It can also be spread to an infant during pregnancy, at the time of birth, or through breast milk (Institute of Medicine, Academy of Sciences, 1986, p. 6).

By sharing unsterilized needles to inject drugs, addicts who had previously accounted for 16 percent of U.S. AIDS cases during the early 1980s (Des Jarlais, Friedman & Hopkins, 1985; Friedman, Selan & Des Jarlais, 1987) now comprise 22 percent of those over the age of thirteen who test HIV positive (U.S. Center for Disease Control, 1990). Any blood remaining on the needle from the first user is injected into the bloodstream of the second user. The sharing of needles is a difficult ritual to stop among drug addicts. They intentionally insert the needle, withdraw some blood, mix it with the heroin, and then inject it back into the bloodstream with the drug. Blood coats the inside of the hypodermic needle, which is then passed to the next user who engages in the same ritual. These drug addicts are most likely to pass AIDS on to children and heterosexuals (Des Jarlais & Hopkins, 1985). Fifty-eight percent of IV drug users tested in New York in 1984 and 10 percent of IV drug users tested in San Francisco have tested positive for the presence of HIV antibodies (Chaisson et al., 1987). Of those IV drug users who also engage in prostitution, the risks of spreading HIV increases. Moreover, some drug users engage in sex for drugs exchanges which further increases the risk of HIV (Inciardi, Pottieger, et. al., 1991). Ninety percent of babies born with AIDS become infected through their mothers' IV drug use (Osborn, 1989).

Many AIDS victims become extremely susceptible to tuberculosis, a deadly lung disease. Their impaired immune systems are unable to ward off the disease. They, in turn, infect others, since tuberculosis is spread by droplets carried through the air when the infected person coughs. Health care workers and others in close proximity to TB patients are at risk for contacting the disease, which spreads quickly through institutions, such as prisons, where a large number of inmates enter the system HIV positive. When these inmates develop AIDS, they easily contract TB as well and then spread the disease to others. In early 1992, it was reported that 15 to 25 percent of the inmate population tested positive for TB exposure (Sullivan, 1992).

Even more startling is the development of a new strain of TB that is drug resistant. Although the drug-resistant strains may still be cured with early diagnosis and treatment, the death rate is high (about 80 percent). Doctors are unsure in many cases whether the high death rate is due to a deadlier strain of TB or lack of prompt medical attention.

Preventing the Spread of AIDS

There is no cure for AIDS, and there are few avenues of recourse in the fight against its spread. AIDS prevention has become politicized and the goals of AIDS prevention programs sometimes conflict with the goals of other political agendas. For example, the free distribution of sterile needles to IV drug users is one way to curb the spread (Des Jarlais, Friedman, et al., 1987). Such a program may take a number of approaches. Addicts may be required to turn in a dirty needle in order to receive a clean one, or clean ones may be distributed freely. However, it is important to note that only a few experimental programs are legal in the United States, and some individuals have been arrested for distributing clean needles. In eleven states mere possession of a hypodermic needle without a prescription is considered illegal. Others have objected to these programs, arguing that free needles "encourage drug use," an illegal activity, although there is no scientific evidence to support this view. On the contrary, Walters, Estillo, et al., (1994) found that a needle-exchange program in San Francisco did not increase the frequency of injection or the initiation of new users.

New Haven, Connecticut, has implemented an experimental needle-exchange program where users were required to turn in a used needle in order to receive a clean one. Sixty percent of the participants were infected with the AIDS virus when they joined the program (Needle-swap program is working…, 1991). After eight months of operation, the Yale University researchers reported a 33 percent reduction in new AIDS cases among the project's 700 participants (Needle-swap program is working, 1991; Yale study reports…, 1991). When researchers collected the used needles, they tested them for the presence of the HIV virus. Of all the needles distributed by the New Haven needle swap program, which were then returned by users, 50 percent were found to contain HIV positive blood. This figure compares favorably with the HIV positive figure of 68 percent for returned needles that were not originally distributed by the researchers. When they gathered discarded needles from "shooting galleries" the HIV positive rate was 92 percent (Needle-swap program is working).

Until 1992 it was a felony in Connecticut to possess a hypodermic needle without a prescription. As a result of the New Haven pilot study, the law was changed and needle-exchange programs spread to Hartford. Massachusetts is currently toying with the idea of officially supporting Boston's needle-exchange program and eliminating the felony charge for possession of a hypodermic needle. The needle-exchange program in Boston had simply skirted the law. Other areas with needle-exchange programs include Honolulu, Hawaii; Portland, Oregon; Seattle and Tacoma, Washington; and Boulder, Colorado (Needle swap program is working, 1991; Yale study reports…, 1991).

Another approach has been to educate IV drug users about sterilizing needles. In some cases, street workers have taught IV drug users how to sterilize their needles by washing them in a solution of ordinary bleach and water or by boiling them. Some street workers have passed out bleach kits to addicts and have shown them how to use the kits. The education of actual and potential substance abusers and others who exhibit high-risk behaviors is a third recourse (Institute of Medicine. National Academy of Sciences, 1986, p. 27). It has been shown that AIDS education can affect people's behavior as evidenced by the gay population. This group has organized and provided support for its members to reduce high-risk behaviors (Friedman et al., 1987). Friedman and his coworkers also report that IV drug users in the Netherlands have organized and attempted to influence other IV drug users to take precautions when injecting drugs. To a lesser extent and through more informal educational channels, IV drug abusers in New York have become more aware of the dangers of sharing needles. Some drug dealers are offering free needles to customers who buy $25 or $50 bags of heroin. Others have run two for one sales, and one dealer was observed hawking needles while chanting, "Get the good needles, don't get the bad AIDS. Get the good needles, don't get the bad AIDS" (Des Jarlais & Hopkins, 1985; Freidman et al., 1987, p. 207).

AIDS in Prison

A report released by the National Institute of Justice indicated that "as of October 1, 1986, there have been 1,232 confirmed AIDS cases among inmates in 58 responding federal, state, and local correctional systems" (Hammett, 1987, p. 4). This figure represents a 61 percent increase since a similar survey was conducted eleven months earlier (Hammett, p. 4).

Hammet (1987) states that the New York correctional system reported that 92 percent of inmates who died from AIDS had admitted to IV drug use. In a statement made by Federal Bureau of Prisons director, J. Michael Quinlin to the Congressional Black Caucus, IV drug use appears to be the leading cause of AIDS in newly committed inmates. "[Out of] 33 inmates with end-stage AIDS…32 were IV drug users while the other was both an IV drug user and a homosexual" (Quinlin quoted by Criminal Justice Newsletter, 1987, p. 1).

Although the rate of transmission of AIDS in prison appears to be low, a New York report notes, "the long incubation period, the existence of the asymptomatic HIV carrier state, small number of long-term inmates, and absence of data on antibody status make this finding inconclusive" (Hammett, 1987, p. 6). The fact that many inmates entering the prison system may have been IV drug users suggests that prison offers an environment highly conducive to the spread of AIDS. Inmates still shooting drugs in prison will be more likely to share needles since they will be particularly scarce. Moreover, even if inmates know they should sterilize their needles, they do not have access to the necessary equipment to boil them nor the bleach to sterilize them. Ear piercing and tatooing are also popular prison behaviors. Again, inmates would have to share bloody needles when they engage in these prohibited activities, thus increasing the probability of contracting or spreading AIDS. Homosexual behavior is another feature of prison milieu that would promote the spread of AIDS. Heterosexual inmates frequently engage in homosexual behavior as a means of coping with heterosexual deprivation or as a power tool. Given these conditions, prisons may well be prime incubators for AIDS. It is also important to note that 99 percent of inmates will eventually return to the free society.

Treatment of Opiate Addiction

The treatment of opiate addiction must take into account users' differences in background, motivation for use, personality, and body chemistry. Each of these conditions will have an impact on what form(s) of treatment will be best suited to each user and which will most likely achieve success. One group of users, for example, may be "iatrogenically" addicted. Iatrogenic addiction refers to a state of drug dependence that results from physician supervised treatment for a medical disorder. These individuals generally become dependent on narcotics after aggressive, long-term administration of the drug for pain, gastrointestinal distress, or cough suppression. They frequently do not fit our preconceptions of drug users; they may be middle or upper class, live in nice neighborhoods, hold professional positions of employment, and have no personal or family history of drug or alcohol abuse. On the other hand, most opiate dependence is initiated on the street with experimental or recreational use that is frequently associated with other lifestyle factors (such as criminality or dysfunctional home environment) that operate to reinforce further drug usage. These two groups of users must receive treatments that address their very different problems.

Opiate Antagonists

Agents called "pure narcotic antagonists" have been used in the treatment of opiate addiction. Narcotic antagonists such as naloxone and naltrexone have also been used to help us understand the mechanisms of action among various opiates as well as the three types of opiate receptors (kappa, mu, and sigma). Opiate antagonists have no ability to produce euphoria or other morphine-like effects, such as analgesia. Instead, they block all three of the opiate receptors (see Figure 7.2). When opiates are introduced to the body, they are unable to have any effect because all of the receptor sites are blocked by the opiate antagonists. The opiates are immediately displaced and the brain is starved for the "missing" opiates. In a normal, drug-free individual, the use of antagonists will not produce noticeable effects. However, when administered to a narcotic-dependent individual, they will quickly induce withdrawal and the user will experience untoward effects.

Two drugs in particular, naloxone and naltrexone, have only antagonistic effects on opiates—they do not potentiate any of the morphine-like effects of opiates. Consequently, neither drug is likely to be abused. Naloxone has been used to reverse the toxic effects of opiates, such as the respiratory depression that accompanies overdose or that we observe in babies born to drug-addicted mothers.

Naltrexone is similar to naloxone with the exception that naltrexone is absorbed more efficiently by oral administration and is longer acting. This drug has been used more extensively in the treatment of opiate addicts because they can be maintained with chronic naltrexone therapy. While an individual is maintained on naltrexone, the simultaneous administration of an opiate, such as heroin, will not produce the desired effects. The use of either antagonist in treatment requires the recovering addict to be motivated to continue taking the drug until drug cravings can be controlled. This process may take quite some time, and many addicts do not demonstrate the willpower to see it through.

Methadone Treatment

Methadone clinics have been the most widely available medical treatment for opiate addiction for the past two decades. Methadone is a synthetic opiate produced originally by the Germans during World War II. Methadone treatment programs are designed to use the synthetic opiate as a substitute for the street drug, usually heroin. Its relative success is based on the properties of methadone, including its ability to relieve pain, be effective with repeated administrations, be administered orally (to avoid the use of needles), produce less euphoria than heroin, and prevent the onset of withdrawal symptoms in addicts for an extended period of time (Jaffe & Martin, 1985).

Methadone's effects last for about twenty-four hours—four times as long as those of heroin. Consequently, the methadone patient is not prone to drastic mood and behavioral changes that characterize those who use injectable shorter-acting opiates. In theory, other benefits of an orally administered opiate include the removal of users from their drug and crime-infested neighborhoods and the elimination of the behavioral habit of injecting drugs, which can be profoundly reinforcing in and of itself. Programs designed to accomplish these goals, however, must provide intensive guidance and counseling to prevent users from returning to their environments and drug using peers and to break old behavioral habits. Otherwise, the mere administration of a substitute drug will not influence the many confounding conditions in a user's lifestyle.

Once users are weaned from the opiate they were previously injecting, the program should encourage them to slowly reduce the dosage of methadone to eventually withdraw altogether from narcotics. Withdrawal symptoms associated with methadone cessation are less severe than morphine withdrawal symptoms. Unfortunately, many addicts simply continue to use methadone indefinitely or either supplement it or replace it entirely with injectable street opiates.

Reports of lower rates of drug use and criminal activity during methadone treatment are widespread and, as already mentioned, the treatment ideally eliminates the risk of exposure to contaminated needles and helps to break a behavioral habit of IV drug use. Nevertheless, methadone clinics are controversial. Methadone treat-

Figure 7.2   *Naltrexone blocks natural opiate receptors so that when an opiate like heroin is taken, it is ineffective and withdrawal ensues.*

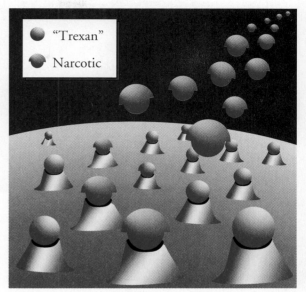

Reprinted with the permission of The DuPont Merck Pharmaceutical Company.

ment has been criticized for condoning the maintenance of another addiction while patients still have ready access to illegal supplies. Also, a relatively low long-term abstinence rate has been reported (Callahan, 1980; Rasor, 1972). Most important, a majority of methadone clinics do not even attempt to wean their clients from the drug. Only the heavily financed, state-of-the-art clinics systematically do this in conjunction with a structured program of counseling. With these two components missing, many of these programs will fail to achieve their initial goals.

Buprenorphine Treatment

The drug buprenorphine is under study for its ability to treat opiate addiction (Mello and Mendelson, 1980; Reisinger, 1985). Buprenorphine is an opiate analgesic that blocks the natural opiate receptors in the brain. Thus, it is capable of blocking the reward value of self-administered opiates to reduce craving and, at the same time, prevent the patient from experiencing withdrawal symptoms, which frequently cause users to return to their drug of

A methadone clinic dispensing the drug to a patient.

abuse. Buprenorphine has a long range of action, avoids the use of needles, and, unlike methadone, has a low level of physical dependence. Researchers hope that buprenorphine will enable users to eventually break both the behavioral and pharmacological aspects of the drug habit.

Clonidine Treatment

Clonidine is a specific adrenergic agonist that helps to alleviate the discomfort of opiate withdrawal (Gold et al., 1980) and has been used in clinical settings for that purpose (Jaffe, 1985). During opiate withdrawal, particular areas of the brain experience an increase in neuronal firing that appears to be partially responsible for withdrawal symptoms. Clonidine reverses excessive firing of neurons that are involved in opiate reception. The greatest effects of clonidine have been reported in the limbic system, where mood states and autonomic functions are regulated (Kimes et al., 1990). Clonidine also helps to alleviate the diarrhea and shakes associated with withdrawal.

Therapeutic Communities

Therapeutic communities (discussed more thoroughly in Chapter 15) were initially developed to treat heroin users.

The premise behind this approach was that a residential treatment center that removed addicts from the drug subculture was necessary to prevent relapse. As individuals become addicted to heroin, they associate more and more often with other drug users and obtain their drugs from the black market. Thus, no matter where addicts came from, who their parents are, or in what social class they were raised, they tend to eventually drift into an underground subculture—the heroin addict's entire life revolves around the use and acquisition of heroin. Therapeutic communities are designed to remove the addict from their subculture and place them in a situation where drug use is not tolerated and other values replace those of the drug subculture. Typical heroin addicts awaken in the morning and crave a fix. Their first goal of the day is to satisfy craving for narcotics and relieve withdrawal symptoms. Following the fix, addicts then begin to plan for the next fix, and so on. The addicts may engage in criminal activity, hustle money from family or friends, exchange in sex for drugs, or sell drugs for a dealer in exchange for a fix. Some dealers will give addicts enough heroin to get them started for a day's worth of work. The day's activities, therefore, center around either getting more of the drug or doing the drug. Acquiring drugs requires extensive planning and negotiation since most addicts seeks the best quality drugs for the least cost. (Preble & Casey, 1969).

The therapeutic community must resocialize addicts to live a life without drugs and their accompanying rituals—the rituals and the paraphernalia associated with drug use become a part of the drug habit and can lead to relapse. In order for treatment to be successful, addicts must completely abandon their old life on the streets and acquire new habits, associations, and attitudes. Ex-addicts are essential personnel for the treatment staff. Only they are familiar with the addicts' excuses for failing to fulfill their responsibilities and are considered to be best able to provide peer support toward a drug-free life. Those who have worked with addicts are accustomed to the question, "Have you ever used drugs?" If the answer is no, addicts commonly reply, "Then how can you know what it's like and what I'm about?" Working with ex-addicts provides the patients with someone to relate to. Counseling is also quite beneficial for ex-addicts, further reinforcing their recovery from drug addiction. The overall goal of therapeutic communities is to replace the deviant rituals and values with nondeviant ones.

Opiate Treatment and Crime

Criminal behavior is significantly reduced during drug treatment for opiate addiction, and the longer addicts stay in treatment, the longer they remain drug free upon discharge (Johnson et al., 1986; Nurco et al., 1989). As Faupel (1981) points out, however, although the literature documents a reduction in crime during treatment, the issue remains controversial. Unfortunately, due to our present emphasis on the use of criminal sanctions to deter drug-related crimes, users are less likely to seek treatment and will be more likely to continue drug use for lack of viable alternatives. This may be particularly true for mothers and pregnant addicts who are frightened that if they seek help, their children will be taken from them or they will be arrested. Drug treatment programs have additional advantages in that the costs of such programs are insignificant relative to the costs of (1) incarceration; (2) continued criminal activity during nontreatment periods; (3) lack of productivity of addicts and their need for welfare and medicare; and, (4) children born to addicts with disabilities and insurmountable social disadvantages. The provision of treatment, in lieu of a criminal sanction, may entice more addicts to enter treatment facilities willingly.

≡ Summary

Opiates or narcotic drugs possess the desirable properties of anxiety and pain relief, which contribute to their abuse potential. They are powerfully addictive as a function of both their ability to enhance feelings of well-being and calmness and their potential to substitute for natural chemicals in our brain. The discovery of receptor sites in the brain that have an affinity for externally taken opiates shed light on mechanisms of addiction and helped us to understand how some drugs compromise our free will decisions to use or not to use. Once a user has experienced the effects of opiates, it becomes increasingly difficult to abstain due to their intense reward value in the brain and in the psyche. The brain's natural supply of opiate-like chemicals or neuropeptides diminishes as it adapts to the influx of external chemicals, which satisfy if not exceed the need for these substances. Once the brain becomes accustomed to the presence of an opiate and reduces its production of neuropeptides, a deficiency state is created. This process encourages the user to continue opiate administrations to avoid the withdrawal symptoms that result from the deficiency. Once a user is truly addicted in this way, the drug may no longer provide the high that was initially pursued. Instead, continued drug usage becomes an attempt by the user to regain some semblance of normalcy and to avoid painful withdrawal symptoms. At this stage, the drug is talking, not the user. Without professional help, opiate addicts have tremendous difficulty discontinuing use for any period of time.

Heroin addiction, in particular, has been a phenomenon largely restricted to lower socioeconomic groups. Although professional classes do become addicted, the overwhelming majority of addicts are poor or socially disadvantaged. Many believe that heroin use is a cultural phenomenon for those who have no other social outlet or hope for their future. Addicts tend to live in crime-infested neighborhoods with ready drug availability. Those unfamiliar with such downward social mobility may be unsympathetic to heroin addicts, scorn them, and attest that they freely chose their lifestyle. Nothing could be further from the truth. Children who eventually become heroin addicts never said, "I want to be an addict when I grow up." No one aspires to get caught up in the tragedy of opiate abuse. Rather, heroin addiction is a lonely, one-way street for many who desperately want to find another path but do not have access to the social means for an alternate lifestyle.

CHAPTER 8

Stimulants: Cocaine

Objectives

1. To explain how raw coca leaves are processed into cocaine.
2. To discuss the different forms of cocaine, including crack.
3. To show the extent and prevalence of cocaine use in the United States.
4. To illustrate the ways in which cocaine can be administered.
5. To describe the mood-altering effects of cocaine.
6. To demonstrate the physiological effects of cocaine.
7. To explain cocaine's addictive nature by understanding the impact of cocaine on the reward center of the brain.
8. To present the negative physical and psychological side effects of chronic cocaine use.
9. To identify and discuss the effects of cocaine on the fetus.
10. To present a profile of the person most likely to abuse cocaine.
11. To describe the relationship between cocaine use and criminal behavior and antisocial lifestyles.
12. To present treatments for abuse of cocaine and discuss their effectiveness.

1914
Cocaine

[Cocaine] may produce the wildest form of insane exaltation, accompanied by the fantastic hallucinations and delusions that characterize acute mania.... He imagines that he hears people taunting or abusing him, and this often incites homicidal attacks upon innocent and unsuspecting victims.... [Cocaine] produces several other conditions that make the "fiend" a peculiarly dangerous criminal. One of these conditions is a temporary immunity to shock—a resistance to the "knock down" effects of fatal wounds. Bullets fired into vital parts, that would drop a sane man in his tracks fail to check the "fiend"—fail to stop his rush or weaken his attack. (E.H. Williams, 1914)

Myths and misperceptions about cocaine have abounded for at least a century. Early in the twentieth century, there were claims that cocaine produced insanity and criminality. But there were also claims that cocaine was beneficial to the health and well-being of its users; cocaine was an original "health-giving" ingredient in Coca Cola during this time. Even Sigmund Freud, the late and legendary psychiatrist, called cocaine a "magical drug" that produced euphoria and a feeling of competence that exceeded any other human experience. He recommended it to his patients and used it in therapy to enable patients to express themselves better and confront their inner beings. Overall, prior to the early 1980s, cocaine, used even for recreational purposes, had been thought of as a relatively benign and safe drug. Socioeconomic classes not normally associated with drug abuse would partake of this drug as it was considered "clean," easy to use, nonaddictive, and beneficial to intellectual functioning. Only in recent years has cocaine been proven a dangerous and addictive drug.

Animal studies documenting that cocaine is powerful enough to cause rats to self-administer a drug other than morphine, even in the absence of measurable withdrawal symptoms, have demonstrated both the dangers and addictive properties of cocaine (Kornetsky & Esposito, 1979; Leith & Barrett, 1981; Petersen & Stillman, 1977; Wise, 1984). Because animals learn so rapidly to work very hard to

obtain cocaine, it has been suggested that this drug is particularly habit forming and pleasure producing. Laboratory animals will take large quantities of cocaine when access is unlimited. Sleeping and feeding habits become altered in an effort to obtain the drug and health begins to deteriorate. The animals (generally rats) will live for no more than three weeks. They succumb to drug-induced convulsions and respiratory viruses that their immune system cannot resist.

Primates also find cocaine irresistible (Aigner & Balster, 1978). When two levers are offered, one for food and the other for cocaine, monkeys continue to press the cocaine lever and ignore the offering of food and water. They will also ignore females in heat, which is particularly unusual behavior for Rhesus monkeys. Eventually, they too collapse in seizures and die. In recent years, we have also witnessed the same type of behavior among humans. Although we do not understand why some will quickly become addicted to cocaine and others will not, those who are most vulnerable to cocaine abuse will self-administer the drug despite the damaging consequences.

Cocaine is classified as a central nervous system stimulant, along with amphetamines, nicotine, and caffeine. All of these stimulants increase behavioral and mental activity, reduce fatigue, and increase alertness or enhance mood. Cocaine and amphetamines, in particular, share many of the same effects and are sometimes used illegally for similar reasons; they both contribute to weight loss, alertness, and euphoria. (Figure 8.1 illustrates cocaine's chemical resemblance to other stimulants.) They differ, however, in their molecular structure and with respect to how they are abused and by whom. Nicotine and caffeine are more different in molecular structure and, as a consequence, exert their effects on the brain in quite a different manner. They are not necessarily abused for the same reason or by the same individuals that become involved with cocaine or amphetamines. In this chapter, we discuss cocaine separate from other stimulants because of its widespread abuse and several unique properties that distinguish it and give us cause for concern.

Types of Cocaine

Cocaine is obtained from the coca plant, which flourishes in the climate of some Latin American countries. Peru, Bolivia, Ecuador, and Colombia supply the vast majority of cocaine although Bolivia may be the leader in the amount of cocaine base produced and exported. It is estimated that about 80 to 90 percent of the cocaine sold by the Colombian drug cartels originates in Bolivia (Levine,

Figure 8.1   *Chemical Structures of Several Stimulants Showing Similarities and Two Endogenous Compounds, Norepinephrine and Dopamine. Imipramine produces a calming or sedative effect in normal individuals but acts as a stimulant or mood elevator in depressed individuals.*

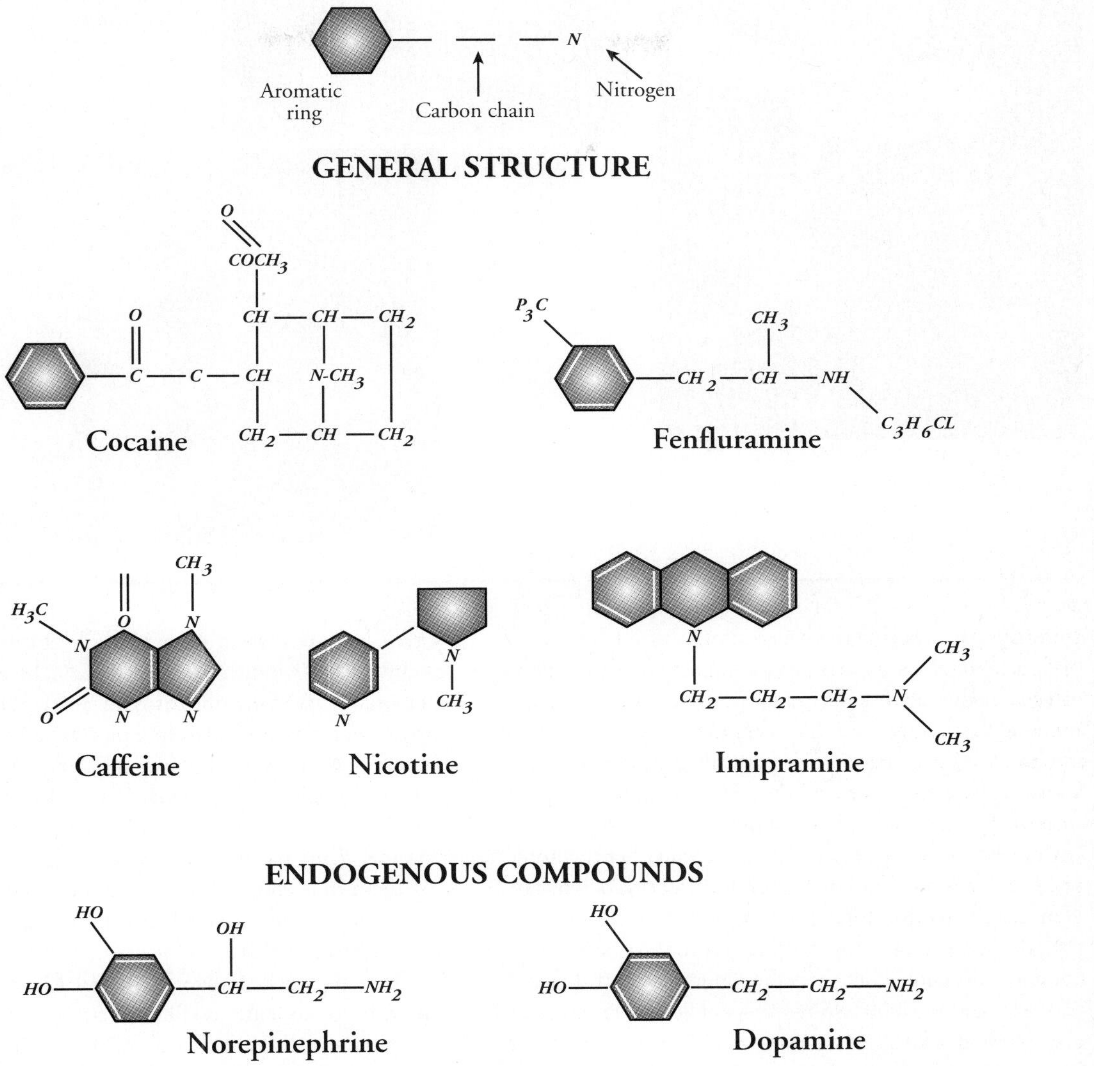

GENERAL STRUCTURE

ENDOGENOUS COMPOUNDS

Source: U.S. Government

1990). Most of the cocaine supplied by these countries was processed in the jungles of Colombia for export to international markets until about 1990. As a result of a governmental crackdown in Colombia, many Colombian traffickers moved their processing sites to remote jungle regions along Colombia's borders with Ecuador, Venezuela, and Brazil (Drug traffickers shift processing…, 1991). In 1988 alone, between 250 and 400 metric tons of cocaine were processed in South America (U.S. Attorneys, 1989).

Cocaine is sold as a water-soluble hydrochloride salt (HC1) for sniffing or injecting. HC1 is the refined version of cocaine sulfate and other alkaloids that are derived

A. *Coca flower*
B. *Coca leaf and flower*
C. *Cocaine hydrochloride*

(Courtesy of the Drug Enforcement
Administration)

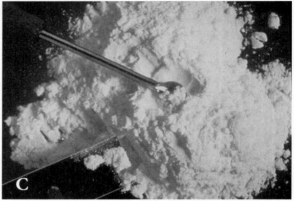

from the coca leaf. In the clandestine jungle laboratories of South America, coca leaves are mixed with an organic solvent, such as kerosene or gasoline. They are soaked and mashed thoroughly and the remaining liquid is filtered out to make coca paste. The paste is easily processed to form cocaine HC1. The cocaine HC1 is then smuggled into the United States for retail sale.

In 1990, it was reported that the United States' supply of cocaine was more prevalent and the price was down. The National Narcotics Intelligence Consumers Committee (NNICC) cited by Cooper, 1990, estimated the value of cocaine at its entry point into the United States at the end of 1988 to be $11,000 to $34,000 per kilo, the lowest price ever. In 1984, a kilo sold for between $40,000 and $50,000 (Cooper, 1990). Although government seizures of cocaine have increased dramatically, the reduction in price indicates that more cocaine is entering the country. In addition, the purity level of the drugs sold on the streets has increased from about 10 to 20 percent purity to approximately 70 percent. Increased purity levels and a decrease in average price are classic indicators of increased cocaine trafficking activity (Cooper, 1990; U.S. Attorneys, 1989).

Crack, a form of cocaine that has been processed for smoking, has become increasingly popular in recent years.

Crack is derived from cocaine HCl by mixing the compound with baking soda and water. Once the water is evaporated, the mixture turns to a crystalline chunk or "rock" that may be heated in a pipe especially designed to smoke cocaine. When the user inhales the vapor, the drug rushes to the brain to produce a remarkable high or rush. Due to the low price and ready-to-smoke form of crack cocaine, many users begin their cocaine use with it, causing them to become addicted in a much shorter period of time than it would have taken with intranasal use (Gawin & Ellinwood, 1988).

With its small dosage units and low cost, crack has opened up an entirely new, lucrative market of low-income users. Indeed, there is evidence that its manufacture was directly aimed at increasing the market for cocaine by providing a low-cost version of the drug. While an ounce of cocaine HC1 worth $1,000 converts to 25,000 milligrams of crack with a street price of $2,500, the real profit in crack is generated by its remarkably high sales volume. Crack's profitability, simplicity of processing, and ease of transportation, combined with the user's need for more frequent hits than with other forms of cocaine, have made crack cocaine popular with pushers and have provided them with a new, easily saleable product that creates a heavy and constant repeat demand (U.S. Attorneys, 1989, p. 8).

Originally, crack was distributed primarily by local dealer networks who bought the traditional cocaine powder from wholesalers, converted it to crack, and then sold it to users. This system of local preparation has given way to the involvement of larger organizations in the direct processing, distribution, and sale of crack. Intense competition for market share and turf has led to violent crack wars in major distribution areas (U.S. Attorneys, 1989, p. 8).

Prevalence of Use

The groups most vulnerable to cocaine use include adolescents and young adults who demonstrate higher than average levels of tobacco, alcohol, and especially marijuana use. Youths with conduct problems in early public school are at higher risk of heavy marijuana use; it is predicted that these adolescents may be more vulnerable to eventual cocaine use. (See O'Malley et al., 1985 for review.) Unfortunately, the risk of becoming a cocaine user does not decrease after the teen years. Initiation to cocaine use occurs anytime from adolescence to adulthood, whereas the chances of beginning use of other commonly abused drugs (e.g., LSD or marijuana) falls drastically after the age of twenty-four.

According to the 1993 *National Household Survey on Drug Abuse,* about 23,494,000 Americans above the age of twelve used cocaine (including crack) at some time in their lives. About 4,530,000 used cocaine during the past year and about 1,307,000 used during the past month. About 1,484,000 Americans over the age of twelve reported using cocaine twelve or more times during the past year and 476,000 reported using the drug once a week or more. Table 8.1 shows the percentage of each age group

Table 8.1   *Cocaine: Percent of Population Reporting Use of Cocaine Ever, Past Year, and Past Month (1993) by Sex and Age Groups for Total Population*

	Ever Used	Used Past Year	Used Past Month	Used 12 or More Times During Past Year	Used Once a Week or More
	RATE ESTIMATES (PERCENTAGES)				
AGE					
12-17	1.1	0.8	0.4	0.3	0.1
Male	0.9	0.6	0.4	0.2	0.1
Female	1.4	0.9	0.4	0.4	0.1
18-25	12.5	5.0	1.5	1.6	0.6
Male	14.0	6.4	1.7	2.2	1.9
Female	11.1	3.7	1.4	1.0	0.4
26-34	25.6	4.4	1.0	1.0	0.4
Male	30.2	6.4	1.6	1.7	0.7
Female	21.2	2.4	0.4	0.4	0.1
35+	8.5	1.1	0.4	0.5	0.1
Male	12.1	1.8	0.6	0.8	0.2
Female	5.3	0.5	0.2	0.3	0.1
Total	11.3	2.2	0.6	0.7	0.2
Male	14.5	3.2	0.9	1.1	0.4
Female	8.5	1.3	0.4	0.4	0.1

Note: Cocaine includes crack.

Source: Adapted from Substance Abuse and Mental Health Services Administration. *1993 National Household Survey on Drug Abuse.*

broken down by sex who reported using cocaine ever, during the past year, during the past month, twelve or more times during the past year, and once a week or more. The group most likely to have tried cocaine is the twenty-six to thirty-four age group (See Table 8.1), but of those reporting use of cocaine once a week or more there were little differences among the age groups twelve to seventeen (0.1 percent), eighteen to twenty-five (0.6 percent) and twenty-six to thirty-four (0.4 percent).

The prevalence of cocaine use continues to increase in certain subpopulations in this country while for the groups included in the annual survey of high school seniors, college students, and other young adults (Johnston, O'Malley, & Bachman, 1993), the annual rates of cocaine use (including crack) have declined since 1986. Extensive media coverage concerning the hazards of cocaine during 1986 and 1987 probably account for this decline as young people began to see experimental and occasional use as more dangerous. In 1993 the decline continued, with annual prevalence of 3.1 among seniors, 5.9 percent among young adults, and 3.0 percent among college students (see Figure 8-2).

The perceived risk of using cocaine generally and crack in particular, has continued to increase among both seniors and young adults. The belief that peers disapprove of drug use has also been fostered. Perceptions that cocaine has become more available rose steadily from 1984 to 1989; however, students reported a 4 percent decrease of perceived availability of cocaine in 1990. Nevertheless, the downward trend occurred at a time when cocaine appeared to be easily available. Therefore, the substantial downturn in use was probably not due to lack of availability.

Unlike other illicit drugs, use of cocaine in a person's lifetime increases with age. More than 40 percent of those aged twenty-seven had tried cocaine. Annual prevalence and thirty-day prevalence (use during past month) is also higher for the upper age categories. Cocaine is a drug that is used much more frequently among people in their twenties than among those in their late teens.

In all populations and age groups studied, males are generally more likely than females to use cocaine. However the trend is still declining for both groups. Figure 8.3 shows the decline trend for male and female college students since 1980.

Figure 8.2   *Cocaine: Trends in Annual Prevalence Among College Students vs. Others (1-4 Years Beyond High School)*

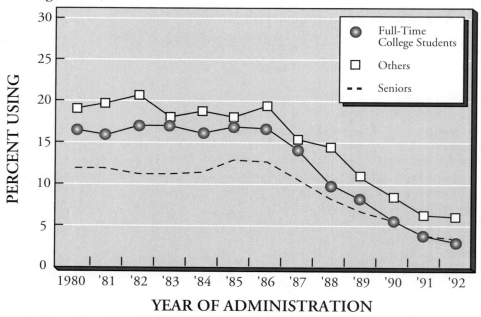

Source: Johnston, L.D., O'Malley, P.M. & Bachman, J.G. (1993). *National Survey Results on Drug Use from Monitoring the Future Study, 1975–1992.*

Figure 8.3   *Cocaine: Trends in Annual Prevalence Among Male and Female College Students*

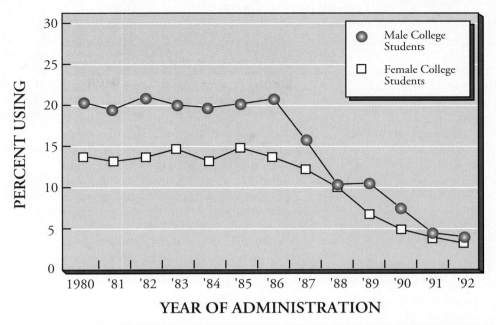

Source: Johnston, L.D., O'Malley, P.M. & Bachman, J.G. (1993). *National Survey Results on Drug Use from Monitoring the Future Study, 1975–1992.*

About 3,749,000 Americans over the age of twelve have tried crack. About 996,000 used the drug during the past year and about 417,000 reported having used the drug during the past month. Those in the twenty-six to thirty-four age category are most likely to have tried crack (4.2 percent), but those in the eighteen to twenty-five age category are as likely to have used during the past year (1.0 percent)(see Table 8.2). There was little difference between the eighteen to twenty-five population and twenty-six to thirty-four population in terms of use during the past month, which indicates regular use of the drug. Those over thirty-five were least likely to have tried crack (0.9 percent). Males were more likely than females to have used crack in every age category and use pattern.

Questions about crack cocaine were not included the Johnston, O'Malley, and Bachman surveys until 1987. In 1992, 2.6 percent of all seniors indicated they had tried crack. More than half of those (1.5 percent of all seniors) reported use in the last year, but only 0.6 percent of all seniors reported use in the last month. Among those seniors who used cocaine in any form during 1992 (3.1 percent of all seniors) about 36 percent used it in crack form, usually resulting from an addiction to it in powdered form.

Use of crack among high school seniors has declined since 1987. In 1987 lifetime prevalence for seniors was 5.4 percent as compared to 2.6 percent in 1990 and annual prevalence declined to 1.5 percent (down from 3.9 percent in 1987). Similar declines occurred among young adults and college students. Among young adults one to ten years past high school, lifetime prevalence declined from 6.9 percent in 1988 to 5.1 percent in 1992, and annual prevalence declined from 3.1 percent in 1988 to 1.4 percent in 1992. College students showed an annual prevalence of crack use of 0.4 percent in 1992, which indicated a sharp decrease from 2.0 percent in 1987. Their annual prevalence is now a fraction of that observed among their age-mates not in college (1.4 percent).

Johnston, O'Malley, & Bachman (1993, p. 6) suggested that the particularly intense media coverage of the hazards of crack cocaine probably had the effect of "capping" a possible epidemic by deterring many would-be users and by motivating many experimenters to desist use. While 2.6 percent of seniors report ever having tried crack, only 0.6 percent report use in the past month, indicating non-continuation by the majority of those who try it. This decline appears to hold true for middle-class youth.

Table 8.2   *Crack: Percent of Population Reporting Use of Crack Ever, Past Year, and Past Month (1993) by Sex and Age Groups for Total Population*

	Ever Used	Used During Past Year	Used during Past Month
	RATE ESTIMATES (PERCENTAGES)		
AGE			
12-17	0.4	0.2	0.1
Male	0.2	0.1	0.1
Female	0.5	0.4	0.2
18-25	3.5	1.0	0.4
Male	4.6	1.6	0.5
Female	2.5	0.5	0.3
26-34	4.2	1.0	0.3
Male	5.9	1.5	0.5
Female	2.5	0.4	0.4
35+	0.9	0.2	0.1
Male	1.5	0.5	0.2
Female	0.4	-	-
Total	1.4	0.5	0.2
Male	2.6	0.8	0.3
Female	1.1	0.2	0.1

- No estimate reported

Source: Adapted from Substance Abuse and Mental Health Services Administration. *National Household Survey on Drug Abuse:* Population Estimates 1993.

Unfortunately high-risk persons who live in poor, crime-ridden communities continue to be relatively immune to influences of the media.

Routes of Administration and Elimination

In order to obtain the full effects of cocaine, users generally inject or inhale the drug. Coca leaves may also be chewed or sucked, a common method in South America, so that the cocaine is absorbed slowly into the mucous membranes. Taken orally, the digestive tract slows the rate of absorption and the effects are weakened, but blood levels remain more constant and the physical and psychological detriments are lessened. Recreational cocaine users, including those who are considered chippers (occasional users), will generally inhale cocaine in its powdered form. The powder will be poured on a smooth, flat surface, such as a mirror, and shaped into thin lines that can be easily inhaled. This way the user can gauge approximately how much has been used by counting the number of lines inhaled. One end of a straw or rolled paper currency is placed in close proximity to the powder and the other end in a nostril to inhale the powder through. This method is efficient, as the nasal membranes are quite absorbent and quickly transport the cocaine to the brain. Those who are vulnerable to the rapidly addicting properties of cocaine and who graduate from chipping to chronic abuse frequently begin to smoke or inject cocaine to achieve more powerful effects.

Before the advent of crack, those who preferred to smoke cocaine chemically altered HC1 to form cocaine base or "free base" to further enhance its potent effects on the brain. This smokable form of cocaine is much purer. Cocaine free base is manufactured by separating the pure cocaine molecule from the HCl compound by extracting the cocaine into an organic substance like ether. When this

Inset 8.1

THE TRACKS OF MY TEARS

Comedian Richard Pryor has entertained the world for almost three decades and particularly engages his audience when he tells the story of how his cocaine habit nearly killed him when he was thirty-nine years old. Now fifty-five, Pryor lives to act as a constant reminder that cocaine can kill in more than one way. According to police, Pryor was sitting in his luxurious home in suburban Los Angeles preparing to free base cocaine when a volatile solvent exploded and engulfed him in flames. An elderly aunt who was in the house quickly smothered the flames with a blanket. But Pryor, who was in agonizing pain, threw off the blanket and bolted out of the house. The police found Pryor wandering half a mile away, his body so burnt that they first thought he was wearing makeup. When the officers attempted to stop him, Pryor muttered, "I can't stop. If I stop, I'll die." One officer walked with him until an ambulance arrived. Before getting into the ambulance, Pryor said, "I done wrong. They told me not to smoke that stuff." Doctors initially put his survival odds at one in three. When he responded well to treatment, however, his doctor said, "He's lucky to be alive. He's been through a hell of a lot."

free base is ignited and smoked, the effects are greatly increased as the pulmonary system rapidly diffuses and absorbs the cocaine for rapid delivery to the brain in a more concentrated fashion. Consequently, the likelihood of abusing this form of cocaine is as high as the IV method due to its profound rewards. Unfortunately for some users, igniting a volatile substance like ether can cause an explosion. The current prevalence of cocaine smoking has resulted in a tremendous increase in hospital and outpatient admissions for cocaine abuse (Gawin & Ellinwood, 1988). Smoking free base cocaine became less popular when users found that they could more easily make "crack" cocaine.

All forms of cocaine easily cross the blood-brain barrier although the free base or crack forms are more lipid soluble and thus transport even more easily. Once in the body, supplies become concentrated in the brain, spleen, and kidneys. The half-life of cocaine is unusually short-about forty minutes—and is a function of the acidity of the urine; the more acidic, the faster cocaine's excretion.

Active Properties of Cocaine

Cocaine has been incorrectly classified in some circles as a narcotic because it has sedative (sleep inducing) and anal-

gesic (pain relieving) properties. Cocaine has a tendency to block the transmission of action potentials so that messages are not conveyed from one neuron to another. The result of this blockage is a blunting of pain perception. Consequently, cocaine acts as a local anesthetic. Because large doses of cocaine are necessary to produce this effect, it is not used for this purpose. Other synthetic substitutes, such as procaine, are used instead because they lack cocaine's stimulating properties.

In actuality, cocaine is a CNS, psychomotor, and behavioral stimulant. Physiologically, it constricts blood vessels, increases heart rate, raises blood pressure, dilates pupils, and increases body temperature. Psychologically, it elevates mood, producing euphoria and alertness, and reduces fatigue. The social effects reinforce cocaine use by enhancing confidence, friendliness, calmness, disinhibition, self-admiration, interest, and anorexia (an eating disorder). High doses, however, can cause irritability, anxiety, and psychotic behavior. The physiological effects are largely due to the release of the neurotransmitter, norepinephrine, while the psychological effects are largely due to increased activity of the neurotransmitter, dopamine (see Figure 8.4).

Similar to PCP and amphetamines, cocaine mimics stimulation of the sympathetic nervous system by initiating f/f/f responses to stress with the release of norepi-

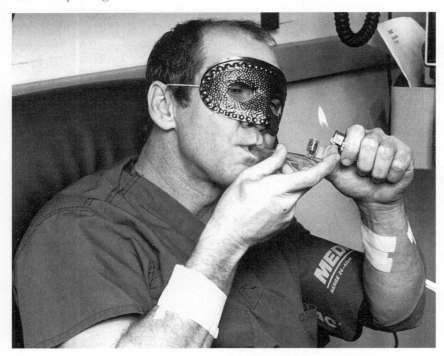

Smoking crack cocaine from a pipe (the user is masked to conceal his identity).

Figure 8.4   *The Dopamine Hypothesis of Cocaine Reinforcement.*

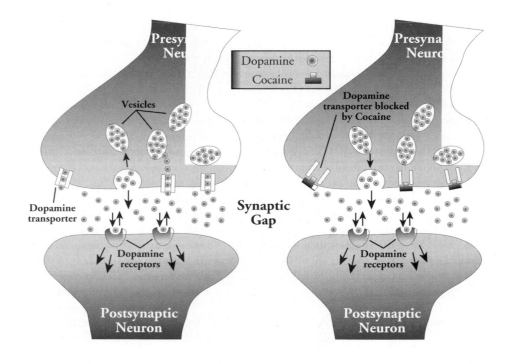

nephrine and dopamine. Thus, the natural effects of these transmitters are enhanced by blocking their reuptake. The user consequently experiences arousal, agitation, and a rush of euphoria, causing habit formation, particularly due to the increase in dopamine activity.

Neurobiological and Psychoactive Properties

Almost immediately upon inhaling cocaine, there is a feeling of numbness that users call freeze. This is quickly followed by an energy that makes users feel they can perform unusual acts of strength and intellectual prowess. Thoughts are perceived as clearer than normal and a feeling of confidence, well-being, and exhilaration cause users to believe they can perform tasks more efficiently and skillfully. As mentioned previously, it is these very perceptions that are reinforcing in a social or work environment. This high lasts for about twenty minutes and is rapidly replaced with a mild feeling of depression. In chronic users, the depression may be unbearable and severe. When cocaine is either injected or smoked in a free base form, a rush is experienced within a few seconds that has been described as a euphoria

more intense than a sexual orgasm. The experience of rush is a strong physiological reinforcement that sometimes entices recreational users to become more devoted to the drug. A psychological and physiological desire to avoid the onset of depression further encourages users to readminister doses of cocaine in a consecutive fashion during a binge.

The behavioral and psychological state produced is a function of neurochemical actions that are similar in many respects to all behavioral stimulants. They each activate the sympathetic nervous system. Specifically, all behavioral stimulants directly influence monoamine synapses, serotonin, epinephrine, norepinephrine, and dopamine. However, the mechanisms by which they affect these synapses differ. Cocaine, in particular, prolongs the amount of time that dopamine talks to the next cell when released, making it a reuptake blocker. Normally, neurotransmitter substances are reabsorbed by the sending cell after they exert their effects. Instead, cocaine blocks the reuptake of the neurotransmitter so dopamine clings to the next cell's receptor, thus providing stimulation beyond normal levels. The results of this action are reward and pleasure.

Stimulation of dopaminergic systems, supplied by cocaine use, produces one of the most powerful and rewarding experiences possible (Ritz et al., 1987). Figure

Figure 8.5 *Reward System of the Brain*

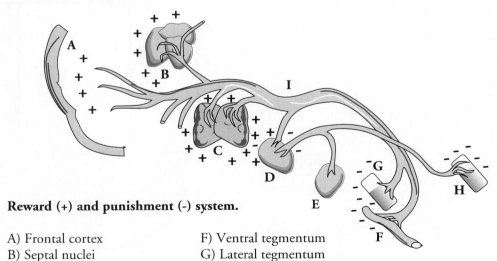

Reward (+) and punishment (-) system.

A) Frontal cortex
B) Septal nuclei
C) Hypothalamus
D) Mammillary body
E) Interpenduncular necleus

F) Ventral tegmentum
G) Lateral tegmentum
H) Periaqueductal gray matter
I) Medial forebrain bundle

Source: Valzelli, Raven Press, 1981

8.5 illustrates the pathways of the brain's reward system, believed to be involved in cocaine's pleasurable effects.

Drugs that block dopamine activity attenuate the reward value of cocaine and are presently being tested in the treatment of cocaine users, as we will discuss later in this chapter (Estroff & Gold, 1985; Kleber & Gawin, 1986). Such treatments suppress feelings of euphoria and the subjective experience of pleasure. Because dopamine arouses and reinforces behavior, the user is strongly motivated to pursue cocaine's high in the same way that individuals are motivated to experience natural reinforcers, such as food, water, and sex.

When certain areas of the pleasure center within the limbic system are stimulated with an electrical probe, the result is intensely pleasurable and reinforcing. Normally, these areas are stimulated by the satisfaction of natural drives, such as hunger, thirst, sex, and others associated with survival and social reward. Behaviors that allow an individual to satisfy these drives are, thus, pleasurable and subsequently reinforced.

When these areas are artificially stimulated, however, natural drives may be overwhelmed by the experience. (Figure 8.6 illustrates how primates quickly learn in the laboratory to self-administer cocaine to the neglect of other needs.) Although there is no natural drive for electrical stimulation, a drive may be created due to its intrinsic reward value—the sheer pleasure derived from the stimulation. Animals given two levers to press, one for food and one for electrical stimulation of the brain, will choose the lever delivering stimulation for the profound pleasure experienced. They may eventually die of dehydration and starvation as the natural drives to eat and drink become superseded.

As far as we know, electrical stimulation and drugs that act on these pleasure centers are the only forms of stimulation that provide reward in the absence of a natural drive. Cocaine in particular exerts its effects by increasing dopamine activity in these brain areas, sometimes result-

Figure 8.6   *Primates Who Self-Administer Cocaine May Do so Until They Die*

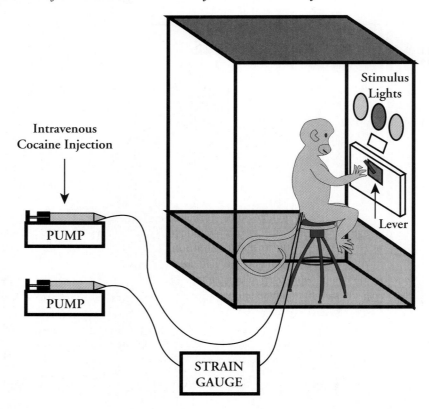

ing in the self-administration of cocaine despite the destructive consequences. The same scenario described above has been observed when the lever delivers cocaine instead of electrical stimulation.

Animals will continue to press this lever to the neglect of food, water, and sex and soon die of seizures, dehydration, or upper respiratory infections that their bodies can no longer resist (see Figure 8.7). Humans who use cocaine on a chronic basis frequently manifest these same behaviors as they begin to neglect social and biological needs and ignore the onset of physical and social problems simply due to the profound reward value of cocaine. The desire to care for one's children, for example, can be quite a powerful natural drive. Mothers addicted to cocaine frequently report that when their own children become an interference with "using," they are shipped off to grandma's house or left on a neighbor's doorstep. One man, while high on cocaine, threw his small son into a television set, killing him, simply because the boy was standing in front of it. When addicts are "straight," the love for their children returns, which can be quite painful as they realize their neglect. The guilt and regret can be incapacitating, which

can actually complicate treatment efforts; their feelings of inadequacy surface while self-esteem falls even further.

Performance levels may be improved with the use of cocaine when the performance decrements are due to boredom or fatigue. There is, however, a decline in selective attention and brain resources available for information processing following cocaine use. Thus, the acquisition of new information or behaviors becomes impaired. Users report that their behavior and ability are enhanced due to elevations in mood and performance although this effect is more perceived than real. At any rate, the belief that cocaine facilitates social behavior and performance levels further increases the popularity of its use.

In contrast to heroin which has built-in controls for its use, cocaine use is unlimited. Rats, for example, will limit the amount of heroin they use to no more than is necessary to produce a high. Thus, heroin does not debilitate the body, and the user will eventually fall asleep. Cocaine, on the other hand, stimulates the body and permits, if not encourages, further drug use. Also, due to the short duration of cocaine's effects, users believe that it is necessary to continue use in order to maintain the high and delay the

Figure 8.7   *Rat Self-Administering Cocaine*

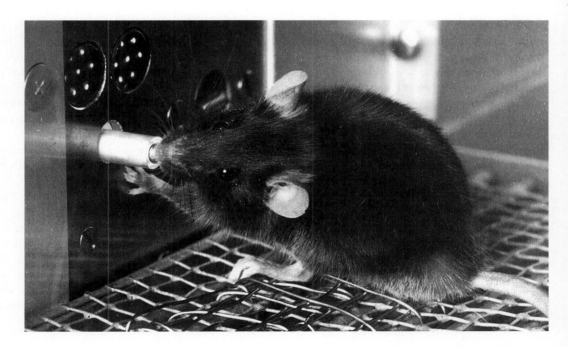

Figure 8.8   *Cumulative Number of Fatalities in Rats from Intravenous Cocaine and Heroin Self-administration During Unlimited Access to Drugs. Percentage of animals lost are depicted as a function of days of continuous testing. Solid circles indicate deaths in cocaine group; solid squares, deaths in heroin group.*

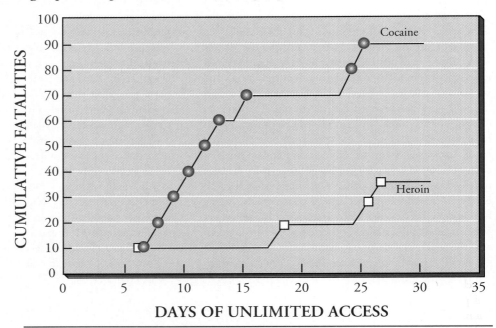

Source: Bozarth, American Medical Association, 1985

onset of depression that will follow soon after the last line, puff, or injection (see Figure 8.8.).

Tolerance, Dependence, and Withdrawal

Cocaine is now known to be one of the most powerful chemical rewards in the brain, even more so than heroin. Heroin had been considered more dangerous than cocaine, and it is more often associated with crime and decadence. Heroin's addictive properties are well documented; the physical dependency that results is marked by readily observable symptoms. Because of the more subtle and seemingly indirect effects of cocaine, it was once believed to be only psychologically addictive, with no development of tolerance and withdrawal symptoms. Thus, treatments for cocaine abuse have been primarily psychotherapeutic in nature. Heavy usage today, however, shows both the tolerance and withdrawal properties of cocaine.

Plasma levels of cocaine are directly related to the subjective experiences produced by the drug. In fact, the rate of change in plasma levels is more correlated with the psychological effects than with the absolute plasma levels of cocaine. Cocaine is rapidly metabolized by the brain from the bloodstream and then travels back to the blood. Due to the rapidity of this process, the high lasts only about fifteen to twenty minutes.

When cocaine is sniffed, it takes three to five minutes to reach the brain. When it is orally ingested it takes about fourteen seconds and when free based it takes about six seconds. Crack is similar to the freebased form. Tolerance develops rapidly, possibly after a single binge of two hours to two days. By the end of a day, the user may need three grams to feel high, a dose that would have been lethal at the start of the drug-taking session. As the concentrations of cocaine in the body increase, tolerance continues to build. Since the user must take the drug every twenty minutes to maintain the high, compulsion quickly results.

Tolerance to cocaine develops and diminishes rapidly. During a single binge, if a user sniffs cocaine every half hour or so, the sensations of rush, euphoria, and enhanced well-being will gradually decrease. After repeated episodes of such use over a period of several hours, these feelings will disappear altogether. It is at this point that the user will generally abstain for a while in order to obtain some rest and nourishment. Twenty-four hours later, this acute tolerance will be gone, and the user finds that cocaine will again provide the pleasurable experience he or she wants.

Although, for the most part, acute tolerance quickly disappears, longer-lasting effects known as reverse tolerance or sensitization have been observed when cocaine is used chronically. With tolerance, the user no longer experiences the same intensity of effects with each subsequent dosage; with sensitization, certain effects are actually exacerbated by repeated administration. Stereotyped behavior, for example, is seen in both rats and humans after chronic cocaine administration. Stereotyped behavior is characterized by repetitive movements that occur without purpose or function. In humans, these are generally simple tasks that are performed over and over again, such as rearranging furniture, continuous cleaning of the same object, or repeatedly taking apart and putting together a radio. If the person is interrupted during stereotyped behavior, he or she may become agitated and want only to return to the action. Related to this effect is an increase in spontaneous motor movement. There is some evidence that these long-term effects are due to the influence of cocaine on dopaminergic systems.

Another result of chronic abuse is called the kindling effect. The seizural threshold in the brain is lowered. Cocaine stimulates areas of the brain, such as the nucleus accumbens (Zito et al., 1985), deep within the cortex and limbic systems. It is this stimulation that is in large part responsible for the pleasure derived from cocaine use. After repeated stimulation, the brain becomes sensitized and neurons can begin to fire spontaneously, causing a seizure (see Figure 8.9).

Kindling produces no measurable tissue damage, however the lowered threshold for convulsive seizures appears to be permanent. The sudden occurrence of seizures or death in those who use only small amounts of cocaine, on a regular basis may be explained by this effect (Post et al., 1987). Consequently, there is a gradual increase in sensitivity of the brain to cocaine. Even when the user has not yet experienced a seizure, it may occur at any time. There is no evidence that kindling is due to an accumulation of the drug in the body or brain, since cocaine has a very short half-life, even when administered repeatedly. Instead, investigators believe that kindling may be the result of per-

manent alterations that occur within the monoamine neurotransmitter system and/or the receptor sites that cause an increased sensitivity to the drug over time.

Interestingly, the kindling effect in brain regions, such as the nucleus accumbens, is also associated with the profound craving experienced by cocaine addicts following withdrawal. This complication contributes substantially to relapse in those attempting to refrain from cocaine use. Raising this seizural threshold and, simultaneously, reducing craving is the focus of many pharmacologic treatment strategies at present.

Withdrawal symptoms have been described briefly above as including feelings of depression, lethargy, irritability, and long periods of sleeping and eating. These symptoms are primarily psychological. However they are no less real than purely physical symptoms because they are a result of neurochemical changes in the brain. These brain changes contribute to the abuse potential of cocaine, craving and relapse, aggressive or criminal behaviors (to obtain more drug), and sometimes suicide.

Another particularly disturbing long-term effect of cocaine use is the development of chronic depression or anhedonia, the inability to experience pleasure. These conditions may result when regulatory mechanisms that provide a system of checks and balances in the brain perceive that too much dopamine is available and that the neurotransmitter system is overactive. Autoreceptors that reside on sending cells signal the nerve to stop firing in order to bring the situation under control. With chronic use of dopaminergic stimulants, such as cocaine, autoreceptors become highly sensitive and may continue to signal a cease-fire. Consequently, less dopamine reaches the receiving cells, and activity in reward areas decreases (see Figure 8.10). In individuals who use cocaine regularly, the dopaminergic system may become chronically downregulated and the user may suffer from depression and underarousal even when not using cocaine (Van Dyke & Byck, 1983).

At present, it is unknown whether the neurotransmitter system ever completely recovers, and investigators speculate that some individuals may never again feel the full range of emotional highs and lows that once were possible.

Medical Complications

Some side effects associated with cocaine include blurred vision, coughing, headaches, tremors, weight loss, dry skin, hypertension, and sleep disturbances (see Table 8.3). Upper respiratory infections are also common as the immune sys-

Figure 8.9   *The Percentage of Amimals in Each Inbred Strain Experiencing Cocane Induced Seizures Following Each of the 10 Daily Injections of Cocaine. Each point represents the data from 8-20 animals initial sensitivity to cocaine-kindle seizures upon repeated exposure.*

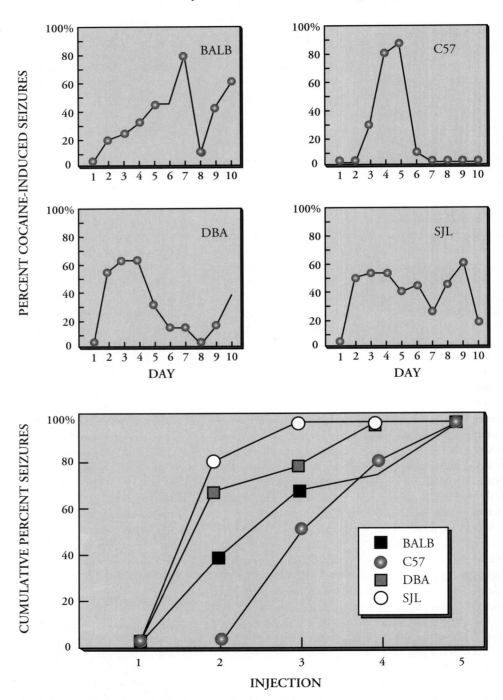

Source: Marley, Witken, and Goldberg, Elsevier, 1991

Figure 8.10   *Autoreceptor Influence on Dopamine Down Regulates Activity Levels when Overstimulated by Cocaine*

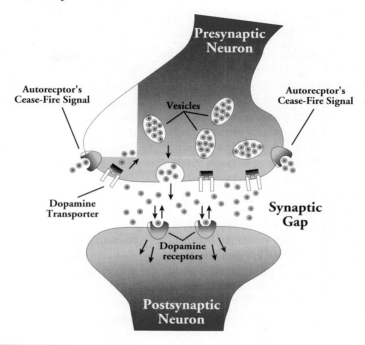

tem is compromised so that the body no longer has the ability to ward off infection. Inadequate nutrition and poor sleep habits contribute to the possibility of infections. There are also a number of changes in the endocrine system, for example, elevated levels of prolactin, a stress hormone, that may be observed for a prolonged period of time. Those who sniff the drug commonly suffer damage to the membranes of the nose and sinus tract. Some chronic sniffers eventually wear away the soft tissue in the nose, causing a hole to form that can only be repaired with plastic surgery. Unfortunately, the discomfort from sniffing cocaine is relieved by further use, which acts to numb the pain and the condition worsens.

The above symptoms are considered relatively minor because they are not immediately life threatening or damaging beyond repair. More serious toxic effects are possible when the user injects the drug with a hypodermic needle (see chapter 4).

A rise in blood pressure may be life threatening either over a period of several years or during the present drug-taking session. Internal bleeding sometimes results from the constriction of the vascular system because of high blood pressure. Cocaine's direct effects on the brain, along with the increase in blood pressure, can also cause fre-

quent headaches. In more severe cases, and without warning, cocaine may cause a seizure (due to the kindling effect described above) or a stroke (due to the increase in blood pressure and hemorrhaging of blood vessels). Strangely enough, a seizure or stroke may occur several days following the last dosage, even though the cocaine itself is no longer in the body. Researchers have found that one of the by-products of cocaine, benzoylecgonine, can remain in the brain for a long time and constrict the arteries in a powerful way. There is further evidence that chronic cocaine use may cause cerebral atrophy. Brain scans of habitual users have shown a substantial number of them to have brain damage that appears to be permanent.

Many casual users report they can feel their heart pounding during cocaine intoxication. This feeling is a common reaction and may not become complicated beyond that sensation. On the other hand, cocaine can cause sudden death by triggering an irregular heart rhythm called ventricular fibrillation. When blood pressure rises under normal circumstances, the body's protective response is to lower heart rate. Cocaine prevents the decline in heart rate, placing the user at risk for sudden death due to cardiac arrhythmia. Thus, acutely intoxicated patients should be

Table 8.3   *Cocaine: Possible Side Effects*

MINOR	MAJOR
Blurred Vision	Complications from injection
Coughing	Hypertension
Headaches	Internal bleeding
Tremors	Severe headaches
Weight loss	Seizure
Dry skin	Stroke
Hypertension	Obstructed blood flow
Insomnia	Cerebral atrophy
Upper respiratory infections	Ventricular fibrillation
Hormone disturbances	Ischemic attacks
Damage to nasal membranes	Infarction of spinal cord & brain
Irritability	Intraparenchymal &
Paranoia	subrachnoid hemorrhage
Agitation	Sudden death

treated as if they are having a heart attack and receive immediate medical attention. Len Bias, a renouned basketball player, died suddenly from ventricular fibrillation when celebrating being drafted into the NBA. It was latter discovered that he had been using cocaine.

George and Goldberg (1989) recently reported that the vulnerability of self-administering lethal doses of cocaine and the sensitivity to the effects of cocaine on the heart are related. Rats that would not self-administer cocaine at the levels normally required to achieve euphoria were unusually sensitive to cocaine's cardiac effects. There was speculation that sensitivity to cocaine in humans may vary in a similar way. Individuals who do not experience the euphoric effects of cocaine to the same extent as others do, may be more likely to administer higher doses to achieve euphoria or rush. If they are also more cardiac sensitive to the drug's toxic effects, they may be at particular risk of sudden death.

Other significant neurological complications have been noted in chronic cocaine users. These conditions have increased in frequency due to the recent availability of crack. Vascular complications, including transient ischemic attacks (lack of blood supply), infarction of the spinal cord and brain (tissue death due to loss of blood supply), and intra-

parenchymal and subarachnoid hemorrhage (bleeding within in an organ or within the covering of the brain) are known to develop from damage to blood vessels and to other neurochemical events triggered by cocaine (Mody et al., 1988).

Overdose may occur either from recreational use or by body packing, the act of stuffing a condom with cocaine and swallowing it for easy and undetectable transport. There are numerous instances of condom breakage. The cocaine then leaks into the digestive system, causing an immediate overdose, characterized by headache, high fever, respiratory depression, unconsciousness, and cardiac failure leading to death. Anticonvulsant and aychotic medications may be helpful, but if too much time elapses before treatment and recovery, the individual may either die or suffer from permanent brain damage due to oxygen loss.

Fetal Cocaine Syndrome

Effects of cocaine on the fetus and later behavior have been studied extensively over the past five or six years because of the alarming increase in the number of women using cocaine during their child-bearing years (Spear et al., 1989; Smith et al., 1989; Madden et al., 1986). Estimates on the number of infants exposed to cocaine while in the womb range from 91,000 (General Accounting Office, 1990) to 158,400 (Gomby & Shiono, 1991) to 240,000 (Besharov, 1989).

The placental barrier supplies nutrients to the fetus and, in most cases, provides protection from harmful substances. However, many substances that are present in the mother's blood may become available to the fetus, including cocaine and other psychoactive drugs. The higher the concentration in the mother's blood, the higher the concentration in fetal tissue. The risk of miscarriage throughout the pregnancy is elevated by related complications, such as precipitous labor, abruptio placenta, hemorrhage, anemia, increased blood pressure, and decreased uterine blood flow.

Studies have reported that there are basically two types of infant behaviors observed in cocaine exposed babies: they either act excitable, irritable, jittery, and inconsolable, or they are sluggish, depressed, and withdrawn.

It has been suggested that the hyperactive behaviors are due to the direct effects of cocaine on the fetus and the hypoactive behaviors are due to indirect effects and low birth weight. Of course, the precise consequences of cocaine exposure on any particular baby depends greatly on when in the pregnancy the fetus was exposed and how much was used.

Normal weight cocaine-exposed babies apparently cry more often and with longer duration and more variability. This is considered excitable behavior for an infant and may be due to increased respiratory effort, laryngeal tension, and constriction in their upper airways (Lester and Dreher., 1989). It is believed that these symptoms are due to cocaine's ability to prevent norepinephrine and dopamine from being absorbed, so they build up at the postsynaptic receptor sites. As these neurotransmitters accumulate, they activate the nervous system and trigger crying. Vasoconstriction, increased blood pressure, and rapid and irregular heart beat are also frequently observed.

On the other hand, low birth weight cocaine-exposed babies tend not to respond readily to environmental stimuli and stressors. It takes longer for them to begin to cry and the crying has a low intensity. Such depressed behavior in an infant may be a result of cocaine's ability to impair the availability of blood and oxygen to the fetus, resulting in hypoxia and retarded growth.

If the mother had used cocaine throughout her pregnancy, but stopped just prior to giving birth, the excitable behavior may be due to the infant's experience of withdrawal symptoms. If the mother had used a great deal of cocaine just prior to giving birth, the baby may be suffering from seizures that cause the excitability. Early maternal usage patterns are important in determining the infant's behavior. First trimester use is associated with stunted growth. Continued usage is associated with more direct effects on the fetus in terms of nervous system development, which occurs throughout pregnancy.

Cocaine using fathers may also contribute to cocaine-related problems in their offspring. A study conducted by Yazig, Odem & Polakoski (1991) presented evidence indicating that cocaine may bind to the male user's sperm and enter the mother's egg during the process of fertilization. The study suggests that birth defects in children could be related to cocaine use on the part of the father. It is also possible that the male's sperm could attach to any cocaine present in the reproductive track of the female and be carried into the egg.

The cost of caring for infants exposed to cocaine in the womb is high. When these babies are born, they require longer hospital stays at an additional cost of $5,200 more per infant than those not exposed to cocaine. Sometimes, an additional stay may be required (averaging $3,500 per infant) while the child awaits review by social services or placement in a foster home. In 1990, it was estimated that an additional $500 million was required for increased medical costs for these infants. This figure reflects only the hospital costs and does not include the costs of rearing these children to adulthood (Phibbs, Bateman, & Schwartz, 1991).

What we do not understand at this time is why some babies born to cocaine abusing mothers do not display detectable abnormalities. Many appear to be normal; they act and look fine. Now that an increasing number of these children are school aged, we are able to observe other, more subtle deficits that result from early cocaine exposure. In many of these children, language development lags behind, and attention deficit disorders are common. They are more distractible and have more difficulty learning in traditional settings.

Babies who were cocaine exposed tend to be more difficult to manage and many addicted mothers may not be able to cope with their babies' special needs. Neglect, abuse and abandonment are, thus, becoming more commonplace. Once such a child begins to demonstrate a learning disability or behavioral problem, appropriate intervention initiated by the parent/guardian is sorely needed and, if not available, the child will inevitably fail to adapt well in his or her environment. Obviously, being reared in a drug-infested environment with drug-using role models is not an optimal situation for any child, much less a child impaired by early exposure to cocaine.

Vulnerability to Cocaine Abuse

Not everyone who uses cocaine engages in compulsive use. However, no criteria exist that can reliably predict who will become a compulsive user. Therefore, we must assume that anyone who tries cocaine is at risk. Some investigators believe that preexisting differences in genetic, biochemical, physiological, psychological, and social factors play a role in determining whether an individual will discontinue use after a short time, remain a recreational user, or become a chronic, hardened user. Unfortunately, no reliable indicators of vulnerability to cocaine abuse have been identified although there is a general consensus that controlled use may become compulsive use when access to cocaine increases and dosages rise, or when a more efficient route of administration is used, such as IV or smoking (Gawin & Ellinwood, 1988).

Several other hypotheses are presently under investigation. Recent reports suggest that an individual is less likely to develop compulsive drug-using behavior if he or she has access to and values more socially acceptable activities that provide pleasure and is free from an environment conducive to drug-taking behavior. Those who live in drug-infested neighborhoods, who lack social support groups and/or legitimate opportunities for advancement, and who suffer from poor self-esteem or underlying psychopathology are at obvious risk for compulsive drug use. For these people, there are no real incentives not to use.

Several studies support the notion that there are specific psychopathologies that may increase the risk for eventual cocaine use (Gawin & Ellinwood, 1988; Kleber & Gawin, 1986; Newcomb & Bentler, 1986; Weiss, Murin, et al., 1983). Among adolescents, for example, depression has been found to lead to increased cocaine use over a one-year period (Newcomb & Bentler). Other independent studies show that adult cocaine users have a preponderance of mood disorders, such as depressive and bipolar (manic-depression) disorders (Weiss et al., Gawin & Kleber, 1985, 1986a). There is also a relative lack of cocaine users with panic disorder, which is not surprising given reports that cocaine may precipitate panic attacks (Aronson & Craig, 1986).

Because depression is characterized by low levels of dopamine and norepinephrine (Green & Costain, 1981; Maas, 1975; Schildkraut & Orsulak 1977; Snyder, 1980), the use of cocaine may help to enhance activity of these neurotransmitters, at least initially. When depressed patients are given low to moderate doses of cocaine, their moods becomes elevated. However, most found that symptoms of depression were worsened after receiving larger doses of the drug. It is possible that a subgroup of depressed patients who obtain symptom relief from cocaine are more likely to seek the drug again, leading to a heavier pattern of abuse. Consequently, like opiate and alcohol users, some cocaine users may also have peculiarities in brain function that predispose them to drug abuse. Therefore, many substance abusers may be self-regulating painful emotions, unpleasant realities in their lives, or psychological disorders with drugs (Khantzian, 1981; Rounsaville, Weissman, et al., 1982).

There may be a similar association between attention deficit disorder (ADD) and cocaine abuse (Khantzian, 1985). ADD, characterized by hyperactivity, impaired concentration, inattention, and impulsivity has been found in some studies to be more prevalent among delinquent and criminal populations (see Farrington, 1987; Hinshaw, 1987; Loeber & Dishion, 1983; Satterfield, 1978) than the rest of the population. Those with ADD have reported temporary improvement of their distractibility and impulsiveness in the early stages of cocaine use (Weiss et al., 1988). A dopamine deficiency has been found in ADD, and dopamine agonists have been successful in the treatment of ADD (Cocores, Dackis, et al., 1986). There is also

evidence that cocaine withdrawal in ADD individuals is exaggerated due to the decline of dopamine function associated with both preexistent and cocaine withdrawal-induced deficiencies (Cocores, Davies, et al., 1987).

Also intriguing is the finding that cocaine abusers have more affective disorders among first-degree relatives when compared with first-degree relatives of other drug-dependent patients (Nunes et al., 1988; Weiss et al., 1988). There is also an increased incidence of drug abuse and alcoholism among cocaine-addicted family members (Miller, Gold, et al., 1989). Although not direct evidence of a genetic influence, a familial relationship may influence cocaine dependence in offspring in one of three ways: (1) there may be a general vulnerability to drug dependence that may not be specific to a particular drug, (2) familial environmental and shared experiences may contribute substantially to drug dependence, or (3) genetic similarities in psychiatric disturbances, such as affective disorders, may place offspring at risk for cocaine dependence.

It is possible, therefore, that cocaine users who are afflicted with other psychiatric disorders that are either preexisting or comorbid (simultaneous) may be self-medicating. Unfortunately, because both psychiatric disturbances and cocaine abuse generally do not occur until late adolescence or early adulthood, it is difficult to ascertain whether one predated the other to determine whether one was a cause of the other. Another factor complicating our efforts to recognize the coexistence of psychopathology is that as drugs become more available in our society, nondrug-related psychopathology becomes less of a risk factor for cocaine dependence as social factors take precedence (Weiss et al., 1988).

Because psychopathology and cocaine use tend to coexist in many users, characterizing them according to their psychiatric or psychological symptoms may facilitate treatment efforts. Numerous reports show that cocaine abusers with psychiatric comorbidities respond much more favorably to treatment efforts when therapies appropriate for their underlying disorder are incorporated (Gawin & Kleber, 1984; Khantzian et al., 1984; Weiss & Mirin, 1986). The relapse rate among patients undergoing such pharmacotherapy appears to be significantly reduced.

Lifestyles of the Crack Addict: Prostitution and Violence

As mentioned earlier in this chapter, the use of crack cocaine has led to the development of a subculture of crack users whose lives revolve around the use and purchase of the drug. Social relationships are altered as users become hooked and interact exclusively with those who use and sell. Basic needs and caring for children become secondary to the drug that, in a sense, becomes their lover. Many crack users report that they are not addicted and can stop at any time; however, they are either unwilling or not ready to do so. One woman in a city jail reflects on her crack habit in a typical way:

> I can't wait to get outta here and git back to my crack. My man's waiting for me too—we do it together. I got custody of my three kids, but they little and don't do any yet. I don't let them touch it. And if the mother fuckers git near my crack I wop 'em good. I ain't addicted. I can stop anytime. But I don't want to cause nothin' makes me feel so good. If my man ever stops using it or tells me not to, he's outta here. Nobody interferes with my crack.

Crack houses became popular in recent years as users attempted to gain more control over the danger and uncertainty that abound in the open street market. Both users and sellers frequent these crack houses—some of them may live there if they have no other shelter. Dealers come and go and are considered a nuisance in the neighborhood. Property values quickly decline where crack houses are located, particularly because there is no upkeep on these houses and they quickly become dilapidated. Police raids on crack houses are common since they may "sweep up" a number of users and sellers in a single operation.

Compared with the heroin subculture, which has been around for a long time, the crack subculture is highly unstable. There are no normative rules or restrictions on crack's use or distribution due to its relative novelty. Heroin dealers do not generally eat up their profits by using the drug themselves, while crack dealers use crack with a passionate obsession. As a result, crack dealers are not as shrewd or successful as heroin dealers and do not have the same profit margin.

Perhaps the most disconcerting travesty of the crack subculture is the propensity for child abuse and neglect. We discussed previously how crack affects the developing fetus and child in terms of its medical effects. We did not, however, mention the impact of the socialization process on children of crack addicts. Because crack-using parents must take a hit every twenty minutes or so to remain high, their day is virtually devoted to the use and purchase of the drug. Child care takes a backseat while the parent is absorbed in daily or, more accurately, hourly drug-related rituals. Children commonly remain unclothed, undiapered, unfed, and unloved for days at a time. These sorely neglected children are not toilet trained, do not learn how to eat with a fork and spoon, and do not learn basic social and academic skills. Once they are school aged, there may be no one to take them to school or give them breakfast, they still may not be entirely toilet trained, they do not know the alphabet or how to spell their names, and do not recognize simple colors or shapes and other skills that most three-year-olds are capable of. Those who do attend school find no reinforcement or encouragement at home for learning and attaining an education. Many of them are also physically and sexually abused. Thus, aside from the impact of in utero exposure to cocaine, these children are further disadvantaged in the social and educational realms.

Prostitution, another aspect of the crack subculture, has become a permanent fixture in many crack houses (Inciardi, Lockwood, et al., 1993). Although the relationship between drug addiction and prostitution is not new, the women who exchange sex for crack are a new breed of prostitute. Women have traditionally used prostitution as a source of income to purchase drugs as well as other goods. In the crack houses, the women barter sex for crack. The sexual exchange often occurs in a designated room after a use fee is paid to the owner of the crack house. Sex may occur in the main smoking rooms as well. Some women work for the house and offer free sex to valued customers (Inciardi et al., 1993, p. 71). Many of these women and girls remain in the crack house for extended periods of time, providing sexual favors to multiple customers simply to acquire a continuous supply of hits. Heroin using females, on the other hand, do not need a fix so often. As a result, female heroin users do not engage in as much sex and use a portion of their earned money for commodities other than drugs.

There appears to be a relationship between crack use and hypersexual behavior (Inciardi et al., 1993). Although some users report a heightened sexual response under the influence of cocaine, others find it impedes sexual functioning. However, crack's disinhibiting effects seem to invite women to use sex as a means of acquiring the drug, resulting in multiple sexual contacts. Many women report that they were willing to engage in the most degrading of sex acts as long as they were fed a supply of crack. Rarely are condoms used as protection against AIDS. Therefore, the hypersexual behavior associated with crack has proba-

Inset 8.2

LIFESTYLES OF THE RICH AND FAMOUS

Jeff was a good-looking all-American high school student from Florida who liked to enjoy himself. He liked to attend parties, meet girls, and get high on marijuana. He had never been in any serious trouble and did relatively well in school. His worst crime was his hedonism—he had a passion for women and spent much of his time looking for ways to feel good. At a loss for what to do after high school ended, he joined the Army. During this time, Jeff discovered cocaine. He liked it right away and primarily sniffed the powder form. Within months, he was given a dishonorable discharge although none of his friends were quite sure why. Shortly after his return home, he quickly became bored and moved to California. It was there that his life changed dramatically. He began using cocaine by freebasing it, and he became rapidly addicted. He attended orgies, visited adult book stores, and even took a job as a male stripper. Searching for pleasure in any form, he became bisexual. Jeff's cocaine habit grew to the point that he began dealing to support his habit. Eventually, as his habit consumed him, he began ripping off his customers by selling them cocaine diluted with laxative and other non pharmaceutical, readily available fillers. While on a major drug buy for a friend, he took the friend's money—$50,000—and disappeared. A contract was put out on his life. He strayed from city to city, and his living conditions deteriorated as did his health and his looks. Still hooked on cocaine, he began to associate almost exclusively with transvestites (cross dressers) and was arrested during a raid on an adult bookstore for having a homosexual encounter in a peep show booth. He was essentially hedonistic, and at this point in his life, given the drug-infested lifestyle he now maintained, he pursued anyone or anything that could meet his needs for pleasure with drugs or sex. He stole from friends, lived in shacks ridden with cockroaches and dirt, and associated only with other drug users. When he eventually returned home to Florida, he was a wreck—depressed, sickly, and hopelessly addicted.

bly made a significant contribution to the AIDS epidemic. Inciardi et al. (1993) also found that female crack users had a much higher incidence of sexually transmitted diseases, such as genital herpes, gonorrhea, syphilis, and genital sores.

A more disturbing behavioral effect of cocaine is the tendency toward aggression or, in some cases, violence. Although it is less likely that an individual without preexisting aggressive or violent tendencies will become truly dangerous during cocaine intoxication, those users with aggressive tendencies or who use the drug in a violent social context may be more likely to become dangerous during or immediately after cocaine use.

As with stimulants/amphetamines, the initial feelings following cocaine use are vitality, assertiveness, and alertness. Feelings of irritability, nervousness, and frenzy frequently ensue after prolonged use. Cocaine addicts may become hypervigilant, highly suspicious, unpredictable,

belligerent and even violent. Crack is even more likely to be associated with psychotic symptoms and thoughts or acts of violence (Honer et al., 1987). The suspicious, paranoid behaviors and thought disorders of chronic cocaine users may last beyond the immediate effects of the drug and eventually lead to psychosis. These frequent consequences of chronic cocaine use are mediated primarily through the dopaminergic system, which is centrally involved in psychotic syndromes.

The user begins to crave cocaine following acute withdrawal from the drug. Some clinicians believe that the hunger for cocaine may be more powerful than the hunger for heroin (Cohen, 1987). Some addicts will do almost anything for a fix, which indicates that the drive for cocaine is at least as intense as that of an individual undergoing heroin withdrawal. Cocaine craving is associated with irritable feelings, agitated behavior, a depression, discomfort, and a perceived need for more drug. Many chronic users have developed a compulsive use pattern difficult to break, and they begin to stalk the drug. Users have been known to scrape residual cocaine powder from mirrors, dollar bills, pipes, and other paraphernalia in a desperate search for a high. Others may hit the streets, looking for friends who use or sellers in the area who can supply even a small quantity. If money is scarce, other means may be used to obtain the drug, such as sex or violence. Because of the depression, agitation, and irritability that have set in, it is during this stage of withdrawal that some users may resort to prostitution, stealing, or aggressive and perhaps violent means of cocaine acquisition (Estroff & Gold, 1985).

Direct effects of cocaine, however, cannot be held completely accountable for the drug-crime connection. The emergence of a powerful drug market and a dedicated drug-using subgroup has dire sociocultural consequences that contribute to crime and violence. Such violent subcultures associated with cocaine use are more likely to form in large inner-city areas where the propensity for violence already exists. In Washington, D.C., for example, the entry of crack cocaine into the drug scene in recent years has been associated with a dramatic increase in violent crime. The murder rate in our nation's capitol has exceeded the rates of the other cities that previously held the record: Miami and New York City. Popular media sources such as *The Washington Post* (Gugliotta & Isikoff, 1990) have noted that, although drug use is abating in some areas, the legacy of the crack epidemic is a violent subculture that is now fueled by the large numbers of weapons available. There are reports of a new street ethic favoring the use of violence, particularly murder, to prove one's manhood and become an accepted member of the street or gang culture. According to these reports, the use of firearms has become the most popular method to solve disputes and establish a trafficker's territory. High profits from the sale of cocaine and crack have fueled aggressive competition among sellers. At present, many of those involved in violent acts are not even using drugs, and an increasing number of violent crimes are not associated with the drug market. Officials are puzzled by this trend toward purposeless, senseless violence just for the sake—or perhaps excitement—of it. The preoccupation with violence within the crack culture is apparent; a violent reputation for a dealer to exert control over turf has become necessary and desirable. Consequently, the pharmacologic properties of cocaine associated with an increased tendency to violence are not solely responsible for violent behavior. The cocaine market has spurred the emergence of perhaps an even more insidious violence market that now exists independent of drug-related activities.

Treatment

Treatment for the acute effects of cocaine must begin with a period of detoxification and, in more serious cases, medicinal control of cocaine's physical complications. Medications with anticonvulsant properties (i.e., diazepam or phenytoin) and antipsychotic agents (i.e., chlorpromazine) may be given to help control the patient and the likelihood of seizures. Once the patient is out of immediate danger, tranquilizing drugs may be given for several days.

If a cocaine addict is not aggressively treated, the likelihood that he or she will return to the drug is quite high. Because craving and depression are experienced immediately following the last dose, the first inclination is to readminister cocaine to relieve the dysphoria and satisfy the craving. Furthermore, cocaine addicts have a tendency to be irritable, paranoid, and uncooperative. For these reasons, cocaine users are extremely difficult to treat for any period of time. Motivation must be quite high and environmental circumstances must be conducive. Time is the essential ingredient for effective treatment. Regardless of whether the treatment is pharmacological, behavioral, or psychotherapeutic, the success of any treatment effort relies on the willingness of the individual to be patient until the remedy can take effect. Due to the nature of both the drug and the lifestyles of many cocaine addicts, such patience is not common and cocaine users have a high probability of dropping out of any treatment program in its very early stages.

Initial outpatient treatment for the first stage of abstinence commonly includes multiple weekly contacts with a practitioner or group setting. Peer support groups, family therapy, behavioral reconditioning, urine surveillance, educational meetings, and individual counseling may all be important depending on the individual needs of the patient. It is absolutely crucial that the addict is not exposed to situations and people previously associated with drug-taking behaviors. Interactions should be restricted to appropriate role models who are, obviously, drug free and can provide support, supervision, and alternate activities. In optimal circumstances, hospitalization will only be necessary if these efforts continue to fail. Strategies for treating the second stage of abstinence, or the prevention of relapse, are described below.

COCAINE AND VIOLENCE

The Case of Reciprocal Paranoia

Mike and Joe had been snorting cocaine for a couple of years. They were small-scale dealers, second-order relatives, and good friends. As time went on, Mike noticed occasions when he got "sick in the head" and experienced strong beliefs that people were going to kill him and his family. He also had compelling thoughts that he should kill Joe and the others who were plotting to do him in. These ruminations only occurred when he was on cocaine. He bought a rifle to protect himself, and when he was "sick", he usually stayed home, afraid to go out, with a weapon always close by. One day Joe angrily accused Mike of turning his wife onto cocaine and of having sex with her. So far as can be determined, this was an incorrect accusation. Nevertheless, it made Mike even more suspicious during his paranoid intervals that Joe intended to harm him. Mike came to the conclusion that it was Joe who was playing around with his wife (probably a delusional notion).

One day after having sniffed some cocaine, Mike got his rifle and drove his car to Joe's house. Joe happened to be in the front yard. He walked over to the car. Joe was heard to say "Go home, take a rest. You're upset." Mike fired. The bullet ruptured the subclavian vessels and Joe [bled to death].

Mike then proceeded to a pool hall where Joe's brother and another man, whom he did not like and who he owed money, were known to hang out. He fired a number of shots into the pool hall, killing an adolescent and severely wounding a man, neither of whom were the intended victims. Mike said later that he wanted to kill Joe's brother, because he knew he would surely avenge his brother's death.

Since being jailed, Mike has had no further episodes of paranoid thought disorder. Cocaine and benzoylecgonine were present in his blood and urine at the time of arrest. Cocaine and benzoylecgonine were not present in Joe's blood, liver, or brain at the time of his autopsy.

The Case of Pathological Jealousy

Jim was a compulsive free base smoker. He no longer seemed to get much pleasure from using but nevertheless persisted, despite obvious severe weight loss, visual hallucinations that were very disturbing, and an inability to work satisfactorily. He was fired from his job but did not mind because it gave him the opportunity to stay home and watch his wife. According to Jim, she was exceedingly skillful at contacting a series of lovers in the hall and laundry room of their apartment building. Her protestations only served to reinforce the conviction that she was consistently unfaithful. He was never able to catch any of her lovers in the act, but he had seen strange men in the building. Furthermore, he blamed his impotence on her promiscuity.

After Jim made a serious threat with a kitchen knife, his wife, Joan became very upset and called a psychiatrist to ask for help. She wanted Jim "put away." It was explained that under state law, he might be detained for three days since he was mentally intact except for his single delusion. She would have to sign a complaint, and Jim would be even more suspicious and angry with her when he was released. It was suggested that she contact the police. She already done this, but the police were unwilling to make an arrest without evidence of actual harm. Jim was also unwilling to obtain treatment; he claimed that it was Joan who needed treatment. It was suggested to Joan that she leave the city and go to a place where Jim could not find her. The proposed solution was not a good one, but better alternatives were not obvious since it was believed that Joan was in a very precarious situation.

Acute Paranoia Can Be Harmful to Your Health

The victim, Henry, was a nasal cocaine user and a dealer. Often when he used cocaine even in moderate amounts, he had illusions (heard a car backfire and believed that people were shooting at him), hallucinations (heard voices and sounds coming from the attic), and delusions (people were trying to steal his cocaine). He was not suspicious about his common-law wife or his three-year-old child, and when he was off cocaine for a few days, the paranoid notions subsided.

One evening he went out to the local bar, had a drink, and met two strangers who seemed to be compatible. He invited them home for some more beer, and they had a good but noisy time. His wife complained that they were waking the sick baby, and when they did not quiet down, she left for her parents' home with the child.

Henry continued to snort coke and drink some beer. By this time the guests were quite drunk. Suddenly, Henry grabbed his shotgun, which was kept under the bed and ordered the two strangers out, while asking what they were doing there. Instead of leaving, one of the guests seized the shotgun and blew a hole in Henry's chest. When apprehended, the guests had over 0.2 percent BAC [blood alcohol content] but no cocaine in their urine. At the autopsy, Henry's blood and urine were positive for cocaine and benzoylecgonine. Blood alcohol was 0.08 percent, and small amounts of diazepam were found in his blood and urine.

Pharmacologic Treatments

Because long-term abstinence from cocaine after chronic abuse is marked by neurochemical changes that resemble the biochemistry of depressive disorders, most treatment strategies are presently focusing on restoring the brain's chemistry to its predrug condition. Cocaine addiction is in large part a chemical disease that throws the whole reward system off balance. In order to target both the depression and the craving that are primarily responsible for the user's return to the drug, the clinician frequently combines traditional psychotherapeutic and behavioral approaches with pharmacological treatments that are commonly used for depression and seizural disorders (associated with craving).

The second phase of withdrawal from cocaine, as described above, is marked by the onset of craving for the drug, which motivates the user to replenish his or her supply. Following acute withdrawal symptoms, powerful craving for cocaine sends most users back into the world of drugs. They feel that they need the drug to be normal again and to eliminate the symptoms of irritability, depression, fatigue, dysphoria and the absence of pleasurable feelings from daily activities. These symptoms, particularly craving, which profoundly contributes to the relapse rate, are the focus of contemporary treatment approaches. The primary objective is to promote extinction of the conditioned response to using cocaine by blocking its rewarding effects and reducing craving.

Treatments for cocaine abuse that show some measure of success are modeled after information on neurotransmitter involvement and an understanding of the reward and pleasure centers of the brain (Kleber & Gawin, 1986). The most efficacious efforts have focused on the dopamine system. When the nervous system is repeatedly stimulated by cocaine, its adaptive response is to downregulate activity. In particular, autoreceptors function to control the supersensitivity of dopaminergic receptor sites that has developed from chronic cocaine use. Even after drug use has been terminated, the brain's autoreceptors will continue to compensate for the increased levels of activity by depressing activity and, consequently, depressing mood and the ability to experience pleasure. This effect is generally seen several days after abstinence when anhedonic symptoms peak.

With this information in mind, pharmacologic treatments for cocaine addiction focus on eliminating the drug's reward value by blocking dopamine receptors that are targeted by cocaine. If another substance with an affinity for dopamine receptors is already at the receptor site, cocaine will not be able to exert its stimulatory effects. Certain antidepressants that act in the brain by blocking dopamine receptors (e.g., desipramine and bromocriptine) are being used in both animal and human clinical and experimental trials with much success. Mammals who readily self-administer cocaine reduce their cocaine intake under the influence of these dopamine blocking agents (deWit & Wise, 1977; Risner & Jones, 1980). Human users also experience fewer withdrawal symptoms and a reduction in cocaine use when receiving these antidepressants (Dackis & Gold, 1985; Gawin, 1986; Kleber & Gawin, 1986; O'Brien et al., 1988). Furthermore, these medications directly influence the neurochemical systems responsible for any preexisting or resulting affective disorder to treat comorbid psychiatric disorders that may threaten the success of the treatment program.

Amantadine hydrochloride is another drug that augments the release of dopamine and is currently being used to treat the depression of cocaine abstinence. Users previously unable to abstain have been better able to stay off the drug while taking amantadine. In a sense, this is a type of replacement therapy.

A recent breakthrough in the treatment of cocaine users has occurred with the discovery that carbamazepine (Tegretol), an anticonvulsant, alters receptor function in the center of the brain responsible for pleasure and craving. Ongoing studies have found evidence that the drug helps to attenuate the craving that occurs after withdrawal (Halikas et al., 1989). Craving is thought to result from the biochemical instability that develops because of the depletion of natural brain chemicals in pleasure areas of the limbic system, such as the nucleus accumbens. Each time an individual uses cocaine, there is a small but progressive increase in sensitivity with the pleasure center, resulting in a lowering of its seizural threshold—the kindling response. This effect appears to be associated with drug craving. Carbamazepine works by raising the seizural threshold so that the brain may become less sensitive to cocaine's effects and craving will be reduced. Although this effect is not well understood at present, the use of this therapy shows substantial promise.

Lithium carbonate, a drug commonly and effectively used to treat manic-depression, has also been reported to block cocaine and amphetamine induced euphoria (Gawin & Kleber, 1983; Van Dyke & Byck, 1983). Lithium has been used with some moderate success in cocaine abusers by lowering relapse rates.

Another form of therapy to emerge as a possible adjunct to traditional treatments is the use of neurotransmitter precursor therapy (see Chapter 4) that facilitates the synthesis of neurotransmitters. Cocaine places an initial strain on various neurotransmitter systems, causing a hyperstimulation of that system followed closely by a depletion of electrochemical activity. Because several neurotransmitters, including dopamine, are synthesized from components of our diet (e.g., amino acids) called precursors, it is possible to revitalize the transmitter system without introducing a drug. NPT involves the administration of dietary precursors that facilitate the synthesis and activity of the transmitters depleted by chronic cocaine use. Tyrosine is a dietary precursor to dopamine and norepinephrine and has been shown to elevate them when given orally (Fernstrom, 1981a). In principle, NPT will help to restore depleted transmitters to therapeutic levels. Clinical trials with NPT have tried to elevate levels of dopamine, serotonin, and norepinephrine and, consequently, reduce the depression associated with cocaine withdrawal. The success of cocaine treatment programs have been enhanced when NPT is used in conjunction with traditional and other appropriate psychiatric therapies (Gold, Pottach, et al., 1983; Trachtenberg & Blum, 1988; Wilbur, 1986). Patients report that these precursors reduce craving for cocaine somewhat and block the euphoric effects when cocaine is used simultaneously.

Psychotherapeutic and Behavioral Treatments

Supportive measures such as counseling, group therapy, exercise, resocialization, aversion therapy, avoidance strategies, psychological strengthening and self-help groups are an essential component of drug abuse treatment. Pharmacologic approaches should never be used alone; other forms of therapy to change behavioral habits, lifestyles, and thinking patterns must accompany medicinal therapies. Simply giving a pill will certainly not change the behavioral repertoire of an individual whose life now revolves around a drug with the abuse potential of cocaine. It is clear that cocaine abuse, like other varieties of drug abuse, is maintained by numerous conditions, each interacting with the other. They include individual susceptibilty, setting, behaviors revolving around use of the drug, and the immediate and delayed rewarding consequences.

To address the many conditions that reinforce cocaine abuse, several approaches may be taken. The first approach attempts to change the environment to modify factors that promote cocaine use and maintain dependence. Health education, behavioral modification, self-help programs and others should be available and customized for individual needs. Additional emphasis should be placed on two strategies in particular: (1) the primary prevention of cocaine abuse, by identifying those contextual and environmental conditions that promote it; and (2) relapse prevention, by identifying those cues and reinforcers that make it difficult to maintain a drug-free existence.

One particular method for a subpopulation of cocaine users is presently being tested and shows promise as an effective behavioral therapy (Higgins et al., 1991). Cocaine addicts are given financial rewards for abstinence. Those attempting to kick the cocaine habit are given vouchers for commodities and desirable activities each time they deliver a clean urine sample, indicating that they have not used cocaine in recent days. The objective is to replace cocaine's reinforcing effects with other pleasures seen as desirable by the addict. The purchases made possible with the vouchers are designed to ease the user back into a drug-free lifestyle. This system of rewards rather than punishing previous drug use has been successful in preliminary trials. Obviously, this strategy may be more effective in those who are not also involved in drug dealing. The financial rewards of dealing may outweigh the relatively small incentives provided by a voucher.

The second approach, possibly complementing the ones described above, requires that health officials, clinicians, parents, and users recognize the powerful hold cocaine has over those who become compulsive users. Cocaine's seduction can be overwhelming, and that force should not be overlooked. We frequently underestimate the disruption to lifestyle and health that cocaine is responsible for. Users commonly find that the drug enables them to confront and cope with (in their perception) daily stressors and that their lives become organized around its use. Allowances for the time to readapt to a new way of living need to be made, and entirely new patterns of learning need to be established that do not involve external dependencies. Programs that support behavioral change and readjustments have the most promise for successful abstention.

Third, programs must also include behavioral substitutes and alternative means to obtain stimulation and contentment. Relaxation techniques, meditation, exercise, and other activities help to compensate for the hole left for an ex-user. Sometimes, depending on the personality of the patient, exciting or thrill-seeking activities such as sky-diving or sports may be a suitable substitute. Ex-users frequently become involved in helping others with their addictions, either as a professional or as a concerned individual. These people find that conveying their experiences and relating to others in need is especially gratifying. Taking on this type of role further benefits them by encouraging them to succeed as an example to those who are presently addicted, and by being constantly reminded of what can happen if they relapse.

Finally, it is particularly important that the cocaine abusing individual be evaluated for an underlying psychiatric, medical, or psychological disorder. Even once an individual learns to abstain from abusing cocaine, in the presence of a disorder that has remained untreated, the chances for relapse are high. Not all cocaine abusers have an underlying disturbance that predated their drug use by any means, but most will have psychiatric or psychological problems after withdrawing even after several months. Long-term abstinence from cocaine is associated with severe depression, for example, so treatment efforts must focus on the individualized needs of the user.

■ Summary

Only recently have we begun to truly understand the power of cocaine over the user's mind and body. Some say that only the initial decision to use cocaine is a purely voluntary option; subsequent uses increase the power of the drug over the user's decision-making ability. This may be especially true for crack, a form of cocaine that is particularly potent and addictive. A user may become addicted to crack after a single overnight binge, which results in both tolerance and withdrawal symptoms. Although the tolerance for cocaine subsides quite rapidly, withdrawal symptoms may be profound enough to compel the user to continue administering the drug. Although the withdrawal symptoms are not visibly physical as are those produced by heroin, the psychological manifestations of cocaine withdrawal (e.g., depression, irritability, and craving) are a direct result of brain chemistry changes that act as potent reinforcers. Until recent years, we did not recognize cocaine addiction due to the elusiveness of these symptoms.

It is clear that many users fall victim to the power of cocaine. What is not at all clear is why many people do not become addicted and may either discontinue use or simply chip the drug. Researchers are attempting to elucidate those conditions that make certain users vulnerable to cocaine dependency while others seem relatively insulated from becoming compulsive users. Although we do not yet have the answers, we do know that people with assets and options in their life are much less likely to become dependent on any drug, including cocaine. Those individuals with high self-esteem, who have access to alternative lifestyles, job opportunities, channels for social mobility, and a strong family structure and values are somewhat protected from drug dependency. On the other side of the coin, those who come from disadvantaged communities, who have few choices in life, low self-esteem, and dysfunctional families have less reason not to use drugs. These conditions are, obviously, pervasive in inner-city neighborhoods and may contribute to extensive cocaine use that we observe in those areas, a fact highlighted by the finding that middle-class youth are using cocaine less frequently, while inner-city youth have stepped up their usage. But some people from middle and upper classes use cocaine, sometimes compulsively, as well. We suspect that in more privileged communities, drug abuse may be more directly a result of underlying psychopathology and family disorganization.

Cocaine dependency may be crippling on a physical level and is responsible for numerous health-related conditions, including infections, heart disturbances, internal bleeding, headaches, hypertension, seizures, cardiac arrest, stroke, hemorrhaging, and other neurological and cardio-

vascular disorders. Although those who use cocaine have an increased likelihood of suffering these effects simply as a function of repeated exposure, it is noteworthy that even a single administration can result in one of these potentially fatal problems. Very much like a game of Russian Roulette, every time that trigger is pulled—including the first time—the gun may fire unexpectedly. No one is immune. And of even more concern is exposure of unborn children to cocaine. Although some researchers may argue that the results of cocaine exposure to a fetus are unclear and unpredictable, evidence is compelling that a pregnancy is seriously jeopardized and that the resulting child is likely to suffer deficits in learning, thinking, decision making, judgment, and behavior controls. Coupled with the reality that cocaine-using mothers are much less capable of providing the emotional or basic needs that youngsters require, these children must endure unusual hardships. We may eventually find ourselves caring for them in hospitals and correctional institutions.

Equally important is the effect of cocaine on a social or personal level. Users frequently lose productivity, neglect social and basic needs, lack self-support, become dependent, and display an increased incidence of antisocial activity. Consequently, as a society, we suffer the burden in terms of both economic and social costs.

CHAPTER 9

Stimulants: Amphetamines

Objectives

1. To discuss the nature of amphetamine use in the United States.
2. To understand the properties of amphetamines, including the process by which the body responds to them, their effects on brain function, and the development of dependence.
3. To identify the legitimate medical uses of amphetamines.
4. To discuss the effects of amphetamines on mental state and performance and to highlight the dangers of its use.
5. To describe the relationship between amphetamine use and antisocial and violent behavior.
6. To discuss the possibility that some individuals are more likely to abuse amphetamines than others.
7. To present various treatment modalities.

timulant drugs are alike in many of their effects, including increasing behavioral and mental activity and alertness. In normal individuals, stimulants tend to elevate mood, increase performance levels, and reduce fatigue. There are many forms of stimulants. Some are available over the counter (OTC), some by prescription only, and others are used primarily within the illicit drug market. Even though certain stimulants can be purchased OTC, there is some controversy about whether they are entirely safe. For example, phenylpropanolamine (PPA), the active ingredient in many over-the-counter cold medicines and diet pills, suppresses appetite to achieve weight loss. There are numerous reports of users, mostly women, who have become addicted to PPA and found it difficult to discontinue the weight control therapy. Phenmetrazine (Preludin) has also been used extensively as an appetite suppressant in the treatment of obesity, but due to the high risk of drug abuse and dependence, it is no longer used for weight loss purposes.

Methylphenidate (Ritalin) and pemoline (Cylert) are prescription stimulants that are commonly used in the treatment of hyperkinesis in children. And finally, amphetamines and cocaine (discussed previously) are the stimulants that are most likely to be abused by an illicit drug-taking population. Although amphetamines are abundant in the illegal drug market, a great deal of amphetamine abuse has been created by physicians attempting to manage patients' weight or fatigue, a condition known as "iatrogenic addiction." Nevertheless, not all stimulants are alike in the way they are structured, their more specific mechanisms of action, subjective and behavioral effects, pharmacology, metabolism and elimination, abuse potential, and medical uses. This chapter is devoted to discussion of amphetamines; the stimulants cocaine, nicotine, and caffeine are covered in separate chapters.

Extent of Use of Amphetamines

In 1993, about 12,524,000 Americans over the age of twelve reported that they had used amphetamines without a doctor's prescription at some time in their lives (Substance Abuse and Mental Health Services Administration, 1994). Only 719,000 reported that they used the drug during the past month. This drug appears to be most popular among those aged eighteen to twenty-five with about 1 percent reporting use during the past month (see Table 9.1).

The annual high school survey (Johnston, O'Malley & Bachman, 1993) shows a continued downward trend for amphetamine use (see Figures 9.1 & 9.2). Stimulant use

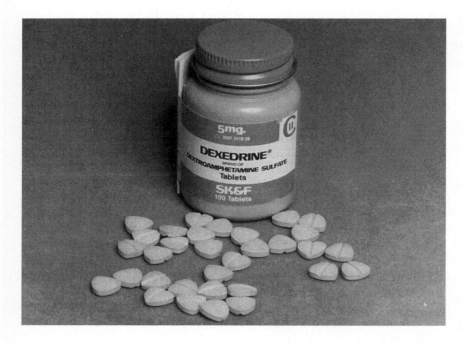

One kind of amphetamine in pill form.

Table 9.1   *Stimulants: Percent of Population Reporting Use of Stimulants, Ever, Past Year, and Past Month (1993) by Sex and Age Groups for Total Population*

	Ever Used	Used During Past Year	Used During Past Month
	RATE ESTIMATES (PERCENTAGES)		
AGE			
12-17	2.1	1.6	0.5
Male	2.0	1.6	0.8
Female	2.2	1.6	0.2
18-25	6.4	3.0	0.9
Male	7.2	4.4	1.3
Female	5.7	1.6	0.4
26-34	10.5	1.7	0.5
Male	12.1	2.3	0.8
Female	8.9	1.2	0.2
35+	5.3	0.5	0.2
Male	7.0	0.4	0.2
Female	3.8	0.5	0.1
Total	6.0	1.1	0.3
Male	7.4	1.5	0.5
Female	4.8	0.9	0.2

Source: Adapted from Substance Abuse and Mental Health Services Administration. *National Household Survey on Drug Abuse:* Population Estimates 1993.

peaked in 1981 among high school seniors (about 26 percent showing annual prevalence), college students (about 22 percent) and other young adults (about 29 percent). Since 1982, annual prevalence has fallen from 20 percent to 7 percent among seniors and from 21 percent to 4 percent among college students. This 4 percent figure is about the same for both male and female college students. The downward trend for amphetamine use since the early 1980s corresponds with an increase in cocaine use; cocaine is believed to have replaced amphetamines in many drug-using circles during that period.

Characteristics

Amphetamines were developed from ephedrine, originally derived by the Chinese from ephedra vulgaris, a type of shrub, for use in treating asthma. Ephedrine acts on the bronchi, blood pressure, blood vessels, and central nervous system. Many over-the-counter medications for colds and the flu contain ephedrine to symptomatically treat congestion and swelling of sinus passages. Due to its remarkable similarity to amphetamine, there is some slight CNS stimulation even with over-the-counter drugs, which is why some manufacturers add a depressant.

Amphetamines come in three molecular structures. D-Amphetamine indicates a "right-handed" molecule and l-amphetamine is "left-handed." Benzedrine, for example, is a drug that contains a combination of the two molecules, while dextroamphetamine (Dexedrine) is strictly right-handed. The "handedness" of a molecule is identified by its isomer (referring to the relative positions of atoms within a molecule) and determines the chemical's physiological and psychotropic properties. A d-isomer has much more CNS potency than a l-isomer, and for that reason, most serious drug users prefer d-amphetamines. Methamphetamine, the third type of amphetamine, is even more potent. Table 9.2 lists amphetamines, their street names, and their beneficial effects.

Methamphetamine is basically amphetamine with the addition of one methyl group (the process of methoxylation). Methoxylation was developed in pharmacology to prolong the circulation of many chemicals in the bloodstream. It functions by reducing the ability of the kidney

Figure 9.1   *Stimulants: Trends in Annual Prevalence Among Male and Female College Students*

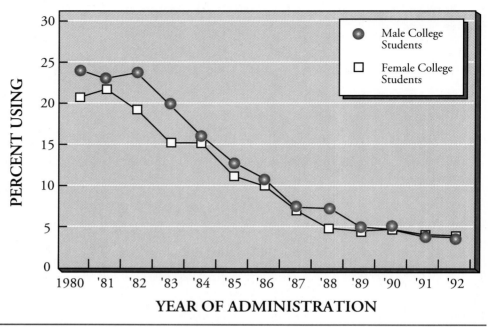

Source: National Institute on Drug Abuse, *National Survey Results on Drug Use from the Monitoring the Future Study, 1975-1992*

Figure 9.2   *Stimulants: Trends in Annual Prevalence Among College Students vs. Others (1-4 Years Beyond High School)*

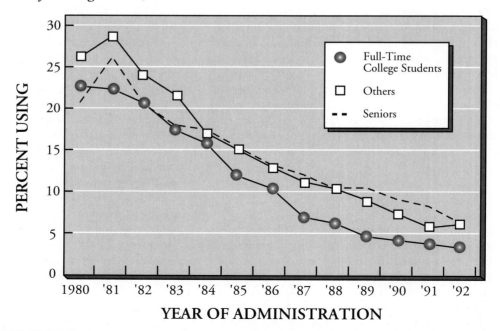

Source: National Institute on Drug Abuse, *National Survey Results on Drug Use from the Monitoring the Future Study, 1975-1992*

to secrete the specific chemical, thereby allowing it to circulate in the bloodstream at higher concentrations for any given dosage. This was performed initially with the sulfa drugs and was later applied to amphetamines. Although all amphetamines are highly lipid soluble and, thus, easily cross the blood-brain barrier, this alteration to produce methamphetamine enables it to cross more readily, further enhancing effects on the CNS.

Methamphetamine is one of the oldest and most popular of the illegally manufactured and distributed drugs. Almost all methamphetamine available to traffickers is produced in illicit domestic laboratories. However, a new, smokeable form of crystalline methamphetamine (ice) has been introduced to the United States from Asia, originally entering the country through Hawaii (U.S. Attorneys, 1989). Ice threatened to quickly become a major drug of abuse in this country with even more insidious properties than crack cocaine.

Physiology and Metabolism

Amphetamines may be administered either orally or intravenously and are absorbed quite efficiently from the gastrointestinal tract when taken by mouth. Levels of activity and stomach contents will help to determine rate of absorption. Taken in pill form, the effects are initially experienced in thirty to sixty minutes and reach a peak between two and three hours later. The half-life for amphetamines is ten to twelve hours. Therefore, it is possible to maintain a constant and stable blood level when the drug is taken every four to six hours. Amphetamines' effects are largely due to their ability to displace natural chemicals in the brain, which become depleted as a result of amphetamine use. As a consequence, when another dose of amphetamine is taken within four to six hours, later drug effects will be reduced because lesser amounts of these neurochemicals are present.

The preferred method of administration for therapeutic purposes is oral in order to minimize potency and stabilize blood levels. When amphetamine is administered by IV injection, effects are experienced within minutes. IV injection is the preferred method for recreational drug users who desire the rush of sensation described as euphoric and intensely pleasurable. Obviously, many users seek this experience repeatedly. The biggest danger of street use of amphetamines relates to the processing of tablets into an injectable form. Many commercial amphetamine tablet makers use inactive substances

known as binders to mold the amphetamine into pill form because the molecular structure of amphetamine powder has a tendency not to mold well. As such, when a tablet is liquified and injected, the inactive substances will not dissolve and can clog capillaries, posing an extreme danger to the user. When these tablets are administered orally, the binders are safely excreted in the feces.

Amphetamines are eliminated from the body unchanged about two days after the last administration. They are first metabolized by the liver, then become concentrated in the brain, spleen, and kidneys, and are finally excreted in urine. The more acidic the urine, the more complete the elimination process. A smaller amount of amphetamine leaves the body through sweat glands and saliva. Urine surveillance techniques have been developed to identify the presence of amphetamines from twenty-four to forty-eight hours after drug use. It is necessary, however, to eliminate the possibility that another legitimate product with amphetamine-like properties has been used, such as ephedrine or phenylpropanolamine. These products, among others, can be responsible for a false positive test result.

Table 9.2   *Amphetamines: Names and Uses*

DRUGS	STREET NAMES	MEDICAL USES
Biphetamine	Bennies	Anesthetic
Delcobese	Speed	Weight Control
Desoxyn	Black Beauties	Narcolepsy
Dextroamphetamine	Crystal	Attention Deficit
(Dexedrine)	Dexies	Disorder
Obetrol	Uppers	Fatigue
Benzedrine	Brain Pills	Asthma
Ephedrine	Jolly Beans	Manic Depressive
Methylphenidate	Pep Pills	Psychosis
(Ritalin)	Crank	Nasal Congestion
Pemoline	Wakeups	Migraine
(Cylert)	Cartwheels	Orthostatic
Phenylpropanolamine	Ups	Hypotension
Phenmetrazine	Ice	Mood &
Methanphetamine	Hearts	Performance
(Preludin)	Crossroads	Enhancement
	Truckdrivers	

Pharmacological Aspects

Amphetamines exert profound effects on the brain because they resemble several chemicals that are naturally present in both the central and peripheral nervous systems. Remember that the more similar in chemical structure a drug is to a naturally occurring substance in the brain, the more potent its physiological and psychological effects. Addiction is also more likely to develop. In particular, amphetamines resemble dopamine and norepinephrine, the catecholamine neurotransmitters that are fundamentally excitatory with respect to their CNS effects. Consequently, amphetamines act at the receptor sites of these neurotransmitters to excite the brain.

Stimulation from amphetamines occurs when the drug acts on catecholamine systems and the presynaptic neurons recognize and attempt to store the amphetamine molecules. This process causes catecholamines to be released into the synapse, act on the adjacent cell's receptor site, and increase activity levels. Furthermore, amphetamine molecules can block the reuptake of catecholamines, causing them to exert their stimulatory effects in the synapse for a longer period of time. Amphetamines may also act directly on the postsynaptic norepinephrine receptor, simulating the action of norepinephrine or dopamine. It is believed that amphetamines specifically influence norepinephrine pathways extending from the locus ceruleus (within the limbic system), which are known to be responsible for alertness, wakefulness, and arousal. They further stimulate the reticular activating system to enhance feelings of alertness while reducing fatigue. Amphetamine stimulation of dopamine pathways in the limbic system is likely to produce subjective feelings of euphoria and an increase in motor activity. Dopamine terminals, particularly in the nucleus accumbens within the limbic system, appear to be involved in the pleasure derived from amphetamine use and the proclivity of animals and humans to self-administer the drug (Gold et al., 1989). Amphetamines suppress appetite specifically by influencing centers of the hypothalamus.

When high doses of amphetamines overstimulate these systems, excessive, repetitive movements characterized as ritualistic and stereotyped behavior are observed. Tachycardia (rapid heart rate), dilated pupils, and increased reflexes are likely to result from increasing doses. Tremor, loss of coordination, nausea, headache, and sometimes even cerebral hemorrhage and neurological damage may develop from excessive doses. High concentrations of amphetamines are believed to increase the

activity of the neurotransmitter serotonin, sometimes resulting in paranoid psychosis. For unknown reasons, some amphetamine users who experience psychosis do not completely recover and are left with a psychiatric illness. Whether this state is caused by the use of amphetamines in these individuals or by a preexisting, underlying disorder that was merely triggered by the drug is unknown (Green & Costain, 1981).

So far amphetamine's actions throughout the CNS have been discussed, but they also have potent peripheral effects. Amphetamines are considered to be *sympathomimetic agents*. They have the ability to mimic the activity of what was introduced in Chapter 3 as the fight, flight, and fright (f/f/f) mechanism. The sympathetic nervous system, one part of the autonomic nervous system in the periphery, is activated by epinephrine, dopamine, and norepinephrine to produce the physiological manifestations and subjective feelings of stress (increased blood pressure, heart rate, skin conductance, blood flow to muscle groups, and so forth). Amphetamines, due to their structural similarity to these substances, exert identical effects on the f/f/f mechanism, in principle preparing the individual to mobilize into action. Consequently, irritability, insomnia, anxiety, and a general feeling of being in the midst of a crisis is experienced.

Tolerance, Dependence, and Withdrawal

Amphetamine use for any purpose, including therapeutic, can rapidly contribute to the development of tolerance in the course of four to six weeks. For this reason, when used therapeutically for weight loss, dieters should discontinue use after a couple of weeks so that tolerance does not develop and an increased dose does not become necessary for effective treatment. By the time tolerance does develop, it is likely that the user has simultaneously developed a psychological tolerance to the pleasure experienced both by the weight loss and the mood elevation. A user may develop an extreme compulsion to continue taking the drug for the pleasurable and euphoric effects it produces. Thus, psychological dependence alone may lead to the abuse of amphetamines.

When used in high doses, as frequently occurs for recreational purposes, tolerance may develop in the course of a one day binge. This form of tolerance is called tachyphylaxis. Once amphetamines cause catecholamines to be released from storage, supplies of these neurotransmitters may become exhausted and the next dose of amphetamine will not produce such profound results. Consequently, a larger dose becomes necessary to achieve the desired drug effects. At this point some hard-core users will switch from oral administration to IV administration in order to heighten the drug's effects. A single episode of drug taking may continue for several days, known as a speed run, and be stopped temporarily only due to extreme fatigue and hunger.

Amphetamine use also causes cross tolerance with other drugs that similarly mimic the sympathetic nervous system, such as cocaine. Why tolerance to amphetamines develops so rapidly and why cross tolerance occurs with sympathomimetic agents remains unknown. It is widely believed that tolerance develops because of the profound increase in neural stimulation. In an attempt to compensate, the brain's cells respond by reducing their level of activity, causing the user to seek more of the drug. Furthering the development of tolerance, amphetamines are so quickly eliminated that neurons may feel starved for stimulation and the user may need larger doses to achieve a desired effect.

Whether amphetamines are truly addicting has been a source of controversy for many years. Initially, experts doubted amphetamines produced physical dependence as the obvious withdrawal symptoms commonly associated with alcohol, barbiturates, and opiates were not observed. As investigation continued, it became apparent that amphetamines do, in fact, produce a consistent array of withdrawal symptoms that immediately follow termination of the drug. Furthermore, after the user recovers from the initial withdrawal symptoms (such as prolonged periods of sleeping) he or she experiences extreme depression and dysphoria. These symptoms may cause the user to crave more of the drug and reinstate its use. The onset of withdrawal symptoms and the relief of these symptoms with continued drug use indicates that amphetamines can lead to physical dependence. Table 9.3 illustrates that while opiate withdrawal is not much more than like a case of the flu, withdrawal from amphetamines can be quite devastating due to the intense depression that follows.

Nevertheless, withdrawal from amphetamines is more benign than withdrawal from alcohol or barbiturates. There are several stages of withdrawal that begin with a crash and end with long-term withdrawal that typically involves residual symptoms that last for weeks or months. Amphetamine treatments must take into account the varying stages of withdrawal to be effective (Gawin & Ellinwood, 1988). The initial phase of withdrawal is

Table 9.3   *Amphetamines: Effects and Withdrawal*

Possible Effects	Effects of Overdose	Withdrawal Syndrome
Increased Alertness	Agitation	Apathy
Excitation	Increase in Body Temperature	Long Periods of Sleep
Euphoria		Irritability
Increased Heart Rate	Hallucinations Convulsions	Depression Disorientation
Increased Blood Pressure	Psychosis Possible Death	Fatigue Craving
Insomnia		Increased Appetite
Loss of Appetite		

marked by feelings of unusual hunger, anxiety, lethargy, and depression. The rebound effect of an increased need for sleep accompanies this phase. It may take many weeks for the user to return to normal sleep patterns. In the meantime, sleep may be rich with dream activity. During the initial sleeping phase there is little to no craving for the drug. Following this period, however, the individual may experience a profound craving for more amphetamines or stimulants. This craving is referred to as the intermediate withdrawal phase. For several days to weeks, the individual experiences anhedonia (an inability to experience pleasure) and decreased mental and physical energy. These symptoms increase the likelihood of relapse since the drug user may wish to regain the drug-induced psychological and physical strength.

The final phase, long-term withdrawal, is characterized by a more normal state reflecting the user's mood and behavior prior to use of the drug. Although desires to repeat the drug experience are somewhat muted, the individual may still crave amphetamines for months or even years after abstinence. Unfortunately, there are several inducements to relapse, including long-lasting changes in brain function that sometimes occur and exposure to environmental cues that were previously associated with drug-taking behaviors. Both of these conditions may contribute to a perceived need for the drug.

These processes of tolerance and withdrawal are responsible for the habit-forming nature of these drugs. Whether amphetamine use will become habit-forming or dependence-producing depends greatly on the dosage level and the route of administration; using a high dose intravenously, for example, is most likely to cause compulsive use.

Medical Uses of Stimulants

Amphetamines have a wide variety of medicinal uses for a number of clinical conditions, including asthma, obesity, narcolepsy (a rare disease marked by daily episodes of sudden and uncontrolled sleep), attention deficit disorder and hyperactivity, manic-depressive psychosis, nasal congestion, migraine, and orthostatic hypotension (see Battaglia & De Souza, 1989). Stimulants are administered for asthma and nasal congestion because they produce bronchodilation—dilation of the air passages in the lungs. Although there are a few medical uses for amphetamines

that are still accepted, the incidence of side effects is noteworthy. Headaches, dry mouth, weight loss, and gastrointestinal problems are commonly reported.

Fatigue and Narcolepsy

Use of amphetamines to produce insomnia is common for those taking long trips, such as truck drivers, or for long hours of studying. All stimulants will suppress rapid eye movement (REM) sleep if the individual actually does fall asleep. Consequently, sleep will not be restful and the user will not awaken feeling refreshed. Figure 9.3 illustrates that as sleep progresses and deepens, brain waves slow. Although not depicted here, REM sleep appears much like an awake state in that the brain waves quicken.

Figure 9.3   *Stages of Sleep. Stage W indicates drowsy wakefulness immediately preceding the onset of stage 1 of sleep.*

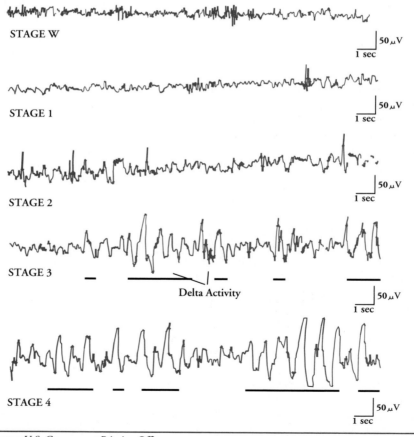

Source: U.S. Government Printing Office

Amphetamines artificially stimulate deep sleep, slowing brain waves, but not completing the full cycle by enabling the user to experience REM. After the drug wears off, REM sleep will increase dramatically for a period of time as will brain wave activity. See Figure 9.3 for a depiction of the normal sleep cycle.

Those suffering from narcolepsy may be helped with amphetamines. In fact, the only known treatment for narcolepsy is to keep patients awake during the day with stimulants so that they may sleep more soundly at night and prevent injuries and accidents that occur when they unpredictably fall asleep throughout the day. Before using this treatment, however, it is important to determine whether the patient is, in fact, sleeping effectively through the night. Some individuals who appear to have narcolepsy actually have a form of sleep apnea characterized by tiny seizures that awaken them, sometimes hundreds of times a night, without their knowledge. Thus, during the day they tend to be overly tired and subject to sudden episodes of sleep. The treatment in these cases would be quite different—stimulants are contraindicated for a seizure-prone patient.

Mood and Performance

Stimulants directly elevate mood by their action in the central and peripheral nervous systems. People report that they feel good, that their well-being is improved, and their ability to interact socially is enhanced when using stimulant drugs. Consequently, those who suffer from intermittent or chronic depression may be more likely to abuse amphetamines to lift their spirits temporarily. Their minds feel clear and alert, and their motivation to work and perform is heightened. Some users believe they can actually perform better—more efficiently and productively—when using stimulants. Studies have supported these claims under controlled situations designed to measure performance abilities. Compared with trials when a placebo is used, stimulant trials are associated with elation, positive moods, energy, talkativeness, and better task performance for both intellectual and motor skills. Improvements in performance are most pronounced when the individual is in an initial state of fatigue. With more complex tasks, however, performance levels may decline with higher doses of stimulants due to the increased difficulty in concentration, increased impulsivity, and impaired decision-making ability. Thus, stimulant effects on performance vary tremendously depending on

the dose and the task. For example, at low doses a student may be able to study for a longer period of time without sleep. However, if he or she were attempting to calculate complicated mathematical equations, stimulants may interfere more than benefit.

Athletes have been known to use various stimulants to improve their athletic performance. They may be able to run longer, lift more weight, swim faster, and accept more painful blows due to increases in energy and endurance. Athletes should be aware, however, of the adverse side effects that can in the long run be devastating to their athletic careers and their personal lives. Furthermore, athletes should be cautious about the use of cold medicines, many of which contain ephedrine, that may produce a positive urine test for a banned substance.

Obesity

Amphetamines have been used pervasively in the past for the treatment of obesity, however there are several reasons why such treatments are frowned upon today. This class of drug specifically acts on the eating centers of the hypothalamus, which normally inform us when we are hungry, by suppressing appetite. Weight loss theoretically follows. Because amphetamines produce rapid levels of tolerance, this effect is quickly attenuated unless dosage levels increase, and weight loss cannot be easily maintained. Furthermore, because the CNS stimulation and appetite suppression effects cannot be separated, the risks have been deemed greater than the benefits.

Phenylpropanolamine (PPA) has replaced the use of amphetamines in the treatment of obesity. It is a mild stimulant that acts on the adrenergic system, has a low potency, and low abuse potential. Nevertheless, an investigation of PPA is presently being conducted by a House Subcommittee. Experts have testified that there is evidence that PPA produces only minor weight loss, encourages eating disorders, has adverse effects, and may not promote the loss of fat only, but may also induce tissue and protein loss. These experts further claim that unrestricted use of PPA should be curtailed, particularly by minors. In spite of this information, the Food and Drug Administration is recommending continued use of PPA in both cold medicines and diet pills. Whether or not PPA or amphetamines are available for weight loss, patients who are overweight should be encouraged to find nonpharmacologic means of treatment. Eating disorders cannot be easily or effectively managed with a magic pill and treatment approaches should focus on underlying psychopathological or behavioral disorders and medical disturbances, when indicated, to achieve a comprehensive treatment program. Optimal programs for overweight individuals include exercise, low-fat diets, behavioral conditioning, and positive redirection strategies. More important, individuals should be encouraged to identify their best weight, which may not be within the range of average weight charts. Some people feel more comfortable at a lower or higher weight than those specified in these charts, given their genetic constitution, bone structure and density, age, and other background factors. In the absence of weight-related health problems, people should not be encouraged to lose weight just to please others or to meet the expectations of society set by glamour magazines and other media.

Hyperkinesis

The amphetamine derivatives methylphenidate (Ritalin) and pemoline (Cylert) have been found to have beneficial effects in many cases of hyperkinesis (previously called "minimal brain dysfunction" or MBD). Those afflicted with this syndrome generally demonstrate emotionality, behavioral hyperactivity, short attention span, distractibility, impulsiveness, and perceptual and learning disabilities (see inset describing DSM-III-R diagnostic criteria for hyperactivity). Boys suffer from the disorder at least three times more often than girls. For a long time, it was ill-understood why some children with average to high IQs performed so poorly in their academic pursuits and acted several years younger than they actually were. Eventually, investigators and other concerned individuals began to recognize these impairments as a problem within the nervous system rather than viewing those afflicted as problem children.

In spite of our relative ignorance about the cause(s), some treatments have been designed that, when used properly, improve the symptoms of hyperkinesis. At least 50 percent of those children correctly diagnosed with hyperkinesis have experienced improvements in behavior and learning ability with the use of stimulants. Adult hyperactivity may be similarly treated. Benefits from these drugs are substantially enhanced with the conjunctive use of remedial educational tools, family counseling, behavioral modification techniques, and other psychological and medical strategies as indicated in each case.

Although the exact reasons why a stimulant would calm an overactive child are unknown at this time, there is evidence that the brains of hyperkinetic individuals are underactive. In particular, the reticular activating system and adjoining areas show a decreased level of activity. If this proves to be true, then the sufferer's behavioral hyperactivity may be a result of an increased need for environmental and neurological stimulation. Characteristic behaviors of hyperkinesis are excessive motor activity and sensory stimulation, which may function to increase CNS activity that is otherwise lacking. Stimulants, such as Ritalin, would, therefore, negate the need for these excessive behaviors by directly enhancing levels of neural arousal. By using a stimulant drug, the hyperkinetic patient would actually have less need for external stimulation and become calmer and more receptive to learning experiences. In the proper doses, these drugs also tend to increase attention spans and learning abilities by activating brain regions responsible for integrating thoughts and ideas, allowing them to piece together informational segments to produce a coherent whole picture, a task they show difficulty in performing. The result may be to further relieve the child's anxieties and frustrations concerning his or her academic abilities. Similarly, adults anxious about their performance (i.e., studying or acting) report an improvement in their ability to concentrate, attend, and work efficiently after using a mild amphetamine or other stimulant.

There is increasing awareness that dangers exist in the use of stimulants to treat hyperkinesis, such as possibility of temporary impaired growth rate. Also, there is a large number of children who have been inappropriately diagnosed as hyperkinetic. Many of them suffer from other underlying disorders, such as depression or anxiety, and others may suffer from another form of learning disability, such as attention deficit disorder without hyperactivity. Their treatments will vary tremendously as a function of the particular problem. Another group of so-called hyperkinetic children may have a conduct disorder or may be acting out due to problems at home. It is of dire importance that stimulants are not overused in an attempt to simply control children who are perceived to be out-of-control.

Psychoactive Properties

Amphetamines have properties similar to LSD and mescaline and it is believed that their hallucinogenic effects, similar to LSD and mescaline, are due to stimulation of serotonin receptors, thus contributing to some of the psychoactive properties of amphetamines (Battaglia &

Inset 9.1

DSM-III-R DIAGNOSTIC CRITERIA 314.01
ATTENTION-DEFICIT HYPERACTIVITY DISORDER

Note: Consider a criterion met only if the behavior is considerably more frequent than that of most people of the same mental age.

A. A disturbance of at least six months during which at least eight of the following are present:
1.   often fidgets with hands or feet or squirms in seat
2.   has difficulty remaining seated when required to do so
3.   is easily distracted by extraneous stimuli
4.   has difficulty awaiting turn in games or group situations
5.   often blurts out answers to questions before they have been completed
6.   has difficulty following through on instructions from others, e.g., fails to finish chores
7.   has difficulty sustaining attention in tasks or play activities
8.   often shifts from one uncompleted activity to another
9.   has difficulty playing quietly
10. often talks excessively
11. often interrupts or intrudes on others, e.g., butts into other children's games
12. often does not seem to listen to what is being said to him or her
13. often loses things necessary for tasks or activities at school or at home
14. often engages in physically dangerous activities without considering possible consequences, e.g., runs into street without looking

B. Onset before the age of seven

C. Does not meet the criteria for a Pervasive Developmental Disorder

CRITERIA FOR SEVERITY OF ATTENTION-DEFICIT HYPERACTIVITY DISORDER:

Mild: Few, if any symptoms in excess of those required to make the diagnosis and only minimal or no impairment in school and social functioning.

Moderate: Symptoms or functional impairment intermediate between "mild" and "severe."

Severe: Many symptoms in excess of those required to make the diagnosis and significant and pervasive impairment in functioning at home and school and with peers.

De Souza, 1989). Nevertheless, alterations in psychological processes are largely due to the influence of amphetamines on norepinephrine systems. Low to moderate doses produce a feeling of alertness, well-being, euphoria, confidence, wakefulness, increased behavioral and motor activity, improved mental functions, decreased fatigue, and high energy levels. Even at low doses, the user may also become irritable, agitated, and anxious, and may experience blurred vision, raised blood pressure, and insomnia.

Chronic use of low doses generally produce bizarre personality changes. When amphetamines are injected, the user will also experience a rush of pleasurable sensation.

When an amphetamine, most particularly methamphetamine, is illegally administered IV, street users refer to it as speed. Those who are street wise will often also add an opiate (i.e., heroin) to the injection to minimize the toxic symptoms of amphetamines. This process is called speed-balling. The term originated in the 1920s and '30s when the drug

DSM-III-R, 292.11, DIAGNOSTIC CRITERIA FOR AMPHETAMINE DELUSIONAL DISORDER

The essential feature of this disorder is an Organic Delusional Syndrome, with rapidly developing persecutory delusions as the predominant clinical feature, developing shortly after use of amphetamine or a similarly acting sympathomimetic.

Associated Features. Distortion of body image and misperception of people's faces may occur. Initially, suspiciousness and curiosity may be experienced with pleasure, but may later induce aggressive or violent action against "enemies." The hallucination of bugs or vermin crawling in or under the skin (formication) can lead to scratching and extensive skin excoriations [abrasion of the skin].

Course. Delusions can linger for a week or more, but occasionally last for over a year.

Impairment and Complications. Impairment in social and occupational functioning is usually severe. The person may harm himself or herself or others while reacting to delusions.

subculture in this country was becoming familiar with IV techniques and began to inject a combination of cocaine and heroin. Because amphetamine users so often use other depressants (i.e., alcohol or barbiturates) in conjunction with amphetamines, the withdrawal symptoms from amphetamines are substantially amplified, contributing to profound feelings of depression, fatigue, and sleepiness.

Larger doses of amphetamines, particularly when injected, produce a psychotic state featuring confusion, disorientation, compulsive behavior, hallucinations and delusions, suspiciousness, and sometimes aggressive and socially inappropriate behaviors. Psychosis frequently develops immediately following rush and is characterized by a manic paranoia that offsets to some degree the good feelings experienced during rush. This reaction strongly resembles paranoid schizophrenia, a type of psychosis that is unusually unstable, aggressive, and dangerous. (Most other forms of schizophrenia are not commonly associated with violent behavior.) The inset describes DSM-III-R diagnostic criteria for amphetamine-induced delusional disorder, which is related to violent psychosis.

Methamphetamine

Methamphetamine is a particularly insidious and dangerous form of amphetamine. It has been used extensively over the past three decades for both legitimate (certain emergency room situations) and illegitimate purposes. As it was thought to be nonaddicting and relatively safe, prescriptions for methamphetamine were not difficult to obtain. Because the drug has more potent effects on the CNS and fewer peripheral effects than amphetamines, users tend to prefer methamphetamine for recreational purposes. A methamphetamine epidemic spread through Japan after World War II when it was sold in the open market and Japanese teenagers began to abuse this drug extensively. Those arrested were usually between the ages of twelve and twenty-five, and the psychiatric syndromes resulting from methamphetamine use ranged from psychopathy to manic-depression and apathetic exhausted states. Surprisingly, female users outnumbered the males, and they tended to be more aggressive and difficult to manage in correctional institutions. The imposition of strict laws and enforcement policies, however, eliminated the problem in Japan (McKim, 1991).

Use of the crystallized form of methamphetamine, known as ice, crank, crystal, crystal meth, or glass on the street—because of its clear, crystal-shaped appearance—was a national source of concern. (The street names crank and crystal were used before the crystallized form of methamphetamine was introduced; however, these names stuck.) In the mid 1980s, ice became a popular drug of abuse in Hawaii although it was not recognized as a problem until 1987. In Honolulu, there are several ice over-doses a day at the Queens Hospital and approximately 25 percent of newborn infants have traces of ice in their bodies. Local Filipino gang members were the primary suppliers of ice and supplies were 98 to 100 percent pure.

Methamphetamine is generally ingested in pill form, snorted, or injected IV. Ice, however, is smoked and may be profoundly addictive. Ice can be smoked in public with relative ease as it is odorless. A glass pipe called a bong, characterized by a circular bowl with a pipe stem with no screens or coolants, is used to ignite and administer the ice. Bongs are also used to administer many other drugs, including marijuana, hashish, and cocaine.

When the drug is heated, it first becomes liquid and then vapor. The openings in the bong must be sealed, usually with a finger, so that the vapor is not released. One of the telltale signs of an ice user is a burn mark on the finger(s) used to cover the bong holes. Once a gas is formed, it is inhaled by the user, and it rapidly enters the bloodstream. Large doses are eliminated in the urine continuously for up to seventy-two hours after ingestion, depending on the amount used. When the drug cools, it will revert to its solid crystal state in a reusable, easy to transport form.

Ice can be manufactured easily in local clandestine laboratories since none of the ingredients need to be imported. Furthermore, there is no need for needles, the drug effects are rapid, it is difficult to detect, easy to transport, and very inexpensive. Moreover, methamphetamine has a much longer duration of action (up to twelve hours) and even more profound effects than crack cocaine. For these reasons experts feared that crystal methamphetamine would soon become a major drug of abuse. Methamphetamine did reach the northeast region of this country and was beginning to gain popularity within a few drug subcultures.

Long-term physical effects of ice are not yet fully known as large-scale use has yet to surface. Nevertheless, due to the potency of ice and the factors mentioned above, it has the potential to be more dangerous than injectable methamphetamine and crack cocaine. Symptoms of abuse include social deterioration, such as absences from work or school; paranoia; schizophrenia; and unpredictable, uncontrollable, delusional, irrational, illogical, and often violent behavior. When an individual binges on ice for several days, the results will be insomnia, depleted energy, nutrient deficiencies, and other signs of physical exhaustion. Also, ice produces a high degree of tolerance and psychological dependence, leading to psychosis, anxiety, depression and fatigue.

Crash may last for twenty-four to thirty-six hours. Withdrawal symptoms are similar to those produced by other amphetamines, most notably severe depression and fatigue. Depression can become so profound that suicidal

Methamphetamine and its crystallized form "ice."

A bong or water pipe used for smoking ice.

tendencies may surface, as life no longer seems worth living due to the lack of ability to experience pleasure or any sense of well-being. Eventually, toxic effects resulting from chronic use may include restlessness, tremors, mania, irritability, delirium, panic, paranoia, palpitation, cardiac arrhythmias, hypertension, circulatory collapse, and others.

Recommendations in the treatment of ice poisoning revolve around the use of antipsychotics (i.e., haloperidol) to control the behavior and anticonvulsants to control the seizures. The patient should be kept isolated in a dark, cool, and quiet room. Finally, to decrease the half-life of the drug, it may help to acidify the urine. Some users may not ever fully recover from their binges and may experience convulsions, coma, and even death. Consequently, using this drug to lose weight, work throughout the night, study, or increase energy levels is a dangerous proposition. Needless to say, the chronic, IV use of amphetamines or the smoking of ice contributes to a deteriorated lifestyle, loss of employment, impaired family and personal relationships, serious mental and physical health problems, self-destructive behavior, and sometimes, due to aggressive and violent behavior, contact with the legal system.

Because law enforcement officials recognized the dimensions of ice use, given their history with crack cocaine, the threat of ice's spread has been substantially curbed. By the time officials had realized that crack was a real problem, it was too late—the drug had infiltrated all

the major markets in the United States and had reached epidemic proportions before criminal justice professionals began to take a serious look at the situation. In the case of ice, on the other hand, officials were better prepared and were able to implement preventative measures prior to a full-blown epidemic. A national comprehensive approach, involving law enforcement and the community, was quickly applied and there is strong evidence that widespread distribution and use of ice has been effectively suppressed (see Chaiken, 1993).

Aggression and Criminal Behavior

Amphetamines gained a bad reputation during the 1960s when a mainstream drug culture emerged. The hippies of this generation experimented with drugs, such as marijuana and LSD that in general were not associated with violence or criminal victimization of others. Those who did experiment with amphetamines and eventually used them on a more or less chronic basis, however, commonly experienced what is called amphetamine psychosis. This type of psychotic state is identical to a severe case of paranoid schizophrenia; the user has auditory and visual hallucinations, delusions that he or she is being persecuted, delusions that creatures are crawling on the skin (formication), and delusions that he or she is immortal or invulnerable. Frequently these users become easily provoked to violence. Psychosis and/or violence can occur even in individuals without any history of such behavior. When amphetamines are administered by IV, paranoid psychosis is more likely to result and the paranoid delusions that characterize this state may lead to violent behavior (Ellinwood, 1971; Siomopoulos, 1981).

Unlike heroin users, speed users frequently came from middle-class backgrounds and, thus, lacked the skills necessary to hustle drugs in order to support a compulsive drug habit. Combined with the hostility, hyperactivity, suspiciousness, paranoia, and other personality changes, this lack of street savvy was problematic to amphetamine users, and their behavior was even more likely to be erratic and explosive in attempts to obtain the drug.

Investigators and criminal justice workers at that time determined that amphetamines, more than most other drugs, were directly related to aggressive behavior (Ellinwood, 1972). Surveys conducted in the late 1960s through the 70s found that a surprising number of both juvenile delinquents and prison inmates committed their violent crimes when using amphetamines (Hemmi, 1969; Simonds & Kashani, 1979). Individuals under the influence of amphetamines were reported to be frequently subject to unexpected and extreme changes in social behavior. Not only did they manifest explosive acts of aggressive behavior, but they also tended to withdraw from appropriate social interactions. It has been speculated that these two drug effects are a result of a complex interaction between environmental, psychological, pharmacological, and genetic conditions (Miczek & Tidey, 1989).

Aggressive behavior following the withdrawal from opiates is characterized by the enhanced activity of dopamine receptors. There are suggestions that the aggression-inducing effects of amphetamines may also be due to dopamine release (Gianutsos & Lal, 1976). Consistent with these observations, administration of amphetamines along with a dopaminergic blocking agent, such as haloperidol (Haldol), attenuates aggressive behaviors.

Psychopathology and Theories of Vulnerability

Cohen (1969) suggested that there were three major reasons for the abuse of psychoactive drugs, including amphetamines. The first motivation is to seek relief from tension or depression and escape from a stressful environment. This need for relief is called the dysphoric syndrome characterized by anxiety, agitation, irritability, unhappiness, and helplessness. The second reason is the avoidance of aphoria, the lack of feeling or the inability to feel. This condition prevents sufferers from becoming involved with others in a manner that is satisfying and meaningful. And finally, the search for euphoria is a compelling motivation to use stimulant drugs. Amphetamine users report that sensory experiences are enhanced, and they can escape the realities of a mundane or unpleasant lifestyle. Because these reasons also lie behind many forms of drug use, most amphetamine abusers are polydrug users and have experimented with a number of different substances, sometimes in combination with amphetamines. It is interesting to note, however, that amphetamine use is frequently not entirely enjoyable because of the panic, irritability, paranoia, depression, and fatigue that accompany its use. Thus, the question of why some individuals continue to abuse these substances or use them as their drug of choice arises. The answer has yet to surface, but there is speculation that it may eventually be found in a better understanding of long-term drug effects on the brain and in particular psychological and sociological orientations of users that may make them particularly vulnerable to amphetamine abuse.

Studies are showing that individuals have differential responses to the use of amphetamines; not everyone in every situation will experience the same drug effects (Lasagna et al., 1955). Subjective drug effects are largely contingent upon the situation in which the drug is administered, the psychological set of the user, the dosage, route of administration, and duration of use. With respect to personality traits, for example, normal subjects with neurotic and obsessive-compulsive tendencies (called psychasthenic traits) have more positive reactions to amphetamines, particularly to perceptions of enhanced alertness, better mood, and less tension (Idestrom & Schalling, 1969).

Several studies reported by the National Institute on Drug Abuse (Spotts & Spotts, 1980) reported that amphetamine users showed evidence of abnormal personalities prior to their drug addiction. Preexisting psychopathology, psychosocial dysfunction, and academic problems preceded their drug use. Parents of users concurred with these observations and further reported that there were early childhood problems in the histories of their amphetamine-abusing children. Most of these users came from broken homes and environments that were considered high risk in terms of abuse, neglect, drug-infestation, familial alcoholism, crime, and other family and community disadvantages. Many were found to have parents, particularly mothers, who abused such drugs as tranquilizers, sleeping pills, or diet pills in excess.

In sum, these studies concluded that the amphetamine abusing population is predominantly made up of insecure and uncertain youth who have problems getting along with others, have poor interpersonal relationships, feel powerless and inferior, and are impulsive and immature. Their inability to cope with everyday stressors and their own emotional problems frequently leads them to use amphetamines, which make them feel more competent and less concerned with their problems. Also, belonging to a drug-using group provides them with a support group of peers who come from similar backgrounds and suffer from similar psychopathologies.

A related study of delinquents who use amphetamines reported that there are two types of users: the malignant and the benign (Scott & Willcox, 1965). The malignant group is more inclined to quickly increase the dosage, use a variety of forms of amphetamine in a reckless manner, take the drug throughout the week, turn to stronger drugs, and damage their social and physical health. Their home backgrounds are considered disadvantageous; they lack self-confidence in relationships, and are fearful and overly dependent on a parent. These delinquents commit crimes parallel to their drug use, not as a result of it; in other words, their criminal behavior would continue whether using amphetamines or not, but the behavior and drug use exacerbate one another. The benign group, on the other hand, does not tend to increase the dose and uses amphetamines only on the weekends. Their relationships and personal histories are considered healthy. It appears that those individuals with dysfunctional backgrounds and poor coping skills are at increased risk for both drug abuse and delinquent behavior. Similar studies with adults agree that these typologies are accurate and indicate the degree of risk a user faces for addiction and criminal activity is contingent on a number of background and personality factors. Thus, a combination of social and psychological factors appear to be contributory.

Mental disorders that *result* from amphetamine abuse include predominantly psychopathy and psychosis/schizophrenia. Individuals appear to be differentially at risk, however, for these disorders. A preexisting tendency toward a mental problem (i.e., symptoms of paranoia or psychosis) may determine, in part, what the final outcome of their amphetamine abuse will be. In a study of psychiatric patients (Hekimian & Gershon, 1968), diagnoses that predated their amphetamine addiction predominantly were for schizophrenic symptoms, neurosis, and psychopathy. Although some patients reported beneficial subjective drug effects, all of them were considered by psychiatrists to be generally worse off as a result of drug consumption, including an exacerbation of paranoid psychoses or overt psychopathic behaviors. It is interesting that depression played a major role in all forms of substance abuse, but that schizophrenia was especially prevalent in the histories of amphetamine addicts. Furthermore, separate studies have reported a greater incidence of schizophrenia in the families of amphetamine users than in the general population, suggesting the possible involvement of genetic predisposition to both psychopathology and drug addiction. What precise roles these preexisting psychiatric disorders played in the eventual development of amphetamine dependence and mental disorder is unclear. There is speculation that the presence of a particular disorder may increase the likelihood of the habitual use of a particular drug *and* the onset of a long-term psychiatric problem. Consequently, personality or psychiatric disturbance may play a significant role in drug addiction and the particular drug of choice may be only a symptom of an underlying disturbance.

Related to influences of personality traits and psychiatric conditions, there is evidence for a biological contribution to the development of amphetamine abuse. The overwhelming incidence of underlying depression in many drug users, including amphetamine addicts, suggests that there is an increased need for nervous system stimulation in some users. Amphetamine users, in particular, frequently respond with high activity levels and confrontation in stressful situations, rather than the withdrawal and avoidance characteristic of many opiate users. Heightened levels of anxiety may actually be sought out by those prone to amphetamine abuse in order to stimulate their autonomic nervous systems. Theoretically, the presence of an underaroused nervous system would exaggerate this tendency to seek stimulation. If this hypothesis proves true, then a biological predisposition (not independent of other risk factors) to amphetamine abuse may be established for some individuals.

Further studies have shown that lesions of specific areas within dopamine forebrain projections have been associated with an increase in the self-administration of amphetamines (Deminiere et al., 1984; Deminiere et al., 1988), suggesting that some specific abnormality within the dopamine system could sensitize individuals to the reinforcing actions of behavioral stimulants. It is unknown at this time what inherent or acquired condition may cause a dysfunction in these dopamine projections to increase the risk for amphetamine abuse, however, investigation into such biological contributors continues. Eventually, the dynamic interaction between biological systems, psychological states, and environmental conditions that precipitate or exacerbate drug abuse behaviors may be more fully understood.

Treatment

There are very few therapies that have been systematically tested for their success in the treatment of amphetamine addicts. Much of the problem stems from the high dropout rate of users in these studies so it is difficult to follow them to evaluate their progress. Amphetamine users generally seek treatment when they are in a crisis period with their drug use; once the crisis is over, they tend to disappear. Also, because they are frequently in a state of agitation and paranoia, they refuse to sign consent forms and participate fully in treatment protocols. Not only may the user be at fault for the high dropout rate, but the possibility must also be considered that their rejection of treatment may reflect a problem with the treatment modalities themselves.

Obviously, the first step in treatment is to detoxify them from the drug immediately so that the direct effects of the drug can be treated. This may require a hospital stay in some cases, particularly if there is a threat of overdose or a severe psychotic reaction. Withdrawal symptoms may be eased either by tapering the user from the drug slowly, or in more hard-core, chronic users, administering a medication that will keep them calm and help them to sleep. For those who are iatrogenically addicted and took only low doses of amphetamines on a chronic basis, it is best to wean slowly and then remove the drug entirely. This strategy is very much dependent on the level of motivation the user has to abstain. For all amphetamine users, counseling, psychotherapy, and/or behavioral therapy are essential components of any treatment program.

For cases of acute intoxication and anxious states produced by amphetamines, the most often used medicinal treatments include haloperidol (Haldol: a dopaminergic blocking agent), promethazine (a tranquilizer that suppresses brain centers responsible for abnormal emotions and behavior), and chlordiazepoxide (Librium: a tranquilizer that alters functions of the limbic system controlling emotions). The opiate receptor antagonists, such as naloxone, have been found to reduce the rewarding properties

of electrical brain stimulation by amphetamines and to counteract increased levels of motor activity in animals (Miczek & Tidey, 1989). Although the use of opiate antagonists in humans may be somewhat promising, they have not been shown to block amphetamines' effects on social and aggressive behaviors.

Chronic intoxication in more serious cases can be treated with long-acting neuroleptics (drugs used to treat psychosis). All pharmacologic treatments should be accompanied by counseling, psychotherapy, and the appropriate diagnosis and treatment of existing physical disorders. Such a comprehensive approach to treatment is particularly important for amphetamine users who frequently suffer from underlying psychopathology and social dysfunction. Also useful is urinalysis monitoring, according to many clinicians, due to the high relapse rate. There is a general consensus that treatment may be more difficult with amphetamine users than with opiate users as there is no safe substitute drug, such as methadone or buprenorphine. And, unfortunately, the prevalence of psychosis among amphetamine users further complicates treatment strategies.

Behavioral Approaches

Behavioral treatments for amphetamine abuse are similar to those used in cocaine addiction. The user should be highly motivated and must make a total commitment to abstinence for treatment to have any chance of success. Also important is an emphasis on the total refrain from using any other drugs—frequently individuals in recovery inadvertently search for replacement drugs to provide them with the stimulation they feel is lacking. Thus, they are quite vulnerable to becoming dependent on other drugs of abuse.

Treatment strategies that may or may not be used in conjunction with a pharmacologic agent, depending on the individual circumstances, involve counseling and psychotherapy. Attempts are made to resolve or at least understand any personal problems that may have led to the initial decision to use amphetamines so that the patient will be further invested in the treatment process. Generally, treatment professionals attempt to remove the addict from situations and peers that have become associated with using the drug. Behavioral modification programs can be effective for some motivated users by breaking associations with drug cues that frequently entice users to return to the drug and by learning new behavioral patterns that do not revolve around amphetamine use. Encouragement can also be received from attending sessions with Narcotics Anonymous.

▤ Summary

Although many types of amphetamines are legal drugs, they have high abuse potential and are addictive, potent, and potentially dangerous when used without the supervision of a professional. Individuals who use high doses of amphetamines on a regular basis for recreational purposes frequently encounter problems with their toxic side effects and may find it difficult to discontinue use at will. Moreover, the behavior and social life of a chronic recreational user is at risk of deteriorating and becoming out of control. Typical problems may be as seemingly benign as irritability, weight loss, and insomnia or as insidious as psychosis, seizures, and heart arrythmia. Toxic effects can persist for weeks, if not months after discontinuation. In spite of these possible complications, users are frequently drawn to amphetamines for the intense euphoria, bursts of energy, and feelings of well-being and power that they provide.

Amphetamines do, nevertheless, have a proper place in medicine. Some may be effectively used to alleviate fatigue, minimize narcoleptic attacks, quell migraine headaches, and treat asthma, obesity, and the symptoms of certain learning disabilities. When taken under a doctor's supervision for short periods of time, amphetamines can be used quite successfully. Even under optimal conditions, however, amphetamine use can be problematic in some patients who become hooked and go beyond what the doctor ordered. Iatrogenically addicted patients comprise a large population of amphetamine users in this country. Still, these individuals tend not to be the users worthy of our legal attention. Rather, it is the group of street users who engage in other forms of drug use in combination with destructive and sometimes criminal activities that cause society the most grief. These amphetamine users can be dangerous and resistant to treatment efforts. It is important, therefore, that new treatment modalities be developed that more specifically target the underlying disorders and medical problems these users suffer from that contribute to their continued drug usage.

CHAPTER  10

Stimulants: Nicotine and Caffeine

Objectives

1. To show the prevalence of tobacco and caffeine use in the United States.
2. To differentiate among different types of tobacco and how they are used.
3. To show how tobacco use has been encouraged and maintained through advertising and government involvement.
4. To describe the properties and effects of nicotine within the body and brain.
5. To illustrate the process by which nicotine becomes addictive.
6. To identify those biological, psychological, and behavioral effects of tobacco use.
7. To discuss the negative effects of nicotine on the fetus, those exposed to secondhand smoke, and the mentally ill.
8. To discuss the special problems associated with smokeless tobacco.
9. To present and assess the effectiveness of treatment programs for nicotine addiction.
10. To describe the process by which caffeine is used in the body.
11. To discuss the various ways in which caffeine alters physiological functions, mental abilities, and performance.
12. To discuss the possible adverse effects of caffeine.
13. To explain how caffeine interacts with other substances.

Nicotine and caffeine are two of the most widely used and abused stimulant drugs in the world. They are found in several substances that we are exposed to daily, and there is very little regulation over their use. Consequently, many of us are exposed to these compounds without even being aware of it. This, obviously, is of most concern when the consumer is a child. Large amounts of caffeine are consumed by children in sodas, candy, and chocolate milk, while tobacco products are readily absorbed by children whose parents smoke cigarettes in their presence. In recent years, there has been increasing attention to this problem, called passive smoking, as a result of findings that several childhood illnesses are directly caused by inhaling tobacco products.

Both drugs are considered general cellular stimulants because of their direct effects on the activity levels of nerve cells. Caffeine exerts its action within nerve cells to increase their rates of cellular metabolism. (Many other central nervous system stimulants act at the synapse between neurons.) Nicotine, one of the most active ingredients in tobacco, stimulates acetylcholine synapses within the brain and peripheral nervous system. As a consequence of their mode of action, both drugs can reward experienced users by perking them up, decreasing fatigue, enhancing alertness and, for those who are dependent, avoiding withdrawal symptoms. These drugs are discussed with respect to their sites of action, pharmacological and psychological effects, side effects, dependence and tolerance, and influence on fetal development.

Nicotine

Within the last decade or so, researchers have been working actively to understand why millions of people find tobacco rewarding and have such difficulty abstaining from its use. With the exception of caffeine, tobacco is the most widely used psychoactive habit in civilized society. At the present time, it is clear that the primary ingredient, nicotine, is greatly responsible for its reinforcing properties. There is virtually no therapeutic value for nicotine, probably due to its unpredictable properties. On the one hand, it has some stimulant effects, and on the other, it exerts some depressant effects. In either event, its effects are potent and its powerfully addictive qualities make this drug most attractive to many (even though initial experiences are generally quite unpleasant!). Moreover, smoking tobacco in the form of cigarettes has taken on social significance in that youth find status and feel a sense of early adulthood when they are seen smoking cigarettes. It is apparent that the widespread use of tobacco, particularly among the young, is unfortunate since hundreds of studies have concluded that nicotine is highly addictive and is in products, such as cigarettes, that contain substances that

The most widely used drugs, caffeine and nicotine, in their most common form.

are also carcinogenic. We will concentrate on the actions of nicotine in the following sections; however, it is important to note that more than 3,000 chemicals become active once a tobacco product is ignited. Some of these substances include benzene (found in gasoline), formaldehyde (used to preserve dead body parts), cyanide (used to induce death in the gas chamber), cadmium (a toxic metal found deep within the ground), arsenic (rat poison), and ammonia (found in toilet bowel cleaner).

How Cigarettes Became a National Habit

The setting was Barnes Hospital, St. Louis, in 1919. The patient died from a disease so rare that medical students were brought in to observe the autopsy. The disease was lung cancer. One of the students who was present remarked later that he did not see another case until 1936 when, suddenly, he saw nine patients with cancer of the lung within a six-month period. To him, this constituted an epidemic with an unknown cause although he observed that all of his patients had smoked cigarettes heavily. At the beginning of this century, most people chose cigars over cigarettes and smokers were predominantly male. In 1904, a New York woman was arrested for smoking in her car and female schoolteachers were dismissed if caught smoking!

When World War I began in 1917, however, this intolerance about smoking began to change. Cigarettes were distributed free to troops in France, and they became important for morale. Production of cigarettes increased expotentially during 1910 and 1919. The consequences of this growing trend were noticed by physicians in the 1930s as cases of lung cancer began to appear. Initial efforts to rid the body of this cancer included the removal of a lobe of the lung. Because physicians did not yet know that the chest cavity must be drained after such an operation, patients died from infections fairly rapidly.

In 1933, an obstetrician, James Lee Gilmore, suffered from a persistent cough and fever. A physician friend took a chest X-ray and found a cancer in the upper-left lobe. Chest surgery was performed to remove the tumor, but once inside, the surgeon found that the entire lung would require removal. Although no patient had ever survived such an operation, he felt he had no other alternative. The patient tolerated the operation well, and it became a more popular procedure.

A study in 1932 found that the tar in cigarettes was responsible for lung cancer and another study in 1950 reported that most lung cancer patients had a longtime history of cigarette smoking. These were the first major studies to make this connection. The author of the 1950 study was the chest surgeon Evarts Graham, who quit smoking once he saw the findings. Yet, in 1951, he was diagnosed with lung cancer and died within the year. His patient, Gilmore, survived him by more than half a decade.

Before we knew the dangers of smoking, cigarette companies regaled consumers with the supposed beneficial effects of nicotine. Advertising campaigns claimed that physicians endorsed certain brands as being less irritating or smoother than others. Even though physicians widely objected to such advertising, they were opposing the commercialization of professional opinion rather than the specific claims. Cigarette companies continued to publicize that their particular brands did not irritate the throat, were sleek and attractive to the smoker, and increased popularity and relaxation.

In the early 1950s, further medical studies began to draw a connection between smoking and illness. Now, instead of insisting that smoking promoted health, companies took a defensive posture and stated that smoking did not contribute to disease and that the link was unsubstantiated. In the interim, the number of people diagnosed with, and dying from lung cancer increased dramatically. In 1930, the death rate from lung cancer among men was less than 5 per 100,000 population per year. By 1950, it had quintupled to more than 20; today, it is above 70. Most people with lung cancer eventually die from it. Even today, less than 10 percent of lung cancer patients can be cured. Lung cancer is presently the leading cause of cancer deaths in the United States, and 85 percent of lung cancer is caused by cigarette smoking. Until around World War II, smoking was still considered socially unacceptable for women. At present, the rate of lung cancer among women has skyrocketed.

World War II saw another tremendous increase in cigarette smokers. (Wars always seem to be associated with an increase in addictive behaviors.) Cigarettes were readily available and sold either tax-free or distributed free. Entertainers advertized cigarettes on their television shows and in commercials. Arthur Godfrey, for example, ended his cigarette-sponsored show with a "Buy-'em-by-the-carton" message. (In 1959 this message was dropped when Godfrey was found to have lung cancer and underwent removal of a lung.)

The tide began to turn for the cigarette market in 1955 when the Surgeon General, Leroy E. Burney, invited members of several national health institutes and organizations to discuss the research on smoking and health. The group agreed that smoking was directly related to lung cancer and an official national position was established. In 1970, cigarettes could no longer be advertized on television. But cigarette manufacturers continue to argue that no conclusive evidence exists to support the link between smoking and lung cancer, despite the thousands of studies. This short history illuminates how a national epidemic can occur when a strong lobby, the media, and the government promote the use of a dangerous substance. Just think what we could do to prevent smoking and other forms of drug abuse if these three forces banded together! (See the December 1992 issue of *American Heritage Magazine,* John Meyer, MD, for a more detailed history.)

Prevalence of Tobacco Use

In 1993, 50,114,000 or 24.2 percent of Americans over the age of twelve reported that they smoked cigarettes dur-

ing the past month (see Table 10.1). A little over half of these smokers were over thirty-five; 11,183,000 fell into the twenty-six to thirty-four age category. About 34.5 percent of children in the twelve to seventeen age category tried cigarettes at some time in their lives, and 9.6 percent used cigarettes in the past month. Males are more likely than females to use cigarettes in all age groups and in all use patterns, except for those who reported use during the past month in the twelve to seventeen age category (9.3 percent of males and 10.0 percent of females) (Substance Abuse and Mental Health Services Administration, 1994.)

Smokeless, or more accurately spit tobacco seems to be gaining popularity among young males (see Table 10.2). About 12.7 percent of males ages eighteen to twenty-five and 3.9 percent of males ages twelve to seventeen reported using spit tobacco during the past month compared to 5.9 percent of all males over the age of twelve. Spit tobacco is clearly preferred by males. A total of 23,554,000 of males over the age of twelve have tried the drug at some time in their lives compared with 2,939,000 females over the age of twelve. An examination of the used in past

---

Table 10.1   *Cigarettes: Percent of Population Reporting Use of Cigarettes Ever, Past Year, and Past Month (1993) by Sex and Age Groups for Total Population*

	Ever Used	Used During Past Year	Used During Past Month
	RATE ESTIMATES (PERCENTAGES)		
AGE			
12-17	34.5	19.1	9.6
Male	34.0	18.0	9.3
Female	35.0	20.3	10.0
18-25	66.7	38.3	29.0
Male	69.2	41.4	30.9
Female	64.3	35.3	27.2
26-34	74.0	35.1	30.1
Male	77.1	36.7	31.4
Female	71.0	33.6	28.8
35+	77.9	27.4	23.8
Male	86.4	31.6	26.7
Female	70.3	23.7	21.3
Total	71.2	29.4	24.2
Male	76.6	32.4	26.2
Female	66.3	26.6	22.3

Source: Substance Abuse and Mental Health Services Administration. *National Household Survey on Drug Abuse: Population Estimates 1993.*

Table 10.2   *Smokeless Tabacco: Percent of Population Reporting Use of Cigarettes Ever, Past Year, and Past Month (1993) by Sex and Age Groups for Total Population*

	Ever Used	Used During Past Year	Used During Past Month
	RATE ESTIMATES (PERCENTAGES)		
AGE			
12-17	8.7	4.8	2.0
Male	14.6	8.4	3.9
Female	2.5	1.1	-
18-25	19.7	8.9	6.4
Male	34.7	17.0	12.7
Female	5.1	1.1	0.2
26-34	18.4	5.6	4.4
Male	33.9	11.1	8.9
Female	3.5	0.3	0.1
35+	10.1	2.2	1.9
Male	19.4	4.3	3.7
Female	2.0	0.3	0.3
Total	12.8	4.0	2.9
Male	23.7	7.8	5.9
Female	2.7	0.5	0.2

Source: Substance Abuse and Mental Health Services Administration. *National Household Survey on Drug Abuse: Population Estimates 1993.*

month category reveals that 5,875,000 males over the age of twelve have used spit tobacco whereas only 220,000 females have used the drug during the past month. As we will learn later, spit tobacco is responsible for a number of fairly insidious and frightening cases of mouth cancer in young men, leading quickly to death in some instances.

Cigarette smoking among American college students declined modestly in the first half of the 1980s. Thirty-day prevalence fell from 26 percent to 22 percent between 1980 and 1985, but has been relatively stable since then (it was 24 percent in 1992). The daily smoking rate fell from 18.3 percent in 1980 to 12.7 percent in 1986, and has been fairly level through 1990. Since 1990 it has risen from 21.1 percent to 14.1 percent in 1992. While the rates of smoking are dramatically lower among college students than among those not in college, their trends have been similar (see Figure 10.1). Unfortunately, among high school seniors, the trend line for daily use of cigarettes during the 1980–1986 interval was much less steep (Johnston, O'Malley & Bachman, 1993).

Between 1980 and 1988, cigarette smoking has consistently been higher among females than males in college,

despite decreases for both sexes during the first half of the decade (see Figure 10.2). The gap between the sexes has narrowed some, however, because smoking by females has declined a bit more than by males. There was a fairly stable period from about 1984-1990, but college students of both sexes have shown slight increases in use between 1990-1992 (Johnston, O'Malley & Bachman, 1993). Also noteworthy is that the use of other drugs, such as caffeine and alcohol, is much more common among smokers than nonsmokers.

Advertising Tobacco Products

Although cigarette manufacturers are no longer allowed to advertise their products on radio or television, the Centers for Disease Control reports the manufacturers spent about about $3.27 billion on print advertisement, billboards, and other forms of promotion in 1988. These advertisements reach children and adults alike and frequently feature young adults who appear healthy, active, and popular. The message and target audiences are obvious.

Figure 10.1   *Cigarettes: Trends in Thirty-Day Prevalence of Daily Use Among College Students vs. Others 1-4 Years Beyond High School*

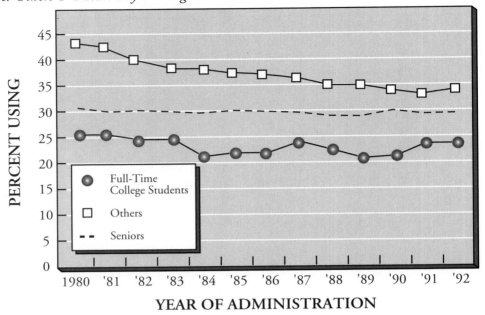

Source: Johnston, O'Malley & Bachman (1993). *National Survey Results in Drug Use from Monitoring the Future Study, 1975–1992.*

Figure 10.2   *Cigarettes: Trends in Thirty-Day Prevalence of Daily Use Among Male and Female College Students*

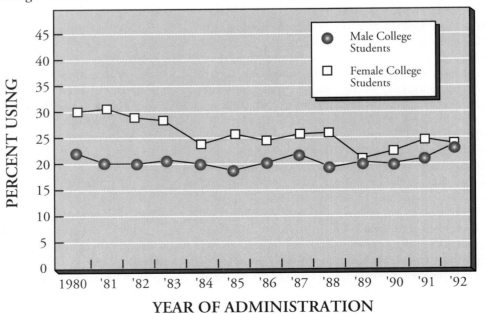

Source: Johnston, O'Malley & Bachman (1994). *National Survey Results in Drug Use from Monitoring the Future Study, 1975–1992.*

Fischer et al. (1991) found that 51 percent of the children aged three to six in their study could successfully identify Old Joe the Camel as being associated with cigarettes. In the same study, 91 percent of the children successfully identified Mickey Mouse as the logo for the Disney Channel. Also, while almost 28 percent correctly identified the Marlboro man, only 23 percent successfully identified the Cheerios logo as cereal. Even more startling was the fact that when the children were divided by age groups, 91 percent of the six-year-old subjects correctly identified Old Joe the Camel as representing cigarettes, which is about equal to the number of six-year-olds who successfully recognized Mickey Mouse.

Spokespersons for the cigarette manufacturers have repeatedly argued that their advertising is designed to induce adults who already smoke to switch brands. However, logic alone would dictate that the tobacco industry must find ways to recruit new smokers since their current consumer population dies off at an astounding rate of more than 400,000 per year (McGinnis & Foege, 1993). DiFranza et al. (1991) argue that the creation of Old Joe the Camel, if not an intentional appeal to children, has had the same consequence. These researchers found that high school students (grades nine to twelve) were much more likely than adults to recognize Old Joe

the Camel as the logo for Camel cigarettes and to find him an appealing character. Moreover, since Old Joe the Camel was first introduced in 1988, Camel cigarettes significantly increased as the cigarette of choice for smokers under age eighteen from 0.5 percent to 32.8 percent. Based on the fact that the total market share for Camel cigarettes is 4.4 percent, DiFranza et al. (1991, p. 3151) computed that only 3.4 percent of that figure accounts for adults. Therefore, children under eighteen are estimated to be spending $476 million per year on Camel cigarettes and account for 25 percent of all Camel sales!

Clearly, the advertising of tobacco products promotes the use of tobacco by minors and initiates new users. It is also clear that advertising is designed to target minorities and women. Ads frequently depict young, healthy African Americans enjoying a smoke at a party and sexy, thin, and athletic young women smoking in bathing suits at beach outings. In order to prevent youngsters and other uninitiated people from using these dangerous products, controls will have to be placed on their advertising. Many have argued that the government has refused to place more restrictive limits on these ads because government subsidies are provided to tobacco farmers and companies. Also, governmental backing of tabacco interests increases lobbyists patronage for supportive legislators.

The mere act of smoking a cigarette becomes a powerful reward as it is associated with the drug's effects.

Mode of Administration

Nicotine may be administered orally, by inhalation, or absorbed through the skin by using a patch. It is possible to inject nicotine intravenously. However, injection is not a route commonly used. Pure nicotine is highly toxic and needs to be diluted to have more comfortable effects. The most popular method is to smoke nicotine-containing tobacco products in the form of a cigarette, cigar, or pipe. This method may be preferred over pure nicotine possibly because other ingredients in tobacco enhance the rewarding aspects of nicotine. Smokers who have attempted to quit by using nicotine gum or patches report that, even though they are obtaining the necessary nicotine to avoid withdrawal, they desperately miss the pleasure of simply holding the cigarette, inhaling, and watching the smoke leave their mouths. Thus, the act of smoking is, in and of itself, rewarding to those addicted. When the smoke is inhaled, it travels, along with particles of ash, to the lungs where it dissolves in the mucous membranes.

Many tobacco users prefer other methods to smoking. Smokeless tobacco is popular in many areas in the form of snuff packaged in a pouch. The tobacco is sniffed into the nostrils; most of the nicotine is absorbed through the membranes of the nasal cavity. Chewing tobacco is another popular way to administer nicotine. With this method, the nicotine, along with other ingredients, is absorbed into the membranes of the mouth. Once the tobacco is adequately chewed, the juice is spit out rather than swallowed. Chewing tobacco dilutes the effects of nicotine because it is not readily absorbed from the digestive tract and it is metabolized quickly by the liver before the nicotine can be distributed throughout the body.

A smokeless cigarette product is presently undergoing trial studies as a possible substitute for conventional cigarettes. The intention is to minimize the toxic effects of the chemicals in the smoke from tobacco that are potentially carcinogenic. Smokeless cigarettes deliver nicotine when air is drawn through but do not contain tobacco. Thus, these cigarettes produce subjective and physiological effects that mimic those produced by administration of nicotine by other, more commonly used, routes. Even though only a relatively small amount of nicotine is detectable in the plasma, smokeless cigarettes seem to provide a high degree of sensory stimulation and may be an adequate alternative for some smokers who would like to reduce their intake of toxins. As of yet, however, this product is not widely used.

Absorption, Metabolism, and Excretion

When nicotine is administered either orally or by inhalation into the lungs, it travels to the stomach where it is absorbed rapidly and completely. Even so, only about 10 to 20 percent of the nicotine contained within the tobacco product is absorbed into the user's bloodstream—enough to provide a powerful effect (Jones, 1987). Similar to alcohol, the body requires about one hour to metabolize nicotine; thus, more than one cigarette an hour will cause the effects of nicotine to accumulate. It is widely believed, in fact, that more nicotine than is necessary to maintain an addiction is administered by hard-core smokers—addicts, in this case, could substantially reduce the amount of nicotine used and not suffer withdrawal effects. This information may be important for the addict if kicking the nicotine habit is desired; the addiction itself is not only physiological but is also behavioral. Thus, realizing that fewer cigarettes may be smoked without suffering ill effects may help to quell the behavioral habit associated with cigarette smoking. A three pack a day smoker could, foreseeably, cut down to one pack—a substantial reduction.

Once the nicotine is absorbed, it travels to the heart and continues on to the brain—inhaled nicotine reaches the brain in approximately seven seconds to provide an immediate response. Concentrations of nicotine in the blood remain quite high until it is pervasively and rapidly distributed to all body organs and fluids. The brain retains a large amount of the nicotine for about thirty minutes when it migrates primarily to the liver, kidneys, salivary glands, and stomach. Nicotine is also evenly distributed to the fetus and milk of a nursing mother so that a breast-fed infant may have the same or higher blood levels of nicotine than that of the mother.

Most of the nicotine is metabolized by the liver (about 80 to 90 percent), although a good portion may be metabolized in the lungs and kidneys. Once metabolized, the inactive by-products travel to the kidneys and are then excreted in the urine. Those with a history of cigarette smoking appear to metabolize nicotine more efficiently than neophytes. This means that those unaccustomed to smoking retain nicotine in their bodies for a longer period. The effects do not last as long for seasoned smokers. Nicotine's effects are likely to last for about one hour after absorption for the regular smoker.

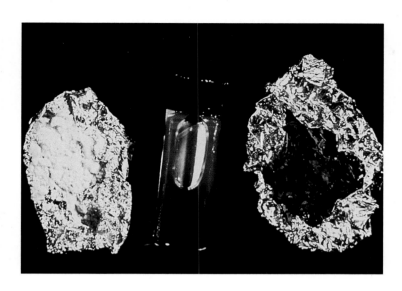

Phencyclidine (PCP) (above)
LSD Blotter Paper (right)
Psilocybin Mushroom (bottom right)
Peyote Cactus (below)

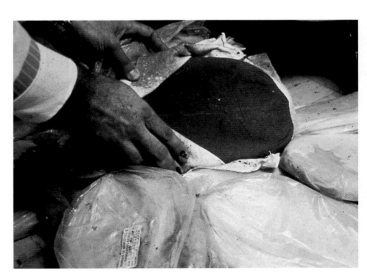

Marijuana (PCP) (above)
Female Marijuana Plant (left)
Hashish (bottom left)
Hashish Oil (below)

Incised Poppy Capsule

Mexican Brown Heroin (top right)
Southeast Asian Heroin (bottom right)
Morphine Preparations (below)

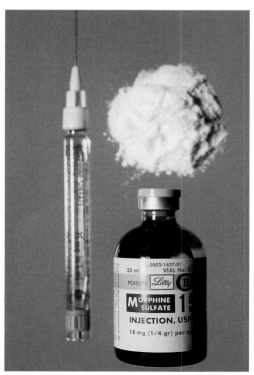

All photos in this section are courtesy of the Drug Enforcement Administration.

Coca Leaf and Flower (left)
Cocaine Hydrochloride (below)

Dexedrine (left)
Valium (below)

Pharmacological Aspects

Nicotine in the peripheral nervous system (PNS) has been studied for nearly a century and was used to help map that system—we have a greater knowledge of the PNS thanks to nicotine. A portion of the peripheral cholinergic nervous system (concentrated in acetylcholine receptors) is thus called the nicotinic nervous system. The second type of cholinergic receptor site is called muscarinic. Figure 10.3 depicts the nicotinic system.

The drug response is complex because nicotine also exerts powerful effects on the central nervous system, the spinal cord, the heart, and other structures and organs. In the CNS, nicotine has been difficult to study. It is clear that nicotine is well absorbed by brain tissue, and we now know that nicotine binding occurs in specific regions where other addictive drugs also bind and alter brain energy use. Because nicotine's effects in these regions are shared by other drugs of abuse, that has given us a clue to the mechanisms behind nicotine's reward value.

Nicotine seems to act somewhat like a neurotransmitter in the CNS, mimicking the action of acetylcholine in the nicotinic cholinergic system. Nicotine has an affinity for receptors in this system, thereby activating centrally located neurons. Because acetylcholine is an excitatory transmitter, related brain activity increases, including activity in the cerebral cortex. This effect may help to explain why smokers actually function better in cognitive tasks when smoking than when they attempt to abstain, as the cortex may suffer from a decrease in activity. At very high doses, nicotine may have the opposite effect, blocking cholinergic transmission and producing depressant effects rather than stimulatory ones. When this occurs, the individual may experience the very untoward symptoms of nicotine overdose. Drugs that block nicotinic receptors such as mecamylamine, block the effects of nicotine and, therefore, have been useful in research. Clinical studies of such drugs suggest that they may eventually be used in the treatment of nicotine toxicity.

Figure 10.3   *Nicotinic System*

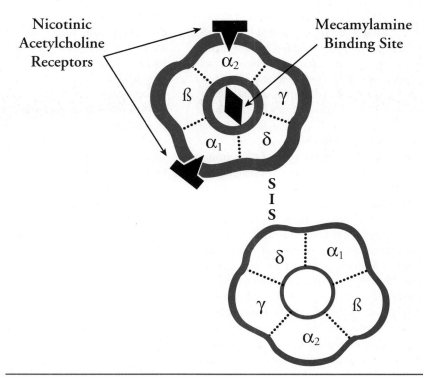

Source: Changeux, Giraudat, and Dennis, 1987

Physical Effects

Physiological alterations in response to nicotine begin with the first nicotine dose. Blood vessels in the skin constrict, reducing blood and oxygen supplies to the extremities. This causes skin temperature to drop and fingers and toes to feel cold to the touch. Constriction of blood vessels may also explain why smokers' skin tends to become quite wrinkled, leathery, and appear older. Because nicotine suppresses urination to some extent, a hormone called the antidiuretic hormone (ADH) is released from the hypothalamus to cause water retention. Centers in the brainstem responsible for vomiting are stimulated. Some cigarette neophytes become nauseated or may even vomit after their first few experiences with nicotine however, this effect tends to diminish with increasing tolerance to nicotine. As with many drugs, unpleasant effects during initial attempts to use nicotine all too often do not deter further tries. Even experienced smokers who have one more cigarette than usual may suffer from some nausea. Respiratory centers in the medulla are stimulated also so that respiration increases. Serious respiratory depression may follow if dosages are high enough. However, this result is unlikely in most smokers, even heavy ones, because the amounts of nicotine administered are not sufficient. An overdose of nicotine will, nevertheless, eventually block respiratory centers in the medulla and centers responsible for muscular activity involved in breathing to cause respiratory arrest.

Nicotine's stimulation of the central cholinergic system causes the user to become behaviorally and physiologically aroused. Nicotinic receptors in the peripheral nervous system are concentrated in areas that control muscle activity. In quite high doses, nicotine is capable of producing tremors and seizures because of this heightened central and peripheral activity state. Direct stimulation of the reticular activating system creates a state of arousal and heightened attention. The adrenal glands are also stimulated to produce epinephrine, thereby activating the f/f/f mechanism much like other sympathomimetic drugs. These effects on the autonomic nervous system cause the release of sugars into the blood, increasing metabolism and fueling the muscles to provide a burst of energy. Blood pressure and heart rate rise, bowel tone and activity increases (serving as a laxative and sometimes causing diarrhea), and gastrointestinal activity increases. Once these effects wear off, however, fuel for cells diminish, resulting in even less energy than before the drug was taken. Also, as CNS activity decreases with withdrawal, physiological, behavioral, and psychological depression may all ensue.

As previously mentioned, labeling nicotine as a stimulant is an oversimplification. Its actions on behavior and physiologic function are either stimulating or depressing, depending on what is measured. For example, although nicotine is a stimulant, many users report feeling more calm and relaxed when they light up and smoke a cigarette. Most smokers, in fact, light up more frequently when they are feeling stressed out. This is probably true for three reasons. First, in addition to CNS stimulation, nicotine activates cells in the spinal cord to reduce muscle tone, thus, serving as a muscle relaxant. Second, if the user is addicted to nicotine, readministering the drug will provide relief from craving and withdrawal symptoms. And finally, the psychological anticipation of the rewarding drug effects alone may create feelings of well-being in nicotine addicts. Just the act of smoking, separate from the effects of the nicotine, has been reported to produce calmness. Thus, expectations and the surroundings play a large role in the actual physiological and psychological effects of each cigarette, whether they are stimulating or depressing.

Psychological Effects

The degree to which nicotine has desirable effects may be a function of either habitual use or its ability to relieve preexisting symptoms—this area has not been well researched. Nicotine appears to diminish responses to stress and to enhance mood, thus reducing anxiety in experienced users (Gilbert, 1979). It also reduces aggressive responses under experimental conditions (Cherek, 1984). The mild to moderate CNS stimulating properties of nicotine reduce fatigue and improve performances that involve speed, reaction time, vigilance, and concentration (Wesnes & Warburton, 1983, 1984). Nicotine may also be a mood regulator because it releases norepinephrine from the adrenal medulla (Gilbert). High doses of nicotine taken only infrequently are even capable of producing hallucinations, apparently a technique used by the American Indians. Nevertheless, this is not an example of a typical use pattern.

As an appetite reducer, nicotine functions in at least three ways: (1) it decreases the efficiency with which food is metabolized (Schecter & Cook, 1976), (2) it reduces the appetite for simple carbohydrates like sweets (Grunberg & Morse, 1984), and (3) it reduces eating at times of stress (Burse et al., 1975). It is no wonder that some individuals attempting to quit the nicotine habit find themselves gaining weight! In addition to an increase in cravings for sweets and the need for a substitute behavioral habit (particularly one that is essentially oral), the associated reduction in metabolic rate contributes to some weight gain. Resting heart rate, one indicator of metabolic rate, actually decreases when a smoker has truly quit. Weight gain is commonly given as an excuse not to quit, even though regular exercise can counteract this effect and increase metabolic rate overall.

Those who use tobacco products are generally seeking the stimulating effects of nicotine on the autonomic nervous system. This stimulation leads to an elevation in mood. Because nicotine is so widely legally available, is inexpensive, and its doses are so easily regulated, it is a very convenient means of self-medication for a dysphoric mood or physical state. Smokers tend to use nicotine to regulate levels of psychological and physiological arousal. For example, smokers may increase arousal during periods of boredom or fatigue by regulating when and how much nicotine they administer. The ability to perform tasks may be manipulated also. The ability to control mood and arousal levels in either direction is a unique feature of nicotine, due to its depressant and stimulant properties. These combined properties probably add to the abuse liability of tobacco products, thus making the treatment of nicotine dependence especially difficult.

Tolerance and Dependence

Nicotine is one of the most powerful and potent addictive drugs used today. In general, cigarette smokers have a very poor success rate when they attempt to quit and, only 2 percent of smokers are able to smoke only occasionally. Most smoke regularly and tend to increase the number of cigarettes over time until they reach a ceiling. Unlike other addictive substances, most smokers find a ceiling or plateau within the first few years of smoking and do not significantly vary from this diet. Once a plateau has been reached, smokers tend to adjust their daily administrations to maintain steady blood levels of nicotine. When a smoker attempts to quit, the craving for a cigarette is profound and, more often than not, leads to eventual reuse. Nicotine may cause mild intoxication and can be quite toxic; less than 1 mg can cause behavioral and physiological effects. Nicotine taken by any route that allows absorption leads to rapid tolerance. Many smokers report that the first or the first few cigarettes of the day provide the strongest effect. Subsequent cigarettes may provide no nicotine kick at all. In such cases, additional cigarettes that

are smoked enable the user to avoid the discomfort of withdrawal and may constitute more of a behavioral habit than a physiological one.

Both physical and psychological dependence develops from nicotine use. This is evidenced by the characteristic abstinence (withdrawal) syndrome (see Table 10.3). Once nicotine receptors become accustomed to the presence of nicotine, tolerance to nicotine is established. Thus, when abstinence occurs, nicotine supplies decline and receptors become hypersensitive. What follows are quick and complex changes in absolute and relative levels of neurohormones, such as norepinephrine and epinephrine. Some evidence suggests that nicotine differentially stimulates the release of more norepinephrine than epinephrine. Elevated levels of norepinephrine relative to epinephrine are associated with pleasurable states of sympathetic arousal, similar to conditions associated with sex or excitement during sporting events. Elevated levels of epinephrine relative to norepinephrine, a state that may be the result of nicotine withdrawal, are associated with uncomfortable states, such as fear, boredom, stress, and anxiety (see, e.g., Pomerleau & Pomerleau, 1984).

Withdrawal symptoms include headache, stomach pain, irritability, difficulty concentrating, gastrointestinal disturbances, drowsiness, and insomnia. Also associated

---

Table 10.3   *Commonalities Between Nicotine and Other Drug Dependence*

- Spread is socially mediated and is persistent.
- Patterns of relapse are similar following treatment.
- User persists in face of damage (individual and social).
- Personality types overlap.
- Centrally (CNS) acting substance is delivered.
- Drug is a reinforcer for animals.
- Deprivation increases drug-seeking behavior.
- Tolerance develops with repeated use.
- Therapeutic effects may be produced.
- Patterns of self-administration and dose-response functions are orderly.

Inset 10.1

NICOTINE DEPENDENCE (305.10 DSM-III-R, APA)

Patterns of Use. At present, the most common form of nicotine dependence is associated with the inhalation of cigarette smoke. Pipe and cigar smoking, the use of snuff, and the chewing of tobacco are less likely to lead to nicotine dependence. The more rapid onset of nicotine effects with cigarette smoking leads to a more intensive habit pattern that is more difficult to give up because of the frequency of reinforcement and the greater physical dependence on nicotine.

Associated Features. People with this disorder are often distressed because of their inability to stop nicotine use, particularly when they have serious physical symptoms that are aggravated by nicotine. Some people who have nicotine dependence may have difficulty remaining in social or occupational situations in which smoking is prohibited.

Course. The course of nicotine dependence is variable. Most people repeatedly attempt to give up nicotine use without success. In some the dependence is brief, in that when they experience concern about nicotine use, they promptly make an effort to stop smoking and are successful, though in many cases they may experience a period of nicotine withdrawal lasting from days to weeks. Studies of treatment outcome suggest that the relapse rate is greater that 50 percent in the first six months, and at least seventy percent in the first twelve months. After a year's abstinence, subsequent relapse is unlikely.

The difficulty in giving up nicotine use definitively, particularly cigarettes, may be due to the unpleasant nature of the withdrawal syndrome, the deeply ingrained nature of the habit, the repeated effects of nicotine, which rapidly follow the inhalation of cigarette smoke (75,000 puffs per year for a pack-a-day smoker), and the likelihood that a desire to use nicotine is elicited by environmental cues, such as the ubiquitous presence of other smokers and the widespread availability of cigarettes. When efforts to give up smoking are made, nicotine withdrawal may develop.

Impairment. Since nicotine, unlike alcohol, rarely causes any clinically significant state of intoxication, there is no impairment in social or occupational functioning as an immediate and direct consequences of its use.

Complications. The most common complications are bronchitis, emphysema, coronary artery disease, peripheral vascular disease, and a variety of cancers.

Prevalence and Sex Ratio. A large proportion of the adult population of the United States has nicotine dependence, the prevalence among males being greater than that among females. Among teenaged smokers, males are affected approximately as often as females.

Familial Pattern. Cigarette smoking among first-degree biologic relatives of people with nicotine dependence is more common than among general population. Evidence for a genetic factor has been documented, but the effect is modest.

with withdrawal is the extreme craving that dependent users experience for a long period of time after quitting. The sense of craving appears to reach a peak within the first twenty-four hours after the last cigarette, thereafter gradually declining over a few days to several weeks. This is evidenced by the difficulty users have abstaining from the drug, even after the first stage of withdrawal has been completed. Former smokers report a recurring desire to smoke for many years, which may be evoked by such smoking-associated activities as eating, socializing, alcohol drinking, and sex. Thus, successful, long-term abstinence is frequently thwarted and relapse rates are high.

Inset 10.2

DIAGNOSTIC CRITERIA FOR 292.00
NICOTINE WITHDRAWAL

A. Daily use of nicotine for at least several weeks.

B. Abrupt cessation of nicotine use, or reduction in the amount of nicotine used, following within twenty-four hours by at least four of the following signs:

1. craving for nicotine
2. irritability, frustration, or anger
3. anxiety
4. difficulty concentrating
5. restlessness
6. decreased heart rate
7. increased appetite or weight gain

Importantly, repeated use may lead to loss of control over subsequent use; in other words, the more frequently nicotine is used the more difficult users find it to abstain without being horribly uncomfortable and dysfunctional. In fact, most smokers surveyed say that they would quit if it would not compromise their ability to function well and feel their usual selves. The most recent edition of the American Psychological Association's DSM-III-R (APA, 1987) contains a diagnostic category called Nicotine Dependence, legitimizing the diagnosis and describing the features of an addiction to nicotine (see Inset 10.1).

According to the APA (1987), many users who attempt to quit after continuous use develop withdrawal symptoms that constitute an organic mental disorder. Because there are so many active substances in tobacco, it is possible that some of tobacco's effects, including the withdrawal symptoms, may partially result from the exposure to and withdrawal from compounds other than nicotine. The DSM-III-R diagnostic criteria for Nicotine Withdrawal are described in Inset 10.2.

The simplest and most graphic evidence that nicotine is a dependence-producing drug is that the majority of people who smoke recognize that smoking is bad for them and say they would like to quit but are unable to do so. Most smokers fail at their first attempt to quit, so the control over their lives has been transferred in part to the perceived need for the cigarette.

The process of becoming dependent on nicotine begins almost immediately as the effects on psychological and physiological processes are rapidly experienced. Smokers know that they are nicotine-dependent when they find that quitting would cause a disruption in lifestyle. At what point this insight occurs differs for each smoker. The question of why some smokers become rapidly dependent on nicotine while others require more experience with the drug or fail to become dependent at all has never been answered adequately. One individual may simply experiment with tobacco as a teenager and never find it particularly appealing or compelling, while another may be immediately reinforced by its use and rapidly develop an addiction. Some smoke for years and quit easily, while others fail miserably at every attempt to abstain. There is speculation that individual differences in brain chemistry, body metabolism, diet, prior learning experiences, personality traits, and other environmental conditions play a role in the propensity to become addicted. The reasons for these differences may relate to their initial reasons for smoking and to the extent to which they are physiologically addicted to nicotine.

People who are dependent on nicotine have reported that their ability to learn, think, perform, reason, drive, and write become impaired if they are unable to smoke. Changes in mood and performance related to withdrawal can be detected within two hours after the last cigarette in a heavy smoker. Physicians and scientists originally believed that these effects were primarily psychological. We now know from laboratory studies that abstinence from nicotine in a dependent user contributes to these impairments by disrupting physiological function of the brain. Airline passengers should be happy that the no-smoking rule does not apply to the cockpit! Readministration of nicotine will reverse or block these deficits in the brain (see Figure 10.4). Given these recent findings, it is not advisable for a chronic smoker to abstain from cigarettes in the face of pressures to think, function, and perform simple arithmetic and logical reasoning. For a period of time, perhaps about two weeks or even two months after quitting, such abilities will be impaired. All such deficits will eventually be restored to normal either after smoking is resumed or once the user has truly quit.

Toxicity

In addition to the possible side effects produced by nicotine, including diarrhea, intestinal distress, increased heart rate and blood pressure, water retention, and possible vomiting, tobacco in any form is quite toxic. There are numerous ingredients in tobacco, such as nicotine, tars, carbon monoxide, benzene, and others that are associated with cancer, lung and upper respiratory disease, heart disease, and a variety of other chronic ailments. Hundreds of thousands of persons die each year from tobacco use. Estimates are that, for every cigarette smoked, about fourteen minutes of the user's life have been destroyed. At this rate, a thirty-year-old who has smoked two packs a day since the age of fifteen would already have lost several years of life. The life expectancy of a thirty-year-old who

---

Figure 10.4   *Performance and Cognitive Impairment with Abstinence. Time course of deterioration and partial recovery on one of the measures (rapid arithmetic) of the computerized cognitive performance assessment battery. The figure shows accuracy and speed scores at baseline (post-abstinence), 10 days of the tobacco abstinence, and 24 hours post-abstinence.*

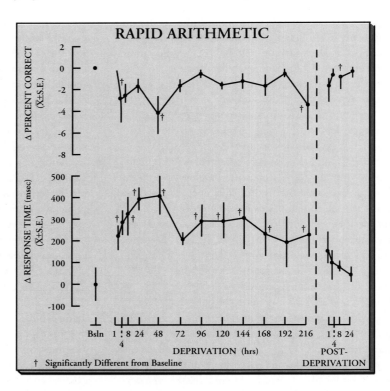

Source: Unpublished data from the Addiction Research Center, NIDA

smokes just fifteen cigarettes a day (less than one pack) is shortened by more than five years. The causes of death related to cigarette smoking are numerous. Heart disease, stroke, and lung cancer are a few of the most common. Reports from the USDHEW (1979) reveal that tobacco-related deaths are most often a result of cancers of the lung, voice box, mouth, throat, pancreas, and bladder; heart attacks and vascular disease; and chronic lung disease such as bronchitis and emphysema. This list does not even include disabilities and illnesses resulting from tobacco use—only mortality! Cigarette smoking is one of the most frequent contributors to poor health, yet it is one of the most preventable causes of death and disability in the United States.

The particular health problems resulting from tobacco use and their level of severity depend on how frequently tobacco is used and in what form (e.g., smoked or chewed), the amount of tar and nicotine contained in the cigarette, how deeply the user inhales, and how long the smoker has used tobacco. Cigarettes with low tar and nicotine can substantially reduce the likelihood of serious health problems. Unfortunately, many who smoke these reduced tar and nicotine cigarettes commonly find themselves smoking more often, eventually accumulating levels of tar and nicotine similar to those of stronger cigarettes. Some of these users even cover the holes above the filters of low tar and nicotine cigarettes with their fingers in a way that lets less ventilation into the cigarette, increasing the dosage of nicotine!

There are several substances of medical importance in tobacco smoke. Tar contains the highest concentrations of carcinogens, contributing to formation of cancers. Numerous other carcinogens and cocarcinogens in tobacco further accelerate the production of cancer. Irritants in tobacco cause coughing and bronchoconstriction after smoke is inhaled. Nicotine principally affects the nervous system and is primarily responsible for a smoker's pharmacologic dependence on cigarettes. And toxic gases in cigarette smoke include carbon monoxide, hydrogen sulfide, hydrocyanic acid, and oxides of nitrogen. These substances reduce the amounts of hemoglobin available for oxygen transport, impairing oxygen release to the tissues and increasing the formation of fat deposits in arteries.

The combined effects of carbon monoxide and nicotine are particularly insidious and damaging to the heart and cardiovascular system. In fact, more people die from heart disease related to smoking than from lung cancer. Carbon monoxide decreases the amount of oxygen that heart muscles receive. At the same time, nicotine increases the activity of the heart, causing it to work harder. Without the necessary supplies of oxygen, damage to the heart muscle may result and the heart may become exhausted, unable to compensate for the drain and pressures. As a result, myocardial metabolism changes, straining and potentially damaging the heart muscle. These compounds also are associated with an increased incidence of aneurysms of the aorta, atherosclerosis and thrombosis in the coronary arteries. As a result, smokers have a much higher risk for heart disease than nonsmokers. The preexistence of high blood pressure or diabetes further heightens this risk. Fortunately, abstaining from cigarettes for about ten years will reverse a great deal of the damage done to the heart (assuming it was not permanent damage) and the risk of coronary heart disease will diminish to that of a nonsmoker. As a consequence, the mortality rate from coronary heart disease declines substantially once smoking cessation has been established.

The smoke from tobacco directly decreases the capacity of the lungs to receive and pump oxygen. Cigarette smokers develop a characteristic cough, find it difficult to breathe, especially with exercise, wheeze, suffer chest pain and lung congestion, and are quite susceptible to upper respiratory infections (URIs). The incidence of bronchitis, sinusitis, and other URIs is quite high among smokers and immune responses generally are compromised, causing them to be at increased risk for all sorts of infections and illnesses. Furthermore, when smokers suffer from URIs, the course of the illness is longer than for nonsmokers. Emphysema (damage to the lungs) develops in many chronic smokers and can be disabling and eventually lethal. This form of lung damage is irreversible and causes the sufferer to have extreme difficulty breathing, low energy levels, and heart strain. Deaths from chronic bronchitis and emphysema are about twenty times more frequent in those who smoke heavily than in nonsmokers. Heavy smokers have been known to actually lose a lung due to collapse and continue smoking.

The tobacco-related disease that receives the most attention is lung cancer—smokers are ten times more likely than nonsmokers to contract lung cancer. Epidemiological studies show that men who smoke more than one pack a day are about twenty times more at risk of developing lung cancer than are nonsmokers. Where filter tips offer some protection, the risk is greatest in those who inhale deeply, take more puffs per cigarette, relight half-smoked cigarettes, and start smoking at an early age. Also, when tobacco is used along with alcohol, the cancer-causing effects of tobacco are exacerbated. Sadly, those

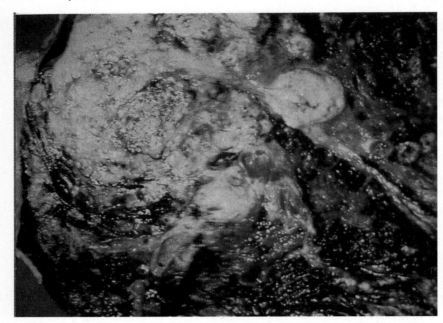

A lung blackened by tobacco use that has become cancerous.

Source: National Cancer Institute

who smoke are more likely to drink alcohol, and those who drink alcohol are more likely to smoke!

Although the link between cigarettes and lung cancer is without question, we still do not understand why not all smokers develop cancer. Actually, only about one tenth of smokers will contract it. One possibility is that the tendency to develop cancer is genetic and only those with a genetic risk will be susceptible to tobacco's carcinogenic effects (Eysenck & Eaves, 1980). There is, by the way, no way to determine if you are one of the unlucky folks at risk. If you have relatives who developed lung cancer, your risk probably increases substantially. Further evidence for how insidiously addictive nicotine is can be seen when smokers are diagnosed with lung cancer and refuse to quit, smoke even while hospitalized, and eventually suffer a painful, agonizing death. Other types of cancer that are associated with cigarette smoking include bladder, kidney, pancreatic, larynx, oral cavity, and esophagus tumors. Smokers suffer from these cancers at higher rates than nonsmokers. Again, the type of cancer that develops may be a function of individual genetically determined differences.

Peptic ulcers occur more frequently and have a higher mortality rate in cigarette smokers than in nonsmokers. In addition, the effectiveness of medical treatment for peptic ulceration is reduced and the rate of ulcer healing is slowed when the patient smokes.

Women who smoke cigarettes and also take oral contraceptives dramatically increase their risk for heart attacks and strokes. The more they smoke, the greater their risk. Furthermore, tobacco-induced lung cancer in women has surpassed breast cancer and is rapidly approaching the male rate.

Smoking and Pregnancy

There is ample evidence to indicate that cigarette smoking during pregnancy compromises the pregnancy, the birth, and the health of the baby. Because smoking is legal and so widespread, problems associated with maternal smoking are common and, thus, particularly disconcerting. Obstetricians and educational efforts should make clear to pregnant women and those who are planning to become pregnant that smoking is contraindicated. Unfortunately, many women do not even realize that they are pregnant until they are halfway through their first trimester, when the major fetal organs are forming. Unless they were informed of the risks before becoming pregnant, a woman who smokes will likely continue to smoke at least during the first few weeks of pregnancy. In response to evidence that maternal smoking constitutes a health hazard, the Surgeon General's warning included on cigarette boxes

Inset 10.3

CONVERSATION WITH A PREGNANT SMOKER

Carla became pregnant when she was seventeen years old. She was not aware that she was pregnant until she was practically through her first trimester. Nevertheless, she wanted to keep the baby and her boyfriend agreed. Together they visited an educational class, designed to inform underprivileged women about stages of pregnancy, fetal development, health care, child birth, and child care. The instructor noticed that Carla was a smoker and inquired about her willingness to quit. Carla did not show any interest in quitting and indicated that she knew very little about health effects of cigarettes on the developing baby. The instructor promptly told her that smoking would likely reduce the weight of her baby, possibly leading to a low birth weight newborn. Carla was very much aware of this effect. In fact, she enthusiastically stated that she preferred a smaller baby because she heard that delivery would be easier. She went on to say that her mother smoked while she was pregnant with her, and the delivery was quick and relatively easy because Carla was born small. Carla, and obviously her mother, were unaware that low birth weight occurs because the fetus does not receive adequate amounts of oxygen and, thus, does not develop as well. Implications that low birth weight may reflect a smaller brain, impaired lung development and other complications were not considered. These facts were explained to Carla who received them with deaf ears. Her youth, lack of maturity, and irresponsibility were all factors in Carla's denial.

now states: "Smoking by pregnant women may result in fetal injury and premature birth." Still, this simple sentence drastically understates the serious implications of maternal smoking.

While nicotine crosses the placenta, its harmful effects are primarily the result of blood vessel constriction in the mother and the consequent reduced oxygen supply to the fetus. This oxygen reduction (hypoxia) is also increased by carbon monoxide interfering with the blood's ability to distribute oxygen throughout the body. It is this lack of oxygen to the fetus that jeopardizes both the pregnancy and the proper development of the baby.

The incidence of spontaneous abortion, (19,000-141,000 per year), stillbirth, and neonatal death (1900-4800 per year) is increased in pregnant women who smoke (DiFranza & Lew, 1994). There is a greater likelihood of premature detachment of the placenta (abruptio placentae), vaginal bleeding, abnormalities in placenta attachment to the uterus (placenta previa), ruptured membranes, and preterm delivery. All these complications of pregnancy carry a high risk of perinatal loss—infants born to mothers who smoke are twice as likely to be stillborn than those born to nonsmokers.

Maternal smoking has been implicated in as many as 14 percent of preterm deliveries in the United States. Prematurity increases the risks for early infant death and for respiratory illness. Recent large-scale studies confirm a positive association between physical defects among newborns and maternal smoking.

The mean birth weight of infants born to mothers who smoke during pregnancy is 7 ounces less than that of infants born to nonsmoking mothers. Reductions in infants' birthweight are proportional to the amounts mothers smoke and are independent of other risk factors and gestational age. The earlier in pregnancy that a woman stops smoking, the better her chances are for delivering a normal-weight baby. It is believed that between 32,000-61,000 infants are born each year with low birth weight that is attributed to the mother's use of tabacco products (DiFranza & Lew, 1994).

These low birth weight babies are also shorter than normal for their gestational age and have smaller head and chest circumferences. Extreme variations in head circumference are somewhat related to intellectual capacity, so there is speculation that these babies may have functioned on a somewhat higher mental level if their mothers had not smoked. In fact, evidence that children who had been exposed to smoke in utero have, on average, lower scores on certain cognitive, psychomotor, language, and academic measures provide support for this speculation.

Children exposed either during pregnancy or in their external environments suffer from more frequent ear infections, upper respiratory infections (including bronchitis and sinusitis), allergies, asthma, and other illnesses. This association may be due to an impaired immune system and underdeveloped lungs from in utero tobacco exposure and to damage from external exposure to smoke's irritants. Maternal smoking has been associated with behavioral problems in children including lack of self-control, irritability, hyperactivity, and disinterest. Finally, it is also believed that between 1,200 to 2,200 deaths each year from sudden infant death syndrome (SIDS) are caused by the mother's use of tobacco (DiFranza & Lew, 1994).

Passive Smoking (Secondhand Smoke)

Passive exposure to cigarette smoke (experienced when someone is smoking in the same room) results in quite high blood levels of nicotine in those who happen to be in the room. The consequences of secondhand smoke are insidious. Nicotine concentrations may reach levels high enough to trigger bronchoconstriction in asthmatics and angina in patients with coronary artery disease. Between 2,500 and 3,300 lung cancer deaths a year have been attributed to environmental tobacco smoke, according to the Environmental Protection Agency (EPA). Besides lung cancer, secondhand smoke causes other respiratory problems in nonsmokers, including coughing, phlegm, chest discomfort, and reduced lung function. The EPA further reports that cigarette smoke is the biggest source of indoor air pollution, and increaingly, regulations are being imposed to resrict use in public areas. Secondhand tobacco smoke is believed to cause thirty times as many lung cancer deaths as all other cancer-causing air pollutants that are regulated by the EPA.

Wives of smokers have been found to have a higher risk of both lung and cervical cancer than wives of nonsmokers (Humble et al., 1985; 1990; Slattery et al., 1989). Respiratory disease and infections are more common in children whose parents smoke (Jarvis et al., 1985; Mason et al., 1985). Up to 300,000 cases of respiratory infections occur in children under eighteen months of age, landing about 15,000 of them in the hospital. These children tend

to suffer from more ear infections, bronchitis, asthma, reduced lung function, sinusitis, and other sometimes severe illnesses. Mothers who smoke ten or more cigarettes a day can actually produce as many as 26,000 new cases of asthma in their children every year. Infants are three times more likely to die of sudden infant death syndrome if their mothers smoked during and after pregnancy.

In the workplace, health hazards are also present. Exposed workers are approximately 34 percent more likely to develop lung cancer. Estimates are that for every smoker in the workplace, at least $1,000 a year is lost due to decreased productivity and increased health care costs. Needless to say, smoking may increase a company's premium costs for life and health insurance or a company's liability because of potential lawsuits brought by nonsmoking employees.

Unfortunately for those near a smoking individual, the airborne particles from the smoke are unfiltered, unlike the bulk of the smoke inhaled by the smoker (if that person uses filtered cigarettes). Thus, carcinogens and irritants found in sidestream smoke are in higher concentrations and the effects can be unexpectedly hazardous.

Smoking and Mental Illness

Because smoking is unusually common among mental patients, the effect of nicotine on their treatment and prognosis has become an important issue. The prevalence of smoking among outpatients is estimated at 52 percent. People with schizophrenia are apparently more likely than anyone else to smoke; 86 percent of them are smokers. This phenomena helps to explain why many psychiatric hospitals issue cigarettes at least once an hour to patients who are behaving acceptably. They may even supply cigarettes to patients who cannot buy their own. Cigarettes are frequently withheld as punishment for unacceptable behavior, and unlimited smoking is permitted by patients who show improvement in behavior. As you can see, manipulating supplies of nicotine acts as a powerful reward and punishment system in controlled settings.

Recently, these practices have been questioned, not only because of the obvious health hazards, but also because nicotine stimulates certain chemical reactions in the body that alter the molecular structure of some medications. Some antipsychotic drugs produce a much higher degree of drowsiness and low blood pressure among nonsmokers than among heavy smokers. Smoking may also reduce the blood levels of some neuroleptic drugs

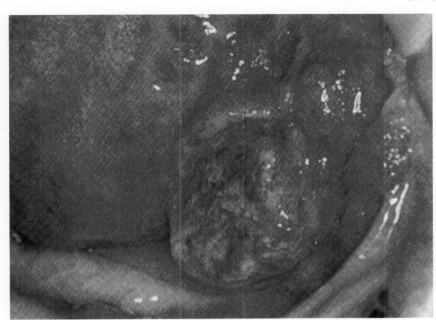

Oral cancer.

Source: U.S.Department of Health and Human Services

used to treat psychosis. Smokers tend to need higher doses of these drugs than nonsmokers to achieve similar levels of improvement.

Nicotine tends to increase the activity of dopamine, which is elevated in schizophrenia and lowered by the use of antipsychotic medications. Consequently, smoking may worsen some forms of mental illness and may even interfere with treatment efforts to control symptoms of mental disorders. One particularly worrisome effect is on tardive dyskinesia (TD). TD is a condition caused in some patients by the use of antipsychotic drugs. It involves uncontrollable movements of the lips and tongue and sometimes also of the arms and legs. The patient may drool and make abnormal sounds. The condition generally disappears when the medication is withdrawn, although for some patients it is permanent. Smoking only one half pack a day increases the risk of developing TD, especially for women.

On the other hand, smoking is not bad in all instances. Because nicotine has anticholinergic properties, it may actually decrease the side effects of some antipsychotic medications, such as rigidity, tremor of muscles, shuffling walk, expressionless face, restlessness, and dystonic reactions (muscle spasms of the face and neck). Nevertheless, the availability of medications intended to minimize side effects lessens the argument in favor of smoking by men-

tal patients. Some psychiatric hospitals are presently considering a ban on smoking by their patients, in spite of fervent opposition by both patients and some staff members.

Smokeless Tobacco

There is a great deal of concern recently about the widespread use of smokeless products, including snuff and chewing tobacco. The adverse health consequences of these products has led the Surgeon General to request a report on the toxic effects of spit tobacco and whether it may produce dependence (Connolly et al., 1986). When snuff is moistened, it contains between 12.0 and 16.6 mg of nicotine per gram. Plug tobacco contains 24.5 mg per gram. Because nicotine is approximately five to ten times more potent than cocaine in producing measurable subjective effects, these amounts are substantial. And there are other ingredients that highlight spit tobacco's dangerousness: polonium-210, a nuclear waste product; cadmium, used in car batteries; lead, a nerve poison; uranium-235, used in nuclear weapons; formaldehyde, used in embalming fluid; and nitrosamines and benzopyrene, which are cancer-causing agents. Not surprisingly, the conclusions from the report to the Surgeon General (USDHHS, 1986) indicate that not only is the use of spit tobacco a hazard to health, it is also addictive and dependence producing.

Usual use of spit tobacco results in plasma nicotine elevations comparable to those produced by cigarette smoking (Gritz et al., 1981; Russell et al., 1981) although nicotine levels rise more slowly. Those who use these products administer large amounts, demonstrate regular use patterns, and experience subjective and behavioral effects. Nicotine absorption from spit tobacco appears to be somewhat similar to that produced by nicotine gum. The implication of this may be that persons dependent on spit tobacco may be more effectively treated with nicotine gum than cigarette smokers.

Studies have documented that spit tobacco has dependence potential (USDHHS, 1987, p. 108). During abstinence, subjects who received moist snuff showed significant signs and symptoms of nicotine withdrawal, such as decreased resting pulse rate as well as a reduction in changes in resting pulse, an increase in craving to reuse tobacco, an increase in eating, sleep disruptions, and confusion.

Oral conditions are common among those who use chewing tobacco. About one-half of spit tobacco users exhibit white lesions in their mouths on the tongue and cheeks, called leukoplakia. Potentially life-threatening oral lesions may also result. The risk for developing oral cancer is much greater among tobacco users than among nonusers. In combination with alcohol use, the risk is even greater. Other conditions directly caused by smokeless tobacco products include tooth loss, tobacco stains, tooth abrasion, bleeding, bad breath, and fungal infections.

Treatment

Categorizing nicotine simply as a stimulant led to the use of amphetamines and other stimulants as treatment for smokers. These strategies were modeled after drug replacement therapies, such as methadone for heroin. For nicotine, however, the effort failed largely because the treatment actually increased the desire and tendency to smoke. So rather than replace the tobacco, the drugs promoted smoking.

The U.S. Surgeon General's declaration in 1990 that nicotine is addictive provided additional fuel to the development of pharmacological smoking-cessation aids to ease withdrawal. New forms of treatment have included using a nicotine gum or nicotine patch. Both forms contain doses of nicotine nearly equivalent to what the smoker normally inhales throughout a twenty-four hour period; thus, someone who smokes only a few cigarettes a day will receive a dosage much smaller than someone who smokes two packs a day. The gum looks like Dentine, however, patients are not always enamored with the taste. It is also hard to chew and can make people's jaws and mouth sore. Nicotine gum is most effective when chewed slowly, and then held between the teeth and gums for a

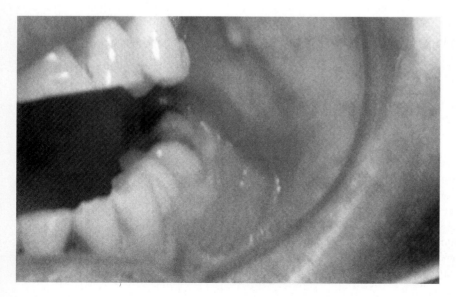

Snuff dipper's pouch.

Source: U.S. Department of Health and Human Services

Inset 10.4

A TEST FOR NICOTINE ADDICTION

	0 Points	1 Point	2 Points
1. How soon after you wake up do you smoke your first cigarette?	after 30 minutes	within 30 minutes	—
2. Do you find it difficult to refrain from smoking in places where it is forbidden, such as the library, theater, doctor's office?	No	Yes	—
3. Which of all the cigarettes you smoke during the day is the most satisfying?	Any other than the first in the morning	The first one in the morning	—
4. How many cigarettes a day do you smoke?	1–15	16–25	26+
5. Do you smoke more during the morning than during the rest of the day?	No	Yes	—
6. Do you smoke when you are so ill that you are in bed most of the day?	No	Yes	—
7. Does the brand you smoke have a low, medium, or high nicotine content?	Low	Medium	High
8. How often do you inhale the smoke?	Never	Sometimes	Always

More than 6 points-very Addicted
Below 6 points-Low to Moderate Addiction

Source: American Lung Association; Fagerstrom Test

time and chewed again. This way, the nicotine is released gradually rather than in a sudden jolt. The downside of the gum is that some patients find themselves addicted to the gum itself and find it difficult to eventually give it up.

Nicotine patches were developed because many who had used the gum complained that they were not strong enough to satisfy their craving and because it does not break psychological and behavioral habits that revolve around smoking—putting something in their mouths

and self-administering nicotine. The patches are round or rectangular adhesives that are attached to a nonhairy, nonoily area of the body—often the back or an arm. These transdermal patches deliver a steady dose of nicotine throughout the day, thus reducing the smoker's craving for the drug. The patch's long-term success rate is still under debate, but early studies indicate that the patch more than doubles the six-month quit rate over a placebo. Similar to the gum, however, some people find it difficult

Table 10.4   *Description of Life Skills Training Program*

SESSION	MATERIAL COVERED
Orientation	General introduction to the program, saliva collection, and administration of pretest questionnaire, overview of forthcoming sessions
Smoking: Myths and realities	Common attitude and beliefs about smoking, prevalence of smoking, reasons for and against smoking, the process of becoming an addicted smoker, and the decreasing social acceptability of smoking
Smoking and biofeedback	Effect of smoking on carbon monoxide levels and heart rate are demonstrated using ecolyzer and cardiotachometer
Self-image and self-improvement	Self-image and how it is formed, the relationship between self-image and behavior, the importance of a positive self-image, and ways of improving self-image
Decision making and independent thinking	A general decision-making strategy, decisions making and sources of influence affecting decisions, resisting persuasive tactics, and the importance of independent thinking
Advertising techniques	Use and function of advertising, ad techniques, identifying techniques used in cigarette advertising and how they are designed to affect consumer behavior, alternative ways of responding to these ads
Coping with anxiety	Situations causing anxiety, demonstration and practice of techniques for coping with anxiety
Communication skills	Verbal and nonverbal communication, techniques for avoiding misunderstanding, basic conversation skills, giving and receiving compliments, making introductions
Social skills A	Overcoming shyness, initiating social contacts, giving and receiving compliments, basic conversational skills
Social skills B	Boy-girl relationships, nature of attraction, conversing with the opposite sex, asking someone out for a date
Assertiveness	Situations calling for assertiveness, reasons for not being assertive, verbal and nonverbal assertive skills, resisting peer pressure to smoke
Conclusion	Brief review, conclusions, saliva collection, posttest questionnaire

Source: Botvin et al. 1983. Copyright 1983 Plenum Publishing Corp.

to wean themselves from the daily nicotine fix. It can also irritate the skin and disrupt sleep if left on all night.

For both forms of replacement, addicts continue to receive their dose of nicotine while they learn to disassociate the act of smoking with other activities such as drinking a cup of coffee, eating, having sex, talking on the phone, and driving. Although the nicotine addiction remains, the patient will, theoretically, lose the behavioral habit and learn new ways of relaxing and coping with stress. The patient is then gradually weaned from the nicotine supplied in the gum or patch. This form of replacement therapy is not, by any means, a magic bullet. Counseling and behavior change is essential when using nicotine replacements. Studies showing low success rates

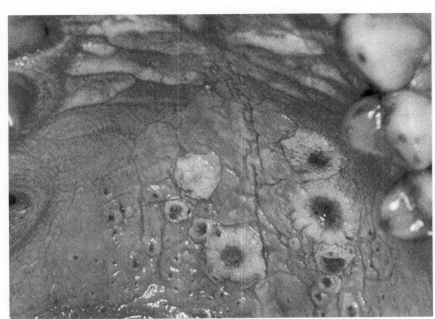

Smoker's palate.

Source: U.S.Department of Health and Human Services

included smokers who did not participate in counseling or other therapeutic programs to support their nicotine cessation. Preliminary testing has demonstrated that long-term relapse rates are substantially lowered when use of the patch is associated with some sort of behavioral modification program. But even with group therapy, only about 35 percent of exsmokers who used the patch to quit can be expected to stay off cigarettes for a year or more. In fact, some patients actually continue to smoke while chewing the gum or wearing the patch, simply because the habit itself is so compelling.

Other forms of behavioral therapies have also been used to treat cigarette smokers. Aversion therapies literally flood users with nicotine and smoke by having them smoke a large number of cigarettes during a short period of time. Smokers are supposed to find this saturation of cigarette smoke so unpleasant that they give up the habit. Sometimes the cigarettes that are smoked, as many as two or three packs in only a few hours, are kept in ashtrays until their accumulation produces a foul odor and a reservoir of ashes and butts. Also, some programs have patients dump their cigarette butts, ashes and all, onto their heads for added effect! Other behavioral approaches have included marking the number of cigarettes smoked each day and learning to reduce the number gradually by increasing the amount of time before the first cigarette is

smoked in the morning, between the end of a meal and the first cigarette and so on.

Obviously the best policy is one of primary prevention; target those who are likely to eventually smoke and prevent its initiation. Educational campaigns in school systems such as the life skills training program—on billboards, in advertisements, through physician assistance, and the curtailing of the tobacco industry's messages are all recommended approaches.

Interestingly, youth generally do not respond to warnings about eventual cancer and heart disease, which seems to be far in the future and not believed to be applicable to them. Instead, they respond better to information suggesting that it causes bad breath, wrinkled skin, and other aesthetic disadvantages. Also important in reducing the number of smokers in this country has been the vocal opposition to public smoking. This has led, for example, to smoking restrictions during airflights and isolated areas in restaurants and other public places for smokers. Youths who receive social pressure not to smoke and who learn the skills necessary to say no also have lower rates of smoking. Attempting to enforce existing laws that limit access of tobacco to minors may also prove successful. Banning vending machine sales has been considered, for example, as have applying sanctions to those store owners who allow minors to purchase cigarettes. Raising taxes on cig-

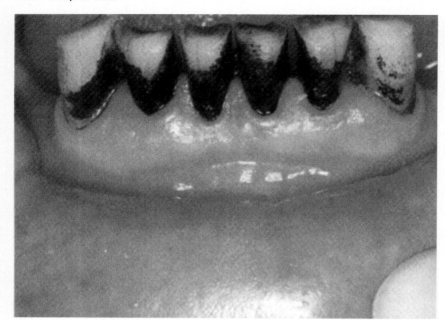

Tobacco stains.

Source: U.S. Department of Health and Human Services

arettes may reduce smoking, particularly among adolescents. Such a tax may not only deter smokers, but may also be used to fund health care and treatment efforts. Reports estimate that a 10 percent increase in cigarette prices would decrease consumption by 3 to 5 percent, although accurate predictions are impossible. While light smokers and youngsters about to initiate cigarette smoking may be deterred by the high prices, those already addicted will probably pay whatever is necessary to maintain their habit.

No matter what the approach, global or individual, smokers can quit if so motivated. Smoking does not, however, become less interesting, addictive, or pleasurable for these users, so we cannot rely on them maturing out of smoking. Quitting requires determination and work (Schelling, 1992).

Caffeine

Caffeine is such a popular drug in the United States that many folks feel they are unable to fully awaken and function in the morning until after their first cup of coffee. If you have ever lived with one of these people, you probably know not to attempt a conversation before that first cup. Many people continue to drink caffeinated beverages throughout the day to maintain a steady caffeine buzz. In addition to coffee, caffeine is also found in and added to numerous sodas, chocolate, appetite suppressants, analgesic preparations (along with aspirin), cold remedies, cocoa, and tea. It is estimated that over three billion pounds of coffee per year are consumed in the United States alone. In addition, children and adolescents drink uncounted gallons of caffeine-containing cola drinks. Citizens of the United States consume a total of about 15 million pounds of caffeine from coffee alone (Julien, 1988).

Concentrations of caffeine vary depending on the product and how it is produced. Table 10.5 provides a summary of average caffeine amounts found in various beverages, foods, and medicines.

Caffeine is an alkaline and a member of the family of xanthines, otherwise known as methylxanthines. Xanthines include stimulants that either occur naturally or are artificially synthesized. Caffeine and two other xanthines—theophylline and theobromine—occur naturally and are commonly self-administered. Along with caffeine, these xanthines are found in a number of plant species, but the most common sources are coffee, tea, and cocoa. Theophylline is used to stimulate respiration, particularly for those suffering from asthma and other allergic conditions. Quite large amounts of theobromine are found in chocolate so that, in combination with caffeine, the total

Table 10.5   *Common Sources and Amounts of Caffeine*

	Average	Range (mg)
Coffee (5 oz)		
Brewed, drip	115	60–180
Brewed, percolator	80	40–170
Instant	65	30–120
Decaffeinated	3	2–5
Tea (5 oz)		
Brewed, domestic	40	20–90
Brewed, imported	60	25–110
Instant	20	25–50
Iced (12 oz glass)	70	67–76
Coca Beverage (5 oz)	4	2–20
Candy		
Milk Chocolate (1 oz)	6	1–15
Dark Chocolate (1 oz)	20	5–35
Candy Bar (8 oz)	20	10–25
Sodas		
Coca Cola	45	-
Pepsi Cola	30	-
Over-the-Counter Analgesics	-	15–70
Over-the-Counter Stimulants No-Doz or Vivarin	-	100–200

amount of xanthines is nearly equivalent to that of a cup of coffee. (Chocolate, by the way, also contains a chemical stimulant called phenylethalamine, which is produced naturally by the brain, particularly during activities associated with pleasure, such as sex. No wonder so many people love chocolate!)

Mode of Administration

There are several possible ways to administer caffeine, although the oral route is most commonly used because it produces the least discomfort. When caffeine is medically indicated, it may be given orally in a purified or pill form, which in some patients causes nausea and gastrointestinal distress. Caffeine may also be injected or given by rectal suppository.

Absorption, Distribution, Metabolism, and Elimination

When caffeine is consumed, it travels to the stomach where it is retained in a water soluble form. Caffeine is more water soluble than the other xanthines and is absorbed faster. Nevertheless, its absorption is still quite slow, and it enters the bloodstream incompletely. Due to delays in the stomach, much of the caffeine passes through the intestinal walls to enter the blood so that the caffeine will eventually be completely absorbed. A full stomach will delay the absorption of caffeine into the bloodstream, as with alcohol. Even so, it is still quite lipid soluble and readily dissolves in many bodily tissues. Caffeine enters biological membranes with ease, and is rapidly and pervasively absorbed and distributed.

Blood levels of caffeine reach their peak between thirty and sixty minutes after ingestion although, as many of you coffee drinkers know, caffeine's effect can be felt right away. Absorption and peak blood levels vary substantially from one individual to the next, thus it is difficult to predict what the individual response time will be (Dews, 1984). This means that the half-life of caffeine is subject to individual variability, averaging about five hours in adults. Caffeine readily penetrates the brain and cerebral spinal fluid and is distributed throughout all body water and to all bodily organs. It also crosses the placental barrier to effect the fetus.

The liver is primarily responsible for metabolizing caffeine, and 99 percent of the caffeine filtered by the liver is reabsorbed in the kidney so the by-products may be eliminated. Ninety percent of the caffeine consumed is excreted. But only 1 or 2 percent of the caffeine is excreted unchanged; the rest is converted to active and inactive metabolites. The ability to eliminate caffeine is slower in pregnant women, the elderly, and infants. In fact, infants up to the age of seven to nine months cannot efficiently metabolize caffeine, and so its average half-life is about 4 days. Older children, on the other hand, dispose of caffeine two or three times more rapidly than do adults. Caffeine levels in the breast milk of a nursing mother may actually be higher than her own levels, making it readily available to the newborn. Interestingly, those who smoke cigarettes excrete caffeine more quickly —their clearance values are doubled. As mentioned previously, cigarette smokers use more caffeine and coffee drinkers are more likely to smoke cigarettes.

Pharmacological Aspects

Caffeine's primary effects are exerted on the CNS, heart, kidneys, lungs, and arteries carrying blood to the brain and heart. Because it is a powerful stimulant of nerve tissue, the cortex of the brain is activated first, and then the brainstem. These effects vary from person to person and children are more susceptible than adults to the excitation from caffeine. Increased cortical activity results in initial feelings of arousal, alertness, quickened and clearer thought processes, restlessness, and an alleviation of drowsiness and fatigue. Because of these effects, coffee drinkers frequently report that a morning cup of coffee enables them to function more effectively. Research has shown, in fact, that 100 to 200 mg of caffeine actually improves certain mental skills under conditions of fatigue and improves mood, particularly in those who are accustomed to caffeine intake (Jacobson et al., 1991; Jacobson & Thurman-Lacey, 1992). These improvements occur without the corresponding impairments in coordination, motor activity, and intellectual processes that result from other stimulants, such as amphetamines and cocaine, that affect the medulla. Accordingly, under conditions of boredom, fatigue, or repetitive task performance, caffeine may actually minimize problems with performance. There is some evidence, however, that recently acquired motor skills in tasks involving delicate muscular coordination and accurate timing may be adversely affected. Some tests have shown certain abilities, such as tactile discrimination and acoustic associations, to be somewhat impaired two hours after using usual amounts of caffeine (Hrbrek et al., 1971). Also, individuals sensitive to caffeine's effects may experience insomnia, restlessness, excitement, agitation, tense muscles, and tremulousness.

Very high doses (more than twelve cups of coffee a day) can lead to more disconcerting effects, manifested as agitation, irritability, shakiness, tremors, anxiety or panic, rapid breathing, and cardiac tachyarrythmia (when the heart beats fast and irregularly). It takes even higher amounts (about 3 grams or thirty cups a day) to stimulate the spinal cord—doses that generally exceed even heavy coffee consumption. In such cases, convulsions and possibly death may result.

Caffeine increases cellular metabolism in the brain and nervous system by indirectly augmenting activity of a chemical called cyclic adenosine monophosphate (cyclic AMP), which has an important role in brain function. As a result, more energy is created and the rate of cellular activity increases. Very high concentrations of caffeine, not normally found in human subjects, are required for this action. It is clear, however, that behavioral stimulation by caffeine is not entirely a function of this process and that other mechanisms are also responsible for caffeine's actions.

More recently, smaller amounts of caffeine have been found to act as an antagonist to adenosine receptors in the brain (Second International Caffeine Workshop, 1980). Adenosine is believed to be an inhibitory neurotransmitter with depressant, hypnotic, and anticonvulsant properties. It suppresses the release of several excitatory neurotransmitters and inhibits spontaneous firing of neurons. All of these actions are counteracted by caffeine. Caffeine is thought to block the interactions of adenosine at the receptor site. Evidence for this blocking effect is provided, first, by findings that adenosine may have a regulatory role in the function of the testes. Adenosine receptors are dense in the testes and appear to play a role in the maturation of sperm. Caffeine is well known to enhance sperm motility (Dews et al., 1982). Secondly, it is believed that caffeine exerts its stimulant effects by blocking adenosine receptors in the brain. Caffeine has the ability to block increases in motor activity produced by adenosine agonists and to block the ability of adenosine to lower blood pressure. In part, the lethargy and headache associated with caffeine withdrawal may be due to the lowering of blood pressure resulting from higher levels of adenosine activity.

There appear to be a few other mechanisms that are altered by caffeine to produce behavioral stimulation. Caffeine enhances the release of the neurotransmitters, norepinephrine, epinephrine (two catecholamines), and acetylcholine from brain cells and the adrenal gland. These transmitters are suppressed by adenosine. Catecholamine release explains the tendency of caffeine to stimulate the heart and increase heart contractions and the amount of blood pumped by the heart. Arteries that supply blood to the heart also dilate, thus the heart works harder and receives more oxygenated blood. On the other hand, caffeine decreases the amount of blood that reaches the brain by constricting cerebral blood vessels. This is good news for the migraine headache sufferer. Migraines are considered vascular headaches because the cerebral blood vessels become dilated and put pressure on nerve endings, causing head pain. (Although migraine sufferers feel like their brains are about to explode, the pain is not actually in their brain but surrounding it.) Caffeine counters this dilation, bringing relief on a short-term basis. For this reason, many over-the-counter analgesic preparations (also containing aspirin) contain caffeine. Continual use of caffeine will backfire, as the cerebral vascular system becomes spastic, constricting when caffeine is used and dilating excessively when caffeine's effects wear off. This is a type of rebound effect. As a result, the migraine-prone person finds instant relief in taking caffeine and so is reinforced by its use. The more often the individual resorts to caffeine, however, the more spastic the vascular system becomes, contributing to even more headaches.

Finally, caffeine blocks benzodiazepine receptors, disabling natural benzodiazepines (e.g., GABA) to exert an effect. Because the presence of natural benzodiazepines contribute to feelings of relaxation, and externally administered benzodiazepines (e.g., Valium or Xanax) are used to control anxiety, it is not surprising that caffeine can cause anxiety. This effect is generally only seen with relatively high doses of caffeine, equaling between five and ten cups of coffee. When doses of caffeine are high enough, the combined effect of these neurochemical responses result in a state similar to that experienced under conditions of acute stress. Consistent with this state, levels of the natural opiate, endorphin, also increase. Individuals prone to panic attacks may trigger an attack from smaller doses of caffeine as their brains may be more sensitive to the blockage of natural benzodiazepine receptors.

Peripheral Physical Effects

Xanthines, including caffeine, relax the muscles of the lung's bronchial tubes, opening them up for deeper breathing capacity. Because of this action, xanthines have been used in the treatment of asthma to open airway passages in children and adults and to aid deep breathing in babies who are experiencing difficulties. Children who suffer from apnea, a syndrome characterized by the intermittent cessation of breathing during sleep, receive xanthines to prevent the lapses in breathing and, potentially, reduce the likelihood of sudden infant death syndrome (sometimes associated with apnea episodes). Patients who have overdosed on a barbiturate and are suffering from respiratory depression have also been treated with xanthines due to their ability to dilate bronchial tubes. The xanthine theophylline is administered more frequently as a therapeutic agent in these syndromes because it is more effective than caffeine.

Caffeine increases gastric secretions in the stomach and intestines and, as a consequence, may contribute to or worsen an ulcer. It exerts a diuretic action on the kidneys, causing the user to need to urinate more often and lose total body water. For this reason, caffeinated beverages should not be calculated into the total amount of fluids recommended for daily consumption (approximately eight cups a day)—it should actually be subtracted due to its diuretic effect. Individuals who exercise are advised to drink large amounts of fluid, but it is important that they do not include caffeine-containing fluids, which cause their bodies to dehydrate.

As mentioned above, increases in the release of adrenal hormones associated with caffeine intake stimulate the sympathetic nervous system, raising heart rate, blood pressure, and respiration, and creating perceptions of anxiety, nervousness, and irritability in some users. Caffeine relaxes the smooth muscles of the body, and strengthens and increases activity levels in striated muscles, making the user feel energized.

Caffeine and the other xanthines can produce insomnia, particularly when caffeine is consumed shortly before bedtime. It takes longer to fall asleep and total sleeping time will be reduced for most users. Over-the-counter remedies designed to increase wakefulness generally contain caffeine. These preparations are actually preferred because caffeine is the only known stimulant drug that does not alter the sleep cycles. Amphetamines disrupt sleep cycles and, thus, contribute to a worsened state of fatigue in the long run. For some unknown reason, some individuals are able to take caffeine immediately before retiring and not experience any disruption in sleep. It is unclear whether these individuals metabolize caffeine differently, are less sensitive to or more tolerant of caffeine, or differ in their brain chemistry in a way that reduces caffeine's actions. In any event, individuals who can tolerate larger amounts of caffeine and do not experience adverse effects with respect to sleeping or nervousness are more likely to become heavy coffee drinkers.

Caffeine stimulates the body to dump sugar into the bloodstream. When blood sugar climbs, appetite is depressed. But the effect is temporary. When the concentration of blood sugar falls, hunger begins again. Taking more caffeine will increase blood sugar again, and so on. Withdrawal symptoms are partially caused by a decrease in blood sugar surges. Those interested in losing weight may find caffeine temporarily suppresses appetite, but when they attempt to quit, weight gain occurs. It should be noted that some of this effect is behavioral—without a coffee cup in hand, candy or other munchies may be substituted to satisfy oral needs. This is further incentive for some to continue using it.

Tolerance and Dependence

There is very little tolerance produced by caffeine in usual doses. Larger doses, however, administered over a long period of time do produce slight tolerance. Individuals who do not drink coffee experience observable signs of low tolerance to caffeine's effects. They tend to feel irritable, nervous, jittery, and nauseous, and they develop stomach distress and insomnia when they ingest caffeine equal to one or two cups of coffee. Regular coffee drinkers, however, report that they feel more normal and do not suffer from the ill effects of nondrinkers. This may be due to tolerance and possibly also to the relative insensitivity to caffeine preexisting in these individuals. Thus, individual differences may help to predict who is most likely to drink coffee regularly and who does not have such a predisposition.

Caffeine produces noticeable symptoms of withdrawal, suggesting that caffeine induces physical dependence. An individual who has a steady diet of caffeine will experience the following symptoms when the caffeine consumption suddenly stops: headache, fatigue, irritability, nervousness, and lack of energy. These symptoms will subside after a few days. As mentioned previously, a rebound headache is associated with caffeine cessation as a function of increased adenosine activity, a rise in blood pressure, and dilation of cerebral blood vessels that press on nerve endings surrounding the brain to produce pain. The number of adenosine receptor sites apparently increases in a regular coffee drinker as the brain attempts to compensate for continual suppression of adenosine activity. Thus, when caffeine is discontinued, adenosine activity increases beyond the precaffeine condition. Caffeine dependence may explain why some people wake up so dysfunctional and irritable until they have their morning cup of coffee. The severity of these symptoms is a function of how much caffeine is ingested daily and how long the individual has been using caffeine. Withdrawal symptoms begin within twenty-four hours of the last dose and can persist for several days (Griffiths & Woodson, 1988).

Adverse Effects

Behavior and Learning

There is evidence that large amounts of caffeinated foods and beverages are being ingested by children, primarily in the form of cola drinks and chocolate. Although the effects are variable from person to person, in general, children are more susceptible than adults to the excitation of caffeine. Unusually sensitive individuals, perhaps including children, may experience insomnia, restlessness, excitement, tense muscles, and tremulousness (Rapoport et al., 1984). Because children who suffer from attention deficit disorder, hyperactivity, and other forms of behavioral and learning difficulties display some of these same symptoms, it may be contraindicated for these children to consume caffeine. Consequently, it is appropriate that the role of caffeine in relation to school performance and learning disorders be reviewed (Powers, 1975).

The behaviorally stimulating effects of caffeine are clear-cut; however, it is not so clear to what extent caffeine produces measurable changes in behaviors, moods, and learning abilities. Avram Goldstein et al. (1965, 156) summed up the findings well, and their conclusions remain current:

> *Adequately designed experiments have shown unequivocally that caffeine (and also amphetamine) counteracts the decrement in various kinds of performance that is caused by fatigue or sleep deprivation. The evidence is much less convincing (and often contradictory) as to whether or not these drugs are capable of enhancing performance over control levels. There is also some indication that caffeine can increase the normal threshold frequency at which flicker fusion occurs but carefully designed experiments have also yielded negative results. In the case of tasks requiring motor coordination, monitoring (alertness), or intellectual activity, the preponderance of data is negative.*

In general, the consumption of usual amounts of caffeine produce only subtle effects, just above a detectable range or often not detectable at all. Some people are aware of caffeine's effects on a particular function, while others do not recognize any effect. The effects are more readily and consistently observable under conditions of fatigue, boredom, or sleeplessness. Thus, only behaviors that are already impaired due to the presence of a subnormal condition will be influenced. Caffeine will not, however, bring performance up to levels considered to be supernormal.

Behaviors that may be susceptible to caffeine's influence include motor coordination or activity, vigilance, memory, mood, reaction time, and continuous performance abilities. Various studies by Rapoport and her colleagues (e.g., 1984) tested these functions in boys around ten years of age and adults. Increases in motor restlessness and vigilance were reported. Improvements in vigilance and alertness were particularly discernible in those with a history of low to moderate caffeine intake who were administered low doses of caffeine. Nevertheless, there are numerous other studies that did not find measurable improvements in behavioral functioning.

Caffeinism is the occurrence of side effects associated with the chronic consumption of caffeine in divided amounts over the course of the day. Children who ingest caffeine regularly in this manner and those who do not were compared to evaluate possible differences in the symptoms experienced. Self-reports by the children and their mothers indicate that insomnia, nervousness, stomachaches, and nausea are suffered among those children who habitually use caffeine but only in low doses. Other symptoms include flushing, loss of appetite, irregular heartbeat, and feelings of being cold. Those children who regularly consume high doses of caffeine did not show signs of caffeinism. This finding may seem counterintuitive, but these differences may be due to the development of tolerance.

Caffeine may influence changes in behavior and mood in those individuals who are sensitive to these effects by altering neurotransmitter activity. Caffeine appears to raise serotonin levels and has little influence on dopamine or norepinephrine activity. Caffeine's alteration of behavior may be more significantly affected by the inhibition of adenosine, discussed previously. Because adenosine is an inhibitory neurotransmitter, the effects would be stimulatory. On the other hand, caffeine has many of the same stimulant properties as amphetamines, only to a lesser degree, which do raise catecholamine levels. Other neurotransmitter alterations that result from caffeine intake are not well understood. Obviously, any change in neurotransmitter levels as a result of caffeine intake will occur in all who use it—so why do only some individuals display

signs of sensitivity? Similar to individual differences in the way other drugs take effect and are metabolized, we do not know what makes us differentially vulnerable to caffeine's effects. For example, in a small group of those who use caffeine, a panic attack may ensue. Generally, individuals susceptible to caffeine-induced panic attacks suffer from an underlying anxiety disorder and require only a trigger to unleash the attack. Whatever the case may be, speculations are that these individual differences contribute to the likelihood that someone will consume caffeine, the amounts taken, and the consequences.

It is interesting that some mental patients experience a therapeutic effect from caffeine. In particular, those patients who suffer from lassitude, depression, hypoactivity, and in some cases, hyperactivity, seek the stimulating effects of caffeine. A problem may arise for depressed or hypoactive patients self-medicating with caffeine— because their activity levels are normally low, they may be unaccustomed to behavioral stimulation and not know how to adequately regulate their behavior. In extreme cases, the result may be impulsive, psychotic, or even violent. For example, a young man with severe learning disabilities and depression, who could barely function on his own, was restricted from using caffeine by his parents. They had noticed since childhood that caffeine "made him crazy", and so it was forbidden. He had a hankering for the substance, however, and whenever they were out of the house, which wasn't often, he would consume large pots of coffee. On several of these occasions, he was found attempting to jump off a bridge in a psychotic rage. A couple of times he threatened to strangle his mother during an caffeine-induced episode. Without caffeine, he was withdrawn and pathologically passive.

Those with hyperactivity, whether children or adults, may use caffeine for the properties it has in common with Ritalin, a stimulant drug commonly used in the treatment of hyperactivity. Individuals with anxiety disorder or who are prone to panic attacks, on the other hand, frequently find caffeine to exacerbate or trigger an anxious episode, worsening their preexisting syndrome. In some cases, these people report that no other treatment will relieve these symptoms until caffeine is removed from the diet, at which time, anxiety, panic, and rapid or irregular heartbeat will subside. The fact that high doses of caffeine interferes with the activity of benzodiazepine receptors in the brain (which operates to calm and reduce anxiety states) helps to explain this phenomenon. In sum, because mental illnesses are associated with irregularities in neurotransmitter activity and because drugs used in the treatment of mental illness alter this activity, caffeine may exert an unpredictable effect on such patients.

Fibrocystic Breast Disease

It has been observed that the removal of caffeine from the diet leads to the reduction in severity, and sometimes complete resolution, of fibrocystic breast disease. High levels of cyclic nucleotides (natural substances that control biological processes, including growth) are found to be elevated in women who suffer from this disorder. Researchers believe that xanthines may inhibit mechanisms for the disposal of cyclic nucleotides so that they accumulate and contribute to the growth of breast cysts.

Cancer

Most studies indicate that caffeine does not have carcinogenic properties. The incidence of neoplasms (tumors) does not appear to be related to caffeine consumption. Interestingly, however, animals administered high doses of caffeine had fewer tumors than those receiving placebo (Dews, Grice, et al., 1984). Those receiving lower dosages had the highest incidence of malignant tumors. In spite of these studies, researchers have concluded that caffeine, particularly in amounts likely to be consumed by humans, does not enhance, promote, or cause neoplasms.

Cardiac Effects

Although there is widespread belief that caffeine may increase the risk for heart disease or heart attack, there is no consistent evidence to support this claim. Further research is needed to clarify the role of caffeine in cardiac problems. Patients prone to a rapid and/or irregular heartbeat, however, frequently report the condition is triggered or exacerbated by caffeine.

Caffeine Poisoning

Doses of caffeine that exceed usual use can produce caffeine poisoning. The symptoms of such poisoning include tachycardia, convulsions, restlessness, excitement, urinary frequency, tinnitus (ringing in the ears),

nausea, vomiting, and tremors. Generally recommended treatments involve substances like diazepam (Valium) to calm the patient or Ipecac that will induce vomiting to rid the body of caffeine.

Teratogenic Effects

Effects of caffeine on reproductive function and fetal development in humans are presently under scrutiny and are difficult to evaluate. Epidemiological analyses of available data on caffeine use during human pregnancy have yet to yield a significant relationship between measures of caffeine consumption and low birth weight or congenital malformations. Clinical studies of caffeine's teratogenic effects have been hampered by the number of other drugs (e.g., tobacco or alcohol) that women who use caffeine also frequently use during pregnancy. Warnings have been widely posted against the use of caffeine during pregnancy because we simply do not know whether caffeine can adversely influence the development of a fetus. Accordingly, some clinicians contend that it is best not to take the chance with any drug that has known effects on the brain.

There is no evidence of mutagenesis or chromosome damage from amounts of caffeine generally consumed by humans. Nevertheless, very high levels have been shown to damage chromosomes in animals. One study of male rats given caffeine before they mated showed an abnormally high death rate among offspring. Still, the clinical significance of these experiments in animals are unknown, but the permanent effects upon reproductive function warrant further human studies. There are other mechanisms by which caffeine can produce damage to a fetus. Most of this research pertains specifically to animals although there may be some application to human fetal development. In particular, animal studies indicate that exposure to caffeine in utero can delay the rate of growth of a fetus and a newborn. This effect may be the result of elevations in catecholamines that constrict blood vessels in the mother, reducing oxygen and blood supply to the fetus. Furthermore, indirect effects on offspring may occur only when caffeine levels rise above a high threshold. At this point, adrenal steroids in the blood increase and may affect fetal development. Finally, women who consume large amounts of caffeine while pregnant may take in less food and water, possibly delaying development of their fetus.

Drug Interactions

Caffeine interacts with several other substances (over-the-counter, prescription, and illicit) to influence their effects. Caffeine somewhat decreases the effects of alcohol (although it is important to note that drinking coffee to get sober is ineffective and may contribute to a worse hangover—alcohol and caffeine both dehydrate). Simultaneous cocaine use may cause overstimulation. Using marijuana along with caffeine may increase the effect of both drugs. Of particular concern is the possibility of rapid heartbeat when these drugs are used together. This possibility is further increased when using tobacco along with caffeine. Such effects are generally only experienced by those with a preexisting vulnerability to tachycardia (rapid heartbeat). The use of oral contraceptives may increase caffeine effects, while certain antidepressants used along with caffeine place the user at risk for dangerous rise in blood pressure. The combined effect of caffeine with sympathomimetics (with adrenalin-like effects) contribute to overstimulation and caffeine increases the effects of thyroid hormones. Tranquilizer effects will be reduced.

Treatment

There is no convention to abide by for the treatment of caffeine dependence. Given the withdrawal symptoms described above, caffeine-dependent individuals do become quite uncomfortable when they attempt to abstain. Frequently, coffee drinkers are advised to give up their caffeine intake by their physicians or even family members if they have trouble sleeping, are jittery or nervous, or suffer from certain types of cardiac conditions that involve disruption of heart rhythms. As always, it is much easier to simply tell someone to quit than to actually accomplish this feat, particularly if the withdrawal period is unpleasant. Those interacting with the individual trying to quit may also suffer a bit, given that for a couple of weeks they may have to put up with the abstainer's irritability, agitation, and general malaise. Since the most common symptom of caffeine withdrawal is headache, pain relieving compounds such as aspirin are generally recommended. For those who suffer from migraine headaches, a more potent pain reliever that affects the vascular system may be recommended. Most important, those trying to avoid caffeine should not turn to other addictive drugs for assistance.

Nicotine, Caffeine, and Crime

Nicotine and caffeine have a noteworthy lack of association with crime, despite their powerful psychoactive effects. Thus, even though their pharmacologic properties are strong, particularly nicotine, the criminal association is not there. This fact is likely due to two conditions. First, although they alter cognitive processes, they do not substantially impair mental functioning, produce high levels of euphoria, or severely change behavior. And second, nicotine and caffeine are legal substances. It may be argued that their legal status alone may drastically reduce their propensity to increase risk for criminal behavior.

≡ Summary

Although nicotine and caffeine were included in the same chapter, this was only a matter of convenience. They are quite different drugs, with extreme variations in the likelihood of a user becoming dependent, the degree of tolerance, the abuse potential, physiological and psychological effects, and most notably, their toxicity and potential to produce health problems. Damage from nicotine use far outweighs the consequences of using caffeine, even in large doses. At the same time, nicotine is both one of the most highly abused drugs in this country and one of the most devastating. Its addictive properties are believed to be more powerful than those of heroin, making it an extremely difficult drug to wean oneself from. The use of tobacco products has definitely been related to cancer, heart disease, oral pathology, fetal toxicity, and a host of other serious problems. Nevertheless, millions of people continue to smoke, and the younger one begins to smoke, the more cigarettes he or she is likely to smoke later in life (Taioli & Wynder, 1991). Thus, nicotine use particularly among the young, is worthy of our concerted attention. A number of treatments have been developed and tested, but with only little to moderate success.

On the brighter side, half the men who ever smoked in this country have quit, and nearly half the women have followed suit (Schelling, 1992). When World War II ended, about three-quarters of young men smoked cigarettes. The number is now less than a third and continuing to decline. Fifty million folks have quit and another fifty million who were projected to become smokers since 1945 have not. Analysts credit this nationwide trend to increased knowledge about tobacco's insidious effects and a bit more government involvement in regulating smoking behavior. More people now know about the risks than ever before, and surgeon generals have taken an active stance against the use of tobacco. Unfortunately, those who are uneducated and who belong to lower socioeconomic groups remain our largest smoking population.

With respect to caffeine, results of hundreds of studies continue to surprise us. Given that it is a stimulant, we would expect it to be more influential in certain forms of heart disease, cholesterol levels, activity and performance levels, psychological state, and other health and behavioral conditions. There is no evidence, to date, however, that caffeine is a particularly hazardous drug. Notwithstanding, it is clear that caffeine is potentially quite addicting when withdrawal symptoms are examined. The unpleasant side effects of removing coffee and other sources of caffeine from the diet affect even those who ingest the equivalent of only a cup or two a day! Heavy coffee drinkers, in particular, suffer from a variety of ills during withdrawal, including headaches, depression, and anxiety that can last as long as a week after they stop drinking. But even much lighter drinkers report dire withdrawal symptoms. In conclusion, it is apparent that no matter how relatively benign a psychoactive drug may be, we must always consider the many facets of their appeal before we imbibe.

CHAPTER 11

Central Nervous System Depressants

Objectives

1. To provide a classification scheme of the various central nervous system depressants.
2. To show how prevalent depressant use is in this country.
3. To identify the various medical uses for depressants.
4. To compare and contrast the various types of depressants.
5. To illustrate the various properties of depressants and their effects on brain function and behavioral response.
6. To explain how depressants can become addictive.
7. To describe those characteristics that may increase an individual's vulnerability to use depressants.
8. To describe the relationship between depressant use and criminal and antisocial behavior.
9. To discuss treatment strategies for abuse of depressants.

rugs that depress the central nervous system are classified as sedative-hypnotic compounds or depressants. Numerous drugs with various chemical structures fall into this category; they all function to sedate, relax, relieve anxiety, release inhibitions, depress sensitivity to environmental stimuli, reduce reaction time and physical activity, and increase impulsivity. They also create difficulties in concentration and impair motor coordination. In some populations, depressants actually produce the opposite of expected reactions. The elderly, children, and sometimes those with manic or violent tendencies may actually experience excitation, anger, hostility, and aggressive feelings from depressants. This paradoxical effect will be discussed in more detail later. At higher doses, anesthesia results along with sleepiness, lethargy, and possible unconsciousness (known as general anesthesia), coma, or death. These symptoms may occur due to the depression of the brain (medulla), which controls our respiratory system.

Depressants include barbiturates, nonbarbiturate hypnotics, antianxiety drugs or benzodiazepines, and a host of miscellaneous compounds, including alcohol and general anesthetics (see Table 11.1). Individual depressants may be referred to as sedatives, tranquilizers, hypnotics, or anesthetics. These compounds are similar based on either their active properties, purposes of usage, or ability to produce depression. They differ only in terms of their individual potency (which to some extent is a function of the dose taken) and how the body processes them with respect to their differing chemical structures. Although potency is an important consideration in determining the dosage for a desired effect, therapeutic potential, adverse effects, and safety are even more important determinants in choosing a depressant for medical purposes.

Extent of Use of Depressants

Data reported for 1993 indicated that about 9,457,000 (4.6 percent) Americans over the age of twelve have used tranquilizers at some time in their lives without a prescription from their doctor (see Table 11.2), and 7,127,000 (3.4 percent) Americans over the age of twelve used sedatives without a prescription from their doctor (see Table 11.3). About 1.2 percent of Americans over age twelve reported use of tranquilizers and 0.8 percent reported use of sedatives during the past year. Only 0.3 percent of Americans over the age of twelve reported using sedatives or tranquilizers during the past month. (Substance Abuse and Mental Health Services Administration, 1994).

Table 11.1   *Classification Scheme of Depressants*

BARBITURATES	HYPNOTICS	NONBARBITURATE BENZODIAZEPINES	MISCELLANOUS
Amobarbital	Chloral hydrate	Lorazepam	Meprobamate
Butabarbital	Ethchlorvynol	Flurazepam	Buspirone
Cyclobarbital	Methaqualone	Diazepam	Tybamate
Lotusate	Glutethimide	Chlordiazepoxide	Antihistamines
Pentobarbital	Methyprylon	Alprazolam	
Secobarbital	Ethinamate	Oxazepam	
Hexobarbital	Paraldehyde	Clorazepate	
Phenobarbital		Midazolam	
Mephobarbital		Trizolam	
Allobarbital		Paxipam	
Methohexital		Temazepam	
Metharbital		Clonazepam	
		Halazepam	
		Quazepam	

Table 11.2   *Tranquilizers: Percent of Population Reporting Use of Tranquilizers Ever, Past Year, and Past Month (1993) by Sex and Age Groups for Total Population.*

	Ever Used	Used During Past Year	Used During Past Month
AGE	RATE ESTIMATES (PERCENTAGES)		
12-17	1.2	0.7	0.2
Male	1.0	0.7	0.3
Female	1.4	0.7	0.3
18-25	5.4	1.9	0.7
Male	5.8	2.7	0.8
Female	4.9	2.0	0.5
26-34	7.1	1.9	0.5
Male	8.0	2.2	0.6
Female	6.2	1.6	0.5
35+	4.2	1.7	0.1
Male	4.6	0.7	—
Female	3.8	1.2	0.2
Total	4.6	1.2	0.3
Male	5.0	1.1	0.3
Female	4.1	1.3	0.3

- no estimate reported
Source: Adapted from Substance Abuse and Mental Health Services Administration. *National Survey on Drug Abuse: Population Estimate 1993.*

Table 11.3   *Sedatives: Percent of Population Reporting Use of Sedatives Ever, Past Year, and Past Month (1993) by Sex and Age Groups for Total Population.*

	Ever Used	Used During Past Year	Used During Past Month
AGE	RATE ESTIMATES (PERCENTAGES)		
12-17	1.4	0.8	0.2
Male	1.2	0.7	0.2
Female	1.6	0.9	0.2
18-25	2.7	1.1	0.6
Male	3.4	1.6	0.9
Female	2.0	0.6	0.4
26-34	4.8	1.0	0.3
Male	5.5	1.2	0.4
Female	4.0	0.7	0.2
35+	3.6	0.6	0.1
Male	4.4	0.4	—
Female	2.8	0.8	0.2
Total	3.4	0.8	0.3
Male	4.1	0.7	0.2
Female	2.8	0.8	0.3

- no estimate reported
Source: Adapted from Substance Abuse and Mental Health Services Administration. *National Survey on Drug Abuse: Population Estimate 1993.*

The Johnston, O'Malley, and Bachman (1993) survey for the year 1992 shows a decreasing trend for barbiturate and tranquilizer use among high school students, college students, and other young adults (see Figures 11.1 and 11.2). Annual prevalence of barbiturate use among seniors in 1992 was 2.8 percent compared with the high of 10.7 percent in 1975. Annual prevalence of barbiturate use was 1.6 percent for young adults and 1.4 percent among college students. Annual prevalence for use of tranquilizers stood at 2.8 percent for high school seniors in 1992 compared to 11 percent in 1977. Annual prevalence has also declined to 3.4 percent for young adults and to 2.9 percent for college students. There is very little difference between males and females in their use of depressants (see Figures 11.3 and 11.4).

Effects of Depressants

We will first discuss those ways in which all depressant drugs behave similarly. Sections that follow address specific differences among categories of depressant drugs: barbiturates, nonbarbiturate sedative-hypnotics, and benzodiazepines.

Active Properties

All CNS depressants share similar properties with respect to the way they behave in the body, their sites of action, and the effect they will have on the condition of each user (see Julien, 1988). To begin, the use of more than one depressant at a time will cause an exaggerated depression, called an additive effect (where one plus one equals two times the effect). For example, the use of a barbiturate with alcohol will increase the sedation caused by the barbiturate and the barbiturate will increase the level of performance impairment produced by the alcohol. Furthermore, if the user is depressed or sleepy prior to taking the drug, it is likely that the depressant will have a far greater effect than it would if the user is in a normal or energetic state. Thus, the preexisting condition of the drug taker must be taken into account in an attempt to predict drug effects apart from the actual drug and dose taken.

Figure 11.1 *Barbiturates: Trends in Annual Prevalence Among College Students vs. Others 1-4 Years Beyond High School*

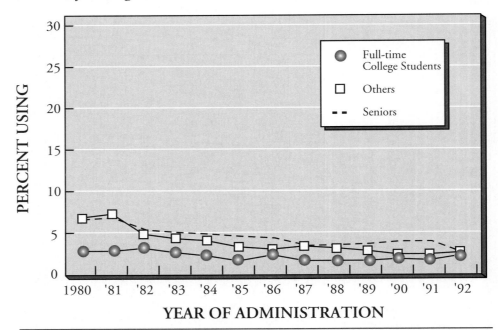

Source: National Institute on Drug Abuse. *National Survey Results on Drug Use from the Monitoring the Future Study, 1975–1992.*

Figure 11.2   *Tranquilizers: Trends in Annual Prevalence Among College Students vs. Others 1-4 Years Beyond High School*

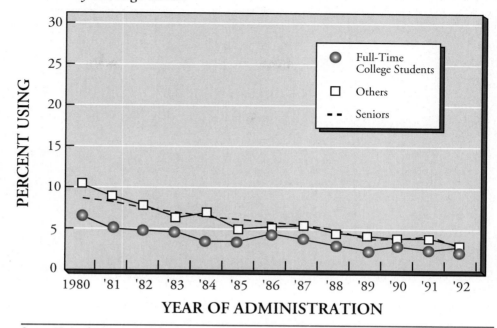

Source: National Institute on Drug Abuse. *National Survey Results on Drug Use from the Monitoring the Future Study, 1975–1992.*

Figure 11.3   *Barbiturates: Trends in Annual Prevalence Among Male and Female College Students*

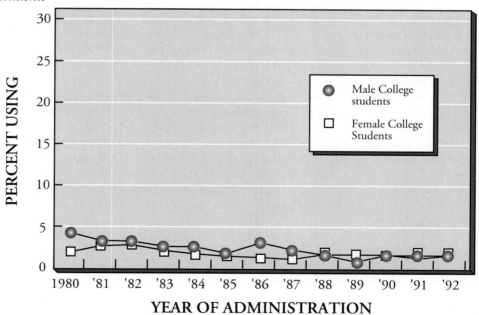

Source: National Institute on Drug Abuse. *National Survey Results on Drug Use from the Monitoring the Future Study, 1975–1992.*

Figure 11.4   *Tranquilizers: Trends in Annual Prevalence Among Male and Female College Students*

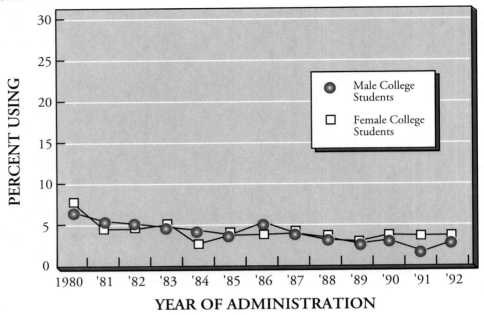

Source: National Institute on Drug Abuse. *National Survey Results on Drug Use from the Monitoring the Future Study, 1975–1992.*

Sedatives also may have synergistic effects, meaning that when a combination of two or more are taken, they will have a multiplicative, rather than a simple additive, effect (where one plus one equals more than two). The term *synergy* can best be described with the following example. If Mary can lift only 40 pounds and Jane can lift only 40 pounds, together they can lift 100 pounds because their combined strength is greater than the sum of their individual strengths. Depressants work in much the same way. In combination, the drugs' effects are much more powerful than one would expect when the individual properties and potencies of each drug are calculated separately and then added together. The actual drugs' effects will be greatly pronounced, unpredictable, and unexpected. For this reason, using a combination of depressants can be a dangerous proposition and possibly even result in death. The case of Karen Quinlan in the 1970s illustrates what may inadvertently happen when the potentially deadly mixture of methaqualone (quaaludes) and alcohol are taken (see the Inset).

The second property of depressants is the ability of stimulants to counteract the action of depressants and for depressants to mitigate the stimulant effect to some extent. This effect is called antagonism. When a depressant, such as

diazepam (Valium), is taken while under the influence of a stimulant, such as cocaine, the effects of the stimulant will be somewhat lessened. Conversely, the use of a stimulant after taking a depressant will somewhat negate the depressant's effects by arousing the individual. Because stimulants and depressants generally act on different sites in the brain, they do not displace each other and, consequently, are not specific blocking agents. One drug simply acts to diminish some of the opposing influences of the other. Taking a stimulant while using a depressant will, in fact, worsen depression in the long term as the brain will attempt to compensate for the overactivity produced by the stimulant by reducing neural activity. Finding medications that can specifically block the effects of a depressant has been difficult. However, the search continues since it would be quite helpful to counteract and prevent the potential life threatening effects of an overdose of depressants.

A third characteristic of depressants is the apparent behavioral excitation that is sometimes observed when one should logically expect behavioral depression. Sedative-hypnotics suppress activity of the brain's neurons. Therefore, the ability of these neurons to perform their particular function is greatly diminished. For exam-

Inset 11.1

THE QUINLAN CASE

Karen Quinlan was an active twenty-one-year-old when disaster struck. She lapsed into a coma in the early morning hours of April 15, 1975, after drinking a few gin-and-tonics and possibly taking some drugs as well. On the night before, Karen accompanied several friends to a roadside tavern where they were to celebrate a friend's birthday. She was seen "popping some pills," reportedly quaaludes, earlier in the day and that evening had several drinks before even reaching the bar. Karen "started to nod out" after only one drink at the tavern, so she was driven home. By the time they arrived, Karen had passed out entirely. A few minutes later, the driver realized that she had stopped breathing and began to give her resuscitation. An ambulance was called and Karen was carried off unconscious to the hospital, never to wake again. Karen spent several years in a coma while her parents fought to discontinue the life support system that forced air into her lungs through an incision in her throat. Karen remained in a "persistent vegetative state" until her death.

ple, receptors intended to register pain would no longer be able to fully process painful stimuli. Pain perception would be dulled, resulting in anesthesia. However, in low doses, depressants suppress the activity of inhibitory systems before they suppress the activity of excitatory systems. Consequently, the brain is relieved of inhibitions and the user appears to be stimulated rather than sedated. Excitatory systems function without the checks and balances provided by the inhibitory systems. In many cases, the user will also report feelings of euphoria. Continued use, however, will eventually suppress excitatory systems and behavior will be more appropriately depressed.

Alcohol users know this effect well. Occasional and regular drinkers frequently do not understand why they become euphoric, energetic, uninhibited, and sexually active when using the depressant, alcohol. Many people believe, because of these effects, that alcohol is a stimulant. The ability of alcohol to initially stimulate behavior is a function of alcohol's initial suppression of inhibitory neural activity. A disproportionate amount of excitatory neural activity remains, which is reflected in behavior and mood. But, as anyone who has used larger amounts of alcohol will tell you, after having several drinks over a period of time, behavioral depression will set in and so, eventually, will sleep.

A fourth characteristic of depressants is the hyperexcitability that follows repeated administrations. After using a single dose, the drug's effects wear off once it is

excreted and the user returns to a predrug or normal state. Larger doses taken over a longer period of time, however, are associated with a compensatory state of excitability once the drug is terminated. The brain attempts to increase activity levels following the drug induced period of hypoactivity. The severity of these symptoms has led us to the conclusion that depressants produce physical dependency. Withdrawal symptoms may include mania, elevated levels of physical activity, and even seizures or death. Dependency on depressants will be discussed further with respect to specific sedative-hypnotic categories.

Finally, depressants produce tolerance and psychological dependency. The liver metabolizes a depressant more quickly and efficiently with repeated doses. Also, brain cells adapt to the drug and learn how to function under its effects. Consequently, depressants become less and less effective over time unless larger doses are taken. Cross tolerance to all depressants may occur. If an individual has been taking diazepam (Valium), for example, the effects of triazolam (Halcion), will be diminished. Cross dependency may also occur. If the user is dependent on one depressant and attempts to terminate the drug, the use of another depressant will relieve withdrawal symptoms. Psychological dependency, of course, enters the picture when there is a preexisting state of dysphoria, such as anxiety or the discomfort associated with a sleeping disorder. Depressants may relieve symptoms of an underlying condition and withdrawal is associated with an exacerbation of these symptoms. Consequently, the user learns to associate the drug with relief and feelings of well-being.

Other qualities that CNS depressants have in common are their ability to depress not only the CNS but also the rate of metabolism in other body tissues. This depression occurs at high doses, while lower doses more specifically influence CNS systems associated with wakefulness. In particular, those systems that are responsible for arousing individuals and alerting them to incoming stimuli are suppressed, including the reticular activating system (RAS) and the diffuse thalamic projection system (which connects the RAS with the hypothalamus and limbic system and is activated by many drugs of abuse). Nevertheless, because depressants reduce neural activity throughout the brain by depressing synaptic transmissions, these drugs have relatively nonspecific effects. For example, they may be used as sedatives, sleeping agents, anticonvulsants, muscle relaxants, amnesics, general anesthetics, and anxiolytics (antianxiety drugs). It would be more clinically useful to discover a drug that had only one effect for one syndrome, for example, a muscle relaxer for strained or tense muscles rather than a drug that will additionally depress other CNS functions and cause drowsiness.

One exception to the tendency of depressants to have diffuse effects is the benzodiazepine group of drugs. They were originally thought to be nonspecific, but researchers have recently discovered that benzodiazepines quite specifically reduce anxiety by targeting those brain areas responsible for the anxiety syndrome. In particular, the activity of gamma-aminobutyric acid (GABA), an inhibitory neurotransmitter, is facilitated by benzodiazepines. GABA is believed to be involved in the regulation of brain excitability, and the heightened activity of GABA contributes to antianxiety effects of the benzodiazepines. Other diffuse depressant effects are not observed with these drugs as they would be if barbiturates or nonbarbiturate hypnotics were used. Consequently, benzodiazepines, such as alprazolam (Xanax), have become an increasingly popular treatment for anxiety.

General Therapeutic Uses

Insomnia

One common reason for using CNS depressants is to treat insomnia. There are many forms of sleeping disorders including narcolepsy and sleep apnea. Insomnia, however, is reported to be the most frequent type of sleep disorder, and those who suffer from it are most likely to use a sedative or hypnotic for relief. The lack of sleep has many causes and may be associated with a variety of mood and behavioral disturbances although causes and effects may be easily confused. For example, an anxiety disorder or depression may antedate the sleeping disorder and, thus, should be considered causal. However, anxiety and depression may result from inadequate sleep, so clinicians may find it difficult to separate the underlying disorder from the actual consequences of sleep deprivation.

Each individual requires a certain amount of sleep each night, and recent estimates indicate that, as a nation, we are obtaining too little sleep. Some investigators and clinicians believe that poor sleeping habits contribute to an inability to cope with daily stressors and to the incidence of psychological disturbances in an otherwise normal population. Depressants are used sometimes too liberally to solve the problem of widespread sleeping disorders. The use of such a drug on a one-time basis, and not repeatedly, is not of concern unless it masks an underlying problem that requires attention. But the continual reliance on depressants for sleep is physically and emotionally a risky business. Furthermore, psychological and physical dependence on depressants may easily develop as users may find that they can no longer fall asleep without them. (See the Inset for some suggestions to aid in sleeping without medication.)

Hypnotic benzodiazepines are most often prescribed for sleep induction as they are less addictive and more effective than the barbiturates. In particular, flurazepam (Dalmane) and triazolam (Halcion) became the drugs of choice as they are relatively short acting, produce little morning hangover, and are associated with less rapid development of tolerance. Dalmane is not used as extensively as it once was, however, because it accumulates in the body over time. Its active metabolite (discussed later in this chapter) stays in the body, causing the hypnotic effect to carry over into daytime hours where it can interfere with daily functioning. For these reasons, Halcion is now more widely prescribed. It is shorter acting, has a short half-life, no active metabolite, and is not expected to accumulate in the system.

Anxiety

Another primary use of CNS depressants is for the relief of anxiety. Most physicians will not recommend drug therapy unless the anxiety is both severe and primary; that

Inset 11.2

RECOMMENDATIONS FOR SLEEP:

The following recommendations are designed to alleviate or minimize the effects of stress. In order to manage sleeping difficulties and help relieve depression and anxiety without the use of drugs; try the following:

1. Just before bed, drink a glass of milk along with a carbohydrate, such as bread or fruit, to increase tryptophan levels and seotonin activity.

2. Go to bed the same time every night and awaken at the same time every morning, even on the weekends.

3. Do not lie in bed for any other reason than sleep.

4. Take several deep breaths once in bed to relax and increase oxygen to the brain.

5. Before bed, sit quietly in a darkened room with no sensory stimulation (no music, sounds, smells…) and repeat a sound over and over until meditation is achieved. Do this every night for at least fifteen minutes.

6. Maintain a low sugar diet and do not drink alcohol close to bedtime.

7. Lose weight. A diet high in complex carbohydrates and low in fat will stabilize weight and blood pressure.

8. Do not drink caffeine after noon and do not drink more than one beverage within two hours before bed.

9. Exercise daily but never immediately before bedtime.

10. Do not think about daily activities or problems once in bed. Clear the mind as much as possible.

11. When sleep does not occur, get out of bed and do something rather than lying in bed.

12. Reduce smoking drastically. Especially do not smoke right before bedtime. Smoking disrupts sleep cycles and steps should be taken to minimize, if not quit, smoking.

13. Stay in bed for the amount of time you feel you are sleeping at night. For example, if you think you are only sleeping 3 hours, then stay in bed for only three hours. The body quickly learns that it is the only chance for sleep during this time and will accommodate this schedule. This may take a couple of days. Then begin to slowly increase the number of hours you are in bed. You will be able to build back up to a normal sleeping pattern.

Inset 11.3

PRODUCT INFORMATION FOR QUAZEPAM (DORAL)

Doral (brand of quazepam). Tablets contain quazepam, a trifluoroethyl benzodiazepine hypnotic agent.

Indications and Usage
Doral tablets are indicated for treatment of insomnia characterized by difficulty in falling asleep, frequent nocturnal awakenings, and/or early morning awakenings...Because insomnia is often transient and intermittent, the prolonged administration of Doral tablets is generally not necessary or recommended. Since insomnia may be a symptom of several other disorders, the possibility that the complaint may be related to a condition for which there is a more specific treatment should be considered.

Drug Abuse and Dependence
Controlled Substance: Doral is a controlled substance under the Controlled Substance Act and has been assigned by the Drug Enforcement Administration to Schedule IV.

Abuse and Dependence: Withdrawal symptoms, similar in character to those noted with barbiturates and alcohol (e.g., convulsions, tremor abdominal and muscle cramps, vomiting, and sweating), have occurred following the abrupt discontinuance of benzodiazepines.

The more severe withdrawal symptoms have usually been limited to those patients who received excessive doses over an extended period of time. Generally milder withdrawal symptoms (e.g., dysphoria and insomnia) have been reported following abrupt discontinuance of benzodiazepines taken continuously at therapeutic levels for several months. Consequently, after, extended therapy, abrupt discontinuation should generally be avoided and a gradual dosage tapering schedule followed. Addiction-prone individuals (such as drug addicts or alcoholics) should be under careful surveillance when receiving quazepam or other psychotropic agents because of the predisposition of such patients to habituation and dependence.

Source: *Physician's Desk Reference*, 1991.

is, there is no underlying disorder responsible for the anxiety (known as secondary anxiety). Frequently, anxiety is secondary to clinical depression and the use of sedative-hypnotics in depression is contraindicated since the syndrome will probably worsen. The preferred therapeutic method is to administer depressants only during periods of acute anxiety, rather than over the long term. This method is recommended not only to prevent the development of dependence but also to allow patients to learn more effective coping skills and respond to conjunctive therapies (relaxation exercises, counseling, or stress management) without relying on a medication. Under these circumstances, individuals are more likely to explore possible environmental reasons for their anxiety.

Treatment of Alcohol Withdrawal

The sometimes dangerous or fatal symptoms of alcohol withdrawal may be treated with CNS depressants. In particular, certain sedatives are effective in minimizing these symptoms by quelling epileptic seizures and hyperexcitability in the brain characteristic of DTs (see Chapter 6). Once the alcohol and its by-products have been metabolized and excreted, sedative dosages may be slowly decreased to make withdrawal more tolerable. One must use extreme caution, however, when combining alcohol with any of the sedative-hypnotics due to the possibility of synergistic effects.

Inset 11.4

PRODUCT INFORMATION FOR DIAZEPAM (VALIUM)

Valium (brand of diazepam/Roche) is a benzodiazepine derivative developed through original Roche research.

Pharmacology

In animals Valium appears to act on parts of the limbic system, the thalamus and hypothalamus, and induces calming effects. Valium, unlike chlorpromazine and reserpine, has no demonstrable peripheral effects.; however, animals treated with Valium do have a transient ataxia at higher doses. Valium was found to have transient cardiovascular depressor effects in dogs. Long-term experiments in rats revealed no disturbances of endocrine function.

Indications

Valium is indicated for the management of anxiety disorders or for the short-term relief of the symptoms of anxiety. Anxiety or tension associated with the stress of everyday life usually does not require treatment with an anxiolytic.

In acute alcohol withdrawal, Valium may be useful in the symptomatic relief of acute agitation, tremor, impending or acute delirium tremens, and hallucinosis.

Valium is a useful adjunct for the relief of skeletal muscle spasm due to reflex spasm to local pathology (such as inflammation of the muscles or joints or secondary to trauma), spasticity caused by upper motor neuron disorders (such as cerebral palsy and paraplegia), athetosis, and stiff-man syndrome.

Oral Valium may be used adjunctively in convulsive disorders although it has not proved useful as the sole therapy. The effectiveness of Valium in long-term, use that is, more than four months, has not been assessed by systematic clinical studies. The physician should periodically reassess the usefulness of the drug for the individual patient.

Adverse Reactions

Side effects most commonly reported were drowsiness, fatigue, and ataxia. Infrequently encountered were confusion, constipation, depression, diplopia dysarthria, headache, hypotension, incontinence, jaundice, changes in libido, nausea, changes in salivation, skin rash, slurred speech, tremor, urinary retention, vertigo, and blurred vision. Paradoxical reactions such as acute spasticity, insomnia, rage, sleep disturbances, and stimulation have been reported; should these occur, use of the drug should be discontinued.

Drug Abuse and Dependence

(Similar to Doral. See Inset 11.3 for details.)

Source: *Physician's Desk Reference*, 1991.

Anticonvulsant Effects

CNS depressants all have some anticonvulsive effects due to their diffuse depression of neural activity. The benzodiazepines, diazepam (Valium), clonazepam (Clonopin), and lorazepam (Ativan), and the barbiturate, phenobarbital (Luminal) are particularly useful in treating epilepsy. Although these drugs are not specifically considered anticonvulsants, they may be recommended for mild cases of petit mal or subcortical (below the cortex) epilepsy, which

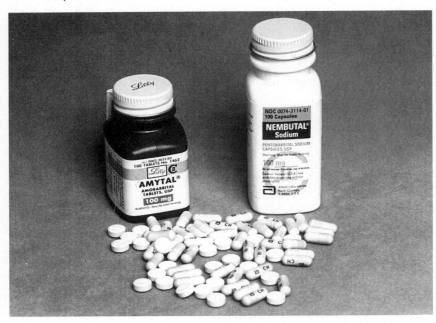

Various types of barbiturates in pill form.

is also sometimes associated with anxiety, irritability, and mood disturbances.

Anesthesia

Finally, sedative-hypnotics are used during surgical and dental procedures for their general anesthetic effects. Larger doses are needed for pain relief but small doses will relieve the anxiety associated with having surgery, thereby reducing the pain to some extent. Those compounds that are short acting and potent are most often given for these purposes. CNS depressant drugs have been given during labor and delivery to calm the mother, reduce the pain, and cause the experience to be more tolerable. However, there are adverse effects on the fetus that contraindicate their use in most cases.

Barbiturates

The barbiturates vary with respect to drug effect, how the drug is administered and at what dosage level, degree of CNS depression, and processes of absorption, distribution, metabolism, and elimination. The initial condition of the user and the setting or circumstances under which

the drug is used also determine what the drug effects will be. All of these factors contribute to how quickly the drug takes effect, its potency, and duration of the effect.

Barbiturates may first be distinguished by their duration of action and their half-lives. The usefulness of each barbiturate is determined, in large part, by the speed of its effect. Long-acting agents (phenobarbital, mephobarbital, and allobarbital), typically at a dosage level between 30-50 mg, are effective for eight to twelve hours and have a half-life of approximately one to six days. Due to their relatively low level of lipid solubility, they do not readily cross the blood-brain barrier, become less concentrated in brain tissue, and have a longer duration of action than the shorter-acting barbiturates. There is little sedation associated with the use of these drugs as they have minimal effects on the reticular activating system when used in low or normal doses. Tolerance and dependence develop less rapidly due to the slow onset and long duration of action. For these reasons, these agents are most useful in the treatment of epilepsy and anxiety disorders. They may also be used in the detoxification of an individual withdrawing from a shorter-acting barbiturate. These drugs are rarely used within drug-abusing populations.

Those that have a duration of action for an intermediate time period (butabarbital, pentobarbital and cyclobarbital) are effective for two to eight hours and have a half-life of between several hours and two days. Short-acting barbiturates (amobarbital or secobarbital) last for one to four hours and their half-life is at most about two days. Both short-acting and intermediate-acting barbiturates are readily absorbed by the gastrointestinal system following oral administration. Absorption is facilitated by drinking plenty of water so that the drug is distributed more widely. Because they are slightly less lipid soluble than the ultra-short-acting barbiturates, they cross the blood-brain barrier a bit more slowly, are not as well concentrated in brain tissue, and have a longer duration of action. Both the short-acting and intermediate-acting barbiturates are most commonly used for insomnia in a dosage range of about 100 to 200 mg. In low doses, they produce sedation while higher doses induce sleep. They may be used orally or by IV, depending on the desired effect. (Both methods are used for recreational purposes.)

Finally, ultra-short-acting barbiturates (thiopental, hexobarbital, and methohexital) have an active duration of five to thirty minutes and have a half-life of several hours. These drugs are so fast acting because they are completely absorbed, highly lipid soluble, and almost entirely protein bound. The active components have an almost immediate impact on the brain, which absorbs a higher concentration of the drug than when a longer-acting barbiturate is taken. As the active drug components leave the brain, they are quickly redistributed to other bodily tissues, resulting in a rapid decline in drug effects. The ultra-short-acting barbiturates are most commonly used IV as anesthetics. They may cause unconsciousness in anesthetic doses in only seconds and consciousness returns in about thirty minutes.

Barbiturates are commonly abused by illicit drug-taking groups and are globally called downers. Particular types of barbiturates are frequently referred to by their color, for example, "blue heavens" for amobarbital (Amytal), "yellow jackets" for pentobarbital (Nembutal), and "red birds" or "red devils" for secobarbital (Seconal). "Goof balls" is another name given to a variety of these depressants due to the condition produced in the user.

Routes of Administration

Barbiturates are taken either orally or by IV. The exact route chosen will depend on the purposes for which the drug is used. If a short-acting effect is desired for anesthesia, then the IV route is preferred. If a long-acting effect is desired to control anxiety or epilepsy, then the drug should be taken orally.

Absorption, Distribution, and Excretion

All the short-acting barbiturates are absorbed readily from the digestive system into the bloodstream after oral administration due to their high lipid solubility. They pass through the blood-brain barrier quickly and exert their effects on the brain. Due to their affinity for fatty tissue, they are rapidly redistributed to areas of the body that have a high fat content so their levels in the brain decline soon after they are administered. As this occurs, they are no longer in the vicinity of their sites of action. This redistribution explains why fast-acting barbiturates are effective for only a few minutes. Once they are deposited in fatty tissue, they are slowly released into the blood and finally metabolized by the liver. Although the drug is no longer active, it remains in the circulatory system at low levels for a much longer period of time.

On the other hand, the longer-acting barbiturates are much less lipid soluble and, thus, cross the blood-brain barrier less readily and do not deposit so entirely in fatty tissue. They remain active in the blood in a more water-soluble form for a longer period of time. Consequently, the exact duration of action depends on how long it takes for the liver to metabolize the drug, rather than on how long it takes to be redistributed to other bodily tissues. The result may be a residual effect of sleepiness or grogginess that may last well beyond the actual effective drug period. Waking up and functioning fully from certain anesthesias may not be so simple even though the actual anesthetic effects have worn off. Sometimes a hangover may still be present after a few days from the small amounts of barbiturates remaining in the bloodstream.

Liver enzymes deactivate and metabolize barbiturates quite efficiently, and the kidneys eliminate the drug from the body. In fact, as repeated doses of barbiturates are taken, more enzymes are induced to increase the metabolic rate of barbiturates and essentially deactivate the drug. It is also possible to increase the rate of barbiturate metabolism when other drugs, such as antipsychotics, nicotine, alcohol, or anesthetics are taken prior to the barbiturate due to the increase in enzyme induction. Barbiturates will similarly increase the metabolic rate of other drugs (e.g., caffeine, general and local anesthetics, and morphine) by inducing liver enzymes that metabolize them. As opposed to the effects of increasing acid levels in the urine on the excretion of some stimulants and hallucinogens, elimination of barbiturates can only be enhanced by reducing acidity of the urine. Because barbiturates are acids, the

Figure 11.5   *Brain Wave Patterns while Awake and Asleep.*

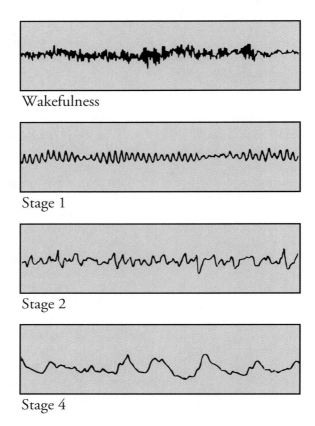

Wakefulness

Stage 1

Stage 2

Stage 4

Changing brain waves trace the patterns of sleep as it passes through REM. The fast and steady alpha rhythm of wakeful relaxation (at top) changes to the erratic, low voltage energy of Stage 1 sleep. Bursts of electrical discharge form "sleep spindles" during Stage 2. Stage 3 sleep (not shown) is characterized by deep delta waves, a slow wave that is first seen during this phase. Slow delta waves then begin to dominate the sleep pattern as seen in Stage 4 sleep.

urine must be made basic to increase the efficiency of the kidneys at excreting them. This technique is especially useful in treating those who have overdosed on barbiturates.

Urine surveillance techniques are quite effective in screening for the presence of barbiturates. The drug may be detected for as little as thirty hours after drug administration to up to several weeks, depending on the compound taken.

Pharmacological Properties

We have discussed the CNS depressants with respect to their pharmacological effects, particularly concerning their effects on the sleep cycle and on facilitating the ability of GABA to inhibit excitatory transmission. The effects of barbiturates are quite similar to other depressants, including the benzodiazepines, with only a few exceptions and distinctions. Barbiturates do not directly influence the amount of GABA released or the interaction between GABA and its receptor. Instead, barbiturates bind to the GABA receptor causing an interference with the ability of the cell to produce action potentials. Because they block the firing of synapses in this way, they are particularly useful for preventing convulsions, which result from repetitive synaptic firing. It should be noted, however, that some barbiturates have the opposite effect and can actually induce convulsions. The ability of barbiturates to directly influence neural cell activity causes them to be especially lethal when taken in high doses; they may inhibit neural activity to a much greater extent, resulting in complete CNS depression that involves both the brainstem and the medulla, which is responsible for breathing. Once respiratory depression occurs, death may be imminent. The benzodiazepines act more indirectly and specifically by modifying GABA activity and, thus, are less dangerous.

At therapeutic doses, barbiturates primarily influence the CNS without producing other unwanted peripheral effects. Brain-wave patterns characteristic of barbiturate use are similar to slow-wave sleep, with high peaks and low frequencies (see Figure 11.5). During normal sleep, the brain cycles between high and low activity levels. Brain-wave patterns during REM sleep demonstrate high activity levels and resemble, to some extent, a waking state. This sleep pattern is generally associated with dreaming. Because barbiturates suppress brain activity and induce slow-wave activity, the sleep produced by barbiturates does not cycle normally to include adequate amounts of REM sleep, which should be about 20 percent. Consequently, dreaming is substantially reduced and the user awakens feeling unrested and fatigued. In order to obtain a satisfying night's sleep, the entire sleep cycle should be experienced during the sleeping session. When the cycle is disrupted, the individual may be less able to function optimally throughout the day. This is one reason why the use of sleeping pills or alcohol may actually exacerbate problems associated with sleep deprivation.

To further complicate matters, some tolerance to barbiturates builds when they are taken over the course of a week or more, and some REM sleep will reappear. When the drug is terminated, the user will experience unusually long periods of REM sleep, as much as 40 percent, for up to several weeks. Even after the individual is no longer taking the drug, sleep will be somewhat disrupted as he or she may awaken several times during the night and the amount of time needed to fall asleep may lengthen. As a result, the individual may be tempted to resume taking the drug.

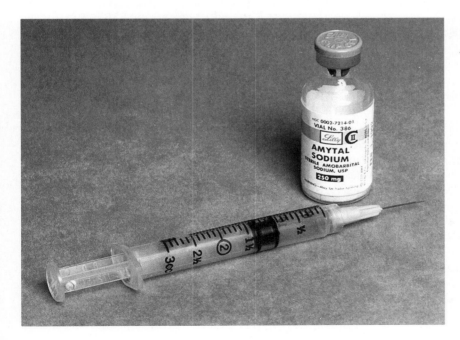

Barbiturate in injectable form.

Psychological and Behavioral Effects

Barbiturate intoxication in many ways resembles alcohol intoxication. Behavior is no longer properly inhibited and the user may be silly and impulsive. Because barbiturates also relieve anxiety, they may produce a mild feeling of euphoria that is quite pleasant and reinforcing. In addition, there is a relative loss of motor coordination and the senses may be dulled. Unfortunately, even when taken in relatively moderate doses, the user may not be aware of the subtle alterations in performance and so should not attempt to drive. Furthermore, due to the relatively long-lasting residual effects of barbiturate use, the individual may be somewhat impaired for up to several days following the last dosage. Unrecognized impairments in mental ability and motor performance may interfere with daily activities. When alcohol or another depressant drug is also present, the effects will be cumulative and the user will be substantially more impaired.

The actual effects depend greatly on the situation and on the initial condition of the individual, both in terms of his or her immediate mood state and innate temperament. When the emotional state of the user is steady and mood is high, barbiturates may simply enhance the initial mood state. When the mood is initially low, however, depression will more likely set in. At a party, one user may become "happy-go-lucky" and have an increased sense of well-being while another, who is alone or not in a situation that is intrinsically joyous, may withdraw, become severely depressed, or even excessively aggressive. This is similar to the use of alcohol—the effects may be unpredictable and unexpected.

Tolerance and Dependence

A single dose of barbiturate is enough to produce some degree of tolerance. Chronic doses can produce tolerance powerful enough to cause a repeated user to be able to tolerate a blood level several times higher than an individual who has taken only one dose. So, a one-time administration of a relatively small dose can cause noticeable mental and physical impairment while a repeat administration several times higher may produce almost no discernible impairment.

Specifically, barbiturates are associated with two forms of tolerance that primarily influence sedative effects: the increase in liver enzymes that metabolize the drug, and the adaptation of neurons in the brain to the presence of the drug (Julien, 1988). Because the ability of the liver to metabolize the drug is enhanced with repeated dosages, each time a barbiturate is taken, more is needed to maintain the same concentration at the receptor site in order to produce the same effect. Achieving a desired effect by simply increasing the dosage is not a simple proposition, however. Receptor sites within the brain adapt to the continual presence of the drug and become less sensitive to its effects. In order to override this process, an even larger dose than one would expect is needed to boost concentrations in the blood sufficiently to activate the receptor. This situation presents an unfortunate risk for those who are not carefully monitored on barbiturates. Although tolerance for the sedative and euphoric effects may develop, there may not be the same degree of tolerance for the respiratory-depressant effects. An individual may continue to take larger quantities of the drug to achieve desired psychoactive effects and not be aware of the increased risk of respiratory depression. Consequently, it becomes easier to accidentally administer a lethal dose of barbiturates.

Because different drug effects develop tolerance at different rates, some effects will disappear quickly while others will remain for a longer period of time before they become extinguished. Motor performance and coordination, for example, diminish rapidly once tolerance develops (over the course of a few days). Sleeping time may increase rapidly but again decrease after barbiturates have been taken over the course of a few weeks. Anticonvulsive effects, however, show virtually no tolerance and, thus, the drug can be taken effectively for several years for the treatment of epilepsy.

Withdrawal from barbiturates, particularly when high doses are used, may produce uncomfortable and perhaps more serious, potentially fatal physical symptoms of dependence. Once an individual has graduated to large daily dosages, removal of the drug may result in convulsions, hallucinations, delusions, severe anxiety, vomiting, nausea, delirium, tremors, and other manifestations of behavioral and physiological hyperexcitability. If the user suffered from a preexisting condition of epilepsy, the consequences may be particularly serious. Withdrawal symptoms may occur within a day following the last dose and may last for up to three days, depending on the half-life of the particular barbiturate. There are major differences between barbiturate withdrawal and opiate withdrawal. Although withdrawal from opiates can produce extremely uncomfortable symptoms, such as shaking, vomiting, and diarrhea, the symptoms are not lethal. For these reasons, withdrawal from barbiturates should only be done under medical supervision.

Normal dosages of barbiturates (about 100 mg) will produce only relatively mild withdrawal symptoms that are not life threatening or particularly serious. A hangover-like effect may follow for hours or days after the drug is stopped. This effect occurs because some barbiturates have a long half-life, and it may take some time before the drug is eliminated. The individual may feel fatigued, sleepy, and perhaps even "out of it." During the withdrawal period, there may be some degree of behavioral and mental impairment in the form of impaired judgment, reduced reaction time, lack of coordination, unsteadiness, and a general inability to concentrate and think clearly. Due to these symptoms, it is unwise to operate machinery or attempt to perform complex tasks the day after drug use. Again, when comparing the difference between opiate withdrawal and barbiturate withdrawal, we find that withdrawal symptoms are more pronounced following relatively small doses of opiates than those following low dosages of barbiturates. Aside from mild symptoms of dependence, barbiturates do not measurably interfere with the functions of the cardiovascular system,

the kidneys, the gastrointestinal tract or other major organs under the influence of normal doses.

Following barbiturate use, sleep is disrupted and unsatisfying, and it may be difficult to fall asleep. Other residual effects develop that may last for as long as a month. Many users find that they cannot easily terminate the drug. These withdrawal effects further encourage barbiturate users to continue taking the drug.

Effects During Pregnancy

Barbiturate use during pregnancy is contraindicated as the drugs readily pass through the placental barrier to influence fetal development. Used during the first trimester, birth defects and malformations are observed in a significant percentage of babies. Some of the most common abnormalities include cleft palate and cleft lip, heart and skeleton malformations, and CNS abnormalities. When taken during any part of the pregnancy, barbiturates may cause delayed growth of the fetal brain and specifically retard development of the genitals and brains of male babies. As adults, these individuals may show irregular sexual behavior. This particular effect appears to be a

At a party, it can be observed that some are "happy-go-lucky" while others are naturally withdrawn and depressed. Taking barbiturates can alter a preexisting mood state.

result of barbiturate's interference with steroid hormones that are largely responsible for the sexual differentiation in males. There is also evidence that barbiturate use during pregnancy may be associated with early learning disabilities and psychological disorders of exposed fetuses.

Finally, babies born to addicted mothers experience withdrawal symptoms several days after birth. These symptoms resemble those suffered by adult users and may be disconcerting and possibly dangerous without treatment. Because these babies have most likely already left the hospital before symptoms occur, they are commonly not treated.

Nonbarbiturate Sedative-Hypnotics

Chloral hydrate, ethchlorvynol, methaqualone (Quaaludes), glutethimide (Doriden), and methyprylon (Noludar) are all examples of nonbarbiturate sedative-hypnotics. The latter two were marketed in the 1950s as new nonbarbiturate drugs for the purposes of sleep and sedation. However, these drugs were produced by making only a very minor modification in the molecular structure of barbiturates and, therefore, differ so negligibly that the brain's receptors probably cannot distinguish between them and the barbiturates (Julien, 1988).

Methaqualone (Quaalude, Sopor, Parest, Mequin) was synthesized in India and found to be an effective hypnotic. Following oral administration, blood levels reach their peak concentration between sixty to ninety minutes later and its duration of action is approximately five to eight hours. In 1959 it became an established, although not yet popular, treatment for insomnia in Great Britain, even though at the time no one was certain of its safety. By the mid 1960s, methaqualone became recognized as a "safer" nonbarbiturate sedative than many on the market, and a global campaign was issued to physicians to improve its sales—it worked. Millions of prescriptions were distributed by the early 1970s in Great Britain. Unfortunately, the illicit drug market became interested in methaqualone at the same time, so its popularity also grew among heroin users and even high school students. At the same time, the drug was being "discovered" by many countries, including Germany, Japan, and the United States. Major epidemics of methaqualone abuse broke out in each of these countries during the 1960s and 70s. All the while, the safety

and abuse potential of methaqualone had yet to be established by government regulatory agencies. Package inserts indicated that there were many unknowns, however there were no restrictions on its prescription or use.

Eventually, it became clear that methaqualone was a highly addictive and dangerous drug. Many countries had already tightened down on its use, and the United States finally removed it from the market in 1984 due to its increasing popularity among drug abusing populations and its established abuse potential.

Methaqualone is no longer available by prescription, and it is viewed by the regulatory powers in the same light as the scheduled drugs marijuana, cocaine, and opium. Street availability, however, is a different matter, which is a source of concern due to its high degree of physical and psychological dependence. Sold under the street names of ludes and sopors, the drug is considered an excellent substitute for alcohol due to its disinhibitory and euphoric properties. Many users combine it with alcohol or other drugs to enhance the drug effect—a dangerous proposition to say the least. It also acts as a sexual enhancer due to its ability to uninhibit and relax. However, in a pharmacologic sense, it is actually a sexual depressant, making it more difficult to become sexually excited and achieve erection or orgasm. The perception of increased sexual freedom is strictly a myth, but a myth powerful enough to override, to some extent, the drug's pharmacologic properties.

Other effects of methaqualone include the drug's ability to suppress muscle spasms, control seizures, anesthesize, and suppress coughing. High doses reduce the amount of time spent in REM sleep, but low doses appear to increase REM sleep. Users frequently suffer from morning hangovers after an evening binge. There may also be some nausea, diarrhea, sweating, restlessness, anxiety, and loss of appetite (Corry & Cimbolic, 1985).

Drugs in this category of CNS depressants are used for the same overall purposes as barbiturates. Similarly, they have the ability to impair behavior and performance, produce side effects and symptoms of toxicity at high doses, and induce tolerance and other signs of dependence. Methaqualone, in particular, is capable of causing death via respiratory depression, and concoctions produced by street manufacturers tend to be impure, containing other more dangerous drugs or contaminants. As described previously, when methaqualone is mixed with another depressant such as alcohol, the consequences may be debilitating or even fatal.

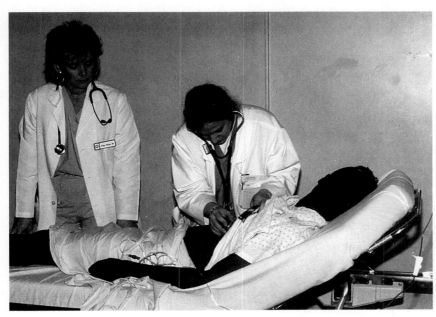

A barbiturate user being wheeled into an emergency room after taking an overdose.

Meprobamate

Meprobamate (Equanil, Miltown) belongs in a separate category of CNS depressants; it is neither a barbiturate nor a benzodiazepine. It is known as an anxiolytic or tranquilizer and in 1952 was developed as an alternative to other CNS depressants in large part for muscle relaxation. By 1955, physicians were prescribing it readily and the public believed it to be the ultimate happy pill because of the euphoria it produced. Meprobamate has both sedative and antianxiety properties and so, in low doses (800-1800 mg daily), can be used during the day for relaxation and coping purposes. At night, the drug may be used in somewhat larger doses as a sleeping agent. Daily doses of more than 3,200 mg for more than a couple of months are known to result in physical dependence. Although its effects are relatively long lasting, it is not as effective or safe an antianxiety drug as the benzodiazepines, and so is presently not used as liberally as it once was.

Meprobamate is not administered IV as it is so well absorbed when taken orally. It readily crosses the blood-brain barrier and is quickly distributed throughout the brain to influence its function. Because it must be fully metabolized by the kidneys before it is excreted, meprobamate's action lasts ten hours or more. Similar to the users of other nonbarbiturate sedative-hypnotics, meprobamate

users will experience tolerance, withdrawal symptoms, psychological dependence, and potentially dangerous consequences when high doses of the drug are terminated. Nevertheless, as compared with the barbiturates, meprobamate is not as potent and not as likely to cause respiratory depression.

Benzodiazepines

Benzodiazepines are a relatively new addition to the family of CNS depressants. The first benzodiazepine, chlordiazepoxide (Librium), was marketed in 1960 and rapidly became the leading psychoactive drug for the treatment of anxiety. Physical, and to some extent psychological, dependence were not initially observed with Librium. Later reports do document the development of withdrawal symptoms in those who took the drug for a year or more. Nevertheless, the overall efficacy, safety, and relative lack of dependence from Librium use were higher than for the barbiturates. In the early 1970s, Librium was replaced with diazepam (Valium) as a smaller, but more potent, dose could be taken with a more rapid onset. Presently, there are fourteen different forms of benzodiazepine available, including oxazepam (Serax), flurazepam (Dalmane), lorazepam (Ativan), clorazepate monopotassium (Azene),

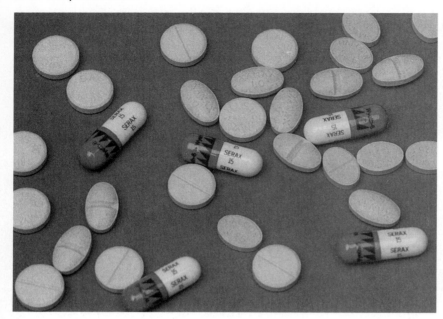

Benzodiazepines in pill form.

clorazepate dipotassium (Tranxene), temazepam (Restoril), and alprazolam (Xanax).

The benzodiazepines specifically influence the activity of GABA and are, thus, thought to be more effective in the treatment of anxiety than are the barbiturates. They additionally have a much larger margin of safety, so it is more difficult to administer a lethal dose. (For that reason, they are not widely used to attempt suicide.) When used along with alcohol, however, they become much more potent and dangerous—the synergistic effect described earlier. Finally, they are quite toxic to a developing fetus, particularly when used by the mother during the first trimester of pregnancy. There is an increased risk of congenital abnormalities and malformations with the use of these minor tranquilizers during the first trimester. Consequently, the prescribing physician must inquire about the patient's childbearing potential prior to administering this type of therapy.

Two benzodiazepines are especially popular in our society: diazepam (Valium) and chlordiazepoxide. Valium is a fast-acting, long-lasting antianxiety agent that is slowly metabolized and produces active metabolites that remain in the system. Due to these features, it is associated with high psychological dependence but only rarely produces notable withdrawal symptoms. Valium, in fact, has been so overprescribed and so overused by both pre-scribing physicians and patients seeking easy solutions to complicated lifestyle problems, that the federal government (Food and Drug Administration) has recently made it more difficult to obtain a prescription. The prescribing physician must register the order with several different authorities (local and federal) so that the availability of Valium can be more closely monitored and supervised.

Absorption, Distribution, and Excretion

Similar to the barbiturates, benzodiazepines are highly lipid soluble and readily pass through the blood-brain barrier to reach high concentrations in the brain and influence its function. Although there is tremendous variability in the extent to which each of the benzodiazepines are soluble, nearly all of them are absorbed efficiently and completely when taken orally. Several of the benzodiazepines, including chlordiazepoxide, diazepam, midazolam, and lorazepam, may also be injected for the purposes of general anesthesia, immediate suppression of seizures, or before and during surgical procedures. Intramuscular injection causes the drug to be more slowly absorbed due to the high degree of protein in muscle tissue; benzodiazepines tend to bind to protein.

How quickly each benzodiazepine is absorbed and becomes active varies tremendously and may depend to some extent on the particular user (the same dose may cause different blood levels in two different people). Some may require only minutes to feel an effect while others may not obtain a peak level of activity for several hours. Consequently, the drug of choice will depend on the therapeutic purpose; if the user wants to medicate an anxiety disorder or an epileptic condition then he or she would desire a long-lasting effect with less immediate punch. In this case, diazepam may be most useful. For sleep, on the other hand, a shorter acting, more immediate effect would be desired with a lesser chance of residual effects in the morning. In this case, triazolam may be the drug of choice.

In choosing a benzodiazepine for therapeutic purposes, one must also consider the manner in which the drug is metabolized before the body eliminates it. Blood levels of the drug drop rapidly after it has been distributed and then the decline slows during the metabolic process. Drug effects, however, are not limited to the half-life of the specific drug taken. Many of the benzodiazepines, particularly the older ones, produce chemically active by-products or metabolites that cause drug effects to endure well beyond the life of the drug originally taken. Diazepam, for example, has a half-life of only a few short hours: however, its metabolites remain active for approximately twenty hours. Although lorazepam reaches peak concentrations after about two hours and has a half-life of approximately twelve hours, its major metabolite, lorazepam glucuronide, has a half-life of about eighteen hours. When these drugs are administered repeatedly, the blood levels of metabolites are likely to be even higher than blood levels of the drug after several days. Because benzodiazepines and their metabolites have relatively long half-lives and are quite slowly eliminated from the body, it is possible to detect the use of these drugs for weeks and perhaps months after the drug has been discontinued. The newer benzodiazepines, such as oxazepam, lorazepam, and triazolam, do not have active metabolites.

Pharmacological Effects

The benzodiazepines exert their effects nearly exclusively within the CNS. The peripheral properties that they possess, such as muscle relaxation, appear to be indirectly due to effects on the brain. Consequently, we do not see the same degree of impairment experienced by barbiturate users, and the drugs can be more safely used in the treat-

ment of patients with neurological disorders, such as brain injuries, Parkinson's disease, or muscular problems associated with multiple sclerosis. These drugs primarily influence the midbrain, limbic system, and brainstem reticular activating system and are active in the hypothalamus (Braestrup & Neilson, 1983). Because of their dampening of hypothalamic activity, the autonomic nervous system does not receive the same degree of communication and, consequently, does not initiate f/f/f responses as it would normally. This may be, in part, how benzodiazepines help to alleviate anxiety.

In particular, benzodiazepines potentiate the activity of GABA and adenosine, both inhibitory neurotransmitters. There is some speculation that the brain possesses a natural benzodiazepine-like substance that is intended to regulate and control anxiety reactions. This would explain the existence of benzodiazepine receptors that have a particular affinity for these drugs. Furthermore, drugs that have an opposite effect on these receptors, for example caffeine, actually elicit anxiety and stimulate behavior. These receptors are found throughout the brain, with the highest concentrations in the frontal and occipital cortex, hypothalamus, cerebellum, hippocampus, and other areas associated with GABA activity. As we will discuss below, the ability of benzodiazepines to reduce anxiety is believed to result from its influence on structures within the limbic system.

Adverse Effects

As mentioned previously, the benzodiazepines are considered safer and less toxic than the barbiturates. Even in large doses, respiratory depression is unlikely. Even experiences of a morning hangover or undue sedation are minimized when benzodiazepines are taken. Depending on the specific drug they take, the dosage, and the frequency of administration, users may experience some fatigue, reduced reaction time, confusion, difficulty in concentration, dizziness, unsteadiness, or even memory loss. Adverse effects will also vary tremendously depending on the constitution, age, and personality of the user. Those with a preexisting anxiety disorder may actually demonstrate performance improvements, particularly in those areas that were disrupted by their anxiety. Those with normal levels of anxiety and elderly people are more likely to experience untoward side effects, such as difficulties in comprehension, short-term memory loss, and motor incoordination. Users may not be aware of these subtle impairments produced by usual dosages. Higher doses will cause more noticeable, dysfunctional effects, possibly for a long period of time. Also similar to the barbiturates, the sleep cycle is disturbed and REM sleep is suppressed. A rebound effect of increased REM sleep occurs following drug cessation; however, the influence of benzodiazepines on sleep cycles is somewhat less than with the barbiturates.

It is important to note that, like the barbiturates, benzodiazpines can cause the nervous system to become generally depressed, resulting in what is called brain syndrome. This syndrome is characteristic of several psychiatric and neurological disorders, such as schizophrenia, depression, Alzeheimer's disease, Korsakoff's (see Chapter 6), and other forms of dementia. Individuals suffering from these disorders or from benzodiazepine-induced brain syndrome show a flat affect and are unable to respond to environmental stimuli adequately. There is disorientation, amnesia, intellectual impairment, lack of judgment, motor incoordination, moodiness, and dulled senses. Unlike the chronic brain syndrome cases that result from a psychiatric or neurological disturbance, the depression of brain function with benzodiazpine use is reversible.

Beneficial Uses

Benzodiazepines are particularly useful agents in the treatment of anxiety disorders, panic, and phobias. They are also commonly administered for insomnia, seizures, and withdrawal from other depressants, such as alcohol, to minimize tremors, agitation, DTs, and hallucinations. When an anxiety disorder is present, the individual should first be evaluated to determine whether environmental causes (i.e., loss of a parent, divorce, difficulties at work) or other primary physical conditions (i.e., neurological disturbance) are contributory. If so, intervention efforts should focus on other forms of medicinal and psychotherapeutic methods. In cases where there is no other identifiable cause and the patient finds anxiety to be disruptive to normal functioning and lifestyle, a benzodiazepine may be helpful. Benzodiazepines do not produce good feelings in individuals with normal levels of anxiety. In fact, normal individuals report unpleasant effects and dysphoria, and tend to refuse opportunities to take the drug again (see McKim, 1991). Thus, it appears that benzodiazepines have a specific anxiolytic effect that may only be beneficial for those with an anxiety disorder.

When an anxiety disorder is endogenous, researchers and clinicians now believe that the f/f/f or stress mechanism is overactive. As a result, excessive amounts of epinephrine, cortisol, and other stress hormones are released, producing the subjective experience of anxiety and sometimes panic. There is quite a bit of speculation that the origins of this disturbance are in the limbic system, thalamus, and hypothalamus. Diazepam, for example, acts directly on these structures to induce a calming effect without any measurable influence on the peripheral autonomic nervous system or endocrine function. Chlordiazepoxide also acts directly on the limbic system to relieve tension and reduce fear and aggression. Similarly, other anxiolytics exert their effects centrally to tranquilize the nervous system. Thus, it is unclear whether anxiety is elicited centrally, peripherally, or both.

The benzodiazepines are additionally used widely for sleeping disorders such as insomnia. Flurazepam is used most commonly in the United States for this purpose. Similar to the barbiturates, these drugs increase total sleeping time, shorten the time it takes to fall asleep, and decrease the number of awakenings during the night. Unfortunately, there is also a suppression of REM sleep. The sleep cycle is disrupted and rebound REM occurs following the last dose. As a result, sleep during and after drug use may not be particularly satisfying. Unlike the barbiturates, however, we do not see the tolerance to these effects with benzodiazepines, so increased dosages over time become unnecessary.

Trials with benzodiazepines have been conducted both clinically and experimentally to determine whether there is a therapeutic effect in the treatment of aggressive or violent patients. Suggestions have been made that they are particularly useful in treating acute episodes of violence by sedating the patient (Yudofsky, 1987). Unfortunately in some cases, high doses are required to achieve this effect and, thus, reduced aggressiveness is accompanied by uncomfortable or debilitating sedation, confusion, dependency, and the exacerbation of depression when it is also present. Although there is evidence that benzodiazepines are effective in the treatment of aggressiveness (Lion, 1979), others have observed what is called a paradoxical rage effect characterized by increased hostility, aggressiveness, and violence. Investigators are presently searching for particular antianxiety agents that are less likely to produce paradoxical rage. Despite the occurrence of this phenomenon in some cases, many clinicians continue to find some benzodiazepines helpful in treating aggressive patients when their symptomatology includes paranoia, suspiciousness, explosive personalities, impulsiveness, and irritability.

Tolerance and Dependence

Acute tolerance to benzodiazepines has been demonstrated in animal studies (Barnett & Fiore, 1973) that showed an attenuated response to a repeated dose two hours later. Studies suggest that acute tolerance may develop due to the presence of active metabolites that compete with the second administration of the drug at the receptor site, reducing its ability to exert an effect. Drug effects are consequently less potent and a larger dose is needed to achieve a full effect.

Benzodiazepines produce chronic tolerance when taken repeatedly although not to the same degree as barbiturates. The reason for this may be related to the fact that relatively small amounts of liver enzymes are induced by repeated doses of these drugs. The development of tolerance differs across different drug effects. For example, depressant drug effects diminish first as tolerance develops while the suppression of certain behaviors or moods (e.g., anxiety) remains relatively untouched. Thus, the individual's behavior and mood may become uninhibited, relaxed, and carefree while not restrained by the initial depressant effects of the drug. As a result, the tolerant individual will be more likely to express latent desires or hidden feelings that would otherwise be suppressed by either the initial state of anxiety or by the depressant drug. This may explain why some individuals become hostile or show signs of rage and violence under the influence of a benzodiazepine. Tolerance to antianxiety effects of the drug develops more slowly, and there is no evidence of tolerance to the sleep-inducing effects.

Withdrawal symptoms have been documented following relatively large doses taken over a period of time. They may include many of the symptoms experienced by barbiturate users, such as sleep disturbance, tremors, muscular and abdominal cramps, sweating, agitation, vomiting, and possibly convulsions. Other side effects commonly experienced are largely behavioral, including a drunken-like state, poor concentration, confusion, mood swings, anger or aggression, and mental and physical impairment. Lower or normal dosages of benzodiazepines taken symptomatically are generally believed not to produce seriously untoward levels of tolerance and dependence. However, after usual doses are terminated, subtle withdrawal symptoms may occur in some individuals that go unrecognized, largely due to the delay in time between drug cessation and symptoms. Withdrawal symptoms may include an increase in anxiety, sensitivity to environmental stimuli (such as bright lights or loud sounds), perceptual impairments, difficulty in concentration and memory, sleep disturbances, and incoordination among others. In many users, the problems they originally intended to correct with benzodiazepines simply become exaggerated during withdrawal. Because these drugs calm the nerves, induce sleep, increase feelings of well-being, decrease disinhibition, and sometimes induce euphoria, psychological dependence is of most concern. Consequently, one of the most important considerations when evaluating patients to determine whether benzodiazepines are indicated for their condition is their preexisting psychological state.

Buspirone

Buspirone is a novel nonbenzodiazepine anxiolytic agent. It is unrelated to the benzodiazepines in both structure and pharmacologic properties. We include a short description of this drug because of its proven efficacy and safety in the treatment of anxiety disorders and of alcoholism. Clinical studies have shown buspirone to have a level of efficacy comparable to diazepam or clorazepate. It alleviates anxiety without causing sedation or measurable functional impairment. Furthermore, it appears to have unusually specific anxiolytic effects without having anticonvulsant or muscle relaxant properties.

There is no interaction with other central nervous system depressants as opposed to the benzodiazepines and barbiturates. Instead of uniformly influencing GABA and monoamine activity by facilitating GABA and inhibiting monoaminergic systems, buspirone suppresses serotonergic activity while enhancing dopaminergic and noradrenergic cell firing. Researchers believe that this drug specifically alters the activity of those neurotransmitter systems that regulate anxiety responses in such a way that other processes, for example, attention and arousal, are not affected (see Eison & Temple, 1986).

One of the most attractive qualities of buspirone is its apparent lack of abuse potential (Rickels, 1983; Griffiths et al., 1986). Studies have shown that, when buspirone is compared with diazepam or with a placebo, subjects do not experience euphoria, withdrawal symptoms, or sedation-anxiolytic properties that are desirable in the treatment of subjects who may be addiction prone, such as alcoholics. Furthermore, there are no measurable effects on blood pressure, pulse or respiratory rates, or body temperature. For these reasons, buspirone may soon become one of the widely prescribed drugs for patients suffering from anxiety, panic attacks, phobias, and alcoholism.

Vulnerability to Abuse

Addict Populations

Those who abuse CNS depressants do not differ significantly between barbiturate and benzodiazepine groups with respect to origins of the addiction, characteristics of the user, and individual risk factors for abuse. Individuals with a history of depressant use or drug abuse generally are most likely to self-administer the drug readily, as opposed to individuals who are naive to drug abuse. In initial trials, individuals naive to depressant use commonly report dysphoric drug effects and do not choose to readminister them (Griffiths et al., 1979; deWit et al., 1989). After repeated administration, however, a compulsion to continue use develops, which may be due to both physiological reasons, as yet undelineated, and psychological dependence.

The largest group of depressant abusers are the iatrogenically addicted. Use of depressants in these individuals is, in fact, legal—for a legitimate medical problem—and the addiction developed over time as a result of an initial physician's prescription. Most often, the original use was as a sleeping aid or for anxiety. Barbiturates are more more likely to be abused by street users than benzodiazepines although benzodiazepines are becoming more and more popular among the iatrogenically addicted as physicians increasingly recognize their potential for treating anxiety disorders. Nevertheless, the fact that so many are addicted to barbiturates suggests that benzodiazepines are still being underused and barbiturates are still overused; benzodiazepines are safer and more effective for anxiety than barbiturates. As a dependence on depressants develops, a small but significant percentage of users continue the drug on their own initiative and beyond what would be considered therapeutically necessary. At this point, the effects for which the drug was originally used, that is, sleeping, have worn off and the user is obtaining reinforcement from the drug's other properties-relaxation, well-being, euphoria, and so forth. Furthermore, continued use may

Simulation of a woman at a pharmacist's counter attempting to obtain an illicit prescription to feed her habit.

actually exacerbate the sleeping disorder by suppressing REM during usage and increasing rebound REM sleep when the drug is not used, contributing to disrupted sleep patterns. The user, consequently, may experience grave difficulty in abstaining. Unfortunately, users are frequently not aware of these psychologically and physically addictive properties and are not carefully monitored by their physicians. Thus, their motivation to quit altogether may be lacking.

A second depressant-abusing population includes the street users who seek the effects strictly for recreational purposes. The pattern of abuse is disturbingly different from those who are iatrogenically addicted, however, as they tend to use them in larger quantities and in combination with other drugs, including alcohol. Due to these tendencies, street users are more likely to administer a fatal dose. Serious IV drug users may inject depressants, particularly barbiturates, to achieve a rush that is somewhat similar to that experienced from heroin. Those also using stimulant drugs, such as cocaine or amphetamines, sometimes cut the stimulant with a depressant to, in a sense, balance out the effect.

Risk Factors

There is some evidence that certain subpopulations of users and potential users are at risk for depressant use because of an underlying psychological, psychiatric, or medical condition. For example, alcoholics are frequently (although not always) polydrug abusers. A study conducted by Jensen et al. (1990) indicated that alcoholic subjects suffering from panic attacks were more likely to abuse anxiolytic or benzodiazepine drugs than panic-inducing drugs, such as stimulants or marijuana. Nonanxious alcoholic subjects were less likely to abuse opiates and sedatives and more likely to abuse marijuana at a younger age than those with anxiety. These findings are consistent with the self-medication hypothesis discussed in earlier chapters, especially Chapter 5.

There is evidence that those most likely to abuse CNS depressants are more severely maladjusted than other drug users (Spotts & Shontz, 1984). Of course, we do not know whether the maladjustments predated their drug use or was a consequence of it. Treatment protocols would need to address the possibility of underlying psychopathology in these drug users. Further studies of temperament and personality suggest that those most likely to abuse depressants have lower arousal-seeking tendencies

and higher external stimulus screening ability than those who prefer stimulants (Kern et al., 1986). CNS depressant users may be somewhat less likely to find high external stimulation rewarding and may seek a reduction in exposure to environmental stimuli so that they may function and cope more effectively. The use of CNS depressants by this group may allow them to become more extroverted than their temperament initially provided for (Spotts & Shontz, 1984) with an increased ability to absorb and act on their environments.

The Role of CNS Depressants in Criminal Activity

Barbiturate use appears to play an active role in victimization. In a study by Goodman and his colleagues (1986), barbiturates were detected in 7.9 percent of homicide victims who were tested. Black victims within this population were positive for barbiturates in 10.4 percent of those tested. Barbiturate use was found to be greatest in black female victims (15.1 percent). The precise role that barbiturates play in homicide victimization is quite unclear at this time, however the authors speculated that specific behaviors associated with the drugs' use may contribute to homicidal attack.

With respect to the victimizer, the link between depressant use and criminal behavior lies primarily in the fact that so many street drug users include depressants on their shopping list. Downers and other depressants are very much a part of the drug underworld, which is already invested in criminal activity. Heroin users commonly shoot barbiturates along with heroin to prolong their high or to extend their heroin supply. Barbiturates are also used in combination with amphetamines or cocaine, even though their effects are contradictory. The barbiturate tends to relax the high from stimulants so the user may avoid some of the more unpleasant side effects. Methaqualone was very popular in drug-abusing crowds during the 1960s and '70s to exaggerate the effects of alcohol or for the aphrodisiac properties that people ascribe to it. One female college student with high grades in a criminology program, exemplifies how depressant use can relax values and impair judgment. This particular student began to use methaqualone regularly along with whiskey. She quickly deteriorated, finding the high enjoyable and all consuming, and began dealing drugs (even to a college professor!) as her associations with the drug subculture increased. Her grades dropped dramatically, and she became incapable of coping with life's daily stressors. After sleeping with a number of people indiscriminantly, she contracted a sexually transmitted disease and eventually moved to St. Petersburg, Florida, where she now sells suntan lotion and drugs. This story illustrates how depressant users may find their decision-making ability compromised and may eventually become associated with crime in an effort to purchase and use the drug. These tendencies further invest the user in a criminal subculture, accentuate the effects of other drugs of abuse, and compromise the ability to cope and succeed using mainstream methods.

Treatment

Treatment strategies for addiction to CNS depressants do not differ substantially across particular drug categories; those regimens for barbiturate and benzodiazepine addicts are essentially the same. The first step is to detoxify the individual. Because of the potentially serious complications resulting from depressant withdrawal, such as convulsions, it is important that the patient not be left to deal with this stage of detoxification alone. Longer-acting drugs should be substituted for previously maintained shorter-acting drugs during withdrawal to help curb the

behavioral habits and reduce their potency. The drug dosage should be very gradually reduced and then withdrawn completely under close medical supervision. Most often, this may be accomplished as an outpatient, however some individuals may require hospitalization depending on their medical, psychiatric, and drug history. In conjunction with medical attention, counseling or psychotherapy is necessary to increase psychological strength and an understanding of the drug withdrawal process. If panic attacks, psychotic episodes, irregular heart beat, or high blood pressure occur, medications such as betablockers may be helpful.

The second step is to assist individuals toward the end of the withdrawal phase so that they are able to withstand the psychological and physical pressure to resume drug use. The perceived need for the drug and the physical dependence are associated with an exacerbation of many of the symptoms that originally caused patients to become addicted. It is important at this stage to provide medical and group or family support in addition to formal counseling or therapy. There are no well-established treatments for depressant dependence once the user has been detoxified. No substitute drugs (such as methadone for heroin) exist that do not also produce dependence and that are not also associated with side effects and tolerance. Those who

A group counseling session for drug abusers.

are iatrogenically addicted must rely on either their own motivation or the curtailing of prescriptions by their physicians. Because those physicians who originally prescribed the medication are frequently not aware of the condition and have not monitored the situation closely from the beginning, the patient must largely rely on his or her own willpower. This can only come once the patient has been sufficiently informed of the dependence-producing properties of depressants and given conjunctive therapy. Thus, the treatment protocol must emphasize education, counseling, relaxation exercises or stress management, and perhaps biofeedback. Unfortunately, due to the high level of physiological and psychological dependence and the reliance on barbiturates for sleep, relapse rates are higher for barbiturate users than for benzodiazepine users.

Another treatment consideration is both the pre- and post-drug condition. Spotts and Shontz (1984) showed that the heavy, chronic use of barbiturates and sedative-hypnotics is associated with long-term psychological problems. There was evidence that these drug abusers experienced or perceived conditions of abandonment, rejection, expectations of failure and defeat, self-destructive tendencies, and feelings of hopelessness. The use of depressants appears to exacerbate these problems; users demonstrate the loss of desirable characteristics and an exaggeration of unwanted or unpleasant traits. This study emphasized the

need for intensive psychotherapy to address these compounded difficulties.

Finally, with respect to psychological state of the depressant user, the chronic administration of barbiturate anticonvulsants to control seizures has been shown to contribute to the development of depression, particularly in children (Ferrari et al., 1983). These effects were present even when there were no signs of a preexisting problem. In cases where depressant therapy is essential, the treatment practitioner must take into account the possibility of psychological or psychiatric complications that require attention.

▤ Summary

Drugs that depress the central nervous system fall into several categories: barbiturates, nonbarbiturate hypnotics, benzodiazepines (or anxiolytics), and a miscellaneous group of compounds. Although each varies in its site of action, its specificity and its pharmacological properties, the drugs have a great deal in common. All depressants have either additive or synergistic effects and can be dangerous when used in combination. They interfere with sleep cycles and can lead to both physical and psychological dependence in varying degrees. Depressants lower

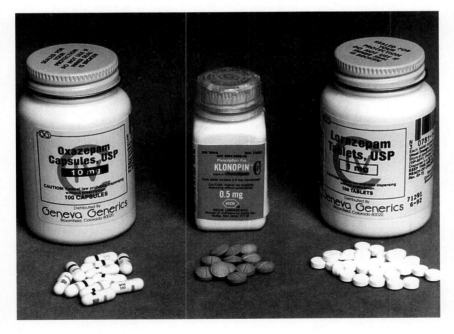

Benzodiazeunes with anticonvulsant effects.

inhibitions and, in large enough doses, will lower brain-stem activity, possibly resulting in coma or death. Also, a state of neurological and behavioral hyperexcitability may follow termination of depressant use, encouraging users to readminister the drug and necessitating the use of other drugs to facilitate withdrawal.

Insomnia, anxiety, alcohol withdrawal, epilepsy or CNS instability, and painful medical procedures are all conditions under which an individual may take depressants. Which type of depressant taken is a function of what the condition calls for, the desired duration of action, the particular effects, and the calculation of risks and benefits. In particular, choosing a barbiturate will very much depend on whether the patient/user is seeking a long-term or short-term effect. Dental procedures require only short acting drugs, while anxiety relief will require longer acting depressants. Those who use depressants recreationally will most likely opt for longer acting drugs that relieve behavioral inhibition, reduce anxiety, and induce pleasure. Most recreational users of barbiturates get into trouble with these drugs when they mix them with other depressants such as alcohol. The result may be debilitating, if not fatal. Regular or even intermittent use during pregnancy is also hazardous and may produce birth defects in the newborn.

In many ways, the development of benzodiazepines has been a real boon to thousands of patients wanting to avoid the untoward side effects of barbiturates. Barbiturates, so far, are irreplaceable in the operating room, however for those suffering from anxiety and sleep disturbances, benzodiazepines offer a safer and less addictive alternative (although their abuse potential remains well documented). Benzodiazepines have less general effects and, thus, are responsible for more specific and controlled effects. They are the preferred class of drugs for psychiatric mood disorders, including phobias and panic attacks, and for detoxification purposes. We should remember, however, that the pharmacologic treatment of psychiatric and psychological disorders cannot be entirely effective without the assistance of behavioral and psychotherapeutic measures. Consequently, depressant drugs should only be used in such patients as a last resort and in conjunction with more conventional therapies.

Depressant abuse does not discriminate between social classes, racial groups, or any other population characteristic. Experimenting with depressants exponentially increases our chances of becoming addicted and should be avoided unless indicated by a medical professional. As with any drug having abuse potential, existing psychological disturbances, traumatic childhood experiences, or the presence of severe social stressors all increase the risk for depressant abuse. Individuals who are less stable and who have difficulty coping with life's various pitfalls may find some escape in a depressant fog. For this reason, the focus of treatment efforts for individuals who are abusing depressants must be comprehensive, not only with respect to their drug abuse but also with an eye to underlying mechanisms and problems that may be contributory.

CHAPTER

12

Psychedelic Drugs

Objectives

1. To provide an overview of the extent to which psychedelics are used in the United States and to describe legitimate uses among religious and cultural groups.

2. To classify psychedelics according to their molecular structure and psychoactive properties.

3. To discuss the various ways in which psychedelics influence different chemical systems in the brain to produce their psychoactive effects.

4. To provide a detailed discussion on widely abused psychedelics and a summary view of those psychedelics less widely used.

5. To identify the numerous and varied effects of psychedelics, including hallucinations, which are a function of the specific chemical system in the brain that is affected.

6. To present the biological, psychological, and behavioral effects of psychedelics.

7. To discuss the characteristics of PCP users and those traits that may increase their risk for drug abuse.

8. To overview existing treatment strategies for PCP abusers.

Psychedelic or hallucinogenic drugs include a number of compounds that have the ability to alter visual, auditory, olfactory, somatosensory (touch), and other sensory perceptions. Included in this class of drugs are LSD, peyote, mescaline, DMT, STP, and PCP. Generally, these drugs are manufactured in clandestine laboratories for the illicit drug trade. Phencyclidine (PCP) can be easily produced in the simplest of laboratories. Virtually all PCP is produced in illicit domestic laboratories, and estimates indicate that almost 80 percent of the PCP found in this country originates from laboratories in California (U.S. Attorneys, 1989, p. 15). During the late 1980s and early 1990s many reports of toad licking among young people and its allegedly fatal consequences appeared in the popular press (If asked to lick a cane toad, 1990). Some believe that the chemical known as bufotenine which can be found in the paratoid glands on a green and red toad called a cane toad has psychedelic properties. Licking or eating the cane toad's paratoid glands will produce hallucinations in the user. Others believe these popular press reports are exaggerated and argue that bufotenine may be toxic to humans but has no psychedelic properties (For a complete review of the toad licking phenomenon see Lyttle, 1993).

Psychedelic drugs generate hallucinations that prevent users from making a realistic appraisal of their environment, providing a true escape from life's realities. Hallucinations produced by these drugs are, for the most part, mild visual distortions. Sufficient doses of a hallucinogenic drug alter judgements about what is really there and what is not. The effects of psychedelics range from alterations in cognition and perception to profound changes in behavior that may be quite disruptive to both the user and his or her surroundings. Depending on the exact substance taken, a state resembling amphetamine psychosis may develop. There are, however, notable differences in the type of psychosis that occurs. As we shall see, behavioral states induced by psychedelics possess some aspects of psychosis, while other aspects of these behaviors are quite dissimilar from amphetamine-induced states. Although each drug in this category causes hallucinations and alters reality, the precise psychological effects that any given user experiences will depend on the drug taken, dosage level, environmental circumstances, preexisting psychological state and behavioral tendencies, and present mood.

Because the term hallucinogen does not accurately portray the active properties of these drugs, many prefer not to use it; relatively high doses are needed to produce hallucinations and the drugs have other psychoactive effects. Therefore, the term psychedelic may be a more accurate description. This term refers to the common ability of these drugs to alter perceptions of reality and change thought patterns. Many other drugs in high doses will also produce hallucinations, but they are frequently a result of the drug's toxicity (i.e., the person has taken more than the recommended dose or is having an unusual adverse reaction) rather than its psychoactive properties. Psychedelics can be distinguished from other drugs that cause hallucinations by their ability to produce these effects in relatively small doses and without many toxic effects. Users perceive that the mind becomes capable of experiencing a range of perceptions that were not possible in a nondrug state. Hence, users refer to psychedelics as mind expanding. Individuals who use psychedelics for their mind expansion capabilities report a freedom from social restrictions. They feel they are able to more fully experience their environments and others around them without being limited by social conventions and imposed inhibitions on their behavior. In reality, rather than being truly mind expanding, psychedelics stimulate sensory mechanisms so that even simple and mundane events are experienced as unique and pleasantly meaningful. Users become passive observers of their inner thoughts and their enhanced sensory environments. Once the drug has worn off, however, the psychedelic user realizes that the drug did not, in fact, contribute to great works of art or truly profound thoughts.

Extent of Use of Psychedelics

LSD was a particularly popular drug during the 1960s and has recently reemerged as the drug of choice among certain groups of users in the southeastern United States (U.S. Attorneys, 1989). Flower children reminiscent of the 1960s are again visible, wearing clothes that characterized the generation of war protesters and peace advocates. At concerts, and all night parties called raves youth high on psychedelics can be seen floating around the crowds, picking invisible flowers out of the air, and displaying the peace sign with their fingers. College students, military personnel, and blue-collar workers make up most of the psychedelic-using population although use among children and youth is also increasing. Particularly disconcerting is the administration of LSD in the form of skin patches to youngsters unaware that they are about to "go for a ride." Because the effects of psychedelics can be so

Table 12.1 *Hallucinogens: Percent of Population Reporting Use of Hallucinogens Ever, Past Year, and Past Month (1993) by Sex and Age Groups for Total Population.*

	Ever Used	Used during Past Month	Used during Past Year
AGE	RATE ESTIMATES (PERCENTAGE)		
12-17	2.9	2.1	0.5
Male	3.4	2.4	0.6
Female	2.4	1.7	0.4
18-25	12.5	4.9	1.3
Male	15.2	6.8	2.1
Female	9.9	3.0	0.6
26-34	15.9	1.2	0.1
Male	19.7	2.0	0.2
Female	12.2	0.4	—
35+	6.6	0.1	—
Male	10.0	0.2	—
Female	3.7	—	—
Total	8.7	1.2	0.2
Male	11.8	1.7	0.4
Female	5.9	0.6	0.1

- no estimate reported
Note: Hallucinogens include LSD and PCP as well as other hallucinogens.
Source: Adapted from Substance Abuse and Mental Health Services Administration. *National Household Survey on Drug Abuse: Population Estimates 1993.*

profoundly conscious altering, such a drug experience without prior knowledge can be devastating.

In 1993, 8.7 percent of Americans reported that they had ever used LSD (see Table 12.1). The twenty-six to thirty-four year-old age group was most likely to have tried psychedelics previously (15.9 percent), but the twelve to seventeen and eighteen to twenty-five age groups were most likely to have used in the past year or in the past month. These reports support the notion that psychedelic use is presently increasing.

During the early 1980s, one of the largest declines observed among college students was for LSD. Annual prevalence fell from 6.3 percent in 1982 to 2.2 percent in 1985. This figure rose to 3.9 percent in 1986, remained fairly level throughout 1989, and then increased significantly to 5.7 percent in 1992. Those young adults not in college have shown fairly parallel trends, as have high school seniors. (See Figure 12.1). College males are more likely than college females to use LSD as annual prevalence for males is 7.4 percent vs. 4.3 percent for females (See Figure 12.2).

Religious Uses and Cultural Trends

Prior to the 1960s in the United States, psychedelics were primarily used by religious groups and as part of cultural practices among isolated groups of people. Although some psychedelics are derived from plant sources and were used for thousands of years, they were not commonplace nor widely familiar to the general public. It was not until the drug revolution of the 1960s that they were "discovered" and became quite popular. Synthetic psychedelics were then produced and became readily available to those who desired a state of altered consciousness. The hippies of this generation found that an enhanced awareness of and sensitivity to one's environment could be achieved under the influence of psychedelics. Users feel they are more able to introspect and understand, with unusual clarity, the meaning of the universe and the purpose for life. What is real becomes secondary to the underlying meaning or expanded experience. Users believe that psychedelics allow them to perceive supernatural forces that were previously hidden

Figure 12.1   *LSD: Trends in Annual Prevalence Among College Students vs. Others 1-4 Years Beyond High School*

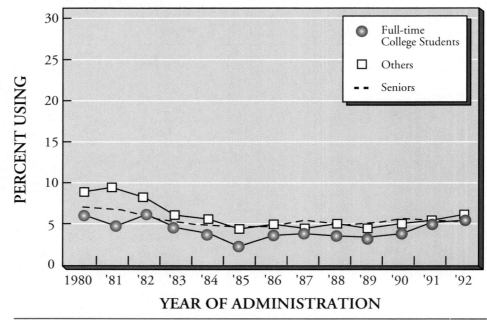

Source: Johnston, O'Malley and Bachman (1993). *National Survey Results on Drug Use from Monitoring the Future Study, 1975–1992.*

Figure 12.2   *LSD: Trends in Annual Prevalence Among Male and Female College Students*

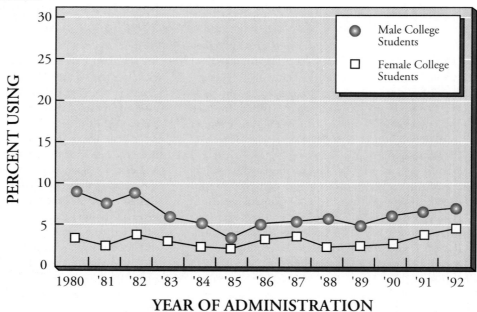

Source: Johnston, O'Malley and Bachman (1993). *National Survey Results on Drug Use from Monitoring the Future Study, 1975–1992.*

and to discover truth in a philosophical sense. They feel as though they become one with their surroundings as the boundaries between them and the environment fade; the ability to distinguish self from others or one object from another diminishes. This effect leads users to report feeling a union with the earth or with the cosmos.

Even though many users desribe the psychedelic experience as pleasant, if not beautiful (in the aesthetic sense) or euphoric, each drug-taking session differs, and some may be tainted with paranoia or disturbing perceptual alterations. During the late 1960s and '70s, these episodes became known as bad trips or bummers. A psychotic-like state may characterize these trips and, for that reason, psychedelics have also been referred to as psychotomimetics because the behaviors and thoughts induced are reminiscent of psychotic symptoms. At other times, users may believe they are witnessing the devil or the end of the universe as we know it. They may perceive their friends as enemies or monsters, or they may feel pain that is not actually present. Others report feeling detached from their bodies and out of control over their ability to respond to external demands. During such delusions and hallucinations, users have been known to harm themselves and others.

Apparently, psychological drug effects during any particular trip are at least partly a function of the initial mood state. Experienced users generally recognize that if you are in the company of friends and your mood is normal or elevated prior to taking the drug, you will likely have a pleasant experience. However, in the presence of strangers—an uncomfortable situation—or in an initial depressed or hostile mood or a high level of anxiety the experience will more likely be dysphoric.

Nevertheless, psychedelics in normal doses frequently produce a rewarding experience that is likely to be repeated—a drug that produces pleasant effects is much more likely to be used (and abused) than a drug that consistently causes psychological or physical discomfort—a fact that is evidenced by the thousands of years of psychedelic use. Psychedelics alter brain chemistry in such a way as to reinforce their continued use, even in the absence of addictive properties.

Classification

Psychedelics are so widely variable in their molecular structures, neurochemical influences, and psychoactive effects that classification of these drugs differs remarkably from classification schemes for other types of drugs and may, as a consequence, be confusing. Fortunately, most of them either resemble or act on particular neurotransmitter systems to exert their particular effects, distinguishing them from each other and simplifying their classification to some extent. Only a few psychedelics influence the brain in unknown ways; no neurotransmitter has yet been identified as structurally similar to these agents to explain the behavioral alterations that result from their use. They do seem to have in common the ability to induce anesthetic action in varying degrees. We will discuss four classes of psychedelic drugs based on the neurotransmitter system affected: serotonin, norepinephrine, acetylcholine, and a miscellaneous category for those that do not fall elsewhere (see Table 12.2). Those with known neurotransmitter influences act either by increasing the amount of the transmitter at the synapse within the brain and increasing its activity or by blocking the chemical's transmission, thereby reducing its activity.

Those psychedelics that primarily exert their effects by acting on serotonergic systems are called indolealkylamines and include lysergic acid diethylamide (LSD), psilocybin, psilocin, ololiuqui, dimethytryptamine (DMT), harmine, bufotenin, and ibogamine. The norepinephrine psychedelics are called phenylethylamines because they are most similar to the catecholaminergic neurotransmitters, norepinephrine and dopamine, and have actions that are somewhat amphetamine-like. This group includes mescaline, DOM, MDA, TMA, MMDA, DMA, myristin, and elemicin. The third category of psychedelics is structurally related to acetylcholine and actually consists of two subtypes: those that decrease acetylcholine activity, known as anticholinergics, and those that increase its activity, including both acetylcholinesterase (AChE) inhibitors and acetylcholine agonists. The first subtype includes atropine and scopolamine. The second subtype includes muscarine, physostigmine, diisopropyl fluorophosphate (DFP), malathion, parathion, sarin, and soman. There will be only limited mention of the latter five drugs as they are toxic and used primarily as insecticides. Our final miscellaneous category will discuss phencyclidine (PCP) and ketamine. Special attention will be given to the actions of PCP due to its widespread abuse in the United States and its association with violent behavior. Marijuana, also commonly known as a psychedelic when used in large doses, has been given a separate chapter because of our extensive knowledge of the drug and its long-term popularity among many subcultures in our society.

Inset 12.1

THE HARVARD DRUG SCANDAL: TIMOTHY LEARY AND RICHARD ALPERT

On May 27, 1963, The President of Harvard University announced that an assistant professor of clinical psychology and education had been fired. It was the first faculty firing in ten years. Dr. Alpert and his associate, Dr. Timothy Leary, now famous for his celebration of psychedelics, had been supported by the Harvard Center for Research in Personality to investigate new drugs. Alpert had become interested in the psychological effects of psychedelic drugs. Although the research began respectably, this marked the beginning of the emergence of a cult of chemical mystics, leading to a series of investigations and the subsequent downfall of both Alpert and Leary.

Alpert and Leary ordered psilocybin from Sandoz, Inc., intending to study the mental and emotional effects that appealed to intellectuals and artists. They were sure that negative reactions to the drug were a result of the method of administration and if taken in an aesthetic setting with the expectation of having a wonderful time, the results would be different. Both investigators were overwhelmed by the consciousness-broadening powers of the drugs. They were convinced, even prior to doing the research, that psilocybin was the solution to all of humankind's ills due to the insight one achieves from its use. Happiness and visionary experiences could be easily gained from taking psychedelic drugs.

During the course of the so-called experiments, an increasing number of students began to try to locate mescaline and requested participation in the research. No one was terribly alarmed until two undergraduate students ended up in mental hospitals after taking the drugs. Chemical supply houses began to pop up in order to meet the growing demand, some charging only a dollar for a sugar cube containing mescaline. Alpert and Leary were unscathed, insisting that government did not have the right to deny citizens the freedom to explore their own consciousness. Once the media got hold of the story, violent reactions ensued, including a battle within the university to terminate both faculty. Finally, one student talked, indicating that Alpert had given him psilocybin during a personal session. That was the final straw for Harvard.

Alpert and Leary were not stopped by this move, however, and went on to author several books and articles on the pleasures and benefits of psychedelic drug use. Nowhere in these works, needless to say, is any mention of the countless numbers of hospitalizations and ill effects that are attributable to these drugs.

Serotonin Psychedelics

In Chapter 3, we discussed the functions of the neurotransmitter serotonin, particularly with respect to its regulatory role in the body's maintenance of temperature, sleep cycles, eating behaviors, impulsivity and aggression, and sensory perception. The possible involvement of serotonin in certain mental illnesses became a topic of interest in the late 1950s when researchers discovered that reserpine, an antipsychotic used in the treatment of schizophrenia, lowered serotonin levels in the brain. Investigators entertained the theory that elevated levels of serotonin activity may be, at least in part, responsible for the symptomology of schizophrenia (a form of psychosis), especially the sensory alterations commonly reported. When it was discovered that certain psychedelics were structurally similar to serotonin and that they mimicked schizophrenic states, support grew for this idea. In fact, due to the increasing popularity of LSD during the 1960s and the obvious similarity of its drug effects to the symp-

Inset 12.2

"EXPERIENCING A LIVING HELL": BAD TRIPS

Bad Trip #1

We skipped school and decided to drop some acid. I was afraid, but since I had done mescaline before, I thought it wouldn't be much different. Instead of eating the whole cube of sugar, I kinda munched on it, hoping I wouldn't get too much acid all at once. Before too long, I started to see things that weren't there. People's faces were distorted and everything seemed really funny. I remember hanging on a light pole and twirling around and around, laughing hysterically as if I couldn't stop. But when it started to get dark, everything changed. The sun was setting. I looked up at the sky and was totally awestruck. God was coming out of the red and orange clouds—it was glorious. I felt my soul come out of my body and fly up to the sky. It was as if the world would be saved. But as I watched, the sky became darker and darker and I realized something was very wrong! Suddenly, God was swallowed up into the darkness along with my soul. I screamed in terror—I felt my blood go cold and my body numb. The life in me was being squeezed out and lifted into the dark hole in the sky. The world was ending, and we were all about to die.

Bad Trip #2

I was standing outside in the dark tripping on acid real bad. A branch poked me in the eye and I thought my eye came out. I could still see out of it—you don't realize while you're high that you couldn't possibly see if your eye came out! Anyway, I could still see out but it looked like shreds of skin hanging over my eyes. I kept asking my friends if my eye was still there and no one would tell me. I was afraid to look in a mirror. I totally freaked out.

Table 12.2 *Classification Scheme of Hallucinogens*

AFFECTED NEUROTRANSMITTER SYSTEM				
Serotonin	Norepinephrine	Acetylcholine		Miscellaneous
		Antagonists	**Agonists**	
LSD	Mescaline	Atropine	Muscarine	PCP
Psilocybin	DOM	Scopolamine	Physostigmine	Ketamine
Psilocin	MDA	Hyoscayamine	DFP	
Ololiuqui	TMA		Malathion	
Dimethytryp-	MMDA		Parathion	
tamine	DMA		Sarin	
Harmine	Myristin		Soman	
Bufotenin	Elemicin			
Ibogamine				

toms of schizophrenia, hallucinogenic properties of these drugs were studied to illuminate the mechanisms behind certain mental illnesses, such as psychosis. Further evidence accumulated for the role of irregularities in serotonergic systems in both the development of schizophrenia and hallucinogenic drug effects. We know now that many of the hallucinogenic drug effects, such as visual disturbances and certain perceptual changes, are not characteristic of true schizophrenia and, thus, the mechanisms may be similar, but not identical.

Stimulation of serotonergic systems induced by psychedelics is responsible for the sensory and mood changes experienced by the user. The excitatory behaviors, mania, irritability, and agitation that are frequently elicited by psychedelics that stimulate catecholamine systems (norepinephrine) are not observed with these drugs. It is believed that serotonin psychedelics stimulate presynaptic receptors for serotonin and decrease its reuptake from the synapse, causing serotonin activity to increase (see Figure 12.3). Serotonin and this class of psychedelics are essentially inhibitory in terms of neural activity within the forebrain and midbrain, and this inhibition is probably the underlying mechanism for mind-altering effects. Antipsychotic drugs (e.g., haloperidol) successfully prevent psychedelic effects from occurring, presumably because they bind to the same receptors as the serotonin psychedelics and do not permit the psychedelics to exert their effects on the receptor. For this reason, antipsychotics can be used somewhat effectively to treat those suffering from a bad trip.

Lysergic Acid Diethylamide (LSD)

LSD is a chemical compound that was first synthesized from ergot, a natural component of a fungus (Claviceps purpurea) that grows on grain, such as rye, primarily in Europe and North America. Before the hallucinogenic properties of LSD were known, the natural compounds that resemble LSD were virtually untested. Eating grains infected with the ergot fungus, however, was associated with a disease called ergotism. Symptoms of this disease range from tingling sensations in the skin, muscle spasms, convulsions, insomnia, and impaired thinking to swelling and burning limbs and numbness. There is some speculation that ergotism may have precipitated the Salem witch trials as there is anecdotal evidence that those considered witches may have been poisoned by ergot, explaining their erratic and bizarre behavior (see Caporael, 1976; Gottlieb & Spanos, 1976).

In 1938, Albert Hoffman from Sandoz Laboratories in Switzerland, among other researchers, was inadvertently searching for beneficial uses (e.g., to induce uterine contractions in labor) of ergot derivatives when they found lysergic acid to be ergot's active ingredient. Most of the lysergic acid derivatives do not produce psychedelic effects, but they do constrict blood vessels, which is why they are now primarily used in the management of migraine headaches and post-partum hemorrhage. No particular benefits were yielded from the derivative, referred to as LSD, in animal studies, and it was soon placed on a back shelf. The psychedelic effects of LSD went unnoticed—how can one determine from a rat that it is hallucinating or experiencing sensory distortions?

LSD was nearly forgotten until 1943 when Dr. Hoffman accidently ingested a small quantity in his laboratory after getting some on his fingers. Unsure of what was happening to him, he described the sensory alterations that overcame him as fantastic and compelling (See Inset 12.3).When he again used LSD, it was under controlled laboratory circumstances in a conscious attempt to more fully evaluate the drug's effects. Not knowing the dosage required to induce psychedelic effects, he ingested several times more than is necessary (0.25 mg; minute amounts are effective). The sensory disturbances were even more profound during this trial and he had a bad trip. Everything around him became deformed and he experienced synesthesias, when the senses become confused or mixed up so that words are observed in visual form, such as colors, sounds are perceived as smells, or musical tones can be touched. He reported that his perception of space and time became disoriented and he developed a fear of losing control over his mental processes. At one point, he thought he had died and projected out of his body. Although these powerful sensory distortions consumed him, he was aware of what was happening to him, as if he could observe the experience from another location outside of his body. He was lucid enough to keep a detailed diary of the account.

LSD became a clinical enigma and was administered during clinical trials to human subjects to further investigate its properties during the late 1940s and '50s and 1960s (See Neill, 1987). Research laboratories around the world conducted trials with LSD in the belief that it might serve as a model for a better understanding of the chemical and physiological basis of psychosis and other mental illnesses. It was discovered during these investigations that LSD mimicked the action of serotonin to produce its effects. This discovery, in turn, illuminated the

Figure 12.3 *Indolealkylamines*

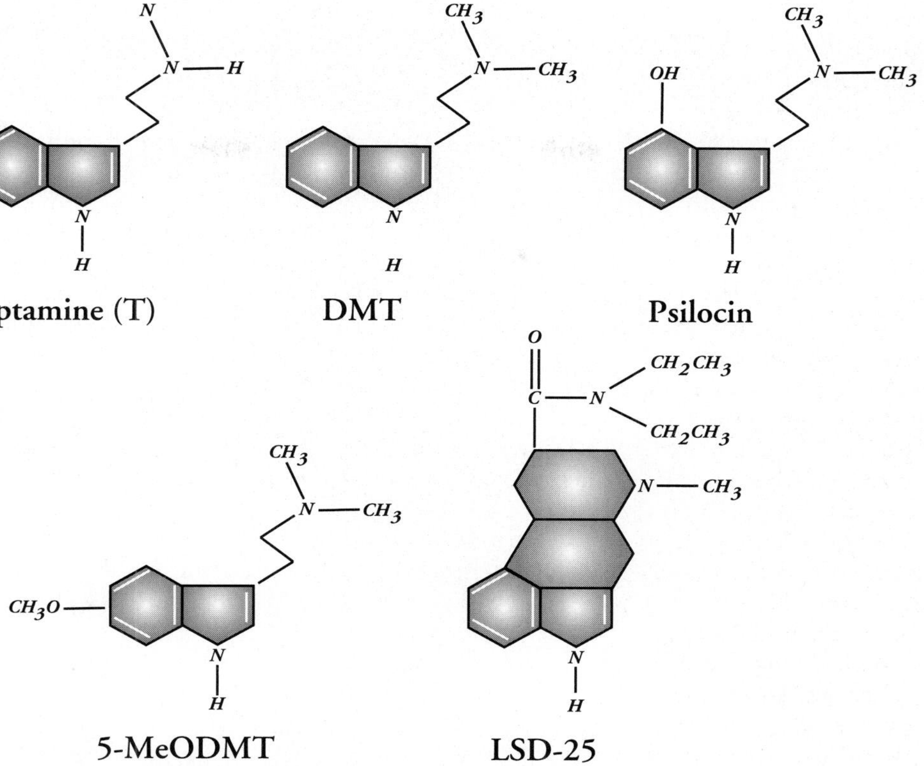

Tryptamine (T)   DMT   Psilocin

5-MeODMT   LSD-25

Source: U.S. Government

role of serotonin in certain mental illnesses, such as schizophrenia. The drug effects of LSD and the symptoms of this disorder are remarkably similar. In some cases, LSD has even been used in clinical settings by therapists who wish to release the inhibitions of their clients and elicit more free thinking and exploration of their problems. It was thought to tap into the subconscious mind, a particularly frustrating task for many therapists. Although some clinicians believe it has utility as a modern truth serum and helps patients to express themselves, this remains a controversial technique. LSD was also used in experimental trials to treat alcoholism (Grinspan & Bakalar, 1987) and enhance creativity.

Because these initial experiments were conducted largely with college and medical students, youths who were becoming involved in the drug revolution during the 1960s became increasingly aware of LSD's power. Simultaneously, Timothy Leary, a Harvard professor of psychology, became a prominent spokesperson for LSD, further extolling its virtues and encouraging its use (see

Inset 12.1). This era was marked by a quest to explore oneself and the universe among a large subgroup of youth; thus, LSD became a popular drug of abuse. It was believed that LSD freed the user from socially conforming thoughts and allowed him or her to observe the truth and its inherent meaning. The hallucinations and sensory changes were frequently pleasurable and more experienced users were able to manipulate these rapidly changing perceptions to some extent. Psychedelics were seen as mobilizers of social change in the pursuit of happiness, peace, and inner tranquility.

In 1966 Sandoz Pharmaceutical Company recalled LSD and refused to further sponsor research on the drug as it had reached illicit drug markets on the street. Many felt that the research had not contributed substantially to an understanding of the drug or its effects and was best regulated by the federal government. To complicate matters further, a report of the Rockefeller Commission on the CIA revealed in 1975 that human research by the CIA and the Army was being conducted in a highly unethical

Inset 12.3

DISCOVERING LSD: ALBERT HOFMANN

Albert Hofmann, M.D., the discoverer of LSD who accidentally self-administered the drug reports the following drug experiences.

The psychic changes and the accompanying unusual states of consciousness produced by psychotomimetics differ so greatly from the ordinary experiences of the outer and inner world that they cannot be described with the aid of words customarily used in the normal daily pattern of the outer and inner universe.

The profound transformation of the conception of the universe under the influence of psychotomimetics, toward either the diabolical sphere or celestial transfiguration, is explained by changes in perception of space and time, the two basic elements of our existence. The experience of corporeity and the spiritual being is also profoundly altered. The subject leaves the familiar world behind and while retaining full consciousness enters a pseudo-dream world ruled by other standards, other dimensions, and a different time.

Time often seems to stand completely still. The familiar surroundings appear in a new light. Forms and colors are changed or have detached, radiating their own intense entity. Colors are usually more intense, transparent, radiating from the inside. The condition elicited by psychotomimetics is generally accompanied by visual and auditory hypersensitivity, which may even lead to illusions and hallucinations.

Reprinted from Hofmann, 1968

Dr. Hofmann's original report, written shortly after his inadvertent experience, was translated and excerpted as follows.

Last Friday, April 16, 1943, I was forced to stop my work in the laboratory in the middle of the afternoon and to go home, as I was seized by a peculiar restlessness associated with a sensation of mild dizziness. Having reached home, I lay down and sank in a kind if drunkenness which was not unpleasant and which was characterized by extreme activity of imagination. As I lay in a dazed condition with my eyes closed (I experienced daylight as disagreeably bright) there surged upon me an uninterrupted stream of fantastic images of extraordinary plasticity and vividness and accompanied by an intense kaleidoscope-like play of colors. This condition gradually passed off after about two hours.

As a result of Dr. Hofmann's curiosity about what he may have taken, he later designed an experiment and administered a larger dose. His laboratory notes read:

As far as I remember, the following were the most outstanding symptoms: vertigo, visual disturbances; the faces of those around me appeared as grotesque, colored masks; marked motor unrest, alternating with paresis; an intermittent heavy feeling in the head, limbs and the entire body, as if they were filled with metal; cramps in the legs, coldness and loss of feeling in the hands; a metallic feeling on the tongue; dry, constricted sensation in the throat; feeling of choking; confusion alternating between clear recognition of my condition, in which state I sometimes observed the manner of an independent, neutral observer, that I shouted half insanely or babbled incoherent words. Occasionally I felt as if I were out of my body.

The doctor later found a rather weak pulse but an otherwise normal circulation.

Die Geschichter des LSD-25, (1975). *Triangel Sandoz Z. Med. Wiss.*, 2, 117.

manner. The report documented that in 1953, a bio-chemist by the name of Frank Olson was given LSD by the CIA in his after-dinner drink without his knowledge. Two weeks later he committed suicide. Dr. Olson developed a panic reaction and was sent to a psychiatric hospital where he jumped from his hotel room window on the tenth floor. President Ford became aware of the incident and apologized to the Olson family. Nearly twenty years after the suicide, the Olsons finally received some compensation for his death. This information led curious journalists and congressmen to discover that the army had been conducting human experiments with LSD for the purposes of war and interrogation. Many of the subjects did not volunteer for the research or found that they could not terminate their participation if they so desired. None were informed of the true nature of the experiment. These revelations caused the public and government to shun these drugs and prohibit their use under all circumstances in the fear that they might be used as mind control instruments by unscrupulous parties. Consequently, propaganda and media campaigns began to highlight and exaggerate the dangers of LSD and other psychedelics.

As quickly as LSD reached its peak of popularity in the street drug subculture, its use began to decline. It is unclear why, although the propaganda about LSD's adverse effects (flashbacks, chromosome damage, self-destructive behaviors, psychosis, and bad trips) seemed to have had some impact on its use. LSD has virtually no utility in medical practice, however it continues to be used in the laboratory to further elucidate the role of serotonin in brain functions generally and mental illnesses specifically.

Interestingly, in very recent years, LSD seems to be making somewhat of a comeback in certain drug circles. Teenagers and college students appear to be in the process of rediscovering LSD, and its use has risen slightly. In some circles, youths administer the drug through the skin by simply attaching a small tatoo containing high doses of LSD. There are even reports of children being unwittingly turned on by older youths who place these tatoos on them for their own vicious enjoyment. In the 1960s, rumors abounded that rock guitarist Jimi Hendrix placed LSD in this headband before a concert so that it would soak into his skin while he played. We cannot predict at this time whether LSD will become as popular as it once was in the 1960s, but we can speculate that its popularity may be due, in part, to recognized dangerous side effects of other popular drugs (e.g., methamphetamine or cocaine) that have infiltrated our present drug market. Perhaps the middle-class youth who are not considered

serious drug users are searching for relatively safe methods of altering their consciousness.

Absorption, Metabolism, and Elimination

LSD is odorless, colorless, and tastless and is generally administered orally in very tiny amounts. Because it is so quickly absorbed and distributed throughout the way, the drug is almost never injected. Drug effects are observed within thirty to sixty minutes and last for approximately ten to twelve hours. Since only miniscule amounts are needed to produce profound psychedelic effects, use in pill form is really impractical. Instead, an almost imperceptible amount is usually placed either on a sugar cube or a small square of paper that can be easily digested. The drug can also be absorbed directly through the skin, explaining the use of tatoos. LSD is then rapidly distributed throughout the body and brain, easily crossing the blood-brain and placental barriers. Relative to other bodily tissues, the brain does not receive a great deal of the drug, but due to its extreme potency, only a few micrograms are necessary to produce psychedelic effects while most other drugs require milligrams or even grams to produce a desired effect. Blood levels decline relatively rapidly following administration. The liver receives the largest amount of LSD and metabolizes and excretes it in an inactive form.

LSD is quite difficult to detect using conventional screening devices due to the small quantities that are present in the body. It is difficult, if not virtually impossible, to identify in the urine; more sensitive instruments must be employed for this purpose. Radioimmunoassay (a technique whereby a radioactively labeled substance, in this case LSD, interacts with its antibody to produce radioactivity that can then be measured) is used when urine samples can be obtained within thirty hours after the drug's ingestion. Due to the extreme variability in concentrations of LSD obtained on the street and the lack of purity, screens should also attempt to identify other drug substances in the suspected user.

Pharmacological Properties

Similar to other psychedelics, LSD influences activity in the forebrain and midbrain. In addition, it appears to alter the activity of the reticular activating system (RAS) in the brainstem, causing the user to show signs of arousal and alertness. Because the RAS is no longer capable of filtering environmental input, a flood of information reaches consciousness, possibly explaining reports that LSD expands the mind. There are some subtle changes in physiological processes caused by LSD due to its sympath-omimetic properties. Changes in autonomic responses occur, observed as a slight rise in body temperature, dilation of the pupils, increases in heart rate and blood pressure, a rise in blood glucose levels reducing appetite, and sweating and chills. Less frequently, the user may suffer from headache, nausea, vomiting, and goose pimples. These side effects are relatively minor and, although they may be noticeable, they are generally not powerful enough to make the LSD trip an unpleasant one or prevent LSD reuse later on.

Ironically, although low doses of LSD produce incredibly powerful psychoactive effects, LSD has not been associated with deaths due to overdose, and it is relatively nontoxic in the sense that there is no known permanent damage to organ systems. Even when LSD is taken repeatedly in large quantities in either laboratory or recreational settings, there are no indications of permanent brain damage. Although LSD use may, consequently, seem relatively benign, the psychological and social complications that may develop must not be taken lightly. Furthermore, the occurrence of self-destructive behavior or suicide based on alterations in perception that occur is a possibility. These adverse effects will be discussed in a following section.

Psychological Effects

Shortly after LSD administration, the user may feel dizzy and the temperature of the room or area may become uncomfortable. Users experience dry mouth and a sensation that something is about to occur. Such symptoms indicate that the autonomic nervous system is being activated. These feelings may be disconcerting to the uninitiated user, but they quickly pass or at least fall into the background of the perceptual changes that develop. Changes in emotional reactions, mood, body sensations, distortions of time and space, and illusions and hallucinations follow the autonomic responses and are so intense that they overwhelm the relatively minor physical effects. As the trip progresses, users commonly report a separation from their body; literature at the time called this phenomenon astral projection. This occurs when the individual believes his or her persona or spirit leaves the body so that it can observe events from another vantage point. The situation becomes surrealistic and depersonalized in this state and users may not be entirely aware of what they are doing or where their body is at any given point. They may lose control of both their behavior and their thoughts—an experience desired by some and frightening to others. Toward the end of the trip, perceptual and mood changes

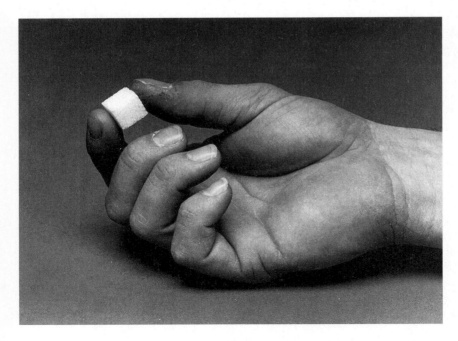

Sugar cubes can be laced with LSD for easy administration.

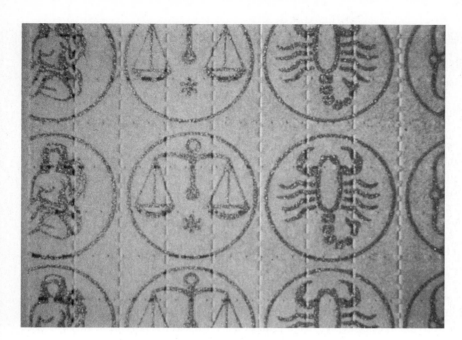

LSD blotter paper.

Courtesy of the Drug Enforcement Administration

gradually return to normal and the user may become depressed, feel fatigued, wish that it had not ended, or develop a feeling of anticlimax.

Only within a certain range are the psychological effects of LSD predictable. Each drug experience will be different from the one before, with the exceptions being that hallucinations and sensory alterations will always occur. But for different users and different situations, these effects do not occur in the same form, within the same context, with the same emotional state, or with the same intensity.

Several factors are influential in the LSD experience. The temperament and personality of the user determine in known and unknown ways how well the individual will respond and what the likelihood of a bad trip will be. For example, a calm and stable person is more likely to remain calm and stable while experiencing sensory distortions, while an anxious and moody person is more likely to become distressed at the sensory changes, increasing the probability of a negative experience. Anticipation of drug effects will also influence psychological effects. Those unfamiliar with and perhaps fearful of LSD use may become distraught over the feeling they are losing control of their thoughts. On the other hand, an experienced drug user may be more capable of controlling and directing

those hallucinations to more pleasant thoughts. Another influential force involves the reasons for using the drug. When the motivation is to elevate a low mood or relieve anxiety, in some cases the outcome is actually an exaggeration of that initial mood state. Further determining the drug experience is the setting in which the drug is used and others who will be interacting with the user during the trip. Both of these conditions should be accepting of drug usage and reinforce positive images of the experience. If the user is with others who do not approve or who are unfamiliar or irritating, the experience may be one of negative images and feelings. In any event, LSD effects will include rapid mood changes and evoke intense emotional and perceptual alterations, both pleasant and unpleasant.

Those experiences that LSD users have in common include dramatic perceptual changes, particularly of visual images. At times, a user will see images, such as faces, tunnels, patterns or shapes, that are not actually present. Other times, the user may find that real objects become distorted, and experience moving or waving walls, colors appearing brighter than actuality, seeing trails of images behind moving objects or solids appearing as liquids. Users also become disoriented in time and space; the perception of time may be significantly retarded so that one hour feels like eight hours or estimations of distance may be substantially off target. Body sense is frequently altered as users may not feel a limb or they may envision frightening facial distortions. Synesthesias, mentioned previously, may also occur causing the senses to blend and become confused. For example, lights may be perceived as sounds and colors may be tasted.

Emotional responses to these perceptual changes are equally exaggerated. The perception (or illusion) of a colorful landscape may elicit extreme emotions of intense joy and appreciation. Or witnessing the sun setting may cause a user to become frightened in the belief that it may never rise again or that the event is due to God's wrath. If thoughts of loss or death cross the user's mind, he or she may quickly slip into a bad trip because of heightened feelings of fear or depression. Most likely, these intense emotional reactions are due to LSD's activation of the sympathetic branch of the autonomic nervous system, causing the heart to pound and beat rapidly and breathing to become shallow. If this response precipitates a panic attack, again the experience may quickly deteriorate into a highly unpleasant one.

Tolerance and Dependence

Tolerance to the psychological and physiological effects of LSD develops rapidly (three to four days when used in repeated daily doses), so the user needs to increase the dose to obtain the same effects. Because so little of the drug is necessary to produce psychedelic effects, only tiny increases are required. Cross tolerance to certain other psychedelics may also be observed; higher doses of these other agents may be necessary to produce desired effects. Tolerance disappears just as rapidly as it develops, so a user can return to initial dosages on a weekly basis.

Physical dependence on LSD has not been reported, even after repeated use over a long period of time. This indicates that LSD is not an addictive drug and that the threat of withdrawal symptoms would not influence a user's choice to either continue or discontinue using LSD. Instead, users report that they have outgrown the drug or drug use overall, that they want to avoid bad trips or possible social or psychological complications, or that they have found other drugs to be more desirable than LSD and have graduated. Psychological dependence, on the other hand, does occur in some users who become partic-

A psychedelic drawing by someone under the influence of a hallucinogen trying to capture on canvas the experience of a trip.

ularly enamored by the drug's effects although most eventually simply tire of it or switch to less powerful and more acceptable drugs, such as alcohol.

Adverse Effects

In large part, the possibility of serious adverse effects of LSD use are speculative rather than factual. There is no evidence of permanent physical damage to the body or brain even after chronic, high dose usage. Moreover, there does not appear to be any long-lasting psychological impairment once the drug has been terminated. In fact, some individuals may actually show moderate improvements in the ability to appreciate sensory experiences, such as in the perception of art, colors, tactile contact, and so forth.

As a method in the 1960s and early 70s to dissuade youth from using LSD, propagandists began a campaign claiming that LSD causes chromosomal abnormalities in users that may be transferred to future generations. The idea was that LSD use in adolescence may be so insidious as to even alter chromosomes of later offspring, even when the drug is no longer being used. It is true that chromosomal breakage was observed after applying LSD to cells in the laboratory, however many other drugs (even aspirin and caffeine), X rays, and illnesses, such as infections and fever, also cause chromosomes to break. One study found an increase of white cell chromosomal damage in LSD users. Nevertheless, white cells are involved in immune system function, not reproduction, and the preponderance of studies did not replicate these findings. There is no evidence that such chromosome breakage affects the user or leads to birth defects, either in offspring who are directly exposed to LSD or in those whose mothers took LSD in the past. The occurrence of fetal abnormalities or malformations is the same for offspring of LSD users as is reported for the normal population. Other drugs that LSD-using mothers frequently take concomitantly, along with poor prenatal care, are much more responsible for the fetal abnormalities that do occasionally occur. Although no gross defects have been noticed in LSD exposed offspring, more subtle alterations in psychological and behavioral features as a result of brain chemistry changes remain possible. This hypothesis has not been tested.

Although there is a great deal of propaganda and misunderstanding about LSD, there are adverse effects that are noteworthy and should be taken seriously. Long-term use of LSD may interfere with an individual's personal and psychological growth. The perceptual and emotional alterations that result may become distracting so that the user is no longer able to cope effectively in the real world. Those who have used LSD extensively, known as acidheads, show a lack of motivation, indifference, and sometimes antisocial or asocial behavior. As situations arise, the user may be inclined to simply escape from daily stressors and withdraw into a world of hallucinations and unrealistic images rather than confront and resolve these issues. This complication is of particular concern when use begins at an early age, for example, when a teenager is in the midst of learning coping skills, developing lifestyle patterns, and making decisions that could have a long-lived impact. As a consequence, developmental delays in emotional maturity may surface.

A related adverse outcome is sometimes observed in those with preexisting tendencies toward mental disturbance, including psychosis, depression, paranoia, or anxiety. It is possible for a seemingly normal individual to become psychotic following LSD use when the predisposition is present. Repressed emotions are unleashed during the LSD experience that the user may not have encountered previously. The reasons for this may be twofold: psychological defenses and adaptive skills break down and/or chemical changes in the brain may be sufficient to trigger the imbalance of an already precarious biochemical system of checks and balances. A subgroup of users, for example, develop schizophrenia after only a few drug experiences, possibly due to their genetic predisposition toward this mental illness. Others continue their drug usage without undue, chronic effects on mental state, perhaps due to the absence of genetic susceptibility.

Flashbacks are also well known to those who have used LSD repeatedly and occur after a period of nondrug use. They are characterized by many of the drug's direct effects, including hallucinations, sensory alterations, and other psychotic and nonpsychotic symptoms. They may be as intense as the actual drug experience or they may be quite subtle, a feeling of mild disorientation or spatial misperception. Years after their last LSD experience, regular users commonly report the sudden onset of an LSD trip. Without warning, the ex-user may become disoriented, confused, and perhaps psychotic. The walls may begin to wave, shapes may become distorted, and other features of a real drug trip may be felt. This type of recurrence may be mild or so profound that the individual is certain that someone laced their coffee with the drug. The underlying mechanisms to explain the occurrence of flashbacks are unknown, however there is speculation that they may be due to either psychological breakdowns in coping skills or subtle chemical changes triggered by previous LSD administrations. There is even speculation that LSD may be stored in the brain for long periods of time, and when large amounts are suddenly released or metabolized into the brain's chemical pool, the result is an active LSD type experience. Flashbacks are most commonly precipitated by anxiety, fatigue, acute changes in the environment (i.e., lighting), stress, or the use of marijuana. They may occur for months if not years following the last administration.

While there is no evidence for an increased incidence of fetal abnormalities in exposed offspring, we do know that LSD readily crosses the placental barrier to reach the fetus. Long-term psychological, neurological, and cognitive studies have not been conducted to determine whether fetal effects of LSD do occur and have simply gone unnoticed due to the absence of more obvious, gross structural deformities. As we have found that maternal doses of alcohol too small to cause gross signs of fetal alcohol syndrome are, in fact, associated with cognitive and behavioral impairments in offspring, the same may be true for LSD. Thus, LSD should not be used during pregnancy.

Psilocybin and Psilocin

Psilocybin and psilocin are close relatives of both LSD and serotonin in terms of their molecular structure. These two related psychedelics differ from each other only in that psilocybin contains phosphoric acid, which is separated from the psilocybin after ingestion, yielding psilocin, the active ingredient. These psychedelics are a natural ingredient of fifteen species of mushrooms that grow all over the world, including Central America and the northwestern region of the United States. Genuses of mushrooms that contain psilocybin or psilocin include *Psilocybe, Conobybe, Paneolis,* and *Stropharia.* Albert Hoffman, the busy scientist who discovered LSD, isolated the active ingredients from the Psilocybe mushroom in 1958. Like LSD, they are absorbed effectively from the gastrointestinal tract when taken orally. However, they are not nearly as potent—it takes about 100 to 200 times more drug to produce psychedelic effects. Generally, the mushrooms are eaten raw or cooked into a tea for drinking. Each mushroom type within a species contains variable amounts of active ingredient, so users must be aware of which type of mushroom they possess to calculate how many to eat. Two to five *Psilocybe cyanescens* mushrooms contain an effective dose, while a whopping ten to forty *Psilocibe semilanceata* mushrooms must be ingested to produce psychedelic effects. It is also important that the user be familiar with mushroom types

generally, as many mushrooms resemble the psychoactive ones but are extremely poisonous.

The same physiological and psychological effects are experienced with psilocybin and psilocin as with LSD, including hallucinations, illusions, disturbances of time and space, and so forth. They occur more quickly, appearing within ten to fifteen minutes, and the effects do not last nearly as long as LSD, which may be effective for up to twelve hours. The effects of psilocybin and psilocin last between two and six hours. Because so much more psilocin is needed for a psychedelic effect as compared with LSD, it is much easier to find a desirable dosage at any particular drug-taking session. The user may eat only a few mushrooms, containing up to 4 mg active ingredient, for an initial high with a pleasant feeling of relaxation and mild euphoria. Or, the user may eat several more to obtain a heightened psychedelic experience. Cross tolerance develops between psilocybin, LSD, and mescaline (a catechol psychedelic), consequently it will require more of these other substances to obtain psychedelic effects if one has been using psilocybin. The user must not take psilocybin for about five days for tolerance to disappear.

Higher doses, from 4 to 8 mg, result in perceptual and mood changes similar to LSD, and hallucinations may be achieved in some individuals if the dose is adequate. We see the same initial symptoms of sympathetic nervous system arousal that LSD causes, and, due to the high lipid solubility of psilocybin, CNS effects may be observed once psilocybin has been converted to psilocin. Approximately 25 percent is excreted in the urine basically unchanged while 5 percent is metabolized. We do not know what happens to the remaining psilocybin in the body.

Psilocybin and psilocin have been an integral part of religious ceremonies and considered sacred in Mexico and Central America for centuries. We are most familiar with their use in Mexico where they are referred to as magic mushrooms or God's flesh due to the spiritual and mystical hallucinogenic overtones the drug produces. Figurines and statues were even designed in their likeness to honor the mushrooms. Religious users believe they can know God or come closer to God under the influence of psilocybin.

In this country, "shrooms" are grown illegally and usually in small quantities for recreational purposes. They can even be grown in a closet if properly cultivated. In the 1960s, these mushrooms became more popular (again, thanks in part to Timothy Leary) among users looking for a natural high. They were not nearly as popular as LSD, however, because of the time and effort it took to manufacture them and the larger dosages needed for effective-

Psychedelic mushrooms are fairly distinctive, but can be confused with poisonous mushrooms.

Courtesy of the Drug Enforcement Administration

ness. LSD was cheaper and easier to produce, and the drug effects were similar. Youngsters in our culture eat mushrooms or drink their tea in social settings, along with alcohol, to enhance the mood. During the early 1970s, the use of psilocybin declined along with the hippie generation, and we have never witnessed a real epidemic phenomenon or a large subculture invested in its use. Nevertheless, there is some evidence that psilocybin use is resurging somewhat, presumably due to the fact that it is natural and that it can be grown easily throughout the country, without having to rely on middlemen or drug traffickers or to deal with the difficulties of importing other drugs, such as cocaine. Unfortunately, however, a large percentage of street supplies are not actually psilocybin mushrooms at all; they are domestic mushrooms laced with LSD or PCP. When psilocybin is sold as a liquid or powder, it is frequently another psychedelic or a completely inactive substance.

Other Serotonin Psychedelics

Two of the remaining serotonin or indole (referring to indolealkylamine) psychedelics, DMT and Morning Glory, will be discussed in a single section since they are not widely used or abused in the United States.

Bufotenine, Harmine, and Ibogamine are other indole psychedelics that have not been well studied, are not widely used, and sometimes have uncomfortable side effects that limit their reinforcing qualities.

DMT

Dimethyltryptamine (DMT) mimics serotonin activity by acting on presynaptic receptors. DMT was synthesized during the hippie era along with LSD but never really gained prominence. Although it is not at all currently popular in the United States, it is a very important hallucinogenic agent in many other parts of the world. DMT occurs in many plants, particularly in snuff, natural substances that are inhaled to produce an effect. Cohoba and Yopo snuffs contain this active agent and are primarily used by South Americans and Caribbean Indians; sometimes witch doctors use it for the diagnosis and treatment of certain diseases and to perform magic. DMT is not effective when taken orally as it is not absorbed into the bloodstream; thus, it must be smoked, inhaled, or injected intramuscularly. Other methods of administration include dipping parsley, tobacco, or marijuana cigarettes in DMT to be smoked. Once administered, hallucinations, confusion, and sensory alterations, especially visual distortions, result. Excitable behavior and euphoric sensations may simultaneously occur. The duration of effect is only one to two hours, and since lunchtime for white-collar workers is about the same length of time, the experience has been referred to as the businessman's trip.

Morning Glory

The seeds of the morning glory plant *Rivea corymbosa* contain a psychoactive agent called ololiugui. Albert Hoffman, had a hand in discovering several of the serotonin psychedelics, examined the seeds of the morning glory plant and found it to contain several active alkaloids along with d-lysergic acid amide. D-lysergic acid amide is about one tenth as potent as LSD (not to be sneezed at considering the potency of LSD) producing both intoxication and hallucinations. Use of ololiugui is largely associated with ceremonial rituals in attempts to communicate with the supernatural and with God(s). Limiting the widespread use of ololiugui are the autonomic effects of nausea, vomiting, increased blood pressure and heart rate, sleepiness, headache, and other untoward side effects. These effects seem to be more intense than with the previously described psychedelics and make Morning Glory a less attractive recreational substance.

Norepinephrine Psychedelics

Otherwise known as catechol or phenylethylamine psychedelics, norepinephrine psychedelics structurally resemble norepinephrine, dopamine, and amphetamine. This category includes mescaline, DOM (or STP), TMA, MDA, MMDA, DMA, myristin, and elemicin. Their psychological effects are quite similar to the indole psychedelics, with the exception that they also produce excitable and sometimes agitated behaviors due to their more direct stimulation of the central and autonomic nervous systems and the reticular activating system. In addition, they differ from the indole types in their potency, onset, and duration of action.

Mescaline (Peyote)

Mescaline, both naturally occurring in mushrooms or ground into capsules, was extremely popular during the 1960s when LSD reached its peak. Mescaline was considered to be a more natural psychedelic than LSD (which is synthetic) and was preferred by those who referred to themselves as flower children who reaped the bounties of the earth. Mescaline is reemerging in the 1990s as a pop-

ular drug although it does not seem to be as readily available as it was in the '60s. Instead, LSD, a more powerful drug, has earned more popularity points than mescaline.

The peyote cactus (*Lophophora williamsii*) is spineless, carrot shaped, and entirely psychoactive. Peyote is native to Mexico and the southwestern United States. Only the part of the plant that is above ground is edible and the upper part holds a small crown that is frequently eaten. The crown can be sliced and dried to form a hard brown button that may be softened in the mouth and swallowed to produce an effect. The taste is bitter and its odor is fairly offensive. More than one button may be necessary to achieve a full desired effect. Cakes, tablets, or powder may be manufactured from these buttons for ingestion as well. The powder form is water soluble and may be either ingested or injected. Indians who ritualistically eat peyote harvest these plants in ceremonious fashion, sometimes for over a month, so that they can be preserved for years to come.

Psychoactive Effects

Hallucinations, illusions, and spatial distortions similar to those produced by the indole psychedelics are characteristic of a mescaline experience, which may be somewhat less powerful because mescaline is frequently taken in lower doses. There is relatively no impairment of senses other than visual, and users remain aware of their condition and surroundings. The initial experience is characterized by physical symptoms, including elevated heart rate and blood pressure, perspiration, tremors, pupil dilation, a rise in body temperature, behavioral excitation, and sometimes, anxiety —all indications of autonomic nervous system arousal. There is also some CNS stimulation as evidenced by increases in electroencephalographic measures (a measure of brain wave activity). Euphoria and intense visual images closely follow these physical symptoms and become the most prominent aspect of the drug-induced experience.

There is a great deal of confusion in the literature about whether peyote and mescaline are equivalent. In fact, mescaline is only one of more than thirty psychoactive alkaloids present in peyote. Mescaline was identified as a component of peyote in the late 1800s by German pharmacologists when it became known to be specifically responsible for the intense colors and other visual effects experienced by users of peyote. Not until the early 1900s, however, was its chemical structure identified as being similar to norepinephrine. Mescaline was subsequently synthesized for experiments on visual perception.

Those who take peyote or synthesized mescaline will sometimes discover that not all experiences are positive or beautiful. Many users report that they suffer from nausea and violent vomiting after ingesting mescaline that may last for a full twenty-four hours. Headache and lasting indigestion may accompany these adverse effects and prevent the individual from trying the drug a second time. Some of those that suffer from unpleasant effects do not even experience the visions and hallucinations that others find reinforcing. We do not know whether some people are especially susceptible to these side effects, perhaps due to individual differences in metabolism or sensitivity, or whether they were simply unfortunate enough to have experienced these effects after the first try while others may not suffer them until a later drug-taking session.

Metabolism and Pharmacological Properties

Mescaline is most often taken orally and is quickly and completely absorbed from the digestive system. Even so, only a small portion of what is ingested is able to cross the blood-brain barrier to produce psychoactive effects in the brain. Consequently, high doses of mescaline are required to achieve a desired effect. Concentrations in the brain reach their peak between thirty minutes and two hours following administration. Its half-life is only a few hours, and the duration of its effect is up to twelve hours. There are indications that a small amount of mescaline may remain in the body for as many as twenty-four hours. Low doses of about 3 mg/kg body weight are sufficient to produce feelings of euphoria while larger doses (5 mg/kg) will produce more intense hallucinations and visual changes. Tolerance to mescaline does develop, but more gradually than with LSD, and there are no signs of withdrawal symptoms or dependence. Mescaline is apparently not metabolized to a great extent and is largely eliminated in the urine in an unchanged form. The drug is not considered to be toxic, even when high doses are taken, as no organ damage results.

Mescaline resembles norepinephrine and one would assume that its effects are largely due to its influence on the catecholamine neurotransmitter system (See Figure 12.4 for the molecular structure of mescaline relative to norepinephrine-like drugs, such as amphetamines). However, there is evidence that the primary underlying mechanism for mescaline's action is via its influence on serotonin neurotransmission, much like the indole psychedelics, particularly when it is used in higher doses. This may explain why the psychological effects of mescaline and other catechol psychedelics so closely resemble those of, for example, LSD. Furthermore, chlorpromazine, an antipsychotic medication that acts to reduce serotonin activity, effectively blocks mescaline intoxication. And finally, cross tolerance develops between mescaline and LSD.

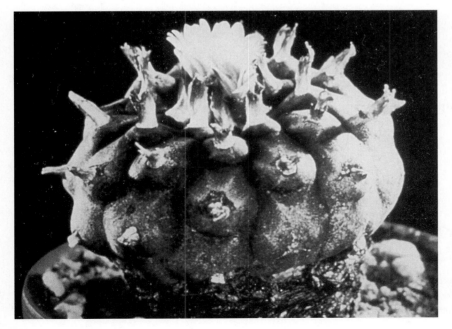

Peyote cactus.

Courtesy of the Drug Enforcement Administration

Designer Drugs: Synthetic Mescalinelike Psychedelics

There are a number of synthetic drugs in this category that are related to amphetamine and possess hallucinogenic properties (DOM, MDA, TMA, DMA, DOET, DOAM, and MMDA). Due to a structural change in the molecule, these drugs act more like mescaline than like amphetamine and, consequently, have only moderate stimulant properties (see Figure 12.5). Low doses produce some amphetaminelike effects while higher doses produce more LSDlike effects. They were first synthesized in an attempt to find medically beneficial properties, however no such uses were discovered and their use has since been restricted to drug subcultures. Although they are considered psychedelics, they are substantially more toxic than LSD or mescaline, particularly when taken in higher doses, and can produce unpleasant side effects such as headaches, nausea, vomiting, and shakiness. Initial low dose effects produce behavioral excitation and sensory hallucinations. As the dose is increased, the individual may become severely hyperactive and excited. Body functions are also affected in ways similar to those impairments produced by toxic doses of amphetamines. Tremors, convulsive movements, and collapse may be followed by death if doses are high enough. One of these designer drugs was sold under the guise of being a heroinlike drug in California. Unfortunately for many, it was later discovered that the drug destroyed an area of the brain (basal ganglia) that controls motor movement. These unsuspecting users in their early 20s developed Parkinson's disease, and their condition is believed to be irreversible. None of these compounds are produced legally for any medical purpose and, thus, there is no way to know the purity of the drug or what dose is being purchased on the street.

DOM (STP)

DOM was originally synthesized in an effort to find a treatment for schizophrenia in 1964. The manufacturing method was published in readily accessible chemical journals, and illicit manufacturers were able to follow the instructions to produce the drug for street use. By 1967, DOM became known to the drug-using public, most notably in San Francisco, for its hallucinogenic properties

Figure 12.4   *Phenethylamines*

Amphetamine

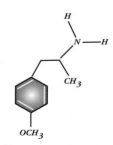

p-Methoxyamphetamine

Methamphetamine

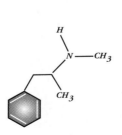

Mescaline

Source: U.S. Government

and abuse liability. DOM stands for 2,5-dimethoxy-4-methylamphetamine, but is called STP on the street, reportedly to signify either "serenity, tranquility, and peace" or "super terrific psychedelic."

Similar to mescaline, physical symptoms develop prior to the psychological effects. Indications of autonomic arousal may be observed between the first and second hour after administration, including pupil dilation, increased heart rate and blood pressure, sweating, tremor, nausea, bronchodilation, anxiety, and tingling in the arms and legs. Three to five hours after ingestion, these symptoms reach a peak and then subside rapidly after seven to eight hours.

In low doses, DOM acts much like an amphetamine, producing behavioral stimulation, euphoria, talkativeness, concentration difficulties, and sometimes anxiety. Higher doses (over 5 mg) produce hallucinogenic effects similar to those seen with mescaline and LSD that may last for up to twenty-four hours if enough is taken (over 10 mg). Initially, stimulant effects will be experienced followed closely by visual perceptual alterations, time and space distortions, and euphoria. Memory of the experience will not be impaired once it ends. Even higher toxic doses may produce seizures that could become fatal.

MDMA (Ecstasy)

MDMA or 3,4-methyenedioxymethamphetamine was synthesized by a German pharmaceutical firm, patented in 1914, and evaluated for possible use as an appetite suppressant (Nichols & Oberlender, 1989). Many of the other designer drugs were manufactured exclusively for illicit use, but MDMA was synthesized without any legal or illegal purpose or utility. It was not until the 1970s when it suddenly became known to the drug subculture and took on a purpose. During the mid 1980s, MDMA became known as ecstasy and had found popularity on the streets. In fact, no other amphetamine derivative has enjoyed the same degree of popularity as MDMA. The reason for this appears to be its special pharmacological properties that are particularly rewarding to the user.

MDMA does not produce hallucinations in low doses. Rather, it heightens awareness of self, one's emotions, and sensory experiences—a state somewhat similar to that produced by marijuana or phencyclidine. Its euphoric properties that cause both animals and humans to self-administer this curious drug appears to be related to MDMA's influence on dopaminergic neurons (cocaine and amphetamine exert the same influence; see Asghar &

Figure 12.5 *Designer Drugs*

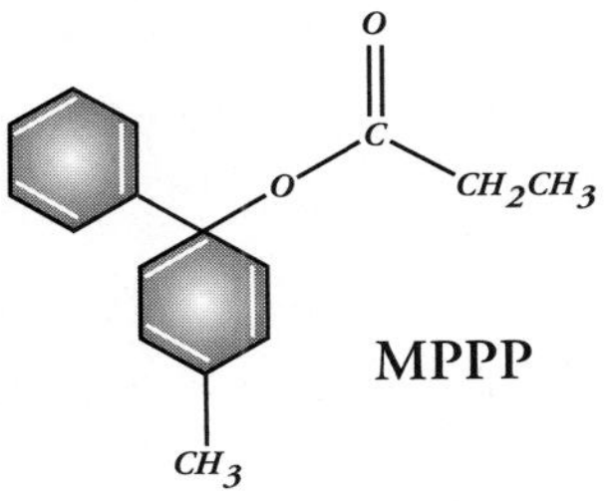

MPPP

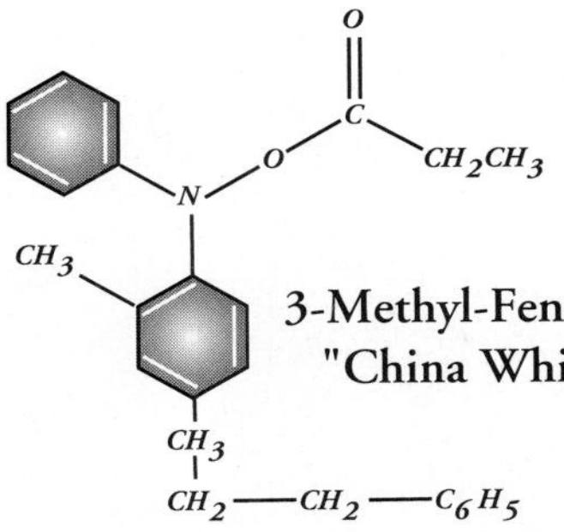

3-Methyl-Fentanyl "China White"

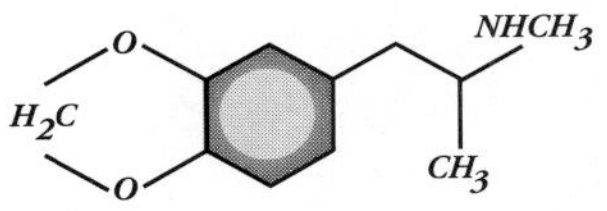

3, 4-Methylenedioxymethamphetamine
(MDMA, "Ecstasy")

Source: U.S. Government

DeSouza, 1989) although MDMA's primary influence is on serotonin. For this and other reasons, MDMA is quite different from other psychedelics and designer drugs. Physical effects include increased heart rate, dry mouth, sweating, and other indications of elevated autonomic activity. Peak effects occur approximately two hours after oral administration. Most of the drug is eliminated unchanged in the urine.

Because of its widespread availability to drug-abusing populations and evidence that a dose only four times that of the normal dose was neurotoxic (it causes a dramatic decline in levels of brain serotonin and permanently destroys serotonin neurons), the Drug Enforcement Administration (DEA) proposed that it become a scheduled drug. This action caused a number of psychiatrists to come out of the woodwork and divulge that they had been using MDMA in psychoanalytic protocols. They lobbied against the DEA proposal by testifying that MDMA was not truly a psychedelic and that it had a spe-cial ability to enhance empathic responses and emotional communication on the part of their patients, thus enhancing treatment results. Nevertheless, MDMA was eventually scheduled and is no longer available commercially. Unfortunately, the use of this drug remains a serious problem in some drug-using groups due to its potential toxicity.

Other Designer Drugs

MDA, DOET, MMDA, PMA, and other amephetamine derivatives produce hallucinogenic effects. MDA, MDMA, and other designer drugs have been placed on Schedule I, which indicates that the drug has a high abuse potential and no recognized therapeutic benefits. There are problems with controlling their availability on the streets, as some of them are not specifically scheduled. Miniscule changes in molecular structure create "new" drugs not yet

Illicit clandestine PCP laboratory.

Courtesy of the Drug Enforcement Administration

identified or scheduled. Also, there are so many of them entering and leaving the drug market, and they are easily manufactured in clandestine labs by neophyte chemists. Users experience positive mood changes, a state of relaxation, insight, euphoria, and heightened awareness without alterations in perception and thought disturbances that characterize other hallucinogenic experiences. TMA, however, produces some disconcerting symptoms, including extreme anger and sometimes aggression, possibly resulting in violent behavior.

Myristicin and Elemicin

Two spices, nutmeg and mace, widely available in grocery stores contain active ingredients with psychoactive properties. Nutmeg is extracted from the dried seed of the nutmeg tree (*Myristica fragans*) and mace is extracted from the seed coat of the same tree, found largely in tropical Asia. The active components, myristicin and elemicin, are phenylethylamines structurally similar to mescaline and produce somewhat similar effects. Between one and two teaspoons may produce symptoms of euphoria and sensory alterations, behavioral stimulation and excitation, visual hallucinations, difficulty assessing reality, feelings of being detached from one's body, and sometimes psychosis.

They generally only become drugs of abuse when nothing else is available; in the past their primary utility was for the medical treatment of various disorders in India and Malaya. They are most often brewed in tea to be ingested. Onset of action is quite slow relative to other psychedelics (from two to five hours), however the duration of effect is much longer (up to twenty-six hours). Most experienced psychedelic users try to avoid these substances as they produce adverse side effects, such as anxiety, vomiting, nausea, headache, dizziness, and tremors. These autonomic effects may be so great as to discourage first time users from a second try.

Psychedelics Influencing Acetylcholine

As previously mentioned, there are two subtypes of psychedelics that act on acetylcholine (ACh) neurons: those that decrease its activity, or anticholinergic drugs, and those that increase its activity, or acetylcholine agonists. Those drugs that increase ACh activity may influence this system by directly stimulating ACh receptors to mimic the action of this neurotransmitter. Another mechanism to increase activity is by inactivating the enzyme that is responsible for degrading ACh, acetylcholinesterase (AChE), causing ACh levels to rise. On the other hand, drugs that decrease ACh activity generally work by blocking the receptors for ACh so that the neurotransmitter is not allowed access to its receptor. Each category of psychedelics that act on ACh to either increase or decrease its activity is discussed in the following sections.

Cholinergic (ACh) Agonists

Active ingredients of the mushroom fly agaric (*Amanita muscaria*) and its relative *Amanita pantherina* are ibotenic acid, muscimol, and muscarine, all of which possess psychoactive properties. The mushroom is found largely in wooded areas in the United States and throughout Europe; the Scandinavians were believed to have used these mushrooms for their psychological effects in centuries past. They are large with a bumpy top and come in various colors, from white to scarlet. The name fly agaric was apparently given to the *Amanita* mushroom because of its insecticidal effects. When given to flies, they become so stuporous and dazed that they can be killed without much effort. Unfortunately for the untrained user, some species of *Amanita* are highly toxic. Even the psychedelic mushroom taken in large quantities is toxic; lower doses produce those effects that psychedelic users seek.

Ibotenic acid and muscimol have not been widely studied, and consequently their mechanism of action is not well understood. There is some evidence that they resemble the serotonin psychedelics and may actually belong in a preceding section of this chapter. However, muscarine is known to specifically act on muscarinic cholinergic (ACh) receptors in the body and brain due to its chemical resemblance, increasing ACh activity directly. Other active ingredients in *Amanita* may be responsible for many of the psychedelic effects, in concert with muscarine. Effects of muscarine on body systems outside the brain include increased blood pressure, reduced heart rate, profuse salivation and sweating, pupil constriction, and contraction of the bladder muscle. The CNS effects include anxiety, agitation, vivid dreaming and sometimes nightmares, incoherence, difficulty in concentration, stupor and slowed responses, hallucinations, muscle spasms and twitching. Secondary symptoms that occur later may include behavioral excitement along with hallucinations, sensory distortions, hyperactivity, and then finally, sleep. Obviously the intense unpleasant peripheral body effects may become a deterrent to further use. Nevertheless, some individuals will use these mushrooms recreationally, over-looking the negative side effects, in order to obtain sensory alterations, euphoria, and giddiness.

Once orally administered, the active ingredients of *Amanita muscaria* are readily absorbed and produce an effect within an hour. They are eliminated in the urine in their active form. Because the urine becomes, in a sense, an active drug, the Siberians were known to obtain a psychedelic effect by drinking the urine of another who had ingested the mushrooms (Julien, 1988). Reportedly, the drugs remain effective even after the fourth or fifth person has passed on urine to be shared. Other ancient modes of administration are to eat the mushrooms raw, cook them, or drink their extracts in water or milk.

Acetylcholinesterase (AChE) Inhibitors

AChE is an enzyme that stops the neurotransmission of ACh in the body and brain. Drugs that inactivate AChE are called anticholinesterase or acetylcholinesterase inhibitors. Because these drugs disable the enzyme responsible for decreasing ACh activity from functioning, the result is an increase in activity of ACh. This causes ACh to build up in the brain and overstimulate brain cells. Physostigmine is the best known AChE inhibitor. It is a natural constituent of a bean found in Nigeria, used primarily as a poison. English pharmacologists who later studied the bean found physostigmine to be the active ingredient and began searching for medical uses. Eventually, it was used for the treatment of glaucoma as it reduces pressure in the eye responsible for onset of the disease. Because it also increases muscular contractions, physostigmine was used to treat myasthenia gravis, characterized by muscle weakness. Other AChE inhibitors have recently been synthesized that have long-lasting, if not permanent, effects. They are used as agricultural insecticides but are known to be toxic to humans; consequently, their use is limited. Some of these agents are even being stored for eventual use as a chemical weapon.

These AChE inhibitors are rarely abused for recreational purposes due to their extreme toxicity, severe side effects, and limited reinforcing qualities. The increase in ACh is associated with the following peripheral effects: bladder and intestinal muscle contraction, decreased blood pressure and heart rate, pupillary and bronchial constriction, extreme salivation and perspiration, respiratory muscle paralysis, possibly causing respiratory failure or even death. CNS effects include agitation, anxiety,

nightmares, delirium, and insomnia. Higher doses may produce behavioral depression, sleepiness, incoordination, slurred speech, confusion, convulsions, coma, and eventually respiratory failure (Julien, 1988).

Anticholinergic Drugs

Drugs that suppress the transmission of ACh by occupying but not stimulating their receptors are atropine and scopolamine. These drugs are present as the active ingredients of various plants that have been cultivated and widely used for centuries, usually as a poison. The ancient Romans and Egyptians administered small quantities of atropine (from the plant Belladonna, meaning "beautiful woman") to their women for pupil dilation, which was thought to be appealing and sexy. The duration of action is between two to eight hours and depends on the dosage used. Unfortunately, to produce psychedelic effects the user may come dangerously close to a damaging or lethal dosage.

In recent decades, atropine and scopolamine have been used to induce intoxication, frequently by rolling the source plant into a cigarette to be smoked. Because of their utility in the treatment of asthma, these cigarettes were at one time widely available in drug stores; however, due to their abuse potential, they are hard to come by now. In other parts of the world, plants containing these active agents are used to prepare drinks to induce intoxication, and sometimes Asians lace marijuana and opium with atropine to enhance drug effects.

Atropine and scopolamine produce effects quite the opposite of those observed with the AChE inhibitors. Heart rate and blood pressure increase; salivation and sweating is suppressed; pupils dilate; urinary, bladder, and gastrointestinal tract tone is reduced; and acid scretion is inhibited (thus explaining its medical use in the treatment of ulcers). CNS symptoms include agitation, delirium, disturbed thought patterns, incoordination, speech impairment, hyperactivity, and visual and auditory hallucinations. Low doses of scopolamine and atropine have differential effects on the CNS and periphery. Scopolamine depresses the activity of the reticular activating system so that the CNS overall becomes underaroused. Associated with this effect are brain wave patterns that resemble early stages of sleep and behavioral effects include sleepiness, confusion, inattention, euphoria, and delirium. There is also some memory loss, and dreams will not accompany sleep. In higher doses, respiratory failure or cardiovascular collapse may occur.

Inset 12.4

POISONING THE BRAIN

David Garabedian went on trial in Massachusetts early in 1984. He was doing his best to adjust to prison life. Five years ago he committed a brutal murder. Some scientists make the extraordinary claim that something in his hypothalamus caused him to bring tragedy to the Muldoon family. Mr. Garabedian, a 22-year-old lawn care specialist , has a reputation as a quiet, almost passive man. But he admits that he killed 34-year-old Aileen Muldoon in March in the yard of her suburban home. Garabedian had been doing a survey for a lawn care company when he argued with the victim, strangled her, and threw several large rocks at her face.

Garabedian said that the pesticides he worked with poisoned his brain causing his violent behavior-a unique defense. But the jury did not believe that as chemical was to blame. He was convicted of first degree murder and sentenced to life in prison. The tragedy hit the Garabedian home too. The tragedy came as a surprise to David's family. David had always been mild tempered. His mother insisted that there had to have been some sort of outside influence to make him do what he did because the behavior was so uncharacteristic. Even the defense attorney felt strongly, knowing his life history, that he could not have done this without a reason. "From the moment of his birth until the incident in question, he was a perfect, moral person. He never had any violence in his background. All of a sudden in a ten day period when he was exposed to these chemicals, he lashed out at his sister, which was totally out of character, and then brutally killed Aileen Muldoon. But for the chemicals, I have no question in my mind that David Garabedian would not have committed this act."

David was responsible for mixing and pouring these chemicals. He reportedly began to feel strange. He said the smell of the chemicals was strong. He began to urinate frequently, had diarrhea, started drooling, suffered frequent headaches, and had bad nightmares, Like the acetylcholinesterase-inhibiting hallucinogens, the pesticide mixed by David poisons cholinesterase, the enzyme that degrades acetylcholine in the hypothalamus. Acetylcholine is in the area of the brain that is believed to coordinate aggression and attack behaviors. Exposure to a concentrated amount of this pesticide can weaken a man and even kill him. These chemicals are used as nerve gases. A slight poisoning may go unnoticed, but a massive poisoning can alter behavior dramatically. They may have caused David to experience overwhelming rage, a feeling that David probably had never experienced in his whole life. Without the behavioral controls for this emotion, given his passive nature, he may not have been able to modulate his reaction to the anger he felt. Consequently he murdered an innocent woman.

Atropine does not, apparently, influence cortical brain wave activity (EEG) or behavior in the same way as scopolamine. In fact, there is very little of the impairment related to scopolamine associated with moderate atropine use. For this reason, atropine has been studied by the U.S. Army as a possible antidote in chemical warfare to the AChE inhibitors that enemies threaten to use. Both agents do, however, cause delirium and euphoria, depending on the dosage taken. They may produce amnesia and interfere with intellectual functions, but neither cause sensory alterations or mind expansion as do the other psychedelics. Due to their limited psychedelic effects, amnesia for the experience, and significant side effects, they are not as widely abused as the aforementioned psychedelics.

Miscellaneous Psychedelics

The pharmacology of two psychedelics—ketamine and phencyclidine (PCP)—has yet to be fully understood, thus there is no precise category to place them. These drugs, also known as psychedelic anesthetics, were introduced into medicine in the 1950s and 1960s for their anesthetic and analgesic properties. Structurally, they more closely resemble the psychedelics and do not induce anesthesia in the same way the sedative-hypnotics do, thus they were not included in the discussion of either general anesthetics or sedative-hypnotics. Both drugs cause users to feel depersonalized or dissociated from their bodies, minds, and surroundings. Heart rate, respiration, and blood pressure are not significantly affected by either drug in moderate doses. Higher doses are associated with agitation, CNS seizures, and muscle rigidity. They appear to influence a number of neurotransmitter systems and may not have specific transmitter effects that explain their various psychoactive properties the way the other psychedelics do. Also, antagonists traditionally used to block the effects of drugs that influence certain neurotransmitter systems do not antagonize the effects of PCP or ketamine. Because ketamine is not a primary drug of abuse and is used most often as an anesthetic for children (it has more depressant activity than PCP with fewer long-term reactions), we will not include additional details about its actions or properties. Instead, we will focus on PCP, which is a major drug of abuse in certain regions of this country with particularly insidious effects.

Phencyclidine (PCP)

Recent observations indicate that phencyclidine (PCP) has become increasingly visible as a primary drug of abuse, and alarmingly, a subpopulation of drug users report that PCP is their single drug of choice (Bolter, 1980; Linder et al., 1981; Smith and Wesson, 1980). Individuals involved in the chronic use of PCP have been described as atypical in terms of their psychiatric status, personality and family dynamics (Domino, 1978; Linder et al; Pradhan, 1984). For the most part, PCP is used among lower class white youths and has never gained a high status among other drug-taking populations. Drug

users frequently report that they will only use PCP when no other drug is available. In many cities during the 1970s and 1980s, PCP intoxication was the most prevalent drug-related admissions into emergency rooms and the extreme drug effects presented a problem for those working the ER (see Figure 12.6).

Initial effects of PCP are generally characterized as euphoric and intensely rewarding. Continued usage, however, is described as having unpredictable and frequently distressing effects as usual use produces occasional episodes of substantial dysphoria (Fauman & Fauman, 1980; Pradhan, 1984; Smith & Wesson, 1980). Also, memory loss or impairment induced by PCP experiences is common whether the experience is pleasurable or agonizing. Thus, the preference to self-administer chronic doses of the drug is not well understood, and preexisting individual differences must be considered to eventually explain the preference to use PCP and its differential drug effects.

PCP was first marketed as Sernyl, an analgesic for humans and animals. Initial animal studies with PCP indicated that it produced analgesia but not sleep or muscle relaxation, which are desirable when undergoing surgery. Instead, the animals appeared to be awake but lacked concern for the pain and the procedure—they were apparently dissociated from their surroundings. Human trials showed that Sernyl was an effective anesthesia and analgesia while not significantly affecting blood pressure, heart rate, or respiration. Later, patients were found to have no memory of the experience, even though they appeared awake during the entire session. These were considered, initially, to be beneficial effects relative to other existing anesthetics.

After their operations, however, patients experienced unusual psychological reactions to PCP that were disconcerting and unpredictable, including behavioral excitation, uncontrollable outbursts, delirium, confusion, schizophrenic symptoms, psychosis, aggressive behavior, mania, dyskinesis and hallucinations. In some individuals, these side effects lasted for days or weeks after use. Further investigations revealed that PCP substantially alters perception, produces thought disorders, memory impairment, hostility, uncooperative behaviors, and apathy. Human experiments with Sernyl were quickly terminated due to these untoward post-operative effects, and currently PCP is not even used for veterinary purposes in most states. The drug, however, became particularly popular within certain drug subcultures during the 1960s due to these same untoward effects and hallucinogenic properties and continues to be illicitly self-administered.

Absorption, Metabolism, and Elimination

PCP is readily available and can be easily manufactured in clandestine labs. It is commonly used in the form of cigarettes, referred to as angel dust, hog, or green (in some cities, users are called greenbeans), mixed with mint leaves, parsley, or marijuana. Lately, tobacco cigarettes are dipped in a PCP solution and dried for smoking. This form is preferred as the bottle of PCP can be dropped and the solvent will rapidly disappear (conveniently gotten rid of during drug raids). PCP may also be taken orally in a capsule or tablet, inhaled in powder form or, very rarely, injected.

Once ingested, PCP passes rapidly from the blood to bodily organs. It is fat soluable and deposits in the nervous system for a long period of time. Although psychological effects last only about six hours, PCP's half-life is three days, which means that if several doses are taken in the course of a few days, the drug will accumulate and produce more extreme effects. Furthermore, there is speculation that flashbacks may occur, possibly for months and years after chronic PCP use, due to long-term CNS stores of PCP that recirculate on occasion. Eventually, the liver metabolizes PCP, and it is excreted in the urine. The duration of PCP storage in the body is unknown. Because PCP leaves the blood so

early, it is difficult to detect using blood analyses. Urinalyses and brain analyses (performed post-mortem) are better methods for drug detection and identification.

Pharmacological Properties

PCP is considered a CNS depressant and stimulant; the exact action depends on the dose and species that takes the drug. The effects are primarily in the limbic system, affecting emotional behavior, and cortical areas, influencing higher intellectual functions. PCP acts on receptor sites for numerous different neurotransmitter systems; with respect to the level of neurological activity PCP initiates, it lights up the brain like a Christmas tree. Whether there are specific PCP sites, however, or just artefactual binding sites masquerading as PCP receptors is presently unknown, however there is strong evidence now that there are specific PCP receptor sites present in the brain that PCP acts on directly (see Figure 12.7 for the molecular structure of PCP). This observation has lead researchers to believe that there may be an endogenous substance similar to PCP that would account for PCP's drug effects. In either event, a number of neurotransmitters are at least indirectly stimulated by PCP, including

Figure 12.6 *District of Columbia Drug Abuse Warning Network (DAWN) Emergency Room Mentions for PCP/Combinations, 1982-1985.*

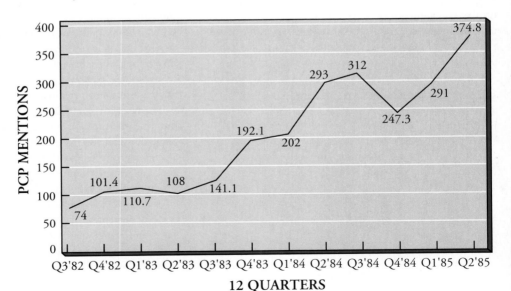

Source: McFarland, 1986,

acetylcholine, serotonin, dopamine, GABA, and natural opiate (neuropeptide) systems (Jaffe, 1987, pp. 565-566).

As specific receptor sites for various neural systems are related to the specific symptoms of PCP use, it is instructive to identify those biochemical systems that are targeted by PCP in order to understand PCP's effects. PCP has peripheral sympathomimetic effects that are responsible for the stimulation of autonomic responses (Domino, 1978, p. 1980). Consequently, regulatory systems involved in stress responses and arousal levels are altered and the user will experience, both physiologically and behaviorally, agitation, excitation, and feelings of internal crisis or stress. This state of high arousal and anxiety is frequently associated with exaggerated responses to situations and events, and sometimes results in aggressive, assaultive, or violent behaviors. There also appears to be a simultaneous release of ACh, which may contribute to aggressive responding.

Other behavioral symptoms of PCP use are associated with dopaminergic activation and include conceptual disorganization, posturing, stereotypic and psychotic symptoms, and delusions and hallucinations. Either PCP binds to sites on dopaminergic terminals or PCP blocks the uptake of dopamine, decreasing the number of binding sites. In either case, the resulting excessive amount of dopamine will eventually downregulate the dopamine system, causing a low level of dopaminergic activity and possibly behavioral or psychological depression and a zombielike manner.

The interaction of PCP with opiate receptors causes PCP to mimic the action of opiates. Drugs that activate natural opiate systems, or opiate agonists, help to relieve the PCP symptoms of hyperexcitation, anxiety, tension, and thought disorder. PCP affects enkephalin-mediated behavior in its production of analgesia. Opiate antagonists (e.g., naloxone), inhibit some of these PCP effects that act on natural opiate receptors.

There is evidence that potassium channels in the brain are also influenced by PCP. Potassium channels are responsible, in part, for the transfer of information between nerve cells. Specifically, PCP blocks these channels to further exaggerate the typical PCP effects of hallucinations, catatonia, aggression, and symptoms of schizophrenia. Because normal brain functioning depends on accurate signaling between nerve cells, when the signals are disrupted, messages to adjacent neurons become garbled. Behaviors and thought processes of PCP users reflect this neural interference. Similarities between symptoms of PCP use and of some psychiatric illnesses (e.g., schizophrenia) indicate that potassium channel defects or alterations may play a role in certain mental illnesses.

Psychological Effects

In low doses, PCP elicits feelings of euphoria, drunkenness, numbness, excitement, and agitation. The user may appear blank or zombielike, however some users become more agitated than they do withdrawn. Those who are high on PCP will display slow and disjointed thinking patterns, short attention span, a lack of direct or organized thought, paranoia, poor memory, and problems with their speech. Thinking may become so disrupted that the user develops suspiciousness and hostility, frequently accompanied by aggressive or violent behaviors—a state that closely resembles paranoid schizophrenia. With increasing dosage, numbness, rigidity, and loss of muscular coordination will also result. Users become incoherent, incommunicative, stuporous, and disoriented with feelings of being disassociated from their own bodies. Sensory mechanisms are blocked so that incoming stimuli are dampened and sensory impulses distorted. Different from LSD, which characteristically produces visual images and hallucinations, PCP is much more associated with distortions in body perception. Blackouts and possibly even convulsions and coma may result if doses are high enough. Although we are not aware of any reliable statistical data providing evidence for irreversible brain damage due to PCP usage, neuropsychological impairments have been observed that may reflect, at a minimum, a temporary organic brain syndrome (S.Cohen, 1977; Smith &

Figure 12.7

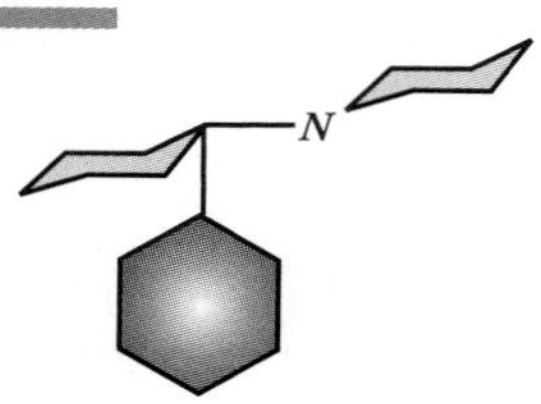

Phencyclidine (PCP)

Source: U.S. Government

Wesson, 1980). Further study is needed to determine whether impairments are transient or longstanding.

Some users become unusually aggressive or violent when under the influence of PCP. Because they are paranoid, they may overreact in an emotional way to relatively benign circumstances. These individuals, even when they are slight of build or normally weak and passive, can really present a problem when they react violently because of the analgesia involved—if they get into a physical fight, they are likely to do much more damage to themselves and others because they do not feel pain. Police commonly report that PCP users are unrestrainable; they resist arrest and cannot be easily managed. There are incidences when several large weapon-carrying policemen were required to restrain, with a great deal of difficulty, one scrawny PCP user. Due to the influence of PCP on the f/f/f system, users may become unusually strong and capable of much more destruction than they would be normally. (These effects are somewhat similar to those seen in individuals who are in a severe crisis and must perform superhuman feats to reverse the crisis. For example, a woman whose child is trapped under a car can actually lift the car under the influence of a heightened autonomic nervous system response. The same heightened response is initialized by PCP.) As a result of this influence, PCP users are known to be at risk for self-mutilation. Again, the combination of analgesia and thought disorders can be deadly, causing users to gouge their eyes out, cut off limbs, jump out windows, and so forth. They are also more prone to accidents, as pain is our warning not to engage in certain damaging acts. Without it, we have no measure of the potentially harmful consequences.

Long-term effects of PCP on psychological functioning may take several forms, depending on the preexisting state of the user. The psychosis that accompanies PCP intoxication may be so profound that it causes chronic problems with coping skills, maturation, and especially a return to normal thinking patterns. Emotional states may be so exaggerated during PCP intoxication that the individual may suffer from residual emotional disturbances, such as anxiety or panic, for some time following the PCP experience. Once a chronic PCP user has terminated his or her drug use, depression may set in. Due to the extreme excitation in the brain induced by PCP, many neurotransmitter systems may downregulate for a period of time before they regain their balance. This process is associated with psychological depression that may require months, if not years, of pharmacologic and psychological therapy to correct. Ironically, the severity of PCP's effects may cause

some individuals to develop a psychological dependence on the drug, particularly when the user is attempting to avoid real-life situations that may be disturbing. PCP is viewed by these users as the perfect escape from reality, relieving them of their preexisting anxieties and causing them to forget their troubles. The onset of psychological dependence obviously complicates therapeutic measures and increases the relapse rate.

Finally, some individuals who use PCP, even only occasionally, may become overtly and chronically schizophrenic. We do not understand this development or why only a small subgroup of users appear to be vulnerable to this effect, but clinicians speculate that there was a preexisting tendency to schizophrenia in these users. Apparently, PCP acts on those neural sites responsible for the development of schizophrenia to trigger a preexisting disorder. Identifying those individuals at risk for this particular drug effect is problematic at present as we are not able to identify those who will eventually become schizophrenic. Perhaps further study of PCP's effects will help to illuminate the mechanisms behind this mental illness.

Vulnerability to PCP Use

A few studies have identified psychological traits—antisocial personality disorder (ASP), psychopathy, schizoid or schizoaffective symptoms, risk taking and impulsivity—that appear to antedate PCP usage, possibly indicating a vulnerability to abuse (Fauman & Fauman, 1980; Siegel, 1980 Smith & Wesson, 1980). These traits may predispose an individual to experiment with potentially dangerous substances that other individuals avoid. For example, ASP, thrill seeking, or other character disorders may be associated with the initial desire to use PCP, a notoriously dangerous drug. Consequently, these syndromes would be more common among PCP users. These studies have not determined whether residual psychological or psychiatric disturbances are a direct result of PCP intoxication or if PCP-precipitated adverse reactions are accentuated by an underlying psychological condition.

Significant drug experimentation among individuals who tend to be aggressive and have symptoms of ASP has been well documented (Kofoed & MacMillan, 1986; Robins, 1966; Satterfield, 1978). One criterion for ASP is drug experimentation at an early age (before the age of fifteen). Individuals with this syndrome have been considered risk takers, impulsive, aggressive, and thrill seekers (Quay, 1965; Schuckit, 1985; Zuckerman, 1978). As PCP causes the release of epinephrine (adrenalin), resulting in the f/f/f response, such physiological stimulation

Inset 12.5

RUSTY: THE STORY OF A PCP USER

I started getting high when I was ten—my sister used to get me high on pot. Then I started drinking. When I was about twelve or thirteen years old I started smoking PCP, and I fell in love with it. I took it from my sister without knowing what I was taking. I liked it the very first time I took it, and I could tell it was different from other drugs. It made me feel kinda powerful, more confident and comfortable with other people. When I'm not using it I feel alone—you know, alienated in a way. It gave me a sense of worth.

With PCP, there is just a small crowd of users, like a little network. I think a lot of PCP users are the same. None of us ever knew where to fit in and then we ran into each other and formed this little clique. We're like a bunch of loners. A lot of us don't have any parents, no kind of authority in our lives, so we ran wild. A lot of us were running the street at ten and twelve years old.

Using drugs made me feel like I fit in because it gave me a common ground—other drug users have a reason to want you. I was really shy when I was straight, and using drugs was an ice breaker. So you always had a friend—if you wanted to get high, you knew who to go to. It was a pretty neat lifestyle. I never really fit in even with drug users all the way. I fit in with PCP addicts the most. I always thought heroin addicts were dirty—the needles and all—they were the worst. I did it one time for a little stretch, but then I got out of it.

PCP users don't do anything else but alcohol. You might see them do a little cocaine here and there when it's a gift or something, They won't spend their money on it and they won't do it unless somebody comes over and says "here." It's strictly PCP and alcohol. Once I got into PCP I didn't want to do anything else. If you like it you like it, if you don't you can't stand it.

The money was a good thing too. You don't have to work. You can make a lot of money off of selling drugs. In the 1970s it was everywhere cause we were making it locally. But now, it comes from California, and they sell it in the liquid form. The bikers in the 90s had a lot of it. I remember my sister doing it with them. They used to make bags full of it.

I felt different as a child 'cause of my family situation. I didn't have no father and my mother died young. I always felt out of place and let down. I'd have parents' day at school and have nobody show up. My grandmother took care of me until I was fourteen, but she worked every day, not like she would have come if she could. She couldn't bring up all the kids and still pay for everything. I think I was a little different from the people I ran around with, not 'cause I was better than them, but because I think I had more values and morals than any of them do because she did plant a lot of that in my head. I got teased and picked on half my life, so that kinda put me in my own little spot. In my neighborhood, the kids were all older, so when I finally started growing up the only people I met were doing drugs so it was OK. They were a bunch of misfits too. I had a lot of fun, but I wish I had done a lot of things different. I'm still friends with a lot of them, but since I went to drug rehab, we don't hang out anymore. The ones that are really my friends have been there for me and don't push drugs on me. The other ones still ask me to set up a deal for them and say "Come one, I know you still get high."

I like the feeling of PCP. It makes me feel numb. It's like an escape from reality. I don't think about nothing that's going on. I escape from reality. I don't worry about anything—all the little things you gotta do on a daily basis. I don't worry about working or anything else, just what's going on at the time. I feel happy in a way although I'm not really happy. There was a lot of really good things that came with it—money, women...I've hallucinated a few times and had some really weird experiences. Some people just think they're the devil, but I always go back and forth from the Lord to the devil. But usually I thought I was the Lord and the whole world revolved around me. Or if I was with a female I thought we were Adam and Eve and the world was just beginning. This must sound really, really crazy, but I used to wonder when I was so high on the stuff if I was close to dying—'cause that's usually when I was getting really bad on it and had a lot in my system. I'd be really flipping. I'd be so dehydrated that blood would come up out of my mouth. I know when I am getting really bad on it. I forget to drink and eat and sleep. I'd get high and think if I went out one window I'd go to heaven and the other window I'd go to hell. I'd always go to heaven. I remember standing out in a parking lot swearing up and down that I was Jesus Christ. And a guy hit me in the face—you can't feel no pain on PCP—and told me to come in the house , and I just stood there telling him I was Jesus. I really believed it . I'd wake up flipping out or start sweating at work and come back thinking that everybody was the devil and that I was the only good person there. I didn't like getting that bad.

It's nothing like LSD. When you trip on LSD, you see things that aren't there—you see trails, things are blurry, you see different colors. When you trip on PCP you don't really see things, you just imagine yourself in a different perspective. I thought I was the Lord, but I didn't picture myself looking like Jesus or what God would look like. So you don't really see things, your thinking is different.

When you come off of it, you're still dinged out, and real light-headed. You're not normal but you're not high. You just get kinda dingy for a couple of days. You'll be a little clumsy, forgetful, and I'd stutter a lot. Just slower really. I could still function. I could go to work high on it. I didn't realize at the time how much slower and awkward I was . Even now, I still stutter from it and my short-term memory is pretty bad. I can remember things back when I was really little, but things I've done just a couple of hours ago I'll forget, or if someone tells me something I'll forget it. I used to be a lot more witty or faster. A lot of times now I have to think what I'm going to say. I can't think as quickly and my speech—I have a lot of problems—there's a lot of words I can't say and I start stuttering. I don't remember doing that when I was growing up, unless I was really high.

The possibility of going back to jail and my health helped me to get off PCP. When I got out of jail and I was clean, I got to looking at myself and my life, and I didn't like it. I was tired of going to jail. I used to use drugs in jail, but the last few times I didn't want to. Jail was somewhere to go to sleep and eat and to clean up for the next summer. And then every time I got out of jail, I'd get healthy, look good, get a job, good things would happen and I'd feel good. Then I'd start using, lose my job, get in trouble and end up back on my ass. I don't want to roll into a drug rehab center at forty or fifty years old, living in some room, not making anything or having anything.

I want to be happy and secure, but I can't do it with PCP. They told me at drug rehab that it was a disease. Before I thought it was just the way I grew up. Drug rehab gave me some time under my belt so I could clean up and turn my head. When I was in jail, even though I was clean I wasn't growing or focusing on anything positive. All we talked about was when we'd get back to drugs. Rehab helped show me things that I could have, and if I do certain things my life would get better. They pointed me in the right direction and showed me how to take care of myself better. They wash your brain out and put the right things in it—it's not brain washing the way most people think of it. I was taught how to ask for help and not be so shy and break out of my shell. They gave me something to believe in. I thought alcohol and drugs were going to be my life. I'm more likely to do drugs when I'm drinking 'cause I don't really think. Rehab made me realize it doesn't have to be like that. It made me feel really good because they respected me and had confidence in me and trusted me. Some people don't really want it and don't have enough upstairs to make it happen. Someone told me the drugs didn't fuck me up, but I'm fucked up. That's when I really decided to change myself. This time I shut up, quit thinking I know it all and I listened. I've never been clean this long. The green has held me back all my life. Never committed any crimes when I was straight. The green gives you an excuse for anything you do. Now when I screw up, It's my fault! And I can think straight.

Inset 12.6

THE FUTURE FOR NATHAN

Nathan was, by all appearances, a normal healthy teenager. With the exception of his parent's divorce, his family life was good and he was close with his mother and sisters. They were well to do, and they wanted for nothing. He performed well in school, excelling in basketball due to his height. He suffered no unusual medical or emotional problems, until suddenly, when he was sixteen years old, he began to act strangely. Nathan had contracted some sort of viral infection that produced flu-like symptoms, something akin to mononucleosis. Blood tests for mono were negative, however, despite the persistence of a low grade fever, swollen glands, sore throat, and malaise. No one, including his doctors could fathom what he had. Nevertheless, it was not severe and everyone figured that it would eventually pass. Nathan had a different idea, though. Because he was feeling so miserable and needed a pick-me-up, he allowed his friends to persuade him to try some angel dust. He did not have any real experience with drugs and did not know what to expect. Nathan tried it several times over the next two weeks hoping that it would alleviate some of his symptoms.

During the third week, it became readily apparent to those around him that something was definitely wrong. Nathan had stopped taking PCP due to its unpleasant effects. Yet, he was listless, withdrawn, paranoid, and would sit and cry for hours for no obvious reason. He began to hallucinate and reported to his physician that he felt like he was going crazy. His affect was flat and he avoided eye contact. Nathan's thoughts became disjointed and disorganized and he seemed to be disoriented.

As the months passed, Nathan's symptoms progressed rapidly in the absence of any more PCP use. A psychiatrist was called upon for a complete evaluation and a diagnosis of schizophrenia was formulated. At this point, Nathan was experiencing irrational beliefs and the continuity of his thoughts was noticeably impaired. His motor activity ranged from low to excitable and much of it was out of his conscious control.

Today, fifteen years later, Nathan is entirely debilitated by his disorder. He can no longer count to ten or carry on a conversation. Although he is only rarely violent, he is irrational and needs constant supervision. He picks at the air as if he is plucking flowers. Nathan never finished high school and is cared for by his mother at home. Studies of his brain have found several peculiarities although no one has been able to specifically state what they reflect.

Clinicians who have examined him now believe that he had the inherited propensity for schizophrenia. Like other schizophrenics, a stressor in the environment is generally responsible for triggering the disorder, which had been previously dormant. Schizophrenia generally makes itself known in the late teens to early twenties and is usually chronic. In Nathan's case, we speculate that PCP triggered a latent schizophrenia state and damaged neural systems, explaining the abnormalities seen in his brain studies. Although the effects of PCP are quite similar to those manifested with schizophrenia, only a few unfortunate individuals with a preexisting tendency become schizophrenic after using the drug.

The real tragedy is that Nathan will never again be a normal healthy individual, able to care for himself and lead a productive life. No one can predict who will suffer long-term damage from PCP and who will escape such a fate.

may be quite rewarding to sensation-seeking individuals, particularly those with an underaroused autonomic nervous system. Thus, PCP may be an attractive drug to these individuals who may also have higher preexisting levels of aggression and ASP than other drug users. A question to be answered in future research is; Does PCP unleash ASP and/or aggressive tendencies in individuals with certain preexisting personality traits?

Further observations indicate that the incidence of family histories of psychiatric and behavioral disturbances, most particularly, drug abuse, alcoholism, criminality, schizophrenia, and affective disorders, is greatly increased among PCP users (Fauman & Fauman, 1980). The relative contribution of environmental influences and possible genetic involvement in PCP usage has not been assessed in the literature although investigators recognize that the effects of PCP result from a complex interaction among physical, psychological, and sociocultural variables (Smith & Wesson, 1980). Disorganized or dysfunctional family structures seem to frequently characterize the home lives of PCP users. In fact, many PCP users were initially familiarized with PCP or other drugs by their parents and siblings. Family contributions to PCP use, whether genetic or situational, appear to be substantial and should be examined with respect to vulnerability issues.

Chronic use of PCP has been repeatedly associated with psychotic behaviors and extreme violence to self and others in individuals both with and without histories of violent behavior (Aronow et al., 1980; Fauman & Fauman, 1980; Linder et al., 1981; Smith & Wesson, 1980). Violent reactions appear, according to some anecdotal reports, to be an extension of PCP toxic psychosis that affects some users (Fauman & Fauman, 1978, 1980). However, as only a subpopulation of users manifest violent behavior, additional research is needed to determine what triggers it and what causes those specific individuals to be particularly susceptible to that effect. Although investigators recognize that the effects of PCP result from a number of dynamically interacting forces (Smith & Wesson, 1980), aggressive behavior during PCP intoxication may be somewhat selective due to differential physiological and biochemical influences. The frequency and intensity of a violent response may further be predicted by identifiable personality variables.

Attempts have been made to identify the risk factors for assaultive behavior under the influence of PCP (McCardle and Fishbein, 1989). PCP use alone does not seem to be associated with an increase in hostile behavior. Instead, PCP use is evidently related to increased levels of hostility when several factors are considered: (1) youthfulness of the user; (2) early age of first PCP experience; (3) frequent PCP use; 4) psychiatric history, related and unrelated to PCP use; and (5) higher levels of suspicion and assaultive behavior when not using PCP. Younger PCP users and those who initiated PCP use at a younger age are more assaultive even when not under the influence of PCP. The youthful user also has higher levels of irritability when PCP intoxicated.

Aggressive behavior is a product of the complex interaction between the drug, personality, background, and drug history of the user and the social circumstance in which the behavior occurs. These individual differences may also be important contributors to the PCP experience; they may help to determine who may be likely to aggress during PCP intoxication (Fauman & Fauman, 1978, 1980; McCardle & Fishbein, 1989). It has also been proposed that individuals with higher levels of testosterone, a male hormone, may be more sensitive to PCP-induced aggression (Marrs-Simon, 1988). Furthermore, PCP increases brain serotonin activity during acute use, possibly leading to a downregulation of sertonin activity following chronic PCP use. If this is shown to be the case, we would expect antisocial or violent tendencies to worsen in the chronic PCP user. Finally, clinical impressions are that many PCP users remain "functional" after several years of abuse while other users develop early onset of schizophrenia and other long-lasting impairments. These observations suggest that the consequences of PCP use, independent of the drug's purity and varying strengths, are at least partially determined by factors other than the drug usage alone.

Treatments

Treatments for PCP use focus primarily on the acute drug effects in an effort to control the psychotic behaviors and sometimes convulsive seizures. For toxic psychosis, major tranquilizers and antipsychotics, including haloperidol (Haldol), are generally administered. Haloperidol is a specific dopamine receptor blocker and helps to calm a psychotic patient. Another antipsychotic medication, chlorpromazine, is also used to block dopamine receptors and has been shown to have more rapid effects on the symptoms of psychosis arising from PCP use. Meperidine is an opiate receptor agonist that improves the hyperexcitation and thought disorders that result. It is the only drug that we know of that helps to relieve the conceptual disorganization that PCP users' thought processes suffer from. Meperidine is preferred to the antipsychotic medications for long-term treatments. Another long-term treatment involves the administration of haloperidol along with a sedative-hypnotic or anxiolytic, such as diazepam (Valium) or buspirone (Buspar). Experimental trials with the calcium channel blockers have shown they are somewhat effective at displacing PCP binding; however, they have not been used extensively in treatment protocols.

Finally, Amantadine, an antiviral drug with CNS effects, shows promise in the acute and chronic treatment of PCP users. Amantadine releases dopamine and helps relieve the tremors and twitches of Parkinson's, which chronic PCP users sometimes suffer. There are no known side effects from this drug. Some patients may, however, experience a worsening of mental symptoms when a psychiatric disorder is preexisting. Investigators have speculated that Amantadine may act on the PCP receptor complex; in other words, both the medication and the drug may influence the same neural systems. Consequently, Amantadine may exert a therapeutic influence by displacing PCP binding.

Because PCP users so frequently suffer from underlying psychological disorders and commonly come from dysfunctional homes, long-term treatment must target sociopsychological precipitants of their drug use. Behavioral, vocational, and psychotherapeutic strategies are recommended for this group of users to instill adaptive coping skills, teach methods of positive redirection, gain insight into their problems, and learn more appropriate behavioral patterns. Special treatments should be designed for female PCP users given their common history of abuse and neglect which may play a role in their preference for PCP—a drug with the profound ability to alter consciousness, provide a feeling of power, and offer escape.

▤ Summary

The psychedelics comprise a diverse group of drugs with a wide range of pharmacological properties, sites of action, and psychedelic effects. They are classified for practical purposes on the basis of their mechanisms of action. It is unknown whether their effects are largely a result of altering the activity of serotonin, norepinephrine, acetylcholine, or another not well understood mechanism (the miscellaneous category). The focus of this chapter was on LSD and mescaline due to their pervasive popularity in the past and their increasing use in the 1990s among teenagers. LSD, in particular, is a powerful drug that produces states somewhat similar to those observed in schizophrenia. Consequently, it has been used extensively not only as a drug of abuse but also as a research tool. Because of the present fear of such drugs as cocaine, many adolescents and young adults are turning to LSD as their drug of choice. We also focused on PCP because of the persistent and atypical subgroup of drug users that continues to engage in PCP use despite its dire consequences.

Psychedelics vary widely with respect to their destructiveness—LSD and mescaline are not known to produce any permanent physical damage while PCP and the anticholinergic psychedelics exert potentially dangerous effects. Although several of these drugs that are most frequently used recreationally are considered quite safe relative to other drugs of abuse (e.g., cocaine or amphetamines), the source of their damage potential is found primarily in the psychological and social aspects of daily functioning. Regular users tend not to mature sufficiently while users with psychological dysfunctions tend not to confront their problems directly and never learn to overcome them. Furthermore, regular use of any of these drugs can lead to profound personality changes and sometimes chronic psychiatric disturbances in those who were previously unimpaired.

CHAPTER 13

Marijuana and the Cannabinoids

Objectives

1. To provide a historical overview of marijuana use in this country.
2. To describe how marijuana is cultivated and marketed.
3. To show how prevalent marijuana use is in the United States.
4. To understand how marijuana influences brain function and behavior by identifying its sites of action and drug properties.
5. To present the physiological, psychological, and behavioral effects of marijuana use and to identify aspects of the social context that promote those effects.
6. To discuss the potential for tolerance and dependence.
7. To provide a detailed and critical discussion of the potential negative effects of marijuana use.
8. To assess the significance of amotivational syndrome as a result of marijuana use, particularly among youth.
9. To identify the potential medical benefits from marijuana.
10. To discuss the evidence that some individuals may be more vulnerable to marijuana abuse than others.
11. To summarize treatments available for those with marijuana-related problems.

1936
Marijuana

Those addicted to marijuana, after an early feeling of exhilaration, soon lose all restraints, all inhibitions. They become bestial demoniacs, filled with the mad lust to kill... (Kenneth Clark cited by Sloman, 1983).

In spite of the fact that marijuana use is pervasive throughout the history of humankind—written records of marijuana use have been discovered that date back to 2700 B.C.—the drug gained a very bad reputation early in the twentieth century. Whether it was fact or fancy, the U.S. government, with the support of the scientific world, commenced a media bash against marijuana. Perhaps because marijuana was being used in the lower social classes, the government felt it necessary to discourage its use and employed a massive media campaign to convey the impression that marijuana caused insanity, immoral acts, and crime. In spite of these efforts, marijuana remains way ahead of the pack in its popularity—it is the most extensively used illicit drug in this country, in spite of a slight gradual decline in use over the past two decades. Nevertheless, marijuana is not a completely safe drug, as

many today believe. Although it is certainly less hazardous than cocaine, heroin, or PCP, and it does not have the same association with criminal activity, marijuana does have its disadvantages. This chapter provides an objective examination of marijuana's relative risks and benefits.

Until the early 1970s, it was widely believed that marijuana plants could be classified into three different species. Although this may not seem remarkable or even important, it became a legal issue worthy of debate in 1971 when a defendant was charged with marijuana possession. Only *Cannabis sativa,* the type of marijuana plant most often used, was mandated illegal, and the defendant claimed that the marijuana in question was of another species altogether, and thus, not technically illegal. A number of studies were promptly conducted that concluded that there is only one species of Cannabis. There does appear, however, to be more than one variety or type within this species (see McKim, 1991).

Notwithstanding, literature on marijuana refers to the Cannabis plant as originating from three separate varieties: *Cannabis sativa, Cannabis indica,* and *Cannabis ruderalis.* Hence, marijuana is also referred to as Cannabis or a type of cannabinoid (other street names include pot, weed, and grass). *Cannabis sativa,* grown by George Washington to make rope (and evidently also for its pharmacological qualities as well), is the hemp plant from

Female marijuana plant.

Courtesy of the Drug Enforcement Administration

which the active ingredient of marijuana is most commonly extracted for use in the United States. The plant grows throughout the world and fares the best under conditions of hot, humid, tropical weather. Although marijuana is primarily cultivated in Mexico, Jamaica, Thailand, Colombia, Laos, and Belize, about 25 percent of illegal marijuana is grown in the United States (U.S. Attorneys, 1989). It accounts for the largest cash crop in North Carolina, Kentucky, California, and Tennessee (Denton, 1990). Worldwide cultivation of marijuana is estimated to have increased from 7,070 to 10,925 metric tons in 1985 to as many as 19,870 tons in 1988 (U.S. Attorneys, 1989, p. 11).

There is evidence that the plant originated in Asia. It has since been widely cultivated for its pharmacological properties, including sedation, hallucinations, and euphoria. *Cannabis indica* is also cultivated for its psychoactive properties. *Cannabis ruderalis* is found mostly in Russia. No matter what conditions under which they are grown, each variety of marijuana plant is associated with a different concentration of active ingredient. Each also differs in its potency from one season to the next, depending upon the weather.

The active compound responsible for marijuana's effects is delta-9-tetrahydrocannabinol (THC). THC was first isolated in 1964 and, although there are at least 419 individual compounds in marijuana and more than eighty active drugs called cannabinoids, THC is most active in the brain and body. There is some evidence that other chemicals in marijuana may also exert psychoactive effects to a lesser degree. THC is most abundant in the gummy resin within the flowers of female Cannabis plants although smaller quantities are present in the leaves and the stalk. Marijuana may consist of any part of the Cannabis plant that produces physical and psychological changes in its users. Marijuana's THC content varies greatly, generally ranging from 0.5 to 11 percent with 2 to 5 percent as an average concentration range.

Other types of Cannabis products are hashish, charas, ganja, bhang, and sinsemilla. These tend to be more potent than marijuana as the THC concentrations are higher, ranging from 10 to 50 percent. Charas is composed of pure resin extracted from the surface of leaves and stems. Because hashish comes from the dried resin of the female flowers, it contains large amounts of THC (up to 14 percent) and, like charas, induces quite powerful effects. Ganja is made up of dried plant materials from the flowers of female plants. The least potent form of Cannabis is bhang, which includes parts of the entire plant minus the top leaves. Sinsemilla, a high-quality marijuana, is produced in the United States. Its popularity has risen over the past two decades due to its potency, with THC concentrations reaching as high as 10 percent. Sinsemilla is made by removing the male plants from the fields to prevent pollination of the female plants, as pollination leads to seed production, causing them to become less potent. Prevention of the pollination process increases THC levels. Although the average range of THC concentration in marijuana commonly available has remained relatively constant over the past 150 years, new practices have emerged that enhance the potential to cultivate much more powerful forms of marijuana (Mijuriya & Aldrich, 1988). For example, growers attempt to increase the THC content in marijuana by using hydroponic techniques, where plants are grown in nutrient rich water rather than in soil. To decrease the possibility of detection, many growers have developed elaborate methods of indoor cultivation (U.S. Attorneys, 1989, p. 12).

Due to its large bulk and distinctive odor, marijuana is difficult to smuggle undetected into the United States. Traffickers must be particularly creative in disguising their product. For example, more than three tons of hashish were hidden in drums containing olives from Lebanon with an estimated street value of $90 million (Hashish seized in…, 1991). Traffickers have also begun to harvest only the top 10 to 15 inches of the flower, with the seed still intact in the closed pod. The advantage of this technique is that the top portion, known as the "cola," or tail, has a higher concentration of THC and can retail at a price three times higher than the compressed brick variety of marijuana. Instead of smuggling multi-ton loads of compressed bricks, traffickers can increase profits with smaller loads of "cola" (U.S. Attorneys, 1989).

Domestic marijuana growers are likely to cultivate the plant in national forests and other public lands to eliminate the possibility of government confiscation of their land. Community attitudes in many of these rural areas where marijuana is grown range from merely tolerant to actively supportive as many residents work for the growers on a part-time basis and are able to supplement their incomes (U.S. Attorneys, 1989).

Prevalence of Marijuana Use

Marijuana remains the most popular illicit drug among high school seniors, but its usage has declined significantly. Data from the *National Household Survey on Drug*

Table 13.1   *Marijuana: Percent of Respondents Reporting Frequency of Use Within Past Year (1993) by Sex and Age Groups for Total Population*

	At Least Once	12 or More Times	Once a Week or More
AGE	RATE ESTIMATES (PERCENTAGES)		
12-17	10.1	4.8	2.8
Male	11.0	5.8	3.5
Female	9.0	3.9	2.1
18-25	22.9	10.1	5.9
Male	28.6	15.1	9.4
Female	17.2	5.2	2.6
26-34	13.8	7.0	3.7
Male	17.6	9.7	5.3
Female	10.2	4.5	2.1
35+	4.0	2.0	1.2
Male	5.7	3.0	1.5
Female	2.5	1.3	0.9
Total	9.0	4.3	2.4
Male	11.7	6.2	3.5
Female	6.5	2.6	1.4

Source: Adapted from Substance Abuse and Mental Health Services Administration. *National Household Survey on Drug Abuse: Population Estimates 1993.*

Abuse for 1993 (Substance Abuse and Mental Health Services Administration, 1994) regarding current prevalence of marijuana use in the United States are presented in Table 13.1.

The eighteen to twenty-five age group is most likely to have tried marijuana at least once. They are also most likely to have used marijuana twelve or more times and most likely to use it once a week or more.

Males tend to be more likely to use marijuana than females in all age categories. In the eighteen to twenty-five age category, males are almost four times as likely as females to use marijuana on a regular basis.

From 1969 to 1979, marijuana use increased each year. Trends in marijuana use since 1975 are best presented in *National Survey Results on Drug Use from The Monitoring the Future Study, 1975–1992* (Johnston, O'Malley, & Bachman, 1993). Use of marijuana by high school seniors hit a seventeen year low in 1992 (See Figures 13.1, 13.2, & 13.3).Whereas in 1975, 55 percent of high school seniors had tried marijuana at some time in their lives, by 1992 only 32.6 percent reported using it. Since 1975

there was a gradual increase in marijuana use until it hit a peak in 1978 and 1980 with 66 percent of high school seniors reporting use. Then a steady decline occurred. Forty percent of seniors reported use in the last twelve months in 1975. This trend reached a peak in 1979 with 51 percent of seniors reporting use the last twelve months, followed by a steady decline until 1992 when 21.9 percent reported use in the last twelve months. 27.1 percent of seniors in 1975 reported use in the past thirty days. This trend steadily increased, reaching 37.1 percent in the year 1978 and 36.5 percent in 1979, and gradually declined until 1992, when only 11.9 percent of high school seniors reported using marijuana in the past month.

Marijuana use among college students also declined significantly. Annual prevalence of use among college students peaked in 1980 with 51 percent reporting use within the last year compared with 28 percent in 1992. Twenty-five percent of young adults reported using marijuana during the past year in 1992.

Daily use of marijuana has also declined since 1980 among all three populations. Daily use is defined as using

Figure 13.1   *Trends in Lifetime, Annual, and Thirty-Day Prevalence of Marijuana Use for Twelfth Graders*

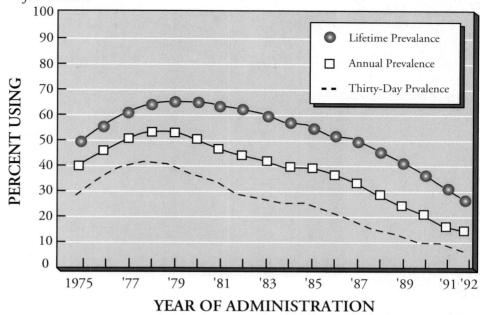

Source: Johnston, L.D., O'Malley, P.M. and Bachman, J.G. (1993). *National Survey Results on Drug Use from the Monitoring the Future Study, 1975–1992.*

Figure 13.2   *Marijuana: Trends in Annual Prevalence Among College Students vs. Others 1-4 Years Beyond High School*

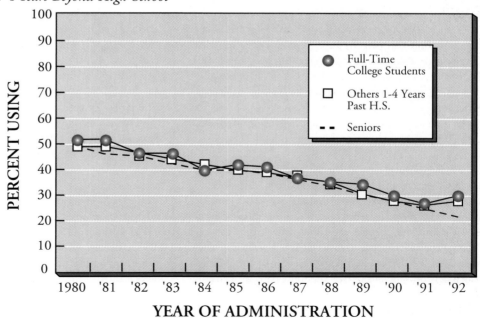

Source: Johnston, L.D., O'Malley, P.M. and Bachman, J.G. (1993). *National Survey Results on Drug Use from the Monitoring the Future Study, 1975–1992.*

Figure 13.3 *Marijuana: Trends in Thirty-Day Prevalence of Daily Use Among College Students vs. Others 1-4 Years Beyond High School*

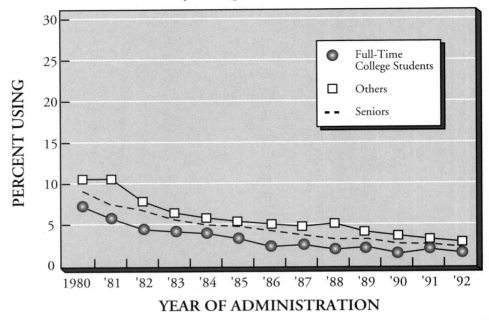

Source: Johnston, O'Malley and Bachman (1993). *National Survey Results on Drug Use from the Monitoring the Future Study, 1975–1992.*

marijuana for twenty or more days per month. Around 1978 and 1979, 11 percent reported daily or almost daily use, and only 35 percent thought marijuana smoking posed a great risk. (In 1984, 67 percent held this opinion.) In 1992, 1.9 percent of high school seniors, 1.6 percent of college students, and 2.3 percent of young adults age nineteen to twenty-eight smoked on a daily basis. Of those high school seniors who reported using marijuana on a daily basis, most began this pattern by the end of the tenth grade.

The reasons for this decrease in marijuana use over the last few decades among youth, particularly in the middle class, are speculative. Nevertheless, we can point to numerous changes in social conditions that may be related to attitudinal changes regarding drug use in general. During the 1960s, drug use was largely experimental and associated with a "free thinking," intellectual and political movement in our society. For the most part, drugs being used by youth were not associated with criminality nor with serious health hazards. Marijuana was the most popular drug of this generation. As this era came to a close, however, only a minority of the children continued to use

marijuana after the age of twenty. Research indicates that youth are more likely to use marijuana than adults and they commonly discontinue use once they have reached adulthood. For those who have never used marijuana, risk for initiation to marijuana use after the age of twenty is quite small. In general, use declines substantially by age 22.5 for both males and females (Kandel & Logan, 1984). In short, as the 60s movement passed (which actually continued on into the 1970s) and the marijuana users of this era aged, fewer and fewer individuals partook of this drug.

In addition to the influence of this movement, research had begun to show that health hazards may be associated with various types of drug use. Marijuana was still considered a relatively benign drug, but many feared unknown harmful effects might be uncovered. This fear has been compounded by the fact that the potency of marijuana has increased over the years. The so-called benign drug of the 60s may bear little resemblance to the much stronger drug of the 80s. Cocaine was once considered a nonaddictive, harmless substance, and people began to wonder whether the same might be true about marijuana. We have no evidence at present to suggest that marijuana and cocaine are in any way comparable in their risks; nevertheless, such fears have been persuasively conveyed to youthful populations.

A third contribution to the decrease in marijuana use may be the emergence of parents' movements to combat drug abuse. These movements do not discriminate against drug types; rather they focus on all drugs that are illegal and some that are legal, such as alcohol. Parents' efforts to curb children's drug abuse have been paralleled in recent years with employers' and law enforcement programs to screen for drug use among workers and motor vehicle drivers. Individuals may now more easily lose their licenses or their jobs if they test positive for just about any illegal substance. These programs are in step with information indicating that illicit drug and alcohol use are frequently the cause of judgment impairments and are sometimes associated with driving or other job-related fatalities.

One other possible reason for the decline in drug use is parents' awareness of the warning signs of drug intoxication due to their own use as teenagers. Twenty years ago, many parents were unfamiliar with the signs and smells of drug use. Today, the youth of the 60s have grown up and have teenaged children of their own; they are imminently better acquainted with drug use cues than their parents were. As a consequence, they may be more attuned to and better equipped to intervene in drug use.

Finally, there has been a recent political shift towards increasing social conservatism. Prior to the 1960s, marijuana use was associated with violence, chromosomal damage, criminality, and mental illness. Thinking became more liberal and tolerant of drugs in the 1960s and marijuana was considered safe and nontoxic. Now, the thinking is more conservative among both the public and politicians. This conservatism and fear of all drugs has led to the clumping of marijuana with other more dangerous drugs. We have become an anti-drug oriented society on a global level, without regard to the specific drug or its effects—beneficial or not. President Bush's refusal in the late 1980s to permit legalization of marijuana for beneficial purposes simply because it is scheduled as an illegal drug is a reflection of this growing conservatism. In concert, several states have repealed laws decriminalizing small amounts of marijuana due to widespread public fervor against all drugs.

Overall, the marijuana use of today is associated with greater use of other drugs and with membership in drug-using groups (Meier et al., 1984). There is even evidence that those who use such drugs actually have stronger alliances with their peers than those who do not use any

drugs. Youth who use marijuana, similar to those who use other drugs, have less involvement in conventional activities, such as, belonging to organizations, attending religious activities, or exercising. It may be suggested that either their drug use becomes a primary focus of their activities or that their use enables them to escape from engaging in activities they lack interest in anyway. Instead, youngsters who use marijuana have a greater incidence of deviant activities, low self-esteem, lowered well-being, and even psychiatric hospitalizations (Kandel, 1985).

Classification of Marijuana

Because marijuana produces such variable effects that are comparable to drugs classified as diversely as hallucinogens, sedatives, and anesthetics, those involved in classification schemes have justifiably been at odds. Early classifications were based more on political and legal foundations rather than on pharmacological properties. In fact, when drugs were initially scheduled for law enforcement purposes by the courts (see Chapter 2), marijuana was classified as a narcotic drug. This was due to the pervasive belief that marijuana use was associated with, if not responsible for, violent crime. These beliefs were primarily a result of political leanings and media blitzes rather than scientific observations. It is now well understood that marijuana does not even resemble the narcotics, either in its pharmacological properties or the criminal tendencies of those who use it (NCMDA, 1972).

Classification attempts based on pharmacological properties are equally as perplexing. Marijuana's effects include both stimulation and depression of the CNS that differs from other drug classes (Consroe et al., 1976). Low-to-moderate doses of THC produce mild sedation similar to alcohol and some anxiolytic drugs (e.g., Valium). Higher doses, however, produce euphoria, hallucinations, and heightened sensory experiences somewhat like those induced by hallucinogens. Sedatives differ from THC as they do not produce these effects. Furthermore, THC will not produce anesthesia or coma in high doses as do the sedatives. There is no evidence that THC produces any cross tolerance with hallucinogens or sedatives, placing THC in a distinct category. Since THC resembles sedatives at low doses and hallucinogens at high doses, it does not fit into any preexisting category. As a consequence, THC is presently considered a unique drug, distinct from other drugs in terms of structural properties and actions, and is discussed as belonging to its own class of psychoactive substances. Until recently, very little has been known about the mechanism of THC's actions in the brain. Because marijuana contains so many chemicals with potential psychoactive properties, it is difficult to separate them and determine their individual and combined influences. Despite new scientific techniques in computer imaging and neurobiological experiments, studies remain inconclusive about which neurotransmitter receptors have an affinity for THC. Further complicating marijuana research is the ability of the surrounding environment and personal expectations to alter the psychoactive effects of THC. However, we do know that marijuana's effects are dose related, like most other drugs, and its effects and risks increase as a function of the amount used.

Administration, Absorption, and Metabolism

The most common route of administration for marijuana is for the user to smoke it in a cigarette or in a pipe. Materials from the Cannabis plant that contain THC are generally hand-rolled in cigarette paper; THC becomes most active when ignited and smoked. When adminis-

tered in another form, such as ingested, its psychoactive effects are relatively small. It is also a well-known practice to separate the resin from the plants by boiling the plants in alcohol, so the solid materials can be filtered out of the liquid. The liquid is then reduced to a thick, sticky substance known as hash oil, containing as much as 50 percent THC or more. By placing a drop of the liquid on a regular cigarette's paper or by dropping some on a hot piece of tinfoil, the smoke may be inhaled to produce intense effects.

Individuals who smoke marijuana find that the intensity of its effects is a function of previous experience with the drug; the more practice a user has inhaling the smoke, the longer the smoke may be held in the lungs. Thus, it follows that if the individual also smokes tobacco cigarettes, he or she may be able to hold the smoke in the lungs longer and deeper than someone who does not have that practical experience. A lengthier stay in the lungs ultimately means a greater amount of THC will be absorbed into the bloodstream. Furthermore, because marijuana has been widely used as a communal activity, the intensity of its effects will also depend on how many other users are sharing the same marijuana cigarette. While one user is holding the smoke in his or her lungs for several seconds, a second user can be inhaling so that less of the smoke from the lighted cigarette

Marijuana is usually hand rolled and smoked like a cigarette called a "joint" or a "doobie."

will be wasted. Finally, only about half of the available THC in a cigarette is supplied by the smoke. For these reasons, one cannot estimate how much THC any given user will obtain from a marijuana cigarette, even when its THC concentration has been calculated.

Because drugs that are inhaled are rapidly and completely absorbed into the bloodstream, the effects of marijuana, including psychological and cardiovascular changes, are experienced within minutes after smoking. Blood levels of THC reach their peak within thirty minutes and subsequently decline as the THC is distributed to other bodily tissues and organs. Interestingly, the subjective experience of being high does not correspond with blood levels of THC. Users often report their peak high as blood levels are declining (see Figure 13.4). This may be due to the possibility that levels of THC in the brain continue to increase after the drug is administered, even though the total amount to reach the brain is quite small. Shortly after it is distributed, most of the THC migrates to the lungs, kidneys, and liver while very little remains in the brain. The effects last between ninety minutes and three hours unless additional cigarettes are smoked. The half-life of THC is approximately nineteen hours; howev-

er, its metabolites that remain in the blood have a half-life of fifty hours. More than forty-five metabolites have been identified, and 11-hydroxy-delta-THC is the most commonly measured in assays to detect the presence of marijuana. There is evidence that many of these metabolites have effects of their own, contributing to the psychoactive properties of marijuana. In order for the THC and its metabolites to be completely eliminated from the body, as many as thirty days may have to pass!

Oral ingestion of marijuana causes absorption to be rather sluggish and incomplete. Because the liver transforms the THC to 11-hydroxy-THC, not much active THC reaches the brain. Therefore, oral administration slowly produces its initial effects within about one hour and will peak after two to three hours. In the late 1960s and early 70s, many users baked marijuana leaves into brownies to be eaten. Sometimes it is also brewed as tea. When THC is heated in this way, much of it will become bioactive and produce notable, albeit somewhat muted, psychoactive effects (burning Cannabis leads to the production of new cannabinoids that increase its potency and effects). These effects may be experienced for more than five hours after ingestion.

Figure 13.4   *Concentration Effect Curve VAS Feel Drug vs. Plasma THC Level*

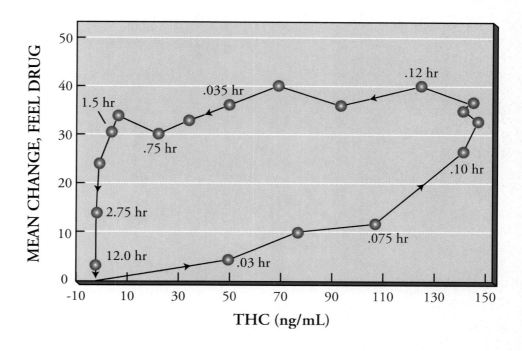

Another disadvantage of ingesting marijuana is the frequent occurrence of nausea, dizziness, vomiting, and hangover. THC may not be safely administered by injection. THC is highly lipid soluble, indicating that fatty tissues of the body absorb it selectively. The brain, adrenal gland, liver, lungs, ovaries, and testes absorb the largest amounts of THC. Within the first three days following administration, about 50 percent of the total THC can be traced in the fatty tissues and organs. As it is slowly released during this interval into the bloodstream and eliminated primarily in the feces (but also in the plasma and urine) the remaining 50 percent can be found in these samples. This means that THC detected in the urine or blood is difficult to associate with psychological and behavioral states, making proof of impairment by virtue of marijuana intoxication complicated. Furthermore, because THC and its metabolites remain in the body for so long, they may have influences on the body and brain that are unknown to us.

Detection of Marijuana Use

Private industry is quite interested in detecting marijuana use as more corporations associate absenteeism, theft, and poor productivity levels with marijuana use. Although the long half-lives of THC and its metabolites make marijuana potentially one of the most easily detectable drugs, detecting traces of THC in the body is, in reality, a tricky business. Because only the metabolites of THC remain after it has been metabolized. Urine tests for metabolites such as 9-carboxy-THC are frequently performed. Detection techniques are unusually complicated and may include either an immunoassay, chromatography, or spectrometry. Within one hour after smoking a single joint, THC metabolites can be found. Those who use marijuana only once in a while will show a positive test result for one to three days after use. However, regular marijuana users will have a positive urine test every time, even if they use it only a couple of times a week. Once heavy or chronic smokers discontinue use of marijuana, their urine tests may be positive for a full month afterward (Schwartz & Hawks, 1985). Because of this observation, one urine test will not reveal the extent or recency of marijuana use. As a consequence, it may be necessary to perform several tests over time to determine how often or how much marijuana has been used by an individual. There are also several adulterants that can be used to disguise THC in the urine, as shown in the photo. Table 13.2 illustrates the results of adding adulterants to urine samples of known marijuana users.

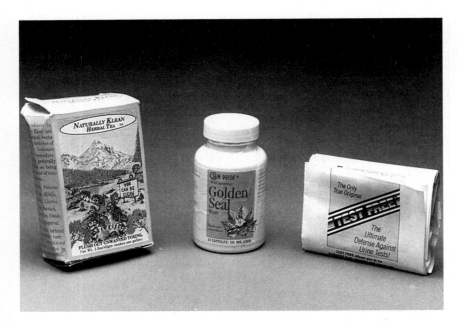

Substances that may be used to adulterate THC to make detection difficult.

Table 13.2 Results of Urinary Cannabinoids Essay: Effect of Adding Adulterants to Known Cannabinoid-Positive Urine Sample*

Adulterant	Amount of Adulterant	Volume of Urine, ml	Test Result for Cannabinoid Using Know-Positive Urine
Salt	0.625 g (0.125 tsp.)	10	+
	1.25 g (0.25 tsp.)	10	+
	2.5 g (0.5 tsp.)	10	-
	3.75 g (0.75 tsp.)	10	-
Vinegar	1 drop	7-10	+
	5 drops	7-10	-
Hypochlorite bleach	1 drop	10	-
	1 drop	5	-
Liquid detergent	1 drop	10	-
	1 drop	5	-
Lemon Juice	1 drop	7-10	+
	1 drops	7-10	+
Liquid Soap	1 drop	5	-
Blood	1 drop	5	-
	1 drop	10	-

Source: Schwartz et al. 1985. Copyright 1985 *American Journal of Diseases of Children.*
*tsp. indicates teaspoon; plus sign, positive test results; minus sign negative test results.

Sites of Action and Pharmacological Aspects

We still do not know exactly how marijuana influences brain systems to create its psychological and physiological effects. We do know that minute amounts of cannabinoids produce notable effects, suggesting that marijuana's effects concentrate on a particular receptor site. Also, if the THC molecule is slightly altered, the drug's effects differ accordingly. This indicates that the structure of the THC molecule determines whether it can influence a receptor site with an affinity for that particular shape. Finally, THC was discovered to change concentrations of cyclic AMP, adenosine monophosphate (a molecule in the brain responsible for neural transmission), within cells, a finding signifying that THC was not just dissolving nonspecifically in cell membranes. Only recently has evidence accumulated showing support for the presence of specific "marijuana receptors" in the brain (Herkenham et al.,

1990). These so-called cannabinoid receptors appear to play an important physiological role in many areas of the brain, but we still do not know what precise functions they serve. Since THC is not normally found in the brain, logic dictates that a naturally occurring substance resembling the molecular structure of THC must be present that regulates pain, learning, memory, and other behaviors related to marijuana's psychoactive effects. Therapeutic uses of cannabinoids in controlling convulsions, nausea, vomiting, and muscle tone disorders lead us to believe that this similar natural brain chemical binds to these receptors to affect these functions.

Marijuana exerts its effects by influencing neural processes throughout the brain but most particularly within the limbic system. Alterations in mood, cognition, and memory produced by marijuana can be attributed to its targeting of this system. The hippocampus and amygdala are especially abundant in THC binding sites, explaining how marijuana relieves anxiety and produces sedation and euphoria. Marijuana's stimulation of the medial forebrain bundle within the limbic system appears to be particularly responsible for the experience of reward and pleasure (Gardner et al., 1988). These structures of the limbic system are equally responsible for time perception. Marijuana use profoundly affects ability to estimate the passage of time, slowing the user's time sense, presumably by influencing the hippocampus and amygdala.

Additional THC binding sites are densely concentrated in the basal ganglia, cerebral cortex, and cerebellum, all regions of the brain responsible for thought processes, including perception, knowledge, and memory (Herkenham et al., 1990). Alterations in memory processes are consistently observed but inadequately understood. It appears that the ability to store short-term memories and transfer them into long-term memory is disrupted as a function of marijuana's influence. Auditory processes may be altered due to the concentration of THC in centers for hearing. Movement control centers in the cerebellum are rich in cannabinoid receptors, explaining marijuana's ability to interfere with coordination. Binding sites are relatively scarce in lower brainstem regions that control heart and lung functions. This relative absence in these areas may explain why high doses of THC are not lethal as are other drugs, such as cocaine and the depressants.

Despite breakthroughs in locating specific marijuana receptors in the brain, we have yet to discover an antagonist for marijuana; there is no known drug that interferes with marijuana's effects. Furthermore, marijuana changes the permeability of cell membranes, similar to the actions of other drugs, such as anesthetics and alcohol, which have more nonspecific chemical properties. As a consequence, it appears that the drug also exerts more global and nonspecific effects, influencing several other brain chemicals and their receptors.

In addition to specific binding sites for marijuana, the drug influences other well-known neurotransmitters to alter brain function and behavior. THC alters the turnover rates for dopamine and serotonin, leading to their release from presynaptic stores. Augmenting dopamine supplies in the brain may especially contribute to the abuse potential of marijuana (Ng Cheong Ton et al., 1988). THC and its chemical associates also influence prostaglandins, acetylcholine, norepinephrine, GABA, and cyclic AMP. We do not know, at present, to what extent each of these neurochemical reactions contribute to marijuana's psychoactive effects. Nevertheless, we may speculate that different mechanisms are responsible for the various effects of marijuana, including its sedative, hallucinatory, and analgesic properties.

Physiological Effects

Marijuana or THC acts much like a depressant in most animals, humans included, by sedating and decreasing motor activity. Reactions to painful stimuli are equally subdued and aggressive behaviors are lessened. Also similar to the depressants is THC's capacity to raise the seizural threshold, block convulsions, dull reflexive behaviors, and impair the ability to carry out complex behavioral activities, although simple motor tasks and reaction times remain relatively unaffected at lower doses. Nevertheless, even at low doses, attention, arousal, and information processing are impaired for several hours. THC, when used in combination with depressants such as the barbiturates or other sedatives, will heighten their effects.

More specific primary effects of THC target the central nervous and cardiovascular systems. Blood pressure and heart rate increase slightly, contributing to feelings of anxiety in users prone to anxiety attacks. Blood vessels in the whites of the eyes dilate about one hour after use, producing bloodshot eyes that may be readily observed by others, even when the subjective effects are imperceptible. The "stoned" look that users manifest is apparently due to a drooping of the eyelids. Blood glucose levels drop, causing the user to experience extreme hunger. (Regular users call this compulsion to eat the munchies.) The mouth becomes dry and on occasion the user may feel nauseated or dizzy, especially when the eyes are closed. Balance and muscle strength may be adversely affected, even at low doses. Headaches can occur at somewhat higher doses. Certain senses become heightened resulting in increased visual and auditory perception. The ability to taste, feel, and smell stimuli in the user's surroundings may also be enhanced. Finally, the perception of time and space is altered, causing the user to perceive the passage of time in slow motion and making it difficult to judge distances. Most users feel somewhat euphoric, relaxed, and at peace.

Higher doses of THC create both disconcerting and dysphoric symptoms in many users. Anxiety and paranoia will increase at this point, and users may feel completely disoriented in time and space, leading to confusion and poor decision-making abilities. Hallucinations and delusions become prominent in their thoughts and sensory perceptions may be overwhelmingly enhanced.

Inset 13.1

GETTING HIGH

Marijuana smokers frequently report increased hunger, dry mouth and throat, more vivid visual imagery, and a keener sense of hearing. Subtle visual and auditory stimuli previously ignored may take on a novel quality , and the nondominant senses of touch, taste, and smell seem to be enhanced. Yet, in usual social doses, marijuana decreases empathy and the perception of emotions in others; clarity of sequential dialogue is impaired, and irrelevant ideas and words intrude into the stream of communication. Altered perception of time is a consistent effect of cannabinoids. Time seems to pass more slowly—minutes may seem like hours.

Higher doses of THC can induce frank hallucinations, delusions, and paranoid feelings. Thinking becomes confused and disorganized: depersonalization and altered time sense are accentuated. Anxiety reaching panic proportions may replace euphoria. Often as a result of the feeling that the drug-induced state will never end. With high enough doses, the clinical picture is that of a toxic psychosis with hallucinations, depersonalization and loss of insight; this can occur acutely or only after months of use. Most users are able to regulate their intake in order to avoid the excessive dosage that produces these unpleasant effects.... Use of marijuana may also cause an acute exacerbation of symptomatology in stabilized schizophrenics, and it is one of the common precipitants of "flashbacks" in former users of LSD.

(Jaffe, 1985, P.559)

Although hospital emergency rooms rarely see individuals suffering from THC-induced psychosis, it does occur, particularly in users who also suffer from schizophrenia or another psychiatric disorder. Marijuana may actually trigger a psychotic episode in a user with a history of this disturbance. More frequently, however, those admitted to hospital emergency rooms claiming to be suffering from THC-related psychiatric problems are actually experiencing toxic psychosis from PCP. Marijuana is sometimes laced with PCP, and the user may not be aware of its presence or willing to acknowledge PCP use to emergency room staff. Overall, the physiological effects of THC are relatively benign when compared to other drugs of abuse, such as cocaine, and no deaths have ever been attributed to marijuana's direct effects when smoked or ingested.

Psychological and Behavioral Effects

In social doses, the user experiences mood changes and mild sedative-hypnotic effects. Marijuana's high is nearly always characterized as pleasant, and when the drug is used in the presence of others, as is common, there is generally a great deal of uncontrolled laughter and highlighted feelings of well-being. This joyful mood may suddenly shift to one of dreaminess and introspection, with a shift just as suddenly back to lighthearted good spirits. Any seemingly neutral comment or occurrence may provoke hysterical laughter that only other users may appreciate. When the marijuana user is alone, the subjective effects of intoxication are likely to be more subtle. Users attest that marijuana enhances creative thoughts and insights that could not be experienced under usual conditions. Artists of various types believe that marijuana causes such tremendous improvement in creative abilities that their productions are unsurpassed by their sober works. Objective research has shown, however, that such creative strides may be a perception rather than a reality.

As the dose or number of marijuana cigarettes increases, the subjective effects become more intense although they still may not be particularly noticeable to others. These effects may be limited to the enhancement of sensory perceptions and emotional responses. The user may even begin to hallucinate and experience a distorted environment. Whether the user is cheerful or contemplative, he or she will generally prefer to remain relatively motionless, as exerting energy for any reason may seem purposeless and cumbersome. Sometimes, simply staring at a television or the surroundings are perceived to provide adequate mental stimulation.

Low doses of marijuana cause the user to focus on an object, conversation, thought, or event in an intense fashion, possibly leading to the experience of euphoria as the user feels that he or she has transcended usual, mundane surroundings. The experience may be much more intense than normal because these senses not only become highly sensitized, but they also are blended together with several external stimuli and internal memories. At this level, thoughts are not so altered that the user feels a loss of control or an inability to cope. Cognitive and motor functions are not substantially altered; nevertheless, recent studies (Yesavage et al., 1985) suggest that smoking marijuana may impair a pilot's ability to fly a plane the following day. Imagine to what extent being high on marijuana might influence a user's ability to drive a car. Although marijuana use does not directly interfere with the physical ability to actually control a car, the user becomes so distracted by irrelevant stimuli that he or she may not notice lights, signs, and other driving cues. Furthermore, judgment is impaired, reaction time may be reduced, and ability to sustain attention is affected so that the driver may fail to attend to a driving-related situation crucial to making an immediate decision and response (Perez-Reyes et al., 1988).

Moderately higher doses produce vivid hallucinations, distorted body images, and psychedelic experiences similar to the weaker hallucinogenic agents, such as mescaline. Users may begin to feel out of control or out of touch with themselves, as if they were not in their own bodies. This sensation is called depersonalization. Some users find this experience exhilarating and exciting, while others may become anxious, panicky, and dysphoric. When depersonalization is accompanied by delusions, hallucinations, and paranoia (effects produced by very high doses of THC), users may become disoriented, confused and extremely uncomfortable. It is at this level of THC intoxication that those who were previously experiencing euphoria will now become panicky and show some symptoms of psychosis.

When marijuana is combined with alcohol, an all-too-common practice especially among young users, the effects become additive, if not multiplicative (Perez-Reyes et al., 1988). Impairments produced by this combination are much greater than when marijuana is used alone in that the performance of complex tasks becomes particu-larly problematic. Driving and operating machinery would become extremely unsafe under these influences.

Influences of the Social Context

The social surroundings influence the subjective effects of marijuana, more so than for other drugs. First of all, because many novice users report no effect from marijuana, Becker (1963) suggested that getting high is a learning experience. For these users, several subsequent tries are necessary before the effects are perceptible, leading Becker to believe that a marijuana user must (1) learn how to smoke the drug properly, (2) learn to recognize the effects as attributable to the drug, since some of the effects are rather subtle, and (3) begin to associate the effects with pleasure in the same way some of us had to acquire a taste for fine brandy or spicy foods. Most researchers now believe that this learning process may have been largely a function of the strength of marijuana used in the 1950s and 60s. Marijuana was not nearly as potent then as it is now; today even first time users are likely to experience the drug effects given the THC content of marijuana sold on the street. Nevertheless, it is true that learning how to smoke the drug is necessary for the THC concentration in the body to reach effective levels.

Other features of the user's social and experiential setting influence subjective effects of marijuana. Previous experiences with the drug will, to a great extent, determine how an individual will feel each time he or she uses marijuana. If they have been primarily pleasurable experiences, subsequent uses should be equally pleasurable. If they have been uncomfortable, associated with panic or anxiety or an otherwise bad experience, subsequent uses may be tainted by that history. Furthermore, instructions and information given to a user will influence their experience. Under laboratory conditions, for example, subjective effects can actually be altered by what users hear prior to or during marijuana intoxication about what to expect. Thus, expectations can completely alter or direct the marijuana experience. Motivation on the part of the user can equally influence the effects. An individual who is excited about the prospect of using marijuana will most likely have a positive experience, while someone who feels pressured to use or is trying to elevate a low mood will likely experience some negative effects.

Marijuana users quickly learn that their existing mood and the mood of those around them can influence their subjective high. If a user is depressed or anxious, marijuana has the reputation of actually exaggerating that mood. Similarly, if the user is already happy, marijuana may further accentuate that state. In the same vein, when marijuana is used in the presence of a hostile or unfriendly crowd, the subjective effects are probably going to be unpleasant. Seasoned marijuana users try to ensure that they "turn on" only with those they know well and under friendly circumstances. It is interesting that marijuana users report an ability to turn on and off their high. For example, when they need to function properly—when questioned by a parent or when they need to "sober up" quickly—they are able to control to some extent, marijuana's effects. One person may be able to really get high on marijuana by subjectively investing in the experience while another may be more inhibited and repress the effects. Nevertheless, even though a user may be able to acquire the perception and appearance of being sober, studies show that users remain impaired and intoxicated.

Finally, there may be certain placebo effects associated with marijuana use. Specifically, regular users report that they are able to experience subjective effects of marijuana by simply thinking about it. They feel intoxicated more readily, for example, after smoking a placebo marijuana cigarette than do novice users. On the other hand, individuals who do not use marijuana or use only rarely do not report such placebo effects.

Tolerance and Dependence

Tolerance does develop to the effects of marijuana in both animals and humans. Psychoactive, harmful, and beneficial effects of marijuana all decrease with repeated use in relatively large amounts. Tolerance to THC-induced cardiovascular and autonomic changes, decreased intraocular (eye fluid) pressure, sleep, mood, and behavioral changes are acquired and rapidly lost after the drug is discontinued (Jones et al., 1981). The development of tolerance differs with respect to the various effects of marijuana; some effects become tolerant rapidly while others may not show tolerance at all. For example, increases in motor activity and heart rate develop tolerance within a few days while the depressive properties of marijuana become tolerant much more slowly. Effects on appetite do not appear to become tolerant after repeated usage. Although it is not well understood, tolerance appears to develop as a function of adjustments made by the brain when THC is continually present rather than from an increased rate of elimination (Jaffe, 1985). Individuals who are exposed to

very heavy doses of THC over time are able to use quantities of marijuana large enough to be toxic to other less experienced users.

On the other hand, there is some evidence supporting the development of reverse tolerance or sensitization to marijuana's effects. The fact that experienced users appear to become high more readily than neophytes indicates that the more exposure an individual has to marijuana, the more rapid and intense its effects may be. On the surface, sensitization theories contradict evidence that the more an individual is exposed to marijuana, the larger the dosages must be to experience subjective effects—an indication of tolerance. Perhaps if one were to distinguish between the physiological and psychological effects of the drug this apparent contradiction would make more sense. Although it may not be this simple, users seem to become tolerant to the physiological effects of THC over time while they become sensitized to the psychological or subjective effects. Because learning and the social context in which marijuana is used play such an important role in becoming high, it is possible that experienced users enhance THC effects according to their expectations and the social cues associated with marijuana use. Also, the accumulation of THC in bodily tissues may contribute to an additive effect, further intensifying the high.

Physical withdrawal symptoms have not been established after regular, social use of marijuana is discontinued. However, those who have been chronically exposed to marijuana in relatively large amounts do demonstrate symptoms of withdrawal, including irritability, nervousness, anxiety, decreased appetite, insomnia, nausea, sweating, and overactivity (Jaffe, 1985; Jones et al., 1981). Time spent in REM sleep, normally suppressed by marijuana, lengthens and increased body temperature, chills, and tremor may occur. These symptoms are similar to the withdrawal syndrome from sedative drugs. When individuals are given high doses on a frequent basis in the laboratory, symptoms of agitation and nervousness appear three or four hours after the marijuana use is discontinued. Twelve hours later, subjects report some flu-like symptoms, including runny nose, hot flashes, sweating, loss of appetite, and diarrhea, in addition to some of the behavioral symptoms mentioned above (Jones & Benowitz, 1976). These withdrawal symptoms may last for a few days.

Most users do not show signs of dependence or addiction to marijuana and may use the drug for years without increasing the dosage or the frequency with which it is used. The relatively small number of marijuana users that develop a regular pattern of high intake reveals, however, that to some individuals, marijuana is psychologically dependence-producing. These users frequently report that they find themselves unable to relax, sleep, or cope with daily realities unless they are high on marijuana. Psychological dependence on marijuana is probably more common than physiological dependence because the relatively low doses used in most social settings are not conducive to withdrawal symptoms. Those who "feel they need it" are generally reacting to stressors in their social environment rather than any physical need that develops to use of the drug.

Toxicity and Side Effects

In the late 1960s and early 70s marijuana was regaled as a safe drug worthy of decriminalization. Evidenced by the large numbers of individuals using marijuana from all social classes, marijuana did not seem to produce the ill effects or criminal tendencies once purported by the government to exist. In fact, if anything, marijuana appears to decrease violent or aggressive tendencies (Tinklenberg, 1974). When users become unusually violent while intoxicated, it is usually attributable to either a preexisting mental illness or other drugs that were taken in combination with marijuana, rather than a function of the marijuana alone. As a consequence, users from all walks of life insisted that criminal penalties for the use of marijuana were unwarranted. Furthermore, marijuana was shown to have several beneficial uses that legitimized its use for some medicinal purposes. Although it is true that marijuana is considered completely nonlethal, has not been associated with criminal tendencies, and does have some therapeutic value in certain cases, the drug is now known to have several adverse effects that are noteworthy. Recent studies are showing that chronic use of marijuana may have potentially toxic effects on several organs, including the brain, heart, lungs, and reproductive systems. Remember, however, that these findings are not definitive. Good studies are hard to come by and there has not been a great deal of research attention paid to marijuana in recent years due to the increased popularity of more dangerous drugs.

Brain Function

Animal and human studies indicate that marijuana may produce changes in brain function that may or may not be reversible (Petersen, 1980; Solomons & Neppe, 1989). Marijuana does cross the blood-brain barrier and neurological dysfunction has been established during acute intoxication using sophisticated techniques. Whether these changes in brain function persist beyond the period of acute intoxication is unknown. Studies employing both the EEG (electroencephalogram) and computerized transaxial tomography (CAT Scan) show relatively long-lived changes to occur primarily in limbic system structures, including the hippocampus, amygdala, and septum. As the dose rises, slow wave activity in the brain increases and beta activity, a fast wave, decreases. Since chronic users show these changes only when the dose of marijuana is increased, there is speculation that the brain becomes tolerant to THC.

Although there is no clear evidence of permanent brain damage, animal studies suggest that intellectual ability may be impaired for months after marijuana use has been discontinued (Fehr et al., 1976). Recent reports do show permanent changes in brain cells within the hippocampus, septal region, and amygdala attributable to THC in laboratory rats and monkeys, providing a hypothesis about why the animals showed consistent deficits in learning certain tasks (Heath et al., 1980). Unfortunately, similar findings from rigorous studies of humans do not yet exist. The implications of these animal studies are that long-term marijuana use may sufficiently sedate the brain to cause significant mental and emotional dullness, apathy, impaired judgment, memory deficits, and loss of motivation and ambition. Furthermore, because marijuana has such a long half-life, regular users may be more or less chronically intoxicated, even when they are not actively high. Consideration of these effects may help to explain the development of "amotivational syndrome" among chronic users. It is not clear at this time whether this state is entirely reversible although improvements have been noted over time once marijuana use is discontinued (Smith & Seymour, 1982). Nevertheless, juveniles who use marijuana extensively may be sedating vital brain functions that would normally still be developing. Again, we do not know whether their brains can play "catch up" when they are no longer using the drug.

Sleep Disturbances

As previously mentioned, THC causes users to feel drowsy and sleeping time actually increases when using marijuana. Sleep cycles may be disrupted, however, from

Inset 13.2

SHOULD MARIJUANA BE LEGALIZED FOR MEDICAL USES?

For more than twenty years, marijuana advocates have been fighting a legal battle aimed at forcing the government to put marijuana in the same category as morphine or cocaine—dangerous but medically useful drugs that doctors can prescribe for therapeutic purposes. But Drug Enforcement Agency officials continue to maintain that the drug has no accepted medical use.

Should marijuana be legalized for medical uses?

YES: Many doctors already recommend that their patients break the law and get marijuana. A recent Harvard survey of oncologists showed that almost half would prescribe marijuana if it were legal. That's because there's is very strong evidence that marijuana works as a medicine. It's effective in controlling muscle spasms for people with neurological problems, in controlling nausea and increasing appetite for cancer and AIDS patients, and in controlling the eye pressure that causes damage in glaucoma.

The Physician's Association for AIDS Care sued the DEA in an effort to free marijuana for medical use. The National Lymphoma Foundation, a major cancer group, did the same thing. During the 1980s we had two and half years of hearings before the DEA's own administrative law judge on whether the medical use of marijuana should be allowed. We put our best case forward. The DEA put its best case forward. And the judge, who was paid by the DEA, ruled in our favor. He said the DEA acted in an arbitrary and capricious manner in classifying marijuana as a drug with no medical use. Still they haven't changed their policy.

Here's how the DEA sees this issue: If they allow marijuana as medicine, there will be thousands more patients using it. People will see that they're functioning fine. And that will raise questions about why marijuana is illegal at all. That's their fear. But I don't think it's a reasonable fear. Right now cocaine and morphine are prescribed legally as medicine. And those legal uses aren't adding in any significant way to the country's drug problems. Marijuana wouldn't either.

Kevin Zeese is vice president and counsel of the Drug Policy Foundation, a nonprofit group in Washington, DC., that favors the medical use of marijuana.

NO: This legalization effort is a cruel hoax being played on very sick people. These patients are being used by the marijuana lobbyists in hopes of bringing attention to what they really want to do, which is to legalize marijuana in general. The way they portray it, the government is the bad guy and they're the good guys. But in fact, their compassion isn't compassion at all.

The marijuana lobbyists have promoted the idea that marijuana is good medicine. To support their claims they've cited pseudo-scientific sources and a number of nameless testimonials. But here are the facts: Twenty years of research have produced no reliable scientific proof that marijuana has medical value. If you call the American Cancer Society, the American Glaucoma Society, The National Multiple Sclerosis Society, the American Academy of Ophthalmology, or the American Medical Association, they'll all say there is no evidence that marijuana is a medicine.

Source: Researched by Valerie Fahey; reprinted from *In Health,* © 1990; by Anthony Schmitz; reprinted from HEALTH, © 1993.

Inset 13.2 (cont'd)

Americans take their medicines in pills, solutions, shots, or drops. But never, ever by smoking. No other drug prescribed today is smoked. And there's no doubt that smoking causes lung cancer. Think about that before you swallow the quack medical claims from the marijuana lobbyists.

Plus, there's new evidence that the active ingredient in marijuana actually reduces your body's ability to fight disease. This is a serious concern for AIDS patients or for people on chemotherapy, whose bodies are already very susceptible to disease. Without reliable evidence showing that marijuana helps, it's irresponsible to advocate its use by serious ill.

William Ruzzamenti is the Drug Enforcement Administration's chief of public affairs and former head of the DEA's anti-marijuana office in California.

either acute or chronic use of marijuana and the individual may experience restlessness and insomnia. These users may find it difficult to fall asleep or dreaming may be delayed or interrupted. Higher doses of THC suppresses total REM sleep so that the individual does not feel rested or refreshed. Instead, slow-wave sleep increases quite substantially. One withdrawal symptom is a rebound increase in REM sleep.

Sexual and Reproduction Functions

Marijuana is thought to alter the hormone production abilities of the hypothalamus, lowering the level of gonadotropin releasing hormone. As a result, the secretion of luteinizing hormone, follicle stimulating hormone, and prolactin by the pituitary is suppressed (Smith & Ashe, 1984). Female hormones, including estrogen and progesterone, decrease as does the male hormone, testosterone, responsible for masculinizing features. Chronic administration in relatively large amounts has been found to decrease the size and weight of the testes in animals. There is strong evidence that sperm count is adversely affected by marijuana use and that reproductive abilities may be compromised, particularly among young male users who already have a low sperm count (Kolodny et al., 1975; Relman, 1982). Caution is particularly advised to this group because chronic marijuana use may influence growth factors related to hormone levels, possibly resulting

in the development of some feminine features (e.g., reduced facial and pubic hair, excessive breast tissue, higher voice, and so forth). The endocrine events that typify puberty are largely a function of a properly functioning hypothalamus and pituitary gland, and the presence of testosterone is instrumental in growth and other developmental phases of adolescence. As a consequence, depriving the body of adequate levels of activity in these operations may lead to delays in critical developmental processes.

A recent study found that the female reproductive system is also quite sensitive to the effects of marijuana (Mendelson et al., 1986). Smoking a single marijuana cigarette after ovulation decreased the plasma level of both follicle stimulating hormone (FSH) and luteinizing hormone, which is essential for maintaining the corpus luteum following fertilization of an egg. Without the corpus luteum, the fertilized egg cannot become implanted and a spontaneous miscarriage will occur. These effects appear to be reversible when marijuana use is discontinued.

High doses of marijuana smoked during pregnancy may further disrupt the development of a fetus (see Table 13.3). THC readily crosses the placental barrier to reach the fetus. Animal fetuses have shown malformations after marijuana was administered to the pregnant female. Human infants may be smaller after marijuana exposure in utero (Tennes et al., 1985), but it should be noted that sufficient data on humans have not been collected to support this finding. Other studies have reported an increased incidence of low birth weight, congenital abnormalities, pre-

Table 13.3   *Percentage of Selected Pregnancy Events. Delivery Characteristics, and Infant Outcomes within Categories of Marijuana Usage during Pregnancy*

Characteristics	Marijuana Usage			
	None	Occasional	Weekly	Daily
Pregnancy Events				
Unplanned pregnancies				
on contraception	14.8	21.4	20.5	17.5
no contraception	23.3	35.5	38.4	48.2
Bleeding in:				
1st trimester	9.5	9.9	8.7	7.3
2nd trimester	3.9	4.0	3.5	2.2
3rd trimester	4.8	4.3	6.1	7.3
Toxemia or eclampsia	3.5	4.4	4.8	3.6
Pre-admission for false labor	8.5	9.9	8.3	12.4
Premature labor	3.7	5.0	7.0	8.8
Delivery Characteristics				
Placenta abrupts	1.1	1.6	2.2	2.9
Premature rupture of membranes	4.3	5.8	7.9	2.9
Breech presentation	4.3	4.7	4.4	2.9
Placenta previa	0.6	0.2	0.4	0.0
Fetal distress	3.1	4.2	3.1	5.1
Infant Outcomes				
Major malformations	2.6	3.2	3.9	3.6
Minor malformations	6.2	7.8	5.2	5.1
Birthweight <2500 grams	7.6	9.8	13.5	11.7
Gestation <37 weeks	7.2	8.2	11.4	11.7
Neonatal jaundice	19.5	19.4	17.0	17.5
Stillbirth	0.6	0.6	1.3	1.5
Neonatal infection	1.0	1.0	2.2	2.9
Special care nursery	17.0	19.2	20.5	13.9
1 minute Apgar score less than 6	7.5	9.4	8.3	13.1
Respiratory problems	5.2	5.3	6.6	5.1

Source: Linn et al. 1983.

Note: Marijuana users were more likely than non-users to have has an unplanned pregnancy, premature labor, and abruptio placenta, and their children were more likely to have a more major malformations.

maturity, and neurological disturbances among babies born to mothers who used marijuana during pregnancy (Fried, 1985; Gibson et al., 1983; Hingston et al., 1984; Linn et al., 1983; Qazi et al., 1985). There is further evidence that heavy marijuana use during pregnancy affects the neurophysiological integrity of the infant (Lester & Dreher, 1989)(see Table 13.4). In order to determine whether these abnormalities are manifested as problems later in development, further research needs to be done. Although these studies attempted to control for the use of other drugs in the subjects, confounding effects of these influences are still possible. In either event, when marijuana is used during pregnancy, testosterone from the mother may become relatively inaccessible to the fetus. When the fetus is male, prenatal exposure to testosterone is critical for the development of the male anatomy, including sexual differentiation of the brain. As a consequence, maternal marijuana smoking may actually impair complete masculinization of a male fetus (Kolodny, 1975).

Table 13.4   *Major Malformations Among Newborns of Marijuana Users and Non-users*

Malformation (type of system)	Marijuana Usage			
	11,178 Non-Users		1,246 Users	
	Number of Malformations	Rate per 1000	Number of Malformations	Rate per 1000
Congenital heart disease	26	2.3	7	5.6
Hypospadias	47	4.2	7	5.6
Clubfoot	41	3.7	6	4.8
Upper alimentary tract	13	1.2	3	2.4
Respiratory tract	6	0.5	3	2.4
Genital	3	0.3	2	1.6
Face, neck and ear	15	1.3	2	1.6
Spina bifida	5	0.5	2	1.6
Hydrocephalus	6	0.5	2	1.6
All other malformations	132	11.7	8	6.7
Total major malformations	294	26.3	42	33.7

Source: Linn et al. 1983.

Cardiovascular System

The effects of marijuana on the cardiovascular system depend entirely on the dosages given. In low doses, heart rate and blood pressure rise, while high doses cause them to decline. These effects can be attributed to the influence of marijuana on the autonomic nervous system. In young healthy users, this may not pose a problem. However, in older users or in users with a history of cardiovascular or heart problems, marijuana may contribute to complications including chest pain (angina). In both groups, the accumulation of carbon monoxide in the lungs may lead to cardiovascular disturbances.

Immunity

Marijuana directly suppresses the activity of the immune system (Relman, 1982). The ability of THC to increase circulating adrenal hormones compromises our ability to fight infection. (One reason why individuals under a great deal of stress frequently suffer from chronic infections and immune system deficiencies is due to the consequent, excessive release of adrenal hormones.) Also, marijuana has been found to lower white blood cell count, thereby reducing infection-fighting activity on a cellular level. For these reasons, marijuana users have a higher incidence of infec-

tions and may be at increased risk for cancer and other diseases. Several other widely abused drugs, including alcohol, depressants, and amyl nitrite, also have immunosuppressant properties and may place individuals already at risk for contracting the AIDS virus in further jeopardy.

Lungs

A number of recent studies have shown marijuana to be carcinogenic in a fashion similar to tobacco (Cohen, 1981; Nicholi, 1983). In fact, the smoke produced by THC is approximately 50 percent more carcinogenic than that from tobacco. Lung capacity is reduced in chronic smokers and their airways have shown obstructions. Examination of individuals simply exposed to the marijuana smoke of others (passive smokers) have shown them to suffer from similar impairments in lung functioning. Because tobacco is inhaled by its users much more often than marijuana is, the risk does not appear to be as great. Nevertheless, THC is held in the lungs, without the use of a filter, for a much longer period of time than is tobacco smoke, so chronic marijuana use may pose a significant danger to the individual. When marijuana is smoked by a tobacco smoking individual, changes in cell structure thought to be a prelude to lung cancer are even more profound. Interestingly, the National Institute on Drug

Abuse has advised users to brew tea with marijuana, if an individual must use it, in order to avoid toxic and possibly cancer-producing fumes.

Additional reports indicate that marijuana smoke leads to the irritation and inflammation of bronchial airways. This effect may eventually result in increased sensitivity to environmental irritants and compromise the body's ability to clear the lungs of contaminants. As a consequence, asthma or emphysema may develop in susceptible users. The gases and materials in marijuana smoke are dense and particularly irritating when smoked frequently. Because marijuana smoke decreases the activity of infection-fighting cells in the lungs, called macrophages, the ability of the body to protect lung tissue from foreign materials is reduced, increasing susceptibility to infection. However, marijuana relaxes the smooth muscles of the lungs and, thus, may have some beneficial effects (discussed later).

Behavioral and Psychological Reactions

Memory

Marijuana has been associated with cognitive alterations, and acute intoxication appears to disrupt memory functions. Early observations of marijuana users noted the fragmentation of thought processes, disturbances of memory, and interruptions in the stream of thought (Ames, 1958). Speech patterns become rapid and disjointed, while mental images and ideas seem to flood the brain as if irrelevant information is not being filtered from relevant information. Consequently, working memory systems fill up with excessive and useless information and then so quickly dissolve that they fail to become fixed in memory stores. The ability to concentrate is notably compromised and, as a consequence, learning new information is severely impaired.

We see the results of this impairment when an individual high on marijuana tries to carry on a conversation. Frequently, the user will stumble, forget what he or she was about to say, and go on to a completely unrelated topic. Fortunately for the speaker, listeners are also frequently high and will not notice that the conversation is going nowhere. To the uninitiated observer, the discourse between users seems nonsensical and purposeless. To the users, the flood of ideas may be so great that a single thought becomes, in a sense, lost in the crowd.

These observations suggest that marijuana produces deficits in short-term memory that may, in fact, be relat-

ed to the disordered sense of time mentioned above. When time sense becomes distorted, new memories may be stored inappropriately and out of sequence. Inversely, because our perceptions of time are, in large part, a function of memory abilities, the passage of time is likely to be incorrectly estimated. Marijuana may also inhibit the transference of short-term memories into long-term storage and be more directly related to concentration difficulties. Equally disconcerting is the difficulty experienced in retrieving long-term memories. When it is necessary to make a decision requiring information about both immediate circumstances and prior experiences, the user may forget what to do in a given situation. For example, a marijuana intoxicated driver may not correctly respond to an oncoming car because he or she is not able to adequately assess the immediate conditions and call up memories that reflect what the consequences might be and how to avoid a potential calamity.

Researchers believe that memory processes become dysfunctional through marijuana's impairment of neural functioning within the limbic system, particularly within the hippocampus, that disable it from performing proper memory functions. There is further evidence that the mechanisms behind such impairment relate to marijuana's anticholinergic effects in the hippocampus (see Drew & Miller, 1974). You should remember from Chapter 3 that acetylcholine is a neurotransmitter involved in learning and memory; interference with the activity of this chemical in certain brain regions, for example by anticholinergic drugs, frequently results in learning and memory deficits.

Amotivational Syndrome

It is difficult to evaluate to what extent performance becomes impaired as any measurable deficits may be partially due to the lack of motivation, interest, attention, and ability to concentrate noted among marijuana users (Solomons & Neppe, 1989). This phenomenon, called amotivational syndrome, contributes to intellectual and developmental delays that are commonly reported. Observations of young marijuana smokers show consistent changes in their lifestyles and behavior. Users commonly become apathetic and lose their motivation to perform competently and achieve long-range goals. They have difficulty concentrating, learning new skills, coping with stressors and daily life events, and they become easily frustrated and develop certain deficits in verbal and writing abilities. Their behavior may be immature and withdrawn, demonstrating little interest in social relationships and activities that do not revolve around their drug use. Nevertheless, due to shortcomings in this research, it is difficult to determine how common amotivational syndrome is among marijuana users, as many of them do not show these tendencies. Also, we are unable to say with any certainty whether these individuals were amotivated initially. If this was the case, their drug use may simply be a result of a preexisting personality pattern rather than a precipitant of amotivational syndrome.

No matter what the primary cause is, when marijuana is used during the formative years of childhood and adolescence, it may substantially interfere with the development of coping skills, responsibility, and social relationships. Because learning and memory functions appear to become impaired, particularly when marijuana is used chronically, teenage use becomes a significant source of concern. In some teenagers, marijuana may serve as an escape from difficult circumstances or a problematic lifestyle. Such users may never learn how to manage their problems and make appropriate decisions. Thus, many clinicians believe that the growth of these youth becomes somewhat stagnated around the time that they began to use marijuana on a steady basis, and they tend not to grow substantially in their social and intellectual development beyond that point.

A recent investigation reported similar influences of daily marijuana use on adult users (Hendin et al., 1987). The daily smokers studied believed that marijuana helped them to function better and improved their self-awareness and relationships with others. In reality, however, more in-depth examination of these adults revealed that marijuana served instead as a buffer, allowing users to simply tolerate their problems rather than take the necessary steps to change or improve their situations. The users further reported that marijuana enhanced understanding of themselves. Conclusions from the research indicated that, in contrast, the drug enabled users to remain detached and avoid conflicts that may have been resolvable.

Psychiatric Illness

There is no evidence that marijuana use can precipitate a mental disturbance or a psychotic reaction. Only when marijuana is used in very large quantities over a long period of time do we sometimes see psychosis related to toxic levels of THC. In such cases, the user may lose consciousness or become delirious and disoriented. Also possible is disturbed and sometimes aggressive behavior or withdrawal and confusion. Once the drug effects wear off, psychotic symptoms will subside. In the same vein, the prevalence of psychosis or other forms of insanity is no greater among marijuana users than in the general population. Rather, individuals with a preexisting psychiatric illness may have an unusually strong or dysfunctional response to marijuana use in that symptoms of their disorder may be triggered or worsen. Schizophrenia, paranoia, delusional thinking, visual and auditory hallucinations, manic, schizo-affective breakdown, and acute brain syndrome are exacerbated by marijuana and sometimes lead to hospitalization (Tunving, 1985). Although the possibility of an otherwise normal person smoking a single joint and becoming mentally deranged is unheard of, it is very common for someone with a history of psychiatric illness to become psychotic after smoking marijuana. Furthermore, marijuana interferes with the effects of antipsychotic medications so that the patient may lose ground in the course of treatment.

Anxiety and Panic Attacks

In many users, marijuana is known to produce pleasurable states and will reduce anxiety in those who are anxious. Nevertheless, high doses of THC may create anxiety in certain users, ranging from mild restlessness to an actual panic attack. Beginners in particular may experience panic. As they undergo various perceptual changes, they may begin to believe they are dying or losing their senses. Anxiety in these individuals is frequently an exaggerated response to the hallucinations and distortions of reality that are experienced. Panic attacks are characterized physiologically by the release of high levels of adrenal hormones, simulating a massive stress response by the body. The behavioral and emotional results of this physiological reaction are feelings of impending doom, fear of losing control, paranoia, derealization, depersonalization, beliefs that reality will not return to normal, and feelings that death may be imminent. The anxiety may persist for from several hours to a few days (Patterson, 1974).

Users report that the setting and those around them determine, to a great extent, whether anxiety or panic will ensue. If they are comfortable in their environment and familiar with the surroundings, anxiety is much less likely to occur. Similarly, if the user is with friends, he or she will feel more relaxed initially and if anxiety begins to surface, the user can fairly easily be talked down by those he or she knows. The user must be reassured that nothing horrible is about to happen and that all things will return to normal when the drug wears off. Being surrounded by strangers in an unfamiliar or unfriendly environment is nearly always the recipe for a bad trip, if the user is so inclined.

Personality traits also appear to predict with some degree of accuracy whether a user will suffer these effects. Individuals with a proneness to panic attacks are unusually sensitive to the anxiety-producing effects of marijuana (Szuster et al., 1988). Because of this reaction, individuals with panic disorder or agoraphobia (fear of crowds) are likely to spontaneously stop using marijuana to avoid increasing their anxiety. In fact, ongoing marijuana use is extremely uncommon in populations with panic or anxiety disorders. On the other hand, depressed individuals have reported a calming effect from marijuana use. In either case, continued use of marijuana throughout adulthood has been associated with a diminution of the more positive effects, such as relaxation, self-confidence, and the perception of heightened mental powers, as well as a greater incidence of anxiety reactions (Millman & Sbriglio, 1986).

Dysphoria

Adverse reactions of discomfort, anxiety and catatonic states with disorientation, paranoid delusions, and hallucinations occur in some users of marijuana. Mood may change rapidly and the afflicted user may become manic or experience concentration difficulties and possible confusion. A few users with dysphoric reactions may even become aggressive or destructive. The severity of the symptoms depends on the concentrations of THC used, and the symptoms generally dissipate after a few hours.

Flashbacks

Flashbacks, most often associated with abuse of hallucinogenic drugs (especially LSD), are the sudden experience of the same sensations that occur with the use of a drug after a drug-free period of weeks or months. Heavy marijuana use is more likely to produce flashbacks than the casual use pattern of most regular users. Therefore, flashbacks from marijuana are rarely reported in this country. In fact, there are some anecdotal reports that the occurrence of flashbacks is more likely related to the use of hashish in those who have experimented with LSD or mescaline.

Medical Benefits

Marijuana is reported to have several medical benefits (Grinspoon & Bakalar, 1987; Roffman, 1982). Because THC acts as an antinausea or antiemetic agent, it has been found useful in the treatment of nausea in chemotherapy patients (Roffman, 1982). Nabilone, a synthetic cannabinoid, is frequently given to chemotherapy patients. It also stimulates appetite so cancer sufferers may not deteriorate from weight loss and malnutrition quite so severely. The use of marijuana by cancer patients has been a controversial subject for many years as the patients and their families have advocated the legalization of marijuana for medical purposes. The development of nabilone has somewhat quieted these discussions. However, there is some evidence that smoking marijuana may produce more effective results.

Studies of marijuana on lung capacity among asthmatic subjects indicate that the drug may have a bronchodilator effect; it may open up the lung's passages so that breathing becomes unobstructed in individuals with a history of asthma. Continued smoking, however, may again decrease lung capacity and exacerbate symptoms of asthma. Thus, marijuana may benefit asthmatics initially and then advance the symptoms of asthma in the long run. These studies are not conclusive, however, and need to be replicated.

Marijuana tends to lower intraocular (in the fluid within the eyeball) pressure, a finding with implications for those suffering from glaucoma (Roffman, 1982), an eye disease typified by increased intraocular pressure that may eventually lead to blindness. In 1975, three years after a report was issued showing that marijuana use was effective in reducing fluid pressure, a man struck with glaucoma was arrested for growing marijuana plants on his back porch to treat his disease (National Drug Reporter, 1977). He argued that it was necessary to smoke five marijuana cigarettes daily to prevent the onset of blindness, inevitable without treatment. Because of marijuana's effectiveness in this case, not only were the charges eventually dropped, but with his physician's support, the U.S. government was also mandated to legitimately supply him with these marijuana cigarettes. Marijuana's effects on glaucoma are relatively long standing and are associated with minimal to no side effects; other medications for glaucoma have rather severe side effects.

Other beneficial effects of THC include some antibiotic properties, mild tumor-reduction activity, anticonvulsant properties, the ability to decrease spasticity, analgesia, and control of certain nervous system disorders, such as multiple sclerosis. Because of these considerations, members of the National Organization for Reform of Marijuana Laws (NORML) have proposed that marijuana be decriminalized, if not legalized. If legalization were achieved, marijuana use and trade could then be more strictly regulated and supervised, increasing the quality of the drug and monitoring the dosages given for medical purposes. Since Schedule I drugs are considered to have

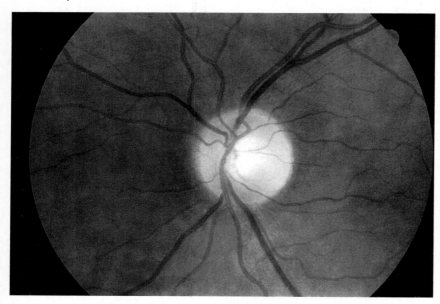

An eye with glaucoma.

the highest abuse potential and possess no medical value, some physicians and politicians have suggested rescheduling marijuana as a Schedule II drug. It may then be used more readily in appropriate cases. Some researchers and clinicians feel that other modern drugs available are just as effective, if not more so, for treating most of these conditions (Nahas, 1984). However, these alternatives often require a hospital stay while the drug is being administered, are extremely expensive, costing as much as six hundred dollars a day, and are only as effective as marijuana for 80 percent of the patients. Use of government-rolled marijuana cigarettes is cheaper, does not require a hospital stay, and has a higher response rate than the alternatives.

Although much attention has been given to marijuana as a medical treatment, it is extremely difficult to acquire this drug legally for medical purposes. Many doctors who recommend marijuana as a treatment for a medical condition, privately advise their patients to buy it on the streets (Trebach, 1987). Only about fourteen people in the United States have legally received government-rolled marijuana cigarettes to treat a medical condition. Permission to receive the drug requires a lengthy process of gaining approval from the Food and Drug Administration (FDA), the National Institute on Drug Abuse (NIDA), and the Drug Enforcement Administration (DEA). The DEA is the agency least likely to grant approval. Although trained in law enforcement rather than medical pharmacology, the official view of the DEA is that marijuana is a dangerous drug with no therapeutic benefit. During his tenure, President Bush further discouraged government agencies to approve marijuana use for medical purposes, despite its documented benefits for certain ailments.

Vulnerability to Abuse Marijuana

Regular marijuana users range tremendously, from the mainstream adolescent or professional to individuals with severe psychopathology. In many users, especially the young, marijuana use begins as a social rite of passage. They may be striving for popularity and acceptance or they may simply be experimenting with altered states of consciousness as part of their youthful curiosity. Others, however, may begin marijuana use in an effort to cope with anxiety, frustrations, feelings of failure or inadequacy, expectations and demands in school or home, or life's daily stressors. In such cases, marijuana may alter their perception of reality sufficiently to allow them a mental escape and downplay the significance of their problems. It follows that a greater number and severity of personal problems, an increased sensitivity to situations, or a lower self-esteem would all be associated with an increased likelihood of drug use generally and perhaps marijuana use specifically. These conditions are strongly correlated with regular use of marijuana, particularly among teenagers.

Many individuals begin using marijuana as teenagers or young adults because of the good feelings it produces and its apparent lack of adverse effects or discomfort. With increasing age, however, chronic smokers frequently report the drug causes them feelings of anxiety, paranoia, or dysphoria. They may decrease their use of marijuana and/or find a substitute for the drug by increasing their use of alcohol or cocaine. We are not able to predict, at this time, who will experience untoward effects and who will continue to enjoy the pleasurable effects of marijuana. Those who learn to dislike the sense of passivity, powerlessness, or lethargy that marijuana induces may become dissatisfied with the drug or actually experience anxiety. On the other hand, individuals who are more gregarious or who seek out social and intellectual stimulation may eventually find marijuana's high to be somewhat unattractive as they crave more of a challenge and less of a solitary existence. It is also possible that the pharmacologic properties of marijuana change as a function of age and that repeated exposure to THC actually alters neurotransmitter activity to influence drug effects. Finally, certain psychological traits may be predictive of marijuana's ability to eventually induce pleasure or discomfort in the chronic user, determining whether the individual will discontinue use or not. The social, psychological, and biological mechanisms to predict vulnerability to abuse marijuana in the aging user remain unidentified.

There is a general consensus among marijuana researchers that the factors predisposing individuals to chronic marijuana use are complex and diverse (see Murray, 1986). Relationships with parents, involvement with drug-using peers, availability of marijuana, family patterns, cultural influences, personality types, and the presence of behavioral or psychiatric disturbances all dynamically interact in as yet unknown ways to eventually contribute to the abuse of marijuana.

An increased incidence of personality disorders has been found among chronic marijuana users, particularly antisocial disorders and criminal records (Stafanis et al., 1976; Weller & Halikas, 1985). Such findings may partially explain high drop-out rates and lower levels of social achievement within this group of users. As with all other drug users, it is difficult to discern whether the psychopathology preceded the marijuana use or whether the marijuana use triggered the psychopathology. It is possible that certain pre-existing personality factors are more responsible for the relatively high failure rate among chronic marijuana users than an amotivational syndrome produced by the drug.

Marijuana has been a staple at parties among adolescents and young adults for decades.

Compulsive or pathological use of marijuana is more frequently related to a pre-existing psychiatric or personality disorder. In particular, those with affective disorders such as depression are found to be quite prevalent among chronic marijuana smokers. There are suggestions that the drug may act as self-medication for symptoms of a disorder, either by reducing the symptoms or enabling the user to rationalize abnormal feelings or behaviors by attributing them to the drug effects (Millman & Sbriglio, 1986). As a consequence, an individual with debilitating depression may actually become more competent and perform at a higher level with more confidence when marijuana intoxicated.

Treatment of Chronic Marijuana Use

In the event of an acute toxic reaction to marijuana, including panic, paranoia, or psychosis, something as simple as reassurance that the episode will pass and support will help (Millman & Sbriglio, 1986) because of a marijuana user's increased suggestibility. If the symptoms are more severe, anxiolytic medications such as benzodiazepines are recommended. In those rare cases where a psychotic syndrome persists, it may be necessary to hospitalize the user and/or administer a tranquilizer.

It is essential that chronic marijuana users receive a comprehensive evaluation for the existence of a major psychiatric or personality disorder. Unless an underlying disorder is addressed, the sufferer will experience great difficulty in remaining abstinent and finding more appropriate coping styles. Treatment, in this vein, must be individualized and specific to the symptoms and problems that characterize the user.

▍ Summary

Marijuana has been around for centuries and no one expects its use to disappear in the near future. People from all walks of life, with variable backgrounds, motivations, and lifestyles, use marijuana. Aside from marijuana's tremendous popularity during the 1960s, when many groups experimented with it, people tend not to begin using the drug once they have reached adulthood. Also, even those who used it extensively as adolescents or in their twenties tend to discontinue its use in later years. Perhaps this trend is due to changes in physiology and drug effects as one ages. Or perhaps the drop out rate for marijuana use is due to the establishment of other priorities, a desire for a more conventional lifestyle, or simply maturation. In any event, there is some speculation that those who continue to use marijuana late into their adulthood may suffer from some underlying psychological disturbance, such as depression, which reinforces the drug-taking behavior. It is also possible, of course, that some users simply like to get high every so often as a recreational outlet.

Marijuana continues to be a staple in the drug-taking diet of more hard-core users. As the majority of serious drug abusers generally abuse multiple substances, marijuana remains part of that lifestyle. No matter what the drug of choice may be, alcohol, heroin, or cocaine, marijuana seems to play the role of sidekick—enhancing, modulating, or prolonging the effects of other drugs. And for some users, marijuana is simply the default drug, used when preferred drugs are not available.

Relative to other drugs of abuse, marijuana is certainly one of the more benign. It is not addictive in a conventional sense and does not produce any fatal consequences. Nevertheless, the prevalent belief that marijuana is a safe drug has mollified many individuals into thinking that marijuana use is perfectly safe. As noted throughout this chapter, this is not the case. Marijuana has potential adverse side effects that are most disconcerting when used by the young. If used during the phase of life when coping skills are developing and when sexual and reproductive maturity is approached, marijuana can thwart these processes. Adolescents tend to use this drug to escape from harsh realities in their lives or to avoid having to make important decisions and own up to them. The consequences can be, for some chronic users, long term and potentially devastating.

On the other hand, marijuana has a few legitimate medical uses. Various medications have been substituted in efforts to substitute legal drugs for marijuana in the treatment of medical problems, however marijuana remains the most effective drug. Many physicians state that it would be their drug of choice in the treatment of certain medical conditions if it were legal. Politicians are considering its decriminalization for medical purposes and, if and when the hysteria about the drug war subsides, marijuana may become a legal course of medical action.

CHAPTER 14

Anabolic Steroids

Objectives

1. To describe anabolic steroids and their users.
2. To discuss why people use and abuse steroids.
3. To present the biological, psychological, and behavioral effects of steroids.
4. To discuss the potential dangers of steroid abuse.
5. To describe how steroid use may be detected.
6. To assess the social and legal impact of steroid abuse.

Anabolic-androgenic steroids are synthetic derivatives of testosterone, a male sex hormone in the family of androgens. Although the female's adrenal gland also produces testosterone, the male's testes produce much larger amounts, which contribute to the development of masculine features. Adrenal androgens are responsible for the development of libido, or sex drive, and the growth of pubertal hair in females. Androgens produced by the male testes have masculinizing effects, including a male pattern brain (the male brain matures somewhat differently from a female as a result of sex hormone exposure), deepening of the voice, large muscle mass, facial hair, increased aggressiveness, and heightened strength.

Approximately seven weeks into a pregnancy, the Y chromosome, present in those who are genetically male, triggers the production of testosterone. Features that differentiate a male from a female then begin to develop. When a male is exposed to normal amounts of testosterone in utero and again during puberty, these features become permanent. If a female fetus is, for some reason, exposed to unusually high amounts of this hormone, the fetus will develop male physical features affecting both the body and brain. The resulting female is more likely to display typical rough and tumble play, be more aggressive and exploratory, and exhibit masculine physical features, rather than a more feminine body type. Sometimes, however, a male or female chooses to take unusually large amounts of synthetic testosterone to either enhance athletic performance or to acquire a more muscular physical appearance. The result may be dramatic and, at times, dangerous (Brower, Eliopulos, et al., 1990).

Prevalence of Use

The inclusion of steroids in the University of Michigan's annual Monitoring the Future Study, did not occur until 1989. Those twelfth graders from the class of 1994 who participated in the survey reported that 2.4 percent used steroids at some point during their lifetime. This figure shows a reduction from 1989 when 3.0 percent reported using steroids, but shows a slight increase from the class of 1993 where only 2.0 percent reported using steroids. Additional findings from the class of 1994 indicate that 1.3 percent reported using steroids during the previous year, 0.9 percent reported using steroids during the past 30 days, and 0.4 reported using steroids on a daily basis. In 1992, of those aged 19-32, 0.3 percent reported using steroids during the past year and 0.1 percent during the past thirty days (Johnston, O'Malley & Bachman, 1993).

There appear to be three categories of people who abuse anabolic steroids. The first group includes athletes who are looking for an extra edge in a competitive sport. The second group is composed of high school kids and those who work out noncompetitively in gyms who hope to transform their bodies and become more "masculine." The third group includes those who want to increase their size and strength to better perform in their daily activities, such as police, bouncers, or gang members. Bodybuilders comprise a major group of steroid users and can be included in each of these three categories; they sometimes engage in competitive bodybuilding, there are some high school youths who attempt to build their bodies noncompetitively, and bodybuilders universally intend to increase their size and strength to perform "better" on a daily basis.

Because testosterone administration builds tissue, increases protein synthesis, and enhances calcium absorption into the bones, many athletes take large amounts of anabolic steroids to increase their muscle mass, energy,

THE FAR SIDE   By GARY LARSON

"Well, Mr. Rosenburg, your lab results look pretty good – although I might suggest your testosterone level is a tad high."

and strength. There is some controversy, however, about the effectiveness of steroids to do so. The 1988 *Physician's Desk Reference,* the standard guide to prescription medicines, includes the warning: *Anabolic Steroids Do Not Enhance Athletic Ability.* Controlled research among male athletes given steroids has generally produced unclear evidence of enhanced strength or performance. Instead, some clinicians and researchers who oppose steroid use insist that these drugs bloat the muscles, causing them to look bigger and weigh more, but do not contribute to increased physical strength. Furthermore, there is evidence of a placebo effect. Those taking steroids believe that their performance and energy will be boosted, thereby giving them a psychological, rather than a physical, edge. These studies and anecdotal reports have been hampered by the fact that it is difficult to locate anabolic steroid users who are willing to confess to such use. The steroid users examined by researchers also tend to be those using much smaller doses than those who are seriously abusing steroids to gain an athletic advantage.

Notwithstanding, bodybuilders who use steroids for several weeks do gain several pounds of lean muscle while bodybuilders who do not use them stay constant in their muscle mass. For this reason, doctors have lost some credibility among athletes interested in "bulking up." Locker room lore spreads the news quickly, even among high school youth, that steroid use boosts athletic performance and a masculine appearance. Thus, steroids have become quite popular in many circles (Buckley et al., 1988). Some athletes who are serious about their steroid use and its perceived benefits engage in stacking: One or more steroids are taken at the same time, totalling ten or more times the recommended therapeutic dose. Steroids may be taken orally or by intramuscular injection. When athletes engage in stacking, they use both methods, which can lead to needle sharing among users.

Rumors of steroid use in athletics first began during the 1936 Olympics. Since then, illicit use of steroids has spread to a multitude of sports, from weight-lifting to horse racing. Steroid use in officially supervised competitive sports has since been banned, and extensive urine tesing for steroids has been regularly instituted since 1976 by Olympic officials. Nevertheless, many athletes, both in professional and amateur competitions, continue to use these drugs to gain a competitive edge. A 1988 survey of National Football League players found that 6 percent of

Body builders have been known to use steroids to bulk up quickly.

players tested positive for steroid use, while another survey the same year showed that 3 percent of college athletes had used the drugs. Ben Johnson, a 1988 Olympic Gold Medal recipient, can certainly attest to both the benefits and the detriments of using anabolic steroids. Although he won the 100-meter run in the Olympics, he was subsequently disqualified when a urine screen provided evidence of steroid use.

Elite athletes are not, by any means, the only ones who turn to steroids to build better bodies and improve performance. An estimated 300,000 Americans who use the drugs include men, women, and teenagers who engage in recreational sports, play on neighborhood teams, or work out at local health spas. Women seem to be an ever-increasing addition to steroid using groups. Recent reports find that steroid use has spread from Olympic, professional, and college levels to the high schools, junior high schools, and even grade schools. These trends indicate that there are a lot of people who believe the benefits outweigh the risks.

There are several reasons the medical profession and the public have become concerned about steroid abuse. First, the advantage it gives in athletic events is obviously unfair and unethical. This situation does not bode well for more honest participants. Many fans, see such artificial means of boosting performance as cheating. Second, it is possible that steroid users and their fans may begin to view drug use in general more favorably. If steroids can enhance performance, then why not use cocaine to enhance mood or hallucinogens to expand the mind? Third, there are numerous documented adverse medical consequences to taking large doses of steroids. Many youth report that they are not terribly concerned about these long-term consequences because the short-term benefits are so rewarding, most adverse effects are reversable, and competition is fierce. Furthermore, many continue to use steroids because they are either misinformed about the risks or they believe the benefits outweigh the risks. Fourth, numerous reports indicate that steroid use can lead to excessive aggressiveness and psychotic violence. It is one thing to feel a burst of energy and a loss of fatigue; it is another to lose inhibitions and self-control. Finally, the large doses of steroids required to achieve desired effects can only be obtained through illegal means (Wilson, 1988). In many cases, the prescribing physician is ultimately responsible.

Tolerance and Dependence

Although there is some preliminary evidence that anabolic-androgenic steroid use is addicting (Moore, 1988; Taylor & Black, 1987), we are unaware of any systematic studies of steroid dependence. Psychological or physical dependence may explain why some users report they are unable to stop using them. Because this research question has important implications for the treatment and prevention of steroid abuse, Brower and his coworkers (1990) conducted a preliminary study to assess steroids' addictive potential. Most of their subjects met the criteria for drug dependence. Furthermore, all subjects reported withdrawal symptoms and features of psychological dependence. Even though these drugs produced adverse reactions, including nervousness, irritability, depression, and a host of other psychiatric and physical symptoms, the subjects continued their use.

The following commonly accepted criteria for psychoactive substance use disorder has been applied to the use of anabolic steroid drugs (Kashkin & Kleber, 1989) as evidence that dependence to these drugs does, in fact, exist: "(1) the hormones are used over longer periods than desired; (2) attempts are made to stop use without success; (3) substantial time is spent obtaining, using, or recovering from the hormones; (4) use continues despite knowledge of significant psychological problems caused by the hormones; (5) characteristic withdrawal symptoms occur; and (6) the hormones are often taken to relieve these withdrawal syndromes". Observations that steroids possess mood-altering properties, resembling that of other psychoactive drugs of abuse, further supports suggestions that steroids contain abuse potential. Kashkin and Kleber suggest that steroid addiction may, in part, be, attributable to an increase in endogenous opiates (e.g., endorphins), causing euphoria, and the discomfort associated with high levels of autonomic nervous system activity when withdrawing from steroids. If this theory is correct, steroid-using individuals would crave the good feelings associated with drug use. They would also continue to use the drug in order to avoid the psychological pain associated with termination of use. Moreover, discontinuing the drugs would result in eventual loss of muscle mass and energy, furthering the perceived need to continue use.

Medical Complications

Recent studies of bodybuilders revealed higher blood pressure, more unfavorable blood-fat ratios, and higher cholesterol levels for steroid users than for nonusers. These effects may contribute to atherosclerosis and other types of heart disease.

Other adverse consequences of steroid use include:

1. *enlargement of the prostate gland, which is uncommon in men age 50; and increased likelihood of prostatic cancer*

2. *liver cancer and other liver malfunctions, such as peliosis hepatitis (the formation of bloody cysts in the liver) and juandice*

3. *inhibition of natural testosterone production in men; shrinking or atrophy of the testicles accompanied by a low sperm count, which can lead to infertility and diminished sex drive; abnormal breast development (gynecomastia)*

Steroid use by female athletes may cause deepening of the voice, the development of facial hair, increased aggressiveness, enlargement of the clitoris, decreased breast size, and menstrual irregularities. Male pattern baldness, attributable in men to their own naturally produced testosterone, may develop in female users. If the woman athlete becomes pregnant while taking steroids, the steroids are likely to have a masculinizing effect on a female fetus, which may result in birth and behovioral abnormalities.

In addition to the hazards that threaten steroid users of any age, steroids can prematurely halt bone growth by closing the growth plates of the long bones in teenagers before they reach full height. Acne, often a teen problem, is worsened by steroid use. As anabolic steroids are synthetic hormones, they may interfere with normal male hormone production, upsetting proper hormonal balance with possible long-term effects on fertility or sexual functioning.

Psychological Effects

Several studies describe the psychological effects associated with anabolic steroid use (see Pope and Katz, 1988), including irritability, euphoria, racing thoughts, confusion, and difficulty sleeping. Other studies, however, report that more serious psychiatric syndromes may develop as a result of steroid use. Clinical studies have identified organic mood disorders, psychoses, aggression, depression, halluci-

nations, hyperactivity, paranoia, psychomotor retardation, chronic anxiety, and suicidal tendencies as symptoms experienced by long-term steroid users (Brower, Blow, Eliopulous, et al., 1989; Brower, Blow, Beresford, et al.,1989; Pope & Katz, 1988; Tennant et al., 1988). However, these psychiatric symptoms were not displayed when subjects were not using steroids. These studies provide fairly clear evidence that the drugs were responsible for the abnormal behavior. It is important to note that the subjects were taking 10 to 100 times the dose used for therapeutic purposes. Such a high dosage is common among steroid abusers, particularly those who stack as many as five or six different steroid preparations. Fortunately, these psychological and psychiatric conditions are often reversed after the drugs are discontinued.

Of particular concern is a type of violence that sometimes accompanies steroid use known as roid rage. Otherwise mild-mannered steroid users have been known to punch holes through closet doors, crash cars for the fun of it, and beat their girlfriends. Violent tendencies in a bodybuilder who can bench press the equivalent of two grown men can be terrifying. Some steroid users report hearing nonexistent voices or the believing they are being robbed blind by friends (Pope & Katz, 1988). Such paranoid delusions can certainly provoke violent episodes in individuals who are already manic or agitated from steroid use and who have histories of involvement in aggressive and competitive sports. Sometimes the violence is self-directed. Bodybuilders have reported feeling invincible and impervious to pain. They convince themselves that they can jump from buildings, drive into trees, or cut themselves without consequence. None of the bodybuilders reported such behavior before taking steroids, and many were shocked by their bizarre actions once they were weaned from the drugs.

Conacher and Workman (1989) report some isolated cases of crimes of aggression. These researchers describe a thirty-two-year-old man who murdered his common-law wife three months after he began using steroids. The user had no previous psychiatric or criminal history. This increase in aggressiveness is consistent with the the fact that steroids are derived from testosterone, long associated with male aggression.

Detection

The metabolites of steroid drugs are detected in the urine as a measure of drug use. Detection times depend upon the specific drug used, the dosage used, and the duration of use. A drug used only once will be detectable for a much shorter time than a drug used over a longer period of time. Generally, the single use of a drug will only be measurable for a few days, while chronic use will result in a positive urine test for a few weeks after discontinuation. Some steroids, for example, nandrolone (Deca-Durabol), can be detected in the urine for about two of months after chronic use.

Another consideration concerning steroid detection is the type of urine test used. The radioimmunoassay (RIA) technique is less sensitive, and the drug will be detectable for a shorter period of time. On the other hand, gas chromotographic-mass spectrometric (GC-MS) detection of anabolic steroids is more sensitive and highly recommended, as it will enable the technician to determine the presence of a steroid drug long after drug use has been terminated. Even with GC-MS, however, after steroids have been discontinued for a few months, the urine will be clear of the drugs. A police officer was temporarily discharged and placed in treatment after testing positive for steroids. Six months after the officer claimed he had stopped using steroids his urine still tested positive. Obviously, this officer was still using steroids, as even GC-MS cannot detect the presence of steroids this long after cessation. The officer was permanently discharged from duty.

Personal, Societal, and Legal Concerns

Recreational use of anabolic steroids has been widely overlooked in political, legal, and medical circles as another form of drug abuse. Perhaps this form of drug use deserves more attention for two reasons: this form of drug use is potentially more harmful to the body than most other popular recreational drugs, and a large underground subculture has emerged revolving around the use of steroids (Fuller & LaFountain, 1987). Approximately 1 million Americans are spending $100 million on black-market anabolic steroids. These data include an estimated 250,000 high school seniors (Kashkin & Kleber, 1989). The current mentality that an athlete should "win at all costs" obviously plays a role on a societal level, and efforts to prevent such drug use should, to some extent, attempt to temper this way of thinking. Moreover, the use of steroids for cosmetic purposes is increasing, focusing our attention on societal pressures to be physically attractive, sometimes to the detriment of our health. High school students are, in

increasing numbers, using steroids to increase their bulk and develop masculine traits more rapidly than they would normally. The occurrence of steroid use among adolescents is of particular concern given their physical and emotional immaturity. Exposure to steroids during stages of puberty may actually interfere with the proper development of sexual and reproductive equipment.

Steroids are legal drugs that have been used for more than fifty years to treat a number of medical ailments, from reproductive problems to severe burns. But taking these drugs to build muscles or enhance athletic performance is an illicit use of the medication. Experts estimate that about 10 to 15 percent of those who use steroids in this manner obtain them from health professionals. The remaining users get them from the black market.

The black market for anabolic steroids has developed to meet the growing demand. Counterfeit black-market steroids are manufactured in underground laboratories and/or imported from foreign countries. They are often produced under unsanitary conditions, exhibit false labels, and contain unknown and possibly hazardous ingredients. Though several U.S. government agencies are coordinating enforcement activity to stop this steroid black market, its estimated value approximates $100 million in illegal sales a year.

Given that performance-enhancing drugs are prohibited by all sport-sanctioning bodies and that athletes obtain them illicitly, many have developed rationales to justify their use. First, athletes attest they cause harm to no one. They believe their drug use is a victimless crime and should not concern anyone. In fact, many athletes argue that steroid use is mandatory if they wish to compete seriously on a professional and national basis. There appears to be a widespread belief among these athletes that their competitors use steroids and that they would be at a disadvantage if they did not.

Steroid users tend to deny that the drugs do any physical damage. The potential health problems are downplayed and, in fact, many users are not even aware that the repercussions could be serious. Moreover, the psychological and emotional changes that result are frequently considered trivial and noninjurious. It is no wonder these attitudes prevail, as their sources of information are predominantly muscle magazines and experienced steroid-taking peers who work out at local gyms.

Finally, these athletes commonly refer to "higher loyalties" and a "code of commitment" to their chosen sport. In other words, many athletes dismiss the illegalities and health risks involved with steroid use as unimportant relative to the higher goals of demonstrating their dedication to and succeeding in their sports. Steroid use is considered a sacrifice that must be made. All in all, steroid-using athletes indicate that this form of drug abuse is widespread. Even among very young athletes (seventeen to twenty-one years old), massive doses are being taken quite casually (see Fuller & LaFountain, 1987 for review).

A link has been found between the use of steroids and other high-risk behaviors, including smoking cigarettes and taking other legal and illicit drugs (Yesalis et al., 1984). Men who reported taking steroids were two to three times more likely to smoke or drink alcohol than males who did not take steroids. Among younger users, the link was even stronger. Youth between twelve and seventeen who took steroids were three to four times more likely to smoke cigarettes and drink alcohol. Whether steroid use leads to taking other illicit drugs or vice versa is not yet known, but investigators believe that these users are also risk takers in other areas of their lives. The side effect of aggressive and sometimes violent behavior, such as fighting or using physical force, is more likely to be tolerated by those who show an existing predisposition toward these and other dangerous behaviors. About 83 percent of younger users, between twelve and seventeen, were prone to become aggressive, while only 38 percent of nonusers reported aggressive acts. Perhaps these findings are evidence for a vulnerability to abuse steroids, a highly dangerous and unpredictable drug, among risk takers.

Is it ethical for physicians to monitor athletes on steroids? Even though doctors widely recognize the serious irreversible effects from steroid abuse, they disagree on how to treat patients who choose to take them. Those who believe it is ethical to monitor their patients argue that physicians confronted by an athlete who uses steroids has two choices: to care for the patient or to refuse care. Taking care of the person includes checking for damage from drug use and providing treatment advice. A physician who decides not to monitor steroid use is, in actuality, deciding not to care for the paient, who may then receive less conscientious care or none at all. This argument revolves around the fact that athletes and others will not stop using the drugs, even if doctors refuse to treat them. Users may feel they are invulnerable. Some physicians argue that they do not condone smoking cigarettes but certainly will take care of smokers if they request medical assistance. Physicians also routinely care for alcoholics, prostitutes, and other drug users in spite of their disapproval of those lifestyles and personal decisions.

Those who do not believe physicians should monitor athletes on steroids contend that too many of them try to take advantage of the system and physicians to gain a competitive edge. These doctors do not want to aid or abet anyone's steroid use. They may make every effort to intervene and help the athlete discontinue use, but they believe providing routine care and monitoring the steroid effects is synonomous with encouraging its use. A further reason for refusing care for steroid use is that some athletes have the knowledge to use official drug-testing regulations during athletic events to manipulate their doses. They are able to figure out exactly how much they can use and when they need to stop so the steroids cannot be detected in their system. These savy users may fall through the cracks, not recognized for the chronicity or severity of their problem. In essence, those who oppose monitoring are, instead, in favor of intervention and rehabilitation for these users.

Treatment

There are no routine treatments for anabolic steroid users. They rarely seek treatment voluntarily and frequently do not receive mandatory treatment when their drug use is detected. Instead professional athletes receive punitive sanctions or are ostracized. Nevertheless, Kashkin and Kleber (1989) propose that a variety of antiandrogens, antiestrogens, or aromatase inhibitors may be useful as treatment strategies to block the psychoactive effects of anabolic steroids. Antidepressants may be used to treat the discomfort of withdrawal and the associated drug craving users experience.

A combination of pharmacological therapy and psychotherapy would be optimal in deterring steroid use. Psychological strategies should focus on ongoing relapse prevention and helping patients to predict risky situations, develop avoidance behaviors, manage stress, eliminate conditioned responses, and learn to withstand craving. These are strategies that have been somewhat successful with cocaine users (Gawin & Ellinwood, 1988; Kleber, 1988).

▤ Summary

There is a great deal of evidence to suggest that the psychoactive effects, withdrawal symptoms, and underlying biological mechanisms of steroid hormones are similar to the properties and complications associated with cocaine, alcohol, or opiate abuse. As a consequence, many experts believe that anabolic steroid abuse can develop into a psychoactive substance-dependence disorder accompanied by the cognitive, behavioral, and physiological symptoms indicative of uncontrollable use of a psychoactive substance in spite of adverse consequences (Kashkin & Kleber, 1989). If steroid use is added to the list of substance-dependence disorders, and accepted by the psychiatric and medical community, we would probably conclude that steroid abusers require treatment rather than simply testing for the drug's presence and assessing penalties. Instead of making the mistake of ignoring the spread of steroid use, as we have done with cocaine and other drugs of abuse, steps should be taken to develop early detection techniques, expand research, and devise treatment modalities. Only by recognizing the scope of the problem early in its development can we slow its spread and apply medical, rather than legal, solutions.

CHAPTER 15

Principles and Practices of Treatment

Objectives

1. To establish that the issues of who should be treated for drug abuse and in what way is not straightforward.

2. To discuss the various controversies surrounding drug abuse treatment.

3. To detail the characteristics of existing treatment.

4. To present several diverse models on which drug abuse treatments are based.

5. To distinguish between those models that assume substance abuse is a result of willful or sinful rational choice, those that contend drug abuse is learned, and those that assume substance abuse is a product of physiological responses.

6. To identify the specific goals of treatment.

7. To provide an overview of the treatment approaches, such as A.A., that are most widely used.

8. To assess the relative impact and success rates of various treatment programs.

Junior Simon, a sixteen-year-old minority boy from a broken home living in a household with below poverty income, stood before a juvenile judge, who sentenced Junior to one year of drug and alcohol treatment, in lieu of incarceration in the state's Training School for Juveniles. This alternative sentence of drug treatment was the judge's most recent attempt to divert Junior from incarceration. Earlier, Junior and three friends had been out cruising and drank several six-packs of beer stolen from one of the friend's parents. In the course of the day, Junior, challanged by his buddies, mustered the nerve to steal a car and try to sell it. Junior broke into a new Jaguar sedan, hot-wired it, and drove it to a neighborhood chop shop that was known to buy cars without question. Junior sold the car to the shop for $1,500 cash. Unfortunately for Junior, the chop shop was a police sting operation, and he was arrested. All four of the boys in Junior's group have been in juvenile court before. This is Junior's fourth time before the same judge. The judge decided to give Junior another chance, even though he displayed an arrogant attitude. The judge was convinced that Junior was under the influence of alcohol and the pressure of his friends. The diversion program set out by the judge mandated that Junior participate in a drug/alcohol abuse treatment group for the duration of his six-year suspended sentence. He was required to attend daily sessions in this group for the first six months, and his attendance at these meetings had to be documented for his probation officer. After that, Junior only had to attend one session a week until his six-year sentence was over. The judge clearly told Junior that failure to comply with this order would result in his immediate incarceration in the training school to serve the full sentence.

Harry McCharin is a very successful businessman. Twenty years ago he opened his first record store and has since developed the business. He now owns a chain of twenty-seven music stores that sell records, tapes, and CDs in Michigan, Ohio, and Indiana. Harry is a happily married man with a family of three children. But Harry has a secret; he uses heroin. He gives himself an injection nearly every day and has had no problem with his health or in obtaining his supply of needles and drugs. He is able to obtain very high grade heroin that is not cut. Other than the risks involved in obtaining drugs and drug paraphernalia, he has not suffered from the use of heroin for the nearly thirty years he has used it. He neither seeks nor wants any help regarding his heroin habit. He likes things just the way they are.

Bernadette Peterson was fifteen years old when she ran away from home in Oswego, New York. She had a long history of problems in school and was truant from school for more than 50 percent of the last school year she attended. She was unable to cope with her parents and their constant fighting over the care of a sickly younger brother. Bernadette ran away to New York City and was quickly taken under the protective wings of a local pimp, Streaker, who provided her with shelter and a sense of security. He also provided this young girl with her first taste of crack. It wasn't long before Bernadette was repaying her debt to Streaker by earning money as a prostitute. Streaker made her increasingly in debt to him by providing ever more crack. Bernadette was on a continuous spiral of increasing drugs and prostitution until one of her customers beat her and cut her face with a razor. The injuries permanently scarred her. Since she was no longer attractive and Streaker could not sell her services, she was quickly turned out on the streets to fend for herself. Bernadette, now nineteen years old, wants help. She entered a women's shelter and attempted to pursue some form of treatment for her crack habit. Unfortunately, there are no openings for services, there are only waiting lists in New York City. The women's shelter can only keep her for a maximum of thirty days, and she now faces the prospect of being on the streets trying to survive.

What does it mean to undergo or provide "drug or alcohol treatment"? Our definition of treatment is as follows: Those activities intended to eliminate the client's physical and psychological addiction to drugs and alcohol; to eliminate the client's abuse of drugs and alcohol and related behavioral problems; and to prevent the clients from returning to addiction and/or abuse, otherwise known as relapse. There is a wide range of treatment interventions offered by a variety of private and public hospitals, special drug and alcohol abuse clinics, self-help groups, and penal and mental institutions. Drug and alcohol abuse treatment is often required by judges as a condition of parole or probation. What is this treatment that so many institutions and professionals talk about? For whom is treatment appropriate: Junior? Harry? Bernadette? What is it that the judge expected Junior to obtain from a treatment program in lieu of incarceration in the training school?

Unfortunately, the answers to these questions are not cut and dry because our understanding of substance abuse and its treatment is not well developed. The application of substance abuse treatment is controversial at best and is conducted by a wide range of providers who function with conflicting ideologies and differing credentials. How a client is treated depends on the assumptions the treatment provider makes about the nature and causes of addiction. If substance abuse is assumed to be a learned problem, then the focus of treatment is to train the client to learn new responses to the circumstances and events that contributed to the onset of the client's problematic substance abuse. From a different perspective, other treatment professionals view substance abuse and addiction as a product of physiological responses of the body, often on the basis of genetic predispositions. These treatment providers, using a medical model, focus on the use of medications to counteract effects of abused substances. They are interested in research to explore genetic codes in an attempt to identify the gene or genes associated with substance abuse. Still other clinicians adhere to the view that substance abusers suffer from some underlying psychological or psychiatric problem and apply counseling and psychotherapeutic approaches. Organizations such as Alcoholics Anonymous (A.A.) and Narcotics Anonymous (N.A.) feel instead that the individual must submit to a higher power that controls their behavior and follow the 12 Step Program described in Chapter 6. Practitioners trained according to a particular theoretical vantage point subscribe to a particular treatment approach founded on their knowledge or beliefs about the origins of substance abuse. Thus, the treatment recommended is tailored to suit an established theoretical orientation.

There is little doubt among the experts that individuals who have problems related to the use and abuse of drugs and/or alcohol need treatment to eliminate or control the problem. But controversy remains as to who exactly requires treatment, what the goals of treatment should be (e.g., never drink again versus moderate, responsible drinking; change in total lifestyle; gaining insight into personal problems), what the best method for treating addiction is, whether one treatment works best for all clients or whether different treatments should be matched with appropriate patients, and whether treatment for alcoholics and drug abusers should be the same or different. Another issue currently a focus of debate is the role, if any, law enforcement agencies should have in the treatment process. The first part of this chapter addresses these issues by presenting the state of our knowledge on each topic, discussing the controversies and highlighting the questions that remain to be answered. The latter part of the chapter will describe particular treatment modalities.

Questions, Controversies, and Concerns

The first question, obviously, pertains to the determination of when treatment is an appropriate avenue. The answer, however, is not so obvious. Would you say that treatment was appropriate for Bernadette? Junior? Harry? Some individuals may not need treatment at all or may not be ready to make the necessary lifestyle changes that treatment often involves. In fact, there is evidence that many people outgrow the drug scene and change their lifestyle to exclude substance abuse without any professional assistance. Others, however, will only respond to a concerted and official effort to stop their drug abuse; for example, Employee Assistance Programs (EAP) serve as an entry point for treatment for many individuals. Still others may use drugs only occasionally and may not find their drug use disruptive or dysfunctional. This point is debatable and depends very much on how drug abuse is defined. Is the elderly lady drinking her daily martini a drug abuser in need of treatment? How about the lawyer who sniffs cocaine on an occasional weekend? We would probably all disagree on what constitutes abuse and what necessitates treatment. Nevertheless, one fact is evident: The individual who actively seeks treatment, recognizes the need for change and desires to be free of drugs is a much better candidate for treatment than the person who resists. This fact does not mean that the person resisting treatment is not in need of it, rather, that the prognosis will be poor.

If the determination has been made that treatment is indicated, what type of treatment approach should be employed? Obviously, quite different approaches should be taken in each case; circumstances, lifestyles, psychological traits, and most likely the origins of the problem differ greatly. There is clear evidence that by any definition no single treatment approach has been proven successful in treating a significant proportion of clients in attendance although most programs have had a degree of success in treating some of their clients.

A second concern pertains to the goals of any given treatment program, which can differ somewhat among programs. The single goal that all programs share is to help the individual stop abusing drugs. But because definitions of drug abuse differ, programmatic techniques vary widely. Just as drug and alcohol abuse is a multidimensional problem, so is treatment. Only when we address these several dimensions can we determine what will be done with the patient in need. Some of the dimensions that must be addressed relate to the precise goals of any given treatment program. Do they include total abstinence from using drugs or alcohol or is social use acceptable? To what extent will a change in lifestyle be required? Must the client avoid his or her entire peer group? What behaviors and habits must be relearned? Perhaps specific goals of the program involve a moral choice for success of the program. Who is to make that moral choice? The individual providing treatment? Probably not. Many assert that agreement between the practitioner and the client requiring assistance are necessary to determine the most appropriate goals of treatment in order to obtain any measure of success. Instead, however, the client is often left out of the decision-making process involving goal selection, and it is simply a function of the theoretical bias of the treatment specialist to define success. For example, in a family situation in which alcohol is a fundamental part of family functions—beer at barbeques and wine at meals—it may well not be acceptable for a client to function in the family without partaking of alcohol. Thus, input from the client is critical so that the goals are consistent with the client's lifestyle, expectations, and motivation level.

A third issue involves the potential of existing treatment strategies to actually succeed in meeting their goals. The impression that clearly successful treatment programs are available is advanced by current advertising practices. Most residential treatment programs experience a high "drop-out rate" (60 to 90 percent) and the few remaining clients generally show a 40 to 60 percent success rate (do not exhibit problem drinking/drug use after a couple of years). Many of the treatment centers (both nonprofit and for profit) recruit clients with advertisements that tend to emphasize the success rate of program completions and ignore the drop-out rate. Thus, a drug or alcohol abuse treatment center that was remarkably successful with the clients who complete their program would have only a 9 percent net success rate (60 percent success rate x 15 percent of those entering who did not drop out). This type of advertising may lead to the mistaken impression that we know how to treat substance abuse.

Many substance abusers repeatedly fail in formal programs. We are familiar with smokers who will assure you that they can quit smoking cigarettes at any time, and they know this because they have quit several times! Some alcoholics report that they have benefitted from A.A. and that it has helped them with their alcohol addiction. Nevertheless, these same individuals, upon further questioning, are frequently found to have been involved in A.A. for a number of years and still have not been able to abstain. Positive results from a treatment program should be attained certainly within a few years. It has been suggested that part of the recovery process involves several cycles of trying and failing to recover (Prochaska & Diclemente, 1984). The question of who is likely to recover and who will be more difficult to treat is an interesting and critical issue requiring address. There is speculation that those more difficult to treat may differ in personal or genetic characteristics from those who recover more readily. Furthermore, some may never face detection or seek treatment for a wide range of reasons (fear of losing a job, fear of legal ramifications, failure to understand treatment as an option). Obviously, the prospects for treatment of these individuals is quite poor.

A fourth question is whether different patients require different treatments. Not all individuals in the population are at equal risk of developing problems with alcohol or drugs, a central tenet of the Diathesis-Stress Model. Wide variations among subtance abuse patients strongly suggest that treatment approaches should be tailored to fit the patient's particular history and present symptoms. There is evidence that certain types of patients should be matched to specific kinds of treatments as a means of increasing the overall effectiveness and efficiency of a treatment system (DeLeon, Gersteint & Harwood, 1990; Institute of Medicine, 1990; Longabaugh, 1986; Lyons et al., 1982; McLellan, 1983; Skinner, 1981 & Solomon, 1981). Consequently, many practitioners recommend that patients be comprehensively evaluated for individual needs at the time of admission so that they may be assigned to the most appropriate and cost-effective treatments. Because substance abusers suffer from such a variety of medical and social problems, it is not surprising that multiple treatments are often used in the same patient. While detoxification is always the initial step in a treatment program, what comes next is a more difficult and complicated question. (See Chapter 18 for more specific information on suggested programs and their objectives.)

The fifth concern requiring address before treatment professionals can agree on a modality is whether treatment can be the same for drugs and alcohol. It was once thought that the treatment for alcoholism must be different from that of drug addiction. Aside from the definitional issues, it is not clear whether professionals should treat addiction to alcohol and drugs differently. It is true that many of the drugs of abuse are illegal, a fact that can, in and of itself, have an impact on the nature and results of a drug addiction. Alcohol is legal and includes a broader group of society's members, while drug addicts have become, by definition, criminals.

A possible basis for the conclusion that the treatment of alcoholics and drug addicts should be similar is the fact that there are numerous other behaviors that have been deemed addictive. For example, there are gambling and sex addictions. Addictions of all types may be similar in that they are all forms of excessive behavior that are considered disruptive and psychopathological. The position that various addictions have a common thread and can be treated similarly presupposes that addictions do not significantly differ in their underlying mechanisms and are all treatable in a psychological environment.

However, drugs of abuse have unique and separate effects on each individual psyche; assuming that the psyche is a composite result of both social and biological conditions. When a drug is taken, the exact effects depend very much on the user's past and present experiences and his or her physical constitution. Learning and childhood experiences, parental conduct, environmental conditions, genetic and biological constitution, setting and circumstances surrounding use of the drug, and psychological traits are only a few of the innumerable conditions that contribute to drug effects. Thus, interventions must include an individualized assessment of unique drug effects to design an effective treatment.

As an example of the dynamic complexity of these effects, let's consider a few ways in which drugs produce various individual effects. Cocaine interferes primarily with dopaminergic systems while heroin acts more directly on the neuropeptide system. Because individuals differ somewhat with respect to their neurochemistry and metabolism prior to drug usage, each drug will influence each user's brain function differently. Thus, cocaine may influence dopamine activity in an individual with previously low levels. This pharmacological effect has an impact on the unique psychological state and behavioral repetoire of the user, producing relatively unpredictable effects and, in this case, possibly causing the individual to be more sensitive to cocaine and more liable to experience severe depression upon withdrawal. An individual using heroin, on the other hand, will experience different drug effects given the different neurological systems that are affected, the user's initial state, and the circumstances. A comprehensive treatment approach must take the medical, psychological, and behavioral consequences of drug abuse into account to be successful. Furthermore, there is some evidence that there may be individual predispositions to abuse particular drugs. If such a tendency does exist, and if

biological or psychological traits are shown to predict a drug of choice, then treatment strategies must incorporate this knowledge into an individual's regimen. Treating all drug addicts as if they were identical may do more harm than good. Instead of lumping all addicts into one group or distinguishing between them on the basis of the drug used, an individualized approach enables professionals to provide a sensitive evaluation of each user's background, personality, medical condition, and future needs.

The controversy about whether alcohol and drug addictions should be treated the same way has been further muddled by the ever-increasing number of polydrug abusers. Typical polydrug abusers consume alcohol along with whatever illicit drugs they prefer. Alcohol is widely taken along with marijuana, cocaine, and heroin, and as mentioned in Chapter 12, those who prefer PCP abuse alcohol more often than PCP, and many are alcoholics. Heroin addicts also frequently inject cocaine, and many use alcohol on a daily basis. Marijuana seems to be a staple in most serious drug abusers' diets. And some users will resort to any mind-altering substance available to them. Consequently, most patients entering treatment programs arrive with addictions to several substances. The new patient's treatment should be less focused on the specific addiction and more on the individual and his or her possible underlying problems. We predict that such an individualized treatment strategy will lead to enhanced success rates.

Finally, the sixth issue pertains to the role of law enforcement agencies in the treatment process. There has been much debate in recent years about whether law enforcement approaches to drug abuse are effective in reducing the demand side of the problem—with the drug abuser as the target—or whether they have been a hindrance. As the perception in this country has grown that the drug problem is out of control, government has launched an all-out campaign to apprehend and incarcerate the user. Overwhelmingly, the evidence suggests that these tactics have failed to reduce demand among hardcore drug-using groups. Instead, drug abuse experts largely agree that the provision of treatment is essential in reducing demand and should accompany law enforcement efforts to reduce supply. What proponents of treatment fear is that many drug abusers are deterred from seeking treatment by the threat of arrest and criminal penalities. This situation may be especially true for pregnant users, some of whom may seek treatment during pregnancy if it were not for the possibility of being incarcerated and of eventually losing their babies to social services. Although most of us do not condone drug abuse and are appalled by the use of drugs during pregnancy—in some states this is now considered child abuse—we need to structure our response according to what works, rather than on vengeance and punishment. If we can more effectively curb drug abuse by providing treatment than we can by imposing penalties, then perhaps more of our national attention should be directed toward making treatment widely available, thereby reducing the role of law enforcement in the treatment process. As discussed in Chapter 17, law enforcement efforts may be more appropriately directed toward interdiction and the control of supply side of the drug problem, rather than the demand side.

Just as we are a long way from fully understanding the nature and causes of addictions, we are a long way from successfully treating all individuals who are exposed to drugs of abuse. We are perhaps even further away from preventing the onset of drug abuse. Students of substance abuse must independently evaluate the results of these different approaches in terms of their success in accomplishing the objectives put forth by their proponents. Before the debate concerning drug treatment can be resolved, clarity about the desired goals of treatment, which individuals should be targeted for treatment, and what modalities are appropriate must be established. For as many causes of drug and alcohol abuse there are, there should be an equal number of different treatment modalities.

Dimensions of Current Treatment Options

It is useful to explore the various types of drug and alcohol treatment along several important dimensions: location, duration, modality, categories of clients, and delivery of services. Costs for the various drug treatments are sometimes quite high, however many insurance companies now defray the cost or cover completely expenses incurred. Many insurers are beginning to cover only outpatient programs because inpatient treatment may be prohibitively expensive.

Treatment Location and Duration

Drug and alcohol treatment can vary from eighteen-month residential treatment programs to one or two brief outpatient intervention sessions in a doctor's office. There are several location types, each differing along a dimension of level of intrusion into the client's life. The duration of the program is closely associated with the location of the program. For example, brief interventions may last a few meetings over the period of four weeks for a total of eight to ten hours of intervention while residential treatment programs may involve the complete and constant participation of the client for as long as one to one and a half years with a total of thousands of hours of treatment.

Residential Treatment

You have probably heard of the Betty Ford Clinic, named after the former First Lady. She endured residential treatment for an alcohol and tranquilizer addiction and, as a result of her experience, established a treatment clinic. This is one of the more exclusive of many such residential treatment centers around the country. Residential treatment programs are usually located in private hospitals specifically designated for alcohol and/or drug treatment or as part of a private mental hospital. Most traditional medical hospital facilities have a few beds assigned for drug or alcohol treatment, but these are usually designated for detoxification or short-term stays. Many states also support local treatment centers that provide residential treatment programs to those who cannot afford the private residential programs. As you might guess, the residential treatment centers with the longest waiting lists are the state-supported programs.

Patients in residential programs reside in housing provided by the hospital or treatment center. They will sometimes share rooms with other patients. The programs are often coeducational. The patients, thus, live, eat, work, and participate in treatment as a group. The patient is immersed in the special environment of the hospital setting and removed from most of the environmental factors that led to drinking or drug abuse. This long-term, immersed environment is designed to help the individual deal with the addiction problem in an isolated environment and should thus be better able to overcome the powerful effects of the addiction to alcohol and/or drugs and the circumstances that led to substance abuse. Relearning behavioral patterns and dealing with underlying problems are generally emphasized in treatment.

Most residential alcohol/drug treatment programs are designed to last as long as one year or more. In some cases, the duration of residential treatment programs is based on the recovery of the patient and can last as long as it takes, even beyond one or two years.

A second, short form of residential treatment is used as a half-way house in many programs or as part of the detoxification process. The residential detoxification programs can last from one to four weeks and most treatment programs include a twenty-eight day counseling program. Although some experimental six-month residential programs are currently under evaluation, most programs are of the very long or very short variety.

Residential treatment centers have been avaliable for alcoholics far longer than for drug addicts. In fact, most residential treatment centers have only recently begun to include drug addicts in their treatment population of primarily alcoholics.

The patient's program in the majority of residential treatment centers begins with an extensive assessment of the patient, including physical and psychological testing, family status (alcohol history of the family is important to treatment), and basic descriptive information. The closer the institution's ties to mental health, the more likely the initial assessment is to include measures of psychological functioning. Once the patient is assessed and assigned to a room, he or she begins participating in the drug treatment. In nearly all cases, treatment consists of group sessions and individual meetings with a personal counselor. Most programs offer social skills training to assist the addict in adjusting to a life without drugs and/or alcohol. The social skills include learning how to make friends, how to interview for a job, and how to communicate ideas and feelings to others. A very few programs also offer vocational programming.

Residential detoxification programs have a similar arrangement in offering group and individual meetings along with the administration of chemical agents to reduce the medical consequences of drug usage by cleaning the body's system of drugs or alcohol. The combination of relatively brief treatments with detoxification is a fairly recent development. More traditional detoxification programs typically involved a three to four day stay in the hospital, until the individual was considered safely out of danger in the course of detoxification. However, the staff of traditional programs report seeing the same patients endure the detoxification process over and over, suggesting that detoxification is not sufficient by itself to rid the individual of the need for more alcohol or drugs. Instead, it appears that individuals detoxify on occasion just to get a clean start on drugs again.

Strengths of the residential treatment environment:

- *The patients are free from daily pressures that could distract them from treatment.*
- *The patients are provided a vast array of medical resources to assist them in overcoming addiction.*
- *The patients' chances of success are enhanced in that they have made a life committment in enrolling in a program that takes them out of their current life pattern.*
- *Patient participation in programs are more readily controlled and consistent.*

Weaknesses of residential treatment programs:

- *They remove patients from the real world, making adjustment after treatment a particularly difficult and risky task.*
- *They require patients to make major sacrifices to job and home life, removing the options for treatment for the poor, single parents, and others.*
- *They have not been proven to be any more effective than outpatient or day treatment programs.*
- *They are the most expensive treatment environment.*

Day Treatment

Many hospitals also conduct day treatment in a hospital setting. In this setting, the patient participates in drug treatment groups and individual counseling during the course of the day. The patient stays at the hospital all day but returns home in the evening. Thus the patient misses work, but still enjoys the comforts of home. In most cases, day treatment lasts six to twelve months and involves a major committment on the part of the patient.

Strengths of the day hospital environment:

- *The patients are free from daily work pressures that could distract them from their treatment.*
- *The patients are provided a vast array of medical resources to assist them in overcoming addiction.*
- *The patients' chances of success are enhanced in that they have made a life committment in enrolling in a program that takes them out of their current life and work pattern.*
- *Patients' participation in programs is more readily controlled and consistent while the patient is in the hospital.*

- *Patients maintain family ties by continuing to live at home.*

Weaknesses of day treatment programes :

- *They remove patients from the real world, making adjustment after treatment a particularly difficult and risky task, especially when they return to work.*
- *They require patients to make major sacrifices to job and in many cases, home life, removing the options for treatment for the poor, single parents, and others.*
- *Many of the potential enviormental stresses associated with home life continue and may interfere with the patients' progress.*
- *They have not been proven to be any more effective than outpatient or residential programs.*
- *They are expensive.*

Outpatient Programs

In contrast with the typical inpatient or day hospital program, the outpatient program allows patients to remain on the job and in the home while attending periodic group and individual meetings (usually two to three per week). Programs of this type are designed to last from six to eighteen months and vary greatly in their scope of intervention and number of contact hours. Some outpatient programs are attached to hospitals while others are within community mental health centers or community substance treatment centers. Independent practitioners that specialize in chemical dependence may also provide services within a private or group practice. Employee assistance programs (EAPs) on occasion employ their own personnel or network with other agencies and individuals to provide drug treatment services. Because EAPs are involved in the screening, assessment, education and monitoring of potential and current employees, they are frequently the point at which individuals with drug problems enter the world of treatment.

In many cases these programs include long-term follow-up functions in that they serve as referral sites for residential programs and, especially with respect to Alcoholics Anonymous, may encourage a lifetime commitment in maintaining freedom from the patient's addiction. Outpatient programs are offered in a wider variety of locations, including storefronts, small treatment centers in community centers, and even treatment on the street.

Methadone maintentance programs are usually part of an outpatient program.

Strengths of the outpatient treatment environment:

- *The patients are involved in their daily work routine and can maintain their careers while in treatment, making the cost of treatment more feasible.*
- *Patients maintain family ties by continuing to live at home.*
- *The costs are relatively small in comparison with residential or day treatment.*

Weaknesses of outpatient treatment environment:

- *Many of the potential environmental stresses associated with home life and job continue and may interfere with patients' progress.*
- *They have not been proven to be any more effective than day hospital or residential programs.*
- *They usually do not have the usual access to medical treatment available in other centers.*

Brief Interventions

One recent trend in the drug/alcohol literature is an attempt at brief intervention. This approach typically takes place in the patients' regular physician's office. Medical practitioners are now being trained to identify the classic warning signs of possible drug or alcohol abuse in treating their clientele and to provide the patient the most current information about the effects of drugs or alcohol on their physical well being. Although this method has not yet been adequately evaluated, it does offer a promising treatment alternative. The intervention method most often associated with drug treatment is called Motivation Enhancement and attempts to present a number of potential incentives to clean up, such as improving health, mental function, social functioning, and job prospects. We should note, however, that most general practitioners are not trained to recognize symptoms of drug abuse and commonly do not ask questions pertaining to that possibility. For example, a common scenario is that of a female patient, a mother and housewife, who has been alcoholic for years and suffers from many related ailments. Doctors too often do not question such a patient about her drinking habits. Many professionals believe that if more physicians were aware of substance abuse and motivated to pursue the topic with their patients, fewer abusers would go undetected.

Strengths of the brief intervention environment:

- *The patients are provided the greatest access to a self-driven treatment program, and it assumes that the patients can take care of themselves given the appropriate information and motivation.*
- *Patients are provided a vast array of medical resources to assist them in overcoming addiction.*
- *Patients maintain family ties by continuing to live at home.*
- *Patients continue to work and are thus able to maintain financial security while in treatment.*
- *It is very inexpensive.*

Weaknesses of the brief intervention environment:

- *They have not been adequately evaluated for effectiveness.*
- *They do not remove patients from some of the major stressors: family and job. This may result in a weakening of the effects of treatment.*

Treatment in Prison

Treatment in prisons could be considered another form of residential treatment. Many states have Alcoholics Anonymous, Cocaine Anonymous, and Narcotics Anonymous available to prison inmates. Some states provide counseling for inmates and a few offer the therapeutic community model. However, few of the nation's prisoners are afforded serious drug treatment in prison. Frohling (1989 cited by Lipton, Falkin & Wexler, 1992, p. 12) estimates that fewer than 20 percent of drug using inmates are serviced by these programs. Yet, many drug users spend some time in prison, since drug use itself is a crime, and many drug users resort to illegal activity to support their drug habits. Another unfortunate reality in prisons is the pervasive use of drugs within the prison itself, whereby an inmate could foreseeably maintain a full-fledged addiction while incarcerated (Purdy, 1995). Once released, without treatment, drug-using offenders are likely to return to their previous drug habits. Moreover, offenders who receive drug treatment have a much lower recidivism rate than those who do not. Therefore, prison seems like a logical place to provide drug treatment (Lipton, Falkin & Wexler). An increasing number of experts are proposing that treatment should be mandatory for drug-abusing offenders (as discussed in Chapter 18).

Reviews of prison-based drug treatment programs (Rouse, 1991; Wexler & Love, 1994) report encouraging results showing positive effects of treatment on recidivism and relapse rates. Moreover, the research evidence indicates that treatment in a correctional institution, regardless of whether it is voluntary or coerced, will reduce drug use and crime, and increase prosocial behavior (Anglin & Hser, 1990; Leukefled & Tims, 1988).

Programs which address the development of cognitive problem solving skills and social skills (Hawkins, Catalano, Wells, 1986; Hayes & Schimmel, 1993; Husband & Platt, 1993; Walters, Heffron, Whitaker, & Dial, 1992) such as stress and anger management skills (Yen, Peyrot & Prino, 1989) are considered to be more effective than programs which only focus on knowledge about the negative effects of drug and alcohol use (Botvin, 1983).

Research indicates that as many as 75 percent of substance abusers may also suffer from depression (Mirin, Weiss & Michael, 1988; Peters, Kearns et al.). Cote & Hodgins (1990) identified 25 percent of their sample of Canadian prisoners suffered from some sort of depression. Many women who abuse crack cocaine are more prone to depression than their male counterparts (Griffin et al., 1989 cited by Wellisch, Anglin & Prendergast, 1993 p.19) and are also likely to be suffering from traumatic stress syndrome related to rape, incest, or other victimization (Daley & Przybycin, 1989, cited by Wellisch et al., 1993, p.19). With regard to female prisoners in general, Wellisch et al. (1993, p.15) report that 35 percent of the women in their national sample were victims of sexual abuse, 50 percent experienced physical abuse and 50 percent reported physical abuse by a husband or boyfriend. Therefore, depression and traumatic stress syndrome should be addressed in all prison based treatment programs, but particularly those for female offenders.

Synopsis

Four styles of drug treatment are available: residential (including prisons), day, outpatient, and through doctor's offices. The residential and day programs can be long term (one to two years) or brief (one to four weeks). While few programs currently exist that fall between these extremes of time commitment, residential treatment centers are exploring six to eight month residential programs. Unfortunately, most of these programs are at the experimental stage, and we know little of their utility. Outpatient programs can last for several months or years. Self-help modalities such as Alcoholics Anonymous may last for the client's lifetime. This contrasts sharply with the new trend of brief interventions (one or two sessions) in the doctor's office.

The advantages and disadvantages of the different types of approaches and modalities show that there is a trade-off between expense and time commitment in programs and the extent to which individuals are removed from the environment in which they developed their substance abuse problem. It should be clear, however, that no program location or duration has been scientifically demonstrated to be more effective than any other.

Treatment Modality

In the 1960s, locally based treatment facilities were constructed and expanded. Not only were there more treatment centers, but there were also more treatment options. Varieties of treatment included detoxification programs, outpatient treatment, inpatient treatment, and prison-based programs, in addition to variations on the methadone maintenance program. The most popular treatment modalities, nevertheless, have been methadone maintenance and the therapeutic community and even other programs incorporate many of the principles and practices of these two models. (Methadone maintenance was discussed in detail in Chapter 7.)

The differences among drug/alcohol treatment alternatives with respect to location and duration have implications for which treatment modality is appropriate. For instance, self-help programs, such as Alcohol Anonymous, occur on a long-term basis in an outpatient setting. Residential hospital programs operate on the assumption that the alcohol/drug addiction is a medical problem requiring medical treatment. Consequently, the typical program involves treatments with a focus on issues similar to those targeted in psychiatric populations. The view is commonly subscribed to, for example, that alcoholism is a disease, as is paranoid schizophrenia.

Alcoholics Anonymous (A.A.) and Other Forms of Anonymity

Perhaps the most famous form of treatment is based on Alcoholics Anonymous (A.A.), as detailed in Chapter 6. A.A. began in 1934 with the initial gathering of founding alcoholics who developed a way of returning to sober life (*Alcoholics Anonymous*, 1976). It has grown from 100 members when their Big Book was first published in 1939 to more than a million members world wide in 1988. A.A. is both an organization designed to assist its members to remain free from alcohol and a deliberately loosely established collection of alcoholics who continually encourage new memberships. The 12 Step Program, forming the foundation of A.A.'s approach, advocates giving the controls to God; thus, enabling the alcoholic to control drinking as a matter of God's will. (For those who do not accept the concept of a higher power, other organizations, such as the Secular Organization for Sobriety, are available.) The 12 Step Program is now also used for other addict populations: Overeaters Anonymous, Gamblers Anonymous, smoking cessation programs, Narcotics Anonymous, and Al-a-Non.

Assumptions and Starting Points

In A.A., alcohol is the problem. Any suppositions about the path that led the individual to alcoholism is irrelevant until the individual gives up the use of alcohol. The basic goal of treatment is to stop drinking altogether and never again take that first drink.

"Once an alcoholic, always an alcoholic" (*Alcoholics Anonymous*, 1976, p. 33) is one of the basic operating principles in A.A.. Thus, the goal of never again taking a drink is part of the recognition of that operating principle. The successful member of A.A., one who no longer drinks, is described as a recovering alcoholic—never as a recovered alcoholic. It is assumed that alcoholics have a special mental and physical reaction to alcohol that renders them unable to resist alcohol once they have begun drinking. Alcoholics in this view cannot be social drinkers. This abusive response to alcohol is out of their control. In fact, the first step in the 12 steps toward recovery from alcohol is for users to admit they are powerless over alcohol. According to A.A., clients must hit bottom before the 12 Step Program can help. This is one of the limiting factors in the A.A. approach. Although this form of treatment is the most widely used for alcoholism, it has never been systematically evaluated. Those who have reviewed the program indicate that the success rate for long-term abstinence is quite low.

The Therapeutic Community

The therapeutic community (TC) is based on a primary residential treatment model and is highly regarded by many treatment professionals. Synanon (Yablonsky, 1965), which began in the 1950s in California, was the original therapeutic community devoted to the treatment of drug addicts. Since then other well-known TCs have emerged, such as Phoenix House (Rosenthal, 1973), Daytop Village (Sugarman, 1974), and Odyssey House, a New York TC for addicts who are pregnant or mothers of very young children.

Charles Dederich, a recovering alcoholic and founder of Synanon, applied many of the self-help principles of Alcoholics Anonymous to the therapeutic community. Former addicts are employed as counselors, administrators, and role models. It is believed that ex-drug users are less likely to be conned by the addicts seeking treatment and more likely to successfully exert the pressure needed for addicts to change their irresponsible behaviors. Moreover, former addicts are likely to benefit from the experience.

The atmosphere in the programs is highly structured, especially for those first entering. The admission process consists of confrontational interviews with staff where prospective residents are forced to admit to their past failures, inadequacies, and irresponsible behaviors. Upon admission to the TC, residents withdraw from drugs without sympathy or handholding. The addict who attempts to gain attention during withdrawal is ignored as staff and residents go about their normal business.

Residents progress through treatment in stages that are clearly set forth when they arrive. Each succeeding stage provides more personal freedom and responsibility. Group counseling or therapy sessions are the foundation for TCs. Methods used in these sessions are confrontational, involving accusations, criticisms, and sanctions, such as wearing a sign that says, "I am irresponsible." The resident is required to remain composed and respond to the criticisms with openness and honesty. Breaking old ways of responding to conflict (which may have included fighting, criminal behavior, drug use, and/or passive aggressiveness) and developing new coping skills are the goals of these methods. Unfortunately, some patients find this confrontational style too threatening or otherwise discomforting and do not respond well.

Although the TC approach is designed to involve several months of participation, drop-out rates are usually high. Patients who remain, without respect to severity of coexisting psychiatric disorders, have better outcomes; improvements in drug use, employment, criminality, and psychological well-being have been reported. Because some who apply the TC approach sometimes construe the method by attempting to break down the defenses of users without rebuilding their characters, a contingency of experts have criticized the method. Many drug abusers have a history of abuse, neglect, and low self-esteem and do not respond well to measures that essentially undermine them further. Rebuilding inner strength and confidence of the user thus become critical in successfully reaching and treating participants.

Therapeutic communities have made several transitions since the founding of Synanon. There is increasing emphasis placed on the reentry phase of treatment, better enabling patients to adjust to their release into their communities by learning a skill, preparing for employment, and, of course, avoiding relapse. Also, the emphasis on confrontational strategies and encounter therapy has declined. There is more of a concentration on professional counseling now than in the past. Efforts are made to connect the patient with community-based counseling and supportive services before release to further reinforce their therapy. These recent changes promise to increase the success rates of TCs.

Contingency Contracting

Contingency contracting involves the establishment of a written contract between the patient and therapist requiring specific behaviors from both. For example, a patient who is both a physician and an addict may give a signed letter to the therapist stating that if this letter has been mailed, the patient has relapsed and should be suspended from medical practice. The patient may also agree to attend specific treatment sessions and to participate in a urine surveillance program at preestablished intervals. The therapist, on the other hand, agrees to certify that the physician is drug-free and able to continue medical practice unless there is evidence of relapse or a failure to provide drug-free urine specimens. Privileges and restrictions are negotiated as the patient attempts to work out various deals with the therapist. Goals of the therapist, theoretically, then become the goals of the patient and external motivations to remain clean and sober become internalized. Obviously, contracting with patients in this way can only work if the patient has something to lose.

Social Interventions

The social milieu can also exert tremendous pressure on individuals to either use drugs or to remain drug free. Although easy to accomplish within the controlled confines of the therapeutic community, we find that other social sanctions against drug use are promising. Massive advertising campaigns to avoid drinking and driving have been effective, not surprising in light of the fact that media is one of the most powerful behavioral influences in modern society. In many social circles it has become customary to have a designated driver who abstains from alcohol. The individual who lights up a cigarette during a social gathering may find him or herself ostracized and exiled. High school students are less likely in 1993 to define drug use as cool than they did in 1973.

Other aspects of the social mileu that are not as far-reaching include the family and peer groups. As established in Chapter 5, in-home experiences and friends profoundly influence drug-taking behavior. Thus, therapeutic efforts should include family members whenever possible to promote lifestyle changes, to educate parents to know the warning signs and what to do about a drug using child, and to enhance communication. Further steps should be taken to educate the patient about how peer group influences can be thwarted. Many who are involved with a group of drug users do not realize that their friendships frequently do not extend beyond their drug use. Once patients attempt to quit or are released from a treatment facility, they quickly find out who their real friends are. Many acquaintances vanish and others make a constant effort to reconnect patients with drug-

Table 15.1   *Pharmacologic Intervention Specific to Neurotransmitters Inhibited or Stimulated by Drugs of Abuse*

Drug class	Toxic or Withdrawal Effects	Treatment
Sedatives/ tranquilizers	Diminished activity of GABA* inhibition	Gradually taper a sedative/hypnotic; substitute phenobarbital or chlordiazepoxide (Librium, Lipoxide, Mitran, etc.), depending on the drug of abuse, to allow restoration of GABA activity
Stimulants	Depletion of dopamine and norepinephrine	Administer bromocriptine (Parlodel), a dopamine agonist. Administer desipramine (Norpramin, Pertofrane), which enhances norepinephrine receptors
Opiates	Norepinephrine release	Administer naloxone (Narcan) to reverse acute intoxication. Administer clonidine (Catapres), which blocks norepinephrine release. Administer naltrexone (Trexan), an opiate antagonist
Psychedelic agents	Enhanced serotonin activity	Place patient in a quiet environment to allow the effects of the drug to wear off. Administer lorazepam (Alzapam, Ativan), an indirect GABA agonist that blocks serotonin effects
Phencyclidine	Stimulation of dopamine and norepinephrine receptors and blockade of acetylcholine	Administer haloperidol (Haldol), a dopamine-2 antagonist. Administer desipramine to prevent postwithdrawal depression

*—GABA = γ-aminobutyric acid
Source: Giannini, 1989.

using friends and activities by bringing drugs to their house, asking them to make a drug buy, borrowing money for drugs, and so forth. The more exposure recovering addicts have to drugs and the drug lifestyle, the greater the risk of relapse.

Pharmacological Strategies

Pharmacological strategies in the treatment of drug abuse include the administration of medications and therapies designed to replenish natural supplies of brain chemicals that are depleted by chronic drug use (see Table 15.1). Because all psychoactive drugs exert their effects by altering the brain's biochemistry, many treatments now focus on how the brain's balance can be restored to a "pre-drug" state. This enables the patient to better tolerate withdrawal, suppress craving, experience less psychological and physical need for the drug, and more effectively avoid relapse.

These strategies are currently being tested in both animals and humans, and are being used in clinical settings throughout the nation. Recent information pertaining to drug effects on the brain have led to the incorporation of biomedical assessments and medicinal regimens into more conventional behavioral and psychotherapeutic approaches. Antidepressants given to cocaine abusers, anxiolytics to certain alcoholics, and buprenorphine to opiate addicts are all examples of the pharmacological approach. Importantly, however, the success of these strategies increase substantially when used in conjunction with other standard individualized treatments that focus on lifestyle changes, attitudes, motivations, and underlying problems, rather than when used alone. Pharmacological strategies are discussed separately and in more detail in each drug chapter.

What Makes Treatment Effective?

Unfortunately, research to evaluate the success rates of various kinds of drug treatments is scarce. What little that has been done indicates that treatment is more effective than no treatment or punitive measures, but which programs are best for which types of drug users is still in question. In essence, studies show that when drug-using offenders enter active treatment, crime rates decline. The longer they are in treatment the less likely they are to recidivate and relapse. Given the methodological weaknesses in

those studies that have been done, few other conclusions can be made (see Faupel, 1981 for review).

Faupel (1981) has outlined two factors believed to be important in making treatment a success. Faupel concentrates on the personal and social aspects of drug abuse and does not consider the medical, biological, and individualistic factors that can make a treatment regimen successful. (Pharmacological strategies hold great promise, but only when used in conjunction with supportive behavioral and psychotherapeutic programs.)

First, Faupel emphasizes the importance of commitment mechanisms employed by the treatment program that enhance the ability of the patient to transform his or her behavior. Commitment must be reinforced in the treatment regimen and requires patients to associate with or attach to a conventional lifestyle. Patients must also disassociate from other commitments, such as the drug subculture or lifestyle. In order to achieve these goals, the treatment program asks members to sacrifice something previously important to them to enforce their commitment to recovery. Addicts must also "renounce [their] past lifestyle and the interpersonal relationships associated with it" (Faupel, 1981). Renouncement means that drug use of any sort is prohibited, as is association with other addicts. Even recollections of what it was like to be high are discouraged. Patients are frequently asked to cut their hair or to alter their appearance in a show of attachment to mainstream society. Finally, patients should develop new friendships to replace their old relationships, a process known as communion. Thus, recovering addicts are encouraged to become attached to others in the treatment group and then to those in conventional society.

The second aspect of treatment that is believed to increase success rates is called social-psychological concomitants (Faupel, 1981). Social-psychological processes help to trigger a motivational response by addicts so that the transfer to a conventional lifestyle can take place. Addicts must invest time, money, emotional energy, status, and security for a treatment program to work. Investments reflect what is at stake for individual patients in making this transformation. Once addicts begin to heavily invest in a different lifestyle, they are likely to experience some conflict or disparity between previous behaviors and the belief systems that are emerging. This conflict is called cognitive dissonance. If addicts can shift their values to parallel conventional standards, then the dissonance should be resolved, further reinforcing acceptance by conventional society and, thus, the transformation. Finally, addicts should be encouraged to restabilize; the self-concept that is emerging, based on conventional values, must be reinforced by the program. This would be the final step in making the transformation from the behavior, lifestyle, and self-concept of a drug addict, to a law-abiding, conventional-minded citizen.

▤ Summary

Providing interventions designed specifically to target the behavioral correlates of vulnerability enhance the prospects that treatment will be successful and make the individual less vulnerable to substance abuse and other forms of psychopathology. Treatment will be successful only to the extent that the predisposition or motivation to use drugs is targeted and eliminated (Tarter & Edwards, 1987). For the most part, drug treatments focus on the symptoms of an underlying problem, concentrating on attitudes and drug-taking behaviors without looking beneath the surface for those conditions that may have been precipitating. Generally speaking, stable, problem-free individuals do not suddenly become drug addicts. Instead, drug abusers tend to manifest difficulties in their personal lives well before the onset of their substance use. For some, the problems may relate to a drug-infested neighborhood or a drug-addicted parent. For others, the problems may be more personal, including genetic propensity and psychological dysfunction. Treatment efforts that identify underlying disorders and their manifestations (such as low self concept) have a far greater likelihood of success than those that ignore individual differences. A combination of pharmacological and behavioral interventions have, to date, been more impressive than those used in the past.

In closing, it should be clear that people initially use drugs to get high and satisfy unfulfilled needs. Although the first decision to use a drug is completely voluntary, subsequent decisions to continue become less a function of free will. Once drugs of abuse have been experienced, the reward value of the drug may become compelling, making it more difficult for the user to say no. In the presence of a biological disturbance and/or a social disadvantage, the reward value of the drug may be even higher, further encouraging drug use. Furthermore, if the drug superficially accomplishes the goal to fill unfulfilled needs, the motivation increases as well. In short, if you like your life without drugs, all theories of genetics and inadequate coping become less influential. If you do not like your life, incentives not to use may not be persuasive. A successful treatment strategy must focus on an indivduals unique deficiencies, sources of unhappiness, and biomedical comdition simultaneonsly.

CHAPTER 16

Drug Trafficking

Objectives

1. To provide a description of the major international drug trafficking organizations.
2. To describe how drug trafficking organizations function and conduct business.
3. To illustrate how various drugs of abuse are smuggled into the United States from their countries of origin.
4. To present the methods used by drug traffickers to launder money.

The term *drug trafficking* refers to the sale and distribution of controlled substances. It represents a major economic activity that occurs outside the law and beyond the public view. Drug distribution organizations function like many of the successful legitimate international corporations, and three well-known Colombian drug kingpins—Jorge Ochoa, and the late Pablo Escobar and Jose Gonzalo Rodriguez Gacha—were even included in the 1989 Forbes magazine list of world billionaires. Their combined worth was estimated at $6 billion.

The scope of the U.S. drug problem cannot be fully understood without some comprehension of the incredible strength, power, and influence exerted by the world's leading drug-trafficking organizations. About $13 billion were allocated during fiscal year 1995 to fight the war on drugs whereas international drug profits are estimated to be in the hundreds of billions of dollars. Interdiction efforts and increased arrests of drug dealers selling ounces of cocaine and heroin did nothing to stop the flow of hundreds of metric tons of cocaine and heroin into the United States. The capture and extradition of dozens of Colombian drug traffickers as well as the deaths of Jose Gonzalo Rodriguez Gacha and Pablo Escobar only resulted in a decrease in the price of cocaine in the United States. The development of an effective American drug policy must be geared to the enormous magnitude of national and international drug trafficking organizations.

The drug trafficking organizations vary widely in size, sophistication, area of operation, clientele, and product. They have differing propensities to violence and differing patterns of interaction with other organizations. Drug-trafficking organizations share the obvious characteristic that they are all engaged in illicit activity and, therefore, do not have access to and are not subject to the normal channels of production, distribution, sales, finance, taxation, regulation, and contract enforcement that affect legitimate businesses. However, these businesses are subject to the same economic laws of supply and demand and the same need for efficiency in operation. Well-established drug trafficking organizations may have a board of directors, a Chief Executive Officer (CEO), and a bureaucracy whose functions and benefits mirror those of executives and middle-level management in a modern corporation, complete with expense accounts, bonuses, and even company cars. On the other hand, the normal commercial concept of contracts, in which disputes are handled by a court of law and restitution is almost always of a financial nature, is twisted in the world of drug trafficking. The rule of law is replaced by the threat of violence and the very word *contract* is often used as a synonym for "death sentence" (U.S. Attorneys, 1989, p. 16).

The larger drug trafficking organizations, like large legitimate businesses, are successful because they are good at what they do. They usually do not make careless errors or take unnecessary risks. Their leaders insulate them-

The arrest of Panamanian Manuel Noriega by Drug Enforcement Administration.

selves and the higher echelons of their organizations from those who actually carry out the risk-taking activities involved in the enterprise (U.S. Attorneys, 1989, p. 17).

Drugs are moved into the United States through several points along the Mexican and Canadian border. The long, deserted Maine coastline also offers traffickers a safe route to transport drugs. Where they enter depends on the drugs involved and which of the major drug cartels is moving them. For example, cocaine has been flown into clandestine airstrips in Louisiana, the Carolinas, Georgia, Florida, and California where it is then shipped to major distribution centers such as Miami, New York City, Los Angeles, and Houston (Morganthau et al., 1989). New Brunswick, Canada, is also being used by Latin cocaine traffickers as a route for smuggling drugs into the United States. Lacking radar to detect the small drug-laden aircraft, and dotted with relatively deserted airstrips, New Brunswick offers traffickers an ideal location for drug-trafficking activities (Weiner, 1989). In general, once the drugs are imported in pure bulk form, they are shipped to local distributors who "step on" or cut the drug into less potent dosages in order to increase its bulk before they distribute it to local dealers. After receiving the drug, the local dealers, who employ sellers and runners, may step on the drug again for sale to street level customers.

The local dealers are the least stable organizations, facing the greatest risks and dealing with the smallest volumes of cash. The large importing cartels deal with millions of dollars per transaction and are the most powerful and stable organizations. The next section examines the major drug trafficking groups as well as some of the smaller street level organizations. In their 1989 report to the president of the United States, the United States Attorneys and the Attorney General of the United States present an excellent overview and rare insight into each of the major drug trafficking organizations. Significant portions of that report appear in this chapter.

Drug-Trafficking Organizations

Colombian Drug Cartels

The Colombian drug cartels exemplify the large, international, well-organized, corporate style trafficking groups. They are structured in what can be characterized as an onion-like layering of organizational power, with kingpins at the center, directing operations but insulated by layer upon layer of subordinate operatives, until one reaches the outside layer, the skin of the organization. Here we find the individuals who deal directly with the production, supply, and sale of the illicit product: the growers, the smugglers, the small-time distributors, and the street pushers. Also important to the strength of this structure and its successful operation are the accountants, the chemists, the lawyers, the paid politicians, and the corrupt customs officials (U.S. Attorneys, 1989, p. 17).

The two largest Colombian cartels are the Medellin cartel and the Cali cartel. They supply about 80 percent of the cocaine distributed in the United States (Harris, 1989) earning several billion dollars a year (Gugliotta & Leen, 1989). During the 1980s and early 1990s the Medellin drug cartel was the most powerful and most publicized group of drug traffickers in the world. Less was known about the Cali cartel, allegedly headed by Jose Santacruz Londono, Gilberto Rodriguez Orejuela and his brother Miguel. The Rodriquez Orejuela brothers claim to run a chain of profitable drug stores but authorities put their illegal drug profits at $8 billion. It is believed that the Cali cartel controls cocaine distribution primarily in New York City (Moody, 1990; Morganthau et al., 1989; Treaster, 1990) and operates with a lower profile and less political violence than the Medellin cartel. Due to their lack of terrorist tactics in Colombia and numerous tips to the Colombian police concerning the Medellin cartel's activities, the Cali cartel operates in Colombia with a minimum of police interference. As a matter of fact, the new president of Colombia, Ernesto Samper, elected in 1994 has allegedly accepted significant campaign contributions from the Cali cartel and has publicly declared that he will not seek to bring its members to justice (Colombian president will not…,1994, June 21).

The Medellin cartel, noted for their terrorist activities and assassinations of political figures, were the most sought after by the Colombian police and United States Drug Enforcement Administration agents. This point is important because it underscores the fact that the Colombian government is more concerned with ending narcoterrorism in Colombia than it is with preventing cocaine from entering the United States (Chernick, 1990).

The Medellin cartel emerged during the 1980s as one of the world's most powerful and profitable criminal organizations, earning several billion dollars a year. The cartel was originally composed of organizations headed by Pablo Escobar Gaviria known as "The Godfather," Jorge Luis Ochoa Vasquez called the "Fat Man," Carlos Enrique

Lehder Rivas, also known as "Joe Lehder," and Jose Gonzalo Rodriguez Gacha nicknamed "The Mexican" (Gugliotta & Leen, 1989).

Pablo Escobar, probably the wealthiest, most powerful, and most wanted cocaine trafficker in the world was born in 1949 to a working class family; his mother was a school teacher and his father a farmer. Before graduating from high school, he began his criminal career in Medellin by stealing headstones from graveyards, sanding the surfaces, and reselling them. During the late 1960s and early 1970s Escobar worked as a bodyguard for a smuggler of stereo equipment and was reported to have kidnaped a Medellin businessman for $100,000 in ransom money. (Note: Kidnaping for ransom has historically been a common crime in Colombia. Individuals may be kidnaped as political statements or by various guerrilla groups to finance their various causes.) He was arrested for car theft in 1974 and again for transporting thirty-nine kilos of cocaine in 1976 (Eddy et al., 1988; Gugliotta & Leen, 1989). The two arresting officers in the drug case were murdered five years after the arrest, even though no judge ever convicted Escobar of the offense. The lack of conviction was probably indicative of Escobar's increasing power and influence as an upper-level drug lord and the judges' fear of retaliation by Escobar's organization.

By the early 1980s, Pablo Escobar emerged as one of Colombia's "leading" businessmen, reputed to be worth about three billion dollars (Poole, 1989). Famous for his gifts to charity, Escobar financed the construction of a thousand units of free housing for the poor. Presenting himself as a servant of the people, Escobar was elected as an alternate to the Colombian Congress in 1982. However, in January 1984, he felt forced to resign amidst unrelenting public exposure of his previous criminal record and allegations concerning his current involvement in drug trafficking by Lara Bonilla, Colombia's Justice Minister (a position comparable to the U.S. Attorney General). On April 30, 1984, while riding to work in his white Mercedes, Lara Bonilla was assassinated (Eddy, 1988; Gugliotta & Leen, 1989). Two men on a motorcycle approached the car from the rear, shot Bonilla through the car window, and escaped into the city traffic.

Jorge Ochoa, a childhood friend of Escobar, heads the Ochoa family organization, assisted by his brothers Fabio and Juan David. During their early years, the Ochoas were known as ranchers who also owned and operated a restaurant. However, they did not make a very good living. Gugliotta and Leen (1989) report that Jorge Ochoa entered the drug-trafficking business because he was dis-tressed by the long hours worked by his mother and sisters in the restaurant.

Ochoa entered the cocaine business during the mid 1970s by distributing cocaine in Miami for his uncle, a mid-level Colombian trafficker. After narrowly escaping arrest in the United States, Ochoa returned to Colombia. Shortly thereafter, the uncle was murdered and Ochoa took over the business. Some have speculated that Ochoa himself was responsible for his uncle's death in order to gain sole control of the business (Gugliotta & Leen, 1989).

During the late 1960s and early 1970s the Colombians limited their scope of operation to purchasing coca paste from Peru and Bolivia and transforming it into cocaine in clandestine laboratories in Colombia. The finished product sold for about $10,000 per kilo to wholesalers, who transported it to the United States. That same kilo then wholesaled again in the United States anywhere from $30,000 to $65,000 and possessed a street value of $135,000. The Colombians recognized they could significantly increase their profit margin if they became involved in the transportation and distribution of cocaine in the United States (Eddy et al., 1988). The American appetite for cocaine seemed insatiable, but smuggling it through customs in suitcases a few kilos at a time was slow, arduous, and risky. A safer, more efficient means of transporting drugs was needed, and Carlos Lehder was the genius who developed the system (Cooper, 1990; Gugliotta & Leen, 1989).

Born in Colombia, Lehder moved to the United States with his mother when he was fifteen years old. He began his criminal career as a car thief and he was later arrested in Miami for possession of 237 pounds of marijuana (Gugliotta & Leen, 1989) and sent to the Federal Correctional Institution at Danbury for four years.

While confined at Danbury, Lehder developed his plan for a highly organized and efficient method to import previously unheard of amounts of cocaine into the United States by private aircraft. Upon release from prison, Lehder lost no time implementing his plan. Recruiting pilots with private airplanes, Lehder set about transforming the planes, removing all but the essential equipment and attaching extra fuel tanks to carry the large shipments of cocaine long distances.

The major obstacle was flying the 1,500 miles from Colombia to the United States. The planes needed a safe place to land and refuel. Lehder thought the Bahamas would do nicely and purchased 165 acres on the island of Norman's Cay in May 1978. The property included several buildings and an airstrip.

Soon planes were landing, refueling, and heading toward the United States on a daily basis. Bribes to the Bahamian government insured Lehder a smooth running operation unencumbered by police interference. The Bahamian banking secrecy laws protected his monetary assets and the banks, which received a substantial counting fee, found it in their best interests to use the utmost discretion when dealing with Lehder and his millions of dollars (Gugliotta & Leen, 1989). Huge amounts of cash, often a million dollars or more, would be brought in suitcases. Banks charged anywhere from two to ten percent just to count the money.

On February 3, 1987, Carlos Lehder was arrested by the Colombian police and extradited to the United States within 24 hours. Extradition occurred quickly because Colombian police feared Lehder's organization would either break him out of prison or bribe enough officials to gain his release, or his attorneys would initiate endless legal maneuvers to prevent his extradition. On July 20, 1988, Lehder was sentenced to life in prison in the United States with no parole plus 135 years (Gugliotta & Leen, 1989).

More is known about the death than the life of Jose Gonzalo Rodriguez Gacha, nicknamed "the Mexican" because of his love for Mexico. Referred to in the press as a former pig farmer (Treaster, 1989a), the billionaire (Poole, 1989) controlled cocaine distribution in southern California and began to compete with the Cali cartel in New York City before his death (Gugliotta & Leen, 1989; Poole, 1989). Some allege that as a result of Rodriguez Gacha's intrusion into Cali territory in New York City, the Cali cartel provided information concerning his whereabouts to the Colombian police. While hiding out in a remote region of Colombia's coastline, Rodriguez Gacha, along with his 17-year-old son and fifteen bodyguards, was killed in a bloody shoot-out with an elite Colombian police unit on December 15, 1989 (Kingpin in Colombian cocaine, 1989; Treaster, 1989a, 1989b). Although The New York Times reported that his death was cheered by the Colombian citizenry (Treaster, 1989a, 1989b), a subsequent article noted that fifteen thousand Colombians gathered during the funeral to mourn his death (Treaster, 1989c). Duzan (1994) notes that the residents of his hometown of Pacho sat in mourning for three days and three nights.

With Rodriguez Gacha dead and Lehder behind bars, the Escobar and Ochoa organizations were clearly the front-runners of the Medellin cartel of the early 1990s. The Colombian government had offered a $400,000 reward for the capture of Escobar (Moody, 1990), but

what Escobar, Ochoa, and other top level traffickers feared most was extradition to the United States, where their influence is minimal and certain lengthy incarceration awaits them. "The Medellin cartel [seem] willing to take whatever steps necessary to be tried in their own country. 'Better a tomb in Colombia than a jail cell in the United States,' is the oft heard quote in Bogata" (Chernick, 1990, p. 37). Their organizations are run from safe houses in the suburbs of Medellin and hide-outs in the jungles of South and Central America where they are protected by rebel groups (Duzan, 1994) or train their own armies. These armies are particularly well equipped and well trained. The New York Times reported that the Federal Bureau of Investigation (FBI) prevented several Colombians, allegedly representing Pablo Escobar, from purchasing twenty-four Stinger antiaircraft missiles to be sent to Colombia (Gerth, 1990b). When the ranch of Rodriguez Gacha was searched after his death, a cache of Israeli Uzi machine guns and other weapons were found. It was also reported that Israeli mercenaries were training Rodriguez Gacha's armies (Gerth, 1990a).

The cartels maintain their enormous power either through corruption or intimidation. In Columbia, when law enforcement and public officials cannot be bribed, they are assassinated. Newspaper editors, reporters, and other journalists who speak against the cartel have met the same fate (U.S. Attorneys, 1989, p. 18). Colombian politicians, judges, and police must live restricted and guarded lives. They travel to and from work in armored cars wearing bulletproof vests and accompanied by several bodyguards. Their families must also be protected from murder and kidnapping (Brooke, 1990). A movie or meal in a restaurant is prohibited. When Dandeny Munoz-Mosquera, a suspected top assassin for the Medellin cartel, was captured in September 1991 by federal drug enforcement agents in New York, Colombia's president Cesar Gaviria Trujillo did not want him extradited to Colombia to stand trial for allegedly killing at least forty Colombian policemen. Munoz-Mosquera had already escaped from prison twice. In April 1991 he walked out of a Bogata prison after paying more than $500,000 in bribes (Treaster, 1991b).

The unimaginable wealth and power of these cartels is expressed in the brazen audacity of their acts. In 1984, the cartels offered to pay Colombia's $9 billion national debt if the government would agree to pardon all cartel leaders and abandon an extradition treaty with the United States (Cooper, 1990, p. 15). In March of 1990, it was reported that the Medellin cocaine cartel had offered members of their death squad $100,000 for each antinarcotics police officer killed and $4,000 for any other police officer killed in Medellin or Bogota (Colombian drug cartel, 1990). In the first six months of 1990, 140 lawmen in Medellin were slain (Moody, 1990). By the time a truce was negotiated with the cartel in early 1991, at least 400 police officers were killed.

The list of other drug-related assassinations in Colombia is extensive. In 1988, the Medellin cartel assassinated the Attorney General of Colombia in retaliation for his vigorous opposition to drug trafficking. The cartels are suspected of being responsible for the murder of eleven Colombian Supreme Court justices, 200 Colombian judges and other court personnel, the Minister of Justice, two newspaper editors, 70 journalists, antidrug political candidates—including a presidential candidate expected to win the 1990 election—and at least 400 Colombian National Police Officers and members of the military and several police chiefs (Cooper, 1990, pp. 17-18; U.S. Attorneys, 1989, p. 19, Duzan, 1994). As a result of these terrorist tactics, no major drug trafficker has ever been convicted in Colombia (Brooke, 1991a).

After sixty-five journalists were killed between 1983 and 1990 (twenty-nine in 1989 alone), and an additional twenty journalists fled into hiding, the Columbian newspapers have been successfully intimidated into backing off on their harsh criticism of the cartels. In September 1989, the Bogota headquarters of *El Espectador,* one of Colombia's largest circulating newspapers, was bombed. The paper was driven out of Medellin in April 1990 (Long, 1990).

Americans working in Columbia are not immune to the violence of the drug cartels. In 1984, the U.S. Embassy in Bogota was bombed. Following that incident, the cartels announced that the kidnaping of any high-ranking agent of the Drug Enforcement Administration was worth $350,000, and in 1985, the cartels threatened to execute five Americans for every drug trafficker extradited to the United States (Inciardi, 1984).

In spite of the rampant violence perpetrated by the cartels, they are becoming more accepted by a significant portion of Colombian society as their well-paid employees assimilate into the middle class. Cartel chiefs control most of the modern office buildings in the city of Medellin (U.S. Attorneys, 1989) and may own as much as one-twelfth of Colombia's farmland (Cooper, 1990), providing much needed jobs for Colombian citizens. Many farmers who grow coca find it is more profitable than growing traditional crops and have enjoyed an increased standard of living. Moreover, growing illegal cocaine is more profitable than growing cocaine for the legal market (Cooper, 1990).

Many Colombians consider the drug cartels a positive force in the country (Duzan, 1994). The cash brought to Colombia from the drug trade has greatly improved its ailing economy. The cartel has funded social welfare programs in the form of legitimate employment, extensive recreational centers, free housing for the poor, charitable gifts to the poor, (Cooper, 1990; Gugliotta & Leen, 1989), street lighting, and thousands of scholarships for grade school, high school, and university students (Brooke, 1991b). *Time* magazine reports, "In Medellin a small boy kicking a ball around a field built by Escobar, called him a hero: 'To me he's more important than God'" (Moody, 1990). It is clear that the Colombian society and economy are dependent upon the flow of drug money from the United States.

However, in 1990, the Medellin cartel claimed it was ready to abandon their business of drugs. They offered to give to the government all the cocaine labs, aircraft, landing strips, explosives, weapons, and hide-outs. They agreed to release hostages and stop the violence against Colombian police, military, politicians, and journalists in return for amnesty and a promise of no extradition to the United States (Chernick, 1990). Many Colombian citizens believe it is better to negotiate with the drug lords and end the violence; however, the United States has always insisted that in order to continue receiving U.S. aid, Colombia must not negotiate with the druglords. Given the tremendous wealth and strength of the armies controlled by the kingpins, the extent of corruption within the Colombian government and military, and the fact that 1 in every 350 Colombians may be involved in the drug trade (Eddy et al, 1988), the refusal to negotiate would only continue the bloodshed in Colombia. Therefore, in late 1990, the Colombian government promised drug traffickers they would not be extradited to the United States if they surrendered to authorities.

The first major drug trafficker to take advantage of Colombia's offer was Fabio Ochoa in December 1990 (Drug-Trafficking Suspect..., 1990, December 19) followed shortly thereafter by Juan David Ochoa and finally Jorge Ochoa. But the major headlines emerged when Pablo Escobar surrendered to Colombian authorities on June 19, 1991, just hours after Colombian law changed to prohibit extradition of drug traffickers to the United States (Gutkin, 1991). As a result of negotiations with the Colombian government, Escobar was incarcerated at a prison he supposedly helped build near his hometown of

Envigado. "The Envigado jail…has private baths, gardens, a soccer field, television and game rooms" (Gutkin, 1991, p. A6). The prison guards (some with criminal records) have reportedly been hand picked by Escobar. An army of 150 soldiers guard the prison's perimeter, presumably to keep out potential assassins rather than to keep inmates from escaping. Other inmates must be screened by a special committee to ensure that none of Escobar's enemies are allowed to penetrate the building. "Sole access [to the prison] is by a steep one-lane dirt road that is passable only by four-wheel-drive vehicles. One mile below the prison, a steel barrier blocks further road access. From their mountain perch, Mr. Escobar's guards can watch through their binoculars any vehicles laboring up the mountain road….Civil aviation authorities have closed the airspace over the jail [to prevent air attacks], and the trafficker is reported to have demanded a radar system and steel roofs" (Brooke, 1991b, p. 4).

On July 22, 1992, the Colombian government sought to move Escobar to a more secure prison after it learned that he continued to traffic cocaine from prison and had ordered the killing of rival drug traffickers who were trying to take control of his business. Escobar learned of the attempt to move him from his plush, custom-built prison and barricaded himself inside while taking several hostages (Treaster, 1992b). When an elite Special Forces unit of the Colombian military was sent to storm the prison, they delayed their arrival by three hours then refused an order to storm the prison for an additional two hours. It is believed that during this delay, the commanding general entrusted with the task of moving Escobar aided his escape by dressing Escobar in an army uniform and hiding him and several of his associates in a military vehicle (French, 1992). Also implicated in the plot to assist Escobar's escape were a major general in the Colombian Airforce, two air force lieutenant colonels, the Deputy Justice Minister (a position comparable to our assistant Attorney General), the prison's warden and the assistant warden (Christian, 1992 Officials fired after escape…, 1992).

In December of 1993, Pablo Escobar was finally tracked to a safe house in Medellin and killed by an elite force of Columbian police. Although his death proved to be a symbolic victory for the Colombian police and the American Drug Enforcement Administration, the real winners of this battle are the Cali cartel.

The Cali cartel, headed by Gilberto Rodriguez Orejuela, Miguel Rodriguez Orejuela, and Jose Santacruz Londono has operated with less violence and a lower profile than the Medellin cartel. A few of their smaller cocaine-refining laboratories have been destroyed (Brooke, 1991c), but the Colombian government failed to arrest any major Cali trafficker and did not officially recognize Gilberto Rodriguez Orejuela as a criminal until 1994. Pablo Escobar had referred to the Rodriguez brothers as "pets of the police" (Brooke, 1991c). The Cali cartel has assimilated into Colombian society and has financed the police stations found throughout Cali in an effort to control street crime. It is believed that the Cali cartel worked closely with the Colombian police in their war against the Medellin cartel. Even their methods of moving drugs represents a lower profile, more conservative approach. "Unlike the Medellin cartel, which prefers fast shipment by plane and speedboat, the Cali traffickers hide their merchandise in freighter cargo containers. Cali cocaine has been found in shipments of lumber, chocolate, coffee, tropical fruit extract and lye" (Brooke, 1991c, p. 6).

Amidst increasing allegations that Colombia's president Ernesto Samper Pizano accepted more than $3.75 million dollars in campaign contributions from members of the Cali cartel during his 1994 election (Colombian press feels heat, 1995; Rohter, 1995) the United States increased pressure on Colombia to fight drug traffickers. Fueling these allegations has been President Samper's lenient dealings with drug traffickers (Brook, 1995).

In early 1995 the United States State Department and White House accused the Colombian government of failing to treat traffickers seriously and threatened to withhold aid and trade benefits (Treaster, 1995, June 12). Moreover, government corruption in Colombia was so extensive that the United States stopped sharing intelligence with Colombian police and military regarding the activities of drug traffickers because they believed it was being passed on to traffickers (Treaster, 1995, June 12).

In response to pressure from the United States, Gilberto Rodriguez Orejuela was finally captured on June 9, 1995, hiding in a closet. The arrest was the result of a 6000 man joint military and police task force (Rohter, 1995).

Twenty-four hours after Rodriguez Orejuela's arrest a bomb exploded during a concert in Medellin killing 30 people (Rohter, 1995, June 12). It is believed that a new reign of violence and terror may begin in Colombia as the government pursues the once protected Cali cartel (Treaster, 1995).

There is increasing evidence that the Colombian drug traffickers have expanded their operations to include the marketing of heroin (Colombian heroin may be increasing, 1991). Paez Indian farmers grow the opium poppies in remote regions of the Andean Mountains. Armed leftist guerrillas guard the farms which are not accessible by roads. The plants are easier to grow than crops such as corn or potatoes and can be sold for a higher profit by the improverished farmers. Since a kilo of heroin wholesales for about 10 times as much as a kilo of cocaine, the Colombian traffickers need only use the same distribution and money laundering methods as they used to market cocaine to reap greater profits.

Colombian cartels operating in the United States use their wealth and power to corrupt and intimidate American law enforcement personnel, public officials, and members of the financial and business community whose cooperation would further the activities of the cartels. They have assassinated one federal judge in Texas (Inciardi, 1984), murdered informers and government witnesses, placed contracts on law enforcement officers, and engaged in violent wars for control of sales territory. U.S. prosecutors have heard accounts of torture and senseless cruelty, fire-bombings of houses and cars, and brutal murders (U.S. Attorneys, 1989).

The Colombian cartels have found southern Florida and central and southern California to be ideal areas for their U.S. operations. These regions of the United States contain a combination of large metropolitan areas and nearby, relatively isolated rural areas with convenient landing strips. They also have long, hard-to-patrol coastlines or border areas, major transportation hubs, populations containing large numbers of transients and immigrants, a well-developed system of international banking, and access to sophisticated communications systems. This combination of elements has proven extremely advantageous to the cartels' operations (U.S. Attorneys, 1989, p. 21).

These operations, from the fields of coca cultivation in South America to the final sale of crack cocaine on a street corner in Des Moines or in a schoolyard in Hartford, represent a massive production, distribution, and sales effort carried out over thousands of miles, employing the nationals of different countries, the resources of many separate, coordinated organizations, and the expertise of hundreds of specialists in all aspects of drug trafficking (U.S. Attorneys, 1989, p. 21).

La Cosa Nostra and the Sicilian Mafia

La Cosa Nostra (LCN), literally translated "Our Thing," was founded in the 1930s. It was an outgrowth of the consolidation of several Italian immigrant gangs, operating the Italian ghettos created by a flood of more than two million immigrants that arrived in the early years of the century. The gangs were originally formed by immigrant criminals who belonged to the three major southern Italian secret societies the Sicilian Mafia, the Neapolitan Camorra, and the Calabrian N'Drangheta. LCN soon emerged as the preeminent American criminal empire, distinct from its diverse Italian antecedents (U.S. Attorneys, 1989, p. 22).

The LCN of today consists of twenty-five known families, with more than 2,000 members and several times that many associates. The families are largely independent, local organizations joined together in a confederation that acknowledges the authority of a commission consisting of the heads of the most powerful LCN families (U.S. Attorneys, 1989, p. 22).

From the outset, certain families had prohibited drug trafficking. LCN has traditionally avoided unnecessarily attracting the attention of law enforcement agencies, and older members were aware that drug trafficking would elicit a strong response from the law enforcement community (U.S. Attorneys, 1989, p. 22). During Prohibition the primary business of LCN was bootlegging illegal liquor, a particularly lucrative racket. However, following the end of Prohibition, this major source of income for LCN dried up and some members looked to importing heroin (McCoy, 1972).

A principal LCN player in the heroin business was Charles "Lucky" Luciano (McCoy, 1972). He also operated a major enterprise in prostitution (employing 1,200 prostitutes in New York City by 1935) and was known to get his employees addicted to heroin in order to keep them working to obtain the drug. By 1936, the Federal Bureau of Narcotics had enough evidence to indict Luciano on narcotics charges but felt they had a better chance of convicting him on charges of forced prostitution. He received a thirty to fifty year sentence (McCoy, 1972, p. 19). However, while in prison, Luciano still controlled all activity on the docks of the New York waterfront. During World War II, the Office of Naval Intelligence (ONI), recognizing Luciano's considerable influence, sought his help in controlling a series of sabotage incidents that occurred on the New York docks. This action allowed him to resume leadership of American organized crime. In addition, Luciano helped the U.S. military secure the cooperation of the Sicilian mafia in Italy to further the Allied war effort. As a result of his wartime cooperation, Luciano was released from prison and deported to Sicily (McCoy, 1972).

McCoy (1972, p. 15) argues quite cogently that following World War II, "there was an excellent chance that heroin addiction could be eliminated in the United States. The wartime security measures designed to prevent infiltration of foreign spies and sabotage to naval installations made smuggling into the United States virtually impossible. Most American addicts were forced to break their habits during the war, and consumer demand just about disappeared. Moreover, the international narcotics syndicates were weakened by the war and could have been decimated with a minimum of police effort." Following Luciano's release, the United States deported hundreds of other known organized crime figures to Italy, and "Luciano was able to build an awesome international narcotics syndicate soon after his arrival in Italy" (McCoy, 1972, p. 24). The population of heroin addicts in the United States increased from about 20,000 following the War to 60,000 by 1952 to 150,000 by 1965 (McCoy, p. 24).

A recent survey of LCN-related intelligence from the Boston FBI files indicates that some New England LCN members have increased their involvement in illegal drug trafficking. This change in favor of drug dealing is probably due to the recent shifting of power among the LCN families. Arrests and convictions of many of its high ranking members has left vacant leadership positions that have been filled by the younger, less-experienced family members. These new leaders are less influenced by family tradition and more driven by the potential for tremendous wealth. Thus the changing LCN membership has given rise to a new and potentially more violent role for the LCN in drug trafficking operations (U.S. Attorneys, 1989, pp. 22–23).

The most obvious drug-trafficking partner for LCN is the Sicilian Mafia, which still flourishes under the original organization founded by Luciano. In New York during the 1970s and 1980s, the Sicilian Mafia conspired with LCN to import and distribute almost 4,000 pounds of heroin and unknown quantities of cocaine, over a ten-year period, realizing $60 million in profits. A famous case, popularly known as the "Pizza Connection" because many of the participants owned pizza parlors, resulted in the imprisonment of more than fifteen LCN/Sicilian Mafia kingpins for twenty to forty-five-year sentences (Blumenthal, 1988; U.S. Attorneys, 1989, p. 23).

Current estimates indicate that LCN and the Sicilian Mafia together are responsible for a significant portion of the total volume of heroin brought into the United States annually. Additionally, it has recently been reported that the Sicilian Mafia is exchanging heroin for cocaine, with the assistance of LCN families. South American cocaine is moving through the United States to a lucrative market in Europe. Heroin purchased by the Sicilian Mafia from the Middle East is moved through Italy to the United States.

This role as middleman in cocaine distribution has led to the development of ties between individual LCN members, and the Colombian cartels. The continuing decline of cocaine prices in the United States has led to expansion in the European and Japanese markets (Drug traffickers shift processing…, 1991). During the summer of 1990, a kilo of cocaine sold in the United States for $10,000 to $20,000 whereas that same kilo sold in Europe for as much as $27,000 to $115,000. As a result, the Colombians have looked to cooperate with the Sicilian Mafia in order to expand their businesses (Cooper, 1990; Johnston, 1990; Europe reportedly biggest…, 1990). In addition, some LCN families have strong ties to Colombian and Cuban drug cartels in the greater Miami area, providing these families with drugs for distribution in the United States. These ad hoc relationships developed on the basis of a common desire to expand both their markets and product lines (U.S. Attorneys, 1989, p. 23).

It is expected that the LCN will further develop their operations to profit from the drug trade. They probably will not initiate direct confrontation with the Colombian or other major drug cartels. Instead, they are prepared to coexist and cooperate with the Colombian cartels and their drug-specific groups and organizations (U.S. Attorneys, 1989, p. 23).

Asian Organized Crime Groups

Although the Asian gangs have traditionally played a limited role in trafficking heroin (Bresler, 1980), they became a major force in the illicit drug market in the United States in the latter part of the 1980s. Primarily of Chinese origin, these gangs operate on both coasts (U.S. Attorneys, 1989, p. 24).

There are two primary classifications of Chinese Organized Crime (COC) groups operating in the United States: American COC and Triads who are based in Hong Kong (Bresler, 1981; Posner, 1988). The Triads have a history hundreds of years old. They were originally formed in China as secret societies whose function consisted of resisting the rule of outside aggressors. Until the later part of the nineteenth century, these societies were primarily legitimate patriotic organizations although the Triads had always engaged in some illegal activity in order to fund their operations. Some Triads have abandoned their political orientation to engage exclusively in criminal enterprises (Bresler, 1980; Posner, 1988).

There are many areas of similarity between Chinese organized crime and LCN. Like LCN, Chinese organized crime grew out of much older secret or fraternal societies that have evolved into criminal groups. Both the Chinese groups and LCN place an unusually strong emphasis on family and on group loyalty, and both practice retribution against those who reveal secrets to outsiders (U.S. Attorneys, 1989, p. 24). It is particularly difficult for American drug agents to infiltrate and gather intelligence on these Chinese organizations. In addition to speaking Mandarin, the organized crime groups also speak four other dialects which compounds an agent's difficulty in gathering information. Both the Chinese gangs and LCN practice the use of extortion and the corruption of public officials to promote their activities, and both gained their initial power and eminence through exploitation of large populations of non-English-speaking immigrants. Finally, both the Chinese groups and LCN have historically been involved in a broad range of criminal activities of which drug trafficking is but one part (U.S. Attorneys, 1989, p. 25).

While Chinese criminal organizations do not approach the operating scope of the Colombian cartels, Chinese American criminals are the largest importers of heroin from Southeast Asia, virtually all of it originating in the Golden Triangle (Myanmar, formerly Burma, Thailand and Laos).

Most of the world's opium originates in the Golden Triangle. Two rebel armies in Myanmar who identify themselves as freedom fighters export about 75 percent of the heroin originating in the golden Triangle (Witkin, 1994; Lintner & Mai, 1994; Lintner, 1994a, 1994b; The Golden Triangle's new king, 1995). Khun Sa, the world's most notorious heroin trafficker is the leader of the Shan United Army. He claims to be fighting for independence for the Shan State and to free his people from an oppressive government known internationally for its human rights violations and opposition to democracy (Lintner, 1994a & 1994b; The Golden Triangle's new king 1995). His heroin trafficking activities provide the funds for his freedom fighting army of 20,000 men and boys. His headquarters, in the Shan State of southern Burma, is well equipped with schools, a hospital, other modern facilities streetlights, and a hydroelectric power station (Lintner, 1994a).

Khun Sa is wanted in New York City on drug trafficking charges. As the United States puts pressure on Myanmar to apprehend Khun Sa, the United Wa State Army, another rebel army headed by Chao Nyi Lai, with peaceful ties to the Myanmar government is increasing its own heroin processing activity. The United Wa State Army, consisting of about 20,000 to 30,000 soldiers (The Golden Triangle's..., 1995) signed a peace treaty with the current Myanmar's ruling junta in 1989. As government suppression increases on Khun Sa, the United Wa State Army has expanded its operation of heroin refineries along the Thai/Myanmar border. It is obvious that the

---

Table 16.1   *Opium Cultivation in the Golden Triangle, 1989-93 (Hectares)*

	1989	1990	1991	1992	1993
Burma	142,700	150,100	160,000	153,700	165,800
Laos	42,130	30,580	29,625	25,610	26,040
Thailand	4,075	3,435	3,000	2,050	2,880
Total	188,905	184,115	192,625	181,360	194,720

Hectare = 2.471 acres
Source: U.S. State Department

government is more concerned with suppressing the drug trafficking activities of those political groups that conflict with its own political views. Other political groups whose views are consistent with the government's are free to traffic in drugs. This scenario appears similar to that which occurred in Colombia when the United States put pressure on the Colombian government to suppress the activities of the Medellin drug cartel during the early 1990s. These governmental assaults on particular drug trafficking groups only serve to strengthen the competition's advantage in the drug trafficking arena.

U.S. foreign policy and drug policy have often conflicted (Weiner, 1994). On the one hand the U.S. has sanctioned Myanmar after thousands of supporters of democracy were either killed or imprisoned in 1988, by the ruling military junta (The Golden Triangle's new king, 1995). On the other hand, the Office of National Drug Control Policy and the State Department's Bureau of International Narcotics Matters strongly support increased aid to the ruling junta to fight the drug trafficking activities of Khun Sa.

The Chinese organizations are a dominant force in heroin trafficking in New York City, New Jersey, and Massachusetts (U.S. Attorneys 1989). They smuggle drugs into the United States in restaurant equipment, mahjongg sets, inside goldfish, in dolls, in golf-cart tires, and inside picture frames. Heroin has also been shipped by parcel post and Federal Express (Maas, 1994).

Jamaican Posses

Approximately forty Jamaican organized crime gangs, known as posses, operate in the United States, Canada, Great Britain, and the Caribbean. Some of the names associated with different posses are Shower, Jungle, Nanyville, Montego Bay, Bibour, Banton, Dog, Southee, and Okra Slime, (McGuire, 1988). The combined membership of these gangs is conservatively estimated to number over 10,000. The majority are convicted felons, illegal aliens, or both. Many of the mid- to high-level positions in the posse organizations are held by individuals who began their criminal careers in Jamaica and who are fugitives from justice there. Americans recruited from black urban areas fill the low-level positions. These gangs generally grew out of specific geographic and political affiliations in Jamaica, but have long since become exclusively profit-oriented organizations trafficking in drugs and firearms (McGuire, 1988; and U.S. Attorneys, 1989, p. 27).

The Jamaican posses, which began as marijuana traffickers, have been active in the United States since about 1984 but have only recently been recognized as a major drug-trafficking force. They are currently most involved in trafficking crack cocaine. Almost all posses have connections in New York and Miami, which have large Jamaican populations (U.S. Attorneys, 1989, p. 28).

The Jamaicans' operations are structured to allow them to be importers, wholesalers, local distributors, retailers, and money launderers. By excluding the middleman, the posses can substantially raise their profit margins. One posse controlling fifty crack houses can make $9 million a month (U.S. Attorneys, 1989, p. 28). McGuire (1988) reports that Jamaican crack houses in Dallas earn as much as $400,000 a day. The Jamaicans purchase cocaine from Colombians or Cubans in Jamaica, the Bahamas, southern California, or South Florida. Recent investigations show that Jamaican criminal groups are establishing new entry routes for drug shipments (U.S. Attorneys, 1989, p. 28).

Distribution of the drugs is directed by key posse members at controlling points. Drugs, drug paraphernalia, and weapons are stored at stash houses, which supply the street level distribution points known as crack houses, gate houses, or dope houses. Those at the controlling points are responsible for resupplying the street-level distribution points, usually located in apartments or rented houses (U.S. Attorneys, 1989, p. 28). The posse members often canvas inner-city housing projects looking for units inhabited by single welfare mothers. Although given no choice to refuse, these women are paid for use of their apartments as gate houses and stash houses and are often required to transport drugs (Surovell, 1990).

Crack houses operated by Jamaican posses are sophisticated distribution operations, often shuttered from outside view with blackened windows. Extensive defensive mechanisms are used, ranging from specially constructed entrance barricades composed of two-by-fours known as New York Stops, to extensive use of lookouts carrying walkie-talkies to warn of police raids. Armed guards or managers, located at the crack houses, keep intruders and law enforcement personnel from entering. Some Jamaican posses have reportedly told their guards to shoot any law enforcement officer who tries to raid them. In many cases, a gun is held to a customer's head until the drug transaction is completed, in case the customer turns out to be a troublemaker, an informant, or an undercover agent. The houses are equipped with secret hiding places for drugs and often have ladders or other emergency exit routes. The location is changed frequently to frustrate police attempts to identify trafficking locations (U.S. Attorneys, 1989, p. 28).

The posses do not restrict their operations to crack houses. In some cases, even more temporary quarters will do. Posse members in Columbus, Ohio; Frederick, Maryland; and Wilmington, North Carolina set up retail distribution networks in economy motels, usually located near interstate highways. It is believed that these operations were a form of market testing; where the market proved lucrative, the Jamaicans subsequently leased rental properties to set up crack houses (U.S. Attorneys, 1989, p. 28).

Unlike most drug organizations, Jamaican posses often do their own money laundering. They have used Western Union for wire transfers of money, purchased legitimate businesses (restaurants, auto repair shops, record stores) as fronts, and bought real estate for quick resale (U.S. Attorneys, 1989, pp. 28–29).

It is believed that the Jamaican posses as a whole have been responsible for at least 1,000 murders in the United States between 1985 and 1989. The posses have demonstrated a willingness to turn to violence and torture at the slightest provocation, which is unusual even among drug traffickers. Victims in some homicides were apparently shot in the ankles, knees, and hips before being shot in the head. Other victims were subjected to scalding hot water before being murdered and dismembered. No one is immune from the violence of the posses. Anyone perceived as a threat to their organization is murdered, including wives, girlfriends, and even children (U.S. Attorneys, 1989, p. 29).

The extensive and brutal violence has effectively imposed a code of silence among anyone associated with the Jamaican posses, making information concerning their organization difficult to obtain. Although a few informants have revealed the existence and operating locations of a few specific posses, a Jamaican criminal, when arrested, will rarely discuss his posse and will even deny that such gangs exist. Because witnesses who have merely been interviewed by the police but who gave no evidence have been murdered, entire neighborhoods have been intimidated and discouraged from cooperating with the police (U.S. Attorneys, 1989, p. 29).

The willingness of posse members to engage police in shoot-outs while resisting arrest makes them even more dangerous. They have not hesitated to issue contracts on police and federal agents who they feel are disrupting their business, even to the point of offering a $25,000 award in Virginia to anyone who killed a police officer. Jamaican criminals have attempted to entrap police by identifying

their telephone and beeper numbers and luring them to staged shoot-outs (U.S. Attorneys, 1989, p. 29).

From the time they enter the United States illegally to the point where they launder their drug profits, members of Jamaican organized crime are adept at avoiding apprehension by law enforcement. They substitute photos or names on valid passports and forge Social Security cards, birth certificates, and INS green cards. Equipped with multiple identities, Jamaican posse members are extremely mobile. In one case, the same passport was used by fifteen different posse members, using the same name but with a different picture each time. Posse members are able to travel freely between the United States, Mexico, and Canada. This mobility is a distinct advantage to the criminal when law enforcement personnel are bound by the constraints of territorial and jurisdictional boundaries (U.S. Attorneys, 1989, pp. 29–30).

Outlaw Motorcycle Gangs

Motorcycle gangs were originally created in California. Although there are more than 500 motorcycle gangs in the United States, the most powerful are the Hell's Angels, the Outlaws, the Pagans, and the Banditos. Highly structured, often national, drug-trafficking organizations, they control most of the amphetamine manufacture and distribution in the United States and have developed working relationships with a number of other drug-trafficking organizations, (U.S. Attorneys, 1989, p. 31).

Although the gangs pursue a wide array of illegal activities such as prostitution, burglary, rape, assault, murder, contract killings, illegal banking, and loan sharking, drug trafficking has emerged as their primary organized crime activity. Each of the major gangs specializes in a particular aspect of the drug trade. For example, the Hell's Angels and the Banditos are heavily involved in methamphetamine manufacturing, distribution, and sales. The Pagans dominate the PCP and methamphetamine trade in the Northeast, while the Outlaws, through their Florida chapters, which may be involved with Cuban and Colombian suppliers, are engaged in cocaine trafficking. The Outlaws also traffic in a bogus form of Valium, manufactured in illegal Canadian laboratories and distributed from a base in Chicago (U.S. Attorneys, 1989, pp. 31–32).

As their structures have become more sophisticated and their activities more widespread, the bikers have developed more sophisticated ways of defending themselves and their activities. The Banditos and the Outlaws carry tape recorders to record conversations with any law enforcement officers who might confront them. They attempt to entice the officers to make statements that will contaminate any case brought against them. The major gangs have begun to exchange computerized information on law enforcement officers and their informants. They have also been known to place operatives in courthouses, prisons, and police stations to gather intelligence on law enforcement operations and planning (U.S. Attorneys, 1989, p. 32).

Gang clubhouses vary in location and layout. They may be located on farms, in the city center, or in residential areas. While the clubhouses are used for business meetings, partying, and working on motorcycles, they must be tightly secured against unexpected police raids or attacks by rival gangs. Some gangs place their houses under twenty-four-hour guard and have steel-reinforced doors and standard chain-link fences topped with barbed wire as a perimeter defense. In many cases, the house itself is also protected by concrete cinderblock walls with built-in gun ports, and guard dogs often roam in the area between the fences (U.S. Attorneys, 1989, p. 32).

Inside the clubhouses, other security measures are taken, including wooden or steel shutters that close from the inside, exterior walls fitted with sheets of armor plating, and electronic security equipment with tracking devices, closed-circuit television cameras, and telephone eavesdropping units. Some gangs have actually planted poisonous snakes in dresser drawers, kitchen cabinets, or boxes, ready to strike out at whoever rummages in their hiding place (U.S. Attorneys, 1989, p. 32).

Law enforcement officials have had some success in turning members who fear that their days within the gang are numbered. They have also exploited intra- and inter-gang rivalries to gain information on gang activities. Law enforcement pressure on the West Coast has succeeded in causing the Hell's Angels to move their methamphetamine manufacturing businesses to other areas. Unfortunately, as is often the case, law enforcement efforts often displace rather than permanently dismantle drug operations (U.S. Attorney's, 1989, pp. 32-33).

California Street Gangs

California is home to one of the most dangerous and menacing developments in drug trafficking, the large-scale organized street gangs. These gangs first appeared in Los Angeles in the late 1960s. Since then, their activities have escalated from the instigation of neighborhood violence to large-scale drug trafficking throughout the United States (U.S. Attorneys, 1989, p. 33).

Although there are many smaller independent gangs in the Los Angeles area, the most successful and dangerous California street gangs are divided into two major organizations, the Crips and the Bloods. Each of these organizations is composed of numerous smaller gangs called sets. It is estimated that there are approximately 190 Crips sets and 65 Bloods sets. Law enforcement officials believe that these approximately 250 sets have a combined membership of approximately 25,000 (U.S. Attorneys, 1989, p. 33).

The sets are structured along lines of seniority and function. They have caste-like subdivisions as delineated below:

1. *original gang members (O.G.)*
2. *gangsters, the hard-core members, whose ages range from sixteen to twenty-two*
3. *baby gangsters, who are between nine and twelve*
4. *tiny gangsters, who are younger than nine.*

While some gangs include members in their late twenties and early thirties, the most violent and active members are those between fourteen and eighteen, many of them "wannabees" who want to prove themselves in order to be accepted by other gang members and who are precisely the ones most useful as soldiers in gang activities (U.S. Attorneys, 1989, p. 33).

The Crips and the Bloods are primarily involved in PCP and crack cocaine trafficking. They operate secret laboratories for drug manufacture in the Los Angeles area, and have become skilled at avoiding detection. Since crack is increasingly the drug of choice in the Los Angeles area the gangs have expanded their operations to meet this demand. A recent FBI investigation has revealed direct ties between the Crips and the Colombian Medellin cartel. Gang members purchase cocaine powder on consignment, indicating a strong relationship between the two groups based on trust (FBI says Los Angeles gang..., 1992). The drug is then processed into crack. Finally, the newly produced crack is given out in multi-ounce quantities by the supplier to street distributors, to be sold to the end user. The street distributors typically carry only small amounts, concealing the rest in convenient locations from which they can quickly replenish their stock (U.S. Attorneys, 1989, p. 34).

California street gang sellers use a number of techniques for distributing crack. Sometimes they employ spotters to direct customers to where the street distributor waits, or they may sell to drivers of passing cars. Another approach is to make the sale from heavily fortified rock houses, to which the customer has only limited access. The customer may have to wait outside until the transaction is completed, with the seller out of sight, or the customer may be admitted only as far as a caged area in the front end of the house. However, crack dealers are moving away from rock houses toward street sales and sales from motel rooms. In the latter case, dealers will usually pay in cash, rent multiple rooms, and use pagers and cellular phones to contact suppliers and buyers (U.S. Attorneys, 1989, p. 34).

The Los Angeles gangs have expanded their drug business to other parts of the country, including Seattle, Vancouver, Denver, Kansas City, Chicago, Nashville, Baltimore, and Sioux Falls. One of the most worrisome aspects of the street gangs is their willingness to direct their violence at each other, at the police, and at members of the public—essentially at anyone who stands in the way of their operations. What makes this violence especially frightening is the amount of firepower at their disposal; they often use semi-automatic rifles and large-caliber handguns. In parts of Los Angeles, the weapon of choice is the AK-47 with a 30-round clip—a large-caliber weapon that dramatically increases the chances of inflicting deadly injury. With so much firepower, gang-related homicides in the Los Angeles area have risen steadily (U.S. Attorneys, 1989, p. 35).

The Street Level Dealer

Once the major dealers deliver the cocaine or heroin to the middle level distributors, the drugs are again stepped on to expand the quantity, at the expense of the quality, to improve the profitability of the trade. These middlemen supply the local dealers who, in turn, further dilute the drug to improve their profits.

The small, local dealer characteristically runs a very well-organized, market-oriented business. Others, not so well organized, quickly lose their business and staff to other dealers (T. Williams, 1989). Of primary concern to the local dealer is the quality of the product purchased from the middle level dealer. The drug should be of sufficient purity to allow it to be stepped-on again without resulting in a final product that customers will find too weak. Many dealers package their cocaine, crack, or heroin in bags with trademarks on them (Goldstein et al., 1984; T. Williams, 1989). Heroin sold in New York City has been marketed under the brandnames of Black Magic,

Chako Fan, Death Row, 888, Fuck Me Please, Good Pussy, 90%, Kojak, The Beast, 32, and The Witch (Goldstein et al.). These trademarks provide the dealer with repeat business and brand recognition associated with high-quality drugs.

The dealer also recruits and maintains an effective sales crew, drawn from the surrounding community of addicts and non-addicts who work for the dealers in a variety of jobs. The very youngest pre-teens are recruited, with the promise of earning large amounts of money to deliver drugs to regular customers and are sometimes used to pick up allotments from the middleman. These very young children are attractive to the dealers because of their loyalty and the fact that they are unlikely to be arrested. Teenaged and young men are drawn to the status associated with the money and possession of the drugs, especially cocaine, because the women are attracted to the money and "coke" (T. Williams, 1989). Many of the sales crew, male and female, begin as users or develop the habit after joining the business. Too much drug use, however, can cost runners their jobs and possibly their lives.

Therein lies another major task of the dealer, "personnel management." the dealer must ensure that members of the sales crew do not lose their effectiveness by using too much of the drug. Heavy drug use increases the probability of an arrest or employee theft. Either way, the dealer stands to lose a significant portion of profits.

The business at the street level requires up-front cash to the middleman, but a consignment arrangement for the local dealer. The dealer allocates a supply of drugs to each crew member with the understanding that he or she will return with a predetermined amount of money. The sales person will try to sell the drugs at a slight mark-up and pocket the difference or use the remaining drugs. The salesperson generally will not be able to step-on the drug again without risk of detection by the customer and the dealer.

A major task of the dealer is to maintain the trust of his customers and suppliers. If the dealer consumes too much of the drug, or the crew is so undisciplined that the brand acquires a bad reputation, the dealer may be cut off from the supplier or the customers may buy elsewhere.

The transactions between the customer and dealer may occur in several ways. First, there is direct delivery to regular customers. Young children deliver the drugs in small packages and pick up payments at prearranged locations. Some deliveries are made to the business offices of some customers. Others sell drugs on street corners and other designated public locations. Because the drug transaction is associated with risks that require trust between the customer and sales crew, customers generally purchase drugs from a favorite dealer.

The dealer will have at least two or three locations in which business is conducted. The multiple locations are necessary to elude law enforcement agencies. There are specific roles played at these locations: In the front room or receiving area, the security crew screens visitors and maintains order during the transactions. In an adjoining room scales are operated by a trusted member of the dealer's crew, or often, the dealer. The person operating the scales is critical because he or she is entrusted with the task of providing accurate amounts of the drug to the customer. The scale operator is rarely seen by the customer or sales crew and typically deals with a second person, who collects money from the customer, carries the funds to the scales, then returns with the drugs. This separation between the person weighing the drug and the customer purchasing the drug is necessary to avoid conflicts regarding the transaction.

While the highly structured organization of the drug dealerships contribute to their stability, they do not endure for more than a few years. Terry Williams (1989), in an ethnographic study of cocaine dealers, reported that most dealers recognized the tenuousness of their trade, and many fantasized about acquiring lots of money and quitting the business after a couple of years. Dr. Williams reported that a few of the successful dealers did, in fact, leave the business with a bit of a nest egg. Most, however, lost their dealerships and their money because of their own drug abuse.

Middlemen may help restore lost drug markets. One former heroin addict (Love, 1990) reported that a community with a dwindling LCN controlled heroin market, which was losing business because new drug users were turning to cocaine and crack was saved by the middlemen. They provided free drugs to their would-be dealers to hold parties where the drugs were given away. These parties continued for more than eighteen months and then suddenly stopped. The sales of heroin quickly approached previous sales levels with this new market of former party-goers. In most other circumstances, it is likely that any dealership lost to one individual will be quickly picked up by another.

The CIA as Drug Traffickers

In its quest to rid the world of Communism, the United States, usually through the covert activities of the Central Intelligence Agency (CIA), has supported political groups whose activities have been funded through drug traffick-

ing. During the Vietnam War, the CIA was involved in drug trafficking possibly to fund secret activities in Laos and Cambodia and to secure the support of various guerrilla groups who opposed the Communists in Southeast Asia (Chambliss, 1990; Kwitney, 1987; McCoy, 1972).

When the United States entered the Vietnam War after France's ignominious defeat at Dien Bien Phu, the U.S. inherited [the French] dependence on opium. The U.S. military and particularly the CIA set about organizing opium smuggling out of Southeast Asia where laboratories sprang up that converted the opium into morphine and heroin (Chambliss, 1990, p. 369).

Using the airline known as Air America, CIA pilots flew raw opium from the hills of the Golden Triangle (Burma, Laos, and Thailand) to heroin laboratories in Siagon, Hong Kong, and Bangkok (Chambliss, 1990, p. 369). As a result, the amount of heroin entering the United States between 1968 and 1972 increased by 50 percent (Chambliss, p. 374).

Scott and Marshall (1991) claim many of the U.S. backed Contras in Nicaragua were extensively involved in cocaine trafficking, which the United States either ignored or, when confronted with the evidence, denied. There were also CIA intelligence links to Mexican drug traffickers whose activities were disregarded because of their sizable "charitable contributions" to the Contras.

Money Laundering

The fact that most drug transactions are carried out exclusively in cash makes money laundering an important part of the drug trafficking industry. The term *money laundering* refers, in its broadest sense, to all activities designed to conceal the existence, nature, and final disposition of funds gained through illicit activities. Essentially, the dirty money (money gotten through illegal activities) is processed in some way to make it appear clean (as though it were acquired through legitimate business).

Money laundering is a highly specialized and complex proposition, especially when large sums are involved. While some drug organizations take care of this aspect of their operations themselves, many turn to those who specialize in this type of service (U.S. Attorneys, 1989, p. 40).

As drug traffickers have become more sophisticated and as federal enforcement agents have become more adept at using financial investigations to pursue them to prosecution, the traffickers have become more conscious of their need to launder illicitly obtained funds. For example, as recently as 1984, one suspected trafficker had never held any legitimate employment, yet during a four-year period he spent more than $400,000 in cash, making no attempt to hide the money. Although he was never charged with a drug violation, he was convicted of tax evasion and sentenced to prison (U.S. Attorneys, 1989, p. 41). Similar tax evasion charges were the only way many of the infamous organized crime figures of the 1930s could be brought to justice.

The most common money scheme involves moving drug profits out of the United States. One route might be for the traffickers to deposit their cash in a foreign bank, route it through various shell corporations, and then return the funds to the United States for investment (United States Attorneys, 1989). Sometimes the money is returned to the United States in the form of a loan, which is never repaid (Inciardi, 1984).

The transfer of funds out of the country is one of the trickiest parts of the money laundering process. In many cases it amounts to a smuggling operation. Currency may be sent out of the country in payment for imported goods that do not exist, that are not shipped, or that are overvalued. Sometimes money is concealed in what appears to be the legitimate export of goods, such as electrical appliances. In one instance, customs officials seized $6.4 million in cash packed in canisters marked bull semen headed for Bogata, Colombia ($6.4 Million in drug, 1990). Packages of cash can also be sent through the mail (U.S. Attorneys, 1989, p. 41) or shipped by commercial or private airlines to those countries whose banking secrecy laws allow the money to be laundered easily (Cooper, 1990, p. 43).

Money laundering within the United States avoids the dangers inherent in a smuggling operation. The principal obstacle is the Bank Secrecy Act, which requires banks and other financial institutions to report all currency transactions of $10,000 or more. Financial institutions must verify and report specific information about the customers' identities, file reports within fifteen days of the transaction, and keep a copy of the reports for a period of five years (U.S. Attorneys, 1989, p. 41).

"Smurfing" is the money laundering technique most closely associated with the Jamaican gangs although it is used by other dealers as well. Operatives, known as "smurfs", go to many different banks and purchase checks or money orders for just under the $10,000 reporting limit. These checks are then mailed or personally delivered to someone who deposits them in various accounts and

then transfers the money to another country (Cooper, 1990, p. 42).

Traffickers often attempt to hide their profits by buying small, legitimate businesses or by investing in personal property, such as gold coins, jewelry, bullion, expensive automobiles, or communications equipment—any item for which there is a cash market. In those cases where legitimate businesses are purchased, the traffickers often are acquiring a long-term money laundering asset that routinely handles large amounts of cash and can be used as a conduit for laundering illicit funds. For example, in Arkansas, the Banditos motorcycle gang invested the profits from its illegal methamphetamine and marijuana trafficking in a string of after-hour nightclubs. These establishments, owned and operated by the Banditos' national leadership, acted as fronts for the gang's drug and prostitution businesses, as well as money laundries (U.S. Attorneys, 1989, p. 42).

Some banking institutions are willing to assist the drug traffickers for a 7 to 10 percent fee of all money laundered (Beaty & Hornik, 1989). The Bank of Commerce and Credit International was one such bank heavily involved in laundering drug money worldwide.

The most sophisticated and hardest to trace method of laundering money is to buy a bank or to take effective control of such a financial institution. Large trafficking organizations, such as the Colombian cartels, have both the wherewithal and the sophistication to attempt such an enterprise. By controlling an institution, traffickers can manipulate the exempt list, of those free from reporting requirements, manipulate transactions with correspondent banks and overnight deposits, and employ all the sophisticated cash transaction procedures available to a modern financial institution to aid in their money laundering schemes (U.S. Attorneys, 1989, p. 43).

Ownership of banks for use in laundering money originated with the Nevada gambling casinos during the 1930s. Money skimmed (not reported to the Internal Revenue Service) was sent to banks in the Bahamas (Block & Scarpitti, 1990). Bahamian banking laws provide absolute secrecy of all transactions, with no income, profit, capital gains, gift, inheritance, estate, or withholding taxes. "Hence, for a small initial cost and annual fee, one may own a bank or company that can receive and disburse large sums of money in complete secrecy and without the threat of taxation" (Block & Scarpitti, p. 334). In some cases, drug dealers use both the banks and the casinos to launder money. According to Block & Scarpitti (p. 341) the casinos provide drug dealers with several secret services, such as changing small bills for large ones, selling money orders or travelers checks, wiring transfers to banks or casinos outside the country, allowing use of safety deposit boxes, and making loans. It is possible that some casinos were even built for the specific purpose of laundering drug money.

Drug traffickers also use cash to buy luxury items such as jewelry and cars as a means of laundering money (Treaster, 1990). The sellers of these items are obligated by law, as are banks, to report any cash transaction in excess of $10,000. Furthermore, these sellers are not supposed to sell items to known drug dealers or to anyone they suspect is paying for the item with drug money. Federal agents have uncovered several car dealerships and insurance agents in New York who not only sold luxury cars to agents posing as drug dealers but also arranged with insurance agents to insure and register the cars using false names. The cash used to pay for the cars was divided into lots of less than $10,000 to be deposited in the bank, phony receipts were prepared, and the dealers failed to report the transactions exceeding as $10,000 to the Internal Revenue Service. It is important to note that the success of drug dealers to not only import, distribute, and sell drugs but also to launder the money often involves the cooperation of those who are not directly involved in the trafficking of drugs but who succumb to the temptation of the fruits of the drug business.

Summary

Drug trafficking is an international operation of enormous magnitude. Efforts by U.S. drug enforcement to stem the flow of drugs into the United States has been largely unsuccessful. The major trafficking organizations include the Colombians, involved primarily in the cocaine trade; the Asians, who traffic in large quantities of heroin; the LCN, who are involved in the importation of heroin; the Jamaicans, who traffic in marijuana and crack; motorcycle gangs, who deal in amphetamines, hallucinogens, and designer drugs; and the street level dealer. The U.S. government and the CIA also had a hand in drug dealings in Southeast Asia during the Vietnam War.

Money made from these illegal enterprises is laundered in a number of ways. Most is sent to foreign banks, where loans are made to the drug traffickers in the form of legitimate businesses. These loans are never repaid. The money is sometimes physically smuggled out of the country and deposited in foreign banks in Panama, Switzerland, or the Bahamas.

The only hope for controlling international drug trade and reducing supplies entering the United States is to eliminate corruption among high-level officials in each of the countries involved and among politically and economically influential businessmen. The assistance or, at the very least, encouragement of corrupted officials ensures widespread drug availability. This is essentially the supply side of the problem, which is believed to directly contribute to the demand side. Global efforts to curb drug trafficking, therefore, involve complete cooperation between the governments of these countries without interference from parties with vested interests and unsavory associates.

CHAPTER  17

The Law Enforcement Response

Objectives

1. To identify methods of foreign intervention to reduce the supply of drugs entering the United States.
2. To describe the extent to which methods of foreign intervention are effective.
3. To identify and discuss the methods of domestic enforcement of drug laws in our streets.
4. To describe when drug tests are most likely to be used and what type of person is most likely to be subjected to testing.
5. To understand the reasons behind the error rate in drug tests.
6. To distinguish between drug testing for purposes of detection and drug testing for purposes of treatment.
7. To understand drug-related corruption of law enforcment officials and the subtle encouragements and rewards for corruption.

overnment efforts to control the multi-billion dollar business of illegal drugs have focused on both supply and demand. Of the billions of dollars spent on the war on drugs, less than 30 percent is allocated for prevention and treatment. The bulk of the money is spent on law enforcement efforts and the incarceration of drug offenders. In 1995, about $13 billion was allocated for law enforcement agencies to fight the drug war by preventing drugs from crossing U.S. borders and by apprehending and prosecuting drug law violators. During the summer of 1990, President George Bush announced appropriations of $450 million to bring the military into the drug war (Waller, Miller, Barry, & Reiss, 1990). Although government seizures of huge amounts of drugs have increased during the 1980s and remained stable through 1993 (see Table 17.1), the price of drugs decreased during this same period, indicating a plentiful supply. Efforts toward reducing demand have included a range of educational prevention programs and increased criminal penalties for possession and use of drugs.

The federal agencies responsible for enforcing drug laws are the Drug Enforcement Administration, the Federal Bureau of Investigation, U.S. Customs Service, and the Bureau of Alcohol, Tobacco, and Firearms. These agencies have adopted several strategies for reducing public demand for drugs as well as reducing the amount of drugs entering the country. Reducing supply has involved crop eradication, efforts at interdiction, increased arrests of drug traffickers through greater use of undercover oper-

ations and drug courier profiling, increased prison sentences for those convicted of drug trafficking, and expanded governmental use of asset forfeiture. Law enforcement efforts to reduce demand primarily involve extensive use of random drug testing in the workplace in addition to apprehension and incarceration.

Government Efforts to Reduce Supply

Crop Eradication

The United States has taken several steps to prevent drugs from entering the country. Many of these policies involve attacking the supply of drugs in their source countries. One such effort known as crop eradication has included the destruction of the opium poppies, coca plants, and marijuana plants in their countries of origin. In the case of marijuana and cocaine, crop eradication has been focused on the Latin American countries (del Olmo, 1987). One of the largest U.S. eradication efforts was instituted in Mexico, "which in 1988 eradicated more than 12,000 acres of marijuana and opium poppy fields in the the ten states along the Pacific Coast" (Cooper, 1990, p. 108). However, Scott & Marshall (1991) claim that Mexico has historically feigned cooperation when in actuality it sprayed the same fields repeatedly, sprayed some fields with water instead of herbicide, and buried the extra sup-

Table 17.1   *Drug Seizures: Combined Drug Seizures of the Drug Enforcement Administration (DEA), Federal Bureau of Investigation (FBI), U.S. Customs Service, and the U.S. Coast Guard in Fiscal Year 1990.*

	1989	1990	1991	1992	1993
DRUG	POUNDS SEIZED				
Total	1,343,204	737,318	926,635	1,093,196	1,019,591
Heroin	2,414	1,794	3,030	2,551	3,345
Cocaine	218,695	235,214	246,324	303,254	238,053
Marijuana	1,070,514	438,248	499,070	783,343	752,114
Hashish	51,581	17,062	178,211	4,048	26,080

Source: Bureau of Justice Statistics. U.S. Department of Justice (1994). *Sourcebook of Criminal Justice Statistics -1993.*

plies of herbicides in the desert. Government officials there benefitted twice from these measures; first by receiving and pocketing funds from the United States and secondly, by receiving bribes from growers to protect their fields from destruction. It was not until the 1985 killing of DEA agent Enrique "Kiki" Camarena Salazar that the State Department finally admitted that drug eradication was not a serious program in Mexico. However, the United States has taken a very lenient stance with regard to active drug trafficking and corruption of Mexican officials so as not to jeopardize the North American Free Trade Agreement (NAFTA) (Golden, 1995).

Although the United States has promoted the use of herbicides, such as paraquat sprayed on marijuana to destroy crops, many countries will cooperate only by sending personnel into the fields to manually remove plants (Cooper, 1990). Manual removal of Andean coca plants proved dangerous to U.S. drug enforcement agents who were killed by snipers in their attempts to destroy crops. Manual eradication of Peru's coca plants was disbanded in July 1991 because of armed guerrilla opposition and government apathy (Brooke, 1991d). However, it appears that a fungus, a strain of fusarium oxysporum, has destroyed a significant amount of Peru's coca fields. Coca growers claim that the United States is intentionally spreading the fungus among the coca plants with helicopters. American officials say the fungus is spreading naturally.

The United States has been pushing for aerial spraying of coca plants with herbicides. However, the chemicals are equally toxic to all vegetation and could contribute to an increase in land erosion. Moreover, the run-off kills fish and other animals, and the chemicals continue to destroy all vegetation for several years. "Citing these environmental dangers, as well as the risk of reprisals against company representatives in the countries where it would be used, Eli Lilly & Co. [the sole manufacturer of the product] announced in May 1988 that it would not participate in the [eradication] program" (Cooper, 1990, p. 109). The United States has also considered releasing millions of malumbia, a white moth that eats the coca plant while in its caterpillar stage, over the coca fields of Peru and Bolivia (Isikoff, 1990). Such a move could prove dangerous, however, to other plant life or result in an influx of large wasps, the natural enemy of the malumbia. Coca growers might react by simply using larger quantities of pesticides to control the insect, which could prove hazardous to the environment. Government scientists are also working on the development of a red dye that kills marijuana plants.

The destruction of processing laboratories and hidden landing strips is another course taken by the United States government to reduce the influx of drugs reaching the United States. However, drug traffickers often move their centers of operation rather than disband them after a lab or landing strip has been destroyed.

Use of the U.S. Military

In 1992, President Bush allocated $1.2 billion to the Pentagon for its role in the drug war. The military has increased its role in protecting the U.S. border, intercepting traffickers on their way to the United States and working with the military in the drug producing countries of Colombia, Mexico, Ecuador, Peru, and Bolivia. U.S. military advisors help train other armies and law enforcement personnel who fight drug traffickers. However, in some cases, U.S. efforts may actually be working *for* the drug traffickers. In Bolivia, 85 percent of the American trained Bolivian army are required to serve only one year in the military. Upon release from service, these soldiers often find work with the drug traffickers who pay high salaries to hire them as security guards. *Newsweek* quoted one U.S. advisor as saying, "With few exceptions, all we're doing is training the bad guys" (Lane, Waller, Larmer, & Katel, 1992, p. 22).

Colombia receives the largest share of U.S. military aid among the cocaine producing countries. However, *Newsweek* reported that much of the money is used to counter leftist guerrilla groups and human rights groups, believe hundreds of Colombian citizens have been executed by government forces without trials (Lane et al., 1992, p. 22).

When Pablo Escobar escaped from Colombian authorities in July of 1992, American military planes joined in the search. The American Air Force and Navy planes used night-vision gear, infrared cameras, and equipment for intercepting telephone communications (Brooke, 1992b, p. A1). The Colombian citizenry, however, does not welcome the U.S. military flying overhead in the early morning hours and have strongly protested their presence. Three Colombian Congressmen, quoted by *The New York Times,* described the flights as "a raping of our air space" (Brooke, 1992b, p. A8).

The United States gives Peru $159 million in drug aid and provides radar stations and intelligence to help the Peruvian Air Force intercept planes carrying coca leaves to the refineries in Colombia. Unfortunately, Peruvian military personnel often bribe their superiors for such choice assignments as the Huallaga Valley, where they charge drug traffickers $5,000 in landing fees (Brooke, 1992a). In a country such as Peru, where 300,000 acres are cultivated for coca and 225,000 peasant families rely on its cultivation for a living (Brooke, 1992a), U.S. "aid" will have little effect on the cocaine industry.

The Posse Comitatus Act of 1878 expressly forbids the military to be used as an agency to enforce criminal laws within the borders of the United States. However, in 1989 the National Defense Authorization Act expanded the role of the military with regard to drug trafficking and allowed it to serve as the lead federal agency for detecting and monitoring aerial and maritime transit of illegal drugs into the United States, to integrate U.S. command, control, communications, and intelligence systems dedicated to the interdiction of illegal drugs into an effective network; and to provide an improved interdiction and enforcement role for the National Guard.

The military can be called upon to support other domestic law enforcement groups. Ships or planes suspected of trafficking drugs must be referred first to civilian law enforcement in order to be searched or seized. The National Guard operates under the control of the states' governors and may support state and local law enforcement efforts. Guard members are not allowed direct contact with suspects but may defend themselves or others from drug suspects (Kaufman, 1992, p. 17). The National Guard is also involved in domestic aerial surveillance of public lands for marijuana crops.

Extradition

Many countries have an extradition treaty with the United States. The purpose is to bring international drug traffickers to trial in the United States, where they face long prison sentences (Cooper, 1990). This policy, however, is often unpopular with the peasants of the countries involved who look to the drug lords for employment and an increased standard of living. Anti-American sentiments are often prevalent in those countries with extradition treaties.

Such sentiments increased following the 1992 Supreme Court decision in the *United States v. Alvarez Machain*, which allowed for the abduction of criminals wanted in the United States from other countries. This case involved a DEA sponsored kidnaping of Humberto Alvarez Machain, a Mexican citizen, to stand trial in the United States for his

involvement in the torture and murder of Enrique "Kiki" Camerena Salazar. Camerena was a special agent for the Drug Enforcement Administration who was working in Mexico at the time of his death. Camerena was kidnaped in 1985 by Mexican drug traffickers in Guadalajara, Mexico. It is alleged that Alvarez, a doctor, prolonged Camerena's life for others to continue his interrogation and torture. An enraged DEA offered a $50,000 reward to anyone who brought Alvarez to the United States. Mexican bounty hunters kidnaped Alvarez from his medical office and flew him to El Paso, Texas, where he was taken into custody by U.S. DEA agents. Two lower Federal Courts ruled that Alvarez could not be tried in the United States because his abduction violated a 1978 extradition treaty with Mexico. However, the Supreme Court ruled that abductions do not violate extradition treaties, and it appears at the time of this writing that Alvarez will stand trial in a Federal Court for his part in the murder (Greenhouse, 1992).

Interdiction

Increased efforts have also been made to decrease the amount of drugs that are carried across U.S. borders. In an unprecedented move in 1987, President Ronald Reagan began to use the military in addition to the civil law enforcement agencies to keep drugs out of the country. Unfortunately, interdiction generally affects the novices rather than the experienced drug smugglers. Hence, increased interdiction efforts tend to eliminate the competition for drug traffickers and the successful traffickers can command higher prices for their products (Reuter, 1990).

Asset Forfeiture

The federal government has always had the right to seize property involved in criminal activity or property acquired through illegal activity without compensating its owner. However, use of this process, known as forfeiture, has increased dramatically as the government seeks additional tools to use against drug offenders. Both the Comprehensive Crime Control Act of 1984 and the Anti-Drug Abuse Act of 1986 provided for greater governmental authority to seize the profits and proceeds of illegal drug trafficking, as well as the currency and property used in connection with money laundering and drug violations (U.S. Attorneys, 1988).

In accord with forfeiture laws, the government brings a civil suit against the property, money, or vehicles believed to be used while committing criminal activity. Any property that was acquired or purchased with money obtained illegally can also be seized. The action is brought against the property (for example, *U.S. v. 320 Main St., U.S. v. Ten Thousand Three Hundred and Fifty Dollars of U.S. Currency,* or *U.S. v. One 1995 Corvette).*

Forfeiture can be brought against the property at any time, even before the suspect is found guilty of a drug offense or anytime thereafter. Moreover, the offender need not be convicted nor even charged with any crime at all, since the contention is that the property "itself" is guilty. Even if the suspect is acquitted of criminal charges the government can still take the property believed to be involved in violation of the drug laws (Troland, Florio, Katz, Lindsay, & Payne, 1988). In the event the offender has been found guilty, it is not considered double jeopardy to initiate forfeiture proceedings against any property involved in the illegal drug activity since the action is a civil one brought against the property. Under the Relation Back Doctrine, the government can seize property believed to be involved in illegal activity even if that property was later sold to an innocent third party after the criminal activity had ceased (Troland et al., 1988). The forfeiture is good against anyone, not just the defendant. If a teenager uses his father's car to transport drugs, the father's innocence or ignorance is irrelevant to the forfeiture procedure since the car is guilty of transporting the drugs.

Although the civil proceedings are brought against the property, an owner's innocence may be used as a defense for the property. The owner does have the option under the innocent party defense to petition the Attorney General of the United States in order to regain the property. However, such a defense can be difficult and costly. The government may use hearsay and circumstantial evidence to establish *probable cause*—the level of proof needed to initiate forfeiture. The defense must prove the case by a *preponderance of the evidence* (a higher level of proof than probable cause, but less than *beyond a reasonable doubt,* which is used in criminal cases). The innocent owner must convince the court that he or she did not know the property was being used illegally or that every means was used to prevent the wrongdoer from using the property for illegal purposes. Consider the following example of a teenager using his parents' home to sell drugs. The parents knew the child had a problem with drugs because they had sought treatment for their child but claim they had no knowledge of his illegal activity.

Could their house still be seized? Yes, and the parents would have to go to great expense in order to convince the court they took every measure to prevent the illegal activity from occurring. There is no guarantee that the court would rule in the owner's favor, and it is entirely possible the parents would lose their house.

Items that can be seized include drugs or the plants from which they will be derived (for example, marijuana plants), the equipment used to manufacture the illegal drugs, and any containers used to store the drugs. Conveyances used to transport drugs including aircraft, motor vehicles, and vessels can also be seized. No exceptions are made for the type of drug, amount, or intended use: A person's aircraft can be seized if it is used to transport large quantities of drugs for resale or if it merely carries one marijuana cigarette for personal use. If a car or plane is used to transport people or money to the site where an illegal drug transaction will occur, it would also qualify for seizure under the forfeiture laws. There are two exceptions to this rule. Common carriers, such as commercial aircraft, are exempt unless the government can prove the owners knew their property was being used to promote illegal drug activity. Also exempt is property that was in the wrongdoer's possession illegally, such as a stolen car. However, the owner of the vehicle must prove to the government that the car was stolen and that he or she had no knowledge of the illegal activity. Simply saying that a friend did not have permission to use a vehicle is not a valid defense (Troland et al, 1988).

Books, records and research used to conduct illegal activity can also be forfeited. In addition, money used to buy drugs, proceeds such as real property traceable to drug deals, and money used to facilitate illegal drug transactions are all subject to forfeiture. Even circumstantial evidence or evasive answers about the source of money or property, or ownership of property or money could result in its seizure. One offender had to relinquish his gold and diamond dental bridge which replaced several of his lower front teeth after he was arrested for possession with intent to sell nine grams of crack. Police made the argument that he probably purchased the bridge with drug money (Jensen, 1995). Finally, real property such as buildings and dwellings used to store drugs or used to engage in drug deals, facilities where drugs are manufactured, or land where illegal drugs are grown can all be seized (Troland et al., 1988).

The Drug Enforcement Administration (DEA), the Federal Bureau of Investigation (FBI), and the Immigration and Naturalization Service (INS) are all active in seizing conveyances and the real property associated with illegal drug trafficking. The U.S. Marshalls Service manages the property and arranges for the liquidation of seized property.

In Michigan, two separate prosecutions resulted in the forfeiture of a controlling interest in a golf course, which had been financed with marijuana proceeds, and the Iron Works Gym, into which cocaine proceeds had been invested. In a third case, a major marijuana and cocaine distributor in southwestern Michigan pleaded guilty to racketeering and income tax evasion and forfeited more than $1 million in jewelry (U. S. Attorneys, 1989, p. 49).

In March of 1991, three fraternity houses were seized by federal authorities in Virginia. Members of the Delta Epsilon, Tau Kappa Epsilon, and Phi Epsilon Pi fraternities at the University of Virginia were accused of using and selling drugs and the houses were seized under federal forfeiture laws (Ayres, 1991).

A former deputy sheriff in Hartford, Connecticut, may lose property worth more than $400,000 after he made two phone calls from the property to negotiate a drug deal with undercover federal law enforcement agents (Routhier, 1992).

As part of Vermont's seizure program, land and buildings used for growing and processing marijuana are tar-geted for forfeiture. This tactic is becoming increasingly effective with the advent of indoor growing operations. Previously, an outdoor grower could reduce the risk of loss through forfeiture by cultivating Cannabis on land rented from an unsuspecting owner. The more sophisticated indoor growing operations, however, often require building modifications, thus reducing the pool of available rentals and forcing the grower to own the site. Forfeiture has become a key instrument in fighting the production of marijuana (U. S. Attorneys, 1989, p. 49).

Not all seized and forfeited property is sold by the government. Some of the property and conveyances are put into service against drug dealers and other organized criminals; some of the cash or forfeited proceeds are used for maintenance and management of the asset removal program (U. S. Attorneys, 1989, p. 49).

As investigators and prosecutors have gained experience with these new forfeiture provisions, each succeeding year brings in increasing amounts of forfeited property and cash. During fiscal year 1993 alone, Department of Justice investigative agencies seized property and cash valued at over $679 million. (See Table 17.2.)

Some of these assets have been shared with state and local governments through the Equitable Sharing Program. During fiscal year 1988, on over 8,200 occa-

Table 17.2   *Asset Seizures of Nondrug Property Made by the Drug Enforcement Agency (DEA) in Fiscal Year 1993.*

Type of Asset	Number of Seizures	Dollar Value
Currency	6,992	249,240,113
Vehicles	4,686	48,679,590
Real Property	1,543	248,870,632
Other financial instruments	578	49,468,389
Vessels	156	9,013,707
Airplanes	46	35,415,750
Other Conveyance	311	2,793,404
Other	2,378	36,067,937
Total	16,690	679,549,522

Source: Bureau of Justice Statistics. U.S. Department of Justice (1994). *Sourcebook of Criminal Justice Statistics -1993.*

sions the profits and proceeds of drug trafficking were shared with more than 1,800 state and local law enforcement agencies that assisted the federal government in the war on drugs. In fiscal year 1986, nearly $50 million was shared. In fiscal year 1987, that amount more than doubled, and in fiscal year 1988, more than $104 million was shared. Shared assets include not only cash but also forfeited property, including cars, boats, and airplanes. Both undercover narcotics agents and senior police officers, usually in administrative positions, are common beneficiaries of confiscated cars. In fiscal year 1988, shared property worth $28 million supplemented more than $76 million in cash (U.S. Attorneys, 1989, p. 50).

In January of 1993, the United States Supreme Court agreed to hear a case concerning whether the government's use of asset forfeiture may in some cases violate the eighth amendment to the U.S. Constitution, which states that there will not be excessive fines or governmental imposition of cruel and unusual punishment (Greenhouse, 1993). The major issue concerns whether the government can seize assets where the value greatly exceeds the severity of the offense. In an action similar to forfeiture, the Bush Administration sought to have suspected drug users and/or dealers automatically evicted from public housing projects on the basis of probable cause, regardless of criminal charges leveled or convictions. However, a federal appeals court ruled against the evictions stating that mere possession of drugs did not "constitute an extraordinary situation" and that the due process clause of the Fifth Amendment to the U.S. Constitution guaranteed notice and a person's right to be heard.

Drug Courier Profiles

In an effort to identify individuals carrying drugs into the country or transporting drugs within the country, law enforcement agencies often rely on what is known as the "drug courier profile." These profiles are used to identify and stop those who are considered suspicious or likely to be engaged in drug trafficking on highways, in train and bus stations, and in airports.

A set of characteristics supposedly associated with drug couriers has been compiled by the Drug Enforcement Administration, and the courts have generally upheld stopping and seizing passengers who fit the profile. The problem is the profile is rather broad and could easily apply to innocent passengers. Characteristics include time

of exit from plane; however, three different cases show the agents stopped one person because he exited first, another because he exited last, and a third because he exited in the middle (Coulter, 1990, p. 1327). Other criteria include flying from or to a source city, using the airport telephones, carrying little or no luggage, acting nervous, or looking suspicious.

No scientific evidence exists to justify use of drug courier profiles. Many of these behaviors are exhibited by innocent travelers who may be unjustifiably stopped and searched by drug agents.

Increased Arrest, Conviction, and Imprisonment

In 1993, the FBI reported an estimated 1,126,300 state and local arrests for drug law violations in the United States. This figure represents a 59 percent increase in arrests since 1984 (see Table 17.3); in 1981, drug arrests were 5.2 percent of all arrests reported to the FBI, whereas by 1992, drug arrests had risen to 8 percent of all arrests. These increases in arrests for all sorts of drug-related violations have occurred at a time when drug use has been declining in the United States (see Chapter 2). At first glance it might appear that increased arrests and penalties explain the decrease in self-reported drug use and serve as a deterrent to drug use. However, closer examination of the statistics show that African Americans are the most likely to be arrested for drug use violations (see Table 17.3). In 1983, 128.5 whites under the age of nineteen were arrested per 100,000 inhabitants. In 1992 that number decreased by 31 percent to reflect arrests of 88.5 per 100,000. These arrest rates are consistent with the decrease in drug use shown by the Johnston, O'Malley, & Bachman (1993) report which indicates that drug use among all age groups, high school students, college students and other adults has decreased since 1981. However, arrest rates for African Americans eighteen and over increased by 85 percent since 1983 and arrest rates of African Americans under eighteen have increased by 171 percent even though the drug use among African American high school seniors also shows a sharp decline since 1981. Even more startling is the fact that among high school seniors, African Americans report the least amount of drug usage when compared with their White and Hispanic counterparts. "Black seniors have consistently shown lower usage rates for most drugs, licit and illicit, than white students; and we know that this also is

Table 17.3   *Arrest Rates (per 100,000 Inhabitants) for Drug Use Violations by Age Group and Race, United States, 1983 & 1992*

	Under 18 years of age			18 years of age and over		
Year	Total	White	Black	Total	White	Black
1983	133.9	128.5	178.3	370.9	289.1	1,079.4
1992	147.3	88.5	483.9	554.7	381.3	1,999.9
Percent Change	10	-31	171	50	32	85

Source: U.S. Department of Justice, Bureau of Justice Statistics (1994) *Sourcebook of Criminal Justice Statistics - 1993*

true at the lower grade levels. In some cases, the differences are quite large" (Johnston, O'Malley, & Bachman, p.16). In view of these arrest statistics, the questions must be raised whether America is waging war against drug use, or war against young African Americans.

The number of suspects prosecuted for drug offenses in federal courts increased from 7,697 in 1981 to 25,663 in 1991. The number of persons convicted of violating Federal drug laws rose to 17,349 in 1991 from 5,981 in 1981. These figures represent a 190 percent increase in convictions. Drug offenses accounted for 19 percent of all defendants convicted in 1981 and 35 percent of all defendants convicted in 1991.

The percentage of offenders convicted of drug offenses sentenced to prison rose from 73 percent in 1981 to 87 percent in 1991. Drug offenders are also receiving longer sentences and are serving a larger percentage of their sentence than in the past.

Drug law violators make up a growing share of the prison and jail populations. Drug offenders accounted for 61 percent of sentenced inmates in federal prisons in 1993. The proportion of drug offenders in state prisons increased from 9 percent in 1986 to 21 percent in 1991. In 1991, 10 percent of the 57,661 juveniles detained in public juvenile facilities were committed for drug related offenses (U.S. Department of Justice. Bureau of Justice Statistics, 1994).

Street Level Narcotics Enforcement

Local law enforcement agencies, particularly in large cities, commonly house narcotics divisions that employ undercover agents assigned to engage in street sweeps or buy/bust operations. Male and female officers attempt to mimic the appearance and behavior of those they are targeting so they are not suspected as police officers. Dealers and users of all sorts generally carry guns, so if an undercover agent is frisked, drug dealers will rarely become suspicious simply because a weapon is found. Because women are less likely to be suspected as police officers, female undercover agents are heavily recruited by many agencies.

Undercover work is not as glamorous as television would lead one to believe. In fact, many undercover officers spend a great deal of down time, when they must simply sit in a van, listening to a wire tap, and wait for something to happen. Officers often speak of the filthy, pathetic conditions under which users frequently live, and they cannot wait to finish their paperwork at the end of a shift in order to shower. Often disturbing is the number of children that live in these same environments that are traumatized when a parent or caretaker is taken away in a drug raid. And finally, officers frequently report that, although there is a great deal of danger involved in the job, the one hazard they fear most is the risk of contracting HIV; during a raid, clothing and other articles must be

Table 17.4   *Estimated Arrests for Drug Abuse Violations for a Ten Year Period 1984-1993*

Year	Total Arrests	Sale/ Manufacturing	Possession
1984	708,400	155,848	552,552
1985	811,400	192,302	619,098
1986	824,100	206,849	617,251
1987	937,400	241,849	695,551
1988	1,155,200	316,525	838,675
1989	1,361,700	441,191	920,509
1990	1,089,500	344,282	745,218
1991	1,101,000	337,340	672,660
1992	1,066,400	338,049	728,351
1993	1,126,300	334,511	791,789

Source: Bureau of Justice Statistics. U.S. Department of Justice (1995). *Drugs and Crime Facts, 1994.*

searched, and a dirty needle may be found only after the officer has been stuck.

Because local drug enforcement involves much more than just undercover work, we take a comprehensive look at the many strategies that comprise street-level tactical operations, including directed patrol, executing outstanding arrest warrants, arresting dealers and users for other offenses, traffic enforcement, roadblocks or checkpoints, simple surveillance and arrest, informant buys, undercover police buys, buy/busts, reverse stings, and crack house raids (see Connors & Nugent, 1990 for a complete description).

Directed patrol focuses specifically on problems or special assignments that are drug related. Once the agency has identified a problem, uniformed officers are directed in how to prioritize their patrol functions. For example, in areas where drug dealers are concentrated, the police may disrupt dealing by making themselves visible and executing arrests. The dealers frequently move to other untapped areas, thus the dealing itself does not cease, it simply moves to another unsupervised location. Potential targets include particular streets or neighborhoods, houses, apartment buildings, and commercial buildings. Or they may target a group, such as sellers, users, or gang members. A particular drug, such as PCP or crack, may instead become the target. Visible police presence is intended to make it difficult

for a street market to operate and to encourage law-abiding citizens to use the streets and feel safe.

Police consider the execution of outstanding arrest and bench warrants an important strategy to affect drug offenses because drug users and sellers are likely to jump bail and fail to appear in court, even for petty citations (e.g., traffic offenses or trespassing). In order to target drug offenders, officers frequent those locations where users and dealers are known to hang out, look for reasonable suspicion, and then check names against a warrant list to see if any violators are present. A valid outstanding warrant is sufficient for an arrest.

Drug trafficking can sometimes be difficult to detect and, even in the case of a known dealer, officers may not be able to impose a drug-related charge. Because drug sellers commonly also engage in other forms of criminal activity, officers may focus on their nondrug-related crimes. Officers may legally harass suspected drug dealers by ticketing and towing them, arresting them for public intoxication, and enforcing trespassing laws, zoning codes, fire and safety codes, health codes, and public nuisance laws. Once the perpetrator is arrested, a search is conducted in the hopes of discovering illegal drugs.

Traffic enforcement is another tactic to interdict drug dealing and identify drug abusers. Stopping a driver for a traffic offense, reckless driving, or even a random traffic stop may lead to a reasonable suspicion that drugs or weapons are present. If the officer smells anything unusual, notices unusual or suspicious behavior, finds that the vehicle is not registered or the tags are expired, or if the driver is resistant, the officer has grounds to search the vehicle.

Roadblocks or checkpoints, when done in accordance with local and federal guidelines, may be used to discourage drug trafficking from entering a neighborhood. Roadblocks may be set up to randomly check vehicle registration and drivers' licenses.

Surveillance and arrest is a simple approach to disrupt open-air drug markets. Officers generally remain in unmarked vehicles until they observe a deal and then arrest the parties involved. Or, the surveillance officer may observe transactions from a remote point through binoculars and call in a jump-out squad to make the actual arrest. The jump-out squad travels in unmarked cars or vans but must be recognized as police officers when they emerge to make the arrest.

Undercover narcotics officers rely heavily on informant buys. Informants are frequently offenders who were previously arrested and are asked to make a deal to receive a more lenient sentence in return for information. Some informants actually volunteer information, even though they were not arrested, to seek revenge against another user, dealer, or lover. Informants are provided money by the police to make a controlled buy as evidence against a dealer. Police use this evidence to request search warrants and gain access to hidden drug markets. Because informants' testimony is rarely used in court, given their lack of credibility, police frequently use informants to gain the trust of dealers. Once an undercover agent has participated in several buys, increasing the quantity purchased each time, the dealer begins to trust the agent and sell to him directly. It is at that point that an arrest is made. Obviously, this can be an extremely dangerous proposition.

Undercover police buys give all the control to the police. However, if the undercover officer makes an arrest, the cover is then blown. Generally another officer will arrest both the undercover agent and the dealer to maintain the agent's cover. Because this sort of transaction is dangerous, the officer wears a wire so a back-up unit can be aware of all activities. Undercover police buys are quite limited in small areas.

Buy/busts occur when the police officer poses as a buyer of drugs. He or she may make several purchases from several dealers while being videotaped by another officer whenever possible. There are several ways to carry out a buy/bust. One way is for the undercover agent to make a drug buy, then move away from the seller for a back-up unit or jump-out squad to make the arrest. Another tactic is for the undercover officer to make a buy and then obtain an arrest warrant on the basis of the buy. The warrant may be executed at another time so that the officer is not placed in danger during the arrest and not directly identified by others in the area. Videotaping of the buy is a valuable tool for use in court to establish probable cause and to use as evidence. In those instances when a buy team is used, officers in unmarked vehicles enter a target area to make a buy. Once they have succeeded, they provide a description of the seller(s) over the radio to a tactical cover team, which then moves in to make an arrest.

When police pose as dealers to arrest buyers we call it a reverse sting. A successful reverse sting occurs when dozens of arrests are made during a single operation. Two issues are raised with this type of strategy. The first is whether the police should be allowed to sell real drugs, which are generally retrieved from the storage room where confiscated drugs are scheduled for destruction. If real drugs are used, they must be carefully weighed, protected, and identified before they are issued. If they substitute other substances, then the buyers are not really buying drugs and charges may not stick. The second issue is entrapment, a defense frequently used by defendants in reverse sting operations. The officers must be thoroughly briefed on entrapment laws so as not to violate them, leading to release of the defendant.

Raids of crack houses and shooting galleries have become commonplace. The first step in a raid operation is to assess the targeted site by determining how many people are involved, whether children are present, who the leaders are, what their histories are, whether weapons are present, and how the suspects will respond to the raid. Both uniformed and undercover agents are sometimes involved. Undercover agents, wearing heavy military-style clothing and thick boots, break down the doors and crawl through the windows to gain entry. Armed with guns, the officers take advantage of the element of surprise by rounding everyone up quickly before the suspects have time to mobilize a defense. Once the situation is under control, uniformed officers enter to help search the surroundings and make arrests. There is constant communication between the inside team and the outside back-up team. Additional officers may be stationed outside to close off the streets and maintain crowd control when the raid is a large-scale operation.

Street sweeps, like raids, are operations that involve massive arrests of drug dealers who are working a particular area. The area clears for a short period of time and then the dealers either return to resume their activity or new dealers enter the area. Street sweeps offer police departments intense positive publicity for a short period of time. The media can show the public that something is being done to fight drug dealing.

Not all street level law enforcement tactics involve arrests. In some parts of New York City touch tone pay phones have been replaced with rotary phones in order to prevent drug dealers from paging runners. Many phones have also been altered to prevent incoming calls (Martin, 1994).

Unfortunately, these solutions are extremely short term for a long-term problem. As most officers will tell you, street level law enforcement tends to have little effect on the extent of drug use or sale. Instead, the courts become burdened with processing these many arrests and the prisons are in crisis conditions of overcrowding as the courts incarcerate the many dealers and users. Although it may be convincingly argued that drug dealing poses hazards to potential victims the crimes of many drug users are not personal or violent offenses. Thus, our jails and prisons are filled with nonviolent offenders who are now spending more time incarcerated than nondrug offenders, many of whom have a history of violent offenses. Furthermore, in order to house drug offenders, others must be released to make room. Decisions regarding who is a good candidate for release are frequently made erroneously.

Drug Testing

Drug testing is another method the government has used to identify and sanction drug users. One area where drug testing has been used extensively is the workplace.

Drug Use in the Workplace

During the Carter Administration, there was much concern in the media about whether the traditional "three martini lunch" consumed by business executives should be allowed as a tax deduction for business expenses. At the time, no one questioned whether business executives ought to be drinking three martinis for lunch and then returning to work; their only concern was over who would pay. It was not until employers began to suspect that employees might be using other drugs on or off the job that drug use in the workplace became a major societal concern.

Despite serious concerns about drug use in the workplace, studies are unclear about exactly what the economic costs are. Some have estimated that drug use in the workplace costs the American economy over $60 billion a year. This figure is cited by many authors (Berger, 1987; O'Hara & Backer, 1989; Stone & Kotch, 1989) who claim that drug use in the workplace presents a serious enough problem that drastic action must be taken to contain it. Despite widespread beliefs that drug use in the workplace is rampant and leads to significant losses, specific studies to support these beliefs are difficult to locate. The study most often referred to was conducted by Research Triangle Institute (RTI) located in North Carolina. The RTI study estimates drug abuse costs the economy about $60 billion per year through absenteeism, disability, theft, and lost productivity. It was shocking to discover that the author of the study, as well as a spokesman for RTI, readily admit that the study has no scientific validity and *"could be off by more than 100 percent"* (Vacon, 1990, p. A6, emphasis added). Not mentioned is that alcohol use and cigarette smoking may also have been included in the $60 billion estimate (Anglin & Westland, 1989). This point is important because most drug tests do not test for alcohol or nicotine (McBay, 1986). Yet these are the drugs used most frequently by workers, and they probably account for the greatest loss to an organization in terms of absenteeism and health care costs. Some vague reference is also made in the popular literature to a study conducted by Metropolitan Life Insurance Company, which estimates drug use costs industry $85 billion (S. Cohen, 1984). This study was not readily available for review.

Even anecdotal evidence was rare, the most popular being the Conrail Train collision that occurred in January 1987. Testimony before Congress by Federal Railway Administrator John Riley revealed that in the Maryland train accident, the Conrail brakeman and engineer were found to have traces of marijuana in their systems (Iuculano). Sixteen people died in this accident and 170 were injured (Taggart, 1989). The two Conrail employees were seen by their supervisor immediately prior to the accident and the supervisor did not detect that they may have been under the influence of drugs (Iuculano, 1989). However, it is important to note that just because traces were found in the urine does not mean that marijuana intoxication was the cause of the accident, since traces of marijuana can be found in the urine several days if not months after the person used the drug. The Federal Aviation Administration reported that 400 pilots of the 47,000 that are licensed to fly passenger planes in the United States have been convicted of alcohol related driving offenses at some time in their lives (FAA publishes figures…, 1991). Although crashes of large passenger planes have not been related to pilot alcohol use, the Federal Aviation Administration did reveal that about 10 of 975 pilots killed in airplane crashes in 1989 and 1990 had been drinking (Wald, 1995).

Is drug use a serious problem in the workplace? Interestingly, Gust and Walsh (1989, p. 4), in their introduction to a NIDA monograph supporting drug testing in the workplace admit that "missing…is the systematic research database on the extent of workplace-related drug use, its impact on performance and productivity." Yet the remainder of the volume is a work supporting drug testing due to the supposed but as yet undetermined amount of loss to the business and economy due to drug use.

We found other estimates of drug use in the workplace to be equally vague. Berger (1987) estimates between 5 and 13 percent of the American work force uses drugs. It is not clear how this statistic is derived and whether the drug use is on or off the job, and she does not include alcohol. Even though alcohol is the most widely abused drug, many of authors treat alcohol as a separate issue (Carter, 1990). The American Management Association (1987) estimates that 2 to 5 percent of American workers use illegal drugs. It is not clear whether these workers are addicts, occasional users, or frequent users who display no addiction.

On the other hand, estimates of alcoholism (as opposed to workers who use alcohol) are at about 10 percent. Again there is no estimate concerning the number who drink on the job. We must be wary of quotes like "most cocaine users work" (Scanlon, 1986, p. 3) since we do not know what percentage of workers this figure represents. In other words, 50 percent of cocaine users could represent anywhere from .01 percent of the workforce to 99 percent of the workforce. As we do not know, the figure is meaningless.

R.F. Cook (1989) examined a sample of 1,716 working adults. He found that, in the past year, 18 percent had used marijuana and 6 percent had used cocaine. During the past 30 days, 11 percent reported using marijuana and 2 percent used cocaine. Most likely to use cocaine are young (eighteen to thirty-four-year-old) males, with no differences found with regard to level of education. Cocaine use appeared to be experimental in nature with few hard-core

users. Young males, eighteen to thirty-four years of age, in skilled trade occupations without a high school degree were most likely to use marijuana. However, it must be kept in mind that these respondents were not admitting to drug use on the job, only to drug use in general.

A study of truck drivers detected extremely small amounts (well below the legal limit) of alcohol in less than 1 percent of the drivers tested, 3 percent showed evidence of being either frequent users or recent users of marijuana, 2 percent were positive for cocaine, and 1 percent for amphetamines (Lund, Preusser, & Williams, 1989).

Anglin & Westland (1989) analyzed data from commercial laboratories that compared drug use rates among several different populations. These populations included those who were employed, medical personnel, criminals, and drug treatment patients. These researchers found that specimens of employed individuals had the lowest positive rate for drugs.

However, even if drug abuse in the workplace represents a smaller number than previously thought, those employees can be responsible for a tremendous amount of corporate loss. Myers (1986, p. 5) believes that 20 percent of the work force causes 80 percent of the problems. Cowan (1987, p. 315) contends that alcoholic or drug abusing employees are 3 times more likely to be late to work and are 2.2 times more likely to ask to leave early or to take time off. They are also 3 times more likely to use sick leave, 3.6 times more likely to be involved in an accident, and 5 times more likely to file a claim for workman's compensation. Employees might also steal to support a drug habit.

The most logical conclusion to be drawn concerning drug use in the workplace is that we do not know the extent to which workers use drugs. We also do not know to what extent drug users are impaired on the job. We do know that some drug using employees (particularly those who use alcohol to excess) can present serious problems for an organization.

Many people feel that extensive use of drug testing is the only way to control drug use in the workplace. It can adversely affect health, safety, security, and productivity as well as public confidence and trust (Walsh & Gust, 1986). Detection of drug users, followed by their rehabilitation or even their discharge, is believed to have a beneficial effect on productivity, safety, and worker effectiveness. Nevertheless, given the expanded use of drug testing in the workplace, administrators frequently do not have comparative information about the use and accuracy of urinalysis technologies. Agencies implementing drug-testing programs may have concerns about the relative accuracy of different tests and whether accuracy varies by type of drug. In addition, drug-testing technologies may vary in ease of use, suitability for use as a screening test, and relative costs.

Drug testing requires a urine sample from the individual to be analyzed and may be performed using one of three procedures. The first procedure most commonly instituted is drug screening during the preemployment stage. Some employers believe that preemployment screening could save the company a substantial amount of money. A second procedure for drug testing is utilized when a supervisor has reason to believe that an employee may be using drugs. This procedure requires that the employer have evidence of "probable cause"; that is, the employee may show signs of intoxication, lower work performance or productivity, personality or lifestyle deterioration, or unexplained excessive absenses. The third procedure is performed "randomly," meaning that an employee may be required to provide a urine sample at any time on demand. Southern Pacific Railroad (Taggart, 1989) claims to have experienced a dramatic decline in positive drug test results once testing became operational in that organization.

Individuals are tested for the presence of drugs in their system through a urine sample. Although most people are accustomed to providing urine samples when they go to the doctor for a physical examination, they do so in privacy. In order for a urine test for drugs to be truly valid, the Council on Scientific Affairs for the American Medical Association (1987) recommends that someone observe the stream of urine as it leaves the body and enters the container and that the observer be no more than several inches away from the stream. This precaution is necessary to prevent contamination of the sample.

Contamination of the Specimen

One issue involving drug testing concerns the problem of obtaining a urine sample from the person being tested. Anyone who uses drugs and is aware of the company's policy regarding drug testing could easily substitute "clean" urine (with no drugs) for "dirty" urine (which contains traces of drugs). Other ways to beat the test include drinking large quantities of water to dilute urine, drinking lemon juice or vinegar to make the urine acidic, adding Drano to the specimen (Berger, 1987), adding table salt to the specimen, which interferes with the testing process (Morgan, 1987), or sucking on copper shortly before providing the specimen (personal interview with anonymous probationers, 1992). Other more sophisticated drug test evaders have been known to strap a bag of clean urine to their bodies with a catheter running from the bag to the urethra. To the untrained observer it looks as though the urine is coming from the individual being tested (Council on Scientific Affairs, 1987, p. 3111). Therefore, it is necessary to carefully watch the stream of urine as it leaves the body and fills the container. The individual cannot be allowed a modicum of privacy if the specimen is to be intact.

The False Positive and False Negative Test Results

A major concern of those opposed to mandatory drug testing is the issue of the false positive drug test (see Table 17.4). A false positive test is one in which even though the subject has used no drugs and no traces of drugs are in the urine, the test shows the urine as being positive for drugs. Some of the causes of false positives are attributed to technician errors, including mislabeling or mishandling of the specimen.

False positives can also result from ingesting poppy seeds, resulting in a match for opiates (Trebach, 1987), and some herbal teas can create a positive result for cocaine (Seigel et al., 1986). Over-the-counter and prescription medicines may also cause misleading test results. Antihistamines can show a positive result for amphetamines, some brands of ibuprofen can show a false positive for marijuana (Bloch, 1986), and the cancer drug dronabinol creates a false positive for marijuana. Also, cocaine has some legitimate uses in medical and dental exams, and cough syrups containing codeine, antidiarrheal agents, and pain killers can all show a positive result for opiates. There are also numerous legitimate uses for amphetamines. "Confirmed positive test results for amphetamines, barbiturates, opiates, and even cocaine can result from legitimate, therapeutic intervention" (Walsh, 1987, p. 2587). Therefore, highly trained and competent technical personnel must be available to interpret test results and rule out other causes for the positive finding. If a particular test has a false positive rate of 10 percent then out of every 200 drug-free people who provide a clean urine sample, 20 will be falsely accused of drug use.

Also of concern to those who perform tests for the presence of drugs is the false negative. False negative means that drugs are really present in the urine but the test gives a negative result. Some people who are actively engaged in drug use will not be identified by the test.

Table 17.5   *Four Possible Outcomes of the Drug Test*

	Drugs Actually In Specimen	No Drugs in Specimen
Drug Test Reads Positive	True Positive	False Positive
Drug Test Reads Negative	False Negative	True Negative

The ideal situation is for all drug tests to result in either a true negative or a true positive. A true negative means that drugs are not present and the test gives a negative outcome. A true positive means that drugs are present and the test gives a positive outcome. Unfortunately, the ideal situation does not always occur in the real world of drug testing. Many innocent people have suffered tremendous consequences as a result of the false positive drug test (Trebach, 1987). A person may not be hired if the preemployment test comes back positive and may never know that it was because of the test. An employee may be required to receive drug treatment and counseling or may even be fired from a job for suspected drug use when in actuality the employee is drug free. False negatives can create a false sense of security for the employer who believes an employee in a sensitive position is drug free when in actuality the employee is a drug user.

Accuracy of Drug Tests

Drug tests can be divided into two categories: screening and confirmation (Council on Scientific Affairs, 1987). Screening tests include color or spot tests, thin-layer chromatography, and immunoassay tests. Since these tests tend to yield high false positive rates (35 percent) (Council on Scientific Affairs, 1987), a positive test should lead to a second, more accurate and more expensive test known as a gas chromatography/mass spectometry (GC/MS) test with a false positive rate of about 0.01 percent (Council on Scientific Affairs, 1987). The accuracy of this test is still dependent, however, on the level of technical training of the personnel preparing the sample

and interpreting the test. If done properly, these tests run a lower risk of error scientifically speaking even though the potential for human error remains.

A study by the Centers for Disease Control (CDC) (Hansen et al., 1985) examined the accuracy of drug testing labs by sending batches of urine samples to various laboratories. They found that drugs were accurately detected on the average of about 65 percent. An even more startling statistic was that these studies showed a 66 percent false positive rate.

Despite these shortcomings, drug testing is big business for those labs processing the samples or selling test kits. In 1989, five companies generated $173 million, representing 75 percent of the total $230 million market (Clark, 1990). If we are to use drug testing as a means of controlling drug use in the workplace then all efforts must be made to ensure their accuracy. A reputable laboratory must be chosen and a positive test must be confirmed with the more accurate method. Also, employees should have the right to be questioned in case a legitimate use of a medication contributed to the positive test. Unless these precautions are taken, the risks to the employee (invasion of privacy, the possibility of a false allegation, and jeopardy to job security) may exceed the benefits of drug testing.

Preemployment Drug Tests

The most prevalent form of drug testing is preemployment screening. One Fortune 100 company rejected 40 percent of all applicants during a one-year period because traces of drugs were found in urine samples (American Management Association, 1987, p. 7). Not all companies tell applicants they were rejected based on a positive drug test, so an applicant may be innocent and not know why he or she was rejected. On the other hand, some companies such as IBM, do tell prospective job applicants when they receive a positive drug test and allow the prospective employee to explain (Iuculano, 1989). IBM also allows the applicant to reapply in six months with a clean slate (Iuculano, p. 53). For most companies, a positive urine test during preemployment screening results in no job.

On the Job Drug Testing

Of major concern to most corporations considering drug testing are accuracy, privacy, and legality (American Management Association, 1987). The AMA surveyed

1,090 companies, and about 80 percent do not conduct drug tests. (Note that the AMA sent out 10,000 questionnaires and only 1,090 or about 10 percent were returned.) About 21 percent do test before granting employment or for probable cause. Eight percent automatically discharge anyone with a positive drug test. Of the 234 companies who said they perform drug tests, 8 percent do random tests whereas 77 percent test only for probable cause.

The True Positive Drug Test

When an active employee tests positive, most authors (Scanlon, 1986; Walsh & Gust, 1986) and labor unions, such as the AFL-CIO (Iuculano, 1989), argue for an employee assistance program aimed at curbing drug use. The employee assistance program should also deal with other problems that could be the underlying cause of the drug use. Although tests can determine prior drug use, they do not prove intoxication or impaired performance (Walsh & Gust). Thus, it is not generally possible to directly link job performance with present drug use. Despite claims that mandatory drug testing would violate a worker's Fourth Amendment rights (the right to be free from unreasonable searches and seizures), the United States Supreme Court has ruled in *Skinner v. Railway Labor Executives' Association and National Treasury Employees Union v. Von Raab* that mandatory testing may be required for those in safety sensitive jobs, those who carry firearms, and those who are involved in enforcing drug laws (Employee drug testing, 1989; Supreme Court drug test rulings, 1989).

Drug Testing in the Criminal Justice System

Drug testing can also be used throughout the criminal justice process, from the time of arrest through post-conviction supervision (see Figure 17.1). The National Institute of Justice's Drug Use Forecasting (DUF) program administers urine tests to selected male arrestees in twenty-three cities and female arrestees in twenty-one cities. In 1990, the DUF program found that the percentage of male arrestees testing positive for an illicit drug at the time of arrest ranged from 30 percent in Omaha to 78 percent in San Diego. Female arrestees testing positive ranged from 39 percent in Indianapolis to 76 percent in Philadelphia.

Setting Bail

Drug testing at the prearraignment stage of the criminal justice process can be used to influence a judge's decision regarding the amount of bail set for an offender or whether bail should be granted at all. The Office of National Drug Control Policy (1991) argues that drug use may be related to an offender's failure to appear for subsequent court appearances. Prearraignment drug testing can help identify these high-risk individuals.

Monitoring Drug Use

When individuals identified as drug users are released on bail or on post-conviction supervision, the Office of National Drug Control Policy (1991) believes it is important that they be monitored through periodic drug testing as a condition of their release. A positive urine test would then constitute a violation of a release condition and could be met with swift (and progressively more severe) sanctions, such as further confinement. Drug testing, then, can serve authorities as both a risk-assessment tool (at the bail setting stage) and as a supervision and risk-management tool (during the pretrial or post conviction release stage).

Drug Use and Corruption Among Police Officers

As with any war, the war on drugs assumes two clearly delineated sides with opposing goals. On one side are the bad guys who use and sell illicit drugs. On the other side are the good guys who risk their lives attempting to stem the flow of drugs and apprehend the drug user and trafficker. In the war on drugs, the good guys wear the blue uniforms; are associated with such law enforcement agencies as the Drug Enforcement Administration, the Federal Bureau of Investigation; or are enlisted in such military organizations as the Coast Guard.

What happens when a significant number of the good guys use and sell drugs, sell information to the bad guys that enables them to traffic drugs more successfully, or steal drugs from the bad guys and use and sell them themselves? Reiman (1990, citing Trebach) reports that the state and federal courts process more than 100 cases per year for drug related police corruption. This number is probably an underestimation of the problem since many law enforcement agencies use internal affairs departments to investigate such cases. Many are handled at the depart-

Figure 17.1   *Drug Testing in State Criminal Justice Systems*

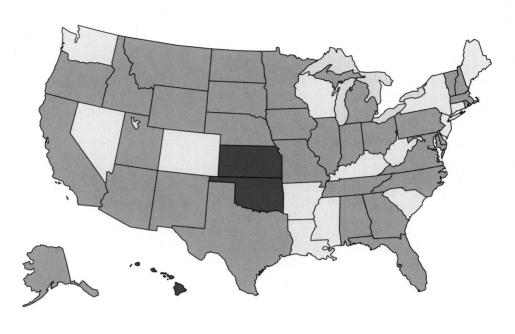

Number of CJS Parts Covered by Testing
■ 0 to 2   ☐ 3 to 4   ■ 5 to 6

NOTE: Drug testing can be used in any of the six parts of the criminal justice system: arrest, pre-trial, probation, parole, jails, or prison. This map identifies how many parts are covered by testing in each state.
Source: Office of National Drug Control Policy (1991, August), *Cost of Drug Testing*, Washington, D.C.

mental level and result in suspension or dismissal of the officer rather than formal prosecution. Hence, no public records are available. As a result it can be difficult to determine who is fighting on which side and for what purpose.

Corruption of law enforcement officers involved in the drug war may be related to several factors. Some either become involved in drug use themselves or succumb to the temptation of the money to be made assisting drug traffickers or becoming drug traffickers themselves (Carter, 1990; Carter & Stephens, 1988). In addition, McAlary (1987) points out that police officers who arrested drug dealers only to find them on the streets again, sometimes within hours of the arrest, experience frustration, resentment, and anger. These feelings have led some officers to steal the dealers' money and drugs instead of arresting the dealers. These officers justified their behavior by arguing that such acts punished the offender and rewarded the officers for their efforts.

The use of alcohol among police officers has long been identified as a major problem. Although serious, possession and use of alcohol is not illegal. However, the involvement of officers in the illegal use and sale of controlled substances, such as marijuana, cocaine (including crack), and heroin is a great concern.

Marijuana is the drug most commonly used by police officers engaged in illicit drug use, followed by cocaine. Some officers use amphetamines to stay awake during long shifts and others have used barbiturates (Carter, 1990). Kraska & Kappeler (1988) reported that 20 percent of police officers in their sample used marijuana while on duty at least twice a month and another 4 percent used it at least once a month. Ten percent were found to have used stimulants or barbiturates while on duty. Officers rarely reported using heroin or hallucinogens (Carter, 1990).

In an effort to conceal their own drug use and prevent blackmail by a drug dealer, police officers who use drugs are more likely to steal drugs or money from dealers rather than act as regular customers. After all, who would believe the dealer who claimed his drugs were stolen by a police officer?

Regardless of the officers' own use, corruption can also be a side effect of officers' prolonged association with drugs. Officers can come to resent the fact that drug dealers make huge amounts of money, have beautiful homes, drive expensive cars, and can hire the best legal counsel to keep them out of jail. The corruption as outlined by Carter (1990, pp. 90–91) manifests itself in the following ways:

- *accepting bribes from drug dealers/traffickers in exchange for "tip" information regarding drug investigations, undercover officers, drug strategies, and names of informants*
- *accepting bribes from drug dealers/traffickers in exchange for interference in the justice process such as nonarrest, evidence tampering, and perjury*
- *stealing drugs from property rooms or laboratories for personal consumption or for sale*
- *seizing of drugs from users/traffickers without an accompanying arrest, with the intent of personal use*
- *robbing drug dealers of profits from drug sales and/or drugs*
- *extorting money (and sometimes property, such as stereos, televisions, and cameras) from drug traffickers in exchange for nonarrest or nonseizure of drugs.*

Officers may steal drugs for personal use or steal money from the dealers for personal use. Typically, officers make arrests and confiscate large amounts of cash. Rather than turn in the full amount, they may choose to keep some for themselves. They rationalize their behavior by thinking, "Why should the drug dealers have all the money and the law enforcers have so little?" Other officers may rob drug dealers of their cash and their drugs, keeping the cash and selling the drugs (officer is accused..., 1993).

The typical drug bribe is $100,000, although sometimes the officer can pick up as much as five years salary in one evening. Carter (1990, p. 94) reports "...ten officers from one police department made two robberies of cocaine from drug traffickers. In just these two robberies, the officers made over $16 million among them."

One federal investigation of Coast Guard personnel stationed in South Florida revealed that about half were directly or indirectly involved in drug trafficking in the mid-1980s (Federal drug probe, 1990). In 1990, additional guardsmen were identified as selling sensitive information "including details about Coast Guard call signs and radio channels" (Federal drug probe, 1990, p. A6) while others were convicted of stealing several kilos of cocaine from a Coast Guard seizure and attempting to sell it to an undercover agent. Other reports of law enforcement corruption have surfaced in Flint, Michigan; Miami, Florida; New York City (Carter, 1988); and the police chief of Brockton, Massachusetts, was sentenced to ten years in prison in 1990 for stealing cocaine from his department's evidence room (Ex-chief of police sentenced, 1990).

Six Brooklyn, New York, police officers were arrested for cocaine trafficking in May and June of 1992. They purchased the drugs on their beat, then sold them in their own neighborhoods in Suffolk County where they lived. In an unrelated incident in July of 1992, Suffolk County police arrested a Queens officer, also for cocaine trafficking (Wolff, 1992).

A two-year federal undercover investigation in southwestern Kentucky resulted in the conviction of the Judge Executive of Morgan County and the Morgan County Sheriff. Both were found guilty of accepting $5,000 monthly payments to protect a large cocaine distribution ring. In the latter part of the 1980s, seven sheriffs and two former sheriffs were convicted in Tennessee for accepting bribes from drug traffickers. Also in Tennessee, a county sheriff and his chief investigator assisted a major marijuana and cocaine distribution ring by selling drugs confiscated from other dealers to members of the distribution ring (U.S. Attorneys, 1989).

A sheriff in Pitkin County, Colorado, upon learning of a federal undercover investigation, placed an advertisement in the local newspaper warning residents of the investigation and advising them to leave the area if they had recently sold drugs to strangers (United States Attorneys, 1989).

A Drug Enforcement Administration team of narcotics agents, known as Group 33, operating in New York City were investigated in 1991. It was alleged "that they beat suspects, snorted cocaine, gambled, had sex with an informant and lied in court" (U.S. narcotics tea, 1991).

A former Drug Enforcement Administration agent was convicted of stealing heroin and cocaine from drug raids, reselling the drugs and laundering the money. At the time of his conviction, the former agent had accumulated $3 million in foreign bank accounts (Ex-agent is guilty, 1991). In Georgia, a United States congressman was convicted of lying to a grand jury in a case growing out of a money laundering scheme (U.S. Attorneys, 1989).

On June 29, 1991, U.S. District Judge Robert F. Collins was the first federal judge to be convicted of accepting a substantial bribe from a drug trafficker in return for a light prison sentence (Federal judge convicted, 1991; U.S. judge is convicted, 1991).

Drug use among government officials has also received considerable attention. In August of 1990, Marion Barry, Mayor of Washington, D.C., was convicted of cocaine possession after the FBI taped him smoking crack in a hotel room with a government informant (Baker, Miller, & Bingham, 1990). Also in August of 1990, Henry G. Barr, a former top aide to Attorney General Dick Thornburg, was indicted on charges that he repeatedly used cocaine over a four-year period and lied about it to receive his security clearance with the Department of Justice. Barr acted as Thornburgh's staff liaison with U.S attorneys' offices, the Federal Bureau of Investigation, and the Drug Enforcement Administration (Ex-top aide to Thornburgh indicted, 1990). Unless we can clean the drugs out of high-level governmental agencies and policy-making bodies, it is unlikely that we will see an end to the drug problem. Individuals with influence and clout who are involved in the drug trade present formidable obstacles to law enforcement efforts.

Although not the same as corruption, there is governmental concern regarding former federal prosecutors who leave their positions only to become defense attorneys for drug traffickers. In June of 1995, former federal prosecutor, Michael Abbell, was indicted on racketeering charges. The government claims that his defense of members of the Cali cartel brand him as an actual member of the cartel (Isikoff et al., 1995).

Abbell went to work for the U.S. Department of Justice in 1967 and was appointed as head of the newly formed Office of International Affairs 1978 where he worked with foreign governments negotiating extraditions of major drug traffickers. In 1984 he was the retained by Gilberto Rodriguez Orejuela, Miguel Rodriguez Orejuela and Jose Santacruz Londono, the three major players in the Cali drug cartel (Isikoff et al., 1995).

▤ Summary

Each year the United States spends in excess of $13 billion to fight the war on drugs. The Drug Enforcement Administratration, the Federal Bureau of Investigation, U.S. Customs Service, and the Bureau of Alcohol, Tobacco, and Firearms are the federal agencies responsbile for the enforcement of drug laws. These agencies have attempted to reduce both the supply of and demand for illegal drugs. The government has attempted to reduce supply through foreign intervention, which includes crop eradication and the destruction of hidden processing laboratories in source countries. In addition, U.S. military advisors provide money, equipment, and training for foreign military and law enforcement personnel to be used against drug traffickers. Extradition and kidnapping of foreign drug offenders to stand trial in the United States are methods used to fight the war on illegal drugs.

Domestic policy includes the expanded use of asset forfeiture whereby the government confiscates any property, cash, or drugs involved in the violation of drug laws. The government has also increased its use of drug courier profiles and has dramatically increased the arrest, conviction, and imprisonment of drug law violators.

Drug testing of those employed in sensitive positions, seeking employment, or convicted of drug-related offenses is also a method to reduce demand. Although errors do exist with regard to the drug tests, more accurate techniques are being developed.

The drug war has taken its toll in the form of drug use and drug-related corruption among law enforcement personnel. Corruption can range from taking money or drugs in return for nonenforcement of laws to actual robbery and murder of drug traffickers by law enforcement officers.

The law enforcement approach to reduce drug trafficking and drug use seems to have negligible effects. Chapter 18 discusses other, perhaps more effective, means to achieve reduction in supply and demand.

CHAPTER 18

Social Drug Policy

Objectives

1. To summarize current drug policy issues with regard to drug use and abuse in the United States.
2. To provide a focus on and prioritize certain drugs, drug users, and drug laws that may be targeted in future policies.
3. To critically assess the current debate concerning drug legalization as an alternative to current drug policy.
4. To analyze and critique the present war on drugs and assess its effectiveness.
5. To examine drug use and abuse as a public health issue as opposed to a legal issue.
6. To make recommendations for a more effective drug policy.

The present war on drugs has stimulated many politicians and investigators to support or criticize current drug policy issues that are already having a profound impact on our criminal justice system.

An ideal policy would strike an optimal balance among all the costs and benefits of enforcing drug laws. The harm produced by excessive drug use must be weighed against the monetary and social costs of enforcing whatever degree of regulation is imposed. Drug abuse is not a victimless act—as a society, we pay the costs of injuries to nonusers and of self-inflicted injuries to users themselves. Loss of productivity, welfare assistance to user's families, and the special education needs of children whose brains have been damaged in utero are only a few of the social costs. (Goldstein & Kalant, 1990)

In spite of the dire consequences of drug abuse, drug policies must not be based on public hysteria and media hype. Instead, they should be founded on scientific knowledge about the nature and extent of drug abuse and rational responses to this knowledge.

We are witnessing a dramatic increase in the number of repeat, and sometimes violent, adult and juvenile offenders involved in drug abuse (Bureau of Justice Statistics, 1989; Chaiken & Chaiken, 1982; Inciardi, 1986). We are not, however, experiencing a global increase in overall drug-taking behavior, with the exception of daily use of crack cocaine. Use among middle class youth is declining (Johnston et al., 1993; Kozel & Adams, 1986; Newcomb & Bentler, 1989). Even though drug abuse is less common in the 1990s than it has been in recent decades, we are seeing it more often associated with serious, violent crime (Chaiken & Chaiken, Elliott et al., 1985; Elliott & Huizinga, 1984; Hartstone & Hanson, 1984).

Drug abuse has a different nature today than it did in the 1960s. Drugs that are most popular now (cocaine, PCP, designer drugs, and methamphetamine) are more dangerous than those predominantely used in the past (LSD and marijuana). Contemporary drugs are more addictive and more powerful. They are also more widely available, cheaper, and easy to use. The present use of drugs in some communities has facilitated the entry of weapons into dispute situations so that the goal to possess and use a weapon has superceded the original goal to obtain and use

drugs. Both drugs and guns give the user/owner a sense of power. Actually having shot someone is viewed as a sign of strength and status in many drug-infested communities. Furthermore, drugs are no longer as socially acceptable in any mainstream segment of our society. They are used primarily by an underclass in our society that is more enmeshed in a criminal subculture than in the past. Some drug use such as smoking marijuana in the 1960s was considered acceptable by mainstream class in the United States and was part and parcel of a political and social movement. Because of sociocultural changes over time, we must now study drug abuse in a different context than we did in previous decades and solutions to the problem should account for those contemporary conditions that characterize today's drug-using population.

Present-day drug offenders are more likely to be incarcerated and will likely spend more time in our criminal justice system, particularly due to relatively high recidivism rates (Bureau of Justice Statistics, 1989). Consequently, policy makers, administrators, and practitioners, particularly in the criminal justice system, should have a better understanding of (1) what conditions lead to drug abuse, (2) what types of people are more prone to abuse, (3) how drug use and crime are linked, and (4) what treatments are available to curb drug craving and relapse. Previous chapters provided the most recent findings with respect to these four issues, so they will not be reiterated here. Instead, this chapter presents an overview of research from the drug abuse field that has direct policy implications, but that unfortunately, many of the general public or policy makers are not aware of or familiar with.

A rational rethinking of drug policy using solid scientific work along medical lines could enable us to understand the actual relationship of specific drugs to drug abuse liability and antisocial behavior. Programs generated from this approach would incorporate well-founded treatments to reduce unwanted behaviors rather than a vague moral condemnation of some drugs and their users. There is no question that certain types of drugs produce behaviors that are antithetical to social life. Some of those drugs are currently illegal (PCP), some are controlled (amphetamines), and some are legal (alcohol). The political decision identifying the criminal justice system as the proper segment of society to control these behaviors has been rooted in fear and misinformation. There may be a more reasonable, productive, and effective approach that neither denies nor downplays the drug problem. Nor does it make claim to the criminal justice myth that the problem can be eliminated. Rather, it suggests that the problem can be more effectively controlled within a public health model—advantageous both for society and for the individuals involved in drug abuse.

The Criminal Justice War on Drugs

Current drug policies are designed to strengthen law enforcement programs in an effort to control drug use and distribution. As a result of these efforts, we have witnessed a vast increase in the number of drug arrests for both possession and distribution. More arrests means more inmates in jails and prisons, leading to overcrowded conditions, just one consequence of increased drug arrests. This situation has also led to the release of offenders who are considered to be "low risk" to make room for incoming drug offenders. Eventually, many of these drug offenders who do not also commit violent crimes are released to make room for their replacements, and so forth. Not only have inmate populations increased, but they have also changed in composition. We now have more nonviolent drug users than ever before housed in jails and prisons.

Another result of the drug war is the disposition of harsher treatments for drug offenders, even for those who are nonviolent, at all stages of case processing as compared with nondrug offenders. Drug offenders are more likely to be charged with a felony, less likely to receive bail, and more likely to be held for pretrial detention (Belenko et al., 1991). These sorts of responses symbolize public contempt for drug offenders. We have largely defined drug-related activities as a moral and legal problem rather than as a health or medical problem. Beefed up law enforcement strategies are intended as a general deterrent —to teach others that drug violators will pay severely for their indiscretions. They are also intended as specific deterrents—to stop drug use, to stop the contagion of use (through the recruitment of new drug users), and to stop drug distribution.

Unfortunately, it is not clear that these strategies work. For the user and seller, the economic gains are great and punishment is viewed as an occupational hazard. The addictive nature of drugs being used today further complicates users' weighing of costs and benefits to obtain the deterrent value from threats of punishment. Many addicts simply lack the cognitive processes and rational choice abilities to calculate the odds that they may get caught and punished. And for many of those who sell, the potential

for high profits outweigh the chances of being arrested and convicted, and there is little otherwise for them to lose. A strict focus on law enforcement neglects the social and economic context in which drugs are used and sold. These conditions must be ameliorated before we can succeed in the drug war.

In order for deterrence programs to be effective, drug users must be rational individuals who premeditate their actions. Or, at a minimum, there should be evidence that drug using offenders rationally choose to use drugs that lead them to crime or reduce their capacity to choose to refrain from crime. Accordingly, policy makers have depicted criminal drug users as sophisticated, clever, and highly organized. Present deterrence programs rely on these assumptions and, consequently, are based on the belief that users will calculate the costs versus benefits of criminal activity and avoid crime due to the threat of apprehension and punishment.

Several studies of drug users do not support these assumptions. Instead, evidence suggests that a large subgroup of drug users are impulsive and sensation seeking (Ahmed et al., 1984; Hesselbrock et al., 1984; Satinder & Black, 1984; G.M. Smith, 1986; Spotts & Shontz, 1984; White et al., 1987), and their crimes are frequently violent and relatively unpremeditated, particularly when cocaine or alcohol is involved (Huizinga et al., 1989; Johnson, Williams, et al., 1990; Johnson & Wish, 1987). Law enforcement deterrence programs that focus on high-tech hardware, more effective police strategies, and elevated arrest statistics will not be effective with this subgroup of offenders. Similarly, stricter sentencing and harsh punishments have not been shown to achieve a deterrent effect among high risk users (Greenberg, 1977; Lipton et al., 1975; Sechrest et al., 1979); the number of serious drug abusers, particularly those involved in crime, has increased despite more intensive law enforcement efforts and lengthier mandatory sentences.

Many researchers and analysts believe that the effect of the criminal justice system's present tactics on the extent of drug-related crime has been simply to escalate its incidence within populations that are beyond our reach. Once war was declared, several predictable developments occurred to further the use of drugs among individuals already at risk for criminal behavior. First, the illegal drug market has been destabilized and an increased number of factions competing to sell drugs have emerged (see Johnson, Williams, et al., 1990). Consequently, the market is now more competitive due to the extremely high profits at stake. An obvious result of this process is vicious

Table 18.1   *Fiscal 1995 Federal Drug Control Budget by Function*

Drug Treatment	$2,874,400,00
Education, Community Action, and the Workplace	2,050,700,000
Criminal Justice System	5,926,900,000
International	427,800,000
Interdiction	1,205,600,000
Research	531,600,000
Intelligence	162,800,000
Total	$13,179,800,000

Source: U.S. Department of Justice. Bureau of Justice Statistics (1995). *Drugs and Crime Facts, 1994*

Table 18.2   *State and Local Spending for Drug Control, Fiscal Year 1991*

Justice	$12,619,000,000
Police Protection	4,223,000,000
Judicial and Legal Services	1,449,000,000
Corrections	6,827,000,000
Other	120,000,000
Health and Hospitals	2,784,000,000
Education	503,000,000
TOTAL	$15,907,000,000

Source: U.S. Department of Justice. Bureau of Justice Statistics (1995). *Drugs and Crime Facts, 1994*.

Third, the focus on drugs as the enemy has further increased drug abuse in some groups by glamorizing the activity. Such focus may cause youths to think of drug use as the forbidden fruit (Farr, 1990), and they may actually be more likely to experiment. Partly as a function of their social immobility and destitution, the use and sale of drugs among inner-city youth have become an escape from seemingly hopeless circumstances and a mechanism by which they can obtain excitement, status, and money. Among middle-class youngsters, the excitement of using an illegal substance is the allure for some. As a whole, adolescents are in a developmental stage of experimentation and they have a high need for stimulation. Activities that result in a fear of detection may provide that stimulation. Many teens will engage in illicit activities for the temporary thrill and eventually outgrow them.

Fourth, crucial resources for managing the drug crisis are funneled almost exclusively into law enforcement efforts to the neglect of efforts to control other criminal behaviors that are at least as dangerous as drug use. These measures are exorbitantly costly, amounting to billions of dollars each year (see Tables 18.1 & 18.2).Moreover, research and treatment programs have become underfunded due to the diversion of scarce monies into law enforcement; in fact, many programs are intentionally dismantled and some are simply terminated because of financial problems. As a consequence, we arrest, charge, and incarcerate large numbers of drug users without the resources to treat them and prevent the future occurrence of drug-related criminal activity. In short, the emphasis on illegal aspects rather than underlying generators of drug abuse may have done more to perpetuate the problem and prevent effective treatment strategies from emerging than to reduce drug-related criminal activities (see Farr, 1990 for further arguments).

An effective drug policy should focus not on criminal justice programs but rather on (1) global economic and social conditions that are conducive to drug-taking behaviors, (2) individuals who are vulnerable to drug use due to predisposing biological and psychological conditions, and (3) direct drug effects on brain function that may increase the likelihood of criminal or violent activity. This strategy pertains to policy focusing on individual drug users, and does not apply to law enforcement efforts to control drug trafficking or distribution, which poses a different set of problems and causes. It is especially important to emphasize this point given that mere drug availability is profoundly influential in drug use nationwide—thus, interdiction efforts and reducing supplies are still paramount to controlling the drug problem. Let us review the

infighting among sellers and between buyers and sellers. Sellers compete ruthlessly for a share of the market. Buyers, on the other hand, have a more difficult time purchasing drugs and resort to both personal and property crimes to obtain purchasing power. Drug traffickers are notoriously violent, intimidating, and corrupting of those they deal with, in large part because of the need to establish and maintain their territory.

facts about drug use and its relation to antisocial behavior and the welfare of society.

Prioritizing Efforts to Thwart Drug Abuse

It is important to specify what types of drug abuse require rigorous attention by policy makers and administrators and what types warrant a lower priority on our list of policy objectives. There is much controversy about what constitutes drug abuse and which drugs of abuse are more of a hazard to users and those around them. The use of any illicit substance is considered by many to be abuse, even when only used occasionally in prosocial situations. Others, however, believe that drug abuse can be identified only when use is chronic, out of the user's control, or associated with antisocial behavior. Further complicating this issue is the fact that numerous legal drugs, such as diazepam, amphetamines, anxiolytics, and alcohol, are abused. It is, therefore, necessary to make a distinction between use and abuse and identify legal and illegal drugs in a discussion of drug abuse policy.

For the purposes of prioritizing our policy decisions, we are concerned with both legal and illegal drugs that have abuse potential and are associated with antisocial behaviors. Categories of drugs should be developed on the basis of pharmacological properties rather than abstract legally administered schedules (which do not reflect a drug's abuse potential or damage potential). The category of drugs that have a high abuse potential includes, for example, opiates, amphetamines, alcohol, cocaine, phencyclidine (PCP), and some designer drugs. These drugs are more likely than others to be abused due to their inherently rewarding effects on brain function and behavior and their potential for psychological and/or physiological dependency. Each of these drugs is also associated with antisocial and criminal behavior; the rate of offending behaviors is increased among groups who use these drugs. Accordingly, use of these drugs deserves a concerted and high-priority effort to eradicate them, for the sake of the individual user and for the sake of society. Other drugs of abuse, such as certain hallucinogens and marijuana, may not require such stringent and costly measures to control their use. Although these drugs do possess some damage potential, they are not deadly to the user or to the rest of society. As a consequence, strict law enforcement efforts to eliminate them may do more harm than good considering that (1) apprehended users take up room in jails and prisons that may be better occupied by antisocial and violent offenders, (2) valuable and scarce resources are appropriated toward these users, (3) eradication efforts will not have an affect on the crime rate (use of these drugs is not associated with antisocial behavior), and (4) these drugs are not, by scientific standards, addictive.

The following questions must be answered in order to more appropriately classify types of drug use that concern policy makers: Are the pharmacological properties of the drug conducive to abuse or dependency? Is the drug associated with antisocial conduct? If so, what are the precipitating social and biological mechanisms? What types of drug abuse are treatable? Strategies to control drug-related antisocial behaviors should focus on answers to these questions.

A Need to Focus on Drug-Related Antisocial and Criminal Behavior

The following six empirical and statistical findings of pharmacologic and characterological phenomena indicate that current programs for dealing with drug abusers are ineffective and require more appropriate remedial actions.

First, there is a prevalence of drug abuse among repeat and violent offenders, both juvenile and adult (Chaiken & Chaiken, 1982; Gropper, 1984; White et al., 1987). It is presently impossible to study the etiology or impact of violence without considering involvement of drug and alcohol use. Certain drugs, especially alcohol, phencyclidine (PCP), and amphetamines, have pharmacologic properties that directly influence areas of the brain responsible for aggressive, impulsive, or compulsive behavior. In addition, there is evidence that individuals who are already prone to criminal or antisocial behavior are more likely to use drugs (Holmberg, 1985; Johnson et al., 1983; Johnston et al., 1986; Santo et al., 1980) and more likely to display extreme forms of antisocial behavior, including violence, under the influence of a drug of abuse (Chaiken & Chaiken, 1982; DeFleur et al., 1969; Fauman & Fauman, 1980; Hartstone & Hansen, 1984; Pihl & Ross, 1987; D.E. Smith & Wesson, 1980). These findings suggest that there is a predisposition to the concomitant development of antisocial behavior and drug abuse among members of a vulnerable subgroup (see Donovan & Jessor, 1984; Elliott et al., 1985; Jessor & Jessor, 1977; Kandel, 1985).

Second, drug users as a group are responsible for the more serious offenses compared to nonusers (Elliott & Huizinga, 1984; Johnson et al., 1983; Johnson & Wish,

1987). Furthermore, a substantial amount of crime is committed during periods of daily, chronic use relative to periods of nonuse or less than daily use (Ball et al., 1983; Farrington, 1983; Gropper, 1984; Hartstone & Hansen, 1984; Johnson et al., 1983; Nurco et al., 1989). Individuals who are presently in drug treatment programs, for example, do not commit as many crimes as those who are not presently in treatment (Gropper, 1984; Nurco et al., 1989).

Third, the crimes of drug users tend to be diverse and random; there is no discernible pattern or specialization among serious drug offenders, even though focal crime types may be identified (Johnson & Wish, 1987). (It should be noted, that not all drug users commit other crimes and not all offenders use drugs.) Drug users' crimes are sometimes impulsive and induced by drug craving, frenzy, or withdrawal. Reports to this effect indicate that there is a relative lack of premeditation or calculation of these criminal acts. Typically, drug users who commit crimes act spontaneously, compelled by acute drug effects, the perceived need to obtain drugs, or drug market competition. If there is no forethought, then traditional strategies of deterrence will fail to suppress criminal activity.

On the other hand, many crimes cannot be attributed to immediate drug effects and, in some instances, are committed by drug-abusing offenders who rationally calculate their crimes and appear to be skilled entrepreneurs. These serious drug abusers that commit crime have a history of antisocial and delinquent behaviors; drug use is one such behavior. Johnson & Wish (1987) found that these users report that drugs or alcohol enabled them to more successfully carry out the crime, rather than cause them to lose control. Their drug-related crimes appear to be an extension of an antisocial orientation, rather than a direct result of drug use (Elliott et al., 1985; Huizinga et al., 1989; Johnson & Wish, 1987; Kandel, 1985; Santoet al., 1980).

This finding brings us to the fourth point, that drug users have a multiproblem lifestyle. Studies have shown that there is a prevalence of early childhood behavioral problems among drug abusers (Alterman & Tarter, 1986; Bush & Iannotti, 1985; Cloninger, Sigvardsson, & Bohman et al., 1988; Hawkins et al., 1986; V.M. Hesselbrock, 1986; Johnston et al., 1987; Kellam & Brown, 1982; Robins, 1966; Workman-Daniels & Hesselbrock, 1987). Such a history includes conduct disorder, hyperactivity, attention deficit disorder, and other learning disabilities and behavioral disorders.

One related study found that a high IQ among so-called high-risk children operated as an insulator against later delinquent behavior (Kandel & Mednick, 1988). Although not directly evaluated in this study, drug abuse may be one type of delinquent behavior that is altered as a function of IQ. Other studies showed a high incidence of dysfunctional family environments among drug users (see Braucht et al., 1973; Penning & Barnes, 1982; Simcha-Fagan & Gersten, 1986), and an intact family may act as an insulator against drug abuse, even in the presence of other risk factors (Adler & Lutecka, 1973; Jessor & Jessor, 1977; Norem-Hebeisen et al., 1984). There is evidence of an increased incidence of psychiatric problems or psychopathology both in the drug abuser and among family members (Alterman, 1988; Anhalt & Klein, 1976; Cristie et al., 1988; Gossop & Eysenck, 1980; Khantzian & Treece, 1985; Robins & Ratcliff, 1979; West & Prinz, 1987). Exposure to child abuse and neglect has also been shown to increase the likelihood of delinquency and criminality (Cavaiola & Schiff, 1988; Gambarino & Plantz, 1986) and substance abuse (Cavaiola & Schiff, Downs et al., 1987; Miller, Downs, et al., 1987).

Fifth, the role of the learning process in drug abuse must not be underestimated. Drug-taking behaviors are acquired and maintained through changes in social relationships. Relationships change gradually as individuals enter into a drug-using environment; users begin to associate more often with other drug users that will support their drug-related activities. This common scenario allows and even encourages users to maintain and perhaps escalate their drug use. They tend to sacrifice their own personal growth for the drug(s), and lifestyles begin to revolve around the purchase and use of drugs (see Johnson, Williams, et al., 1990). In many areas of our inner cities and even in some middle-class homes, children are exposed to the drug subculture at a very early age. Children observe parents as they cook their crack, shoot dope (heroin), and smoke PCP. It is not uncommon for drug dealers to enter and leave their homes freely, and drug raids occur on a regular basis throughout some of these neighborhoods. Lives revolve around the use and purchase of drugs, and this is considered normal. Social support systems and lifestyles devoted to drug use pose a powerful obstacle to abstinence programs.

Compounding these lifestyle contributions to drug abuse are conditioned responses to pain and pleasure. We are conditioned to escape or avoid those situations perceived as painful, and we are attracted to situations perceived as pleasurable. Each situation, painful or pleasurable, becomes associated with environmental cues that are generally present. For example, we will experience pleasure at the mere presence of an associated cue and perhaps crave the actual behavior that will allow us to experience a pleasurable or rewarding response. In the same way, drug users learn to associate the pleasurable drug effect with particular behaviors and paraphernalia and will likely experience craving when the cues are present even in the absence of the drug. Cigarette smokers, for example, commonly report difficulty abstaining when talking on the phone, when others are smoking, after sex, or after a meal, as these are all cues that have become associated with the physiological effects of nicotine. Cocaine users also report extreme drug craving when they see a dollar bill, talcum powder, or a drug-taking peer. These behavioral habits are as difficult to break as the pharmacological habit, and the behavior itself can become addicting. Treatment efforts are frequently frustrated by the presence of social reinforcers that compound and exacerbate drug-taking behaviors.

And finally, the social environment plays a role in the development of drug abuse. Certain neighborhoods are plagued by drug users who are also involved in criminal activity. Specific characteristics of these environments have been identified as possible contributors: poverty, lack of access to social resources, economic and social immobility, poor school systems, filth and deterioration of buildings (Blumstein et al., 1985; Connors & Tarbox, 1985; Farrington, 1985; McCarty, 1985; Robins, 1979; West & Farrington, 1973). Drug use for many in impoverished neighborhoods is appealing; it provides an escape from social realities, it may be the only means of enjoyment or status, and it provides the opportunity to make a great deal of money in an environment lacking legitimate opportunities for mobility. Studies have also shown that users are more likely to raise drug-abusing children (Cotton, 1979; G.M. Johnson, Schontz, et al., 1984; Kandel, Kessler, et al., 1978; Kandel, 1982). Thus, the cycle of drug abuse in certain communities is self-perpetuating.

Unless drug policies focus on the constellation of drug abuse generating conditions, the war on drugs will fail. Drug abusing or addicted offenders will be released from correctional institutions to return to the same biological and socioenvironmental conditions that contributed to their initial problem. Children will continue to be exposed to these same conditions, and we shall witness the eventual onset of drug-abuse behaviors among them. Media blitzes, law enforcement efforts, and "Just Say No" strategies will continue to reach only those populations that are already at the lowest risk for long-term drug abuse. For instance, decreasing levels of drug abuse have been observed among nonaddict, recreational users (National Household Survey on Drug Abuse, 1990)

although no such finding has been reported for the more serious, drug-abusing populations. Indications are that those at high risk for chronic, hard-core drug abuse may have predisposing conditions that contribute to their high risk status.

In short, antisocial traits and behaviors are frequently manifested prior to drug use, possibly placing these individuals at risk for eventual drug abuse. Drug experimentation is prevalent among antisocial or psychopathic individuals, who are also more aggressive and sensation seeking than those without antisocial tendencies. Finally, it is believed that certain neurobiological traits are, in part, responsible for the development of both antisocial and drug-abuse behaviors. Once we have the tools to identify markers for these behaviors, we can incorporate this knowledge into preexisting drug-control strategies to more effectively treat drug users and prevent the eventual onset of drug abuse.

To enhance our law enforcement efforts and educational programs among high-risk populations, existing evidence suggests that if we make drug abuse and addiction a public health issue rather than simply a moral or criminal justice issue, our methods may be more successful. Accordingly, treatments would be based on our knowledge of drug effects on the brain and behavior in conjunction with the socioenvironmental and psychological aspects of drug abuse. Particular recommendations are to investigate and target the rewarding aspects of illicit drug usage, their abuse potential, addictive properties, genetic or psychological predispositions to abuse, and agents that block drug effects.

Medications and therapies that replenish natural supplies of brain chemicals depleted by chronic drug use are currently being tested in animal and clinical trials. Nevertheless, it is clear that even in the presence of a magic pill, the solution to drug abuse and addiction is not a simple one. We cannot entirely blame the drug for the criminal behavior. Most drugs of abuse lessen inhibitions and, in an individual predisposed to antisocial behavior, the drug may act as a catalyst for an underlying tendency. There is a wealth of literature on the incidence of underlying psychopathology among drug abusers, suggesting that the pathological condition preceded both the drug abuse and criminal behavior. Thus, we must consider the possibility of inherent mechanisms that play a role in drug abuse. Furthermore, by the time a drug user is detected, his or her entire lifestyle has become compounded by social and biological forces that may undermine unidirectional treatment efforts. The relative roles of genetic and biological traits, family, social relationships, lifestyle changes, behavioral responses, environmental cues, and numerous other conditions must all be taken into account in the development of an adequate treatment program.

Drug Legalization

As one possible solution to the drug problem, the issue of drug legalization or decriminalization has received considerable attention during the 1980s, and the debate continues into the 1990s. That a focus on law enforcement, punishment, and drug supplies has failed to make a dent in the problem has led some experts to advocate removing or reducing legal penalties much like what we have done with alcohol. Legalized drugs may still be regulated, for example, by restricting their sale in specified locations or use by minors. Decriminalization, on the other hand, would remove serious criminal penalties from drug-related offenses and retain other forms of penalties (e.g., fines) for behaviors involving drug abuse that continue to be regulated; drug offenses would be treated in a manner similar to traffic violations. Although legalization and decriminalization are separate concepts, they will be discussed here interchangeably as they commonly are in public forums.

Arguments for legalization are founded on several assumptions, only some of which have been supported by fact: (1) many drugs are not as harmful as people generally think; (2) illegal drugs contribute to an increased crime rate, including crimes associated with the trafficking of drugs, such as territorial disputes, rival gangs, and corruption of public officials, (3) drug use will not increase if drugs are legalized; (4) the war on drugs has failed; and (5) the drug war has resulted in many undesirable consequences, such as increased government intrusion into the private lives of citizens and the tendency for youth to do what is specifically forbidden.

Harm to the Individual

Some legalization proponents (Barnett, 1987; Szasz, 1974, 1987; Trebach, 1987) have approached the argument for drug legalization on a more philosophical level and question whether the government has the right to tell people what they can or cannot do to their bodies. Even if we accept the premise that drugs can be harmful to the health of those who ingest them, to what extent is the government responsible for protecting people from themselves? Barnett argues that although drugs may be harmful to people, drug laws are also harmful to people. Making otherwise law-abiding drug users criminal and sending them to prison is ultimately more harmful to individuals and costly to society.

Also crucial to the harm argument is the fact that the negative physical effects of illegal drugs have been greatly exaggerated (Barnett, 1987; Farr, 1990; Karel, 1991; Nadelmann, 1989; Trebach, 1987; and as explained in Chapter 2). Although we would not venture to say that there is any such thing as a safe drug, some drugs are more harmful to the user than others. Making some psychoactive drugs legal and others illegal implies that the legal drugs are safer when in actuality they are not. Occasional use of marijuana does not appear to cause any long lasting damage, nor does LSD use. The hallucinogens have no addictive potential. Although crack appears to be a highly addictive drug with deleterious consequences to chronic users (and few legalization proponents support legalization of this drug), occasional cocaine use intranasally does not appear to pose long-term health problems. The key here is the extent to which the drug is used. Extrapolating from the NIDA drug use surveys, Nadelmann (1989, p. 944) argues that only 3 percent of cocaine users appear to be potential problem users. Byck (1987, p. 234) predicts that only one in fifty cocaine users will become a compulsive user. (The distinction between powder cocaine and crack must be made here, as many more who try crack quickly become dependent.) Pure opiates administered in a sterile manner have as their most serious side effects lowered sex drive, insomnia, and constipation, although Wilson (1990) argues that another side effect, so to speak, of opiate addiction is the removal of the user from productive positions in society. On the other hand, many Chinese who were opiate addicted built the transcontinental railroad, and some commentators propose that soldiers in Vietnam were not as severely impaired by the use of opiates as we are led to believe. The argument is set forth that many illegal drugs are no worse than alcohol and nicotine and, in many cases, less addictive and dangerous. Wilson maintains, however, that we would only increase the human misery and deaths already caused by these legal drugs by making other abusable drugs legal. Proponents of legalization can only answer on moral grounds that the individual and not the government should choose which drugs will be used, particulary when alcohol, a most dangerous drug, has already been legalized.

Proponents (Barnett, 1987, 1989) further argue that drug users must deal with criminals. As a consequence, users are introduced into the criminal subculture to obtain drugs; their involvement with the criminal element intensifies, they begin to affiliate themselves with criminals, and they become labeled as criminal because of their illicit drug use. Such a process of investment in the drug subculture contributes to a change in self-concept and reinforces ties with crime, placing them at risk for crime and violence. Another consequence of involvement with an underground drug market is that they may be harmed by drugs that are contaminated or by doses that are not controlled because illegal drugs are not regulated or monitored for safety. Also, when prices are high and purity is low, users are more likely to use IV injection as the preferred method of drug administration to produce a greater effect (Barnett, 1987). IV drug use is more apt to result in added health hazards, such as collapsed veins, abcesses, and, if needles are shared, hepatitis and AIDS. When drugs are in stronger concentrations, users are more likely to engage in safer methods of administration, such as inhalation.

Drug Use and Crime

Those in favor of legalization further suggest that users must pay inflated prices for drugs when they are illegal (Barnett, 1987), thereby driving some otherwise law-abiding drug users to commit crime in order to raise the money needed for drugs. In the absence of legal penalties and with legal routes of distribution, the costs of drugs that are now illicit would be significantly lower, thus reducing the necessity to commit crimes to obtain drugs. Conversely, Inciardi (1992) argues against the proposition that drugs and crime are related strictly as a function of economic need to support drug use. Referring to this proposition as the enslavement theory, Inciardi defines it as the idea that otherwise law-abiding individuals become addicted to drugs and then must turn to crime in order to support their habits. He notes that many hard-core users who regularly commit crimes to support their habits were criminals first and drug users second. The research of Ball et al. (1981) supports the point that many drug users were criminals first but also found that narcotic addicts commit crimes at a higher rate when addicted than during periods of nonuse. It is also important to note that not all drug users commit crimes. Rosenbaum (1991) points out that the employed middle-class drug user more frequently controls his or her habit rather than resort to crime to support the habit.

Increased Drug Use

One argument against legalization is that if drugs are legalized, more people will use them (Inciardi & McBride, 1989; Kondracke, 1988; Wilson, 1990). Wilson argues that the high prices of drugs, the threat of legal sanctions, and the health hazards associated with illegal drug use are all deterrents to many would-be drug users. If drugs were cheap, clean, and plentiful, there would be no deterrent to drug use, as the risks would be minimal. Inciardi and McBride argue that if drugs were legalized, the power of advertising would persuade many nonusers to try them. Those who support legalization respond to this argument by expressing adamant opposition to any advertising of psychoactive substances (Jonas, 1991; Karel, 1991; McVay, 1991; Nadelmann, 1989). The emergence of advertisements, however, may be difficult to quash given that government, or perhaps even private industry, would benefit in tax dollars and other profit-making schemes related to the sale of these drugs. Just think about how difficult it has simply to regulate advertisements of cigarettes and alcoholic beverages.

The argument that drug use would increase is easy to propose but may be difficult to support empirically. When several states decriminalized possession of small amounts of marijuana during the 1970s, there was no measurable increase in use or trafficking (Cuskey, Berger & Richardson, 1978; Maloff, 1981; Single, 1981). When the Netherlands decriminalized marijuana and hashish during the 1970s and allowed them to be sold in coffee houses, consumption decreased (Dutch Ministry of Welfare, Health, and Cultural Affairs, 1985; Nadelmann, 1989). Along the same lines, when New York passed a law in 1973 that increased penalties for the sale of heroin, heroin use did not decrease accordingly (Myers, 1989). The elimination of criminal penalties for drug use may or may not alter the drug-taking habits of our citizens. Although speculations abound on the part of both proponents and opponents, accurate predictions are impossible at this time.

The War on Drugs Has Failed

Wistosky (1991), Nadelmann (1989), and Chapter 17 of this text summarize the vast resources government has allocated to domestic law enforcement, the military, prisons, and intervention in source countries in an effort to stem the flow of illegal drugs infiltrating the United

States. Although we have seen a significant increase in drug seizures, asset forfeitures, arrests, and incarceration of drug users and traffickers, there has been no decrease in the amount of drugs finding their way to American streets. Furthermore, the amount of drugs seized and related drug activities reduced do not even come close to the extraordinary amount of tax dollars spent on these law enforcement efforts. The added costs in crime, corruption of public officials, and narco-terrorism give us additional cause to question our present tactics.

Wilson (1990) does not feel the war on drugs has been lost nor does he feel that $11 billion a year on law enforcement and $2 billion a year on treatment is an unreasonable amount of money to spend in order to contain this problem. He maintains that, although the war has not yet been won, drug abuse has decreased during the past decade and he attributes this decrease to increased law enforcement efforts and incarceration of offenders. Those who oppose Wilson's viewpoint feel that the illegal nature of drug use rather than drug use itself has contributed to the disintegration of America's inner cities (Lapham, 1989; Nadelmann, 1989). Victims of the drug war are those who live in poor neighborhoods where drugs are prevalent and drug gangs rule the streets. Law abiding citizens who do not use drugs are victim to the violence and intimidation of those who deal drugs. These individuals are far more threatening than the drug users themselves (Nadelmann, 1989). Moreover, children in these neighborhoods are often recruited as workers by drug dealers who serve as role models for success (Nadelmann, 1989; Williams, 1989). Often these children begin using drugs after they become employed by drug dealers.

Increased Governmental Intrusion into the Private Lives of Citizens

Some policy analysts argue that the drug war has contributed to the erosion of individual rights and intrusions into individual privacy, such as drug testing (Wistosky, 1991, p. 108). For example, the Comprehensive Crime Control Act of 1984 allowed the government to limit pretrial release for drug offenders. This was accomplished in spite of the historical support courts have afforded pretrial release in an attempt to preserve the dignity of those yet convicted and, especially, to help offenders prepare the best defense for their cases.

Courts have also moved to accept illegally seized evidence in drug cases (Wistosky, 1991, p. 109). Virtually every search and seizure Supreme Court case that expanded police rights since 1980 has involved drugs. Moreover, drug offenses are now the most seriously punished of all criminal offenses (Wistosky, 1991).

Mandatory drug testing can also be viewed as governmental intrusion into the privacy of its citizens. As noted in Chapter 17, drug tests are not always accurate, and an innocent person could lose his or her job because of a false positive. Many opponents of the law enforcement end of the drug war purport that an atmosphere of guilty until proven innocent, rather than innocent until proven guilty, now permeates our legal system.

Legalized Drugs

Before the process of drug legalization can begin, it must be determined which drugs would be legalized and, in what doses, how they would be distributed, to whom they would be sold and, at what age, what cost, and what level of advertising.

Different strategies have been presented for the legalization and distribution of drugs. Karel (1991) proposes that coca tea be sold in supermarkets and marijuana and hashish sold through tobacco or Cannabis shops. Regulated doses of cocaine, in the form of chewing gum, and smokeable or edible opium drugs would be sold in a manner similar to the ATM (Automatic Teller Machine) method of banking. An ATM type card would allow the user to purchase a limited amount of a drug during a specified period. These drugs would be dispensed by a pharmacist. The psychedelic drug user could use his or her drug of choice under the supervision of trained facilitators (Karel, 1991, p. 92) in the controlled environment of a dispensary. (One problem with this strategy is that the recreational nature of drug use, desired by most users, is practically eliminated under such close scrutiny; thus, many users may return to the streets to obtain their drugs.) For addicts, Karel further recommends allowing physicians to use their discretion in prescribing cocaine, heroin, or other opiates to addicts. These drugs would be dispensed through a clinical distribution system similar to our current methods of methadone distribution, where users could also obtain sterile needles. Crack and PCP would not be legalized at all, and all advertising would be prohibited. When drug availability was diverted to the streets from British government run clinics, drug use did, in fact, increase. Furthermore, when British doctors changed their emphasis from maintenance to abstinence, illegal drug use increased and more people were arrested and incarcerated for drug use. These events provide some support for government-controlled drug clinics.

Nadelman (1989, p. 945) suggests that the move toward legalization be a gradual one "with ample opportunity to halt, reevaluate, and redirect drug policies that begin to prove too costly or counterproductive." He suggests beginning with the legalization of marijuana and making currently illegal drugs available for medical treatment.

Counterpoints to the Legalization Argument

Although there are numerous arguments that oppose legalization, only the few most compelling points will be made here. Inciardi and McBride (1989) argue that drugs will never be legalized because the general public is overwhelmingly opposed to the idea. These researchers also contend that clinicians and others who work most closely with the addict population have not come out in support of legalization. It should be noted that many of these researchers are funded by the federal government to carry out their research efforts. To publically support legalization might result in an immediate cessation of federal funds as the government will not fund studies that support legalization. With respect to popular opinion, many citizens and professionals who oppose legalization believe it would send a misleading, and possibly hazardous, message to our youth—that drug use is acceptable, or even condoned, in our society. Some argue that this alone would result in increased drug use in youth.

Another argument against legalization refers to studies that show increased availability of drugs is associated with increased use (see Goldstein & Kalant, 1990). Drugs would likely become more readily available to a wider population through legalization. Furthermore, these drugs may become cheaper. Although this development may reduce the necessity to commit crimes to finance a drug habit, it may make the drugs more accessible to those who presently do not have the resources to locate and purchase drugs. Legalization also places government in the awkward position of having to compete with the black market. There is no evidence that the underground drug trade would die out. Thus, government would have to lower drug prices to out-bid street dealers. As street prices fall, so would government's prices. Eventually, prices may be so low that abusable drugs would become affordable to almost everyone. Since we cannot predict

with any degree of certainty who is likely to become a compulsive user and who is not, we may generate a new breed of drug abusers and addicts.

Those who oppose legalization point out that drugs are not only harmful to the user. These opponents do not view drug abuse as a victimless crime. Individuals using drugs are more likely to commit crimes, including violent ones, to require more welfare assistance for themselves and their families, and to lose productivity. As taxpayers and potential victims, we may be justified in our efforts to enforce laws against drug abusers. Nevertheless, it is important to reiterate that not all drug users commit crimes, and the simple use of drugs in the absence of criminal activity *is* a victimless crime. The propensity to commit crimes under the influence of a drug is a function of the particular drug used and the environment within which it is purchased.

Opponents further argue that drugs do harm the individual and result in other destructive behaviors, such as child abuse and neglect, exposure of unborn children to drugs, violent behavior, and crime generally. Moreover, opponents contend that the criminal sanction deters individuals from illegal use, and legalization of drugs would increase drug use among those who do not currently use drugs. In other words, what are youth to think if the government legalizes drugs? They may perceive that the government implicitly condones the use of abusable drugs.

The Public Health Alternative

It is unlikely that drug legalization will be considered a viable option in the near future. It is equally unlikely that the law enforcement approach alone will suddenly begin to yield impressive results. We have turned this war on drugs over to our political machine to produce answers. The answers we have received in return suggest that we have focused on band-aid measures that hide the problem by focusing on its symptoms rather than its causes. It is important that we now assess our social ills and identify the underlying problems in our society that have contributed to the symptoms of drug abuse, violence, crime, and personal psychopathologies.

> The war against drugs provides [the politicians] with something to say that offends nobody, requires them to do nothing difficult, and allows them to postpone, perhaps indefinitely, the more urgent and specific

questions about the state of the nation's schools, housing, employment opportunities for young black men—i.e., the conditions to which drug addiction speaks as tragic symptoms, not a cause. (Lapham, 1989, p. 45)

The public health approach emphasizes that our inner cities are falling apart and that we have looked the other way as social programs and community resources for those in need have been handily removed. This approach emphasizes the importance of education, prevention, and treatment to target the underlying generators of drug abuse in the United States (Fishbein, 1991; Jonas, 1991; Lapham, 1989; Rouse & Johnson, 1991; Trebach, 1987). The following section on practical implications serves as a guide to accomplishing public health initiatives.

Practical Implications

As mentioned in this chapter, there is no evidence that present tactics of the drug war are effective. Criminal justice sanctions do not deter, treat, or change rates of drug-related crime (Farr, 1990). Scientific findings lead to the following recommendations to institute more appropriate measures to combat drug abuse.

First, we need to prioritize the types of drugs that warrant our attention and should be targeted. This decision is not necessarily based on a drug's illegality. Rather, efforts should be concentrated on those drugs associated with addiction, deteriorated lifestyles, crime, health problems, and death. Alcohol is not an illegal drug, nor is nicotine. Nevertheless, both drugs are highly addictive and responsible for more deaths in this country than any of the illicit drugs. Furthermore, alcohol has been linked with criminal activity and violence to a greater extent than these other drugs. With this in mind, alcohol, cocaine, opiates, PCP, amphetamines, and barbiturates are worthy of our concerted efforts to stringently regulate their availability and use. Law enforcement measures should continue to focus on the supply side of the problem, while medical approaches should focus on the demand side.

Second, the prevalence of underlying psychopathology among drug users strongly suggests that steps should be taken toward the early detection of individuals at risk. In the presence of a deleterious environment (poverty, poor home life, neglect, abuse, drug-infested neighborhoods), the risk for drug abuse among individuals with existing psychopathology is substantially compounded. Two

strategies are proposed for the management of these vulnerable individuals. The first is an individualized approach for those who are already manifesting problem behaviors, including early onset of drug experimentation and psychiatric disorders, such as ASP or affective disorders (see Friedman & Glickman, 1986 for multisite evaluations of this approach). Programs should target those groups considered at greatest risk for drug abuse. Interventions provided early in the individual's development appear to be the most promising (Loeber & Stouthamer-Loeber, 1986). Because the high incidence of cormorbid mental disorders with substance abuse complicates drug treatment efforts (Regier et al., 1990), mental disorders must be addressed in the clinical management of substance abuse.

Individualized treatment and prevention techniques that are currently being evaluated include psychotherapy, counseling and group therapy (C.C.H. Cook, 1988a, 1988b; Gawin, 1989), pharmacologic treatment (Gawin; Gawin & Kleber, 1986b), vocational or educational training (Goodstadt, 1989), behavioral and cognitive therapies (Garrett, 1985; Nathan & McCrady, 1987), and family therapy (Friedman & Granick, 1990; Moos & Moos, 1984). Due to the association between neurotransmitter system dysfunction in major mental disorders and the rewarding influence that drugs of abuse have on these same systems, medications that stabilize neurotransmitter activity may be indicated when comorbidity exists. Psychiatric attention and counseling should accompany pharmacologic approaches to address lifestyle, psychological, and social problems that compound substance abuse problems.

A second approach involving global or community treatment and prevention efforts may be more suitable for populations at risk due to prevailing environmental, family, educational, and pre- and postnatal conditions (see Smart et al., 1990-91 for a specific research agenda). This strategy requires a sensitive evaluation of these conditions without targeting or stigmatizing individuals. Economic, social, educational, and behavioral programs have been implemented to some extent in an attempt to remedy, modify, or at least minimize the impact of environments conducive to drug abuse (McAlister et al., 1980; Shaffer et al., 1983). The establishment of prenatal medical services, funded by Medical Assistance, for underprivileged or drug-using mothers is an example of this approach. Many behavioral and health problems stem from poor prenatal care, and there are an increasing number of babies born drug addicted, infected with HIV, and/or suffering from numerous health problems that, from the time of their birth through adulthood, pose serious complications and disadvantges. For example, congental syphilis has reappeared with a vengeance in the last five years, afflicting thousands of newborns nationwide. Its resurgence is both a social and a medical problem because it is due largely to the use of crack among women who are also exchanging sex for drugs. Without prenatal care, syphillis remains undetected and untreated, and babies are born with skin lesions and neurological, liver, and lung defects, potentially leading to deafness, blindness, bone deformations or permanent brain, liver, and spleen damage. The cost to taxpayers of providing prenatal services on a wide scale in the long run is significantly lower than the costs of disabilities and crime. Success rates for many of these programs are as yet undetermined; they are in preliminary stages of evaluation (U.S. Select Committee on Narcotics Abuse and Control, 1989-1990). Several other strategies have yet to be implemented.

Third, there is convincing evidence that fewer crimes are committed when users are actively in treatment (Gropper, 1984; Nurco et al., 1989). Also, the length of time the user remains in treatment is negatively related to the commission of crimes and the use of drugs once treatment has ended. These consistent findings indicate that treatment should be mandatory for convicted offenders who abuse drugs and that treatment should be made widely available to those who are self-motivated (see Platt et al., 1988; Visher, in press, for reviews). Users are less likely to seek treatment in the presence of a possible criminal sanction and, thus, will be more likely to continue drug use due to lack of a viable alternative. And, because treatment programs are underfunded, understaffed, and overcrowded, large numbers of users are kept on waiting lists for indefinite periods of time. These individuals should be a target of concern, as many remain on these lists for months, lose interest in treatment, and continue their drug-related activities.

Fourth, financial incentives further enhance drug treatment efforts. The costs of such programs are insignificant relative to the costs of incarceration, additional crimes committed during nontreatment periods, welfare expenditures, special education needs of children exposed to drugs in utero, and a general loss of productivity among active drug users (Goldstein & Kalant, 1990). At present, approximately 70 to 80 percent of our federal antidrug money is devoted to law enforcement programs (Weisheit, 1990) that have shown no measure of success. Furthermore, the increase in mandatory sentences for drug offenders, even for small-time users possessing sub-

stances not associated with antisocial behavior (e.g., marijuana) who have not committed a crime against persons or property, are inordinately costly to taxpayers. These offenders clog the criminal justice system and may be more expeditiously and effectively handled outside the system by treatment professionals; the costs of incarcerating such offenders is substantial relative to treatments more compatible with the seriousness of their drug use. Federal, local, and private monies should be funneled into treatment programs that offer some promise of success with drug-abusing populations. Although there is some agreement about appropriate treatments for heroin addicts, there is no consensus on appropriate treatments for cocaine addicts; thus, there is a dire need for research monies with the goal of developing new treatment protocols. The eventual costs of future drug users that are being born to drug-using parents and are reared in drug-infested environments are astronomical. They are at risk of failure in our school systems, and this growing population needs social, psychological, and financial support to control drug-related crimes.

Fifth, types of drug offenders requiring incarceration should be prioritized. The drug offenders with a history of antisocial and violent behavior should be the focus of the criminal justice system. Those offenders who abuse drugs but are not considered dangerous should be mandatorily referred for treatment outside of the criminal justice system. There is some evidence that when serious drug-abusing offenders are coerced by the criminal justice system to receive treatment, they exhibit improvements in terms of less criminality, less drug use, and more employment (Collins & Allison, 1983; DeLeon & Schwartz, 1984). We mandate lengthy prison sentences, dictate who parolees can cavort with and when they can come and go, electronically supervise probationers, and even execute prisoners. Requiring that a drug-addicted offender receive treatment does not, in light of present policies, appear to be cruel or inhumane. All offenders should be screened for drug addiction and underlying psychopathology so they will receive appropriate treatment. Furthermore, drug-abusing offenders should be more intensively supervised after release because their potential for recidivism is quite high.

Sixth, some of the more glaring travesties committed by the criminal justice system and related agencies that directly contribute to drug abuse and criminal behaviors may be immediately remedied. Children subject to abuse, neglect, and abandonment by caretakers, situations related to later problems including eventual drug abuse, should be removed from their environment, or caretakers should be aggressively monitored and treated as indicated. Presently, when a baby is left in a trash can or when a drug-abusing mother neglects a child, social services and other agencies strive to reunite families, frequently in a hostile environment infested with crime and drug abuse. Instead, we should acknowledge that not all biological mothers are capable of nurturing and caring for children. There are large numbers of potential parents willing and able to care for a child or to adopt a baby. This alternative may decrease the growing number of future drug abusers. We should not perpetuate circumstances that knowingly contribute to the problem. Such situations should be more intensively investigated and alternative solutions should be provided for children subject to these conditions; increased availability of foster care or court actions that mandate routine supervision of abusive home environments are two possible routes.

Seventh, we need to address the unique problems of the drug-abusing mother. For example, as mentioned previously, the widespread availability of prenatal care for mothers at risk is particularly crucial if we want to protect their children from the disadvantageous conditions that many are exposed to. What occurs in utero and shortly thereafter are strong determinants of later behavioral problems, including drug abuse and delinquency. Accordingly, enforced mandatory contraception may be considered a viable option for those women who have proven themselves incapable of caring for their children. Grandparents, other relatives, and friends frequently take over child-care responsibilities in these cases. Nevertheless, the impact on the developing child of being separated from parents and having no consistent care-giver is profound. These children are all too often doomed to neglect, abuse, and drug- and crime-infested surroundings. All of these conditions contribute to eventual drug abuse and delinquency. *Unhealthy child care is the only condition leading to drug abuse and delinquency that is entirely preventable.* Many such possible solutions may require serious reconsideration of present legal statutes and recommendations of new legislation that specifically protects children.

Eighth, in order to enhance the efficacy of treatment programs, they must incorporate recent scientific knowledge pertaining to drug effects on the brain; the behavioral, psychological, and social aspects of drug abuse; biomedical assessments; and pharmacological strategies where appropriate (see Kamerow et al., 1986 and Semlitz & Gold, 1986 for discussion and recommendations). In short, the need for further research is paramount.

Research will eventually help us to identify brain mechanisms in drug rewards and explain why some individuals persist in self-destructive activities despite knowledge of the consequences. Also needed is investigation into the failure of our present system, involving society and the family, in inculcating values conducive to prosocial behavior and in opposition to substance abuse. Research is also necessary to test innovative therapeutic approaches to facilitate detoxification, suppress craving for drugs, and to block their brain rewards.

Ninth, the legislature should be guided on an ongoing basis by the best factual information from experts on drugs of abuse, representing such fields as pharmacology, medicine, psychology, psychiatry, criminology, sociology, law enforcement, and education.

And last, but certainly not least, we need the patience to carry out long-term studies and massive educational efforts that do not simply warn of the dangers of being caught but also of the real health and social dangers of using these drugs. Primary prevention, the objective of educational campaigns, is designed to prevent a problem from developing at the outset, so that the number of new cases will be reduced. This concept is the opposite of tertiary prevention tactics, which attempt to manage or control a problem that is already fully developed. Tertiary prevention is the goal of law enforcement and our criminal justice system; to rid the streets of the problem and incarcerate users for purposes of public safety and punishment. Unfortunately, although teritiary prevention tactics are necessary, they are not effective in alleviating the problem; they only move it around, and hide it from the public eye. Primary prevention is thought to have the most potential in dealing with the substance abuse problem. If children learn values inconsistent with drug taking, if they understand the consequences, and if they are given alternative behavioral options (jobs, sports, involvement in the arts, or community service), they are much less likely to turn to drugs for answers. The present federal initiative to create drug-free schools and communities is just one example of a primary prevention program.

If we are serious about drug treatment efforts, we must update our services and individualize them. There is a growing body of literature on biomedical and behavioral treatments that promise to enhance the success of present treatment programs. These treatments go beyond a vague attempt to treat the attitude or moral character of the drug abuser and directly address the socioenvironmental, psychological, and biological bases of the abuse founded on a body of scientific literature generated over the last twenty years.

■ Summary

Exclusive reliance on criminal sanctions will discourage addicts and pregnant users from seeking treatment due to the threat of punishment. Although many citizens and policy makers may not be ready to discard law enforcement measures, particularly for trafficking, a substantial amount of financial and popular support should be redirected to the medical, social, and individual aspects of our drug-abuse problem. The nature of the drug user, the pharmacological aspects of drug abuse, and emerging treatments cited herein and elsewhere are not globally known to the public nor to policy makers. Drug abusers (1) may suffer from underlying disorders that may predispose them to both drug use and crime, (2) may display early warning signs that can be detected and targeted prior to the development of a full-blown problem, (3) are frequently involved in criminal or antisocial activity prior to drug use, and (4) respond with a reduction in use when exposed to a combined pharmacological, psychological, and social therapeutic regimen. The evidence presented condenses to two critically relevant understandings—

- *Although criminality generally precedes drug abuse, the potential for drug abuse exists prior to criminal involvement.*
- *Treatments are on the horizon that promise some enhanced success in reducing both drug abuse and related crimes.*

With these findings in mind, we are persuaded to reevaluate traditional strategies. We must broaden our focus and avail ourselves to up-to-date information on the links between drug abuse and crime. On a global, societal level, the drug war should focus on parents, neighborhoods, education, individual responsibility, and the merits of delaying gratification through legitimate channels. Educational efforts in particular will be instrumental in alerting parents and school systems to warning signs of an eventual problem. Once these markers have been observed in an individual, appropriate early interventions should immediately ensue. These interventions must include a comprehensive assessment of underlying pathologies and treatments that address each aspect of the individual's drug-abuse problem.

Such information also promises to enhance the efforts of our criminal justice correctional system. Effective and well-funded programs should be instituted in our prisons, jails, and prerelease centers. Offenders should be evaluated for their involvement in substance abuse during intake procedures. Those convicted of an offense who demonstrate evidence of drug abuse or addiction should receive mandatory treatment as part of their disposition. When drug using offenders are not considered dangerous and incarceration is unnecessary, diversion programs with intensive treatment must be available. Supervision of these offenders, who are more likely than nondrug users to recidivate, should be constant, intensive, and based upon a view of them as having a serious medical problem rather than as being immoral or criminal. Agents must attempt to identify precursors responsible for the concomitant development of both drug use and criminality, rather than simply a propensity for crime. Strategies to change behavioral habits revolving around usage must be included in treatment efforts. Underlying disorders that may contribute to drug abuse and criminal activity need to be identified and treated. And finally, new pharmacological approaches should be available whenever appropriate.

Street-level drug abusers are not the vicious animals portrayed on television—they are often pathetic individuals, many of whom were physically and sexually abused as children or born to drug-abusing parents. They have no sense of self-worth and feel helpless to change their personal inadequacies and social immobility. Drugs, for these individuals, provide a feeling of power they cannot experience otherwise and allow an escape from adversities. Thus, we not only have an ethical obligation to provide compassionate treatment for their social and medical problems, but it is the only reasonable approach to reducing the demand side of the drug problem.

Policy making, legal decisions, and public opinion should all reflect the knowledge of an inextricable bond between certain forms of drug use and criminal behavior; we cannot focus on one to the neglect of the other. Because drug abuse and addiction have sociomedical origins, we must shift our views of these problems to effectively conquer them. Global social changes and individual medical treatments must be incorporated in our drug war. Furthermore, the need for additional research and prevention efforts is paramount. The lack of parental guidance, the preponderance of drug-intoxicated babies who are at risk for future drug abuse, the prevalence of underlying disorders, the absence of legitimate opportunities, the intense reward value of street drugs, and several other deleterious conditions contribute in important ways to our drug problem. Incarceration alone will not influence or eliminate these precipitating factors. On the contrary, there is evidence that a continued emphasis on law enforcement and incarceration will exacerbate the current situation by allowing these conditions to fester. Our present research base regarding drug abuse, although still in its infancy, indicates that the drug war should be based on scientific data and medicalized. Drug abuse and addiction are health problems, not simply moral issues that we should automatically condemn without providing effective solutions.

GLOSSARY

absorption: occurs when a drug reaches the bloodstream from surrounding tissue or organs.

abuse potential: the ability of a drug to produce pleasure and/or reduce pain, increasing the likelihood that the user will continue to use the drug and eventually become dependent.

acetylcholine: a neurotransmitter in the peripheral and central nervous systems responsible, in part, for memory, learning, and motor coordination.

acetylcholinesterase inhibitors: drugs that increase the activity of acetylcholine transmission.

action potential: an electrical impulse that is released by a neuron, travels down its axon, and changes the electrical field of a neighboring synapse to stimulate the dendrite of an adjacent neuron.

addictive personality: personality traits that may predispose to or place an individual at risk for addictive behaviors, such as drug addiction, eating disorders, compulsive gambling, or other compulsive behaviors.

adenosine: an inhibitory neurotransmitter.

adoption studies: a method to estimate the relative roles of environment and genetics on a trait or behavior by comparing individuals who were raised by adoptive parents with individuals raised by their biological parents.

agonist: a drug with an affinity to a receptor site(s) that can produce effects similar to an endogenous chemical or that causes the endogenous chemical to become more active.

AIDS: auto-immune deficiency syndrome. Transmitted by blood and body fluids, usually in used syringes or during the course of sexual intercourse.

alcohol: otherwise known as ethyl alcohol or ethanol, the most widely abused drug in the United States with nonselective depressant properties.

alcohol dehydrogenase: a liver enzyme involved in alcohol metabolism that converts acetaldehyde to acetate, which is subsequently excreted.

alcoholism: a disease characterized by chronic, excessive use of alcohol, resulting in dependency that impairs social functioning and health.

amotivational syndrome: a condition thought to be associated with chronic marijuana use, particularly among youth, characterized by a lack of motivation and ambition leading to intellectual and developmental delays.

amygdala: an almond-shaped mass of gray matter located in the limbic system. Animal elicits sham rage and attack behavior when stimulated.

anabolic steroids: synethetic derivatives of testosterone used primarily to enhance masculine traits and increase muscle mass.

anhedonia: the inability to experience pleasure.

Antabuse (disulfiram): drug given to alcoholics and problem drinkers that results in the accumulation of acetaldehyde in the body and severe hangover-like symptoms.

antagonist: a drug that attaches to a receptor and blocks the action of either an exogenous or endogenous substance.

anticholinergics: drugs such as atropine and scopolamine, that decrease acetylcholine activity.

anxiolytic: anxiety-reducing property.

asset forfeiture: civil procedure whereby the government may seize any property or money associated with the violation of drug laws.

autonomic nervous system: a portion of the peripheral nervous system that is responsible for functions not generally under our conscious control, for example, heart rate, blood pressure, respiration.

autoreceptors: receptors situated on sending neurons that produce a signal to cease neural firing to regain a balance between excitatory and inhibitory activities. These receptors are particularly active when the suppression of excessive excitatory neurotransmission is required.

axon: a projection from the soma or cell body of a neuron that transmits action potentials to synapses of adjacent neurons.

barbiturates: a subcategory of sedative-hypnotic compounds that share the same molecular structure and are generally used to induce sleep.

bazuko: cocaine paste that is mixed with tobacco and smoked.

behavioral conditioning: learning to associate a stimulus with a response or behavior.

benzodiazepine: a subcategory of sedative hypnotic compounds that relieve anxiety.

blood-brain barrier: the functional barrier between the brain capillaries and the brain tissue that allows some substances from the blood to enter the brain rapidly while other substances either enter slowly or not at all.

booting: a procedure whereby IV heroin users inject the needle into their veins, withdraw some blood, mix it with the heroin and then complete the injection.

brain: the portion of the central nervous system located within the skull, containing two hemispheres and four lobes.

brainstem: that portion of the brain that connects to the spinal cord and controls vital functions and instinctual behaviors.

brain syndrome: a general depression of the CNS caused by chronic, high doses of alcohol or benzodiazepine consumption resulting in disorientation, unresponsiveness to environmental stimuli, mental clouding, impaired memory, decreased judgment, labile affect, incoordination, dulled senses, and sometimes psychosis.

buprenorphine: an opiate analgesic that blocks the natural opiate receptors in the brain, under study as a treatment for opiate addiction.

buspirone (Buspar): a nonbenzodiazepine anxiolytic agent used to treat anxiety disorders and alcoholism without abuse potential.

carbamazepine (Tegretol): an anticonvulsant drug that alters receptor function in brain centers responsible for pleasure and drug cravings.

cartel: a loosely organized group of independent drug traffickers who work together to regulate price, production, transportation, and distribution of drugs.

cellular tolerance: the tendency of cells targeted by drugs to become relatively insensitive to or to compensate for the drug effects so that, to achieve desired drug effects, increased amounts are required.

central nervous system: those nerve cells that make up the brain and the spinal cord.

chipping: the occasional, recreational use of an addictive drug.

chlordiazepoxide (Librium): a tranquilizer that alters functions of the limbic system responsible for controlling emotions; used to control anxiety.

cholinergic agonists: drugs that increase the activity of acetylcholine transmission, having psychoactive properties.

classical conditioning: a type of behavioral conditioning whereby two stimuli, an unconditioned and a neutral stimulus, are presented in the same time frame. The unconditioned stimulus evokes an unconditioned response. By presenting the neutral stimulus followed by the unconditioned stimulus repeatedly, the neutral stimulus evokes a response similar to the original unconditioned response, and the neutral stimulus becomes a conditioned stimulus capable of evoking a conditioned response.

clean urine: a urine sample that is free from drugs.

clonazepam (Clonopin): a benzodiazepine, sedative-hypnotic drug.

clonidine: adrenergic agonist that attenuates the discomfort of opiate withdrawal.

cocaine: a behavioral stimulant, derived from the coca leaf, commonly sold as a water-soluble hydrochloride salt for sniffing or injecting.

cocaine base: form of cocaine that is crudely refined and composed of cocaine sulfate and impurities.

cocaine free base: pure form of cocaine manufactured by separating the cocaine molecule from the hydrochloride molecule of cocaine HCL. When the freebase is ignited and smoked, the effects are greater than the inhaled powder form.

cold turkey: abrupt withdrawal from an addictive drug without the assistance of other drugs to ease withdrawal symptoms; most commonly associated with heroin withdrawal.

comorbidity: common occurrence of two or more maladies. In alcohol, drug, and other addictions, it refers to the presence of a second problem associated with the addiction. For example, a common comorbidity with alcohol is unipolar depression.

congeners: natural by-products of the fermentation and processing of alcohol, responsible, in part, for hangover symptoms.

convulsion: a condition produced by the blockage of inhibitory transmission in the brain, marked by an involuntary, sudden attack of muscle contractions.

corruption: when law enforcement officers use their professional position for personal gain.

cortex: the external gray matter of the brain primarily responsible for higher intellectual functioning.

crack cocaine: derived from cocaine HCL by mixing the compound with baking soda and water. The water is evaporated and the mixture turns to a crystalline chunk or rock that may be smoked in a pipe.

cross dependency: ability of a drug to terminate the withdrawal symptoms associated with discontinuation of another drug on which an individual is dependent.

cross tolerance: the development of reduced sensitivity to a drug due to the repeated administration of another drug to which the user has become tolerant.

cut: ingredients added to a drug to increase its bulk.

deep cover: a drug enforcement agent assumes a new identity as a drug trafficker or buyer, generally for an extended period of time, in order to apprehend individuals involved in illegal drug activity.

delirium tremens (DTs): brain seizures that result from the sudden termination of alcohol intake after long-term, high dosage use.

dendrites: projections from a cell body that receive action potentials from adjacent neurons.

dependency: the development of psychological and/or physical need for a drug to maintain an individual's sense of well-being and avoid withdrawal symptoms.

depressants: a classification of drugs that decrease activity and arousal of the central nervous system and frequently induce sleep.

designer drugs: slang for drugs derived from fentanyl-type opiates with both stimulant and hallucinogenic properties.

diazepam (Valium): a benzodiazepine commonly used for the treatment of anxiety.

dimethyltryptamine (DMT): an hallucinogenic LSD-like drug that mimicks serotonin activity. DMT is found predominantly in South and Central America in the bark of trees of the genus *virola* and used as snuff. In the United States, it is called the businessman's lunch due to its short action.

dirty urine: a urine sample that shows the presence of drugs

DOM (STP; 2,5-dimethoxy-4-methamphetamine): a synthetic designer drug similar to amphetamine.

dopamine: an excitatory neurotransmitter synthesized by catecholamine neurons responsible, in part, for the experience of pleasure.

downers: a slang term for barbiturates.

drug: any chemical substance used to exert its effects on bodily processes.

drug abuse: the use or misuse of a drug for recreational or medicinal purposes to the detriment of the user or others with whom the user comes into contact.

drug addiction: a state of periodic or chronic intoxication produced by repeated consumption of a drug. Its characteristics include an overpowering desire or need (compulsion) to continue taking the drug and to obtain it by any means, the tendency to increase the dose (tolerance), and a psychological and/or physical dependence upon the effect of the drug.

drug courier profile: a compilation of personal characteristics drug enforcement agents use to identify individuals they believe may be transporting drugs through the airports, bus, or train stations or on the highways.

dysphoria: the experience of a physically or emotionally uncomfortable state.

eight-ball: slang for 8 grams of cocaine.

electrical stimulation of the brain (ESB): the use of electrical leads placed within the skull that stimulate portions of the brain to produce an effect.

electroencephalography (EEG): a technique that records the electrical activity of the brain.

endocrine system: a system composed of glands that secrete hormones directly into the bloodstream to exert an effect on another gland or organ.

endogenous: arises from within a given system or structure, as from within the brain or biological group of the body. May refer to either substances found naturally within the body/brain or forms of mental deficiency that are hereditary.

endorphins: refers to naturally occurring proteins, the neuropeptides, that act as neurotransmitters with opiate-like properties responsible, in part, for the experience of pleasure.

enkephalins: refers to naturally occurring proteins, the neuropeptides, that act as neurotransmitters with opiate-like properties responsible, in part, for the management of pain.

epinephrine: also known as adrenaline; a neurotransmitter found primarily in the peripheral nervous system and synthesized and released by the adrenal gland.

etiology: the study of the development of a problem. In the case of drug and alcohol abuse, it is the question of what led the individual to become a substance abuser.

euphoria: an exaggerated sense of physical or emotional well-being, especially when not in keeping with real events.

exogenous: that which originates from outside the body, as in a substance taken into the body from an external source.

family studies: a method to estimate genetic influences on a trait or behavior by comparing its incidence in individuals having relatives with and without that trait or behavior.

fetal alcohol syndrome: abnormalities in facial structure, limb and cardiovascular defects and central nervous system impairments attributed to exposure of the fetus to alcohol ingested during pregnancy.

fight/flight/fright mechanism: refers to the activation of the autonomic nervous system by higher brain centers to mobilize behavioral and emotional responses to an internal or external stressor.

flashbacks: the temporary reexperience of a drug effect some time after the acute drug effects have worn off. Particularly known to occur with some hallucinogenic drugs.

flurazepam (Dalmane): a hypnotic benzodiazepine.

gamma-aminobutyric acid (GABA): an inhibitory neurotransmitter in the central nervous system.

genetics: pertaining to traits or features that originate from the genes and tend to be inherited.

glaucoma: an eye disease characterized by increased intraocular pressure that may lead to blindness.

Golden Triangle: the countries of Burma, Laos, and Thailand; most of the world's opium originates here.

hallucination: perception without an external stimulus, which may occur in any field of sensation: auditory, visual, olfactory, gustatory, or tactile.

hallucinogens: drugs that alter sensory perception and frequently produce hallucinations.

haloperidol (Haldol): a dopaminergic blocking agent used to treatvarious forms of mental illness and to control acute psychosis that results from the use of certain drugs, such as phencyclidine or amphetamines.

hashish: composed of dried resin of the female flowers of cannabis plants with high concentrations of THC. heroin: a partially synthetic opiate produced by modifying the molecular structure of morphine.

high risk studies: a method to estimate genetic influences on a trait or behavior, comparing individuals with and without relatives who possess that trait or behavior, to identify similarities and differences.

hippies: slang used to describe those who participated in the subcultural movement of the 1960s to either change society and its values, or drop out. A large subgroup of hippies were known to engage in experimental and recreational drug use during that era.

hippocampus: a portion of the limbic system largely responsible for memory and emotional state.

hormone: a substance released from an endocrine gland that travels to exert its effect upon a different gland, organ, or structure.

hyperkinesis: a syndrome manifested primarily by children and characterized by hyperemotionality, hyperactivity, short attention span, impulsivity, distractibility, and perceptual and learning disabilities.

hypoglycemia: chronic low blood glucose condition characterized by the enhanced release of insulin, epinephrine, cortisol, and ACTH.

hypothalamus: closely associated with the limbic system, this structure sits near the midbrain and the thalamus. It has many regulatory functions, including hunger, thirst, sleeping, reproduction, mood, and emotions. It also controls the activity of the pituitary gland.

iatrogenic dependence: drug dependence induced and maintained by a physician.

ice: a crystallized form of methamphetamine with addictive properties ingested in pill form, snorted, or injected IV.

indolealkylamines: hallucinogens that exert their effects by acting on serotonergic systems.

inhalation: a method to administer a drug by breathing in a gas, spray, or powder.

innocent owner defense: related to asset forfeiture; the owner of property involved in illegal drug activity may argue that he or she did not know that the illegal activity took place or that he or she did everything possible to prevent the illegal activity from occurring.

instrumental conditioning: a type of behavioral conditioning whereby an individual's behavior is instrumental in the obtaining of reward or the avoidance of or escape from punishment.

interdiction: intercepting and preventing the transportation of of illegal drugs for the purpose of illegal sale and distribution.

intramuscular injection: a method to administer a drug by injecting the substance into the skeletal muscle.

intravenous injection: a method to administer a drug by injecting the substance directly into a vein to rapidly enter the bloodstream.

ketamine: an hallucinogenic drug with anesthetic properties first developed for surgical purposes.

kindling: occurs when the seizural threshold of the brain is lowered from being repeated stimulation so that the area becomes more sensitized and neurons begin to fire spontaneously. The likelihood of erratic electrical discharges and possibly seizures increases.

libido: sex drive.

limbic system: a primitive portion of the brain that interacts with the hypothalamus to regulate emotion, mood, memory, pain, and pleasure. Its primary structures include the hippocampus, amygdala, mammillary bodies, septum, and several other smaller areas. The limbic system is the source of many profound drug effects on emotions and behavior.

lipid (fat) soluble: the property of a drug to dissolve in fatty tissue. Such drugs generally accumulate in the kidneys and are slowly eliminated from the body.

lithium carbonate: a drug commonly and effectively used to treat manic-depression.

lock and key mechanism: describes the ability of an endogenous or exogenous chemical to attach to a receptor site and exert an effect, either excitatory or inhibitory.

locus ceruleus: structure within the mesolimbic system responsible for alertness, wakefulness, and arousal.

lorazepam (Ativan): a benzodiazepine, sedative-hypnotic drug.

lysergic acid diethylamide (LSD): a semi-synthetic hallucinogen.

marijuana: cultivated from Cannabis plants, used for its hallucinogenic and mind-altering properties. The active constituents are primarily the tetrahydrocannabinols.

MDMA (Ecstasy; 3,4-methyene-dioxymethamphetamine): a synthetic designer drug with mescaline-like effects.

meprobamate (Equanil, Milton): a CNS depressant with anxiety-reducing and tranquilizing properties.

mescaline (peyote): a hallucinogenic drug found in the peyote cactus (*Lophophora williamsii*).

metabolic tolerance: the tendency of liver enzymes to become more efficient at degrading a drug with repeated administrations.

metabolite, drug: a by-product, active or inactive, produced after a drug is metabolized.

methadone: a synthetic opiate designed to replace street drugs, such as heroin, primarily used for treatment purposes.

methamphetamine: an amphetamine derivative.

methaqualone (Quaalude): a nonbarbiturate, sedative drug with highly addictive properties.

methylphenidate (Ritalin): prescription stimulants commonly used in the treatment of hyperkinesis in children and, less often, adults.

money laundering: the process of making money gained from illegal activity look as though it was earned through legitmate sources.

morphine: the principle component of the opium poppy with pain relieving and sedating properties.

Naloxone and Naltrexone: drugs with antagonistic effects on opiates, blocking opiate receptor sites and attenuating the drug action.

narcotic: refers to opiate analgesics. Several nonnarcotic drugs are scheduled as narcotics for legal purposes.

neuron: a nerve cell in the nervous system.

neuropeptide: chemical proteins in the nervous system with an affinity for specific receptor sites to exert their effects. Also known as opiate peptides, they generally include the endorphins, enkephalins, and dynorphins.

neurotransmitter: a chemical messenger in the nervous system that conveys information from one nerve cell to another nerve cell or structure.

neurotransmitter precursor: a substance, such as tyrosine or tryptophan, frequently found in food, that helps to synthesize a neurotransmitter..

neurotransmitter precusor therapy (NPT): the use of food constituents, such as amino acids, that act as precursors in the synthesis of neurotransmitters in an attempt to treat certain disorders, both mental and physical, including substance abuse.

norepinephrine: an excitatory neurotransmitter in the central and peripheral nervous systems synthesized by catecholamine neurons.

nucleus accumbens: structure within the limbic system where dopamine terminals are concentrated and involved largely in experiences of pleasure.

opiate: a natural or synthetic drug that has pain relieving properties, similar to morphine, that tend to be addictive.

pathological intoxication: a rare syndrome seen in individuals extremely sensitive to the effects of alcohol, resulting in signs of severe intoxication and impaired behavior after consuming only small amounts.

pemoline (Cylert): prescription stimulant commonly used in the treatment of hyperkinesis in children and adults.

peripheral nervous system: that portion of the nervous system that consists of neurons located outside of the skull and spinal cord.

pharmacokinetics: the study of drug actions with respect to conditions influencing absorption, distribution, metabolism, and elimination.

pharmacology: a field of scientific inquiry that studies the effects of drugs on the brain and behavior.

phencyclidine (PCP): a hallucinogenic anesthetic developed for surgical purposes but now used only by illicit drug users.

phenmetrazine (Preludin): stimulant drug previously used as an appetite suppressant.

phenobarbital (Luminal): a barbiturate with anticonvulsive effects.

phenylethylamines: drugs similar in structure to the catecholamine neurotransmitters with amphetamine-like properties

phenylpropanolamine (PPA): stimulant drug found in many over-the-counter cold medicines and diet pills.

physical dependence: the development of withdrawal symptoms and inability to function normally when a drug is discontinued. Readministration of that drug will terminate withdrawal symptoms.

placebo: a pharmacologically inert substance, thought to be an active drug that may produce effects similar to an active substance due to a belief that it will. May exert this effect by activating neuropeptide systems.

placental barrier: the tissues intervening between the maternal and the fetal blood of the placenta, which prevent or hinder certain substances or organisms from passing from mother to fetus.

prevention: a public health term that refers to interventions designed to prevent individuals from acquiring a disease or illness. In the addiction literature, the term refers specifically to the prevention of addictive behaviors.

primary prevention: a public health term referring to intervention programs aimed at high-risk individuals who do not as yet have any symptoms of the malady. In the addiction field an example is the "Just Say No" campaign that was apparently designed to keep young children from trying drugs.

promethazine: a tranquilizer that suppresses brain centers responsible for abnormal emotions and behaviors, sometimes used to treat acute cases of amphetamine psychosis.

psilocybin: an hallucinogenic drug found in the Mexican mushroom *Psilocybe mexicana.*

psychedelic: term commonly used in the 1960s to denote a hallucinogen.

psychoactive drugs: any chemical substance that modifies emotions, mood, or behavior due to its alteration of brain chemistry and/or function.

psychopathy: a state or condition that characterizes individuals who are unable to experience anxiety or learn from punishment, and who exhibit sensation-seeking and impulsive behaviors.

psychosis: an impairment of mental functioning to the extent that it interferes grossly with an individual's ability to meet the ordinary demands of life, characterized generally by severe affective disturbance, profound introspection, and withdrawal from reality.

psychotomimetic: drugs that produce psychotic-like states and symptoms.

radioimmunoassay: a technique for measuring antibody levels whereby a radioactively labeled antigen is reacted with a serum under study, and antibody activity is determined as a measure of the amount of radioactivity bound to the antibody fraction.

rapid eye movement (REM) sleep: a stage occuring during the sleep cycle characterized by rapid eye movements, fast brain wave activity, and dreaming.

rebound effect: occurs when a drug suppresses symptoms or behaviors temporarily; when the drug is discontinued, the symptoms resurface in an exaggerated fashion.

receptor site: a molecular site on a cell's dendrite that receives a specific brain chemical or drug to produce an effect.

red clause: a line in the advertising contract between a drug company and newspaper that states that all advertising will be pulled if the state in which the paper resided passed any kind of regulatory law related to patent medicines. The clause was underlined in red ink.

reinforcement: a rewarding event or state of affairs that obtains its effectiveness from a prior learning or conditioning experience. When a positive reinforcer is presented as a consequence of a particular response or behavior, the occurrence of that response increases. When a negative reinforcer is presented, the occurrence of the associated response decreases.

relapse: a term used in the drug treatment literature to denote a return to the use of drugs or alcohol after treatment has begun.

relations back doctrine: related to asset forfeiture; authorities may seize property related to illegal drug activities for three years after the illegal activity occurred.

reticular activating system (RAS): a network of fibers that extends up the brainstem almost to the thalamus. It is primarily responsible for arousing the organism to attend to incoming stimuli and is susceptible to the effects of many drugs that alter its control of sleepfulness and wakefulness.

reverse tolerance (sensitization): certain drug effects that become heightened after repeated administration of the drug.

roid rage: jargon for the tendency of some anabolic steroid users to become unusually aggressive and display sudden bursts of explosive violence.

rush: jargon for the sensation of euphoria and extreme well-being felt immediately following administration of a drug of abuse.

sedative-hypnotic drugs: a category of depressant drugs that produce a quieting effect on the central nervous system in a general, nonselective fashion to relieve anxiety, induce sleep, or provide anesthesia.

self medication: to use a drug so that a present dysphoric state is relieved.

serotonin: a neurotransmitter in the brain involved in the regulation of body temperature, sleep, sensory perception, and impulse control.

shooting gallery: a place where drug users can go to inject drugs. Needles and/or other paraphenalia may be borrowed or rented.

skin popping: slang for injecting drugs under the skin with a hypodermic needle.

smurfing: a method of money laundering where many money orders under the amount of $10,000 are purchased from various banks and then deposited into several bank accounts.

speed: amphetamines by street users taken by IV.

speed ball: a mixture of cocaine and heroin or amphetamine and heroin that is injected into the veins.

spinal cord: the part of the central nervous system located within the vertebral canal that regulates spinal reflexes and transmits information between the peripheral and central nervous systems.

stacking: jargon for using more than one anabolic steroid at a time to equal several times the therapeutic dose of steroids and enhance their effects.

step on: a process whereby substances such as baking soda, talc, lactose, and/or quinine are added to a drug to increase its bulk and reduce its purity.

stereotyped behavior: repetitive movements or series of behaviors that occur without purpose or function.

stimulants: drugs that increase behavioral and mental activity.

subcutaneous injection: a method of administering a drug by injecting the substance directly under the skin.

sympathomimetic agents: drugs that activate the autonomic nervous system, arousing the individual, and creating feelings of anxiety and stress.

synapse: a functional gap between two separate neurons where impulses are transmitted between cells in the nervous system.

synergistic effect: with respect to drug effects, when a combination of two or more drugs are taken, the effects will be multiplicative, rather than simply additive.

synesthesias: a condition marked by a confusion or mixing of the senses.

tachyphylaxis: decreasing response to stimulation by a drug as doses of the substance are repeatedly given, leading to the rapid development of tolerance.

testosterone: a male hormone responsible for masculine orientation, male anatomy, sex drive, aggression, and territorial instinct.

tetrahydrocannabinols (THC): the active ingredients of Cannabis plants used for its psychoactive properties in both marijuana and hashish.

thalamus: situated above the brainstem and below the cortex, the thalamus receives incoming stimuli from the spinal cord, through the brainstem, and relays information to the cortex.

tolerance: the need to increase the dosage of a drug to produce the same effect—the user becomes increasingly insensitive to the drug's effects.

toxic: drug effects that are detrimental to the functioning of an organ or group of organs—can be temporary or permanent.

treatment: any intervention by professional therapists or trained lay staff that is intended to modify destructive or harmful behavior. In the case of drug or alcohol abuse, any intervention to render the individual's use of drugs and alcohol as harmless.

triazolam (Halcion): a hypnotic benzodiazepine.

twin studies: a method to estimate genetic influences on a trait or behavior by comparing identical and fraternal twins for the incidence of that trait or behavior.

water soluble: the ability of a substance to dissolve in water.

withdrawal: occurs when a user discontinues drug administration and may include several symptoms of pain and dysphoria, including vomiting, nausea, diarrhea, headache, depression, irritability, anxiety, stomach cramps.

REFERENCES

Ackerman, R. J. (1983). *Children of alcoholics: A guide for parents, educators, and therapists.* New York: Simon & Schuster.

Ackerman, R. J. (1987). *Let go and grow: Recovery for adult children of alcoholics.* Pompano Beach, FL: Health Communications.

Ackerman, R. J. (1989). *Perfect daughters: Adult daughters of alcoholics.* Deerfield Beach, FL: Health Communications.

Adams, S. H. (1924a, March 1). How people become drug addicts. *Colliers, The National Weekly,* p. 9.

Adams, S. H. (1924b, March 8). How to stop the "dope" peddler. *Colliers, The National Weekly,* pp. 13, 31.

Adler, P. T., & Lutecka, L. (1973). Drug use among high school students: Patterns and correlates. *International Journal of Addictions, 8,* 537-548.

Agents arrest car dealers in sales to drug traffickers. (1990, October 4). *The New York Times,* p. B3.

Ahmed, S. W., Bush, P. J., Davidson, F. R., & Iannotti, R. J. (1984). Predicting children's use and intentions to use abusable substances. Paper presented at the Annual Meeting of the American Public Health Association, Anaheim, CA.

Aigner, T. G., & Balster, R. L. (1978). Choice behavior in rhesus monkeys: C versus food. *Science, 201,* 534-535.

Akil, H., Madden, J., Patrick, R. L. & Barchas, J. D. (1976). Stress induced increase in endogenous opiate peptides: Concurrent analgesia and its partial reversal by naloxone. In H. W. Kosterlitz (Ed.), *Opiates and endogenous opioid peptides* (pp. 63-70). Amsterdam: North-Holland Publishing Co.

"Alcoholic Disease" a myth. (1919, August 23). *The Literary Digest,* pp. 79-80.

Alcoholics Anonymous (1952). The twelve steps and twelve traditions. New York: AA World Services, Inc.

Alcoholics Anonymous (1976). New York: Alcoholics Anonymous World Services, Inc.

Alibrandi, L.A. (1978) The folk psychotherapy of Alcoholics Anonymous. In S. Zimberg., J. Wallace, & S. Blume (Eds.), *Practical approaches to alcoholism psychotherapy.* New York: Plenum Press.

Alterman, A. I. (1988). Patterns of familial alcoholism, alcoholism severity, and psychopathology. *Journal of Nervous and Mental Disease, 176,* 167-175.

Alterman, A. I., Bridges, K. R., & Tarter, R. E. (1986). The influence of both drinking and familial risk statuses on cognitive functioning of social drinkers. *Alcoholism: Clinical and Experimental Research, 10,* 448-451.

Alterman, A. I., Petrarulo, E., Tarter, R., & McCowan, J. (1982). Hyperactivity and alcoholism: Familial and behavioral correlates. *Addictive Behaviors, 7,* 413-421.

Alterman, A. I. & Tarter, R. E. (1986). An examination of selected typologies: Hyperactivity, familial, and antisocial alcoholism. In M. Galanter (Ed.), *Recent developments in alcoholism* (Vol. 4), (pp. 169-189). New York: Plenum Press.

American enslavement to drugs. (1919, April 26). *The Literary Digest,* p. 32.

American Management Association. (1987). *Drug abuse: The workplace issues.* New York: American Management Association.

American Psychiatric Association (APA) (1987). *Diagnostic and statistical manual, third edition, revised.* American Psychiatric Association, Washington, DC.

Ames, F. (1958). A clinical and metabolic study of acute intoxication with Cannabis sativa and its role in the model psychoses. *Journal of Mental Sciences, 104,* 972-999.

Amit, Z., Sutherland, E. A., Gill, K., & Ogren, S. O. (1984). Zimeldine: A review of its effects on ethanol consumption. *Neuroscience Biobehavioral Review, 8,* 35-54.

Anglin, M. D. & Hser, Y. (1990). Treatment of drug abuse (pp. 393- 460). In M. Tonry & J. W. Wilson (Eds.), *Drugs and crime.* Chicago, IL: University of Chicago Press.

Anglin, M. D. & Westland, C. A. (1989). Drug monitoring in the workplace: Results from the California commercial laboratory drug testing project. In S. W. Gust & J. M. Walsh (Eds.), *Drugs in the workplace: Research and evaluation data* (NIDA Research Monograph 91) (pp. 81-96). Rockville, MD: National Institute on Drug Abuse.

Anhalt, H. & Klein, D. (1976). Drug abuse in junior high school populations. *American Journal of Drug and Alcohol Abuse, 3,* 589-603.

Aronow, R., Miceli, J. N. & Done, A. K. (1980). A therapeutic approach to the acutely overdosed patient. *Journal of Psychedelic Drugs, 12,* 259-268.

Aronson, T. A. & Craig, T. J. (1986). Cocaine precipitation of panic disorder. *American Journal of Psychiatry, 143,* 643-645.

Aronson, M., Kyllerman, M., Sabel, K. G., Sandin, B., & Olegard, R. (1985). Children of alcoholic mothers: Developmental, perceptual and behavioral characteristics as compared to matched controls. *Acta Paediatrica Scandanavia, 74,* 27-35.

Asghar, K. & DeSouza, E. (1989). *Pharmacology and Toxicology of Amphetamine and Related Designer Drugs* (NIDA Research Monograph No. 94). Washington, DC: U.S. Government Printing Office.

Asnis, S.F. & Smith, R.C. (1978). Amphetamine abuse and violence. *Journal of Psychedelic Drugs, 10,* 371-377.

Ayres, R. D., Jr. (1991, March 23). 11 held and 3 fraternities seize in drug raids at U. of Virginia. *The New York Times,* pp. 1,8.

Bach-y-Rita, G., Lion, J. R. & Ervin, F. R. (1970). Pathological intoxication. Clinical and electroencephalographic studies. *American Journal of Psychiatry, 127,* 698-703.

Bakalar J. B., & Grinspoon, L. (1984). *Drug control in a free society.* Cambridge, England: Cambridge University Press.

Baker, J. N., Miller, M. & Bingham, C. (1990, August 20). Barry beats the rap. *Newsweek,* pp. 43-44.

Ball, D.S. (1978). The experimental reproduction of amphetamine psychosis. *Archives of General Psychiatry, 29,* 35-40.

Ball, J. C., Rosen, L., Flueck, J. A., & Nurco, D. N.(1981). The criminality of heroin addicts when addicted and when off opiates. In A. Inciardi (Ed.), *The Drugs-Crime Connection* (pp.39-65). Beverly Hills, CA: Sage Publications, Inc.

Ball, J. C., Schaffer, J. W., & Nurco, D. N. (1983). Day to day criminality of heroin addicts in Baltimore—A study in the continuity of offense rates. *Drug and Alcohol Dependence, 12,* 119-142.

Ballenger, J. C., Goodwin, F. K., Major, L. F. & Brown, G. L. (1979). Alcohol and central serotonin metabolism in man. *Archives of General Psychiatry, 36,* 224-227.

Banki, C. (1981). Factors influencing monoamine metabolites and tryptophan in patients with alcohol dependence. *Journal of Neural Transmission, 50,* 98-101.

Barbeau, A., Growdon, J. H. & Wurtman, R. J. (1979). *Nurtrition and the brain (Vol. 5).* New York: Raven Press.

Barnett, A., & Fiore, J.W. (1973). Acute tolerance to diazepam in cats. In S. Garattini, E. Mussini, & L.O. Randall (Eds.) *The benzodiazepines* (pp. 545-558). New York: Raven Press.

Barnett, R. E. (1987). Curing the drug-law addiction: The harmful side effects of legal prohibition. In R. Hamowy (Ed.), *Dealing with drugs: Consequences of government control.* Lexington, MA: D. C. Heath and Co.

Bartus, R. T., Dean, R. L., Beer, B., & Lippa, A. S. (1982). The cholinergic hypothesis of geriatric memory dysfunction. *Science, 217,* 408-417.

Battaglia, G. & De Souza, E. B. (1989). Pharmacologic profile of amphetamine derivatives at various brain recognition sites: Selective effects on serotonergic systems. In K. Asghar & E. De Souza (Eds.), *Pharmacology and toxicology of amphetamine and related designer drugs.* (pp. 240-258) (NIDA Research Monograph No. 94). Washington, DC: U.S. Government Printing Office.

Beattie, M. (1989). *Beyond codependancy and getting better all the time.* San Fransisco: Harper & Row Publishers.

Beaty, J. & Hornik, R. (1989 December 18). A torrent of dirty dollars. *Newsweek,* pp. 50-56.

Becker, H. S. (1963). Outsiders: Studies in the sociology of deviance. New York: Free Press.

Beecher, E. M. (1972). *Licit & illicit drugs.* Mount Vernon, NY: Consumers Union.

Belenko, S., Fagan, J. & Chin, K. (1991). Criminal justice responses to crack. *Journal of Research in Crime and Delinquency, 28,* 55-74.

Bell, B. & Cohen, R. (1981). The Bristol social adjustment guide: Comparison between the offspring of alcoholic and non-alcoholic mothers. *British Journal of Clinical Psychology, 20,* 93-95.

Bellak, L. (1979). *Disorders of the schizophrenic syndrome.* New York: Basic Books.

Berger, G. (1987). *Drug testing.* New York: Franklin Watts.

Berkow, R. (1982). *The Merck manual* (14th ed.). Rahway, NJ: Marck Sharp & Dohme Research Laboratories.

Besharov, D. J. (1989, Fall). The children of crack: Will we protect them? *Public Welfare,* pp. 6-11.

Biernacki, P. (1986). *Pathways from heroin addiction: Recovery without treatment.* Philadelphia: Temple Univ.

Bird, E. D., Spokes, E. G., Barnes, J., Mackay, A. V. P., Iverson, L. L. & Shepherd, M. (1977). Increased brain dopamine and reduced glutamic acid decarboxylase and choline acetyltransferase activity in schizophrenia and related psychoses. *Lancet, 2,* 1157-1159.

Block, A. A. & Scarpitti, F. R. (1990). Casinos and banking: Organized crime in the Bahamas. In D. Kelly (Ed.), *Criminal Behavior: Text and Readings in Criminology* (pp. 334-343). New York: St. Martin's Press.

Blum, K., & Trachtenberg, M. (1987, Mar/Apr). New insights into the causes of alcoholism. Professional Counselor, 33-35.

Blum, K., Noble, E. P., Sheridan, P. J., Montgomery, A., Ritchie, T., Jagadeeswaran, P., Nogami, H., Briggs, A. H., & Cohn, J. B. (1990). Allelic association of human dopamine D 2 receptor gene in alcoholism. *Journal of the American Medical Association, 263,* 2055-2060.

Blum, R. H., Blum, E., & Garfield, E. (1976). *Drug education: Results and recommendations.* Lexington, MA: D.C. Heath and Co.

Blumenthal, R. (1988) *Last days of the Sicilians: At war with Mafia—The FBI assault on the pizza connection.* New York: Times Books.

Blumstein, A., Farrington, D. P. & Moitra, S. (1985). Delinquency careers: Innocents, desisters, and persisters. In T. Tonry & N. Morris (Eds.), *Crime and justice* (pp. 137-168). Chicago: University of Chicago Press.

Bohman, M. (1978). Some genetic aspects of alcoholism and criminality. *Archives of General Psychiatry, 35,* 269-276.

Bolter, A. (1980). Issues for inpatient treatment of chronic PCP abuse. *Journal of Psychedelic Drugs, 12,* 287-288.

Born a dope fiend. (1919, July 19). *The Literary Digest,* p. 27.

Botvin, G. J. (1983). Prevention of adolescent substance abuse through the development of personal and social competence. In T. J. Glynn, L. G. Leukefield & J. P. Lundford (Eds.), *Preventing adolescent drug abuse: Intervention strategies* (NIDA Research Monograph No. 47, pp. 115-140). Rockville, MD: National Institute on Drug Abuse.

Bozarth, M. A. & Wise, R. A. (1985). Toxicity associated with long-term intravenous heroin and cocaine self-administration in the rat. *Journal of the American Medical Association, 254,* 81-83.

Brady, J. V. & Lukas, S. E. (1984). *Testing drugs for physical dependence potential and abuse liability.* (NIDA Research Monograph No. 52). Rockville, MD: National Institute on Drug Abuse.

Braestrup, C., & Neilsen. M. (1983). Benzodiazepine receptors. In L. L. Ikersen, S. D. Iversen, & S. H. Soldman (Eds.) *Handbook of Psychopharmacology. Vol. 17: Biochemical Studies of CNS Receptors.* New York: Plenum Press.

Brain, P. F. & Coward, G. A. (1989). A review of the history, actions, and legitimate uses of cocaine. *Journal of Substance Abuse, 1,* 431-451.

Braucht, G. N., Brakarsh, D., Follingstad, D. & Barry, K. L. (1973). Deviant drug use in adolescence: A review of psychosocial correlates. *Psychological Bulletin, 79,* 92-106.

Bray, J. H. & Maxwell, S.E. (1985) *Multivariate analysis of variance.* Beverly Hills, CA: Sage Publications.

Bresler, F. (1981). *The Chinese mafia.* New York: Stein and Day.

British Medical Association. Public Affairs Division. (1986) *Smoking out the barons; The campaign against the tobacco industry.* Chichester, Eng.: John Wiley & Sons.

Brooke, J. (1991, July 14). Cali, the 'Quiet' drug cartel, profits by accommodation. *The New York Times,* pp. 1 & 6.

Brooke, J. (1991, December 22). The cocaine war's biggest success: A fungus. *The New York Times,* p. 15.

Brooke, J. (1995, June 27). Crackdown has Cali drug cartel on the run. *The New York Times,* pp. A1 & A8.

Brooke, J. (1991a, June 21). Drug baron's jailing heartens Colombia. *The New York Times,* p. A8.

Brooke, J. (1991b, June 22). Drug baron's prison has every comfort: Even mom and TV. *The New York Times,* pp. 1 & 4.

Brooke, J. (1992, March 28). Fighting the drug war in the skies over Peru. *The New York Times,* p. 4.

Brooke, J. (1995, January 23). Peru combats drug traffic, Winning U.S. team's praise. *The New York Times,* p. A2.

Brooke, J. (1990, January 5). Police chief's tough (Just ask the death squads). *The New York Times,* p. A4.

Brooke, J. (1992, July 31). U.S. military planes join search for escaped Colombia drug lord. *The New York Times,* pp. A1 & A8.

Brower, K. J., Eliopulos, G. A., Blow, F. C., Catlin, D. H. & Beresford, T. P. (1990). Evidence for physical and psychological dependence on anabolic androgenic steroids in eight weight lifters. *American Journal of Psychiatry, 147,* 510-512.

Brower, K. J., Blow, F. C., Eliopulos, G. A. & Beresford, T.P. (1989). Anabolic androgenic steroids and suicide (letter). *American Journal of Psychiatry, 146,* 1078.

Brower, K. J., Blow, F. C., Beresford, T. P., & Fuelling C. (1989). Anabolic-androgenic steroid dependence. *Journal of Clinical Psychiatry, 50,* 31-33.

Brown, E. M. (1986). English interest in the treatment of alcoholism in the United States during the early 1870's. *British Journal of Addiction, 81,* 545-551.

Brown, G. L., Ebert, M. H., Goyer, P. F., Jimerson, D. C., Klein, W. F., Bunney, W. E. & Goodwin, F. K. (1982). Aggression, suicide and serotonin: Relationships to CSF amine metabolites. *American Journal of Psychiatry, 139,* 741-746.

Brown, G. L., Goodwin, F. K., Ballenger, J. C., Goyer, P. F., & Major, L. F. (1979). Aggression in humans correlates with cerebrospinal fluid amine metabolites. *Psychiatry Research, 1,* 131-139.

Brown, J.W., Mazze, R., & Glaser, D. (1974) *Narcotics knowledge and nonsense; Program disaster versus a scientific model.* Cambridge, MA: Ballinger Pub. Co.

Brown, L. S., Murphy, D. L., Primm, B. J. (1987). Needle sharing and AIDS in minorities. [Letter to the editor]. *Journal of the American Medical Association, 256,* 1474-1475.

Brunner, H. G., Nelen, M., Breakefield, X. O., Ropers, H. H., & van Oost, B. A. (1993). Abnormal behavior associated with a point mutation in the structural gene for monoamine Oxidase A. *American Journal of Human Genetics, 262,* 578-580.

Bruno, F. (1989). Buspirone in the treatment of alcoholic patients. *Psychopathology, 22 (Suppl. 1),* 49-59.

Buckley, W. E., Yesalis, C. E., Friedl, K. E., Anderson, W. A., Streit A. Z. & Wright, J. E. (1988). Estimated prevalence of anabolic steroid use among male high school seniors. *Journal of the American Medical Association, 260,* 3441-3445.

Bureau of Communicable Disease Control, New York State Department of Health. (1986) *AIDS Surveillance Monthly Update.*

Bureau of Justice Statistics, U.S. Department of Justice. (1989). *Drugs and crime facts, 1989.* Rockville, MD: Drugs and Crime Data Center and Clearinghouse.

Burse, R. L., Bynum, G. D. & Pandolf, K. B. (1975). Increased appetite and unchanged metabolism upon cessation of smoking with diet held constant. *Physiologist, 18,* 257.

Bush, P. J. & Iannotti, R. J. (1985). The development of children's health orientations and behaviors: Lessons for substance abuse prevention. In C. L. Jones & R. J. Battjes (Eds.) *Etiology of Drug Abuse: Implications for Prevention* (pp. 45-74). (NIDA Research Monograph Series 56). Rockville, MD: National Institute on Drug Abuse.

Byck, R. (1987). Cocaine, marijuana, and the meanings of addiction. In R. Hamowy, (Ed.), *Dealing with drugs: Consequences of government control* (pp. 221-245). Lexington, MA: D. C. Heath and Co.

Cadoret, R., & Gath, A. (1978). Inheritance of alcoholism in adoptees. *British Journal of Psychiatry, 132,* 252-258.

Cadoret, R. J., Troughton, E., & O'Gorman, T. W. (1987). Genetic and environmental factors in alcohol abuse and antisocial personality. *Journal of Studies on Alcohol, 48,* 1-8.

Cadoret, R. J., Troughton, E., O'Gorman, T. W., & Heywood, E. (1986). An adoption study of genetic and environmental factors in drug abuse. *Archives of General Psychiatry, 43,* 1131-1136.

Cadoret, R., Troughton, E. & Widmer, R. (1984). Clinical differences between antisocial and primary alcoholics. *Comprehensive Psychiatry, 25,* 1-8.

California being enriched by underground and illegal money. (1994, April 10). *The New York Times,* p. 17.

Callahan, E. J. (1980). Alternative strategies in the treatment of narcotic addiction: A review. In W. Miller (Ed.), *The addictive behaviors: Treatment of alcoholism, drug abuse, smoking and obesity.* (pp. 143-167). New York: Perganom.

Canavan, P. (1990). Civil forfeiture of real property: The government's weapon against drug traffickers injures innocent owners. *Pace Law Review, 10,* 485-518.

Cantor, D. S. & Thatcher, R. W. (1986). A report on phosphatidylcholine therapy in a Down's syndrome toddler. *Psychological Reports, 58,* 207-217.

Cantwell, D. P. (1975). Genetics of hyperactivity. *Journal of Child Psychology and Psychiatry, 16,* 261-264.

Caporael, L. R. (1976). Ergotism: The Satan loosed in Salem. *Science, 192,* 21-26.

Carlsson, A. & Lindquist, M. (1963). Effect of chlorpromazine and haloperidol on formation of 3-methantyramine and normetanephrine in mouse brain. *Acta Pharmacologica Toxicologica, 20,* 140-144.

Carpenter, C., Glassner, B., Johnson, B. D. & Loughlin J. (1988) *Kids, drugs, and crime.* Lexington, MA: D. C. Heath and Co.

Carter, D. L. (1990). An overview of drug-related misconduct of police officers: Drug abuse and narcotic corruption. In R. Weisheit (Ed.), *Drugs, crime and the criminal justice system* (pp. 79-109). Cincinnati, OH: Anderson Publishing Co.

Carter, D. L. & Stephens, D. W. (1988). *Drug abuse by police officers: An analysis of critical policy issues.* Springfield, IL: Charles C. Thomas.

Cavaiola, A. A. & Schiff, M. (1988). Behavioral sequelae of physical and/or sexual abuse in adolescents. *Child Abuse and Neglect, 12,* 181-188.

Center for Disease Control. U.S. Dept. of Health and Human Services. (August 1987). Public health service guidelines for counseling and antibody testing to prevent HIV infection and AIDS. *Morbidity and Mortality Weekly Report, 36*, 509-515.

Chaiken, J. & Chaiken, M. (1982). *Varieties of criminal behavior.* Santa Monica, CA: RAND Corporation.

Chaiken, M. R. (1993). The rise of crack and ice: Experiences in three locales. National Institute of Justice, Research in Brief, March. Washington, D.C.

Chaisson, R. E., Moss, A. R., Onishi, R., Osmond, D., & Carlson, J. R. (1987) Human immunodeficiency virus infection in heterosexual intravenous drug users in San Francisco. *American Journal of Public Health, 77*, 169-172.

Chambliss, W. J. (1990). The state and organizing crime. In D. H. Kelly (Ed.), *Criminal behavior: Text and readings in criminology* (pp.367-378). New York: St. Martin's Press.

Chase, S. & Schlink, F. J. (1927). Consumers in Wonderland, III—What we get for our money when we buy from quacks and venders of cure-alls. *The New Republic, 49*, 348-351.

Cherek, D. R. (1984). Effects of cigarette smoking on human aggressive behavior. *Progress in Clinical and Biological Research, 169*, 333-344.

Chernick, M. W. (1990, April). The drug war. *NACLA Report on the Americas, 23*(6), pp. 30-40.

Christian, S. (1992, July 29). Why indulge drug lords? Colombia pressed to tell. *The New York Times*, p. A3.

Clark, J. R. (1990, March 31). Drug testing: The weeding-out process. *Law Enforcement News, XVI*(311), pp. 1, 6.

Cloninger, C. R. (1987). Neurogenetic adaptive mechanisms in alcoholism. *Science, 236*, 410-416.

Cloninger, C. R., Bohman, M. & Sigvardsson, S. (1981). Inheritance of alcohol abuse: Cross-fostering analysis of adopted men. *Archives of General Psychiatry, 38*, 861-868.

Cloninger, C. R., Sigvardsson, S. & Bohman, M. (1988). Childhood personality predicts alcohol abuse in young adults. *Alcoholism: Clinical and Experimental Research, 12*, 494-505.

Cloninger, C. R., Sigvardsson, S., von Knorring, A., & Bohman, M. (1988). The Swedish studies of the adopted children of alcoholics: A reply to Littrell. *Journal of Studies on Alcohol, 49*, 500-509.

Clouet, D. H., Asghar, K., Brown, R. M. (1988) *Mechanisms of cocaine abuse and toxicity.* (NIDA Research Monograph No. 88). Rockville, MD, National Institute on Drug Abuse.

Cloward, R. A. & Ohlin, L. E. (1960). *Delinquency and opportunity.* New York: Free Press.

Cocores, J. A., Dackis, C. A., & Gold, M. S. (1986). Sexual dysfunction secondary to cocaine abuse in two patients. *Journal of Clinical Psychiatry, 47*, 384-385.

Cocores, J. A., Davies, R. K., Mueller, P. S. & Gold, M. S. (1987). Cocaine abuse and adult attention deficit disorder. *Journal of Clinical Psychiatry, 48*, 376-377.

Cohen, A. (1955). *Delinquent boys.* New York: Free Press.

Cohen, S. (1969). Abuse of centrally stimulating agents among juveniles in California. In F. Sjoqvist & J. Tottie (Eds.), *Abuse of central stimulants* (pp. 165-185). New York: Raven Press.

Cohen, S. (1977). Angel dust. *Journal of the American Medical Association, 238*, 515-516.

Cohen, S. (1980). Alcoholic hypoglycemia. *Drug Abuse and Alcoholism Newsletter, 9*(2), 1-4.

Cohen, S. (1981). Adverse effects of marijuana: Selected issues. In *Research Developments in Drug and Alcohol Use, Annals of the New York Academy of Science, 361*, 119-125.

Cohen, S. (1987). Cocaine and violence. *Drug Abuse and Alcoholism Newsletter, 16*, 1-4.

Cohen, S. (1984). Drugs in the workplace. *Journal of Clinical Psychiatry, 45*(12), 4-8.

Coid, J. (1979). Mania a potu: A critical review of pathological intoxication. *Psychological Medicine, 9*, 709-719.

Collins, J. (1981). *Drinking and crime.* New York: Guilford Press.

Collins, J. J. & Allison, M. (1983) Legal coercion and retention in drug abuse treatment. *Hospital and Community Psychiatry, 34*, 1145-1149.

Collins, J. J., Schlenger, W. E. & Jordan, B. K. (1988). Antisocial personality and substance abuse disorders. *Bulletin of the American Academy of Psychiatry and the Law, 16*, 187-198.

Colombia gives rewards in drug crackdown. (1995, April 1995). *The New York Times*, p. A14.

Colombian drug cartel said to pay for killings. (1990, March 31). *The Durham Sun*, pp. A1-2.

Colombian heroin may be increasing: Officials fear traffickers will use network for cocaine to gain a new market. (1991, October 27). *The New York Times*, p. 15.

Colombian president will not take on cartel. (1994, June 21). *The Hartford Courant*, p. A5.

Colombian press feels heat for linking president to drug lords. (1995, April 5). *The New York Times*, p. A7.

The competitive status of the U.S. pharmaceutical industry: The influences of technology in determining international industrial competive advantage. 1983, Washington, DC: National Academy Press.

Conacher, G. N. & Workman, D. G. (1989). Violent crime possibly associated with anabolic steroid use (letter). *American Journal of Psychiatry, 146*, 679.

Connolly, G. N., Winn, D. M., Hecht, S. S., Henningfield, J. E., Hoffman, D. & Walker, B. (1986). The reemergence of smokeless tobacco. *New England Journal of Medicine, 314*, 1020-1027.

Connors, E. F. & Nugent, H. (1990). *Street level narcotics enforcement.* Bureau of Justice Assistance Monograph, Washington, DC: U.S. Department of Justice.

Connors, G. J. & Tarbox, A. R. (1985). Macro-environmental determinants of substance abuse. In M. Galizio & S. A. Maisto (Eds.), *Determinants of substance abuse: Biological, psychological and environmental factors* (pp. 283-314). New York: Plenum Press.

Consroe, R., Jones, B., & Laird, H. (1976). Interactions of delta-9-tetrahydro-cannabinol with other pharmacological agents. *Annals of New York Academy of Sciences, 281*, 198-211.

Cook, C. C. H. (1988a). The Minnesota Model in the management of drug and alcohol dependence: Miracle, method or myth? Part I. The philosophy and the programme. *British Journal of Addiction, 83*, 735-748.

Cook, C. C. H. (1988b). The Minnesota Model in the management of drug and alcohol dependence: Miracle, method or myth? Part II. Evidence and conclusions. *British Journal of Addiction, 83*, 749-761.

Cook, R. F. (1989). Drug use among working adults: Prevalence rates and estimation methods. In S. W. Gust & J. M. Walsh (Eds.), *Drugs in the workplace: Research and evaluation data* (Research Monograph No. 91, pp. 17-32). Rockville, MD: National Institute on Drug Abuse.

Cooper, M. H. (1990). *The business of drugs.* Washington: DC: Congressional Quarterly, Inc.

Coppen, A. (1967). The biochemistry of affective disorders. *British Journal of Psychiatry, 113*, 1237-1264.

Coppen, A., Brooksbank, B. W., & Peet, M. (1972). Tryptophan concentration in the cerebrospinal fluid of depressive patients. *Lancet, 1*, 1393.

Corey, M. A. (1989) *Kicking the drug habit: A comprehensive self-help guide to understanding the drug problem and overcoming addiction.* Springfield, IL: Charles C. Thomas Publisher.

Corry, J. M. & Cimbolic, P. (1985). *Drugs: Facts, alternatives, decisions.* Belmont, CA: Wadsworth Publishing Co.

Cote, G. & Hodgins, S. (1990). Co-occurring mental disorders among criminal offenders. *Bulletin of the American Academy of Psychiatry and Law, 18*, 271-281.

Cotton, N. A. (1979). The familial incidence of alcoholism. *Journal of Studies on Alcohol, 40*, 89-116.

Council on Scientific Affairs. American Medical Association. (1987). Scientific issues in drug testing. *Journal of the American Medical Association, 257*, 3110-3114.

Court rules against drug-related evictions. (1992, March 4). *The New York Times*, p. A14.

Courtwright, D. T. (1982). *Dark paradise: Opiate addiction in America before 1940.* Cambridge, Mass.: Harvard University Press.

Covington, J. (1987, Summer). Addict attitudes toward legalization of heroin. *Contemporary Drug Problems*, 315-353.

Cowan, T. R. (1987). Drugs and the workplace: To drug test or not to test? *Public Personnel Management, 16*, 313-322.

Craig, R. J. (1988). A psychosomatic study of the prevalence of DSM-III personality disorders among treated opiate addicts. *International Journal of Addictions, 23*, 115-124.

Cristie, K. A., Burke, J. D. R., Begier, D. A., Rae, D. S., Boyd, J. H. & Locke, B. S. (1988). Epidemiologic evidence for early onset of mental disorders and higher risk of drug abuse in young adults. *American Journal of Psychiatry, 145*, 971- 975.

Crown, D. F. & Rosse, J. G. (1988). A critical review of the assumptions underlying drug testing. *Journal of Business and Psychology, 3*, 22-41.

Cuskey, W. R., Berger, L. H. & Richardson, A. H. (1978). The effects of marijuana decriminalization on drug use patterns. *Contemporary Drug Problems, 7*, 491-532.

Dackis, C. A. & Gold, M. S. (1985). New concepts in cocaine addiction: The dopamine depletion hypothesis. *Neuroscience and Biobehavioral Reviews, 9*, 469-477.

Daley, B. & Przybycin, C. (1989). Cocaine-dependent women have unique treatment needs. *Addiction Letter, 5*(10).

Davis, K. L. & Berger, P. A. (1979). *Brain acetylcholine and neuropsychiatric disease.* New York: Plenum Press.

Dearth of drink not driving us to drugs. (1925, August 1) *The Literary Digest*, 13-14.

DeFleur, L. B., Ball, J. C. & Snarr, R. W. (1969). The long-term social correlates of opiate addiction. *Social Problems, 17*, 225-234.

De Leon, G. (1986). *Demographic predictors of outcomes in drug abuse treatment, NIDA technical review meeting on matching clients to treatment: A critical review.* Rockville, MD: National Institute on Drug Abuse.

De Leon, G. & Schwartz, S. (1984). The therapeutic community: What are the retention rates? *American Journal of Drug and Alcohol Abuse, 10*, 267-284.

del Olmo, R. (1987). Aerobiology and the war on drugs: A transnational crime. *Crime and Social Justice, 30*, 28-44.

Deminiere, J. M., Simon, H., Herman, J. P. & Le Moal, M. (1984). 6-Hydroxy-dopamine lesion of the dopamine mesocorticolimbic cell bodies increases (+)-amphetamine self-administration. *Psychopharmacology, 83*, 281-284.

Deminiere, J. M., Taghzouti, K., Tassin, J. P., Le Moal, M. & Simon, H. (1988). Increased sensitivity to amphetamine and facilitation of amphetamine self-administration after 6-hydroxydopamine lesions of the amygdala. *Psychopharmacology, 94*, 232-236.

Des Jarlais, D. C., Friedman, S. R., Casriel, C. & Kott, A. (1987). AIDS and preventing initiation into intravenous (IV) drug use. *Psychology and Health, 1*, 179-194.

Des Jarlais, D. C., Friedman, S. R., & Hopkins, W. (1985). Risk reduction for acquired immunodeficiency syndrome among intravenous drug users. *Annals of Internal Medicine, 103*, 755-759.

Des Jarlais, D. C. & Hopkins, W. (1985). "Free" needles for intravenous drug users at risk for aids: Current developments in New York City. [Correspondence]. *The New England Journal of Medicine, 313*, 1476.

deWit, H. & Wise, R. A. (1977). Blockage of cocaine reinforcement in rats with the dopamine receptor blocker pimozide but not with the noradrenergic blockers phentolamine or phenxybenzamine. *Canadian Journal of Psychology, 31*, 195-203.

deWit, H., Perri, J., & Johanson, C. E. (1989). Assessing pentobarbital preference in normal human volunteers using a cumulative dosing procedure. *Psychopharmacology* 99, 416-421.

Dews, P. B. (1984). Behavioral effects of caffeine. In P. B. Dews (Ed.), *Caffeine: Perspectives from recent research* (pp. 86-103). Berlin: Springer-Verlag.

Dews, P. B., Grice, H. C., Neims, A., Wilson, J. & Wurtman, R. (1984). Report of fourth international caffeine workshop, Athens, 1982. *Food and Chemical Toxicity, 22*, 163-169.

DiFranza, J. R. & Lew, R. A. (1995). Effect of maternal cigarette smoking on pregnancy complications and sudden infant death syndrome. *The Journal of Family Practice, 40*, 385-394.

DiFranza, J. R., Richards, J. W., Paulman, P. M., Wolf-Gillespie, N., Fletcher, C., Jaffe, R. N. & Murray, D. (1991). RJR Nabisco's cartoon camel promotes Camel cigarettes to children. *Journal of the American Medical Association, 266*, 3149-3153.

DiFranza, J. R. & Tye, J. B. (1990). Who profits from tobacco sales to children? *Journal of the American Medical Association, 263*, 2784-2787.

Domino, E. F. (1978). Neurobiology of phencyclidine—An update. In R. C. Peterson & R. C. Stillman (Eds.), *PCP phencyclidine abuse: An appraisal* (NIDA Research Monograph Series No. 21). Washington, DC: U.S. Government Printing Office.

Donovan, J. E. & Jessor, R. (1984). The structure of problem behavior in adolescence and young adulthood. Research Report No. 10. Young adult follow-up study. Institute of Behavior Science, Boulder, CO: University of Colorado.

"Dope-cops" at work. (1916, September, 16). *The Literary Digest*. 829-830.

Dorris, M. (1990). *The Broken Cord.* London: Collins.

Dougherty, R. J. (1987). Controversies regarding urine testing. *Journal of Substance Abuse Treatment, 4*, 115-117.

Downs, W. R., Miller, B. A. & Gondoli, D.M. (1987). Childhood experiences of parental physical violence for alcoholic women as compared with a randomly selected household sample of women. *Violence and Victims, 2*, 224-240.

Drejer, K., Theilgaard, A., Teasdale, T. W., Schulsinger, F. & Goodwin, D. W. (1985). A prospective study of young men at high risk for alcoholism: Neuropsychological assessment. *Alcoholism: Clinical and Experimental Research, 9*, 498-502.

Drew, W. G. & Miller, L L. (1974). Cannabis: Neural mechanisms and behavior: A theoretical review. *Pharmacology, 11*, 12-32.

Drug Abuse and Drug Abuse Research II, The Second Triennial Report to Congress from the Secretary, Department of Health and Human Services. 1987 (DHHS Publication No. (ADM) 87-13865). Rockville: MD, Government Printing Office.

Drug abuse the main cause of AIDS in federal prisons. *Criminal Justic Newsletter, 18*(19), 1-2.

Drug addicts in America. (1919, June 25). *The Outlook, 122*, p. 315.

Drug traffickers shift processing from Colombia. (1991, August 19). *The Hartford Courant*, p. C11.

Drug-trafficking suspect surrenders in Colombia. (1991, December 19). *The New York Times*, p. A13.

Durkheim, E. (1951). *Suicide: Study in sociology.* (J. A. Spaulding & G. Simpson, Trans.) Glencoe, IL: Free Press.

Duster, T. (1970) *The legislation of morality; Law, drugs, and moral judgment.* New York: Free Press.

Dutch Ministry of Welfare, Health, and Cultural Affairs. (1985). *Policy and drug users.* Rijswijk, the Netherlands: Ministry of Welfare, Health, and Cultural Affairs.

Duzan, M. J. (1994). *Death beat: A Colombian journalist's life inside the cocaine wars.* New York: Harper Collins Publishers.

Eddy, P., Sabogal H. & Walden S. (1988) *The cocaine wars: murder, money, corruption, and the world's most valuable commodity.* New York: W.W. Norton & Co.

Effects of the Harrison drug law. (1915, September 18). *Survey*, p. 553.

Eison, A. S. & Temple, D. L., Jr. (1986). Buspirone: Review of its pharmacology and current perspectives on its mechanism of action. *American Journal of Medicine 80*, 1-9.

Ellinwood, E. H., Jr. (1971). Assault and homicide associated with amphetamine abuse. *American Journal of Psychiatry, 127*, 90-95.

Ellinwood, E. H., Jr. (1972). Amphetamine psychosis: Individuals, settings, and sequences. In E. H. Ellinwood, Jr. & S. Cohen (Eds.), *Current concepts on amphetamine abuse* (pp. 143-157). Rockville, MD: National Institute on Mental Health.

Elliott, D. S. & Huizinga, D. (1984, April 17-18). The relationship between delinquent behavior and ADM problem behaviors. Paper prepared for the ADAMHA/OJJDP State of the Art Research Conference on Juvenile Offenders with Serious Drug/Alcohol and Mental Health Problems, Bethesda, MD.

Elliott, D. S., Huizinga, D. & Ageton, S. S. (1985). *Explaining delinquency and drug use.* Beverly Hills, CA: Sage Publications.

Employee drug testing. (1989, November). *Monthly Labor Review, 112*, 75-76.

Ellis, L. (1987). Relationships of criminality and psychopathy with eight other apparent behavioral manifestations of sub-optimal arousal. *Personality and Individual Differences 8*, 905-925.

Erickson, K. (1962). Notes on the sociology of deviance. *Social Problems, 9*, 397-414.

Erickson, P. G. (1990). Past, current and future directions in Canadian drug policy. *International Journal of Addictions, 25*, 247-266.

Erickson, P. G., Adlaf, E. M., Murray, G. F., & Smart, R. G. (1987) *The steel drug: Cocaine in perspective.* Lexington, MA: Lexington Books.

Ervin, C., Little, R., Streissguth, A., Beck, D. (1984). Alcoholic fathering and its relation to child's intellectual development. *Alcoholism: Clinical Experimental Research, 8*, 362-365.

Estroff, T. W. & Gold, M. S. (1985). Medical and psychiatric complications of cocaine abuse with possible points of pharmacological treatment. *Advances in Alcohol and Substance Abuse, 5*, 61-76.

Europe reportedly biggest cocaine market. (1990, August 27). *The Hartford Courant*, p. A7.

Ex-agent is guilty on 5 drug charges. (1991, April 17). *The New York Times*, p. A25.

Ex-agent on trial in drug-corruption case. (1990, November 22). *The New York Times*, p. A25.

Ex-chief of police sentenced. (1990, June 29). *The Hartford Courant*, p. A3.

Ex-top aide to Thornburgh indicted. (1990, August 11). *The Hartford Courant*, p. A3.

Eysenck, H. J. & Eaves, L. J. (1980). *The causes and effects of smoking.* Beverly Hills, CA: Sage Publications.

FAA publishes figures on pilots' alcohol-related arrests. (1991, September 24). *The Hartford Courant*, p. A4.

Farr, K. A. (1990). Revitalizing the drug decriminalization debate. *Crime & Delinquency, 36*, 223-237.

Farrington, D. P. (1983). Offending from 10 to 25 years of age. In K. T. Van Dusen & S. A. Mednick (Eds.), *Prospective studies of crime and delinquency* (pp. 17-38). Boston, MA: Kluwer-Nijhoff.

Farrington, D. P. (1985). Predicting self-reported and official delinquency. In D. P. Farrington & R. Tarling (Eds.), *Prediction in Criminology*. Albany: State University of New York Press.

Farrington, D. P. (1987). Stepping stones to adult criminal careers. In D. Olweus, J. Block & M. R. Yarrow (Eds.), *Development of antisocial and prosocial behavior* (pp. 359-384). New York: Academic Press.

Fauman, M. A. & Fauman, B. F. (1978). The psychiatric aspects of chronic phencyclidine use: A study of chronic PCP users. In R. C. Peterson & R. C. Stillman (Eds.), *PCP phencyclidine abuse: An appraisal* pp. 128-139. (NIDA Research Monograph Series No. 21). Washington, DC: U.S. Government Printing Office.

Fauman, M. A. & Fauman, B. F. (1980). Chronic phencyclidine (PCP) abuse: A psychiatric perspective. *Journal of Psychedelic Drugs, 12*, 307-314.

Faupel, C. E. (1981). Drug treatment and criminality: Methodological and theoretical considerations. In J. A. Inciardi (Ed.) *The drugs-crime connection*. Beverly Hills, CA: Sage Publications.

Fawzy, R. I., Coombs, R. H. & Gerber, B. (1983). Generational continuity in the use of substances: The impact of parental substance use on adolescent substance use. *Addictive Behaviors, 9*, 109-114.

F.B.I. says Los Angeles gang has drug cartel ties. (1992, January 10). *The New York Times*, p. A12.

Federal aid in the antidrug war. (1915, April 24). *Literary Digest.* pp. 958-959.

Federal Bureau of Prisons. (1990). *State of the bureau, 1989*. Washington, DC: U.S. Dept. of Justice.

Federal drug probe targets Coast Guard. (1990, May 23). *The Hartford Courant*, p. A6.

Federal judge convicted of bribery. (1991, June 30). *The Hartford Courant*, p. A11.

Fehr, K. A., Kalant, H., LeBlanc, A. E. & Knox, G. C. (1976). Permanent learning impairment after chronic heavy exposure to cannabis or ethanol in the rat. In G. G. Nahas (Ed.), *Marijuana: Chemistry, biochemistry and cellular effects* (pp. 495-506). New York: Springer-Verlag.

Fernstrom, J. D. (1981a). Dietary precursors and brain neurotransmitter formation. *Annual Review of Medicine, 32*, 413-425.

Fernstrom, J. D. (1981b). Effects of precursors on brain neurotransmitter synthesis and brain functions. *Diabetologia,* (Suppl. March 20), 281-289.

Fernstrom, J. D. & Wurtman, R. J. (1971). Brain serotonin content: Physiological dependence on plasma tryptophan levels. *Science, 173*, 149-152.

Ferrari, J. M., Barabas, G., & Matthews, W. S. (1983). Psychologic and behavioral disturbance among epileptic children treated with barbiturate anticonvulsants. *American Journal of Psychiatry 140*, 112-113.

Field, L. M. (1987). Reliability of urine drug testing. *Journal of the American Medical Association, 258*, 2587.

Fields, H. L., & Levine, J. D. (1981). Biology of placebo analgesia. *American Journal of Medicine, 70*, 745.

Fine, E., Yudin, L., Holmes, J., & Heinemann, S. (1976). Behavioral disorders in children with parental alcoholism. *Annals of the New York Academy of Sciences, 273*, 507-517.

Finestone, H. (1967). Narcotics and criminality. *Law and Contemporary Problems, 22*, 60-85.

Finn, P. R. & Pihl, R. O. (1987). Men at risk for alcoholism: The effect of alcohol on cardiovascular response to unavoidable shock. *Journal of Abnormal Psychology, 96*, 230-236.

Fishbein, D. H., Lozovsky, D. & Jaffe, J. H. (1989). Impulsivity, aggression, and neuroendocrine responses to serotonergic stimulation in substance users. *Biological Psychiatry, 25*, 1049-1066.

Fishbein, D. H. & Pease, S. E. (1988). The effects of diet on behavior: Implications for criminology and corrections (Monograph Series). Boulder, CO: The Rand Corporation and National Institute for Corrections.

Fishbein, D. H. & Pease, S. E. (1990). Neurological links between substance abuse and crime. In L. Ellis & H. Hoffman (Eds.), *Crime in biological, social, and moral contexts* (pp. 218- 243). New York: Praeger.

Fishbein, D. H. (1991). Medicalizing the drug war. *Behavioral Sciences and the Law*, 9, 323-344.

Fischer, P. M., Schwartz, M. P., Richards, J. W., Goldstein, A. O., Rojas, T. H. (1991). Brand logo recognition by children aged 3 to 6 years. *Journal of the American Medical Association, 266*, 3145-3148.

Fitzpatrick, J. P. (1974). Drugs, alcohol and violent crime. *Addictive Diseases, 1*, 553-568.

Forsander, O., & Eriksson, K. (1974). Forekommer det etnologiska skillnader i alkoholens amnesomsattningen. *Alkoholpolitik, 37*, 315.

Freemantle, B. (1986). *The fix: Inside the world drug trade*. New York: Doherty.

French, H. W. (1992, July 25). Army general is implicated in Colombian prison escape. *The New York Times*, p. 3.

Fried, P. A. (1985). Postnatal consequences of maternal marijuana use. In T. M. Pinkert (Ed.), *Current research on consequences of maternal drug use* (NIDA Research Monograph Series No. 59, pp. 61-72). Washington, DC: U.S. Government Printing Office.

Fried, P. A. & Oxorn, H. (1980). *Smoking for two: Cigarettes and pregnancy*. New York: The Free Press.

Friedman, A. S. & Glickman, N. W. (1986). Program characteristics for successful treatment of adolescent drug abuse. *Journal of Nervous and Mental Disorders, 174*, 669-679.

Friedman, A. S. & Granick, S. (1990). *Family therapy for adolescent drug abuse*. Lexington, MA: Lexington Books.

Friedman, C. J. & Friedman, A. S. (1973). Drug abuse and delinquency, Part I: Drug abuse and delinquency among lower social class, court adjudicated adolescent boys. In National Commission on Marihuana and Drug Abuse. *Drug abuse in America—Problems in perspectives. Appendix, Vol. 1, Patterns and consequences of drug use*. Washington, D.C.: U.S. Government Printing Office.

Friedman, S. R., Des Jarlais, D. C., Sotheran, J. L., Garber, J., Cohen, H., & Smith, D. (1987). AIDS and self-organization among intravenous drug users. *The International Journal of the Addictions, 22*, 201-219.

Friedman, S. R., Selan, B. H., & Des Jarlais, D. C. (1987, November). The special problems of intravenous drug users as persons at risk for AIDS. *Resident & Staff Physician, 33*(12), 35-44.

Fritschler, A.L. (1989) *Smoking and politics: Policy making and the federal bureaucracy*. Englewood Cliffs, N.J.: Prentice Hall.

Frohling, R. (1989). *Promising approaches to drug treatment in correctional settings*. Denver, CO: National Conference of State Legislatures.

Fuller, J. R. & LaFountain, M. J. (1987). Performance-enhancing drugs in sport: A different form of drug abuse. *Adolescence, 22*, 969-976.

Gabrielli, W. F. & Mednick, S. A. (1983). Intellectual performance of children of alcoholics. *Journal of Nervous and Mental Disorders, 171*, 444-447.

Gambarino, J. & Plantz, M. C. (1986). Child abuse and juvenile delinquency: What are the links? In J. Gambarino (Ed.), *Troubled youth, troubled families* (pp. 27-39). New York: Aldine-DeGruyter.

Gandossy, R. P., Williams, J. R., Cohen, J., & Harwood, H. J. (1980) *Drugs and crime: A survey and analysis of the literature*. Washington, DC: U.S. Government Printing Office.

Gardner, E. L., Paredes, W., Smith, D., Donner, A., Milling, C., Cohen, D., & Morrison, D. (1988). Facilitation of brain stimulation reward by delta 9-tetrahydrocannabinol. *Psychopharmacology, 96*, 142-144.

Garrett, C. J. (1985). Effects of residential treatment on adjudicated delinquents: A meta-analysis. *Journal of Research in Crime and Delinquency, 22*, 287-308.

Gary, L. E. (1986). Drinking, homicide and the black male. *Journal of Black Studies, 17*, 15-31.

Gawin, F. H. (1986). New uses of antidepressants in cocaine abuse. *Psychosomatics, 27*(11 suppl.), 24-29.

Gawin, F. H. (1989). Cocaine abuse and addiction. *Journal of Family Practitioners, 29*, 193-197.

Gawin, F. H., & Ellinwood, E. H., Jr. (1988). Cocaine and other stimulants: Actions, abuse, and treatment. *New England Journal of Medicine, 318*, 1173-1182.

Gawin, F. H., & Kleber, H. D. (1983). Cocaine abuse treatment. *Yale Psychiatric Quarterly, 6*, 4-15.

Gawin, F. H., & Kleber, H. D. (1984). Cocaine abuse treatment: Open pilot trial with desipramine and lithium carbonate. *Archives of General Psychiatry, 41*, 903-909.

Gawin, F. H., & Kleber, H. D. (1985). Cocaine abuse in a treatment population: Patterns and diagnostic distinctions. In H. Adams, & N. J. Kozel (Eds.), *Cocaine use in America: Epidemiologic and clinical perspectives* (pp. 182-192). (NIDA Research Monograph Series 61) Rockville, MD: National Institute on Drug Abuse.

Gawin, F. H. & Kleber, H. D. (1986a). Abstinence symptomatology and psychiatric diagnosis in chronic cocaine abusers. *Archives of General Psychiatry, 43*, 903-910.

Gawin, F. H., & Kleber, H. D. (1986b). Pharmacologic treatment of cocaine abuse. *Psychiatric Clinics of North America, 9*, 573-583.

Gelenberg, A. J., Wojcik, J. D., Growdon, J. H., Sved, Z. G., & Wurtman, R. J. (1980). Tyrosine for the treatment of depression. *American Journal of Psychiatry, 137*, 622-623.

Geller, I., Purdy, R., & Merritt, J. H. (1973). Alterations in ethanol preference in the rat: The role of brain biogenic amines. *Annals of the New York Academy of Sciences, 215*, 54-59.

General Accounting Office. (1990). *Drug exposed infants: A generation at risk* (Publication GAO/HRD-90-138). Washington, DC.

George, F. R. & Goldberg, S. R. (1989). Genetic approaches to the analysis of addiction processes. *Trends in Pharmacological Sciences, 10,* 78-83.

George, W. H. & Marlatt, G. A. (1986). The effect of alcohol and anger on interest in violence, erotica, and deviance. *Journal of Abnormal Psychology, 95,* 150-158.

Gerald, M. C. (1981). *Pharmacology: An introduction to drugs.* (2nd ed.). Englewood Cliffs, NJ: Prentice-Hall.

Gerstein, D. R. & Harwood, H. J. (Eds.). (1990). *Treating drug problems: Vol. 1: A study of the evolution, effectiveness, and financing of public and private drug treatment systems.* Washington, DC: National Academy Press.

Gerth, J. (1990a, May 6). Israeli arms diverted to Colombia drug traffickers. *The New York Times,* pp. A5.

Gerth, J. (1990b, May 7). F.B.I. said to foil missile smuggling to Colombia. *The New York Times,* p. .

Giannini, A. J. & Miller, N. S. (1989). Drug abuse: A biopsychiatric model. *American Family Physician, 40*(5), 173-182.

Gianutsos, G., Hynes, M. D., Drawbaugh, R. B., & Lal, H. (1975). Paradoxical absence of aggression during naloxone-precipitated morphine withdrawal. *Psychopharmacologia, 43,* 43-46.

Gianutsos, G. & Lal, H. (1976). Blockage of apomorphine-induced aggression by morphine or neuroleptics: Differential alteration by antimuscarinics and naloxone. *Pharmacology and Biochemistry of Behavior, 4,* 639-642.

Gibson, G. T., Bayhurst, P. A. & Colley, D. P. (1983). Maternal alcohol, tobacco and cannabis consumption on the outcome of pregnancy. *Australia NZ Obstetrics and Gynecology, 23,* 16-19.

Gilbert, R. M. (1979). Coffee, tea and cigarette use. *Canadian Medical Association Journal, 120,* 522-524.

Goddard, D. (1988). *Undercover: The secret lives of a federal agent.* New York: Times Books.

Gold, L. H., Geyer, M. A., & Koob, G. J. (1989). Neurochemical mechanisms involved in behavioral effects of amphetamines and related designer drugs. In K. Asghar & E. De Souza (Eds.), *Pharmacology and toxicology of amphetamine and related designer drugs* (NIDA Research Monograph No. 94, pp. 101-126). Washington, DC: U.S. Government Printing Office.

Gold, M. S., Pottash, A., Annitto, W. J., Vereby, A. K., & Sweeney, D. R. (1983). Cocaine withdrawal: Effect of tyrosine. *Society for Neuroscience Abstracts, 9,* 157.

Gold, M. S., Pottash, A., Sweeney, D. R., & Kleber, H. D. (1980). Opiate withdrawal using clonidine, a safe effective and rapid nonopiate treatment. *Journal of the American Medical Association, 243,* 343-346.

Golden, T. (1995, July 31). To help keep Mexico stable, U.S. soft-pedaled drug war. *The New York Times,* pp. A1 & A6.

The Golden Triangle's new king. (1995, February 4). *The Economist,* pp. 31-32.

Goldman, B. (1984). *Death in the locker room: Steroids & sports.* South Bend, IN: Icarus Press.

Goldsmith, D. S., Hunt, D. E., Lipton, D. S., & Strug, D. L. (1984). Methadone folklore: Beliefs about side effects and their impact on treatment. *Human Organization, 43,* 330-340.

Goldstein, A., & Kalant, H. (1990). Drug policy: Striking the right balance. *Science, 249,* 1513-1521.

Goldstein, A., Warren, R., & Kaiser, S. (1965). Psychotropic effects of caffeine in man. I. Individual differences in sensitivity to caffeine-induced wakefulness. *Journal of Pharmacological and Experimental Therapy, 149,* 156-159.

Goldstein, A., ed. (1976). *The opiate narcotics: Neurochemical mechanisms of analgesia and dependence.* Elmsford, NY: Pergamon.

Goldstein, P. J., Lipton, D. S., Preble, E., Sobel, I., Miller, W. A., Paige, W., & Soto, F. (1984, summer). The marketing of street heroin in New York City. *Journal of Drug Issues,* 553-566.

Gomby, D., & Shiono, P. H. (1991). Estimating the number of substance-exposed infants. *Future Child, 1,* 17-25.

Goodman, R. A., Mercy, J. A., & Rosenberg, M. L. (1986). Drug use and interpersonal violence. Barbiturates detected in homicide victims. *American Journal of Epidemiology 124,* 851-855.

Goodstadt, M. S. (1989). Drug education: The prevention issues. *Journal of Drug Education, 19,* 197-208.

Goodwin, D. W. (1980). The bad habit theory of drug abuse. (pp. 12-17). (NIDA Research Monograph Series No. 30) Washington, DC: U.S. Government Printing Office.

Goodwin, D. W. (1986). Genetic factors in the development of alcoholism. *Substance Abuse, 9,* 427-433.

Goodwin, D. W., Crane, J. B. & Guze, S. B. (1971). Felons who drink: An 8-year follow-up. *Quarterly Journal of Studies on Alcohol, 32,* 136-147.

Goodwin, D. W., Schulsinger, F., Hermansen, L., Guze, S. B. & Winokur, G. (1973). Alcohol problems in adoptees raised apart by alcoholic biological parents. *Archives of General Psychiatry, 28,* 238-243.

Goodwin, D. W., Schulsinger, F., Hermansen, L., Guze, S. B., & Winokur, G. (1975). Alcoholism and the hyperactive child syndrome. *Journal of Nervous and Mental Disorders, 160,* 349-353.

Goodwin, D. W., Schulsinger, F., Moller, N., Hermansen, L. Winokur, G. & Guze, S. B. (1974). Drinking problems in adopted and nonadopted sons of alcoholics. *Archives of General Psychiatry, 131,* 164-169.

Gordis, E., Tabakiff, B., Goldman, D., & Berg, K. (1990). Finding the gene(s) for alcoholism [editorial]. *Journal of the American Medical Association, 263,* 2094 - 2095.

Gossop, M. R., & Eysenck, S. B. G. (1980). A further investigation into the personality of drug addicts in treatment. *British Journal of Addiction, 75,* 305-311.

Gottheil, E., Druley, K. A., Skoloda, T. E., & Waxman, H. M. (1983). *Alcohol, drug abuse and aggression.* Springfield, IL: Charles C. Thomas.

Gottlieb, J., & Spanos, N. P. (1976). Ergotism and the Salem village witch trials. *Science, 194,* 1390-1394.

Grande, T. P., Wolf, A. W., Schubert, D. S. P., Patterson, M. B., & Brocco, K. (1984). Associations among alcoholism, drug abuse, and antisocial personality: A review of literature. *Psychological Reports, 55,* 455-474.

Green, A. R. & Costain, D. W. (1981). *Pharmacology and biochemistry of psychiatric disorders.* Toronto: Wiley.

Greenberg, D. (1977). The correctional effects of corrections. In D. Greenberg (Eds.), *Corrections and punishment* (pp. 111-148). Beverly Hills, CA: Sage Publications.

Greenberg, S. W. (1981). Alcohol and crime: A methodological critique of the literature. In J. J. Collins, Jr. (Ed.), *Drinking and crime* (pp.70-109). New York: Guilford Press.

Greenberg, S.W., & Adler, F. (1974). Crime and addiction: An empirical analysis of the literature, 1920-1973. *Contemporary Drug Problems, 3,* 221-270.

Greenhouse, L. (1992, June 16). High court backs seizing foreigner for trial in U.S. *The New York Times,* pp. A1 & A18.

Greenhouse, L. (1993, January 16). Court to weigh U.S. power to seize criminals' assets. *The New York Times,* p. 9.

Greenwood, M. H., Lader, M. H., Kantameneni, H., & Curzon, G. (1975). The acute effects of oral (-) tryptophan in human subjects. *British Journal of Clinical Psychiatry, 2,* 145-172.

Griffiths, J. D., Jasinski, D. R., Casten, G. P., and McKinney, G. R. (1986). Investigation of abuse liability of buspirone in alcohol-dependent subjects. *American Journal of Medicine 80,* 30-35.

Griffiths, J. D., Bigelow, G. E. , & Lieberson, I. (1979). Human drug self-administration: Double-blind comparison of pentobarbital, diazepam, chlorpromazine and placebo. *Journal of Pharmacology and Experimental Therapeutics 210,* 301-310.

Griffiths, R. R., & Woodson, P. (1988). Caffeine physical dependence: A review of human and laboratory animal studies. *Psychopharmacology, 94,* 437-451.

Griffin, M. L., Weiss, R. D., Mirin, S. M., & Lange, U. (1989). A comparison of male and female cocaine abusers. *Archives of General Psychiatry, 46,* 122-126.

Grigsby, S. E. (1963). The Raiford study: Alcohol and crime. *Journal of Criminal Law, Criminology, and Police Science, 54,* 296-306.

Grinspoon, L. & Bakalar, J. B. (1987). Medical uses of illicit drugs. In R. Hamowy (Ed.), *Dealing with drugs; Consequences of government control* (pp. 211-219). San Francisco, CA: Pacific Research Institute for Public Policy.

Gritz, E. R., Baer-Weiss, B., Benowitz, V. L., Van Vunakis, H. & Jarvik, M. K. (1981). Plasma nicotine and cotinine concentrations in habitual smokeless tobacco users. *Clinical Pharmacology and Therapeutics, 30,* 201-209.

Gropper, B. A. (1984). Probing the links between drugs and crime. *Research in Brief.* Washington, DC: U.S. Department of Justice, National Institute of Justice (SNI 188) November.

Growden, J. H., Hirsch, M. J., Wurtman, R. J. & Weiner, W. (1977). Oral choline administration to patients with tardive dyskinesia. *New England Journal of Medicine, 297,* 524-527.

Grunberg, N. E. & Morse, D. E. (1984). Cigarette smoking and food consumption in the United States. *Journal of Applied Social Psychology, 14,* 310-317.

Gugliotta, G. & Leen, J. (1989) *Kings of cocaine: Inside the Medellin cartel—An astonishing true story of murder, money, and international corruption.* New York: Simon & Schuster.

Gugliotta, G. & Isikoff, M. (1990). Violence in the '90s: Drugs' deadly residue. *Washington Post,* October 14.

Gust, S. W., & Walsh, J. M. (1989). Research on the prevalence, impact, and treatment of drug abuse in the workplace. In S. W. Gust & J. M. Walsh (Eds.), *Drugs in the workplace: Research and evaluation data*. pp. 13-22. Washington, DC: National Institute on Drug Abuse.

Gutkin, S. (1991, June 20). Colombian drug kingpin surrenders: Medellin cartel head likely to avoid extradition to U.S. *The Hartford Courant*, pp. A1, A6.

Guze, S. B. (1976). *Criminality and psychiatric disorders*. New York: Oxford University Press.

Halikas, J., Kemp, K., Kuhn, K., Carlson, G., & Crea, F. (1989). Carbamazepine for cocaine addiction? [letter]. *Lancet, 1*, 623-624.

Hammett, T. M. (1987). *1986 Update: AIDS in Correctional Facilities*. Washington DC: National Institute of Justice, U.S. Dept. of Justice.

Hansen, H. J., Caudill, S. P., & Boone, D. J. (1985). Crisis in drug testing; Results of CDC blind study. *Journal of the American Medical Association, 253*, 2382-2387.

Hare, R. (1984). Performance of psychopaths on cognitive tasks related to frontal lobe function. *Journal of Abnormal Psychology, 93*, 141-149.

Hare, R., & Schalling, D. (1978). *Psychopathic behaviour*. New York: Wiley.

Harmony, T. (1984). *Functional neuroscience*. (Vol. III. Neurometric assessment of brain dysfunction in neurological patients). Hillsdale, NJ: Erlbaum.

Harper, A. E. & Gans, D. A. (1986). Claims of antisocial behavior from consumption of sugar: An assessment. *Food Technology Overview: Outstanding Symposia in Food Science and Technology, January*, 142-149.

Harris, L. S. (1988). Problems of drug dependence. *Proceedings of the 49th Annual Scientific Meeting, The Committee on Problems of Drug Dependence, Inc.* (NIDA Research Monograph No. 81). Rockville, MD: National Institute on Drug Abuse.

Harris, M. (1989, November). Life styles of the rich and heinous. *Money*, pp. 70-76.

Harris, R. J. (1975). *A primer of multivariate statistics*. New York, Academic Press.

Hartmann, E. (1977). L-tryptophan: A rational hypnotic with clinical potential. *American Journal of Psychiatry, 134*, 366-370.

Hartstone, E., & Hansen, K. V. (1984). The violent juvenile offender: An empirical portrait. In R. A. Mathias, P. Demuro, & R. S. Allinson (Eds.), *Violent juvenile offenders: An anthology* (pp. 83-112). San Francisco, CA: National Council on Crime and Delinquency.

Hashish seized in four-year investigation. (1991, September 1). *The Hartford Courant*, p. A12.

Hatton, C. K. & Catlin, D. H. (1987). Detection of androgenic anabolic steroids in urine. *Clinics in Laboratory Medicine, 7*, 655-668.

Hawkins, J. D., Catalano, R. F. & Wells, E. A. (1986). Measuring effects of a skills training intervention for drug abusers. *Journal of Consulting and Clinical Psychology, 54*, 661-664.

Hawkins, J. D. Lishner, D. M., Catalano, R. F. & Howard, M. O. (1986). Childhood predictors of adolescent substance abuse: Towards an empirically grounded theory. *Journal of Children in Contemporary Society, 18*, 1-65.

Hayes, T. & Schimmel, D. (1993). Residential drug abuse in the Federal Bureau of Prisons. *Journal of Drug Issues, 23*, 61-73.

Heath, R. G., Fitzjarrell, A. T., Fontana, C. J. & Carey, R. E. (1980). Cannabis sativa: Effects on brain function and ultrastructure in rhesus monkeys. *Biological Psychiatry, 15*, 657-690.

Hekimian, L. J., & Gershon, S. (1968). Characteristics of drug abusers admitted to a psychiatric hospital. *The Journal of the American Medical Association, 205*, 125-130.

Hemmi, T. (1969). How we handled the problem of drug abuse in Japan. In F. Sjoqvist & J. Tottie (Eds.), *Abuse of central stimulants* (pp. 147-153). Stockholm: Almquist and Wiksell.

Hendin, H., Hass, A. P., Singer, P. et al. (1987). *Living high: Daily marijuana use among adults*. New York: Human Sciences Press, Inc.

Herkenham, M., Lynn, A. B., Little, M. D., Johnson, M. R., Melvin, L. S., de Costa, B. R. & Rice, K. C. (1990). Cannabinoid receptor localization in the brain. *Proceedings of the National Academy of Sciences, 87*, 1932-1936.

Heroin trail, the. (1974). By the staff and editors of Newsday. New York: Holt, Rinehart & Winston.

Herzberg, J. L., & Fenwick, P. B. C. (1988). The aetiology of aggression in temporal-lobe epilepsy. *British Journal of Psychiatry, 153*, 50-55.

Hesselbrock, M. N., Hesselbrock, V. M., Babor, T. F., Stabenau, J. R. Meyer, R. E., & Weidenman, M. (1984). Antisocial behavior psychopathology and problem drinking in the natural history of alcoholism. In D. W. Goodwin, K. T. Van Dusen & S. A. Mednick (Eds.), *Longitudinal research in alcoholism* (pp. 197-214). Boston: Kluwer-Nijhoff Publishing.

Hesselbrock, M. N., Meyer, R. E., & Kenner, J. J. (1985). Psychopathology in hospitalized alcoholics. *Archives of General Psychiatry, 42*, 1050-1055.

Hesselbrock, V. M. (1986). Alcoholic typologies: A review of empirical evaluations of common classification schemes. In M. Galanter (Ed.), *Recent developments in alcoholism. Vol. 4* (pp. 191-206). New York: Plenum Press.

Higgins, S. T., Delaney, D. D., Budney, A. J., Bickel, W. K., Hughes, J. R., Foerg, F., Fenwick, J. W. (1991). A behavioral approach to achieving initial cocaine abstinence. *American Journal of Psychiatry, 148*, 1218-1224.

Hingston, R., Zucherman, B., Frank, D. S., Kaynes, H., Sorenson, J. R., & Mitchell, J. (1984). Effects on fetal development of maternal marijuana use during pregnancy. In D. J. Harvey (Ed.), *Marijuana '84 :Proceedings of the Oxford Symposium on Marijuana*. pp. 48-53. Oxford: IRL Press.

Hinshaw, S. P. (1987). On the distinction between attentional deficits/hyperactivity and conduct problems/aggression in child psychopathology. *Psychological Bulletin, 101*, 443-463.

Hirshi, T. (1969). *Causes of delinquency*. Berkeley: University of California Press.

Hoffman, A. (1955). Die Ges Chiclite des LSD-25, Triangel Sandoz Z. Med. Wiss., 2, 117.

Hoffman, A. (1968). Psychotomimetic agents. In A. Burger (Ed.), *Drugs affecting the central nervous system. Vol. 2*. pp. 94-111. New York, Marcel Dekker.

Holmberg, M. B. (1985). Longitudinal studies of drug abuse in a fifteen-year-old population. *Acta Psychiatrica Scandinavia, 16*, 129-136.

Hometown mourns Colombian drug dealer. (1989, December 19). *New York Times*, p. A12.

Honer, W. G., Gewirtz, G., & Turey, M. (1987). Psychosis and violence in cocaine smokers. *Lancet II, 8556*, 451.

Hornykiewicz, O. (1978). Psychopharmacological implications of dopamine and dopamine antagonists: A critical evaluation of current evidence. *Neuroscience, 3*, 773-783.

House, T. H., & Milligan, W. L. (1976). Autonomic responses to modeled distress in prison psychopaths. *Journal of Personality and Social Psychology, 34*, 556-560.

Hrbrek, J., Komenda, J. & Siroka, A. (1971). Acute effect of chloroprothixen (5mg), caffeine (200mg), and combination of both drugs on verbal association. *Activas Nervosa Superior, 13*, 207.

Hubbard, R. L., Marsden, M. E., Rachal, J. V., Harwood, H. J., Cavanugh, E. R., & Ginzburg, H. M. (1989). *Drug abuse treatment: A national study of effectiveness*. Chapel Hill, NC: The University of North Carolina Press.

Huizinga, D. H., Menard, S., & Elliott, D. S. (1989). Delinquency and drug use: Temporal and developmental patterns. *Justice Quarterly, 6*, 419-455.

Humble, C., Croft, J., Gerber, A., Casper, M., Hames, C. G., & Tyroler, H. A. (1985). Passive smoking and 20-year cardiovascular disease mortality among non-smoking wives. (letter) *Lancet, 1*, 866-867.

Humble, C., Croft, J., Gerber, A., Casper, M., Hames, C. G. & Tyroler, H. A. (1990). Passive smoking and 20-year cardiovascular mortality among nonsmoking wives. *American Journal of Public Health, 80*, 599-601.

Husband, S. & Platt, J. (1993). The cognitive skills component in substance abuse treatment in correctional settings: A brief review. *Journal of Drug Issues, 23*, 31-42.

Idestrom, C. M., & Schalling D. (1969). Influence of personality on effects of centrally stimulating drugs. In F. Sjoqvist & M. Tottie (Eds.), *Abuse of central stimulants* (pp. 61-69). New York: Raven Press.

If asked to lick a cane toad, just say 'ribit.' (1990, February 1). *The Hartford Courant*, p. A6.

Ijic, R., Stern, P., & Basagic, E. (1970). Changes in emotional behavior after application of cholinesterase inhibitor in septal and amygdala regions. *Neuropharmacology, 9*, 73-80.

Inciardi, J. A. (1986). *The war on drugs: Heroin, cocaine, crime and public policy*. Mountain View, CA: Mayfield.

Inciardi, J. A., & Chambers, C. (1972). Unreported criminal involvement of narcotic addicts. *Journal of Drug Issues, 2*, 57-64.

Inciardi, J. A., Lockwood, D., & Pottieger, A. E. (1993). *Women and crack-cocaine*. New York: Macmillan Publishing Co.

Inciardi, J. A., & McBride, D. C. (1989). Legalization: A high-risk alternative in the war on drugs. *American Behavioral Scientist, 32*, 259 - 289.

Inciardi, J. A., Pottieger, A. E., Forney, M., Chitwood, D. D., & McBride, D. C. (1991). Prostitution, IV drug use, and sex-for-crack exchanges among serious delinquents: Risks for HIV infection. *Criminology, 29*, 221-235.

Inciardi, J. A. (1992). *The war on drugs II: The continuing epic of heroin, cocaine, crack, crime, AIDS, and public policy*. Mountain View, CA: Mayfield.

Innes, C. A. (1988) Drug use and crime: State prison inmate survey, 1986. Bureau of Justice Statistics, U.S. Department of Justice.

Institute of Medicine. National Academy of Sciences (1986). *Confronting AIDS: Directions for public health, health care, and research*. Washington DC: National Academy Press.

Institute of Medicine. (1990). *Broadening the base treatment for alcohol problems*. Washington, DC: National Academy Press.

Isenberg, D. (1992, Fall). Militarizing the drug war. *Covert Action Information Bulletin*, pp. 42-47.

Isikoff, M. (1990, February 20). U.S. drafts insects for drug war. *The Hartford Courant*, pp. A1, A5.

Isikoff, M., Hosenball, M., Cohn, B. Katel, P., & Morganthau, T. (1995). A turn-coat in the drug war. *Newsweek, June 26*, pp. 26-27.

Iuculano, R. (1989). Private sector concerns. In M. Falco & W. I. Cikins (Eds.), *Toward a national policy on drug and AIDS testing* (pp. 43-59). Washington, DC: The Brookings Institution.

Jacobson, B. H., & Thurman-Lacey, S. R. (1992). Effect of caffeine on motor performance by caffeine-naive and familiar subjects. *Perceptual and Motor Skills, 74*, 151-157.

Jacobson, B. H., Winter-Roberts, E. & Gemmell, H. A. (1991). Influence of caffeine on selected manual manipulation skills. *Perceptual and Motor Skills, 72*, 1175-1181.

Jaffe, J. H. (1985). Drug addiction and drug abuse. In A. G. Gilman, L. S. Goodman, T. W. Rall, & F. Murad (Eds.), *The pharmacological basis of therapeutics (7th ed.)* (pp. 532-581). New York: Macmillan.

Jamieson, A., Glanz, A., & MacGregor, S. (1984). *Dealing with drug misuse: Crisis intervention in the city.* London: Tavistock.

Janofsky, M. (1993, December 28). Drug use and worker rights: Campbell soup faces suits and arbitration. *The New York Times*, pp. D1, D13.

Jarvis, M. J., Russell, M. A., Feyerabend, C., Eiser, J. R., Morgan, M., Gammage, P., & Gray, E. M. (1985). Passive exposure to tobacco smoke: Saliva cotinine concentrations in a representative population sample of non-smoking school children. *British Medical Journal (Clinical Research Edition), 291*, 927-929.

Jensen, C. F., Cowley, D. S., & Walker, R. D. (1990). Drug preferences of alcoholic polydrug abusers with and without panic. *Journal of Clinical Psychiatry 51*, 189-191.

Jensen, S. (1995 April 22). Drug suspect has little to smile about after his arrest. *The Hartford Courant*, p. 6.

Jeri, F. R., Sanchez, C., Del Pozo, T., & Fernandez, M. (1978). The syndrome of coca paste. *Journal of Psychedelic Drugs, 10*, 361-370.

Jessor, R. & Jessor, S. L. (1977). *Problem behavior and psychosocial development: A longitudinal study of youth.* New York: Academic Press.

Johnson, B. D., Goldstein, P. J., Preble, E., Schmeidler, J., Lipton, D. S., Spunt, B. & Miller, T. (1985). *Taking care of business: The economics of crime by heroin abusers.* Lexington, MA: Heath.

Johnson, B. D., & Wish, E. D., Ed. (1986). *Crime rates among drug abusing offenders: Final report of secondary analyses of existing data.* National Institute of Justice. New York: Interdisciplinary Research Center.

Johnson, B. D., Williams, T., Dai, K. A. & Sanabria, H. (1990). Drug abuse in the inner city: Impact on hard-drug users and the community. In J.Q. Wilson & M. Tonry (Eds.), *Drugs and crime* (pp. 9-68) Chicago, IL: University of Chicago Press.

Johnson, B. D., & Wish, E. D. (1987). *Criminal events among seriously criminal drug abusers: Final report.* Interdisciplinary Research Center for the Study of the Relations of Drugs and Alcohol to Crime. Narcotic and Drug Research, Inc. and Bureau of Research and Evaluation, New York State Division of Substance Abuse Services. April 14.

Johnson, B. D., Wish, E. D. & Huizinga, D. (1983, November). The concentration of delinquent offending: The contribution of serious drug involvement to high rate delinquency. Paper presented at the annual meeting of the American Society of Criminology, Denver, CO.

Johnson, G. M., Schoutz, F. C. & Locke, T. P. (1984). Relationships between adolescent drug use and parental drug behaviors. *Adolescence, 19*, 295-299.

Johnston, D. (1990, November 5). Miami drug case links Sicily mafia to Medellin. *The New York Times*, p. A15.

Johnston, L. D., O'Malley, P. M. & Bachman, J. G. (1991). *Drug use among American high school seniors, college students and young adults, 1975-1990. Vols. I & II.* Rockville, MD: National Institute on Drug Abuse.

Johnston, L. D., O'Malley, P. M. & Bachman, J. G. (1993). *National survey results on drug use from monitoring the future study, 1975-1992, Vols I & II.* Rockville, MD: National Institute on Drug Abuse.

Johnston, L. D., O'Malley, P. M. & Eveland, L. (1978). Drugs and delinquency: A search for causal connections. In D. B. Kandell (Ed.), *Longitudinal research on drug use.* Washington, DC: Hemisphere.

Joint Committee on New York Drug Law Evaluation (1978). *The nation's toughest drug law: Evaluating the New York experience.* National Institute of Law Enforcement and Criminal Justice, LEAA, Washington, DC: U.S. Department of Justice.

Jonas, S. (1991). The U.S. drug problem and the U.S. drug culture: A public health solution. In J. A. Inciardi (Ed.), *The drug legalization debate* (pp. 161-182). Newbury Park, CA: Sage Publications.

Jones, R. (1987). Tobacco dependence. In H. Y. Meltzer (Ed.), *Psychopharmacology: The third generation of progress* (pp. 1589-1595). New York: Raven Press.

Jones, R. T., & Benowitz, N. (1976). The 30 day trip: Clinical studies of cannabis tolerance and dependence. In M. C. Braude & S. Szara (Eds.), *Pharmacology of marijuana. Vol. 2* (pp. 627-642). Orlando, FL: Academic Press.

Jones, R. T., Benowitz, N. L., & Herning, R. I. (1981). Clinical relevance of cannabis tolerance and dependence. *Journal of Clinical Pharmacology, 21* (8-9 Suppl.), 143S-152S.

Jonsson, E., & Nilsson, T. (1968). Alkoholkonsumption hos monozygota och dizygota twillingpar. *Nord. Hyg. Tidskr., 49*, 21-25.

Judd, L. L., & Huey, L. Y. (1984). Lithium antagonizes ethanol intoxication in alcoholics. *American Journal of Psychiatry, 141*, 1517-1521.

Julien, R. M. (1988). *A primer of drug action* (5th ed.). New York: Freeman.

Kaij, L. (1960). *Alcoholism in twins.* Stockholm: Almqvist and Wiksell.

Kalogerakis, G. (1995, May 1). Retox: It's drugs again. *New York, Vol. 28, No. 18*, pp. 40-47.

Kamerow, D. B., Pincus, H. A., & MacDonald, D. I. (1986). Alcohol abuse, other drug abuse, and mental disorders in medical practice: Prevalence, costs, recognition, and treatment. *Journal of the American Medical Association, 255*, 2054-2057.

Kandel, D. B. (1982). Epidemiological and psychosocial perspectives on adolescent drug use. *Journal of American Academic Clinical Psychiatry, 21*, 328-347.

Kandel, D. B. (1985). On processes of peer influence in adolescent drug use: A developmental perspective. *Alcohol and Substance Abuse in Adolescence, 4*, 139-163.

Kandel, D. B., & Logan, J. A. (1984). Patterns of drug use from adolescence to young adulthood: I. Periods of risk for initiation, continued use, and discontinuation. *American Journal of Public Health, 7*, 660-666.

Kandel, D. B., Kessler, R. C., & Margulies, R. S. (1978). Antecedents of adolescent initiation into stages of drug use: A developmental analysis. *Journal of Youth and Adolescence, 7*, 13-40.

Kandel, E., & Mednick, S. A. (1988). IQ as a protective factor for subjects at high risk for antisocial behavior. *Journal of Consulting and Clinical Psychology, 56*, 224-226.

Kaplan, N. M. (1991). Bashing booze: The danger of losing the benefits of moderate alcohol consumption. *American Heart Journal, 121*, 1854-1956.

Kaprio, J., Koskenvuo, M., Langinvainio, H., Romanov, K., Seppo, S., & Rose, R.J. (1987). Genetic influences on use and abuse of alcohol: A study of 5638 adult Finnish twin brothers. *Alcoholism, 11*, 349-356.

Karel, R. B. (1991). A model legalization proposal. In J. A. Inciardi (Ed.), *The drug legalization debate* (pp. 80-102). Newbury Park, CA: Sage Publications.

Kashkin, K. B. & Kleber, H. D. (1989). Hooked on hormones? An anabolic steroid addiction hypothesis. *Journal of the American Medical Association, 262*, 3166-3170.

Kaufmann, R. (1992, March). The National Guard remains out front in drug war battles. *National Guard*, pp. 16-18.

Kellam, S. G. & Brown, H. (1982). *Social adaptational and psychological antecedents of adolescent psychopathology ten years later.* Baltimore, MD: Johns Hopkins University.

Kent, T. A., Campbell, J. L., Pazdernik, T. L., Hunter, R., Gunn, W. H. & Goodwin, D. W. (1985). Blood platelet uptake of serotonin in men alcoholics. *Journal of Studies on Alcohol, 46*, 357-359.

Kern, M. F., Kenkel, M. B., Templer, D. I., and Newell, T. G. (1986). Drug preference as a function of arousal and stimulus screening. *International Journal of the Addictions 18*, 633-680.

Khantzian, E. J. (1981). Self-selection and progression in drug dependence. In H. Shaffer, & M. E. Burglass (Eds.), *Classic contributions in the addictions* (pp. 154-160). New York: Brunner/Mazel.

Khantzian, E. J. (1985). The self-medication hypothesis of addictive disorders: Focus on heroin and cocaine dependence. *American Journal of Psychiatry, 142*, 1259-1264.

Khantzian, E. J., Gawin, F. H., Kleber, H. D., & Riodan, C. E. (1984). Methylphenidate treatment of cocaine dependence—A preliminary report. *Journal of Substance Abuse Treatment, 1*, 107-112.

Khantzian, E. J., & Treece, C. (1985). DSM-III psychiatric diagnosis of narcotic addicts: Recent findings. *Archives of General Psychiatry, 42*, 1067-1071.

Kimes, A. S., Bell, J. A., & London, E. D. (1990). Clonidine attenuates increased brain glucose metabolism during naloxone-precipitated morphine withdrawal. *Neuroscience, 34*, 633-644.

King, R. (1972). *The drug hang-up: America's fifty year folly.* New York: W. W. Norton & Co.

Kleber, H. D. (1988). Epidemic cocaine abuse: America's present, Britain's future? *British Journal of Addiction, 83*, 1359-1371.

Kleber, H., & Gawin, F. H. (1986). Psychopharmacological trials in cocaine abuse treatment. *American Journal of Drug and Alcohol Abuse, 12*, 235-246.

Kleinman, P. H., Goldsmith, D. S., Friedman, S. R., Hopkins, W., & Des Jarlais, D. C. (1990). Knowledge about and behaviors affecting the spread of AIDS: A street survey of intravenous drug users and their associates in New York City. *The International Journal of the Addictions, 25,* 345-361.

Kligman, D. & Goldberg, D. A. (1975). Temporal lobe epilepsy and aggression. *Nervous and Mental Diseases, 160,* 324-341.

Kofoed, L., & MacMillan, J. (1986). Alcoholism and antisocial personality. *Journal of Nervous and Mental Diseases, 174,* 332-335.

Kolata, G. (1986). New drug counters alcohol intoxication. *Science, 234,* 1198-1199.

Kolodny, R. C. (1975). Research issues in the study of marijuana and male reproductive physiology in humans. In J. R. Tinklenberg (Ed.), *Marijuana and health hazards* (pp. 71-81). Orlando, FL: Academic Press.

Kondracke, M. N. (1988, June 27). Don't legalize drugs: The costs are still too high. *The New Republic,* pp. 16-19.

Kornetsky, C., & Esposito, R. U. (1979). Euphorigenic drugs: Effects on the reward pathways of the brain. *Federal Proceedings, 38,* 2473-2476.

Kozel, N.J., Dupont, R., & Brown, B. (1972). A study of narcotic involvement in an offender population. *International Journal of Addictions, 7,* 443-450.

Kozel, N. J., & Adams, E. H. (1986). Epidemiology of drug abuse: An overview. *Science, 234,* 970-974.

Kreek, M. J., & Hartman, N. (1982). Chronic use of opioids and antipsychotic drugs: Side effects, effects on endogenous opioids, and toxicity. *Annals of the New York Academy of Sciences, 398,* 151-172.

Krivanek, J. (1988). *Heroin: Myths and reality.* Sydney, Australia: Allen & Unwin.

Kwitney, J. (1987). *The crimes of patriots: A true tale of dope, dirty money and the CIA.* New York: Norton.

Laberg, J. C., & Loberg, T. (1989). Expectancy and tolerance: A study of acute alcohol intoxication using the balanced placebo design. *Journal of Studies on Alcohol, 50,* 448-455.

Lal, H., Gianutsos, G., & Puri, S. K. (1975). A comparison of narcotic analgesics with neuroleptics on behavioral measures of dopaminergic activity. *Life Sciences, 17,* 29-32.

Landesman-Dwyer, S., Ragozin, A. S., & Little, R. E. (1981). Behavioral correlates of prenatal alcohol exposure: A four-year follow-up study. *Neurobehavioral Toxicology and Teratology, 3,* 187-193.

Lane, C., Waller, D., Larmer, B., & Katel, P. (1992, January 6). The newest war. *Newsweek,* pp. 18-23.

Lapham, L. H. (1989, December). A political opiate: The war on drugs is a folly and a menace. *Harper's Magazine,* pp. 43-48.

Lasagna, L., von Felsinger, J. M. & Beecher, H. K. (1955). Drug induced mood changes in man. I. Observations on healthy subjects, chronically ill patients, and postaddicts. *Journal of the American Medical Association, 157,* 1006-1020.

Latimer, D., & Goldberg, J. (1981). *Flowers in the blood: The story of opium.* New York: Franklin Watts.

Leary, T. (1968) *The Politics of Ecstasy.* New York: Putnam.

Leathwood, P. D. (1986). Neurotransmitter precursors: From animal experiments to human applications. *Nutrition Reviews, 44(Suppl.),* 193-204.

LeBlanc, T. J. (1925). The medicine show. *The American Mercury, 5,* pp. 232-237.

Leith, N. J., & Barrett, R. J. (1981). Self-stimulation and amphetamine: Tolerance to D and L isomers and cross tolerance to cocaine and methylphenidate. *Psychopharmacology, 72,* 23-28.

Lemert, E. (1951). *Social pathology.* New York: McGraw-Hill.

Lester, B.M., & Dreher, M. (1989). Effects of marijuana use during pregnancy on newborn cry. *Child Development, 60,* 765-771.

Leukefeld, C. G. & Tims, F. M. (1988). *Compulsory treatment of drug abuse: Research and clinical practice.* Rockville, MD: National Institute on Drug Abuse.

Leukefeld, C. G., & Tims, F. M. (1992). Drug Abuse Treatment in Prisons and Jails. (NIDA Research Monograph 118). Rockville, MD: National Institute on Drug Abuse.

Levander, S. E., Schalling, D. S., Lidberg, L., Bartfai, A. & Lidberg, Y. (1980). Skin conductance recovery time and personality in a group of criminals. *Psychophysiology, 17,* 105-111.

Levine, M. (1990). *Deep cover.* New York: Delacorte Press.

Levinthal, C. F. (1988). *Messengers of paradise: Opiates and the brain.* New York: Anchor Press, Doubleday.

Lewis, C. E. (1984). Alcoholism, antisocial personality, narcotic addiction: An integrative approach. *Psychiatric Developments, 3,* 223-235.

Lewis, C. E., Cloninger, C. R., & Pais, J. (1983). Alcoholism, antisocial personality, and drug use in a criminal population. *Alcohol and Alcoholism, 18,* 53-60.

Lewis, D. C. & Zinberg, N. E. (1964). Narcotic usage. II. A historical perspective on a difficult medical problem. *New England Journal of Medicine, 270,* 1045-1050.

Lewis, D. O. (1981). *Vulnerabilities to delinquency.* New York: SP Medical & Scientific Books.

Lieberman, H. R., Corkin, S., Spring, B., J., Growden, J. H., & Wurtman, R. J. (1982). Mood and sensorimotor performance after neurotransmitter precursor administration. *Society for Neuroscience, 8,* 395.

Linder, R. L., Lerner, S. E., & Burns, R. S. (1981). The experience and effects of PCP abuse. In *The devil's dust: Recognition, management, and prevention of phencyclidine abuse.* pp. 103-124. Belmont, CA: Wadsworth Publishing Co.

Lindesmith, A. R. (1947). *Opiate addiction.* Bloomington, IN: Principia Press.

Lindesmith, A. R. (1965). *The addict and the law.* New York: Vintage Books.

Linn, S., Schoenbaum, S. C., Monson, R. R., Rosner, R., Stubblefield, P. C. & Ryan, K. J. (1983). The association of marijuana use with outcome of pregnancy. *American Journal of Public Health, 73,* 1161-1164.

Linnoila, M. (1986). Heredity of alcoholism. *Duodecim, 201,* 1742- 1743.

Linnoila, M., Virkkunen, M., Scheinin, M., Nuutila, A., Rimon, R., & Goodwin, F. K. (1983). Low cerebrospinal fluid 5-hydroxyindoleacetic acid concentration differentiates impulsive from nonimpulsive violent behavior. *Life Sciences, 33,* 2609-2614.

Lion, J. R. (1979). Benzodiazepines in the treatment of aggressive patients. *Journal of Clinical Psychiatry 40,* 70-71.

Lipton, D. S. (1994). Correctional opportunity: Pathways to drug treatment for offenders. *Journal of Drug Issues, 24,* 331-348.

Litner, B. (1994a, January 20). Pusher with a cause. *Far Eastern Ecomonic Review,* pp. 24-26.

Litner, B. (1994b, January 20). Turf war in the triangle. *Far Eastern Economic Review,* p. 26.

Litner, B. & Mai, C. (1994, January 20). Opium war. *Far Eastern Economic Review,* pp. 22-24.

Lipton, D., Martinson, R., & Wilks, J. (1975). *The effectiveness of correctional treatment—A survey of treatment evaluation studies.* Spring, MA, Praeger.

Loeber, R., & Dishion, T. (1983). Early predictors of male delinquency: A review. *Psychological Bulletin, 94,* 68-99.

Loeber, R. L. & Stouthamer-Loeber, M. (1986). Family factors as correlates and predictors of juvenile conduct problems and delinquency. In M. Tonry & N. Morris (Eds.), *Crime and Justice, Vol. 7* (pp 29-150). Chicago: University of Chicago Press.

Long, W. R. (1990, July 8). Drug lords target Colombian media. *The Hartford Courant,* p. A11.

Longabaugh, R. (1986). The matching hypothesis: Theoretical and empirical status. Presented at the Annual Meeting of the American Psychological Association, Washington, DC, August 24.

Love, C. T. (1990). Personal interview with ex-heroin addict. City undisclosed to ensure protection of the source.

Lovenberg, W. M. (1986). Biochemical regulation of brain function. *Nutrition Reviews, 44(Suppl.),* 6-11.

Lucas, S. E. (1985). *Amphetamines: Danger in the fast lane.* New York, Chelsea House.

Lund, A. K., Preusser, D. F., & Williams, A. F. (1989). Drug use in tractor-trailer drivers. In S. W. Gust, & J. M. Walsh (Eds.), *Drugs in the workplace: Research and evaluation data* (NIDA Research Monograph 91, pp. 47-67). Rockville, MD: National Institute on Drug Abuse.

Luria, A. R. (1973). The frontal lobes and the regulation of behavior. In K. H. Pribram & A. R. Luria (Eds.), *Psychophysiological of the frontal lobes* (pp.3-28). New York: Academic Press.

Lyons, J. P., Welte, J., Brons, J., Sokolow, L. & Hynes, G. (1982). Variation in alcoholism treatment orientation: Differential impact upon specific subpopulations. *Alcoholism, Clinical and Experimental Research, 6,* 333-343.

Lyttle, T. (1993). Misuse and legend in the 'toad licking' phenomenon. *The International Journal of the Addictions, 28,* 521-538.

Maas, J. W. (1975). Biogenic amines and depression. *Archives of General Psychiatry, 32,* 1357-1361.

Maas, P. (1994, September 18). The menace of China white. *Parade Magazine,* pp. 4-6.

MacLean, P. (1976). The Triune Brain.

Madden, J. D., Payne, T. F., & Miller, S. (1986). Maternal cocaine abuse and effect on the newborn. *Pediatrics, 77,* 209-211.

Maddux, J. F., & Desmond, D. P. (1989). Family and environment in the choice of opioid dependence or alcoholism. *American Journal of Drug and Alcohol Abuse, 15,* 117-134.

Maletsky, B. M. (1976). The diagnosis of pathological intoxication. *Journal of Studies on Alcohol, 37*, 1215-1228.

Malka, R. (1988). Role of drug therapies in the treatment of alcoholism: Alcohol and anxiety—Alcohol and depression. *Clinical Neuropharmacology, 11(Suppl. 2),* S69-S73.

Maloff, D. (1981). A review of the effects of the decriminalization of marijuana. *Contemporary Drug Problems, 10,* 307-322.

Mannella, J. A., & Beauchamp, G. K. (1991). The transfer of alcohol to human milk: Effects on flavor and the infant's behavior. *New England Journal of Medicine, 325,* 981-985.

Marinacci, A. A. (1963). Special types of temporal lobe seizures following ingestion of alcohol. *Bulletin of the Los Angeles Neurological Society, 28,* 241-250.

Marrs-Simon, P. A., Weiler, M., Santangelo, M. A., Perry, M. I. & Leikin, J. B. (1988). Analysis of sexual disparity of violent behavior in PCP intoxication. *Veterinary and Human Toxicology, 30,* 53-55.

Marsh, D. C., Flynn, D. D., & Potter, L. T. (1985). Loss of M2 muscarine receptors in the cerebral cortex in Alzheimer's disease and experimental cholinergic denervation. *Science, 228,* 1115-1117.

Mason, R. J., Buist, A. S., Fisher, E. B., Merchant, J. A., Samet, J. M., & Welsh, C. H. (1985). Cigarette smoking and health. *American Review of Respiratory Diseases, 132,* 1133-1136.

Martin, D. (1994, January 10). Rotary pay phones return this time to foil drug deals. *The New York Times,* pp. A1 and B3.

Masters, M. R., Ferris, G. R., & Ratcliff, S. L. (1988). Practices and attitudes of substance abuse testing. *Personnel Administrator, 33(7),* 72-78.

Mayer, D. J., Price, D. D., & Raffi, A. (1977). Antagonism of acupuncture analgesia in man by the narcotic antagonist naloxone. *Brain Research, 121,* 386-392.

Mayfield, D. (1976). Alcoholism, alcohol, intoxication and assaultive behavior. *Diseases of the Nervous System, 37,* 288-291.

McAlary, M. (1987). *Buddy boys.* New York: Putnam.

McAlister, A. L., Perry, C. L., Killen, J., Slinkard, L. A., & Maccoby, N. (1980). Pilot study of smoking, alcohol and drug abuse prevention. *American Journal of Public Health, 70,* 719-721.

McBay, A. J. (1986). Problems in testing for abused drugs [Letter to the editor]. *Journal of the American Medical Association, 255,* 39.

McBride, D. C. (1981). Drugs and violence. In J. A. Inciardi (Ed.). *The Drugs-crime connection* (pp. 105-123). Beverly Hills, CA.: Sage Publicaations.

McCardle, L., & Fishbein, D. H. (1989). The self-reported effects of PCP on human aggression. *Addictive Behaviors, 4,* 465-472.

McCarty, D. (1985). Micro-environmental determinants of substance abuse. In M. Galizio & S. A. Maisto (Eds.), *Determinants of substance abuse: Biological, psychological, and environmental factors* (pp. 247-282). New York: Plenum Press.

McCaul, M. E., Svikis, D. S., Turkkan, J. S., Bigelow, G. E. & Cromwell, C. C. (1989). Degree of familial alcoholism: Effects on substance abuse by college males. (pp. 372-373). (NIDA Research Monograph Series No. 195). Rockville, MD: National Institute on Drug Abuse.

McCord, J. (1981). Alcoholism and criminality confounding and differentiating factors. *Journal of Studies on Alcohol, 42,* 739-748.

McCoy, A.W. (1991). *The politics of heroin: CIA complicity in the global drug trade.* Brooklyn, NY: Lawrence Hill Books.

McCoy, A. (1972). *The politics of heroin in Southeast Asia.* New York: Harper & Row.

McCoy A. W. (with Read, C. B., & Adams, L. P. II) (1973). *The politics of heroin in southeast Asia.* New York: Harper Colophon Books.

McFarland, G. C. (1986). Drug abuse indicators trend report. District of Columbia, December 1985. In N. J. Kozel (Ed.), *Epidemiology of drug abuse: Research, clinical and social perspectives,* December 1985. (pp. 236-257). Rockville, MD: National Institute on Drug Abuse.

McGinnis, J. M. & Foege, W. H. (1993). Actual causes of death in the United States. *Journal of the American Medical Association, 270,* 2207-2212.

McGuire, P. C. (1988 January). Jamaican posses: A call for cooperation among law enforcement agencies. *The Police Chief,* pp. 20-27.

McLellan, A. T. (1983). Increased effectiveness of substance abusers treatment: A prospective study of patient-treatment 'matching'. *Journal of Nervous and Mental Diseases, 17,* 587-605.

McKim, W. A. (1991). Drugs and behavior: An introduction to behavioral pharmacology (2nd. ed.). Englewood Cliffs, NJ: Prentice-Hall.

McVay, D. (1991). Marijuana legalization: The time is now. In J. A. Inciardi (Ed.), *The drug legalization debate* (pp. 147-160). Newbury Park, CA: Sage Publications.

Meer, J. (1987). *Drugs & sports.* New York: Chelsea House Publishers.

Meier, R. F., Burkett, S .R., & Hickman, C.A. (1984). Sanctions, peers and deviance: Preliminary models of a social control process. *The Sociological Quarterly, 25,* 67-82.

Melchoir, C. L., & Myers, R. D. (1976). Genetic differences in ethanol drinking of the rat following injection of 6-OHDA, 5, 6-DHT or 5,7DHT into cerebral ventricles. *Pharmacology Biochemistry and Behavior, 5,* 63-72.

Meller, W. H., Rinehart, R., Cadoret, R. J., & Troughton, E. (1988). Specific familial transmission in substance abuse. *The International Journal of the Addictions, 23,* 1029-1039.

Mello, N., & Mendelson, J. (1980). Buprenorphine suppresses heroin use by heroin addicts. *Science, 207,* 657-659.

Mendelson, J., Mello, N., Ellingboe, J., Skupny, A. S., et al. (1986). Marijuana smoking suppressed luteinizing hormone in women. *Journal of Pharmacology and Experimental Therapeutics, 237,* 862-866.

Mendenhall, W. (1989). Co-dependency definitions and dynamics. In B. Carruth, & W. Mendenhall (Eds.), *Co-dependency: Issues in treatment and recovery* (pp. 3-17). Binghamton, NY: The Haworth Press.

Mennella, J. A., & Beauchamp, G. K. (1991). The transfer of alcohol to human milk. *New England Journal of Medicine, 325,* 981-985.

Menon, P., Rando, R. J., Stankus, R. P., Salvaggio, J. E. & Lehrer, S.B. (1992). Passive cigarette smoke-challenge studies: Increase in bronchial hyperreactivity. *Journal of Allergy and Clinical Immunology, 89,* 560-566.

Merton, R. (1938). Social structure and anomie. *American Sociological Review, 3,* 672-682.

Miczek, K. A., & Tidey, J. W. (1989). Amphetamines: Aggressive and social behavior. In K. Asghar & E. De Souza (Eds.), *Pharmacology and toxicology of amphetamine and related designer drugs* (pp. 68-100)(NIDA Research Monograph 94).

Mijuriya, T. H. & Aldrich, M. R. (1988). Cannabis 1988: Old drug, new dangers—The potency question. *Journal of Psychoactive Drugs, 20,* 47-55.

Miller, B. A., Downs, W. R. Gondoli, D. M., & Keil, A. (1987). Childhood sexual abuse incidents for alcoholic women versus a random sample of household women. *Violence and Victims, 2,* 157-172.

Miller, N. S., Gold, M. S., Belkin, B. M., & Klahr, A. L. (1989). Family history and diagnosis of alcohol dependence in cocaine dependence. *Psychiatry Research, 29,* 113-121.

Miller, R. E., & Cappiello, L. A. (1983). Relationships between inmates' past drug practices and current drug knowledge and attitudes. *International Journal of the Addictions, 18,*881-890.

Miller, R. E., Cappiello, L. A., & Golaszewski, T. J. (1983). Instrumentation for the measurement of inmates' drug use, knowledge, and attitudes. *Journal of Drug Education, 13(1),* 63-72.

Millman, R. B., & Sbriglio, R. (1986). Patterns of use and psychopathology in chronic marijuana users. *Psychiatric Clinics of North America, 9,* 533-545.

Mirin, S. M., Weiss, R. D. & Michael, J. (1988). Psychopathology in substance abusers: Diagnosis and treatment. *American Journal of Drug and Alcohol Abuse, 14,* 139-157.

Mizuno, T. I., & Yugari, Y. (1974). Self mutilation in the Lesch-Nyhan syndrome. *Lancet, 1,* 761.

Mody, C. K., Miller, B. L., McIntyre, H. B., Cobb, S. K., & Goldberg, M. A. (1988). Neurological complications of cocaine abuse. *Neurology, 38,* 1189-1193.

Moller, S. E., Kirk, L. & Fremming, K. H. (1976). Plasma amino acids as an index for subgroups in manic depressive psychosis: Correlation to effect of tryptophan. *Psychopharmacology, 49,* 205-213.

Montforte, J. R., & Spitz, W. U. (1975). Narcotic abuse among homicides in Detroit. *Journal of Forensic Sciences, 20,* 186-190.

Moody, J. (1990, July 23). The war that will not end. *Time, 136(4),* 33, 35.

Moore, W. V. (1988). Anabolic steroid use in adolescence. *Journal of the American Medical Association, 260,* 3484-3486.

Moos, R. H. & Moos, B. S. (1984). The process of recovery from alcoholism: III. Comparing functioning in families of alcoholics and matched control families. *Journal of Studies on Alcohol, 45,* 111-118.

Morgan, J. P. (1987). Urine testing for abused drugs: Technology and the real world. In *The drug testing debate: Remedy or reaction?* (pp. 7-10). American Federation of State, County and Municipal Employees, AFL-CIO.

Morganthau, T., Sandza, R., Miller, M., Gonzalez, D. L., Calonius, E., McKillop, P., Rogers, P., Lerner, M. A. & Doherty, S. (1989, November 13). Cocaine's `dirty 300.' *Newsweek,* pp. 36-41.

Muhlbauer, H. D. (1985). Human aggression and the role of central serotonin. *Pharmacopsychiatry, 18,* 218-221.

Murphy, D. L. (1988). Heterosexual contacts of intravenous drug abusers: Implications for the next spread of the AIDS epidemic. *Advances in Alcohol and Substance Abuse, 7,* 89-97.

Murphy, J. M., McBride, W. J., Lumeng, L., & Li, T. K. (1982). Regional brain levels of monoamines in alcohol-preferring and non-preferring lines of rats. *Pharmacology Biochemistry and Behavior, 16,* 145-149.

Murphy, J. M., McBride, W. J., Lumeng, L., & Li, T. K. (1987). Contents of monoamines in forebrain regions of alcohol- preferring (P) and non-preferring (NP) lines of rats. *Pharmacology, Biochemistry and Behavior, 26,* 389-392.

Murphy, J. M., Waller, M. B., Gatto, G. J., McBride, W. J., Lumeng, L., & Li T.-K. (1985). Monoamine uptake inhibitors attenuate ethanol intake in alcohol-preferring (P) rats. *Alcohol, 2,* 349-352.

Murray, J. B. (1986). Marijuana's effects on human cognitive functions, psychomotor function, and personality. *The Journal of General Psychology, 113,* 23-55.

Muscettola, G., Wehr, T. & Goodwin, F. K. (1977). Effect of diet on urinary MHPG excretion in depressed patients and normal control subjects. *American Journal of Psychiatry, 134,* 914-916.

Musto, D. F. (1970). The American antinarcotic movement: Clinical research and public policy. *Clinical Research, 19,* 601-605.

Musto, D. F. (1972). The Marihuana Tax Act of 1937. *Archives of General Psychiatry, 26,* 101-108.

Musto, D. F. (1974). Social and political influences on addiction research. In S. Fisher & A. M. Freedman (Eds.). *Opiate addiction: Origins and treatment.* (pp. 93-98). New York: Halsted Press Division of Wiley.

Musto, D. F. (1987). The history of legislative control over opium, cocaine, and their derivatives. In R. Hamowy (Ed.). *Dealing with drugs.* (pp. 37-71). San Francisco: Pacific Research Institute for Public Policy.

Myers, D. W. (1986). An overview of employee assistance programs. In Commerce Clearing House, Inc. *Employee assistance programs: Drug, alcohol, and other problems.* Chicago, IL: Author.

Myers, M. A. (1989). Symbolic policy and the sentencing of drug offenders. *Law and Society Review, 23,* 292-315.

Myers, R. D., & Melchior, C. L. (1977). Alcohol and alcoholism: Role of serotonin. In W. B. Essman (Ed.), *Serotonin in health and disease, Vol. 2, Physiological regulation and pharmacological action* (pp. 373-430). New York: Spectrum.

Nadelmann, E. A. (1989). Drug prohibition in the United States: Costs, consequences, and alternatives. *Science, 245,* 939-947.

Nagoshi, C. T., Dixon, L. K., Johnson, R. C., & Yuen, S. H. L. (1988). Familial transmission of alcohol consumption and the flushing response to alcohol in three Oriental groups. *Journal of Studies on Alcohol, 46,* 289-297.

Nahas, G. G. (1984). The medical use of cannabis. In G. G. Nahas (Ed.), *Marijuana in science and medicine* (pp. 238-252). New York: Raven Press.

Naranjo, C. A., Sellers, E. M., Roach, C. A. Woodley, D. V., Sanchez-Craig, M. & Sykora, K. (1984). Zimelidine-induced variations in alcohol intake by nondepressed heavy drinkers. *Clinical Pharmacological Therapies, 35,* 374-381.

Narcotics Anonymous. (1988). Van Nuys, CA: World Service Office.

Nathan, P. E., & McCrady, B. S. (1987). Bases for the use of abstinence as a goal in the behavioral treatment of alcohol abusers. In M. B. Sobell & L. C. Sobell (Eds.), *Moderation as a goal or outcome of treatment for alcohol problems: A dialogue. Drugs and society, 1,* New York: Haworth Press.

National Commission on Marijuana and Drug Abuse (1972). *Marijuana: A signal of misunderstanding.* R. P. Shafer, Chairman, New York: Signet, p. 94.

National Defense Authorization Act (1989). (Public Law 100-456), September 29, 1988 (Title XI, 102 STAT.), pp. 2042-2049.

National Drug Reporter. (1977). *Medical therapy, legalization issues debated at Marijuana Reform Conference, 7,* 3-5.

National Institute on Alcohol Abuse and Alcoholism (1989). *Relapse and craving. Alcohol Alert (#6).* Washington, DC: U.S. Department of Health and Human Services.

National Institute on Drug Abuse. (1990). *National household survey on drug abuse: Highlights 1988.* Rockville, MD: NIDA.

Nauta, W. J. (1971). The problem of the frontal lobe: A reinterpretation. *Journal of Psychiatric Research, 8,* 167-187.

Needle-swap program is working. (1991, August 1). *The Hartford Courant,* pp. A1, A7.

Neill, J. R. (1987). More than medical significance: LSD and American Psychiatry 1953 to 1966. *Journal of Pschoactive Drugs, 19,* January - March.

Newcomb, M. D., & Bentler, P. M. (1986). Cocaine use among adolescents: Longitudinal associations with social context, psychopathology, and use of other substances. *Addictive Behaviors, 11,* 263-273.

Newcomb, M. D., & Bentler, P. M. (1989). Substance use and abuse among children and teenagers. *American Psychologist, 44,* 242-248.

Newlin, D. B. (1989). Placebo responding in the same direction as alcohol in women. *Alcoholism: Clinical and Experimental Research, 13,* 36-39.

New York State Commission of Correction.(1986). *Acquired Immune Deficiency Syndrome: A demographic profile of New York state inmate mortalities 1981-1985.* Albany, NY: Author.

Ng Cheong Ton, J. M., Gerhardt, G. A., Friedemann, M., Etgen, A. M., Rose, G. M., Sharpless, N. S. & Gardner, E .L. (1988). The effects of delta 9-tetrahydrocannabinol and potassium-evoked release of dopamine in the rate caudate nucleus: An in vivo electrochemical and in vivo microdialysis study. *Brain Research, 451,* 59-68.

Nicholi, A. M. (1983). The nontherapeutic use of psychoactive drugs: A modern epidemic. *New England Journal of Medicine, 308,* 925-933.

Nicholl, C. (1985). *The fruit palace.* New York: St. Martin's Press.

Nichols, D. E., & Oberlender, R. (1989). Structure-activity relationships of MDMA-like substances. In K. Asghar & E. De Souza (Eds.), *Pharmacology and toxicology of amphetamine and related designer drugs* (NIDA Research Monograph No. 94). Washington, DC: U.S. Government Printing Office.

Norem-Hebeisen, A. Johnson, D. W., Anderson, D. & Johnson, R. (1984). Predictors and concomitants of changes in drug use patterns among teenagers. *The Journal of Social Psychology, 124,* 43-50.

Nunes, E. V., Quitklin, F. M. & Klein, D. J. (1989). Psychiatric diagnosis in cocaine abuse. *Psychiatric Research, 28,* 105-114.

Nurco, D. N., Hanlon, T. E., Kinlock, T. W., & Dyxzynski, K. R. (1989). The consistency of types of criminal behavior over preaddiction, addiction, and nonaddiction status periods. *Comprehensive Psychiatry, 30,* 391-402.

Nyhan, W. L. (1976). Behavior in the Lesch-Nyhan syndrome. *Journal of Autism and Childhood Schizophrenia, 6,* 235-252.

O'Brien, C. P., Childress, A. R., Arndt, I. O., McLellan, A. T., Woody, G. E., & Maany, I. (1988). Pharmacological and behavioral treatments of cocaine dependence: Controlled studies. *Journal of Clinical Psychiatry, 49* (Suppl. 2), 17-22).

Officer is accused of robbing dealers (1993, January 10). *The New York Times,* p. 28.

Officials fired after escape of drug trafficker. (1992, July 25). *The Hartford Courant,* p. A4.

Ogborne, A. C., & Glaser, F. B. (1985). Evaluating Alcoholics Anonymous. In T. E. Bratter, & G. G. Forrest (Eds.) *Alcohol and substance abuse: Strategies for clinical intervention.* pp. 69-83. New York: Free Press.

O'Hara, K., & Backer, T. E. (1989). Index of survey research studies on workplace drug abuse and EAPs. *Employee Assistance Quarterly, 4,* 87-100.

O'Keefe, A. M. (1987). The case against drug testing. *Psychology Today, 21* (6), 34-38.

O'Malley, P. M., Johnston, L. D., & Bachman, J. G. (1985). Cocaine use among American adolescents and young adults. In N. J. Kozel, & E. H. Adams (Eds.), *Cocaine use in America: Epidemiologic and clinical perspectives* (pp. 250-273) (NIDA Research Monograph No. 61). Rockville, MD: National Institute on Drug Abuse.

O'Malley, S. S. & Maisto, S. A. (1985). Effects of family drinking history and expectancies on responses to alcohol in men. *Journal of Studies on Alcohol, 46,* 289-297.

Osborn, J. E. (1989). Medical considerations. In M. Falco & W. I. Cikins (Eds.), *Toward a national policy on drug and AIDS testing* (pp. 26-42). Washington, DC: The Brookings Institution.

Our million drug addicts. (1923, August 25). *The Literary Digest,* pp. 22-23.

Owen, D.E. (1968). *British opium policy in China and India.* Archon Books.

"Patent medicine" advertising. (1927, January). *Hygeia,* p. 44.

Patterson, C. D. (1974). Self-reported unpleasant effects from illicit use of fourteen substances. *British Journal of Addiction, 69,* 249-256.

Pear, R. (1992, June 3). U.S. drug offical urges mayors against needle-swap programs. *The New York Times,* p. B3.

Peele, S. (1986). The implications and limitations of genetic models of alcoholism and other addictions. *Journal of Studies on Alcohol, 47* (1), 63-73.

Peele, S. (1987). A moral vision of addiction: How people's values determine whether they become and remain addicts. Visions of addiction. Part 1. *Journal of Drug Issues, 17* (2), 187-215.

Peele, S. (1989). *Diseasing of America.* Lexington, MA: D. C. Heath and Co.

Peele, S. (1991). What we now know about treating alcoholism and other addictions. *Harvard Mental Health Letter, 8,* 5-7.

Peele, S., & Alexander, B. K. (1985). Theories of addiction. In S. Peele, *The meaning of addiction: Compulsive experience and its interpretation. pp. 47-72.* Lexington, MA: D. C. Heath and Co.

Pekkanen, J. (1973). *The American connection: Profiteering and politicking in the "ethical" drug industry.* Chicago: Follett.

Penning, M., & Barnes, G. E. (1982). Adolescent marijuana use review. *International Journal of Addictions, 18,* 749-791.

Perez-Reyes, M., Hicks, R. E., Bumberry, J., Jeffcoat, A. R., & Cook, C. E. (1988). Interaction between marijuana and ethanol: Effects on psychomotor performance. *Alcoholism: Clinical and Experimental Research, 12,* 268-276.

Pernanen, K. (1976). Alcohol and crimes of violence. In B. Kissin & H. Begleiter (Eds.), *The biology of alcoholism, Vol. 4* (pp. 351-444). New York: Plenum Press.

Pernanen, K. (1991). *Alcohol in human violence.* New York: Guilford Press.

Perry, E. K. & Perry, R. H. (1980). The cholinergic system in Alzheimer's disease. In P. J. Roberts (Ed.), *Biochemistry of dementia* (pp. 135-184). Chichester: John Wiley & Sons.

Pervin, L. A. (1988). Affect and addiction. *Addictive Behaviors, 13,* 83-86.

Peters, B. H. & Levine, H.S. (1977). Memory enhancement after physostigmine in the amnesic syndrome. *Archives of Neurology, 34,* 215-219.

Peters, R., Kearns, W., Murrin, M. & Dolente, A. (1992). Psychopathology and mental health needs among drug-involved inmates. *Journal of Prison and Jail Health, 11,* 3-25.

Peters, R., Kearns, W., Murrin, M., Dolente, A., & May, R. (1993). Examining the effectiveness of in-jail substance abuse treatment. *Journal of Offender Rehabilitation, 19,* 1-39.

Petersen, R. C. (Ed.), (1980). *Marijuana research findings: 1980.* (NIDA Research Monograph No. 31). Washington, DC: U.S. Government Printing Office.

Petersen, R.C. & Stillman, R.C. (1977). *Cocaine: 1977.* (NIDA Research Monograph No. 13). Washington, DC: U.S. Government Printing Office.

Petersilia, J. (1980). Criminal career research: A review of recent evidence. In N. Morris & M. Tonry (Eds.), *Crime and justice: An annual review of research, Vol. 2.* pp. 321-379. Chicago: University of Chicago Press.

Peterson, J. L. & Bakeman, R. (1989). AIDS and IV drug use among ethnic minorities. *The Journal of Drug Issues, 19,* 27-37.

Phibbs, C. S., Bateman, D. A. & Schwartz, R. M. (1991). The neonatal costs of maternal cocaine use. *Journal of the American Medical Association, 266,* 1521-1526.

Pihl, R. O. & Ross, C. (1987). Research on alcohol related aggression: A review and implications for understanding aggression. In S. W. Sadava (Eds.). *Drug use and psychological theory* (pp. 105-126). New York: The Haworth Press, Inc.

Platt, J. J., Buhringer, G., Kaplan, C. D., Brown, B. S. & Taube, D. O. (1988). The prospects and limitations of compulsory treatment for drug addiction. *The Journal of Drug Issues, 18,* 505-525.

Pomeranz, B., Cheng, R., & Law, P. (1977). Acupuncture reduces electrophysiological and behavioral responses to noxious stimuli: Pituitary is implicated. *Experimental Neurology, 54,* 172-178.

Pomeranz, B. & Chiu, D. (1976). Naloxone blockage of acupuncture analgesia: Endorphin implicated. *Life Sciences, 19,* 1757-1762.

Pomerleau, O. F. & Pomerleau, C. S. (1984). Neuroregulators and the reinforcement of smoking; Towards a biobehavioral explanation. *Neuroscience and Biobehavioral Reviews, 8,* 503-513.

Poole, C. (1989, July 24). Gonzalo Rodriguez Gacha: Gacha for warlord. *Forbes,* pp. 122-123.

Pope, H. G., Jr., & Katz, D. L. (1988). Affective and psychotic symptoms associated with anabolic steroid use. *American Journal of Psychiatry, 148,* 487-490.

Porter, L., Arif, A. E., & Curran, W. J. (1986). *The law and the treatment of drug and alcohol dependent persons; A comparative study of existing legislation.* Geneva, Switzerland: World Health Organization.

Posner, G. L. (1988). *Warlords of crime: Chinese secret societies—The new mafia.* New York: McGraw-Hill.

Post, R. M., Weiss, S. R. B., & Pert, A. (1987). Chronic cocaine administration: Sensitization and kindling effects. In E. G. Uhlenhuth, A. Raskin & S. Fisher (Eds.), *Cocaine: Clinical and behavioral aspects* (pp. 107-168). New York: Oxford University Press.

Potter-Efron, R. T. & Potter-Efron, P. S. (1990). *Aggression, family violence and chemical dependency.* New York: The Haworth Press.

Powers, M. W. S., Jr. (1975). Caffeine, behavior and the LD child. *Academic Therapy, XI,* 5-19.

Pradhan, S. N. (1984). Phencyclidine (PCP): Some human studies. *Neuroscience and Biobehavioral Reviews, 8,* 493-501.

Preble, E. & Casey, J. J. (1969). Taking care of business—The heroin addict's life on the street. *The International Journal of the Addictions, 4,* 1-24.

Prinz, R. J., Roberts, W. A., & Hantman, E. (1980). Dietary correlates of hyperactive behavior in children. *Journal of Consulting and Clinical Psychology, 48,* 760-769.

Prochaska, J. O. & DiClemente, C. C. (1984). *The transtheoretical approach: Crossing traditional boundaries of therapy.* Homewood, IL: Dorsey Press.

Purdy, M. (1995, July 2). Bars don't stop flow of drugs into prison. *The New York Times,* pp. 1 & 28-29.

Qazi, Q. H., Mariano, E., Millman, D. H., Beller, E., & Crombleholme, W. (1985). Abnormalities in offspring associated with prenatal marijuana exposure. *Developments in Pharmacological Therapy, 9,* 141-148.

Quay, H. C. (1965). Psychopathic personality as pathological stimulation seeking. *American Journal of psychiatry, 122,* 180-183.

Rapoport, J. L., Berg, C. J., Ismond, D. R., Zahn, T. P., & Neims, A. (1984). Behavioral effects of caffeine in children. Relationship between dietary choice and effects of caffeine challenge. *Archives of General Psychiatry, 41,* 1073-1079.

Ray, O., & Ksir, C. (1990). *Drugs, society, & human behavior.* St. Louis: Times Mirror/Mosby.

Regier, D. A., Farmer, M. E., Rae, D. S., Locke, B. Z, Keith, S. J., Judd, L. L. & Goodwin, F. E. (1990). Comorbidity of mental disorders with alcohol and other drug abuse: Results from the epidemiologic catchment area (ECA) study. *Journal of the American Medical Association, 264,* 2511-2518.

Reisinger, M. (1985). Buprenorphine as a new treatment for heroin dependence. *Drug and Alcohol Dependence, 16,* 257-262.

Relman, A. S. (1982). Marihuana and health. *New England Journal of Medicine, 306,* 603-604.

Restak, R. (1984). *The brain.* Toronto: Bantam Books.

Reuter, P. (1990). Can the borders be sealed? In R. Weisheit (Ed.), *Drugs, crime and the criminal justice system* (pp. 13 - 26). Cincinnati, OH: Anderson Publishing Co.

Richardson, L. A. (1989). Traveling and the fourth amendment in light of *United States v. Sokolow:* The cost of looking suspicious. *Search and Seizure Law Report, 16* (5), 121-128.

Richman, J. (1985). Sociological perspectives on illegal drug use: Definitional, reactional, and etiologic insights. *Behavioral Sciences and the Law,* 3, 249-258.

Rickels, K. (1983). Nonbenzodiazepine anxiolytics: Clinical usefulness. *Journal of Clinical Psychiatry 44* (11 pt. 2): 38-44.

Risner, M E. & Jones, B. E. (1980). Intravenous self-administration of cocaine and norcocaine by dogs. *Psychopharmacology, 71,* 83-93.

Ritz, M. C., Lamb, R. J., Goldberg, S. R. & Kuhar, M. J. (1987). Cocaine receptors on dopamine transporters are related to self-administration of cocaine. *Science, 237,* 1219-1223.

Robins, L. N. (1966). *Deviant children grown up: A sociological and psychiatric study of sociopathic personality.* Baltimore, MD: Williams and Wilkins.

Robins, L. N. (1974). *The Vietnam drug user returns.* Washington, DC: U.S. Government Printing Office.

Robins, L. N. (1979). longitudinal methods in the study of normal and psychological development. *der Gegenwart Vol. 1 Grundlagen und Methoden der Psychiatrie.* 2nd Ed. (pp. 627-689). Psychiatrie Bd., Heildelberg: Springer-Verlag.

Robins, L. N. (1980). Vietnam veterans three years after Vietnam: How our study changed our view of heroin. In L. Brill & C. Winick (Ed.) *The yearbook of substance use and abuse,* vol. 2 (pp. 213-230). New York: Human Services Press.

Robins, L. N. & Ratcliff, K. S. (1979). Risk factors in the continuation of childhood antisocial hehavior into adulthood. *International Journal of Mental Health, 73,* 96-116.

Rockman, G. E., Amit, Z., Brown, W., Bourque, C. & Ogren, S. O. (1982). An investigation of the mechanisms of action of 5-hydroxytryptamine in the suppression of ethanol intake. *Neuropharmacology, 21,* 341-347.

Rockman, G. E., Amit, Z., Carr, G., Brown, Z. W. & Ogren, S. O. (1979). Attenuation of ethanol intake by 5-hydroxytryptamine uptake blockage in laboratory rats: 1. Involvement of brain 5-hydroxytryptamine in the mediation of the positive reinforcing properties of ethanol. *Archives of Internal Pharmacodynamic Therapy,* 241, 245-259.

Roffman, R. A. (1982). *Marijuana as medicine.* Seattle: Madrona.

Rohter, L. (1995, June 13). Colombia vows a crackdown on cartels. *The New York Times,* p. A14.

Rosecan, J. (1983, July 14-19). The treatment of cocaine abuse with Imipramine, L-tyrosine, and L-tryptophan. Paper presented at the VII World Congress of Psychiatry, Vienna, Austria.

Rosenbaum, M. (1995). Difficulties in taking care of business. In J. A. Inciardi & K. McElrath (Eds.), *The American drug scene: An anthology.* Los Angeles: Roxbury Publishing Co.

Rosenbaum, M., & Doblin, R. (1991). Why MDMA should not have been made illegal. In J. A. Inciardi (Ed.), *The drug legalization debate* (pp. 135-146). Newbury, CA: Sage Publications.

Rosenthal, M. S. (1973). New York City Phoenix House: A therapeutic community for the treatment of drug abusers and drug addicts. In L. Brill & E. Harms (Eds.), *Yearbook of drug abuse* (pp. 83-102). New York: Behavioral Publications.

Ross, D. F., & Pihl, R. O. (1988). Alcohol, self-focus and complex reaction-time performance. *Journal of Studies on Alcohol, 49,* 115-125.

Ross, H. E., Glaser, F. B. & Germanson, T. (1988). The prevalence of psychiatric disorders in patients with alcohol and other drug problems. *Archives of General Psychiatry, 45,* 1023-1031.

Ross, M. & Olson, J. M. (1982). Placebo effects in medical reseach practice. In J. R. Eiser (Ed.), *Social psychology and behavioral medicine* (pp. 441-458). New York: Wiley.

Rounsaville, B. J., Anton, S. F., Carroll, K., Budde, D., Prusoff, B. A. & Gawin, F. A. (1991). Psychiatric diagnoses of treatment-seeking cocaine abusers. *Archives of General Psychiatry, 48,* 43-51.

Rounsaville, B. J., Dolinsky, Z. S., Babor, T. F. & Meyer, R. E. (1987). Psychopathology as a predictor of treatment outcome in alcoholics. *Archives of General psychiatry, 44,* 505-513.

Rounsaville, B. J., Weissman, M. M., Kleber, H. & Wilber, C. (1982). Heterogeneity of psychiatric diagnosis in treated opiate addicts. *Archives of General Psychiatry, 39,* 151-156.

Rouse, J. J. (1991). Evaluation research on prison-based drug treatment programs and some policy implications. *The International Journal of the Addictions, 26,* 29-44.

Rouse, J. J., & Johnson, B. D. (1991). Hidden paradigms of morality in debates about drugs: Historical and policy shifts in British and American drug policies. In J. A. Inciardi (Ed.), *The drug legalization debate* (pp. 183-214). Newbury Park, CA: Sage Publications.

Routhier, R. (1992, February 21). U.S. attempts to seize former deputy sheriff's property. *The Hartford Courant,* p. B5.

Roy, A., Virrkunen, M., & Linnoila, M. (1987). Reduced central serotonin turnover in a subgroup of alcoholics. *Progress in Neuro-Psychopharmacology and Biological Psychiatry, 11,* 173-177.

Russell, M. A. H., Jarvis, M. J., Devitt, G., & Feyerabend, C. (1981). Nicotine intake by snuff users. *British Medical Journal, 283,* 814-817.

Santo, Y., Hooper, H. E., Friedman, A. S. & Conner, W. (1980). Criminal behaviors of adolescent nonheroin ploydrug abusers in drug treatment programs. *Contemporary Drug Problems, 9,* 301-325.

Satinder, K. P. & Black, A. (1984). Cannabis use and sensation seeking orientation. *The Journal of Psychology, 16,* 101-105.

Satterfield, J. H. (1978). The hyperactive child syndrome: A precursor of adult psychopathy? In R. D. Hare & D. Schalling (Eds.), *Psychopathic behaviour: Approaches to research.* (pp. 329-346). Chichester, England: Wiley.

Scanlon, W. F. (1986). *Alcoholism and drug abuse in the workplace: Employee assistance program.* New York: Praeger.

Schachter, S. (1971). *Emotion, obesity and crime.* New York: Academic Press.

Schecter, M. D., & Cook, P. G. (1976). Nicotine-induced weight loss in rats without an effect on appetite. *European Journal of Pharmacology, 38,* 63-69.

Schelling, T. C. (1992). Addictive drugs: The cigarette experience. *Science, 255,* 430-433.

Scherer, S. E. (1973). Self-report parent and child drug use. *British Journal of Addiction, 68,* 363-364.

Schildkraut, J. J. (1965). The catecholamine hypothesis of affective disorders: A review of supporting evidence. *American Journal of Psychiatry, 122,* 509-522.

Schildkraut, J. J., & Orsulak, P. J. (1977). Recent studies on the role of catecholamines in the pathophysiology and classification of depressive disorders. In E. Usdin, D. A. Hamburg, & J. D. Barchas (Eds.), *Neuroregulators and psychiatric disorders* (pp. 122-147). New York: Oxford University Press.

Schless, R. A. (1925, February). The drug addict. *American Mercury Magazine,* pp. 196-199.

Schuckit, M. A. (1973). Alcoholism and sociopathy—Diagnostic confusion. *Quarterly Journal of Studies on Alcohol, 34,* 157-164.

Schuckit, M. A. (1982). A study of young men with alcoholic close relatives. *American Journal of Psychiatry, 139,* 791-794.

Schuckit, M. A. (1995). Chasing the dragon. In J. A. Inciardi & K. McElrath (Eds.), *The American drug scene: An anthology* (pp. 144-146). Los Angeles, CA: Roxbury Publishing Co.

Schuckit, M. A. (1985). The clinical implications of primary diagnostic groups among alcoholics. *Archives of General Psychiatry, 42,* 1043-1049.

Schuckit, M.A. (1986). Genetic and clinical implications of alcoholism and affective disorder. *American Journal of Psychiatry, 143,* 140-147.

Schuckit, M. A. (1987). Biological vulnerability to alcoholism. *Journal of Consulting and Clinical Psychology, 55,* 301-309.

Schuckit, M. A. & Duby, J. (1982). Alcohol-related flushing and the risk for alcoholism in sons of alcoholics. *Journal of Clinical Psychiatry, 43,* 415-418.

Schuckit, M. A., Goodwin, D. W. & Winokur, G. (1972). A study of alcoholism in half siblings. *American Journal of Psychiatry, 128,* 1132-1135.

Schuckit, M. A., Gunderson, E. K. E., Heckman, N. A. & Kolb, D. (1976). Family history as a predictor of alcoholism in U.S. Navy personnel. *Journal of Studies on Alcohol, 37,* 1678-1685.

Schuckit, M. A. & Rayses, V. (1979). Ethanol ingestion: Differences in blood acetaldehyde concentrations in relatives of alcoholics and controls. *Science, 203,* 54-55.

Schulsinger, F., Goodwin, D. W., Knop, J., Pollock, V. & Mikkelson, U. (1985). Characteristics of young men at high risk for alcoholism. In U. Rydberg et al. (Eds.), *Alcohol and the developing brain* (pp. 193-205). New York: Raven Press.

Schulsinger, F., Knop, J., Goodwin, D. W., Teasdale, T. W. & Mikkelsen, U. (1986). A prospective study of young men at risk for alcoholism: Social and psychological characteristics. *Archives of General Psychiatry, 43,* 755-760.

Schur, E. (1972). *Labeling deviant behavior.* New York: Harper & Row.

Schwartz, R. H. & Hawks, R. L. (1985). Laboratory detection of marijuana use. *Journal of the American Medical Association, 254,* 788-792.

Scott, P. D. & Marshall, J. (1991). *Cocaine politics: Drugs, armies, and the CIA in Central America.* Berkeley: University of California Press.

Scott, P. D. & Willcox, D. R. C. (1965). Delinquency and the amphetamines. *British Journal of Psychiatry, 111,* 865-875.

Sechrest, L., White, S. O. & Brown, E. D. (1979). *The rehabilitation of criminal offenders: Problems and prospects.* Washington, DC: National Academy Press.

Second International Caffeine Workshop (1980). *Nutrition Reviews, 38,* 196-200.

Seigel, R. K., Elsohly, M.A., Plowman, T., Rury, P. M., & Jones, R. T. (1986). Cocaine in herbal tea [Letter to the editor]. *Journal of the American Medical Association, 255,* 40.

Semlitz, L. & Gold, M. S. (1986). Adolescent drug abuse: Diagnosis, treatment, and prevention. *Psychiatric Clinics of North America, 9,* 455-473.

Shaffer, H., Beck, J. C. & Boothroyd, P. (1983). The primary prevention of smoking onset: An inoculation approach. *Journal of Psychoactive Drugs, 15,* 177-184.

Shannon, E. (1988) *Desperados: Latin drug lords, U.S. lawmen, and the war America can't win.* New York: Viking Penguin Inc.

Shaw, C. R. & McKay, H. D. (1942). *Juvenile delinquency and urban areas.* Rev. ed. Chicago: University of Chicago Press.

Shedler, J. & Block, J. (1990). Adolescent drug users and psychological health. *American Psychologist, 45,* 612-630.

Sheehy, T. W. (1992). Alcohol and the heart: How it helps, how it harms. *Postgraduate Medicine, 91,* 271-277.

Shenon, P. (1995, April 10). Burmese military steps up drive against major drug trafficker. *The New York Times,* p. A5.

Sher, K., Walitzer, K. S., Wood, P. K. & Brent, E. E. (1991). Characteristics of children of alcoholics: Putative risk factors, substance use and abuse, and psychopathology. *Journal of Abnormal Psychology 100,* 427-448.

Shopsin, B. (1978). Enhancement of the antidepressant response to L-tryptophan by a liver pyrrolase inhibitor: A rational treatment approach. *Neuropsychobiology, 4,* 188-192.

Siegel, R. K. (1980). PCP and violent crime: The people vs. peace. *Journal of Psychedelic Drugs 12,* 317-324.

Siegel, S., Krank, M. D., & Hinson, R. E. (1987). Anticipation of pharmacological and nonpharmacological events: Classical conditioning and addictive behavior. In S. Peele (Ed.), *Visions of Addiction. Part I. Journal of Drug Issues, 17,* 83-110.

Siegel, R.K. (1989). *Intoxication: Life in pursuit of artificial paradise.* New York: E.F. Dutton.

Siever, L. J., Coccaro, E. J., Zemishlany, Z., Silverman, J., Klar, H., Losonczy, M. F., Davidson, M., Friedman, R., Mohs, R. C., & Davis, K. L. (1987). Psychobiology of personality disorders: Pharmacologic implications. *Psychopharmacology Bulletin, 23,* 333-335.

Silverman, M., Lee, P. R., & Lydecker, M. (1982). *Prescriptions for death: The drugging of the third world.* Berkeley, CA: University of California Press.

Simcha-Fagan, O., Gersten, J. C., & Langer, T. S. (1986). Early precursors and concurrent correlates of patterns of illicit drug use in adolescence. *Journal of Drug Issues, 60,* 7-28.

Simonds, J. F. & Kashani, J. (1979). Drug abuse and criminal behavior in delinquent boys committed to a training school. *American Journal of Psychiatry, 136,* 1444-1448.

Simrell, E. V. (1970). History of legal and medical roles in narcotic abuse in the U.S. In J. C. Ball & C. D. Chambers (Eds.). *The epidemiology of opiate addiction in the United States.* (pp. 22-35). Springfield, IL: Charles C. Thomas.

Sinclair, J. D. (1987). The feasibility of effective psychopharmacological treatments for alcoholism. *British Journal of Addictions, 82,* 1213-1223.

Sinclair, U. (1950). *The jungle.* New York: The Viking Press.

Single, E. (1981). The impact of marijuana decriminalization. In Y. Israel, R. J. Gibbins, H. Kalant, R. E. Popham, W. Schmidt & R. G. Smart (Eds.), *Research advances in alcohol and drug problems* (pp. 405-424). New York: Plenum Press.

Siomopoulos, V. (1981). Violence: The ugly face of amphetamine abuse. *Indiana Medical Journal, 159,* 375-377.

$6.4 million in drug cash found at Kennedy. (1990 September 18). *The New York Times,* p. B3.

Skinner, H. A. (1981). "Different strokes for different folks": Differential treatment for alcohol abuse. In R. E. Meyer, T. F. Babor, B. C. Glueck, H. H. Jaffe, J. E. O'Brien & J. R. Stabenau (Eds.). *Evaluation of the alcoholic: Implications for research, theory, and Treatment* (pp. 349-367). Washington, DC: U.S. Government Printing Office.

Slattery, M. L., Robison, L. M., Schuman, K. L., & French, T. K. (1989). Cigarette smoking and exposure to passive smoke are risk factors for cervical cancer. *Journal of the American Medical Association, 262,* 499.

Slice of vice. (1986, January 6). *Time,* p. 72.

Sloman, L. (1979). *Reefer madness: Marijuana in America.* New York: Grove Press, Inc.

Smart, R. G., Allison, K. R., Cheung, Y., & Erickson, P. G. (1990-1991). Future research needs in policy, prevention, and treatment for drug abuse problems. *International Journal of Addictions, 25,* 117-126.

Smith, C. G. & Ashe, R. H. (1984). Acute, short term and chronic effects of marijuana on the female primate productive function. In M.C. Braude, & J. P. Ludford (Eds.), *Marijuana effects on the endocrine and reproductive systems* (NIDA Research Monograph Series No. 44, pp. 82-96). Washington, DC: U.S. Government Printing Office.

Smith, D. E., King, M. B. & Hoebel, G. B. (1970). Lateral hypothalamic control of killing: Evidence for a cholinoceptive mechanism. *Science, 167,* 900-901.

Smith, D. E. & Wesson, D. R. (1980). PCP abuse: Diagnostic and pharmacological treatment approaches. *Journal of Psychedelic Drugs, 12,* 293-299.

Smith, D. E., & Seymour, R. B. (1982). Clinical perspectives on the toxicology of marijuana: 1967-1981. In *Marijuana and Youth: Clinical Observations on Motivation and Learning.* Washington, DC: US Department of Health and Human Services, U.S. Government Printing Office.

Smith, G. M. (1986). Adolescent personality traits that predict young adult drug use. *Comprehensive Therapy, 12,* 44-50.

Smith, R. F., Mattran, K. M., Kurkjian, M. F. & Kurtz, S. L. (1987). Alterations in offspring behavior induced by chronic prenatal cocaine dosing. *Neurotoxicology and Teratology, 11,* 35-38.

Sneader, W. (1985). *Drug discovery: The evolution of modern medicines.* Chichester, England:Wiley.

Snyder, S. H. (1977). Opiate receptors and internal opiates. *Scientific American 236,* 44.

Snyder, S. H. (1978). The opiate receptor and morphine-like peptides in the brain. *American Journal of Psychiatry, 135,* 645-652.

Snyder, S. H. (1980). *Biological aspects of mental disorder.* New York: Oxford University Press.

Solomon, S. D. (1981). *Tailoring alcoholism therapy to client needs.* Washington, DC: U.S. Government Printing Office.

Solomons, K. & Neppe, V. M. (1989). Cannabis—Its clinical effects. *South African Medical Journal, 76,* 102-104.

Sorensen, J. R. & del Carmen, R. V. (1990). Legal issues in drug testing offenders and criminal justice employees. In R. Weisheit (Ed.). *Drugs, crime and the criminal justice system.* (pp. 329-359). Cincinnati, OH: Anderson.

Spear, L. P., Kirstein, C. L., Bell, J., Yoottanasumpun, V., Greenbaum, R., O'Shea, J., Hoffmann, H., & Spear, N. E. (1989). Effects of prenatal cocaine exposure on behavior during the early postnatal period. *Neurotoxicology and Teratology, 11,* 57-63.

Spotts, J. W. & Shontz, F. C. (1984). Correlates of sensation seeking by heavy, chronic drug users. *Perceptual and Motor Skills, 58,* 427-435.

Spotts, J. V., & Spotts, C. A. (Eds.)(1980) *Use and abuse of amphetamine and its substitutes.* National Institute on Drug Abuse Research Issues 25. Rockville, MD: U.S. Government Printing Office.

Stafanis, C., Liakos, A., Boulougouris, J., Fink, M. & Freedman, A. M. (1976). Chronic hashish use and mental disorder. *American Journal of Psychiatry, 133,* 225-227.

Stamatoyannopoulas, G., Chen, S., & Fukui, M. (1975). Liver alcohol dehydrogenase in Japanese: High population frequency of atypical form and its possible role in alcohol sensitivity. *American Journal of Human Genetics, 276,* 789-796.

Steinhausen, H., Nestler, J. V., & Huth, H. (1982). Psychopathology and mental functions in the offspring of alcoholic and epileptic mothers. *Journal of the American Academy of Child Psychiatry, 21,* 268-273.

Stevens, J. R., & Hermann, B. P. (1981). Temporal lobe epilepsy, psychopathology and violence: The state of the evidence. *Neurology, 31,* 1127-1132.

Stone, D. L. & Kotch, D. A. (1989). Individuals' attitudes toward organizational drug testing policies and practices. *Journal of Applied Psychology, 74,* 518-521.

Streissguth, A. P., Little, R. E., Herman, C., & Woodell, S. (1979). IQ in children of recovered alcoholic mothers compared to matched controls. *Alcoholism: Clinical and Experimental Research, 3,* 197.

Strug, D., Wish, E., Johnson, B., Anderson, K., Miller, T., & Sears, A. (1984). The role of alcohol in the crimes of active heroin users. *Crime and Delinquency, 30,* 551-567.

Subtance Abuse and Mental Health Services Administration. Office of Applied Studies. (1994). *National household survey on drug abuse: Population estimates 1993.* Rockville, MD: U.S. Department of Health and Human Services.

Sugarman, B. (1974). *Daytop Village: A therapeutic community.* New York: Rinehart & Winston.

Suh, I., Shaten, B. J., Cutler, J. A., & Kuller, L. H. (1992). Alcohol use and mortality from coronary heart disease: The role of high density lipoprotein cholesterol. *Annals of Internal Medicine, 116,* 881-887.

Sullivan, R. (1992, January 25). Federal judge orders rush on prison tuberculosis unit. *The New York Times,* p. 9.

Supreme Court drug test rulings. (1989, June). *Monthly Labor Review, 112,* 43.

Surovell, H. (1990, April). Posse power. *Penthouse,* 36-42, 72-74, 136.

Sutherland, E. H. & Cressey, D. R. (1978). *Criminology.* Philadelphia: Lippincott.

Sutker, P. B. & Allain, A. N. (1988). Issues in personality conceptualizations of addictive behaviors. *Journal of Consulting and Clinical Psychology, 56,* 172-182.

Sutker, P. B. & Archer, R. P. (1984). Opiate abuse and dependence disorder. In H.E. Adams, & P. B. Sutker (Eds.) *Comprehensive handbook of psychopathology.* (pp. 585-621). New York: Plenum Press.

Syndulko, K., Parker, D. A., Jens, R., Maltzman, I., & Ziskind, E. (1975). Psychophysiology of sociopathy: Electroncortical measures. *Biological Psychiatry, 3,* 185-200.

Szasz, T. (1974) *Ceremonial chemistry: The ritual persecution of drugs, addicts, and pushers.* New York: Anchor Press/Doubleday.

Szasz, T. (1987). The morality of drug controls. In R. Hamowy (Ed.), *Dealing with drugs: Consequences of government control* (pp. 327-351). Lexington, MA: D. C. Heath and Co.

Szuster, R. R., Pontium, E. B., & Campos, P. E. (1988). Marijuana sensitivity and panic anxiety. *Journal of Clinical Psychiatry, 49,* 427-429.

Taggart, R. W. (1989). Results of the drug testing program at Southern Pacific Railroad. In S. W. Gust & J. M. Walsh (Eds.), *Drugs in the workplace: Research and evaluation data.* (NIDA) Research Monograph No. 91, pp. 97-108). Rockville, MD: National Institute on Drug Abuse.

Taioli, E., & Wynder, E. L. (1991). Effect of the age at which smoking begins on frequency of smoking in adulthood. (letter) *New England Journal of Medicine, 325,* 968-969.

Takahashi, S., Yamane, H., Kondo, H. & Tani, N. (1974). CSF monoamine metabolites in alcoholism, a comparative study with depression. *Folia Psychiatrica Neurologica Japan, 28,* 347-354.

Tannenbaum, F. (1938). *Crime and the Community.* New York: Columbia University Press.

Tarter, R. E. (1988). Are there inherited behavioral traits that predispose to substance abuse? *Journal of Consulting and Clinical Psychology, 56,* 189-196.

Tarter, R. E., Alterman, A. I., & Edwards, K. L. (1985). Vulnerability to alcoholism in men: A behavior-genetic perspective. *Journal of Studies on Alcoholism, 46,* 329-356.

Tarter, R. E. & Edwards, K. L. (1987). Vulnerability to alcohol and drug abuse: A behavior-genetic view. *Psychological Bulletin, 102,* 204-218.

Tarter, R. E., McBride, H., Buonpane, N., & Schneider, D.U. (1977). Differentiation of alcoholics: Childhood history of minimal brain dysfunction, family history, and drinking pattern. *Archives of General Psychiatry, 34,* 761-768.

Taylor, A. H. (1969). *American diplomacy and the narcotics traffic, 1900-1939: A study in international humanitarian reform.* Durham, NC: Duke University Press.

Taylor, W. N., & Black, A. B. (1987). Pervasive anabolic steroid use among health club athletes. *Annals of Sports Medicine, 3,* 155-159.

Temple, M. & Ladouceur, P. (1986). The alcohol-crime relationship as an age-specific phenomenon: A longitudinal study. *Contemporary Drug Problems,* 89-115.

Tennant, F., Black, D. L. & Voy, R. O. (1988). Anabolic steroid dependence with opioid-type features (letter). *New England Journal of Medicine, 319,* 578.

Tennes, K., Auitable, N., Blackard, C., Boyles, C., Hassoun, B., Holmes, L., & Kreye, M. (1985). Marijuana: prenatal and postnatal exposure in the human. In T. M. Pinkert (Ed.), *Consequences of maternal drug abuse* (pp. 115-123) NIDA

Research Monograph No. 59. (pp. 115-123). Washington, DC: U.S. Government Printing Office.

Terry C. E., & Pellens, M. (1970). The extent of chronic opiate use in the United States prior to 1921. In J. C. Ball & C. D. Chambers (Eds.). *The epidemiology of opiate addiction in the United States.* (pp. 36-67). Springfield, IL: Charles C. Thomas.

Theodore, A. (1988). *The origins and sources of drugs.* New York: Chelsea House.

Tinklenberg, J. R. (1973). Alcohol and violence. In P. G. Bourne & R. Fox (Eds.), *Alcoholism: progress in research and treatment* (pp. 195-210). New York: AcademicPress, Inc.

Tinklenberg, J. R. (1974). Marijuana and human aggression. In L. L. Miler (Ed.), *Marijuana: Effects on human behavior* (pp. 339-358). Orlando, FL: Academic Press.

Tinklenberg, J. R. (1981). Drugs and criminal assaults by adolescents: A replication study. *Journal of Psychoactive Drugs, 13,* 277-288.

Tinklenberg, J. R., Murphy, P., Murphy, P. L., & Pfefferbaum, A. (1981). Drugs and criminal assaults by adolescents: a replication study. *Journal of Psychoactive Drugs, 13,* 277-288.

Towns, C. B. (1916a, October 14). Drugs and the drug user. *Survey,* pp. 47-49.

Towns, C. B. (1916b, October 28). Drugs: A world problem. *Survey,* pp. 87-88.

Towns, C. B. (1916c, November 18). The national drug problem. *Survey,* pp. 169-170.

Trachtenberg, M. & Blum, L. (1988). Improvement of cocaine-induced neuro-modulator deficits by the neuronutrient tropamine. *Journal of Psychoactive Drugs, 20,* 315-331.

Treaster, J. B. (1989a, December 16). A top Medellin drug trafficker dies in a shootout in Colombia. *The New York Times,* pp. 1, 12.

Treaster, J. B. (1989b, December 17). Drug trafficker's death cheers many Colombians. *The New York Times,* p. 43.

Treaster, J. B. (1989c, December 18). Extradition key to Bogota drug raid. *The New York Times,* p. 3.

Treaster, J. B. (1990, September 25). 'Arsenal' in trunks linked to a Colombian drug gang. *The New York Times,* p. B2.

Treaster, J. (1990, October 4). Agents arrest car dealers in money-laundering sting. *The New York Times,* p. B3.

Treaster, J. B. (1991a, June 21). Drug baron's arrest not seen as slowing U.S. cocaine flow. *The New York Times,* p. A8.

Treaster, J. B. (1991b, September 27). In Queens, agents seize suspect in 40 Colombian drug slayings. *The New York Times,* pp. Al, B2.

Treaster, J. B. (1992a, July 23). Colombian drug baron escapes luxurious prison after gunfight. *The New York Times,* pp. A1 & A10.

Treaster, J. B. (1992b, January 14). Colombia's drug lords add new line: Heroin for the U.S. *The New York Times,* pp. A1, B2.

Treaster, J. B. (1995a, June 12). Arrest in Colombia heartens U.S., but officials see little immendiate impact on drug flow. *The New York Times,* p. A8.

Treaster, J. B. (1995b, June 13). New terror campaign by drug traffickers feared in Colombia. *The New York Times,* p. 6.

Trebach, A. S. (1982). *The heroin solution.* New Haven, CT.: Yale University Press.

Trebach, A. S. (1987). *The great drug war: And radical proposals that could make America safe again.* New York: Macmillan.

Troland, M. B., Florio, J. A., Katz, J. V., Lindsay, J. G., & Payne, J. H. (1988). *Asset forfeiture: Law, practice & policy.* Washington, DC: U.S. Department of Justice. Criminal Division. Asset Forfeiture Office.

Tucker, D. (1984). *The world health market: The future of the pharmaceutical industry.* New York: Facts on File Publications.

Tunving, K. (1985). Psychiatric effects of cannabis use. *Acta Psychiatria Scandanavia, 72,* 209-217.

Tweed, S., & Ryff, C. D. (1991). Adult children of alcoholics: Profiles of wellness amidst distress. *Journal of Studies on Alcohol, 52,* 133-141.

Ungerleider, J. R. & Beigel, A. (1980). Drug abuse: Crisis in the treatment arena. *Journal of Drug Education, 10,* 279-288.

United States Attorneys and the Attorney General of the United States. (1989). *Drug trafficking: A report to the president of the United States.* Washington, DC: U.S. Department of Justice.

United States Center for Disease Control. (1990, December). *HIV/AIDS Surveillance.*

United States Department of Health, Education, and Welfare. (1979). *Smoking and health: A report of the Surgeon General.* U.S. Department of Health, Education, and Welfare, Public Health Service, Office of the Assistance Secretary for Health, Office on Smoking and Health. DHEW Publication No. (PHS) 79-50066.

United States Department of Health and Human Services. (USDHHS).(1986). *The health consequences of using smokeless tobacco: A report of the advisory committee to the Surgeon General* (NIH Publication No. 86-2874). Bethesda, MD: Government Printing Office.

United States Department of Health and Human Services. (USDHHS). (1987). *Drug abuse and drug abuse research: The second triennial report to Congress from the Secretary, Department of Health and Human Services* (DHHS Publication No. (ADM) 87-1486). Rockville, MD: National Institute on Drug Abuse.

U.S. Dept. of Justice. Bureau of Justice Statistics (1995). *Drugs and crime facts, 1994.* Rockville, MD: ONDCP Drugs Crime Clearinghouse, National Criminal Justice Reference Service.

United States Department of Justice. (1983, January). Prisoners and alcohol. *Bureau of Justice Statistics Bulletin,* 1-4.

U.S. judge is convicted in New Orleans bribe case. (1991, June 30). *The New York Times,* p. 13.

U.S. narcotics team target of wide-ranging investigation. (1991, August 18). *The Hartford Courant,* p. A14.

United States Select Committee on Narcotics Abuse and Control. (1989-1990). *Efficacy of drug abuse treatment programs.* House of Representatives, One Hundred First Congress, First Session. Washington, DC: U.S. Government Printing Office.

Vacon, B. (1990, May 28). Untruths, unreliable data create obstacles in war on drugs. *The Hartford Courant,* pp. A1 & A6.

Valzelli, L. (1981). *Psychobiology of aggression and violence.* New York: Raven Press.

Van Dyke, C. & Byck, R. (1983). Cocaine use in man. *Advances in Substance Abuse, 3,* 1-24.

vanKammen, D. P., Mann, L. S., & Sternberg, D. E. (1983). Dopamine-B-Hydroxylase activity and homovanollic acid in spinal fluid of schizophrenics with brain atrophy. *Science, 220,* 974-976.

Venables, P. H. (1987). Autonomic nervous system factors in criminal behavior. In S. A. Mednick, T. E. Moffitt, & S. A. Stack (Eds.), *Causes of crime: New biological approaches* (pp. 110-136). Cambridge, MA: Cambridge University Press.

Vesell, E. S., Page, J. G., & Passananti, G. T. (1971). Genetic and environmental factors affecting ethanol metabolism in man. *Clinical Pharmacological Therapeutics, 12,* 192-201.

Virkkunen, M. (1986). Insulin secretion during the glucose tolerance test among habitually violent and impulsive offenders. *Aggressive Behavior, 12,* 303-310.

Virkkunen, M. Nuutila, A., Goodwin, F. K., Linnoila, M. (1987). Cerebrospinal fluid monoamine metabolite levels in male arsonists. *Archives of General Psychiatry, 44,* 241-247.

Visher, C. A. (in press). Linking criminal sanctions, drug testing, & drug abuse treatment: A crime control strategy for the 1990's. *Criminal Justice Policy Review.*

Vodanovich, S. J. & Reyna, M. (1988). Alternatives to workplace testing. *Personnel Administrator, 33*(5), 78-84.

Wadler, G. I. & Hainline, B. (1989). *Drugs and the athlete.* Philadelphia: F. A. Davis.

Waksman, S. A. (1983). Diet and children's behavior disorders: A review of research. *Clinical Psychology Review, 3,* 201-213.

Wald, M. L. (1995, April 9). Was the pilot drunk? DNA might tell. *The New York Times,* p. 25.

Waldman, S., Miller, M., Lerner, M. A. & McKillop, P. (1989, November 13). The drug lawyers. *Newsweek,* pp. 41, 44.

Walker, W. O., III (1989). *Drug control in the Americas.* Albequerque: University of New Mexico Press.

Waller, D., Miller, M., Barry, J., & Reiss, S. (1990, July 16). Risky business. *Newsweek,* pp. 16-19.

Wallgren, H. & Barry, H. (1970). *Action of alcohol, vols. 1 and 2.* New York: Elseview.

Wallgren, H. & Barry, H. (1976). *Action of alcohol, vols. 1 & 2.* New York: Elseview.

Walsh, J. M. (1987). Reliability of urine drug testing. *Journal of the American Medical Association, 258,* 2587-2588.

Walsh, J. M. & Gust, S. W. (Eds.) (1986). *Interdisciplinary approaches to the problem of drug abuse in the workplace* [DHHS Pub. No. (ADM) 86-1477]. Washington, DC: National Institute on Drug Abuse.

Walters, G. Heffron, M., Whitaker, D. & Dial, S. (1992). The Choice program: A comprehensive residential treatment program for drug involved federal offenders. *International Journal of Offender Therapy and Comparitive Criminology, 36,* 21-29.

Walters, J. K., Estilo, M. J., Clark, G. L. & Lorvick, J. (1994). Syringe and needle exchange as HIV/AIDS prevention for injection drug users. *Journal of the American Medical Association, 271,* 115-120.

Webster, B. & Brown, J. G. (1989). Mandatory and random drug testing in the Honolulu police department. *Research in Action*. Washington, DC: National Institute of Justice.

Wegscheider, S. (1981). *Another chance: Hope & health for the alcoholic family*. Palo Alto, CA: Science and Behavior Books, Inc.

Weil, A. (1986). *The natural mind: An investigation of drugs and the higher consciousness*. (Rev. ed.) Boston: Houghton Mifflin Co.

Weiner, E. (1989, December 26). Latin drug traffickers use Canada as new route. *New York Times*, p. A3.

Weiner, T. (1994, October 27). Suit by drug agent says U.S. subverted his Burmese efforts. *The New York Times*, p. A9.

Weingartner, H., Rudorfer, M. V., Buchsbaum, M. S. & Linnoila, M. (1983). Effects of serotonin on memory impairments produced by ethanol. *Science, 221*, 472-473.

Weisheit, R. A. (1990). Challenging the criminalizers. *The Criminologist, 15*, 1-5.

Weiss, R. D., & Mirin, S. M. (1986). Subtypes of cocaine abusers. *Psychiatric Clinician in North America, 9*, 491-501.

Weiss, R. D., Mirin, S. M., Griffin, M. L. & Michael, J. L. (1988). Psychopathology in cocaine abusers. *The Journal of Nervous and Mental Disease, 176*, 719-725.

Weiss, R. D., Mirin, S. M. & Michael, J. L. (1983, May 4). Psychopathology in chronic cocaine abusers. Paper presented at the 136th annual meeting of the American Psychiatric Association, New York.

Weller, R. A. & Halikas, J. A. (1985). Marijuana use and psychiatric illness: A follow-up study. *American Journal of Psychiatry, 142*, 848-850.

Wellisch, J., Anglin, M. & Pendergast, M. (1993). Numbers and characteristics of drug using women in the criminal justice system: Implications for treatment. *Journal of Drug Issues, 23*, 7-30.

Wender, P. H. (1977). Minimal brain dysfunction: An overivew. In M. Lipton, A. DiMascio & K. Killman (Eds.). *Psychopharmacology: A generation of progress* (pp. 1429-1436). New York: Raven Press.

Wesnes, K. & Warburton, D. M. (1983). Smoking, nicotine and human performance. *Pharmacology and Therapeutics, 21*, 189-208.

Wesnes, K. & Warburton, D. M. (1984). The effects of cigarettes on varying yield on rapid information processing performance. *Psychopharmacology, 82*, 338-342.

West, D. J. & Farrington, D. P. (1973). *Who becomes delinquent?* London: Heinemann.

West, D. J. & Prinz, R. J. (1987). Parental alcoholism and childhood psychopathology. *Psychological Bulletin, 102*, 204- 218.

Wexler, H. & Love, C. T. (1994). Therapeutic communities in prison. In F. M. Times, G. DeLeon & N. Jainchill (Eds.), *Therapeutic community: Advances in research and application* (pp. 181-208). (NIDA Research Monograph 144). Rockville, MD: National Institute on Drug Abuse.

White, H. R., Pandina, R. J. & LaGrange, R. L. (1987). Longitudinal predictors of serious substance use and delinquency. *Criminology, 25*, 715-741.

Whitfield, C. (1989). Co-dependence: Our most common addiction—Some physical, mental, emotional and spiritual perspectives. (pp. 19-36)

Whitkin, G. (1994, October 10). The new opium wars: The administration plans to attack the lords of heroin. *U.S. News & World Report*, pp. 39-44.

Wilbur, R. (1986). A drug to fight cocaine. *Science, 86*, 42-47.

Williams, E. H. (1914, February 4). Negro cocaine "fiends" are a new Southern menace. *The New York Times Sunday Magazine*, p 12.

Williams, T. (1984). *The cocaine kids*. New York: Addison-Wesley.

Williams, T. (1989). *The cocaine kids: The inside story of a teenage drug ring*. Reading, MA: Addison-Wesley.

Wilson, J. Q. (1990, February). Against the legalization of drugs. *Commentary*, pp. 21-28.

Wilson, J. D. (1988) Androgen abuse by athletes. *Endocrine Review, 9*, 181-199.

Winick, C. (1963). Physician addicts. *Social Problems*.

Wise, R. (1984). Neural mechanisms of the reinforcing action of cocaine. In J. bowski (Ed.), *Cocaine: Pharmacology, effects, and treatment of abuse* (pp. 15-33) (NIDA Research Monograph 50). Washington, DC.

Wise, R. (1988). The neurobiology of craving: Implications for the understanding and treatment of addiction. *Journal of Abnormal Psychology, 97*, 118-132.

Wisotsky, S. (1986). *Breaking the impasse in the war on drugs*. New York: Greenwood Press.

Wisotsky, S. (1990). *Beyond the war on drugs*. Buffalo, NY: Prometheus Books.

Woititz, J. G. (1990). *Adult children of alcoholics* (expanded edition). Deerfield Beach, FL: Health Communications, Inc.

Wolfgang, M. (1958). *Patterns in criminal homicide*. Philadelphia: University of Pennsylvania Press.

Wood, D., Wender, P. H., & Reimherr, F. W. (1983). The prevalence of attention deficit disorder, residual type, or minimal brain dysfunction, in a population of male alcoholic patients. *American Journal of Psychiatry, 140*, 95-98.

Woolley, D. W. & Shaw, E. (1954). A biological and pharmacological suggestion about certain mental disorders. *Proceedings of the National Academy of Sciences, 40*, 228.

Workman-Daniels, K. L. & Hesselbrock, V. M. (1987). Childhood problem behavior and neuropsychological function in persons at risk for alcoholism. *Journal of Studies on Alcohol, 48*, 187-193.

World Health Organization Expert Committee on Addiction-Producting Drugs. (1964). Terminology in regard to drug abuse. *W.H.O. Technical Report* (Series No. 273, Vol. 9) Albany, NY: WHO Publication Centre.

Wurtman, R. J. & Wurtman, J. J. (1979). *Nutrition and the brain: Vol. 3. Disorders of eating and nutrients in the treatment of brain diseases*. New York: Raven Press.

Yablonsky, L. (1965). *Synanon: The tunnel back*. New York: Macmillan Co.

Yale study reports clean needle project reduces AIDS cases. (1991, August 1). *The New York Times*, pp. A1, B2.

Yazigi, R. A., Odem, R. R. & Polakoski, K. L. (1991). Demonstration of specific binding of cocaine to human spermatozoa. *Journal of the American Medical Association, 266*, 1956-1959.

Yen, S., Peyrot, M. & Prino, C. (1989). A behavioral approach to substance abuse prevention in the correctional setting: A preliminary report. *Journal of Behavioral Residential Treatment, 4*, 53-56.

Yesalis, C. E., Kennedy, N. J., & Kopstein, A. N. (1989). Anabolic-androgenic steroid use in the United States. *Journal of the American Medical Association 270*, 1217.

Yesavage, J. A., Leirer, V. O., Denari, M. & Hollister, L. E. (1985). Carry-over effects of marijuana intoxication on aircraft pilot performance: A preliminary report. *American Journal of Psychiatry, 142*, 1325-1329.

Yeudall, L. T., Fedora, O., & Fromm, D. (1985). *A Neuropsychosocial theory of persistent criminality: Implications for assessment and treatment* (Research Bulletin 97). Edmonton: Alberta Hospital.

Yogman, M. W., Zeisel, S. H. & Roberts, C. (1982). Dietary precursors of serotonin and newborn behavior. In H. R. Lieberman & R. J. Wurtman (Eds.), *Research strategies for assessing the behavioral effects of foods and nutrients: Proceedings of Massachusetts Institute of Technology Symposium*.

Young, J. H. (1961). *The toadstool millionaires; A social history of patent medicines in America before federal regulation*. Princeton, NJ: Princeton University Press.

Young, P. (1987). *Drugs and pregnancy*. New York: Chelsea House Publishers.

Young, S. N. & Sourkes, T. L (1977). Tryptophan in the central nervous system: Regulation and significance. *Advanced Neurochemistry, 2*, 133.

Yudofsky, S. C., Silver, J. M., & Schneider, S. E. (1987). Pharmacologic treatment of aggression. *Psychiatric Annals, 17*, 397-406.

Zinberg, N.E. (1984). *Drug, set, and setting: The basis for controlled intoxicant use*. New Haven, CT.: Yale University Press.

Zito, K. A., Vickers, G., & Roberts, D. C. S. (1985). Disruption of cocaine and heroin self-administration following kainic acid lesions of the nucleus accumbens. *Pharmacology, Biochemistry and Behavior, 23*, 1029-1036.

Zuckerman, M. (1978). Sensation seeking and psychopathy. In R. D. Hare & D. Schalling (Eds.), *Psychopathic behaviour: approaches to research.* (pp. 165-185) Chichester, England: Wiley.